1972 **25th Anniversary Edition** **1997**

UGANDAN ASIAN EXPULSION

90 Days and Beyond Through the Eyes of the International Press

© Expulsion Publications, 1997
All rights reserved

ISBN 0-9658740-0-1

Copyright to each article, photograph and illustration reproduced herein belongs to the individual newspaper, wire service or writer and has been reproduced with their permission. No material in this publication may be reproduced without the written permission of the copyright holder.

Printed in the United States of America

Published by Expulsion Publications
Post Office Box 340547
Tampa, FL 33694-0547 USA

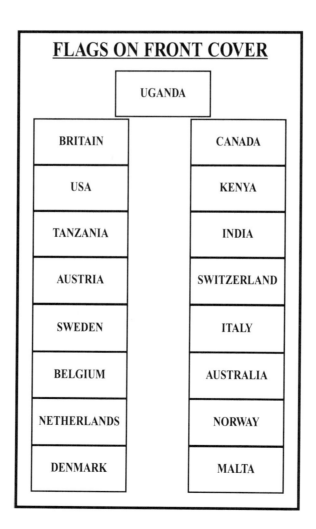

FLAGS ON FRONT COVER

UGANDA	
BRITAIN	CANADA
USA	KENYA
TANZANIA	INDIA
AUSTRIA	SWITZERLAND
SWEDEN	ITALY
BELGIUM	AUSTRALIA
NETHERLANDS	NORWAY
DENMARK	MALTA

Dedicated to my parents

On a personal note:
The following telegram was sent to my sister by my brother on the day of the expulsion deadline. The next day we left under the auspices of the United Nations and spent six months in a refugee camp in Malta.

B & C

POST OFFICE TELEGRAPHS
REPUBLIC OF ZAMBIA

No. 209

DATE

SERIAL No.	OFFICE OF ORIGIN	WORDS	TIME HANDED IN	SCE. INSTRUCTIONS

ZCZC CS483 NAL221 UGN305 KT76 XCP16 ZALX CO
UGKA 039 KAMPALA 39 7 1845

SENT

RECEIVED

AT 0932/8/11/72

FROM LSKA

BY R.CHIBWK

JIWANIS
BOX 1180 CHINGOLA ZAMBIA

— FOLD —

AT

TO

BY

FAMILY DEPARTING WITH UNITED NATIONS DESTINATION UNKNOWN
EVERYONE FINE HERE FI AND MADAT LEAVING FOR LONDON TONIGHT WE
WILL WRITE TO YOU FROM ANY SETTLEMENT CAMP ON OUR ARRIVAL
PLEASE DO NOT WORRY

EQBAL

If the accuracy of this telegram is doubted, inquiry should be made at the office of delivery. This form should accompany any inquiry.

COL 1180

<u>PREFACE</u>

International press coverage of the expulsion of the Asians from Uganda 25 years ago was remarkably extensive around the world. Consider some of the many major news events during the 90 day expulsion period: dock strike and prison riots in Britain, violence in Northern Ireland, Olympic boycott threat by African countries, massacre at the Munich Olympics, Vietnam War peace talks and federal elections in Canada and the United States. As prominent as these events were, coverage of the expulsion was extraordinary.

Passionate front page headlines about the expulsion screamed regularly in most British newspapers. Television news broadcasts added to the intense scrutiny by the media. Editorials in many influential newspapers around the world denounced the expulsion. Protests, petitions and heated arguments were the rage on the streets and in pubs and homes across Britain. Fierce political battles in the Parliament as well as city and town councils added fuel to the fire.

Many believe that President Amin, realising that the world was closely watching the developments in Uganda, may have restrained his soldiers. Despite many of the atrocities committed by Amin's army, the widespread coverage likely prevented what could have been a very bloody outcome. The press is often condemned for its sensationalism; but in this instance, it may have saved lives.

This book is a collection of some of the press coverage. Its purpose is to present the historical event as portrayed in the press and provide fluidity to several dramas as they were unfolding simultaneously in many countries. You will experience the triumphs and tragedies, determination and despondency, courage and fear felt by those being expelled.

The gift of history allows us to gain knowledge about the past and learn from it. It is very important that this piece of history be shared with, and preserved for, our children and the generations to follow as it is a part of us forever.

Z. Lalani

It is a pleasure to extend greetings to all those celebrating the 25th anniversary of the arrival of Ugandan Asians to Canada.

By celebrating the rich heritage of your community through the publication of this book, you are playing an important role in preserving and promoting vital cultural links from generation to generation. Ugandan Asians in Canada can take great pride in the many contributions that they have made and continue to make to the growth and prosperity of our country.

Canada is a nation that derives strength from the diversity of its population, as well as from its traditions of tolerance and mutual understanding. Events such as this anniversary provide a fitting opportunity to celebrate the uniqueness of Canada's multiculturalism.

Please accept my best wishes.

Jean Chrétien

OTTAWA
1997

UNITED NATIONS HIGH COMMISSIONER FOR REFUGEES		HAUT COMMISSARIAT DES NATIONS UNIES POUR LES RÉFUGIÉS
Liaison Office at United Nations Headquarters		Délégation au Siège des Nations Unies

NEW YORK

TELEGRAMS: UNATIONS, HICOMREF New York   TELEPHONE: (212) 963-0032

We were lecturers at Makrerere in 1972, pleased with starting our careers in the pearl of Africa" next door to my husband's home country, Sudan. Life seemed good for us and our young son, full of stimulating opportunities, interesting friends and all the delights of a country with a perfect climate and an endless variety of beautiful places to go and exciting things to do and see.

Then Idi Amin burst the bubble. A slow descent into irrationality took on explosive proportions in the summer of 1972 when Amin decided to "expel the Asians." His actions devastated the Asian community and in turn the economy and infrastructure, as well as life in the towns of Uganda generally.

Many, including us ivory tower academics, were mobilized to assist the humanitarian agencies in a most inhumane task of evicting people from their homes, taking over their property and sending them into unknown places and uncertain futures. Colleagues at the University, our son's teacher and many other friends disappeared over the horizon, while those left behind faced a vacuum in both friendship and services.

It was a frightful time, demonstrating the power ignorant and evil dictators could wield and the disruption they could cause not only to individuals, but even to an entire nation. Many of our friends left Uganda in protest and the remainder of our stay was coloured by what had happened to a group of people, persecuted as a whole because of their ethnic relationship to a small number among them who had been cast as "economic" villains.

Some years later in Sudan, and inspired partly by a lingering uneasiness from those disturbing days in Kampala, I joined the Office of the High Commissioner for Refugees and began a round of emergency assignments in Sudan, Namibia, Sierra Leone, Kenya, Somalia and Bosnia. Repeatedly my work has brought me face to face with masses of people forced to flee their homes, thrown on the mercy of reluctant hosts and an ambivalent international community.

Confronting man's inhumanity to man becomes no easier with repetition, and although I now have more confidence in the humanitarian community's ability to respond to such crises and to provide safety nets, the real truth shouts out from one of UNHCR's posters:

"A refugee would like to have your problems!"

Although from our Ugandan friends we eventually heard many success stories about rapid adjustment to new environments and were told of general satisfaction with re-created lives, there remains for every ex-refugee a sense of fundamental loss, perpetually nagging no matter what the new achievements or new found happiness.

Those who have been, along with those of us who serve, refugees have a duty to keep the notion of loss alive and to address its consequences at all times and in all aspects of our work and lives.

Karen Koning AbuZayd
Chef de Cabinet
UNHCR
8.8.97

UGANDA
1972

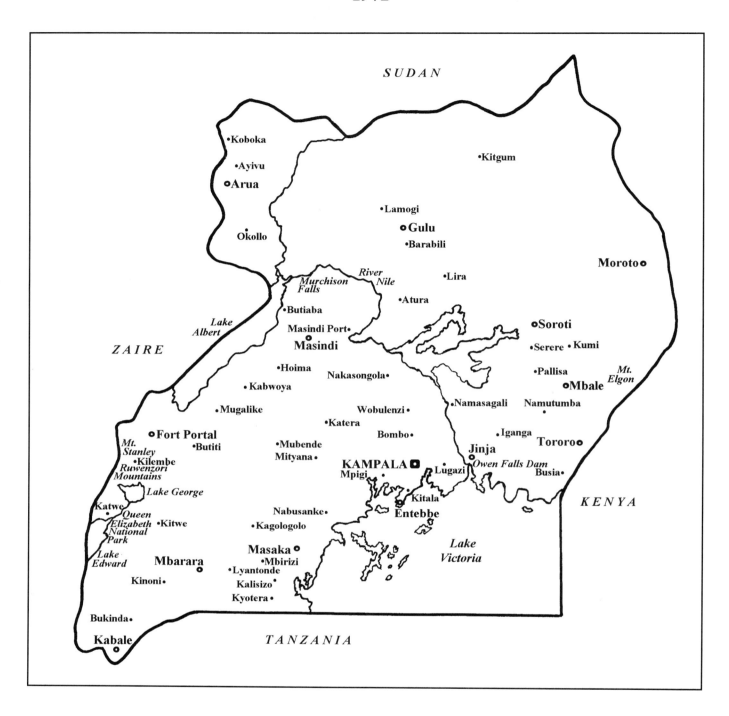

It will be Britain's responsibility
THE FUTURE OF ASIANS IN UGANDA

Reprinted with permission, ©Uganda Argus, August 5, 1972

PRESIDENT AMIN WILL ASK THE BRITISH GOVERNMENT TO TAKE OVER RESPONSIBILITY OF ALL ASIANS IN UGANDA WHO ARE HOLDING BRITISH PASSPORTS BECAUSE THEY ARE SABOTAGING THE ECONOMY OF THE COUNTRY.

The president made this announcement yesterday when he addressed officers and men of the Airborne Regiment at Tororo. He said that there was no room in Uganda "for the over 80,000 Asians holding British passports who are sabotaging Uganda's economy and encouraging corruption." General Amin told the soldiers that he wants to see that the economy of Uganda is in the hands of Uganda citizens, especially "black Ugandans."

He appealed to the troops to assist him in defending the public against "those people who are sabotaging the economy of Uganda." "The troops must be prepared to arrest any saboteurs who are trying to undermine the economy of the country and to confuse the people."

The General also directed the officers and men of the Airborne Regiment to arrest any Israelis who attempt to enter Uganda and warned that if any Israelis enter Uganda and do sabotage to the country, it will be the responsibility of the soldiers.

President Amin, who was on his way to Kampala from South Karamoja, told the officers and soldiers that he had decided to visit them because he had received good news that there is now discipline and co-operation between the soldiers and civilians in Tororo.

Ugandan President Idi Amin Dada

Reproduced with permission, ©United Press International/Corbis Bettman

Britain will reject Amin's ultimatum on Asians

by COLIN LEGUM, our Commonwealth Correspondent
Reprinted with permission, ©The Observer, London, August 6, 1972

PRESIDENT IDI AMIN yesterday gave the British Government an ultimatum to remove all Ugandan Asians entitled to British passports within three months. He said about 80,000 Asians would be affected.

In a broadcast, General Amin announced that he would summon the British High Commissioner in Kampala, Mr Richard Slater, to ask him to arrange for their removal.

His impetuous demand threatens Britain and the Commonwealth with a serious racial crisis. Although the Foreign and Commonwealth Office was not ready to comment yesterday, there can be no question of the British Government agreeing to Amin's demands.

The first step will almost certainly be to seek negotiations with Uganda's military ruler to try to work out a reasonable agreement. His figure of 80,000 Ugandan Asians with British passports will be strenuously contested. Whitehall has never accepted that more than between 25,000 and 40,000 Asians are entitled to British passports.

Britain can look to other Commonwealth countries—especially India and Kenya—to help in the negotiations. It could also, if necessary, remind Amin of Britain's economic aid to Uganda. This is running at £4,500,000 a year with a further agreement for £10 million awaiting completion—and Uganda is virtually bankrupt.

But Britain would have to consider carefully how far she can go in dealing with General Amin. He has recently sought to ally himself with Libya's President Qadhafi and other Arab leaders, and there is a 50-man Ugandan military mission in Russia.

Amin's mood may be gauged from his further decision yesterday to buy out the giant British American Tobacco Company's processing factory and cigarette plant because he alleged that—like the

Continued on Page 2

THREAT OF EXPULSION
Asian Minority Faced With Tragic Dilemma in E. Africa

Exclusive to The Times from a Staff Writer
Reprinted with permission, ©Los Angeles Times, August 7, 1972

NAIROBI, KENYA—For a decade, the 325,000 Asians of East Africa—a shunned minority like the Jews of old Europe—have lived here under both subtle and blatant pressures to get out.

Now, for the first time, a quarter of them face far more than pressure. They are threatened with official expulsion in three months. It could become one of the most dramatic upheavals in recent African history.

On Saturday, President Idi Amin of Uganda announced that the country's 80,000 Asians—residents of Indian and Pakistani descent—would have to leave within three months. In an earlier speech last week, he accused the Asians, who control the commerce of Uganda, of "sabotaging the economy of the country."

Amin referred to them all as British passport holders and said he would ask the British High Commission (embassy) in Kampala to make the arrangements for their departure. Actually, Britain only recognizes 40,000 as citizens. Most of the rest consider themselves Ugandan citizens. The lumping of all together by Amin may mean that he intends to revoke the citizenship of Ugandan Asians and expel them as well.

(In London, David Lans, undersecretary of the Home Office, said Sunday the government's immediate reaction to Amin's statement was, "We are already a crowded island and immigration must and will remain strictly controlled.")

The threat to expel the Asians does not necessarily mean that they all will be gone in three months. Amin is an erratic leader who does not

Continued on Page 2

Ugandan Asian Expulsion: 90 Days and Beyond through the Eyes of the International Press

Continued from Page 1

Britain will reject Amin's ultimatum on Asians

Asian community—it was 'sabotaging the economy of Uganda.'

BAT's chairman in Kampala, Mr R. P. Dobson, said the announcement had come like 'a bolt from the blue.' The firm's territorial director, Mr Patrick Sheely, said the company's 'very profitable' plant employed about 650 Ugandans, and that BAT had always had good relations with General Amin.

General Amin's ultimatum brought an immediate reaction from right-wing Tory MPs.

Mr Ronald Bell, MP for Buckinghamshire South, said in a statement on behalf of the Monday Club's Immigration Committee that President Amin's action 'may serve a useful purpose if it brings to a head a situation which we have spun for ourselves out of a thin air by extreme and sustained folly.'

The statement added: 'These so-called British Asiatics are no more and no less British than any Indian in the bazaars of Bombay. They were either born in India or have retained close connections with India. They have no connection with Britain either by blood or residence.

'The problem of the East African Indians is not that they cannot go back to their own country, but that they don't want to.

'They want to come here, and the whole vast and growing race relations industry shouts in chorus that they have a divine right to come and, by coming, accelerate the colonisation of Britain.'

A different kind of reaction came from another Tory MP, Mr John Hunt, chairman of the all-party Committee on UK Citizenship, who said that he was writing to the Foreign and Commonwealth Secretary, Sir Alec Douglas-Home, to propose a new initiative through a conference of the five Commonwealth countries most immediately concerned with East African Asians—Uganda, Kenya, Tanzania, India and Britain.

Even if there were some prospect of reaching an accommodation with Amin, there are serious fears in Whitehall that Uganda Asians may panic and try to flood into Britain. This would make the present difficulties of trying to deal with the pressures of 'illegal' immigrants—highlighted by the shuttlecocking of Asians around the world—seem comparatively trivial.

The most urgent need, it is now felt in Whitehall, is to instill some confidence into the Ugandan Asian leaders. But this will not be easy since Amin in an earlier speech on Friday instructed his notoriously undisciplined Army to be 'prepared to arrest anyone trying to sabotage the economy and confuse the people.'

Even without this license to arrest on suspicion, Amin's soldiers have been making conditions increasingly intolerable for Asian businessmen and their families. Many are forced to pay regular sums to officers and soldiers for protection; girls have been raped; men and women have been arrested; and a number of prominent leaders of the Asian community have simply disappeared without trace. Among these is the lawyer and former MP, Mr Anil Clerk.

While most Asians in East Africa have been prepared to stay so long as they could work or see any prospect of realising their investments, they have recently begun to put first the safety of their families and themselves.

General Amin's speech is bound to increase the sense of insecurity which has been a major factor in the growing tendency for young Asians with British passports to attempt to enter this country without entry vouchers.

The British Government is known to be greatly embarrassed by its policy of shuttlecocking British Asians around the world as a means of discouraging others from trying to jump the queue of immigrants patiently waiting for their number to come up in the annual allocation of 4,500 vouchers for East African Asians.

Apart from British embarrassment and growing concern about the cost involved in shuttlecocking Asians across the world, there is now a growing realisation that this unpleasant form of deterrence will have to be abandoned because countries are no longer prepared to allow the Asian shuttlecocks to be landed even temporarily.

India now takes a firm stand on this matter. Her policy is to insist on getting a proper agreement about responsibility for British Asians who do not want to live in India.

Most European countries have now taken steps to prevent Asians being dumped at their airports. There are still 59 Asians in a camp in Italy; 21 in France; two in Spain; and 40 in Greece.

An attempt to clarify this aspect of British policy and to press for more positive action will be made this week by a delegation to the Home Secretary, Mr Robert Carr, led by Lord Avebury and Mr Stanley Clinton-Davis, MP.

Continued from Page 1

Asian Minority Faced With Tragic Dilemma in E. Africa

always think his decisions through. Decisions come from him like thunderbolts. His actions are arbitrary and capricious, much like those of the potentates whom the explorers sometimes encountered in 19th century Africa. He could decide to retain the Asians just as easily as he had decided to expel them.

Perhaps more important, the expulsion is sure to be resisted strenuously by the British government. British immigration laws discriminate against citizens who acquired their British passports simply because they were subjects in the old British empire.

Under the British quota system, only 3,000 immigration vouchers are set aside each year for British Asians from East Africa. Faced with mounting protest in Britain against colored immigrants, the British government does not intend to allow in many times the annual quota in a three-month period.

Intense Disquiet

Whatever the outcome, the announcement by Amin is sure to cause intense disquiet and rethinking about the future among the Asian communities in East Africa. Kenya has 140,000 Asians and Tanzania 105,000. Of these, 70,000 are Kenya citizens and 35,000 Tanzanian citizens. Most of the rest have British passports.

The Asians have had contact with East Africa for centuries. Before the 19th century, the East African coast was looked on, not as the eastern boundary of Africa, but as the western boundary of the Indian Ocean. Indian merchants were active in the Arab and Swahili ports and towns of the coast.

More Indians came when the British recruited them at the turn of the 20th century to help build the Uganda railway from Mombasa on the coast to Lake Victoria in the interior.

The bulk of Asian immigration, however, came later during the years of British colonial rule. On their own initiative, thousands of Asians sailed to East Africa to open small shops, work as craftsmen or clerks in the business of relatives.

By the time of black African independence in the early 1960s the Asians had become the middle class of East Africa, controlling the commerce and filling most of the professional, artisan, and clerk posts.

They were middle class in more ways than one. Politically and socially, the British had allowed them more rights than the Africans but fewer rights than the whites.

Considered Home

At independence, many of the Asians had been born in East Africa and almost all considered East Africa home. They had no intention of flying back to the Indian subcontinent.

But they now faced the enmity of their new black rulers. There is an intense hatred of Asians among Africans, even well-educated Africans. Partly this stems from the resentment that the lower classes have always shown toward shopkeepers throughout history. Partly it comes from the feeling among Africans that the Asians fill jobs that Africans have the skills to fill themselves. In the view of Africans, the Asian is simply a foreigner blocking the way.

At independence, a majority of the Asians failed to apply for East African citizenship. They feared the uncertainty of tying themselves to the new African countries.

Late last year, however, President Amin began a series of actions against Asians that failed to discriminate between citizens and noncitizens. All Asians, whether citizens or not, were forced to line up and register for a special government census. He also canceled the applications of 12,000 Asians for Uganda citizenship.

Economy in Danger

The expulsion of the Asians in Uganda, if it takes place, might devastate the economy of Uganda. It has deteriorated steadily since Amin took over the country in a coup in January, 1971. Uganda Africans would not have either the skills or the capital to fill the void left by the departing Asians.

Simply put, the official British attitude has been that it has a responsibility for British Asians, but not right away and not all at once. That attitude could work so long as the East African governments pressured Asians to leave only a little at a time. It can not work if Amin goes through with his threat.

For the Asians, the dilemma is acute and fearful. They not only face the terrors of uprooting themselves from a land that has meant home and security to them. But they have no idea where to go.

Britain does not want them, though it may take a few grudgingly and may even have to take all the citizens but not the others under moral pressure. The Indian government accepts responsibility only for the 30,000 in East Africa who have kept Indian citizenship. Some Asians are looking toward Canada, but it has stringent immigration regulations. Only professionals and young Asians with investment capital will have a good chance to make it.

In a dramatic way, Amin's threat bares the pathos of one more racial plight in Africa.

Calls to London show the desperation of Asians in Uganda

By Peter Evans, Home Affairs Correspondent
Reprinted with permission, ©Times Newspaper Limited, August 7, 1972

The crisis facing British passport-holders in Uganda is not so simple as it seems. Impressions that the Asians are taking calmly President Amin's ultimatum to Britain to remove them are not borne out by anxious telephone calls reaching London. Mr. Praful Patel, secretary of the committee on United Kingdom Citizenship, has received four calls from leaders of the Asian community in Uganda. One spoke of a lot of people thinking of buying airline tickets to get to Britain.

Mr. Patel, who I know from experience on a visit to Uganda has intimate contacts there, has urged leaders to stay calm while the British Government seeks to sort out the problem.

During my stay, many Ugandan Asians felt insecure under President Obote. President Amin's announcement that they would have to leave may have raised hopes that they would, as a result, be allowed to escape increasing pressure against them by quick entry to Britain.

Their new desperation arises from the apparently firm stand by Mr. David Lane, Under-Secretary of State, Home Office, against any further increase in the number of vouchers issued to East African Asians. If he stays firm, and pressure is increased by President Amin, it would be realistic to expect that some British Asians would try to come here.

The Government's firmness springs from an election promise not to allow into Britain any further large-scale permanent immigration. This stand is based on a belief that good race relations depend on the knowledge of the white British majority that they will not be overwhelmed by large numbers of coloured immigrants. It was fear of this among some sections of the population in the early 1960s that led eventually to the new Immigration Act.

Race relations are delicately balanced. The immigrant community is much more cohesive than in the early 1960s and any move that provoked white indignation would now be likely to get a much fiercer coloured response. A big influx of Asians could lead to an inflammation of race relations with dangerous polarization of views. This lies behind Government thinking.

The reaction of Mr. Ronald Bell, Conservative MP for Buckinghamshire, South, in a statement on behalf of the Monday Club, is significant. The statement says: "These so-called British Asiatics are no more and no less British than any Indian in the bazaars of Bombay. They were either born in India or have retained close connections with India. They have no connections with Britain either by blood or residence. The problem of the East African Indians is not that they cannot go back to their own country, but that they do not want to.

They want to come here, and the whole vast and growing race relations industry shouts in chorus that they have a divine right to come and, by coming, accelerate the colonization of Britain."

Again the situation is not so simple as it

Continued on Page 4

Uganda's British Asians

Editorial
Reprinted with permission, ©East African Standard, Nairobi, August 7, 1972

President Amin has decided that Asians in Uganda holding British passports must leave the country within three months. Legally he has every right to do so, but morally and physically he is demanding the impossible.

There are about 55,000 British Asian passport holders in Uganda and most have lived there for many years. As in Kenya they are the descendants of those of their race who built the Kenya Uganda Railway and they have graduated from being labourers and the like to running businesses, large and small.

Undoubtedly there is some truth in the statement by Gen. Amin that the Asians hold the economy of his country in their hands. But with Uganda's economy on a far from sound basis at present this would surely be a strange time to decide that it should change hands overnight.

Continued on Page 4

Street scene in Kampala after the expulsion announcement.
Reproduced with permission, ©Archive Photos/Camera Press

INDIA SAYS NO!

News Compilation
August 7, 1972

India will not accept the bulk of the Asians with British passports who are to be expelled from Uganda, a Government spokesman announced.

Indian policy is that British passport holders of Indian origin are allowed into the country in limited numbers on humanitarian grounds if their passports are endorsed to the effect that Britain acknowledges that the immigrants are a British responsibility.

DECISION ON ASIANS FINAL, SAYS AMIN

Threat to other non-Ugandans

By FRANK ROBERTSON, Diplomatic Staff
Reprinted with permission, ©Telegraph Group Limited, London,
August 7, 1972

MR KIBEDI, Uganda's Foreign Minister, said in London yesterday that his country is determined to expel 50,000 Asian holders of British passports from Uganda within three months. "If they still remain they will soon see what happens to them," he said.

Gen. Amin, Uganda's President, said in Kampala last night that his expulsion decision was final. He also suggested that similar action might be taken against other people living in the country who were not citizens of Uganda.

A statement on this is expected to be issued in Kampala today. There are about 2,000 non-Asian Britons living in Uganda.

Mr Richard Slater, the British High Commissioner in Kampala, pressed for an early meeting with President Amin.

Mr Slater will say that Britain accepts responsibility for the Indians and Pakistanis who claim British citizenship. But he will ask for much more time than the three months given by the president's announcement on Saturday.

Control "Must Stay"

Entry to Britain of Commonwealth immigrants is rigidly restricted. "We already are a crowded island and immigration must and will remain strictly controlled," Mr David Lane, Under-Secretary at the Home Office, said yesterday.

Last week all diplomatic missions in Kampala were asked unexpectedly by the Ugandan Government to state how many of their citizens

Continued on Page 4

Continued from Page 3

DECISION ON ASIANS FINAL, SAYS AMIN

were in the country. On Saturday President Amin announced his expulsion policy on Asians and said that his Government will take over the British-American Tobacco Company's operations in the country.

Before leaving Heathrow yesterday after an unofficial visit, Mr Kibedi said that there was nothing racial in President Amin's actions.

"Ask Canada"

"The Asians in Uganda are British citizens and Britain does not want them. If Britain cannot cope you should ask Canada, Australia or India to help you out.

"These Asians cause us a lot of social and economic problems. They are totally affecting our trade and economy and we must be independent. This may lead to some serious problems for Uganda but they will not be insurmountable," he said.

On Saturday President Amin said that 80,000 Asian holders of British passports in Uganda must leave because they were "sabotaging the economy." The true figure of those with a claim to British citizenship is just under 50,000, including children.

Besides the 50,000 in Uganda, there are 55,000 Asians in Kenya and 22,000 in Tanzania who are eligible for British passports. About 18,000 Asians from these East African states who now are back in India or Pakistan also are eligible.

The present British quota for Asian immigrants from Uganda, Kenya and Tanzania is 3,500 families a year, providing they have British passports. But this figure also includes Asians who have left East Africa for the Indian sub-continent since 1968, when British immigration laws were tightened.

Airlines Warned

A British passport is not enough for those wishing to settle in Britain. They must have a voucher attached and these are allocated on the merits of each applicant's case.

Recently fewer than 50 Asians from Uganda have entered Britain to settle each month, but long queues are expected at Entebbe airport from today. The Home Office has warned airlines to make sure that the papers of Asians travelling to Britain are in order.

In Kampala some Asian holders of British passports said that they were pleased that they had been told to get out, because this would allow them to enter Britain. But most regard Uganda as their home, and do not want to leave.

Some Indian families have been settled in Uganda for more than 200 years. Among present-day descendants are doctors, lawyers, professors and businessmen who contribute enormously to the economy of an almost-bankrupt country which President Amin alleged they were "sabotaging."

In London yesterday Mr Kibedi said that President Amin's action was "inevitable." But he did not say this on Thursday night to Sir Alec Douglas-Home, when he drank convivially with the Foreign Secretary at a reception given by the Uganda High Commissioner at his Hampstead home.

"The matter was not mentioned," a Foreign Office spokesman said.

Last night Sir Alec was at his home in Scotland, but a Foreign Office spokesman said he was being kept informed of developments. His reaction was not known, but at the Foreign Office and the Home Office there was an atmosphere of scarcely-controlled dismay.

"We always thought that Amin was a decent chap. After all, he served in the British Army for more than 15 years, and our relations with Uganda seemed to be going along quite well," one official said.

Impulsive Actions

President Amin was a major-general in the Ugandan Army when he seized power on January 25, 1971. Since then he has often behaved impulsively and at first Whitehall felt that his weekend pronouncements were simply further evidence of his brashness.

Britain has been giving Uganda economic aid at the rate of £4,500,000 a year. Earlier this year Britain agreed to a further loan of £10,000,000 after Uganda's foreign exchange reserves fell from about £18 million to less than £11 million in 1971. Uganda has not yet signed this agreement.

In Kenya a Government spokesman said that President Amin's decision had come as "something of a shock." The repercussions could be far-reaching.

The Indian Government is examining the implications of President Amin's announcement. New Delhi's attitude has been that Indians who hold British passports are the responsibility of the British Government. The Indian policy since the expulsions from African countries began has been that Indian settlers with Indian passports can return and have been taken in.

In London Mr Harold Soref, Conservative MP for Ormskirk and chairman of the Africa Committee of the Monday Club, described President Amin's decision as "discriminatory racialism."

"Britain is under no obligation to accept these people," he said. The Commonwealth secretariat should promote the establishment of race relations boards in Uganda and other developing nations.

Continued from Page 3

Calls to London show the desperation of Asians in Uganda

sounds. Some other Conservative MPs are worried because these Asians are a conscience issue: they have the British passport. Not to honour it devalues British promises.

Moreover, these Asians are on the whole not like many who have come here straight from India. They are by nature self-sufficient and good at trade or qualified in professions. Mr. Praful Patel is himself an example of an articulate, educated and successful British Asian businessman.

As part of the business community himself, he estimates that there are about 20 British Asian millionaires now in Britain. He quotes an estimate given in 1969 by the Indian Deputy Prime Minister that British banks have £240m belonging to British Asians.

Generally the Asians are middle-class traders, business or professional people, though not all are. The danger is that the savings of those in Uganda and elsewhere will be used up and they will be forced to live on the charity of relatives and friends if they are deprived of a livelihood without entry to Britain.

Continued from Page 3

Uganda's British Asians

Of the Asians few are in large-scale business. Those who are, have been citizens for some time and their contribution to the stability of the country is large and sound.

The majority run service and consumer businesses, small but profit-making and employing many African citizens. To tell them to leave, probably with insufficient time to dispose of their assets correctly, is morally unfair.

This new move by the General is the third stage in Uganda's recent critical appraisal of its Asian residents. The first was the ordering of an Asian census and the second the speech in which Gen. Amin called the British Asians "economic saboteurs".

What must come as a shock to the Asians in Uganda are the President's words to the Airborne Regiment in Tororo, urging all Uganda soldiers to watch for and arrest any "saboteurs" trying to undermine the country's economy.

Unfortunate though it may be to say so Uganda's armed forces are hardly free from suspicion when it comes to their dealings with the general public. Disappearances, killings (agreed by judicial finding) and constant references to indiscipline are not the stuff to make civilians, of whatever race, confident about their treatment once in military hands.

Considering all this and then disposing of it on the grounds that a sovereign nation has the right to decide its own destiny and who shall reap the benefits of residence, can it seriously be considered practical to order the uprooting of 55,000 people and their transfer to a new country in three months?

This would be an airlift of gigantic proportions. It has never been easy because of taxation issues to leave East Africa and it has never been easy for those leaving to find buyers with the capital ready to take over their businesses.

The British Government has not yet been officially appraised of Gen. Amin's ruling. It would be amazing, indeed, in the present state of affairs in Britain if the Government there acquiesced in the General's edict without a fight.

The entry voucher system has kept many Asians bottled up in Uganda when they would have been happy to leave. But the uncompromising attitude of India and Pakistan has been of little help. Many who have gone to India have only used it as a staging point before going elsewhere.

A conference of Commonwealth countries affected by the problem of British Asians could help if everybody was prepared to compromise or, at least, attend with an open mind.

Britain is in a very unhappy state. To expect her to absorb 55,000 extra people almost instantly, many of whom would be without resources, is asking for a full-scale confrontation.

If Britain flatly refuses to accept these people, legally her citizens but morally a responsibility shared by Uganda, what then?

The initiative would be placed fairly and squarely on the broad shoulders of Uganda's President. Could the Asians become permanent migronauts—and at whose expense—or would they become another problem for the United Nations, already overburdened looking after refugees?

In a situation such as this the only possible solution is for Britain and Uganda to sit around a table and talk.

Proper arrangements must be made for the Asians to sell and remove their assets. Three months is too short a time for either Britain to accept the influx or for Uganda to deal fairly with these people.

Asians milked the cow: They did not feed it - Gen. Amin

Reprinted with permission, ©Uganda Argus, August 7, 1972

PRESIDENT Amin has disclosed that he would summon the British High Commissioner to Uganda to make arrangements and remove the 80,000 Asian British passport holders within three months.

Speaking on the occasion of International Co-operative Day, the President said that the Asians were sabotaging the economy of Uganda and do not have the welfare of Uganda at heart. He said that nearly all shops in Kampala, Jinja, Mbale, Fort Portal, Arua and many other towns are in the hands of Asians. "It must be clearly understood as guiding principal", said the General, "that Uganda's economy must remain under the control of the citizens of Uganda."

He said that on July 27 BAT wrote to the Government asking for an agreement to be concluded between them and the Uganda Government which would be to the detriment of the tobacco industry and the economy of Uganda. He said BAT would like an agreement which would limit the period between which the Produce Marketing Board could deliver tobacco to their processing plant from July to April. "This", said the General, "means that if there was any tobacco left unprocessed when the agreement expires in April, then such a crop will be left useless in the hands of the Produce Marketing Board." The President pointed out many other difficult terms set by BAT intended to sabotage the economy of the country.

The President saluted the co-operatives, the farmers and the marketing boards for the excellent work they have done and are doing in Uganda's struggle for economic independence. The co-operatives, he said, have enabled the African farmer to process their own crops, which they grow — a thing which in the past was monopolised by foreigners. The co-operatives have taken over coffee factories end cotton ginneries, the industries which are so important for Uganda's foreign exchange, and which must be in the hands of the citizens, he said. Today, through co-operation, small farmers have been enabled to get agricultural loans for hiring tractors or for buying oxen, ox ploughs, insecticides, fertilisers, seeds and other agricultural implements.

"No Asian," said General Amin, "would have loaned money to the small farmers for such increased agricultural production." They were not interested in assisting the farmers to produce more crops.

"They only milked the cow," he said, "but did not feed it to yield more milk."

General Amin said that in order to assess the achievements the farmers have made through co-operatives, one needed to look back at the development of the marketing structure in Uganda. In the past, he said, marketing of cash crops such as coffee and cotton was carried out entirely by Asians. The Asians, he said, had a monopoly of

Continued on Page 6

BRITISH AID TO UGANDA IN JEOPARDY

News Compilation
August 8, 1972

Sir Alec Douglas - Home told the House of Commons that if President Idi Amin continued with his plan to expel Asians with British passports from Uganda, Britain would have to review economic ties with Uganda.

President Idi Amin said that he would be "not at all worried" if Britain discontinued further aid to Uganda. "Britain is also at liberty to recall her military training mission," he added.

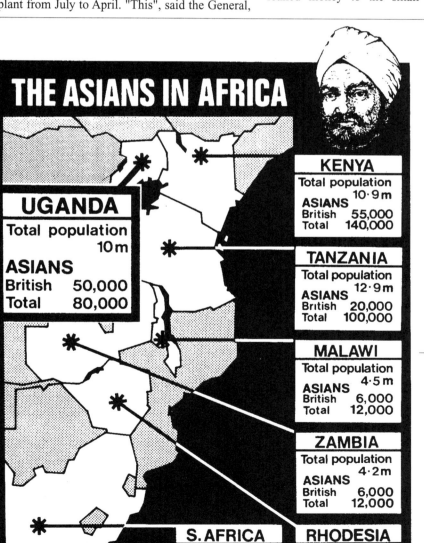

MAXIMUM BORDER SECURITY, SAYS VICE-PRESIDENT MOI

Kenya shuts the door to Uganda Asians

By NATION Reporter
Reprinted with permission, Reprinted with permission, ©Daily Nation, Nairobi, August 9, 1972

THE Kenya Government "will not allow Asian British passport holders from Uganda to flock into the country since Kenya is not a dumping ground for citizens of other countries."

This warning was sounded in Nakuru yesterday by the Vice-President and Minister for Home Affairs, Mr. Daniel Arap Moi, following Ugandan President Gen. Idi Amin's decision to expel Asians holding British passports.

Mr. Moi's statement, reported by the Kenya News Agency, was first broadcast over the Voice of Kenya yesterday afternoon.

He said the Kenya Government has no intention of "providing refuge to the 80,000 Asians holding British passports affected by President Amin's decree".

The Kenya-Uganda border, Mr. Moi said, will be sealed off against would-be refugees from Uganda using Kenya as a "calling station" and maximum border patrols will be deployed to combat "any intended influx".

Continued on Page 8

The Asian dilemma

Editorial
Reprinted with permission, ©Daily Nation, Nairobi, August 7, 1972

WORLD-WIDE interest will naturally centre on this week's meeting reportedly planned to take place between Uganda's President Idi Amin and the British High Commissioner in Kampala, Mr. Richard Slater. The topic will of course be General Amin's decision announced at the weekend that all British Asians living in Uganda must quit the country within three months, and that the British Government must assume responsibility for these British passport holders, estimated by various authorities to number between 40,000 and 80,000.

It is obvious and understandable from enquiries made in both Kampala and London, that British officials are withholding comment until after the crucial encounter. General Amin has already indicated the line he would take. He said in a nationwide broadcast that he would summon the British High Commissioner to tell him that the British

Continued on Page 6

Continued from Page 5

Asians milked the cow: They did not feed it - Gen. Amin

the processing and marketing of these crops, "although they never bent down to dig and did not know the problems of the farmers."

The motive of the Asians, he said, was to make high profits from the farmers' crops with the least investment.

He said that the siting of processing and storage facilities was done at places to suit the convenience of the Asian traders rather than the interests of the farmers. When the Asians dominated the buying, processing and marketing of farmers' crops, he said, they limited the opportunity of Ugandans to aquire knowledge and experience in the field. The foreign language they used and the family involvement in the business made it impossible for the African farmer to know the profit margin and prices.

He said that since the beginning of the co-operative credit scheme in 1961, farmers have been loaned 42,000,000/-. Today, he went on, farmers are being loaned 13,000,000/- each year. The repayment of the loans by farmers to societies and repayment from societies to banks have been very good and is considered to be the best in all developing countries.

The President said that he and his ministers have been looking for markets overseas for Uganda agricultural products but the imperialist Press has wrongly alleged that he said that Libya would buy one million bags of Uganda's coffee for £10,000,000. The General explained that Libya was a coffee quota market country and that Libya has agreed to increase her purchase of Uganda coffee. The General said Libya was prepared to help Uganda financially to enable her to carry out her economic development projects.

In conclusion, the President wished the co-operators success in their operations in the years to come.

Continued from Page 7

Ugandans Hail Move on Asians

"All this was done to frustrate African participation in trade", he disclosed.

He expressed the hope that President Amin's decision will enable Africans to enjoy the same opportunities the Asians have had for years.

"We hope we shall share the same bank facilities previously offered to only Asians as banks will have no other alternative."

But they suggested that the Government make arrangements for foreign currency exchange that would enable African businessmen to import cars and other goods.

A trader at Nakivubo Bus Park said the step taken by General Amin is the only solution to African businessmen's problems. It is far better than a scheme of the former Government on restricted trading areas, he said.

A jaggery trader at Nakivubo, near Shauri Yako Market, said the new measure taken by the government will save the country from corruption.

He said Africans have suffered greatly from the Asians who were underselling them.

Although I believe in competition, this cannot be done with Indians." Indian traders get goods from their kin and brothers—wholesalers—at a lower price than that charged to African retail traders," he said.

And in most cases Africans have been operating their businesses at a loss, he added.

Another trader at Bwaise said, "We are jubilant not because Asians are leaving, but because we are going to get a fair share in the economy of our country. For a long time we have been denied the taste of the fruits of our independence which has been tasted by only a few."

"We don't hate Asians, but their selfish attitude and unbecoming behaviour in trade with Africans."

Mr. Joseph Mukasa of 'Music Craft' near Shauri Yako, Nakivubo, Kampala said, the President's announcement is welcome to every Ugandan interested in African participation in trade and controlling the country's economy.

Africans will now get confidence from the banks operating in Uganda. He said that in the past most Africans started business from scratch as they could not get assistance from banks because they had no securities and guarantors.

This was not the case with Asians, he said.

He hoped that Africans will prosper from this new move, and that the banks will change their attitude towards Africans against when they previously discriminated.

Miss Musoke of Kawempe said, "From now on, the voice of Africans will be heard and Africans will be recognised as masters of their land."

A spokesman of East Buganda Agalyawamu Limited also praised the President's action and described it as "foresightedness."

The new move he said, will boost the country's economy which had been paralysed since the colonial time.

"It is an encouragement for African participation in commerce and trade."

Mr. Tuntua farmer of Kawolo, Kyaggwe, advised African traders to stop talking and start working like the outgoing Asian traders.

"Idle talk and excess drinking should depart with Asians for this is a time to concentrate on trade, and all our talk should be 'Trade'."

Mr. Wako, a wholesaler of Mukono says: "We are prepared for the challenge put before us and we shall always be ready to serve all people efficiently."

A salesman of Kayondo Shoe Shop said, the time was ever over-ripe.

"We have been looking forward to this move for a long time and we are sure the decision taken by President Amin is the decision of every Ugandan."

It is now the task of every Ugandan to see how we can improve our trade, commerce and industry, and also play our full role in the development of the country, he said.

He said the more Africans participate in trade, the more the money will circulate among all citizens in the country.

"Africans should work very hard to make up the time lost."

A prominent African businessman, Mr. Daudi Mukubira reserved his comment until President Amin meets the Indian and British Commissioners to Uganda and the Pakistan Ambassador today.

But he said, "We are working for the best and preparing for the worst. We shall face bravely whatever may result from the President's announcement."

President Amin has met traders from Kenya, Tanzania and Uganda and explained to them the reasons why he had decided to expel the Asians who hold British passports.

Continued from Page 5

The Asian Dilemma

Government should arrange to repatriate the Asians within the time specified.

The silence on the part of the British may be a matter of strategy. They may not wish to say anything which might prejudice the forthcoming meeting. Or it may indicate the awkward dilemma in which the British authorities find themselves. Their task has been embarrassing enough without the prospect of a huge influx of 80,000 British Asians scrambling for entry permits into Great Britain all at the same time. The current voucher system by which a limited number of British Asians are allowed into the country annually has proved completely inadequate.

Now that an ultimatum has been issued by Uganda, the British seem to have lost one of the best chances for solving the issue of Coloured immigration in general and the absorption of British Asians resident in Uganda. Judging by the tone and mood of General Amin's announcement, Uganda's generosity and patience which have so far given Whitehall time to sort out the problem, has run out. Uganda blatantly accuses British Asians of sabotaging the economy and encouraging corruption. And the prospects of Mr. Slater asking the General for a stay of execution don't seem bright, though they may not entirely be without hope. If for nothing other than humanitarian grounds, three months may prove a too congested time in which to wind up and start life anew in alien economic, social and cultural surroundings.

However, despite the outcome of the meeting between General Amin and Mr. Slater, it is certain that the British Government, whose legal and moral responsibility it is to look after and give priority to her citizens—this time British Asians in Uganda—will have to mount a crash programme to cope with the huge number of British Asians who would now rush to enter Britain.

It has been suggested in some quarters, though without very much hope, that some Commonwealth countries can help Britain out of her dilemma. Indeed Canada, for example, has indicated that it would consider the immigration of those Asians with the right skills. However, India, the country of origin of most British Asians, has taken the attitude of East African States which argues that British Asians voluntarily chose to be British and were encouraged to do so by the British Government, and so the responsibility for their future must lie with nobody else except the British Government.

Legally, the Indian and East African Governments are right. Only emotional and far-fetched argument can accuse them of abandoning kith and kin or of racialism. However, the time has come when legal niceties and clashes of interest seem to block the way for an amicable solution.

There is no easy way out and we can only hope that the present pressure from Uganda will invoke humane passions in Africa and the Commonwealth. In Africa, because on a smaller scale, we have to cope with a similar problem of immigrant Africans living, working or conducting business across their borders, while each State rightly avows to give priority to its nationals in employment, trade and industry. And in the commonwealth because the British Asians originated from friendly Commonwealth countries.

For Britain, both legal and moral obligation are binding. For the rest, a token exercise of moral responsibility can help tremendously.

Page 6   *Ugandan Asian Expulsion: 90 Days and Beyond through the Eyes of the International Press*

Ugandans Hail Move on Asians
IT WAS OVERDUE SAY AFRICANS 'GOOD LUCK' SAY THE ASIANS

By CHRIS SERUNJOGI
Reprinted with permission, ©Uganda Argus, August 9, 1972

AFRICAN businessmen in and around Kampala have hailed President Amin's reported final decision to ask the British Government to take over responsibility for all Asians and other non-Ugandan nationals, for alleged sabotage of our economy, according to an opinion survey.

Many Ugandans described the President's announcement as "a great challenge to African traders" as it meant sacrifice, patience, hard work, devotion and dedication.

One trader asked traders to come forward "in full swing" and exploit opportunities opened to them by General Idi Amin and his Military Government.

"It is time for Africans to show their capability and participate fully in the economic development of their country and also see that Uganda is economically independent," he said.

Mr. George Kalamagi, sales manager of the Simba Motors said: "I fully support the President's move, which I think is timely and, if not, overdue."

Efforts

He said that Simba Motors, which has been strongly supporting Government's efforts to bring Africans into trade, and will continue to do so.

Many Indians interviewed declined to make any comment. But two did so.

One said, "I wish African businessmen success."

The other: "We have given our service with a clean heart, and we think Ugandans will accept this. We have no quarrel with anybody and if it is the wish of the Government and the people of Uganda to see us leave, we are prepared to do so."

A motor dealer said the decision taken by President Amin will enable Africans who have been restricted in non-profit making business premises also to occupy premises on busy streets.

Many Africans, he said, are running their businesses in slums or in corners of the city because Indians did not like them to come to the centre.

"Many good premises for trade are rented to Africans at exhorbitant rents of 7000/-, 5000/- or more, while their counterparts are renting them cheaply," he said.

Continued on Page 6

Ugandans celebrate in Kampala after hearing President Amin's announcement to expel Asians from Uganda.
Reproduced with permission ©United Press International/Corbis Bettman

Tanzania says no!

News Compilation, August 10, 1972

Tanzania will not allow Asians expelled from Uganda to settle in the country, the Minister for Home Affairs, Mr. Saidi Maswanya, declared in Dar es Salaam.

He said that "our policy is very clear on this question that Uganda Asians are not our responsibility, and therefore allowing them to settle or giving them refuge was far from thought."

PRESS REACTIONS

News Compilation, August 10, 1972

LAGOS, Aug. 9—President Idi Amin of Uganda should rescind his decision to expel all Asians with British passports in the interest of the black race, the Nigerian newspaper *Renaissance* said today. In a leading article headed "Racial or what?" the newspaper said that the decision was "rash and unrealistic". "The message for the world, it would seen, is that Africans are no less racially prejudiced than Europeans", it went on.

BLANTYRE—The independent *Malawi Times* today said that President Amin's move would help neither his country's economy nor its international image.

LUSAKA—The *Zambia Daily Mail* said in a leading article that the British "outcry" over the issue was "uncalled for". It was the British Government that had encouraged these unfortunate people of Asian origin living in East Africa to take British citizenship.

DELHI—The independent *Times of India* said that the Indian Government "cannot possibly be insensitive to the fact that General Amin's unilateral and uncalled for move is a blatant act of racial discrimination".

TEL AVIV—The Israel newspaper *Maariv* said: "The ruler with the empty coffers is seeking new friends who would be prepared to pump dollars into his treasury."

OSLO—Norway's *Arbeiderbladet,* termed Britain's threat to halt economic aid to Uganda if she expels all British passport-holders an attempted smokescreen. It would mask Britain's commitment towards a group of people who had trusted her work, the editorial said. "The political responsibility in this matter rests with Britain which should take the consequence of her actions of the colonial past. The British have morally, if not legally promised the Asians a right to settle in Britain. Britain should keep the promise." it concluded.

Australia urged to admit 'token number' of Asians

News Compilation, August 10, 1972

AUSTRALIA had no obligation to take in some of the Asians to be expelled from Uganda although the Government should give a sympathetic look at any applications to migrate here, the *Sydney Morning Herald* said in an editorial today.

"Many are well educated and could bring commercial skill and resources. we could accept a token number in line with our country's needs and abilities—but the obligation ends there," the newspaper said.

"Australia has no obligation to help President Amin's Africanisation policies by acting as a receptacle for unwanted minorities," it said.

The editorial claimed that, in part, the unwanted Asians had only themselves to blame for the hostility shown by President Amin.

"A minority more sophisticated than the African, and showing little inclination to assimilate, they established a firm grip on commercial life under colonial rule. That so many retained British passports was seen as 'fence-sitting' on their allegiance to the new nation."

But, the Herald added, neither the Ugandan Government, nor the British Government "which encouraged false hopes", could shrug off the responsibility for shuttlecocking people. Nor indeed, it said, could the United Nations.

Continued from Page 9

SOME WILL STAY, SOME WILL GO

"My Government believes that one of its primary duties is to ensure the welfare of members of the community. This means, therefore, that no one section of the community can be allowed to dominated, control or monopolise the business life of the nation.

"No country can tolerate the economy of its nation being so much in the hands of non-citizens as is the case in Uganda today."

The Asian community, the President said, has frustrated attempts by Ugandan Africans to participate in the economy and business life of their own country.

Asians have used their economic power and family ties to ensure that Ugandan Africans are effectively excluded from participating in the economic life of their own country.

President Amin has directed all his ministers to tour the whole country over the weekend starting on Saturday, and to address and explain to the people the move that has been taken by the Government to expel Asians with British passports

They had refused to identify themselves with Uganda and that is why when, at the time of independence, they were offered a chance to become citizens, the majority of them turned down the offer while a few of them took out the citizenship half-heartedly, and still others retained dual citizenship.

Asians have kept themselves apart as a closed community and have refused to integrate with Ugandan Africans. Their main interest has been to exploit the economy of Uganda and Ugandan Africans. They have been milking the economy of the country by exporting illegally large sums of money from this country.

As the Government of Uganda has an obligation to put the economy of Uganda into the hands of its citizens, said the President, it would be a futile exercise to request British Asians only to leave Uganda, without at the same time requiring the nationals of India, Pakistan and Bangladesh also to leave since their presence is not in the best interests of the economy of Uganda.

"I have, therefore, today signed a decree revoking with effect from today, August 9, 1972, permits and certificates of residence granted to the above categories of persons. They are, however, permitted to stay in Uganda for a maximum period of 90 days from today.

"That means that the persons affected should make arrangements to remove themselves from Uganda during this period.

"I must emphasise that after the expiration of the 90 days period, any of those people who will still be in Uganda, will be doing so illegally, and will face the consequences."

The President made it clear that a Statutory Instrument had been signed exempting certain categories of persons within the nationals affected allowing them to stay in Ugandan accordance with the provisions of the immigration laws.

The persons exempted are those in the employment of Government, Government bodies, co-operative movement, East African Community, international organisations, professionals such as teachers, practising lawyers, medical practitioners, pharmacists, dentists, chemists, auditors, architects, accountants, surveyors, engineers; technicians in industries, commercial and agricultural enterprises; owners of industrial and agricultural enterprises; managers or owners of banks and insurance companies, owners and professionals and technicians engaged in plant, animal, agricultural and forestry departments.

The results from the recent mini-census organised by the Government last year, showed that there are 23,242 Asians claiming to be Uganda citizens. Of these, 8,791 claimed to be Uganda citizens by registration while 14,451 claimed to be Uganda citizens by birth.

However, records available to Government indicate that the number of Uganda citizens of Asian origin is smaller than 23,242.

For that reason, the President had directed the Ministry of Internal Affairs to verify the number of the claims. Therefore, all those persons claiming to be Uganda citizens will be called upon to produce documentary proof in support of their claims of Uganda citizenship.

Measure

"It will be appreciated that the above decisions and measures taken to implement them necessitate taking certain security measures. Therefore travellers to or from Uganda are requested to co-operate with security forces and immigration officers at the points of entry or departure.

"Travellers leaving Uganda by road are requested to have with them their current motor vehicle registration books, valid insurance certificates and valid driving permits to establish ownership of the vehicle and identity of the driver.

"We are not asking the British of Asian origin to leave Uganda because of racism. We are not racists. We have no animosity against Asians or any other foreigners for that matter.

"The Government has taken this decision purely in the interest of the economy of this country. The Government has the support of the entire 10 million Ugandans in the measures it has taken."

When members of the Armed Forces took over on January 25, 1971, the President said, he was charged with the responsibility of ensuring that the economy of this republic is put into the hands of Ugandans.

In reply to questions from Pressmen, the President said that he was not against the British Government, and added that Britain was responsible for the Asians because they were brought in Uganda by the British. He denied that the Government of Uganda was preparing transit camps for the Asians who will still be in the country after the statutory period had expired.

Asked what he would do if some Asians refuse to leave by the given period, the President said: "Wait, you will see. I want to tell them that those who will not leave during the given period, they will be sitting on fire. You will see what will happen. But I advise them to leave before the period expires."

For the purposes of verifying the population of Asians in Uganda, the President said that Mr Oboth-Ofumbi is going to be full Minister responsible for the Ministry of Internal Affairs and that immigration offices in Kampala will be opened daily with effect from today to September 10, inclusive until the exercise is over. In the meantime the President will be responsible for the Ministry of Defence.

Mr Oboth-Ofumbi said the offices will be open daily including Saturdays and Sundays from 7 a.m. to 7 p.m. to take their documentary proof with them to the immigration office in Kampala starting from today until August 19. Eastern Region excluding Jinja urban area from August 20 to 26; Buganda Region, excluding Kampala and Entebbe urban areas from August 27 to 31; Western Region from September 6 to 10.

Asians in Uganda are "London's baby" and Britain should "change its own nappies", the Kenyan assistant Minister of Home Affairs, Mr Shikuku said. Mr Shikuku, who was speaking in his capacity as an M.P., said that he supported President Amin's decision to expel British Asians in his country.

British Minister to visit Amin

News Compilation
August 10, 1972

House of Lords, London—LADY TWEEDSMUIR OF BELHELVIE, Minister of State for Foreign and Commonwealth Affairs, in a statement on events in Uganda affecting Asian holders of United Kingdom passports, said.

On August 9 President Amin confirmed to our High Commissioner that all Asians in Uganda who are holding British passports must leave the country within 90 days. The same order is to apply to Asians in Uganda holding Indian or Pakistan citizenship.

Though he stated that there would be a number of exceptions, including employees of government, professional people, owners of industrial and agricultural enterprises and others, the effect of this order as it stands is that the vast majority of Asians in Uganda who cannot prove that they have local citizenship must leave the country in the stated period.

Our High Commissioner in Uganda was able to see the President beforehand and made strong representation against the proposed expulsion order. He also conveyed to him a message from the Prime Minister.

It is a very serious political situation. To ask any country to suddenly have an influx of people of this magnitude is really extremely damaging to those concerned and also to the country of reception.

In view of the serious situation that would arise if the order were carried out, it had been decided, with President Amin's agreement, that the Chancellor of the Duchy of Lancaster should visit Kampala in the very near future to discuss the whole matter.

Mr Rippon's visit was to see whether the President could have second thoughts. We feel it is inhumane to the people concerned to suggest that people who have spent their lives in Uganda should suddenly be asked to uproot themselves. It is for this reason that Mr Rippon is making his journey.

Mr Rippon will also visit Nairobi and Dar-es-Salaam for discussion with the Kenyan and Tanzanian Governments, with whom we have been in touch. We are also in touch with the Governments of India and Pakistan who now have a common interest with us in this matter.

Continued from Page 5

Kenya shuts the door to Uganda Asians

The Principal Immigration Officer, Mr. Jonathan Njenga, told the NATION later the situation was "quite normal" and had not been "immediately affected by the Uganda situation".

The Ugandan authorities had disclosed that the necessary security checks were in force at the borders.

Travellers arriving in Nairobi by road from the common border areas reported, in the wake of Mr. Moi's statement, that they had noticed "unusual vigilance by border guards".

SOME WILL STAY, SOME WILL GO

BY WILLY MUKASA
Reprinted with permission, ©Uganda Argus, August 10, 1972

ASIANS HOLDING BRITISH PASSPORTS AND NATIONALS OF INDIA, PAKISTAN AND BANGLADESH—EXCEPT THOSE IN ESSENTIAL OCCUPATIONS—WILL HAVE TO LEAVE UGANDA WITHIN THREE MONTHS. THIS FINAL ORDER CAME YESTERDAY FROM THE PRESIDENT, GENERAL IDI AMIN, WHO TOLD A PRESS CONFERENCE AT THE COMMAND POST, KAMPALA THAT HE HAD SIGNED A DECREE TO THIS EFFECT WHICH CAME INTO FORCE FROM AUGUST 9.

Present were the British High Commissioner, Mr Richard Slater; the Indian High commissioner, Mr Dharma Deva; and Pakistan Ambassador, Air Vice-Marshal Khan; and elders of the Asian community.

The move, said the President, had not been motivated by racism as it had been alleged in some quarters, but because the Uganda Government's primary duty is to ensure the well being of her citizens.

The President said he had convened yesterday's meeting because he wanted to announce his final decision on the question of the Asians in Uganda.

He recalled that on August 4, this year, when he was addressing troops at Tororo, he announced the decision of his government asking the British government to take over responsibility for the British citizens of Asian origin living in Uganda, who were "sabotaging the economy of the country" and were practising and encouraging corruption.

He further recalled that in his message to the nation on August 5 on the occasion of the Co-operative International Day he had elaborated on his announcement and made it clear that British citizens of Asian origin whose continued presence in Uganda was no longer in the country's best interests would be given three months within which to leave the country.

Continued on Page 8

Pakistan's Ambassador, Air Vice-Marshal Khan (left) & British High Commissioner, Mr. Richard Slater (right) were among those who attended President Amin's (center) press conference announcing the signing of the decree expelling the Asians.
Reproduced with permission ©Archive Photos/Camera Press

Cold-comfort curry

Amin asks Asians to lunch, then issues new threat

STEPHEN HARPER
Reprinted with permission, ©Daily Express, London, August 10, 1972

Kampala-THE latest blockbuster from General Amin in his "war" to boot the Asians out of Uganda came at a lunch which he gave today for the leaders of the people he plans to expel.

The lunch of curry and cold chicken was served on the flat roof of General Amin's private villa, with the blue waters of Lake Victoria shimmering in the distance.

NERVES

Among the guests were 15 leaders of the 80,000 Asians—mostly Indians and Pakistanis who run much of Uganda's business. The 15 Asian representatives were understandably nervous as they toyed with the curry. The top British diplomat at the luncheon—Mr. Richard Slater, the High Commissioner—looked apoplectic.

A little earlier in the day Mr. Slater had been granted a private interview with General Amin—but the general refused to disclose in advance what he intended to say at the luncheon. The blockbuster came immediately after the coffee. General Amin, a burly figure in dark blue battledress with paratrooper's wings on his breast, pushed back his cup, rose from the table and

Continued on Page 10

PREPARATION BEGINS FOR ASIAN INFLUX

By JOHN KEMP
Social Services Correspondent
Reprinted with permission, ©Telegraph Group Limited, London, August 10, 1972

THE Government is to set up a standing committee of ministers and officials whose job will be to make contingency plans in the event of thousands of Asians streaming into Britain from Uganda.

Mr Carr, Home Secretary, announcing the plan in the Commons yesterday, said that intense diplomatic activity had been initiated by Sir Alec Douglas-Home, Foreign and Commonwealth Secretary, to try to ward off "this threatened very inhumane treatment" of Asians in Uganda.

The standing committee was to be set up to watch day-to-day developments in the situation, said Mr Carr.

They would make sure all action is taken to try to avert the threat hanging over these people and decide "what contingency plans may be made if President Amin does not yield to reason and appeal."

Continued on Page 10

Reproduced with permission, ©Times of India/R.K. Laxman

Continued from Page 11

UGANDA ASIANS JOIN THE QUEUES FOR EXODUS

made up of Asians who are stateless.

Leading Asians in Uganda estimate that the number of their people in "essential occupation" who have been exempted from the decree will amount to no more than 10,000, including wives and families.

The exempted category includes all types of professional people and "owner of industrial and agricultural enterprises and mangers or owners of banks and insurance companies." Most Asians in Uganda are "Dukawallahs"— small shopkeepers who are far removed from any exempted category.

Professional Asians in Uganda said yesterday that they were assuming the exemption would include wives and families, although this point has not yet been clarified by the Government.

In the streets of Kampala, where more than 90 per cent of the shops and businesses are Asian-owned, there was an air of fatalistic resignation following the President's decree.

One shopkeeper said: "We cannot sell because there is nobody prepared to buy."

British officials and Asian leaders have no doubts that most of those displaced from Uganda will seek entry to Britain. But senior members of the Asian community have been quick to point out that educational standards of East African Asians are considerably higher than "others from India and Pakistan who have gone to Britain."

Apart from the shopkeepers, those seeking entry to Britain are likely to include a high proportion of artisans and clerical workers.

President Amin reaffirmed yesterday his determination to expel non-citizen Asians by November 7.

Commenting on London reports of a British move to bring Commonwealth pressure to bear on him, the President said: "I have made up my mind—finish."

The British, he said, were the "Kings of Imperialism" and he was not taking any imperialist advice.

Mr Richard Slater, the British High Commissioner in Kampala, called briefly at the Foreign Ministry yesterday.

It is understood he delivered a message for the President from Sir Alec Douglas-Home.

Radio Uganda, reported that messages of congratulations to the President on his move against the Asians had been received from African businessmen throughout the country. Many business groups were planning celebrations to mark the event, said the radio.

The President has instructed his Ministers to tour the country during the weekend to explain his action.

Strict border control was maintained at all frontier posts in Uganda to prevent illegal removal of property. At Entebbe, Uganda's international airport, all travellers must report two hours before take-off to undergo rigorous baggage searches.

Continued from Page 9

PREPARATIONS BEGIN FOR ASIAN INFLUX

Spokesmen for the Foreign and Home Offices said last night that no details were yet being released of the composition of the Committee, but presumably both Mr Carr and Sir Alec will be involved.

25,000 expected

Mr Praful Patel, secretary of the all-party Committee on UK Citizenship, said last night that of 57,000 Asian holders of British passports estimated to be in Uganda, about 25,000 would probably want to go to Britain and the remainder to India.

Most of those coming to Britain would be likely to have relations or friends living here, and in the short term could probably seek shelter with them.

Figures issued yesterday show that nearly 40,000 foreigners and Commonwealth citizens were granted British Citizenship in 1971.

The Home Office document shows that 28,081 were Commonwealth citizens, including 6,081 Pakistanis, 6,063 Indians, 2,695 Cypriots, 2,571 Jamaicans, 1,769 Guyanese, 1,381 from Mauritius and 961 from Barbados. There were 990 from the Irish Republic.

Among aliens, those granted citizenship were 1,479 Poles, 662 Germans, 485 South Africans and 355 Hungarians.

Few citizens

The number of Pakistanis and Indians in Britain who have taken out British nationality is still a small proportion of the total numbers living here it is thought.

It is estimated that about half a million Indians and another 225,000 from Pakistan and Bangladesh now live in Britain, and the majority hold on to their original nationality.

The majority came on work vouchers issued to Commonwealth citizens in the past 10 years, and after living in Britain for five years, have an automatic right to citizenship.

The numbers seeking British nationality are expected to show a steep rise this year. Pakistan recently agreed to allow dual nationality to Pakistanis in Britain, and many more Indians are being encouraged by community leaders to take out British citizenship.

Only those who take out citizenship will be able to travel freely in the Common Market. Some see it as an "insurance" against being made to leave the country if Britain ever adopted the same policy towards non-citizens as has President Amin.

Continued from Page 9

Cold-comfort curry

strode over to a throne-like armchair.

In a statement which took 20 minutes to read he announced that he had revoked the residence permits of more than 50,000 Asians. He persisted in his original demand that they must be out of Uganda within 90 days, and he added this new threat:—"I must emphasise that after the 90-day period has expired, any of these people still in Uganda will face the consequences. *They will be sitting on a fire, and they will not sit comfortably."*

General Amin spelled out that the Asians who must go included those holding British passports and others whom he described as citizens of India, Pakistan and Bangladesh.

TENSE

The leaders of the Asian community became more and more tense. Then the atmosphere eased a little as the General listed Asians who are to be exempted from his expulsion order.

They include doctors, dentists, lawyers, civil servants, bank managers, and owners of industrial and agricultural enterprises.

General Amin said there were 23,242 Asians who claimed to be citizens of Uganda. They must provide documentary proof—original birth certificates.

The General glowered at Mr. Slater and said Uganda would hold Britain responsible for the removal of Asians with British passports who were not on the exempted list. DANIEL McGEACHIE writes: Whitehall officials believe that if General Amin cannot be persuaded to change his mind, the British Government will have no alternative but to honour its responsibility and allow Asians who have British passports to enter this country. The number in Uganda is estimated at 57,000.

The Government has set up a group of Ministers and officials to consider contingency plans.

Continued from Page 11

UGANDA'S ASIAN ASSET

clannish way) must be set the enormous contribution of the Indians and other Asians to the economies of East Africa. It is not, after all, their fault that they tend to work harder, be more conscientious and thrifty, and are arguably more intelligent, or at least more highly qualified, than the African majority. The Asians cannot help existing where they do and it is absurd and illogical to argue that because they usually prosper others correspondingly suffer. In the average East African township the people are excellently served by the local Asian small shopkeepers and artisans. Where they have perforce left, as in parts of Zambia, in commercial terms they have been sorely missed; the Africans on the whole have not had the capital in any event to buy what were Asians' shops. Britain should use all her influence to persuade Uganda's Ministers, for their own sakes, of these hard facts.

UGANDA ASIANS JOIN THE QUEUES FOR EXODUS

By CHRISTOPHER MUNNION in Kampala
Reprinted with permission, ©Telegraph Group Limited, London,
August 11, 1972

UGANDAN ASIANS, many of them still stunned and bewildered by President Idi Amin's three-month ultimatum for them to leave the country, queued calmly outside official buildings in Kampala yesterday to prepare for their exodus into the unknown.

The largest queues formed outside the city clinic, where families sought vaccinations needed for travel to Britain. The clinic is handling several hundred cases daily. Outside the British High Commission, orderly groups of Asians holding British passports gathered to register as British citizens and seek advice on their status.

There were no signs of panic although British officials expect the number of Asian callers to increase daily following the expulsion order.

Military police were on duty at the Ministry of Immigration building where Asians who have claimed Ugandan citizenship have been instructed to present their credentials for verification.

Rules tightened

Banks reopening after a three-day closure were immediately filled with scores of worried Asians inquiring how much money they could take out with them.

Foreign exchange regulations have been tightened since President Amin's "notice to quit." Previously banks could let emigrants take about £1,000 with them. Now all travel allowance applications must be referred to the Central Bank.

During a census last year 23,000 Asians claimed Ugandan citizenship but in announcing his expulsion decree on Wednesday, President Amin said Government figures indicated that the number of Ugandan Asian citizens was much smaller.

It appeared yesterday that many Asians who called at the Ministry were having their citizenship disputed because they could not produce the correct documentation required.

Officials and diplomats in Uganda trying to make an accurate assessment of the numbers of Asians expected to be involved in the exorcism are being hampered by the lack of reliable registration information.

They agree that the minimum number who will seek entry to Britain within the next 90 days will be 50,000 men, women and children.

This figure could well increase as many claims to Ugandan citizenship are expected to be rejected by the Government. The number of Asians in Uganda is officially estimated at 80,000 of whom 23,000 claim Ugandan citizenship. British officials in Kampala estimate the number of those entitled to British passports at about 55,000.

"Essential jobs"

India, Pakistan and Bangladesh citizens who are also affected by the expulsion order number more than 4,000 according to diplomatic sources in Kampala. The remainder of the 80,000 total is

Continued on Page 10

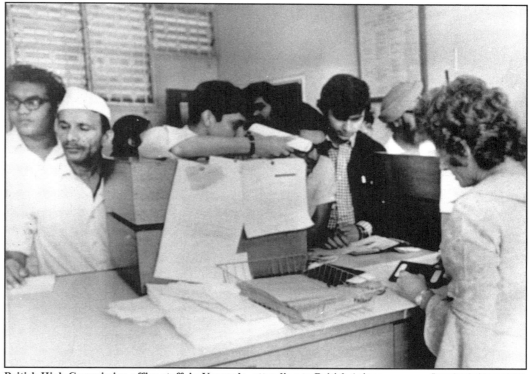

British High Commission office staff, in Kampala, attending to British Asians. Reproduced with permission, ©United Press International/Corbis Bettman

Scene outside the British High Commission in Kampala. Reproduced with permission, ©Associated Press/Wide World Photos

UGANDA'S ASIAN ASSET

Editorial
Reprinted with permission, ©Telegraph Group Limited, London,
August 10, 1972

THERE IS INDEED TRUTH in the criticism of a leading Nigerian newspaper that the decision of President Amin of Uganda to expel all Asians (except certain professional people) with British passports could do a lot of harm to Africa's "image." At least as important, it could do a great deal of harm to Uganda's economy. As Kenya seals its borders against an influx of Asians from Uganda, the President should consider, before it is too late, the benefits which accrue to the Ugandan economy from their presence. No doubt it is partially true, as he says, that the importation of Asians into Africa to—among other things—build Britain's railways there was a mixed blessing for all concerned. Certainly in subsequent decades many of the Asians have been tactless—to put it no higher—in concentrating in what have been virtually ghettoes, set apart from the mainstream of African life. There they have tended to perpetuate their primordial Asian social customs; and in business no doubt they have tended to favour each other.

Yet against these demerits, which are considerable sins in African eyes (although people throughout the world tend to behave in such a

Continued on Page 10

Asians in East Africa: A Plight Rooted in Colonialism

By Ndalo Raburu Kobilo
Reprinted with permission, ©Washington Post, August 12, 1972

The writer, a native and citizen of Kenya, is presently an instructor in history at Federal City College.

NEWS REPORTS that President Amin of Uganda has ordered some 80,000 Asians in his country to depart within three months can hardly have failed to provoke sympathetic consideration in the United States. But I would point out that the question of Asian plight in East Africa is a historic one and deeply rooted in the genesis of the colonial system in East Africa as a whole. It can not be properly analyzed apart from the system itself.

The history of European settlement in East Africa is also the history of Asian settlement there. The coming into power of leaders of independence uncovered its political and socio-economic aspects. The "erratic" leadership of General Amin, if such it is, only capitalized upon an already existing problem that had never been squarely faced.

Throughout their long stay in East Africa, the evidence indicates, Asians never valued East Africa as a possible permanent home. By avoiding social interaction with Africans, they also remained isolated from the European community with which they strive to identify. To some thoughtful Asian leaders, like Nehru, the writing was already on the wall. Following India's independence in 1947, Nehru warned Asians to adjust and identify with the interests of the countries in which they were residents.

There is no substantial indication that Asians in East Africa took the Indian philosopher seriously. In East Africa, the phrase "standing on the wall" became a common vocabulary used to describe the Asian attitude toward African nationalism. They never thought it possible that Africans, by themselves, would ever become heads of state.

IN EAST AFRICA British governors had been replaced by black leaders, and independent East African states began to change passports. Asians, however, still were not yet sure whether independence had been achieved. They still found homage in British citizenship and held on to their old passports. By then, British personnel were already leaving for Europe. Asians remained in East Africa.

Their arrival dates to the 19th century. They were recruited by the British to build the East African railways system to connect East African trade with the rest of the world. At the opening of the Kenya highlands for settlement, Asians had sought equal share with the British. When the British whites pressed their demand upon the Colonial Office in London for representative government in Kenya, as a step to the establishment of a white dominion, Asians demanded equal representation. As the colonial system flourished, Asian businesses began to expand. It was like two partners sharing in the system. But at home, India itself was under colonial rule, and these Asians could not have mistaken the nature of their relationship with either Africans or with Europeans.

The British controlled the entire system politically. Asians controlled the economy—wholesale and retail businesses, industries and shops. In major Asian businesses and industrial houses, Africans were found only as "boi," house servants, or as office boys. The bulk of their buyers were Africans. I would challenge any researcher to come out with facts to show that Africans ever treated Indians with indignity in East Africa.

Asians also maintained control in the job market in East Africa. Outside their own enterprises, Asians were also found in government offices as clerks, accountants, auditors, cashiers. In railways administration, they were ticket examiners, station masters, clerks, cashiers, guardsmen, etc. Socially, they remained a closed community. They never intermingled with Africans in jobs, in social activities, or even on an intellectual level.

Yet the fact that Europeans with whom they were always seeking to identify had never accepted them equally should have served to them as a warning. The failure of the Indian community to relate to Africans served as a deterrent to Asian and African communities coming together.

IF PRESIDENT AMIN'S or any other East African leader's action with regard to the status of Asians in East Africa were to be attributed to a particular leader's personality, we would be doing a disservice to East African history. For example, I would not tolerate an act simply aimed at discriminating against Asians because they are a different people. Nor would I support any attempt to lump together those Asians who, by becoming citizens, have made their home in East Africa, with those who have all along resisted the trend of nationalism. By the same token, Uganda or East Africa as such are not resorting to severe measures which have no precedent. Every country has laws aimed to give prior consideration to its own citizens. For a new nation like Uganda, the need for jobs is a major question of priority to which no leader would be unconcerned. Sometimes it may mean slicing Asian businesses or demanding that such businesses provide for the inclusion of Africans as shareholders. The priority is national and the question is how far Asians are nationally committed to a national spirit that will determine their status.

In December, 1967, Kenya passed a law which required non-Kenyans to obtain a working permit. Early in 1968 Asians rushed with their British passports to catch their flight to Britain. According to The Washington Post, there are now about 140,000 Asians in Kenya, 105,000 in Tanzania, and about 80,000 in Uganda. Amin himself took over the presidency of Uganda only in January 1971. Under the circumstances, and for Amin, there is no doubt that the expulsion of Asians could provide him a political gain.

Americans must be educated to the history that goes into the making of the current symptoms. To say that Asians are simply hated in East Africa would be a wrong assumption. Likewise, it

1968 demonstration in Britain against proposed bill restricting Asian Immigration.

Reproduced with permission ©Archive photos/Express News

would be futile to think that the Asian expulsion is of Amin's own making. There is history behind it. As long as it remains unsettled, there will always be some problem.

My own view would be that the mere expulsion of these Asians may not be the answer. The real needs of economic policy of East African countries would call for a joint approach. This would aim at coordinated operations to ensure Africans jobs in various industries and businesses, and opportunities to become shareholders in enterprises. Fair distribution of the wealth with emphasis on communal rather than individual interests, with governmental guidelines, might be one way. By itself, as a political theme, Asian expulsion is far from a solution.

AMIN SNUBS RIPPON ON ASIANS

Talks delayed as Minister flies out

By PETER THORNTON
Reprinted with permission, ©Telegraph Group Limited, London, August 12, 1972

MR GEOFFREY RIPPON flew to Uganda last night for talks with Gen. Amin on Uganda's decision to expel 50,000 Asians holding United Kingdom passports despite a last-minute snub.

As Mr Rippon was on his way to Heathrow, a Uganda Government spokesman in Kampala said Gen. Amin would be "too busy" to see him until Tuesday.

It had been understood earlier in Whitehall that Gen. Amin was prepared to meet Mr Rippon, who is Chancellor of the Duchy of Lancaster, today.

Mr Rippon, who is going to Uganda as a special envoy in his capacity as a Foreign Office Minister, had expected to be back in London on Tuesday after visits to Kenya and Tanzania.

A report that General Amin could not see him until Tuesday was passed to Mr Rippon as he waited at Heathrow for his plane to Kampala.

Mr Rippon took the news calmly.

Smoking a cigar and smiling, he said: "The meeting will have to be before Tuesday. It has all been arranged and I assume it will take place tomorrow."

The Government is hoping that Mr Rippon can persuade Gen. Amin to have second thoughts about his decision to expel Asians holding United Kingdom passports within 90 days.

A Uganda Government spokesman in Kampala said last night that Gen Amin could not meet Mr Rippon until Tuesday "because of the tight programme of His Excellency the President."

It is understood that one of the President's commitments today is to address a meeting of Ugandan students—at which he will reiterate his determination to expel the Asians.

"Damaging influx"

In the House of Lords earlier yesterday Baroness Tweedsmuir, Minister of State, Foreign Office, made it clear that while Britain accepted its obligation to receive holders of United Kingdom passports, Mr Rippon would ask Gen. Amin for a resumption of the orderly arrangement for immigration.

The present quota for East African Asians is 3,500 a year.

"We do feel it is inhumane to those concerned to suggest that people who have spent their lives in Uganda should suddenly be asked to uproot themselves," Lady Tweedsmuir said.

"To ask any country to have suddenly an influx of people of this magnitude is really extremely damaging to those concerned, and also the country of reception."

Lady Tweedsmuir added that the Government was in touch with India and Pakistan. They had a common interest in view of General Amin's similar threat against Asians of India and Pakistan citizenship. If General Amin persists in refusing to meet Mr Rippon until Tuesday, it is possible he will visit Kenya and Tanzania first.

British envoy Geoffrey Rippon (left) chats with Asians outside the British High Commission in Kampala.
Reproduced with permission ©United Press International/Corbis Bettman

INDIA Visas to check influx from Uganda

"The Times of India" News Service
Reprinted with permission, ©Times of India, August 12, 1972

NEW DELHI, August 11: The government of India has decided to introduce, with immediate effect, a visa system to prevent the entry into India of a large number of British passport-holders (of Indian origin) from Uganda.

Announcing this in the Lok Sabha today, the deputy minister for external-affairs, Mr. Surendra Pal Singh, said: "the government is not oblivious of the fact that many of the affected persons have social, cultural and traditional links with India, and the visa system will make adequate provision for these requirements."

As regards Indian nationals resident in Uganda, the number registered with the Indian High Commission there is about 3,000. Details are being awaited as to how many of these would come within the purview of the Ugandan government's new decisions.

ASSURANCE GIVEN

"We have always viewed with understanding the aspirations of African countries to regulate their international affairs in the best interests of their citizens," Mr. Singh said.

"We are in touch with the Ugandan authorities and I can assure the house that we shall do everything we can to protect the interests of Indian nationals there and ensure that those who might eventually be affected are treated equitably, humanely and with dignity."

On August 4, President Amin of Uganda had announced that British passport-holders of Asian origin in Uganda would be required to leave the country within three months.

On August 9, President Amin called a meeting in Kampala of the high commissioners of the U.K. and India and of the envoy of Pakistan to apprise them of his government's decision.

A full report of the meeting is being awaited from the Indian High Commissioner in Kampala. But certain categories of persons, details about whom have not yet been specified, would be exempt.

He said "as far as British passport-holders were concerned it had been the stand of the government that "U.K. nationals are entirely the responsibility of the U.K. government and are entitled to free entry into the U.K. without discrimination."

Advertisement

PAKISTAN CITIZENS RESIDING IN UGANDA

All Pakistan Citizens are required to register on 12th and 13th August, 1972, Mr Amanullah Khan, Second Secretary, Embassy of Pakistan, will be at HOTEL EQUATORIA on the above days to register Pakistan Nationals.

Pakistan Citizens residing in Uganda who have not yet registered themselves with the EMBASSY OF PAKISTAN at Nairobi for the year 1972 are, in their own interests, requested to contact him along with their passports for registration between 9 a.m. to 12 noon on the above two days.

Signed: **AMANULLAH KHAN**
Second Secretary
Pakistan Embassy, Kenya.

Britain will let Amin's Asians in

by COLIN LEGUM, Commonwealth Correspondent
Reprinted with permission, ©The Observer, London, August 13, 1972

THE British Government has decided to admit all Ugandan Asians entitled to British passports who are under General Amin's three-month expulsion order. The numbers involved may be anything between 25,000 and 50,000, though other Commonwealth countries are being asked to take some of the Asians.

Britain's decision will be conveyed to Uganda's military ruler by Britain's envoy, Mr Geoffrey Rippon, Minister without Portfolio.

At a Press conference in Kampala yesterday afternoon, Mr Rippon confirmed that the Government accepted ultimate responsibility for UK passport holders. He pointed out, however, that there were responsibilities on both sides, and Britain did not expect friendly Governments to act in the way Uganda had done.

'People cannot be treated like cattle,' he said. The British Government would like to discuss the problem as between friends.

Mr Rippon referred to the difficulties of arranging a meeting with President Amin and said he would not be returning to Kampala to see President Amin on Tuesday.

Unless Amin finds time to arrange an appointment for this morning the two men will not now meet.

Asked if he felt he had been snubbed, Mr Rippon replied that 'a snub' did not worry him personally. People must make their own deductions about why General Amin had not seen him. He had changed his mind in the past; he might do so again. 'The great thing was to get the atmosphere and the people calmer.'

General Amin won thunderous applause from a mass rally of university students in Kampala yesterday when he told them he was not going to change his plans for the unwanted Asians.

The President was wearing the uniform of a paratroop general. His speech was noteworthy for a tough warning against robbing and looting the Asian families liable to expulsion.

He disclosed that—in the first substantiated incident of its kind—two police in the small town of Masaka demanded goods worth £200 from an Asian trader.

'They might have killed him,' General Amin said. 'I don't want this to happen again. We have got to buy everything from the Asians and not behave like robbers.'

Mr Rippon went to Kampala to negotiate three main points with General Amin. First, a reasonable extension of the present ultimatum to allow more time for an orderly withdrawal. Secondly, an enlargement of the category of exemptions already made for Asians whose departure would injure Uganda's economy. Thirdly, proper compensation for the property and businesses of British Asians, and their right to transfer their cap-ital over a reasonable period.

These concessions are the most the British Government now thinks can be obtained from General Amin. They accept that he is unlikely to be persuaded over his decision to expel the bulk of the country's 80,000 Asians.

Of these about 3,000 are Indian citizens and a few hundred Pakistan or Bangladesh. Some 23,000 are Ugandan citizens, but their fate is still uncertain.

Some Asians who acquired Ugandan citizenship in earlier years became stateless last week when Government immigration officials cancelled their citizenship certificates because of technical faults. The Asians failed to produce birth certificates or documents showing renunciation of their previous citizenship.

This new category of stateless Asians could become the most difficult to deal with, unless India agrees to admit them on compassionate grounds.

Continued on Page 16

Few havens for Ugandan Asians

Reprinted with permission, ©Times Newspapers Limited, London, August 14, 1972

The crisis in Uganda has given rise to the question whether there is any refuge other than Britain for the dispossessed Asians. Correspondents of *The Times* report reactions.

Roger Choate writes from Stockholm: The Government is maintaining a studied silence on whether Ugandan Asians would be permitted to flock to Sweden in view of the neutral country's liberal laws regarding refugees and military deserters.

For years the Social Democratic Government has practised an open-door policy towards military deserters, and has admitted political dissidents and refugees from East and West.

Diplomatic circles recalled that almost 300,000 deserters and refugees had found sanctuary in Sweden by the end of the Second World War. Since then more than 600 deserters or men evading military service in America, Britain, France, Israel and other countries have settled here.

One sticking point is whether the Ugandan Asians are refugees in the strict sense of the word, in view of the fact that they hold British passports. Government newspapers have been censorious of Britain's immigration policies towards Asians and Africans with British passports, describing them as racist.

Political commentators in Stockholm made it clear that the Government of Mr Olaf Palme views the plight of the Ugandan Asians as an ugly legacy from Britain's colonial past, and declared that London must assume responsibility for their fate.

The country is only now emerging from last year's

Continued on Page 16

DIPLOMATIC SETBACK FOR RIPPON

Kenyatta, Nyerere talks in doubt

Reprinted with permission, ©Telegraph Group Limited, London, August 14, 1972

MR RIPPON, Britain's special envoy on the problem of East African Asians, who left London on Friday hoping for talks with the presidents of Uganda, Kenya and Tanzania, will probably return home tomorrow night without meeting any of them.

Gen. Amin, of Uganda, was not available to see him at the weekend; President Kenyatta, of Kenya—where Mr Rippon arrived last night—was "up country" 100 miles from Nairobi and a meeting with him was in doubt; and President Nyerere, of Tanzania, has told Mr Rippon that he has a previous engagement.

The Foreign Office is considering taking the case of the 50,000 Asians facing expulsion from Uganda to the United Nations, but no decision has yet been reached.

Holiday camps and Army barracks may be used as temporary accommodation for expelled Asians. Most towns in Britain where there are already large Asian populations say they could not cope with a heavy influx of new immigrants.

In an attempt to enter Britain without permits Asians are paying high prices to use an illegal route through Italy, says R. Barry O'Brien.

Amin gets letter

By CHRISTOPHER MUNNION in Nairobi

MR RIPPON, Britain's special envoy on the Ugandan Asian crisis, flew from Entebbe to Nairobi yesterday, having failed in his mission to hold urgent talks with President Amin.

He had hoped to have talks with President Kenyatta on the problem this morning, but the Kenyan leader is visiting an up-country area 100 miles away and Mr Rippon is due to fly on to Dar es Salaam at midday.

But diplomatic sources in Nairobi were still hopeful that a meeting could be arranged.

President Nyerere of Tanzania has said that although he would like to meet Mr Rippon, he has long standing engagements in the country and will not be able to see him in Dar es Salaam.

Apparently unruffled by President Amin's refusal to see him until tomorrow, Mr Rippon disclosed he had left a personal letter for the Uganda President in which he called for talks on the practicalities of the threat to expel at least 50,000 Asians within the next three months.

"I did not come to Uganda to threaten and cajole but to discuss", he said. "We must discuss problems involving tens of thousands of human beings calmly, sensibly and rationally."

Continued on Page 16

Page 14

Ugandan Asian Expulsion: 90 Days and Beyond through the Eyes of the International Press

THESE ASIANS ARE REQUIRED TO REPORT

Reprinted with permission, ©Uganda Argus, August 15, 1972

THE Government has decided that all those Asians who claim Ugandan citizenship and who will not have reported to the Immigration Office by September 10, 1972, to verify their claims will automatically lose their claims for Uganda citizenship and will henceforth be regarded as non-citizens of Uganda.

This has been announced by a spokesman of the Ministry of Internal Affairs who recalls that as previously announced, the verification of claims for citizenship by Asians claiming to be Uganda citizens will end on Sunday, September 10. The timetable for reporting to the Immigration Office per Region and certain urban areas has already been published.

The spokesman also reminds all British citizens of Asian origin, and citizens of India, Pakistan and Bangladesh affected by Decree No. 17 of 1972, that the last date for surrendering all firearms and ammunition they have under the provisions of the Firearms Act to the nearest Police Station is before noon on Wednesday, August 16.

The spokesman further states that as announced on Thursday, August 10, all persons affected by Statutory Instrument No. 124 of 1972 will have to register themselves with the Immigration Office, Kampala, with a view to ascertaining whether they qualify to stay in Uganda under the provisions of that statutory instrument.

The time-table for reporting to the Immigration Office, Kampala, is as follows:

1. Those living in Kampala and Entebbe Urban areas should report between August 15 and 16 inclusive.

2. Those living in the Eastern Region, including Jinja Urban areas should report between Sunday August 20 and 26 inclusive.

3. Those living in Buganda Region but excluding Kampala and Entebbe Urban areas should report between Sunday and Thursday, August 27 and 31.

4. Those living in the Western Region should report between Friday, and Tuesday September 1 and 5 inclusive.

5. Those living in the Northern Region should report between Wednesday, and Sunday, September 6 and 10 inclusive.

Continued on Page 18

Asians reach out for application forms, handed out by a police officer, outside the offices of the British High Commission.
Reproduced with permission
©United Press International/Corbis Bettman

Rippon to meet Gen. Amin in Uganda today

By CHRISTOPHER MUNNION in Kampala
Reprinted with permission, ©Telegraph Group Limited, London, August 15, 1972

In a dramatic switch of policy President of Uganda last night extended a formal invitation for talks with Mr Rippon, Britain's special envoy to Uganda on the Asian expulsion crisis.

The message was relayed to Mr Rippon on board an East African VC-10 airliner flying from Dar es Salaam to London. During a transit stop at Nairobi Mr Rippon who had earlier been snubbed by President Amin, was told the Ugandan leader was prepared to meet him today.

Mr Rippon agreed that he and his party of Foreign Office officials should disembark at Entebbe during a 45-minute refuelling stop to accept the invitation.

He was greeted at the airport by Uganda's acting Foreign Minister. Later, Mr Rippon arrived in Kampala, where he will meet Gen. Amin today.

Continued on Page 18

Schools prepare for 19,000 Uganda-Asian children

By RICHARD BOURNE, Education Correspondent
Reprinted with permission, ©The Guardian, London, August 15, 1972

Plans for the possible reception of up to 19,000 school-age Asians from Uganda are being drawn up by the Department of Education and other Government departments.

Unless the Government decides to direct the arrivals, one London borough could find itself with up to 10,000—an increase of nearly a quarter on a child population which has already risen by a fifth since 1965.

The pattern of settlement of East African Asians suggests that they would concentrate in a handful of boroughs—a clutch round London including Brent, Haringey, Barnet, Ealing, Hounslow, and Harrow, and a few elsewhere, of which Leicester is the most notable.

Miss G. M. Rickus, chief education officer for Brent, said yesterday that she was writing to the Secretary for Education, Mrs Thatcher, about the problems of accommodation that could arise. Brent would be happy to welcome the Asians so long as the central Government authorised the spending of money on emergency buildings, she said. "We have no spare capacity in our schools.

"Out of about 3,000 special vouchers recently available for East African Asians, about 1,300 families came here, and we have spent an extra £210,000 on extensions to secondary schools which are now pretty well filled."

Brent could have nearly 10,000 children arriving suddenly. "We should then need permission to spend just over £500,000, merely to provide for the minimum of hutted accommodation," she added.

Brent, where there are still labour shortages and shops and other businesses have grown up to serve the Asian communities, is likely to maintain its attraction for arrivals. They have mainly settled in Wembley.

The need for teachers will depend on the number of children who do not speak English. In 1968, when non-English-speaking children were

Continued on Page 18

Continued from Page 14

Few havens for Ugandan Asians

economic recession, and unemployment is still regarded as unacceptable by the Social Democratic planners. Immigration in any form is being discouraged, and a sudden influx of new settlers could well produce an adverse reaction from Sweden's equivalent of the Trades Union Congress.

Michael Knipe writes from Cape Town: Appeals to the South African Government to allow "a substantial number" of the Ugandan Asians to settle in the country have been made by two leaders of the Indian community. There is little likelihood of the Government taking such action, however.

The remoteness of the possibility can be judged from the fact that it was only as recently as 1961 that the Government recognized that South Africa's Indians were a permanent part of the Republic's population.

Richard Wigg writes from Buenos Aires: At first sight Latin America theoretically might offer a haven for Ugandan Asians—for over the years several hundred thousand Japanese have built new homes for themselves in countries as differing as Brazil and Peru, Paraguay and Argentina.

Yet subtle and complex immigration restrictions do exist in Latin America. Highly important is the skill immigrants offer. Unfortunately the Asians as businessmen, shopkeepers and doctors face native competition in already over-recruited fields.

Stewart Harris writes from Canberra: Australia will not resettle any significant number of British Asians from Uganda. Last year the total number of coloured people with British passports settling here was about 150 and very few of these were from Africa.

Dr A.J. Forbes, the Minister for Immigration, said firmly: "The question of any action beyond our normal policy has not arisen and we do not expect it to arise."

Our Wellington Correspondent writes: The New Zealand Government will probably respond sympathetically to any appeal to resettle Asian families expelled from Uganda though the number admitted is likely to be tiny in relation to the scale of the problem.

Mr David Thomson, the Minister for Immigration, is to study a request from the National Council of Churches for the Government to make immediate provision on humanitarian grounds for the entry of a limited number of families. The minister has said: "Provided it is a refugee situation, the Government's position has usually been positive."

Our Delhi Correspondent writes: Delhi may allow Ugandan Asians to enter India on "a selective basis", according to informed sources. The case of every entrant will be considered on "its merits".

Rawalpindi Aug 13. The Pakistan Government will wait for fuller details before making concrete decisions in the case of British passport-holding Pakistanis being expelled from Uganda, Foreign Office sources said today.

Continued from Page 14

Britain will let Amin's Asians in

The British Ministerial group dealing with the crisis is believed to have come to the following firm conclusions:—

The situation in Uganda now requires Britain to fulfill the undertaking given to Parliament in 1968 by the Labour Home Secretary, Mr James Callaghan, during the passage of the Commonwealth Immigrants' Act. He said any British Asians evicted from East Africa would be admitted to Britain.

There will be no shuttlecocking of Ugandan Asians who might find their way to British ports.

Under no circumstances will British Asians be left shut up in Uganda with nowhere to go and subjected to the pressures of the Amin regime.

Considerable progress has already been made in British planning for on orderly exodus from Uganda.

The guiding principle is the avoidance, if at all possible, of a sudden mass arrival of Asians within the next three months.

The present plan is to get the co-operation of India and Pakistan for Ugandan Asians to be shipped, in the first place, mainly to India. On arrival there they would be given the choice of staying in India or, within a reasonable time, coming on to Britain or to other Commonwealth countries who are being asked to help.

New Zealand has already responded well to this idea, Canada is also taking in East African Asians, and Australia might be persuaded to follow suit.

The success of this plan depends on India's co-operation. Negotiations now going on in New Delhi give some cause for hope. The first tangible sign is to be found in India's decision that all British Asian citizens must have British visas before being allowed to enter.

Since these visas would have to be issued by the British High Commissioners in East Africa, they would give India the fundamental assurance she has sought—that Britain accepts final responsibility for all British Asians.

This planned exodus, however, can occur only if Uganda's neighbours agree to allow Ugandan Asians to cross their territory to the nearest ports. Kenya and Tanzania both sealed their borders last week to prevent Ugandan Asians escaping into their countries and an airlift from Kampala to India is impracticable because of the numbers involved.

East African Airways, the airline operating domestic services throughout Uganda, Kenya and Tanzania, has announced that all Asians have been banned from using its flights. The move, which applies to Asians regardless of nationality, is part of a campaign by the East African Governments to control the movement of Asians affected by General Amin's expulsion order.

Mr Rippon is visiting Kenya tomorrow and Tanzania on Tuesday to seek the co-operation of Presidents Kenyatta and Nyerere.

Kenya's anxieties are, first, that Ugandan Asians in transit might try to 'disappear' locally; and, secondly,

that the sight of large numbers of Asians passing across Kenya might feed the anti-Asian feelings rampant there. Already there are demands that Kenya should follow Uganda's example.

President Kenyatta is anxious to damp down these pressures against his own more careful policy of co-operating with British in a more orderly departure of the 75,000 British Asians waiting for vouchers in Kenya.

Mr Rippon will be concerned to explain the impossibly difficult situation that would be created for the British Government if Kenya's leaders, encouraged by General Amin's policies, tried to speed up the exodus of Asians from Kenya.

President Nyerere is not under the same kind of pressure as President Kenyatta. He might, therefore, be more willing to allow the exodus to take place through Dar es Salaam. The difficulty of this route is that there is no direct railway line from Ugandan to Tanzania. This would call for a massive airlift.

While Anglo-Tanzanian relations have been seriously strained in recent years, there has in the last few weeks—quite fortuitously—been a rapprochement between the two countries involving negotiations for the restoration of British aid to Tanzania.

Although these contingency plans are now being pressed forward vigorously, the dramatic nature of the exodus would be greatly reduced if General Amin could be persuaded to extend his deadline by anything up to three years. It has been left to Mr Rippon to judge what British concessions of financial aid might be offered to General Amin to secure this badly needed extension.

Apart from this major objective, Mr Rippon's other principle concern is to damp down the signs of panic which have taken hold of Uganda's Asian community and which show signs of spreading to Asians in the rest of East Africa.

Mr Rippon yesterday received a cable addressed to him by 'your Monday Club colleagues'—a pointed reminder of his former influential role in the right-wing Conservative pressure group.

The cable drew Mr Rippon's attention to a proposal sent to Sir Alec Douglas-Home by the Monday Club's Immigration Group for the immediate establishment of a transit and holding centre on any available Indian Ocean dependency 'to cope with any sudden outflow of Ugandan Asians while the British Government brings home to Indian and Pakistan Governments their responsibilities for their ethnic communities in East Africa.'

In London an 'Admit the British Campaign' group marched to 10 Downing Street. While 50 people picketed with placards, a seven year old black girl led a delegation to deliver a letter asking Britain to scrap her entry voucher system for immigrants from East Africa.

The letter warned that when General Amin's deadline expires he 'will do something desperate to send them out of Uganda.' It added: 'We don't believe that the public would prefer to see them suffer violence or starvation.'

Continued from Page 14

Diplomatic setback for Rippon

The problem required many meetings at many levels "Given that a government has a policy which it is determined to pursue it has to be pursued in a humane and orderly manner."

No magic wand

During his flight to Kenya, Mr Rippon reiterated to me that Britain was prepared to accept its responsibility for British passport-holding Asians from Uganda. "However unreasonable and inhumane the policy of

expulsion might be, we have to accept that responsibility.

"Britain will do the best we can but we cannot wave a magic wand. We cannot solve the situation created by the Ugandan Government. We have to do our best to protect them and give them sanctuary."

Mr Rippon did not see any Ugandan official during his 36 hours in Kampala. He said that before he left London on Friday his visit had been cleared and he had been given to understand that he would be welcome.

One of the most disturbing aspects of the situation he had discovered in Kampala was that Asians who had

Ugandan citizenship were having their documents torn up.

"Ugandan citizens do not automatically become United Kingdom citizens because their papers have been torn up. It's not just a case of receiving them in the United Kingdom. It is a question of their rights as British passport holders."

In Kampala yesterday, President Amin startled a conference of Roman Catholic bishops from all parts of Africa when he launched into an attack on "British imperialism." Britain was engineering religious strife in Uganda and deceiving the world he said.

Rippon smooths way for Asians from Uganda

By CHRISTOPHER MUNNION in Kampala
Reprinted with permission, ©Telegraph Group Limited, London, August 16, 1972

TWO hours of "fruitful and friendly" talks between President Amin and Mr Rippon, Britain's special envoy, yesterday failed to change the Ugandan leader's plans to expel 55,000 British Asians within the next three months.

But Mr Rippon flew back to London last night having agreed on procedures aimed at easing the practical problems involved in organising the departures.

These provide for:

Extra British staff to be drafted to the High Commission in Kampala to help with documentation processes; and

Ugandan Government officials to maintain close contact with the commission.

During the talks President Amin indicated that expelled Asians who had not been able to leave by his Nov. 7 deadline would be permitted to remain in transit camps in Uganda until their departures could be organised.

President Amin gave an assurance that the Asians and their property would be guaranteed protection and the they would be compensated for businesses and property they had to leave behind.

Chicken lunch

Relations between Britain and Uganda, which appeared close to breaking point last week, were revived after four days of diplomatic manoeuvring which began with President Amin's snub to the British Minister and ended with an amiable chicken lunch on the terrace of State House in Entebbe.

When Mr Rippon and his party of officials learned that President Amin was not prepared to receive them within 48 hours of their arrival last Saturday they flew on to Kenya and Tanzania, proclaiming their determination to stick to a schedule which would return them to London on Monday night.

But, aware that President Amin had announced on the State radio that he would receive Mr Rippon on Tuesday, Mr Rippon ensured that his return flight from Dar-es-Salaam would be one making a refueling stop at Entebbe, Uganda's international airport. British High Commission officials notified the Ugandan Government of this fact, mentioning that a formal invitation for talks would be welcome.

The invitation was extended late on Monday night and relayed to Mr Rippon, already on his way, in transit at Nairobi. The British party, wearied by 6,000 miles of unsuccessful travelling, disembarked at Entebbe at midnight to an official welcome, leaving their baggage on the London-bound airliner. Yesterday morning they arrived at the official residence for the delayed talks.

Continued on Page 18

NEW WARNING BY MOI

Reprinted with permission, ©Daily Nation, Nairobi, August 16, 1972

THE Kenya Government will take drastic action against any Kenya Asian who is found giving refuge to or harbouring Asians ousted from Uganda, the Vice-President and Minister for Home Affairs, Mr. Daniel Arap Moi, has warned.

Mr. Moi said any British Asian passport holder "who might have sneaked into the country secretly" had done so illegally and his or her presence in the country was illegal and undesirable.

He warned those who might have done so that they must report to the Kenya immigration authorities immediately. Severe punishment would be meted out to the culprits or the parties concerned if they were found out, he said at a fund-raising meeting for Kabunout Harambee Secondary School in Bomet, Kericho District, on Monday.

Mr. Moi emphasised that Kenya's stand on the issue of British Asians, either from Uganda or Kenya, is "crystal clear", adding: "the Government has categorically stated that Kenya is not a dumping ground for people from other countries to come and loiter about."

Continued on Page 18

100 Ugandan Asians Stranded in Tanzania

News Compilation, August 16, 1972

The Tanzanian Daily News reported that about 100 Ugandan Asians with British passports are unable to return to Uganda.

Sources reported to the paper that East African Airways Corporation had directed its offices in Tanzania not to issue tickets to any Asian going to Uganda until further notice.

The newspaper also reported that some Asians from Uganda have been denied entry to Tanzania.

Rippon flies to see Heath today over stalemate
Gun-totin' Amin won't back down on Asians

From BRIAN PARK in Kampala
Reprinted with permission, ©Daily Mail, London, August 16, 1972

Uganda and Britain were as far apart as ever last night after the crucial two-way talks over expelled Asians broke up in stalemate.

Britain's Geoffrey Rippon failed to get any time extension for the 87,000 told to be up, out and far away within 90 days.

Uganda's leader, President Idi Amin, would not give an inch—and hinted that some Asians might be under way much sooner.

And it was that gap, between just when and how you shift so many people without suffering and hardship, that marred any hope of a settlement.

It led, too, to the only sharp note the two men allowed to peep through after their three-hour talks.

Glowering from a red- leather chair emblazoned, God and my country, Amin, wearing a paratroop general's uniform and with a pistol strapped to his waist, snapped firmly: 'I will not accept any delaying tactics.'

Quietly, Mr Rippon from the seat alongside replied: 'We're not concerned with tactics—just reality.'

The General parried questions about how the Asians could be physically moved by coming up with the idea that British battleships—'You have quite a number used in the last war'—should be pressed into the removal business.

'If not that—the Americans have quite a few ships in Vietnam'.

Glimmer

He appeared to give a glimmer of hope when tackling further questions about just what would happen to the very many Asians still expected to be around after 90 days.

He said the British Government and the Red Cross would have to 'make them camp where they can stay while they are waiting to go to Britain and elsewhere'.

Continued on Page 18

Asians quitting Uganda arrive under guard at Mombasa

By NATION Reporter
Reprinted with permission, ©Daily Nation, Nairobi, August 16, 1972

EIGHT UGANDA non-citizens holding Indian passports arrived in Mombasa from Uganda by train yesterday, under strict escort. The Asians, five adults and three children left Uganda following President Amin's quit order to non-citizen Asians.

Guarded by policemen, the Asians were not allowed to talk to people apart from Customs officers and other workmen at the railway baggage hall. They had a few boxes each containing personal belongings.

One of the group, Mr. M. S. Panesar, asked me when I approached him: "Have you got permission from the police to talk to me? You know we have been under constant escort by police and

immigration officers right from the Uganda-Kenya border until we arrived here. You can see them; they are still here."

Mr. Panesar was accompanied by his mother, sister and his brother-in-law, S. Dheraj, who has three children.

A supervisor with the Superior Construction Company, Kampala, Mr. Panesar held a British passport but received a visa for India on Saturday.

He lived in Uganda for 11 years. "I would like to live there but we have now been kicked out and I have to go where I belong," he said.

Mr. Panesar, whose wife is in India, said it was terrible to be ordered out of a country where one lived for years without being given enough time to wind up one's business.

Continued on Page 18

Ugandan Asian Expulsion: 90 Days and Beyond through the Eyes of the International Press

Page 17

Continued from Page 17
NEW WARNING BY MOI

The Vice-President said the Kenya Government, under the inspired leadership of President Kenyatta, conducted its affairs openly without using "underhand methods".

He directed that British Asians who pass through Kenya to their destinations will not be allowed to stop over even to "say hello" to their friends in any of Kenya's towns or centres. "They must take the most direct route to whatever their destinations."

Touching on Asian British passport holders resident in Kenya, the Vice-President said they would also have to leave for their country of citizenship when their time came "and as arranged by the Kenya Government". He stressed there would be no change as far as their position was concerned.

Mr. Moi went on to say that Kenya's borders would continue to be sealed off to ensure that "undesirable elements" did not gain entry into the country.

He appealed to the police, particularly those stationed at the centres near the Kenya-Uganda border, to maintain vigilance and be on the lookout for such elements.

Continued from Page 15
Schools prepare for 19,000 Uganda-Asian Children

still few, the borough set up a language centre designed to do experimental work with Jamaican children. Since then, with the arrival of more Asians, it has doubled its capacity, and a further increase may be necessary if large numbers of Ugandan Asians have difficulties with English.

Mr A. J. Davis, the chief education officer of Leicester said: "We are living with these problems anyway. We have had an average of 100 children coming here from overseas every month this year and about 350 children are unplaced for next term. Any increase on the rate we have been admitting would cause considerable strain but we are not getting dramatic about it."

A couple of months ago, Leicester was allowed to spend an extra £50,000 on minor works to cope with the arrivals. Mr Davis accepted that the Ugandan deportation could result in 2,000 to 3,000 children reaching the borough. "In primary education we would have to put up a systems-built school in two to three months; we have a site available," he added.

Leicester would then need additional teachers with some special skills and it would try hard to avoid letting a few schools have a high percentage of immigrants.

Mr Davis confirmed that he had already held discussions with his senior staff. Other local authorities which may be involved seem to be reacting more coolly. Mr G. F. Crump, chief education officer of Preston—which has 1,550 Asian children, only some of whom have come by way of East Africa—said that the town was "taking note" of the facts of the Uganda expulsions.

The Department of Education said: "Much depends on whether the Government decides to direct the families to particular centres." The Department had already had practice at handling sudden migrations and could authorise quickly money for building and the employment of extra teachers.

Baden Hickman, our Churches Correspondent, writes: Contingency plans for the arrivals in Britain of Ugandan Asians and their families are being prepared by a welfare committee set up by the community race relations unit of the British Council of Churches and a number of voluntary agencies. Yesterday the committee discussed the possible use of church premises as temporary accommodation, and prepared plans for appointing a number of welfare officers.

Continued from Page 17
Rippon smooths way for Asians from Uganda

First came a stroll around the grounds, where the president pointing out to Mr Rippon the trees planted during successive Royal visits to Uganda. Then came lunch and a toast to the Queen and to further fruitful and friendly discussions between the two Governments.

With his senior ministers on one side and Mr Rippon on the other, President Amin then conducted a Press conference in which he professed once again that the British were his best friends but that British Asians would have to leave in his decreed 90-day period.

The operation would be carried out in friendly and fruitful co-operation, he declared.

Did he think it was physically possible to move tens of thousands of people in the prescribed time?

"I think the British have many battleships they used during the war and the Americans have battleships in Vietnam," he replied.

The British Government would have to assist the Ugandans in providing camps for displaced Asians

where they could stay to await transport, he said, adding that Uganda had some new hospitals, not yet in use, which might serve this purpose.

"No delaying tactics"

Mr Rippon, reasserting that Britain accepted responsibility for British passport-holding Asians who would be displaced by the decree, said practical problems would be dealt with as they arose.

The President intervened. "We in Uganda are working day and night on this. I will not accept any delaying tactics."

Mr Rippon, attempting to retain the early cordiality, could not help riposting: "We are not talking about tactics but about reality."

Britain would attempt to deal with the removal as speedily as possible and he had been reassured by the President's insistence that lives and property of Asians would be protected, that property would be valued, and that payments would be made.

Continued from Page 17
Gun-totin Amin won't back down on Asians

He even volunteered an empty hospital 'which can be in use immediately for transit'.

Meanwhile Mr Rippon agreed with President Amin to set up a working relationship to deal with the matters practically.

He said the High Commission staff in Kampala would be strengthened to process Asian applications to enter Britain. And Amin agreed that his Ministers and officials would co-operate.

Mr Rippon expects to return to Uganda in October.

He also said the General had reassured him that the lives of the Asians would not be in danger, and that his Ministers would make arrangements to enable them to sell their property at what he called 'proper prices'.

Decision

Mr Rippon is expected to report personally to Mr Heath soon after he returns to London this morning.

A decision will then be taken on whether a meeting of senior Ministers should be held later today or tomorrow to review plans for handling the refugees.

The fact that the Cabinet's special envoy is going back to Kampala in October suggests that a more reasonable line may still be taken.

In NAIROBI, Vice-President Daniel Arap Moi said drastic action would be taken against any Kenyan Asian giving refuge to the expelled Asians.

Continued from Page 17
Asians quitting Uganda arrive under guard at Mombasa

"My brother-in-law and my sister have left behind their furniture, cars and other household goods, to the value of £2,000 and a house," he said.

"We are now going to start a new life in India, just like beggars."

Indian passport-holder Mr. Adrian Vaz has lived in Uganda for 22 years. His family went to Goa about three years ago," he said.

Mr. Vaz, a former electrician with Kilembe Mines, decided to leave Uganda before the expiry of the quit notice because he could not send any money to his family.

He, too, complained that he left behind property, including money. "I do not have even a traveller's cheque and my ticket to Bombay was paid by my company," he said.

They leave today on board the s.s. Mozaffari for Bombay.

Continued from Page 15
Rippon to meet Amin today

Offhand receptions

Mr Rippon had earlier said he intended to stick to his itinerary which brought him to Uganda on Friday for urgent talks with President Amin. These never materialised and Mr Rippon flew on to Kenya and Tanzania for talks with the Presidents or Tanzania and Kenya.

He was met with very offhand receptions in both of these capitals, not seeing any official in Kenya and having only brief meetings with Tanzanian officials.

But Mr Rippon had deliberately asked for his return flight to London to be switched so that he and his team made a transit stop at Entebbe. The British High Commission in Kampala was advised that he would be "passing through" Entebbe at midnight last night.

On the flight into Uganda Mr Rippon told me: "This was a precaution. We were simply allowing for all contingencies. Call it Plan B if you like."

Continued from Page 15
These Asians are required to report

The Immigration Office will be open throughout the days specified above from seven in the morning to seven in the evening daily, including Saturdays and Sundays.

Application forms for registration will be issued at the Immigration Office and must be filled out on the spot. The details of documentary proofs qualifying them to stay in Uganda are as follows and must be produced by the applicant when reporting to the Immigration Office. All documents must be in their original form and no duplicates, photostat copies or carbon copies will be accepted.

83 Asians headed to Uganda sent back by ship to India

By NATION Reporter
Reprinted with permission, ©Daily Nation, Nairobi, August 17, 1972

EIGHTY-THREE Asians with British and Indian passports who arrived in Mombasa by sea from India on Tuesday on their way to Uganda were refused permission to land and sent back on the same vessel yesterday.

The group, told on arrival they would not be able to re-enter Uganda, is travelling on the s.s. Mozaffari, which sailed from Mombasa for India yesterday by way of Dar es Salaam.

Women were in tears when they learned they could not return to their husbands after holidaying in India. Thirty-six of the passengers held Indian passports, the rest British. They included men, women and children.

The Assistant Commissioner for India in Mombasa, Mr. B. R. Sharma, and officials of the Shipping Corporation of India,

Continued on Page 20

Reproduced with permission, ©Times of India/R.K. Laxman

Ugandan Cites British 'Insult'

By Jay Ross
Washington Post Staff Writer
Reprinted with permission, ©Washington Post, August 16, 1972

Britain has been "insulting" in its dealings with Uganda over the expulsion of British Asians in the East African country, according to Ugandan Foreign Minister Wanume Kibedi.

The foreign minister said in an interview here Monday that Britain did not even inform Uganda that Cabinet member Geoffrey Rippon would visit Kampala to discuss Uganda's action ordering 80,000 Asians with British passports to leave the country within 90 days. Kibedi said he first learned of the visit from a BBC broadcast.

Rippon arrived in Uganda last Saturday, but left for Kenya the next day without seeing President Idi Amin. Rippon did return to Uganda Monday and saw Amin yesterday.

Kibedi, who spent two days here en route home from last week's nonaligned nations' conference in Guyana, said, "Britain has been extremely arrogant over the question" of the expulsion of the Asians. Most are Indians and Pakistanis.

The British Asians are Britain's responsibility, Kibedi said, adding that the two countries had discussed the matter for several years before Amin ordered their expulsion last week.

Britain indicated that it would not change its policy of restricting entry to 3,500 Asian families from East Africa yearly, Kibedi said. Therefore, Uganda ordered the expulsion.

Continued on Page 20

East Asians Without a Country

Editorial
Reprinted with permission, ©Los Angeles Times, August 16, 1972

Eleven days ago the president of Uganda, Gen. Idi Amin, announced that all East Asians who are not citizens of Uganda must leave the country within 90 days. The expulsion order affects at least 55,000 of the 80,000 Indians and Pakistanis who live in Uganda. The figure may be higher, since even Asians with Ugandan citizenship are being harassed by the government and told they are not welcome. The question is, where are these unfortunate people to go?

Continued on Page 20

Kampala fear that more will become stateless

From Our Correspondent, Kampala, August 16
Reprinted with permission, ©Times Newspapers Limited, London, August 17, 1972

Several hundred Asians here have been deprived of their Ugandan citizenship on technicalities during the first week of a "verification campaign" ordered by President Idi Amin. By the time the campaign ends next month more than half Uganda's 23,000 Asian citizens may find themselves stateless.

Ostensibly the verification campaign is designed to weed out Asians who have obtained Ugandan citizenship by corrupt means or who have shown their lack of faith in the country by retaining dual nationality. Few deny that many such cases exist.

However, the way in which the procedures are being applied suggests that from the start the Ugandan authorities have had a rather more general objective in view. As General Amin put it earlier this week: "If all of them go I'll be very, very happy".

Under a presidential directive all Asians here claiming to hold Ugandan citizenship must report to the immigration authorities within the next four weeks to prove their claims. Today, while a queue of Asians two or three abreast stretched several hundred yards down Kampala's main street, Asians emerging from the Immigration Department headquarters told me why their citizenship claims were being rejected.

Many said they had been told that they had renounced their British citizenship more than three months after being registered as Ugandans, which is contrary to Ugandan law. Some admitted that this was so, but claimed that the fault lay with the Home Office in Britain, which had taken several months to process their papers.

Others said they had lost their citizenship because the certificates of renunciation sent to them from London were carbon copies of originals retained by the British authorities.

Yet others had lost their original renunciation papers and could produce only photocopies, albeit authenticated with the Home Office seal. Photocopies and duplicates are not being accepted.

A fourth group said the Ugandan Central registry page number had been omitted from their birth certificates. This, too, was held to be sufficient ground for revocation. Some said their renunciation certificates had been torn up, while others said their Ugandan passports had been confiscated.

General Amin has denied that immigration officials have been destroying Asians' documents. The contradiction may be explained as the result of Asians' exaggerations, or by the fact that while

Continued on Page 20

Moi tells Uganda Asians in Kenya to report

News Compilation, August 17, 1972

THE Vice-President and Minister for Home Affairs, Mr. Daniel arap Moi, said in a statement yesterday that all persons of Asian origin at present in Kenya who are Uganda citizens and those who are holding re-entry facilities to Uganda, are to report in person to the nearest Immigration Department office either in Nairobi, Mombasa or Kisumu with their passports "within three days of this announcement".

"This instruction means all such persons, including those holding entry permits, pupils' passes, dependants' passes, visitors' passes and any other type of pass issued under the Kenya immigrations laws," the statement said.

Council Warning

News Compilation, August 17, 1972

Ealing Borough Council has warned the Government that the borough's housing and educational difficulties will increase if more Asian immigrants are allowed to settle there.

Brent Borough Council has appealed to the Government for help, if necessary, to deal with Uganda Asians flooding into the Wembley area which already has a big Asian community.

Continued from Page 19

83 Asians sent back by ship to India

agents for the ship, went on board yesterday before it sailed to meet the travellers. All of them had valid entry permits, visitors passes or special passes for Uganda. President Amin's decision to expel Asians came while they were on the high seas.

One of the women, controlling tears, said in broken Swahili that her husband and children were in Uganda. "I do not know what will happen to them or when I will see them," she wailed.

Thirty-four year-old Damodar K. Nimavat, a building supervisor with the Madhvani Group in Kakira, Uganda, told me: "I went to India on two months' leave and I was going back to work. I was shocked when I learned that we were not allowed to enter Uganda."

Flanked by his wife, Mr. Nimavat added: "All my life-savings and everything of mine is in Uganda. At least on humanitarian grounds, we should be allowed to go there and wind up our business and collect whatever is of necessity to us."

He holds a British passport. "I do not know where I am going to settle now. I do not have a visa for England and India might throw me out," he said.

A 52-year-old carpenter, Tahel Singh, had gone to India on a four-month visit and was returning to his own business in Kampala. "I do not know what to do next. I did not leave anyone at my workshop and all my property is now lost," he said.

A fitter with Mulco Textiles in Jinja, Mr. N. V. Nandha, said he had been on five months' leave. He had worked with the company for the last six years and had a two-year work permit.

Married with two children, Mr. Nandha said: "I do not know what is going to happen to my provident fund, apart from my personal property in Uganda."

Nine of the passengers were girl students who had completed their studies in India.

Also on the ship as it returns to India are eight Uganda non-citizens with Indian passports who were sent from Uganda to Mombasa under police escort after President Amin's quit order.

Continued from Page 19

Ugandan Cites British 'insult'

A British embassy spokesman in Washington denied Kibedi's allegation about Rippon's visit, saying that he went to Uganda after the visit was approved by Amin.

The spokesman said Britain is "keeping all options open" in seeking a solution that would minimize human suffering. He repeated that Britain accepts "responsibility" for Asians holding British passports, but he added that the arrival of a large number in a short time could cause a strong popular reaction among Britons and damage relations with Uganda.

The Ugandan foreign minister said that, although Asians constitute only about 1 percent of Uganda's population of 10 million, they control about 90 per cent of the country's retail and wholesale commerce. He denied that Uganda's move was racist and said his country was just trying "to assure elementary rights for its people."

"The fault is at the door of Britain because of racialism" restricting entry of British subjects on the basis of race, he said.

"Uganda wants people who are useful to the country but not leeches sucking the blood of the country," Kibedi said.

There has been some dispute over the number of Asians subject to expulsion. Britain has said 55,000 have British passports and another 23,000 hold Ugandan citizenship.

Uganda has ordered 80,000 to leave, and Kibedi said that is the total number of British Asians. He said there are 23,000 who claim Ugandan citizenship. But he said these claims are subject to verification since some Asians have forged documents.

The foreign minister said exceptions to the expulsion will be made for British Asians who are in government, the professions or farming.

Accusing Britain of "economic blackmail" by threatening to cut off its aid to Uganda, the foreign minister said the annual British aid of nearly $12 million was "peanuts." Britain is free to cut it off, he said. British Foreign Minister Sir Alec Douglas-Home has said that Britain would "review" its aid to Uganda in light of Amin's eviction of the Asians.

It has been reported that Uganda is receiving aid from Libya and Saudi Arabia and that the expulsion of Israeli advisers and military men last spring and Amin's recent criticism of the United States were linked to that aid. But Kibedi denied that there is any Arab aid. There has been speculation that Amin, who ousted President Milton Obote in a military coup in January 1971, is using foreigners as scapegoats to divert attention from internal problems. He has faced economic difficulties and political dissension.

Uganda reportedly spent $100 million on defense in the last fiscal year, proportionately more than any other country in Africa. Lately, there have been reports that Uganda is having difficulty buying arms because it cannot pay.

Amin publicly demanded U.S. withdrawal from Vietnam when the new U.S. ambassador, Thomas Melady, presented his credentials last month. Last week, the government recognized the Provisional Revolutionary Government of South Vietnam (the political arm of the Vietcong).

Kibedi said, however, that relations with Washington are good and that Uganda is calm and on the road to recovery from its economic problems last year after Amin's takeover.

Continued from Page 19

Fear that more will become stateless

General Amin believes the revocation to be justified, the Asians do not.

Whichever view is accepted, and it can be argued that cases of bribery by some Asians in the past explain the present toughness towards all Asians, the net result is going to be immense hardship.

A 15-year-old Asian boy explained to me on the steps of the British High Commission here that he and his brothers and sisters were Ugandans by birth but that his parents, who were Ugandans by registration, had lost their citizenship. Would his parents be allowed to go to Britain and take himself and their other children with them, he wanted to know.

The same story was repeated over and over again. A stateless teacher with a Ugandan sister. An elderly British Asian couple with stateless children. A stateless doctor, educated at Oxford, with British parents.

The only hope for these people is that either Uganda will relent or Britain will agree to absorb them together with the 50,000 or so British passport holders here. Neither possibility seems likely.

Continued from Page 19

East Asians Without a Country

Nearly all non-citizen Asians in Uganda hold British passports. They were given the opportunity for citizenship, along with other Asians in East Africa when Britain ended colonial rule in the early 1960's. The fact that most Asians opted for British citizenship instead of adopting the nationality of the countries they were living in added to the resentment that has long been held against them in East Africa.

The resentment is founded on economic envy and racial differences. Like the Overseas Chinese of East Asia, the Indians and Pakistanis of East Africa are strongly represented in retail trade, commerce and the professions. Their success has inevitably added to their unpopularity. So has their separateness. In addition to accusing the East Asians of economic exploitation and corruption, Amin has also made an issue of their refusal to intermarry with Africans. It is a curious point in an area where intertribal marriage, let alone interracial ones, are often frowned upon.

Amin's action is not the first threat against Asians in East Africa, and it may not be the last. Kenya, Tanzania and Malawi all have sizable Asian minorities. Again, many of these persons are non-citizens with British passports. They are vulnerable to racial and nationalistic antagonisms. And they contribute to what is a very serious problem for Britain.

The moral responsibility of Britain to those who hold British passports is clear, though it is far from simple. For more than four years London has strictly controlled immigration of Asians and Africans, a policy begun by the former Labor government in the face of rising, domestic racial tensions. Those tensions—economic and social—remain, and given the present high rate of unemployment in Britain, they could be brought to the flash-point if a major influx of Asians were to be permitted. The situation is not helped by India's lack of interest in receiving uprooted East Asians, or for that matter, by their uninterest in going anywhere except Britain.

Britain's efforts so far have concentrated on gaining time by having Amin modify or delay implementation of his expulsion order. As yet, there are no signs of success. The East Asians of Uganda remain under a suspended sword, and so does Prime Minister Heath's government in London.

Page 20   *Ugandan Asian Expulsion: 90 Days and Beyond through the Eyes of the International Press*

Uganda Asians rush to report to Kenyan authorities

By NATION Reporter
Reprinted with permission, ©Daily Nation, Nairobi, August 19, 1972

THE Nairobi Immigration Department yesterday was "rushed" by Uganda Asians currently in Kenya who were responding to the order by Vice-President Mr. Daniel arap Moi that all Uganda citizens of Asian origin at present in Kenya, including those holding re-entry facilities to Uganda, must report to the nearest immigration office with their passports within three days from last Wednesday.

They included wives of Kenya Asians who are Uganda citizens and have been staying in Kenya on dependants' passes. They also included Asians holding British passports who have been ordered by President Amin to return to Uganda.

Mr. M. Lalji, a Uganda Asian with British passport, said his wife and son are Kenya citizens. Relating some of his problems, he said he had been refused a ticket to Uganda by East African Airways and firms operating passenger buses to Uganda.

The Mombasa Immigration Office reported an "influx" of Uganda citizens of Asian origin.

An Immigration Officer in Mombasa, Mr. Tom Kifworo, told a KNA reporter that an increasing number of Asians had been reporting to his office in response to the Vice-President's directive.

Most of these people were wives of Kenya citizens holding Uganda passports while others were holiday-makers or just visitors on short-term passes, he explained.

Mr. Kifworo thought that if the number of Asians checking in at the Mombasa office continued to rise, it might not be possible to complete their processing within the three-day deadline.

Meanwhile, long queues of Asians were yesterday morning seen outside the immigration office in the town where officials busily processed their documents.

Asians expelled from Uganda could be 'a benefit to Britain'

News Compilation, August 17, 1972

Uganda Asians expelled by General Amin could be a benefit to Britain Mr John Ennals, Director of the United Kingdom Immigrants Advisory Service, said yesterday. After a meeting in London at which 20 organizations connected with community relations and immigrant welfare agreed to cooperate in helping to settle any Uganda Asians, Mr Ennals said many of the people affected spoke English and had skills which could be very useful in Britain.

The organizations which attended the meeting at the National Council of Social Service included the Race Relations Board, the Community Relations Commission, the National Council of Social Service, the British Council of Churches, the Joint Council for the Welfare of Immigrants,

Continued on Page 24

Thousands rendered stateless as faults are found in their papers
Asians queue to beat citizenship deadline

News Compilation, August 19, 1972

Kampala—Several hundred Uganda Asians tonight prepared to camp outside the immigration department here, some of them for the second night running, in an attempt to beat the Government's deadline for the verification of their Ugandan citizenship.

Under a directive from President Amin, all Asians here holding Ugandan passports must produce their original citizenship documents to the immigration authorities by the middle of next month to have their claims checked. The exercise is being carried out by regions. For the Kampala area, where most of the Asians live, it is due to end tomorrow night. Any Asian holder of a Ugandan passport who has not reported by then will automatically lose his citizenship.

Some applicants were asked to produce additional documents and told to return tomorrow. Others, and these were the majority, were shown faults in their papers. Of the 23,000 Asians who claim to be Ugandan citizens, more than half are being told that their citizenship is invalid on some technicality or other. They are rendered stateless.

Another category of Asians holding British or Indian citizenship formed a short queue. They were applying for exemption from the expulsion decree, under which 60,000 Asian non-citizens must leave Uganda within the next three months.

When the expulsion policy was announced just over a week ago General Amin said professional people and owners of agricultural and industrial enterprises would be able to claim exemption. Yesterday he said he had reconsidered that decision. Asian professional people would also have to leave, because "they could not serve the country with a good spirit after the departure of other Asians."

Long lines of Asians formed at the British High Commission, where extra staff are dealing with a flood of passport applications. Additional officers will start arriving from London at the weekend.

Officials today were making contingency plans to cope with the mass of work that will arise once the British Government announces officially that it will admit Ugandan holders of British passports. About 40,000 British Asians will want to move themselves and as many of their belongings as they can take with them in a few weeks.

Reports continue to arrive of suicides by Asian traders up country and here in Kampala. How many are attempting to take their own lives is not known, but in the past week at least five have succeeded.

CARR GIVES PLEDGE TO AID ASIANS
Guidance and help for immigrants

By FRANK ROBERTSON, Diplomatic Staff
Reprinted with permission, ©Telegraph Group Limited, London, August 19, 1972

MR CARR, Home Secretary, announced yesterday that the Government will establish a special board to look after the expelled British passport-holding Asians who will be coming to Britain from Uganda.

The board, an executive agency of Government, will be set up "in days, not weeks." It will use public money and consist largely of civil servants.

Mr Carr said: "This is a problem we are determined to handle in a humane and orderly way. That is the guts of everything we are trying to do."

Arriving Asians would be generally free to settle where they chose.

However, every care would be taken to ensure that they did not impose "an excessive strain on community relations, or housing, schools or other facilities in particular areas," Mr Carr said.

Persuasion would be used and co-operation sought. The board would "guide, help, inform and persuade the immigrants in their best interests."

Fighting for time

Mr Carr said: "We feel that the 90 days imposed by President Amin is totally inadequate if the people concerned are to be dealt with in a reasonable, orderly and humane manner. In Uganda, above all, we are fighting for time.

"As far as possible we want to continue the voucher system from Uganda, since this guarantees orderly handling. We are trying to convince President Amin of this."

The board will co-operate closely with local authorities, voluntary organisations and immigrant communities. Mr Carr said that the role of the voluntary organisations was "immensely important."

"It will be one of our primary objectives to see that they are given a chance to make their contribution," he said.

The board will work closely with the team of British experts going to Uganda to establish the number of Asians entitled to enter Britain.

Commonwealth talks

Discussions were taking place with Commonwealth and other countries to ensure that Asian British passport-holders from Uganda "who wish to go to countries other than Britain should be allowed to do so."

But Britain would not shirk her responsibilities. The Government's aim was "to ensure that the Government of Uganda will see that the United Kingdom passport-holders in their country receive the fair treatment which is their due.

"This means that if they are expelled they must have time to settle their affairs in an equitable way and take out their assets"

Mr Carr said the Government had no plans to

Continued on Page 24

Ugandan Asian Expulsion: 90 Days and Beyond through the Eyes of the International Press

Uganda ditches her middle class

CHRISTOPHER MUNNION reports from Kampala on some implications of Gen. Amin's expulsion order

Reprinted with permission, ©Telegraph Group Limited, London, August 19 1972

AN AFRICAN youth approaches a young Asian sitting on a brand new bicycle and offers to buy it "before you leave." Two well-dressed Africans stroll into an Indian outfitters and take note of the contents, informing the startled owner that they are stocktaking in anticipation of buying his store when he goes.

Minor as they may appear, these cameos of covetousness in Kampala this week give some indication of the large-scale human drama about to unfold in Uganda as some 50,000 Asians prepare to abandon livelihoods, homes and businesses as a result of President Amin's expulsion decree.

When Mr Rippon returned to London on Tuesday having failed to persuade President Amin to alter either the expulsion policy or the 90-day ultimatum, the Asians of Uganda knew their fate was unquestionably sealed. Reaction among them ranged from the suicide of two businessmen to lavish spending sprees in Kampala restaurants and nightclubs as wealthier families set out to spend what they will not be able to take with them.

The writing has been on the wall for the 80,000-strong community since independence and most Asians have long since accepted that they would have to leave Uganda sooner or later. The General suddenly decided that it had to be ruthlessly soon, and it is the time factor which has take the Asians by surprise.

Not a small proportion of them have made provision for such a move, however. Illicit transfer of funds overseas—one of the key points in Amin's allegations of economic sabotage—has been conducted on a large scale over many years. Their close-knit but far-flung family system provides contacts and a promise of shelter rarely found among displaced persons.

It was not without significance that by far the largest queues in Kampala this week were not at the British High Commission but outside the Ugandan immigration headquarters where Asians claiming Ugandan citizenship or exemption as "essential service" personnel were asked to call.

The mood of most of those in the lines was not so much to seek permanent security in Uganda but to seek time outside the Nov. 7 deadline in the hope of putting their affairs in order. In brief, the great majority of Ugandan Asians wish to leave the country.

These facts may assist to put the crisis in perspective but they cannot minimise the massive human and logistical problems which the exodus must involve.

According to a Ugandan census conducted last year, 23,000 Asians laid claim to Ugandan citizenship. President Amin made it clear that his administration regarded this figure as excessive and the point is being proved by the rigorous check on credentials which threatens to whittle down the total of those accepted as citizens to no more than a few thousand.

The categories exempted in the initial decree—the professions, senior technicians, engineers, managers and owners of large businesses and industries—have yet to be specifically defined, but Asian leaders estimate the total will be no more than 10,000 people including wives and families (if these are allowed to stay).

Moreover, Gen. Amin has now decided to withdraw the professional classes from the exempted categories, a move which will halve the health facilities in Uganda and render much trade, commerce and industry unworkable.

To those who fail to attain exemption or Ugandan citizenship must be added about 10,000 stateless Asians. President Amin clearly expects Britain to assume responsibility for all these people with the exception of the few thousand who have Indian, Pakistani or Bangladesh citizenship.

The Indian Government angered many Ugandan Asians by imposing visa restrictions specifically aimed at preventing an influx from East Africa. A great number of Asians in Uganda—some estimate as many as half of those who will be displaced—would choose to go to the sub-continent, irrespective of the passports they hold.

But even when and if the Asian community is finally assessed, sorted and categorised, there remains the problem of fair disposal of assets built up over three generations.

What will be a "fair" price for a business which is one of thousands and suddenly dumped on a market, which, if it exists at all, is sorely under-capitalised?

Frozen funds

Even if the disposal should be reasonably achieved, the displaced owners have little prospect of getting their compensation outside Uganda. The allowances per migrating family remains at £2,800—although all applications now have to be approved by the Central State Bank, which means that if 10,000 families leave within the next few months with their full entitlement Uganda's total foreign reserves of £15 million would barely meet half of the foreign allowance demand.

This point was discussed by Mr Rippon and President Amin last Tuesday and it appeared the General had agreed that, where allowances and compensation could not be paid in full, money owing would be frozen in Uganda and paid eventually with interest.

"Eventually," of course, is about as specific a word as one could find for any large disbursement of foreign exchange from Uganda. The parlous economy—the blame for which Amin is now placing squarely on the Asians—will take a further knock of inestimable proportions when the exodus has been completed.

Apart from the skills and enterprise and the flair for trade and commerce which the Asian community bestows on the country, the average Asian family is an employer of labour on no small scale. The East African Asians, in fact, constitute the middle class of the societies in which they live.

Most of those from Uganda who will choose to stay in Britain will be in the younger age brackets, with a good average education. Westernised in manner and with a range of competence in clerical, mechanical and construction work. A great many of the breadwinners will be the *dukawhallas*—the small shopkeepers—against whom Amin's purge is primarily directed. The shortage of capital will handicap them in new enterprises, but, having established successful businesses in areas where few customers had heard of the cash economy, they are unlikely to be daunted for long.

In addition, as the General narrows down the list of exemptions to his decree, there will be a fair proportion of doctors, dentists, architects, accountants, lawyers and engineers whose value to any community is unquestionable.

Arrayed against the potential effects on the Ugandan economy of the Asian departure, even the physical problem of moving 50,000 people half-way across the world at short notice and in short order seems less than insoluble.

An airlift would meet only a fraction of the need. Ships are the obvious choice, but the Kenyan Government's co-operation would be required in transporting the families from landlocked Uganda to Mombasa.

The attitude of Uganda's neighbours, Kenya and Tanzania, to the Asian expulsion is a crucial one. Between them they have 70,000 British-passport-holding Asians.

In Kenya, where the Asian community is no more popular with the African people than in Uganda, the Government appears to be satisfied with the British voucher system under which some 6,000 Asians leave the country each year. The same attitude prevails in Tanzania, where President Nyerere would shy from any anti-Asian move which might conflict with his views on discrimination in other parts of the continent. In any event, last year's property acquisition legislation in Tanzania has despatched some 20,000 Asians, most of them British citizens, to Canada and the United States.

President Amin has given assurances that the lives and limbs of the displaced Asians will be protected. He rammed the point home last week by announcing that his Army had shot two corrupt policemen who had robbed and beaten an Asian trader.

But the Ugandan leader has also warned that non-citizen Asians remaining after his deadline will be "sitting on fire," and with almost daily verbal attacks broadcast on the Asian community the potential threat of violence as the ultimatum expires cannot be taken too lightly.

ASIANS UNWELCOME UNLESS CITY IS GIVEN AID

—Labour leader

Reprinted with permission, ©Leicester Mercury, August 19, 1972

ASIANS from Uganda will not be welcome in Leicester in present circumstances, says the leader of the City Council, Alderman Edward Marston.

He declared today: "They will not be welcome until the Government assures us that they will provide money and materials such as prefabricated buildings for schools, and make all the necessary arrangements themselves for housing these people."

But Conservative Alderman Harold Heard, a former Education Committee chairman, said: "One cannot reject human beings. If they come here we will have to do what we have always done and try and absorb them".

Meanwhile the Conservative Monday Club, whose chairman is Leicestershire County Councillor Jonathan Guinness, issued a statement reminding the Prime Minister of the 1970 Tory pledge that "there will be no further large scale permanent immigration" and urging the Premier "to have over-riding regard for the feelings of the British people for whom he holds in trust his power and authority."

Alderman Marston said he would not be calling on the City Council to protest to the Government against the possibility of large numbers of Asians coming to the city because he had not yet received any information from the Government.

GREAT STRAIN

"They could merely turn around and say 'What are you talking about?'" he says. But a special meeting of the Council General Purposes committee will be convened once information is to hand."

Alderman Marston explained: "Up to last night we had not received any information at all from Whitehall, whether anyone is expected to come to Leicester or what assistance they can give.

"The main reason that the Ugandan Asians, or anyone else. will not be welcome is that our services are working to the utmost of their capacity—health, welfare, and housing in particular."

MUST PAY

"They are already under a great strain to retain their present services."

Councillor Mrs. Dorothy Davis, Chairman of the Education Committee, said an Asian influx would put another heavy strain on Leicester's stretched education resources and would require "unique" emergency measures.

The city had found school places for 5,500 immigrant children in the last four years and at present 400 or so children were waiting to be admitted to schools.

But Councillor Mrs. Davis added: "I would not like to give the impression that the education service has closed its eyes to this problem.

"Conventional school places cannot be found in a hurry. You cannot build schools overnight.

"If in fact they come, we shall be able to do something, but of course we shall expect the Government to pay for it".

Buildings other than conventional schools would have to be found. "The provision would not be ideal but we would do the best we could", Councillor Mrs. Davis added.

Continued on Page 24

Let's all be frank about the Asians

Editorial
Reprinted with permission, ©The Observer, London, August 20, 1972

THE GOVERNMENT is to be congratulated on its decision to set up an executive board to organise the resettlement of the Ugandan Asians who have British passports. But this welcome evidence of forethought and planning still leaves many unanswered questions. This is understandable. No one knows yet the exact dimensions of the influx into this country; that depends partly on the dialogue that may now hopefully continue with President Amin and partly on the contribution that other countries, notably India, Pakistan and Bangladesh, may make.

It depends above all on the wishes of the Ugandan Asians themselves. How many want to come here? How many would prefer to go to the Indian sub-continent? How many will in the end be allowed to or will want to stay in Uganda when their large contribution to that country's professional and commercial life is more realistically measured? While these questions remain

Continued on Page 24

First, simple decency

Editorial
Reprinted with permission, ©The Globe & Mail, Toronto, August 19, 1972

Canada has now been formally asked by the British Government to help with the resettlement of the 50,000 to 80,000 Asian people to be expelled from Uganda over the next two and a half months. The request, says a spokesman for the external Affairs Department, is "under consideration". There can be no question about the conclusion to be reached through this consideration. Elementary decency demands that Canada not only accept several thousand of these refugees, but also help with the formidable logistical task of getting them out of Uganda safely.

Legally, the problem belongs primarily to Britain and the British Government has fully accepted responsibility in principle. In practice, however, it is clearly impossible for Britain to manage such a large and sudden influx to its crowded island, where there are dangerous racial tensions resulting from past waves of

Continued on Page 26

Plan to settle Asians praised

News Compilation, August 19, 1972

Immigrant groups last night welcomed the government decision to set up a board to handle the resettlement of Uganda Asians and to accept unequivocally the responsibility for them.

The Government also announced yesterday that a team of Whitehall experts in immigration procedures, employment and property valuation will be sent to reinforce the staff of the British High Commission in Kampala.

At a press conference in London yesterday Mr Carr, Home Secretary, said contingency plans for the Asian arrivals would be drawn up. The emphasis would be on their dispersal to areas where they would place minimum strain on housing and education.

Special transit centres would be set up only as a last resort, and only if an unexpectedly large number of people were involved.

Mr Carr said the board would work closely with local authorities and voluntary organizations. It would consist of civil servants as well as representatives of interested bodies. "We have set it up because we do not yet know how large or over what period the movement of people will be", Mr Carr said.

"The board will have to operate through persuasion and cooperation, since we cannot direct people where to go. They will show what opportunities are available and where. Dispersal would be in their own interests as well as ours."

Mr Praful Patel, secretary of the All-Party Committee on United Kingdom Citizenship, said last night that the decision was "in the highest traditions of justice and fair play so often shown by the British people.

"The decision to accept responsibility for these people is a tremendous credit for the Government. It vindicates our trust in them.

"The creation of the board means that our efforts can be coordinated for the first time. There have been complaints from immigrant groups in the past that they have not been consulted but this move may mean the start of a new epoch."

"A Foolish Move"

Toronto, August 18, 1972

An editorial in the *Toronto Sun* called External Affairs Minister Mitchell Sharpe's offer to open Canada's door to Asians expelled from Uganda an "irresponsible, unrealistic, emotional, short-sighted and foolish act for a statesman".

It challenged if the Asians would be happy in Canada and if they would benefit Canada. The editorial claimed that "by bringing in large numbers of Asians, it will increase welfare rolls and increase immigration problems when relatives start 'visiting'".

Ugandan Asian Expulsion: 90 Days and Beyond through the Eyes of the International Press   *Page 23*

Continued from Page 21

Ugandan Asians could be 'a benefit'

and representatives from immigrant organizations and religious communities.

"We found a complete identity of purpose", Mr Ennals said.

Plans were suggested to provide reception centres at all main airports and shipping ports manned by British volunteers and Asians. The centres would find out where the Uganda Asians wanted to settle and what work they wanted. Many would join relatives as a first step to finding somewhere to settle and it was expected that the reception centres would be able to give advice on education and housing.

Mr Ennals said that of the 25,000 expected to choose Britain as their new home, about half would be traders and the remainder divided equally between skilled and semi-skilled people. "From information we have, between 7,000 and 8,000 families might be expected to arrive and we anticipate about 80 per cent of them will already have family or friends in this country", Mr Ennals said.

Offers of help had come in from many parts of the country.

Mr Praful Patel, secretary of the all-party committee on United Kingdom citizenship, said that a breakdown of the numbers of British Asians in Uganda showed that 1,867 were classed semi-skilled, 2,032 skilled or technical assistants, 1,493 were in the professional or senior management class, and 5,000 were small traders or industrialists.

"We know that 57,000 Asians in Uganda hold British passports but there is good reason to believe half of these will opt to go to India, the pattern of immigration in the past five years shows this. These people are the skilled, the professional and the very articulate. They are hard working and will not be any burden to our social services. Far from it, they will be an asset to the country", Mr Patel said.

Continued from Page 21

Carr gives pledge to aid Asians

set up reception centres or transit camps. But if too many came too soon he warned that "some sort of holding operation" in Britain might be needed.

It was hoped that by the time the expelled Asians began arriving, arrangements for their resettlement would have been completed.

Urban aid

The new Board would examine whether urban aid programme funds might have to be increased for areas affected by an influx of immigrants.

Mr Carr said that Britain could not accept responsibility, as an individual nation, for Ugandan Asians who might be stateless as a result of Uganda's policy. But the special British team in Kampala would do everything possible to investigate the claims of those who appeared "to fall between two stools."

Asked if he could give a categorical assurance that the immigrants will have "total freedom to choose where they will settle" in Britain, Mr Carr replied: "Definitely."

As he was speaking, members of the Nation Front demonstrated at the entrance to Downing Street, 100 yards away. They carried placards stating "We support Enoch." and "Start repatriation now."

Continued from Page 23

Let's all be frank about the Asians

imponderable, it makes sense for the Government to plan for the reception of the largest number of Asians that might be expected in the shortest possible time.

Mr Heath has a political problem on his hands: how best to deprive Mr Enoch Powell of the chance to stir things up to his Government's embarrassment. For though Mr Powell is an isolated figure politically these days, his speeches have a resonance in the country that the party chiefs, now planning their autumn conference, are well aware of. In the past, silence on racial issues has tended to play into Powell's hands. It fed his suspicion—a suspicion he found that he shared with many others—that there was a conspiracy of silence about the darkening of our industrial cities and the transforming of our national identity. And, indeed, he was right—to the extent that liberals of all parties, for the best of motives, hardly dared talk about race for fear of awakening racial feelings. Such a policy was only justifiable—if it was justifiable—by success. If it merely bottled feelings up until Mr Powell came along and released them, then it was neither successful nor justifiable.

It is important not to make this mistake again, particularly as we are dealing with a relatively small number of people, most of whom speak good English and are educated and trained in various skills and many of whom have relatives already in this country. It would be a pity to allow Mr Powell to muddy the waters by arousing fears that are without much substance. That is why Mr Carr's firm and frank publicity for the contingency planning that the new board is to undertake is so welcome.

For although the problem of admitting, in a short time, large numbers of these Ugandan Asians is perfectly manageable provided proper planning is done, it is not going to be easy. Where are they to go to? Obviously, they must be free to go where they will: those who have friends and relatives here will want to join them. There can be no direction and there should be no incarceration in camps either in this country or abroad. But it is only sensible for the board to point out very clearly where job opportunities are better and where the shortage of housing and school places is less acute.

In the last resort, however, as Mr Carr very fairly

recognised, it must be left to the immigrants themselves to decide where to go. Their choice would be eased, of course, if they were allowed to bring funds out of Uganda with them. President Amin is unlikely to be at all generous in encouraging such a flow of capital, for this was, apparently, one of the reasons he decided to expel them. But could not the British Government make some arrangement with him for having the money withdrawn in instalments from Uganda, and meanwhile advance loans to the Asians to be repaid as their own funds are released?

It would be a mistake, however, to imagine that, whatever inducements are offered to encourage these immigrants to disperse themselves about the country for their own good and for that of the rest of the community. Ultimately they will not choose to concentrate in the cities and towns where their own people live. Successive waves of immigrants have always initially done this, whether they are Jews, Cypriots, West Indians or Asians.

There are dangers and difficulties in such concentrations that it is open to men like Mr Powell to exploit. But we should not expect minorities to forsake the comfort that comes from living among their own people. We should not mistake their successful integration into our community with complete assimilation. The former involves our showing respect for their differences, while insisting on absolute equality of rights and opportunities; while the latter attempts an unacceptable and self-defeating uniformity. Assimilation is no longer expected of a Welshman, and is positively rejected by many American Negroes: why should it be thought suitable for a Hindu or Muslim from East Africa?

Diversity in unity is the right aim and it should be achievable over a period. It calls for flexibility in policy: there should be a maximum of public education in mutual respect and a minimum use of force, such as is involved in the American practice of 'bussing' young children to enforce racial mixing in schools. The Ugandan Asians will bring to our community, among their many assets, a social cohesion of real value. Their precarious, yet successful, position in Uganda should have given them a self-confidence that will help them here.

Continued from Page 23

ASIANS UNWELCOME UNLESS CITY IS GIVEN AID

"We are already considering what can be done if this happens but we have no firm plans. Until we have a better notion of what to expect, firm plans cannot be made".

FEARS SHARPENED

The Monday Club statement said there had for some time been widespread anxiety about the implementation of the Conservative pledge.

"Fears have been greatly sharpened by indications that, against the undoubted wishes of the people, there may be an intention to admit many thousands of Asiatic people from Africa.

"The Monday Club urges the Prime Minister, in the interests of the country and the Conservative Party, to have over-riding regard to the feelings of the British people for whom he holds in trust his power and authority".

Mr. Guinness was not available for comment after the statement was made, because he is on holiday in Spain, but the national director of the Monday Club, Commander Michael Woolrych, who is at present in Leicestershire, told the Leicester Mercury that the Club felt that although it could be said there were "special aspects" of this particular case, the problem did not stop there.

"The Government have allowed far too many immigrants in under one guise or another and they have not stood up to their undertaking to stem the flow".

RECALL MPs

Mr. John Biggs-Davison, Conservative MP for Chigwell, Essex today called on the Home Secretary to see that Parliament was in session before the Government decided to admit additional Uganda Asians. Parliament should be recalled necessary.

Mr. Biggs-Davison said: "MPs, particularly those with constituencies whose housing, employment and social problems would be aggravated, should be enabled to give their views before Ministers resign themselves (or rather, us) to importing a horrifying problem for this and future generations."

Now all Uganda Asians are ordered out

Reprinted with permission, ©East African Standard, Nairobi, August 20, 1972

President Amin of Uganda has now ordered the expulsion of all his country's 80,000 strong Asian community—including 23,000 people who thought they had secured Ugandan nationality.

Announcing his latest decision, the Ugandan leader said that even those Asians who opted to become citizens of the country around the time Uganda became independent ten years ago would have to leave.

Gen. Amin had said earlier they could remain in Uganda provided they produced proof of their citizenship. For as many as 10,000 of those who claim Ugandan nationality the situation is especially precarious. They might fail to substantiate their claims because of an elaborate screening of papers being carried out.

If they are unable to substantiate their claims they will not only have to quit the country by the general expulsion date of November 9 but would technically become stateless. Those Asians who prove Uganda citizenship will be able to leave the country later.

Diplomats in Uganda think that those who could become stateless would probably have a case in international law for reverting to their previous established nationality—in most cases British.

Uganda's Asian citizens were stunned and bewildered by Gen. Amin's decision.

"It doesn't make sense, it doesn't make sense," said one 20-year-old Asian who was born in Uganda. "The only thing to do is to take a one-way ticket to India."

Gen. Amin's latest move came three days after he said professional people in the Asian community would also have to leave. He had previously said that such people, who include doctors, teachers and lawyers would be exempted from the general expulsion order.

The President has also stated he is going to return refugees living in Uganda to their respective countries. These would comprise about 100,000 from Rwanda, 80,000 from Southern Sudan and some from Zaire and Burundi. No deadline for the expulsion of these people has yet been given.

Many of the Asian Ugandan citizens are expected to turn for help to Britain, which is already coping with the needs of about 57,000 non-citizens holding British passports.

Some of the Asians hope the U.N. will come to their rescue.

President Amin at the weekend told a mass rally at Rukungiri in western Uganda: "I have decided that *even Asians with Ugandan citizenship will have to leave the country.*

Continued on Page 26

Preparing for the Uganda Asians

INQUIRY by CYRIL DUNN and LAURENCE MARKS
Reprinted with permission, ©The Observer, London, August 20, 1972

IN THE Sikh and Hindu temples and the Muslim mosques of Britain, as well as in the less exotic committee rooms of our domestic voluntary bodies, plans are being laid this weekend to help the Asian families about to be driven from their homes in Uganda.

For the first time in this country's experience of Commonwealth immigration, the flight of the Asians is being treated as a catastrophe demanding a humane response. On Friday the Government itself officially accepted leadership of the operation.

Nobody yet knows precisely how many of these British Asians are coming. Complex arithmetic taking many social and political factors into account now puts the likeliest total at 30,000 to 35,000. This is small beside the number of Jews who fled before World War II, or of Displaced Persons who looked for a new life here after it.

The danger is that most of the Ugandan Asians could reach these shores en masse, within a short space of time. This might well happen if General Idi Amin, the burly Nubian who now rules Uganda, sticks rigidly to his 90 day deadline, set for 5 November.

Continued on Page 28

Two Asian women who are among the thousands performing the heart-breaking task of packing up their belongings in Kampala. Reproduced with permission, ©United Press International/Corbis Bettman

Plight of the 23,000 Ugandans made stateless

By Phillip Short, Kampala
Reprinted with permission, ©Times Newspapers Limited, London, August 20, 1972

THE UGANDAN leader's latest move against the Asian community was foreshadowed by President Idi Amin a few days ago when he told me at his home in Kampala that he looked forward to the day when there would be no more Asians in the country.

I asked him if he thought this would come about within the next 10 or 15 years. "Yes," he said, "the only Asians then will be Asian tourists." At the time he declined to say whether he would enforce the departure of Ugandan citizens, but now, evidently, the prospect of years of waiting has become too much.

The past few days have been a time of great uncertainty for the 23,000 Asians with Ugandan passports. It looked at first, after President Amin's original announcement about the expulsion of Asians with British and other passports, as though the Ugandan passport holders would be unaffected.

Of the 80,000 or so Asians in Uganda, Britain has accepted responsibility for about 50,000 British passport holders, and India and Pakistan have agreed to admit their own nationals. Now a new and entirely novel problem has been posed—the forced exodus of about 23,000 people, who will almost certainly become stateless.

Continued on Page 26

Continued from Page 23

First, simple decency

Commonwealth immigration. If the Commonwealth still means anything at all, this is a problem for co-operative Commonwealth action.

In urging this, we are not thinking merely in terms of helping Britain. Nor is it a matter of making a pious demonstration of Canadian largess. The simple fact is that by his brutal decision, President Idi Amin has created a situation of human injustice and mass suffering that demands the concern of the whole civilized world. If the Commonwealth cannot act, then it should come before the United Nations.

Gen. Amin has been utterly unyielding to British efforts to negotiate at least the 90-day deadline of his order. It must be accepted that he is finally determined to carry it out, and that any Asians who remain in Uganda after the deadline has expired will be at least in concentration camps and probably in danger for their lives as well.

In a word, this is an international emergency. Since Canada has the capacity to act, it has a moral obligation to participate in the rescue operation, and quickly. There is no time now to be concerned with arguments about the responsibility of the Asian community itself for its predicament.

This is the first consideration. The second is what to do about Uganda under Gen. Amin, for it would be galling simply to have to accept the consequences of his racism.

It seems likely that one effective way to turn the policy against him will be to carry out the order as completely and rapidly as possible. For although a tiny percentage of the total population, the Asians manage a large part of the Ugandan economy. It has been calculated, moreover, that the money they can take with them, even under present restrictions, will leave Uganda with a massive balance of payments problem.

No doubt Gen. Amin will try in one way or another to deprive the departing Asians of their property rights. In response, Britain and all other countries will be fully justified in using all possible pressure, including withholding of foreign aid, to prevent his doing so. This is a matter both of justice and self interest, so that the refugees will have the resources to establish themselves in the new homes that must be found for them.

Finally, there is the question of Uganda in the Commonwealth. South Africa was expelled for its racism. Is Uganda then still to be tolerated as a member?

Nixon Renominated

News Compilation, August 23, 1972

The 1972 Republican National Convention renominated President Richard M. Nixon and Vice President Spiro Agnew to lead the Republican party in the upcoming elections.

Demonstrators outside the convention hall were disorderly and disruptive. Police arrested 1,129 on the final day of the convention.

Continued from Page 25

Now all Uganda Asians are ordered out

"This will be carried out as a second phase operation after the present one involving Asians holding British passports and nationals of India, Pakistan and Bangladesh," he said.

The Ugandan leader explained that he had decided on the expulsion orders in the light of sabotage which the Asians have now started or planned to carry out in the country."

President Amin has said he wants Asians to leave the country because they are sabotaging the economy and keeping Africans out of commerce.

Gen. Amin said all Asians would have to register their buildings, industries and businesses with the authorities by the end of this month.

He said their sale would be centrally controlled by the Government, and no private transactions would be allowed for anything except personal effects.

Asians were also prohibited from transferring their businesses and properties to relatives without special Government permission, Gen. Amin said.

He said certain "inconveniences" would inevitably follow from his Asian policy, but these would be "only short-lived if all the people are determined to do their best in whatever they will be doing and never give up."

Gen. Amin said university students would be directed to replace Asian teachers, and motor manufacturers in Europe would be asked to send technicians to keep the country's garages going.

Hundreds of African traders shouting anti-Asian slogans on Saturday paraded through Kampala, in a demonstration backing President Amin's decision.

Representing traders' associations from all over the country, they brandished placards urging support for Gen. Amin's policies. Many of the Asians to be expelled are themselves traders. Gen. Amin has accused them of "economic sabotage". Priority in buying out their businesses is to be given to Black Ugandans, Gen. Amin said.

The demonstrators, marching behind a police band, gathered in the central city square to hear a leading Kampala businessman, Mr. Haji Musa Sebatuka, attack the British for coming to Uganda "under the guise of protecting the Africans—but instead of protecting them they brought in the Asians to exploit them."

Meanwhile transporters in Nairobi said yesterday they were still complying with Kenya Government instructions not to carry any Asian holding a British passport into Kenya.

Akamba Road Services said that "because of too much trouble" at the border they were not carrying any Asians at all in their buses to and from Uganda.

E.A.A. have stopped carrying Asians from Uganda into either Kenya or Tanzania "irrespective of their nationality" and the Railways Corporation has continued to intensify checks at railway entry points.

Continued from Page 25

Plight of the 23,000 Ugandans made stateless

But then, as the programme of citizenship verification got under way, it became clear that more than half of the 23,000 would have their citizenship revoked and become stateless.

The verification programme will now be seen was a preliminary to the President's announcement yesterday. About one in two failed to prove citizenship, often because of trivial objections and on minor technical points.

As the deadline neared in Kampala yesterday about 600 Asians queued outside the Immigration Department. Those who failed to get inside will have their citizenship automatically revoked. Many of those who did go through the checking process fared no better.

Asians have been losing their Ugandan passports on any one of several grounds. The commonest is that they renounced their British citizenships more than three months after being registered as Ugandans, so failing to fulfill a condition stipulated by law. Many of those now stateless for this reason claimed the fault lay with the nationalities department of the Home Office in London, which had taken several months to process their renunciations. Some of them were able to produce documents to prove this.

Others said immigration officers refused to accept duplicates of their renunciation certificates, even though they bore the official Home Office seal and were certified as authentic copies. Under President Amin's directive, no duplicates or photostats were admissible because of the danger of forgery.

Still others omitted to take the oath of allegiance to Uganda, while a fourth group were rejected because their birth certificates were incomplete. Others again, and there may be a substantial number, were said to have obtained their citizenship by official corruption or bribery.

Some Asians have claimed that their renunciation or registration certificates were ripped up in front of them. President Amin has denied this, but doubt remains because journalists have been barred from the Immigration Department precincts. By and large, it seems the letter of the law was being fulfilled. Asians were not being deprived of their citizenship by disregard of regulations, but by the rigorous application of them.

The slightest flaw in their papers was deemed enough for their passports to be confiscated. A number of people have been made stateless for no other reason than that the page number was missing from their birth certificates—a circumstance taken as meaning that the certificates might have been fraudulently obtained.

Almost all the Asians queueing outside the Immigration Department yesterday had spent the night there, and for some it was the second successive night. Some said they had queued on each of the previous four days, but each time had just failed to reach the front of the queue before the door closed.

A boy of 13, queueing with his seven-year-old sister, said he had come at 6:30 am each day for three days. He did not say why his parents had not come with him, but presumably they felt that he had a better chance of getting his papers approved if he was alone.

The fate of those who believed they had Ugandan status is now joined with those whose papers were not approved, and those who did not even get the chance of approval. For all these, the future is uncertain. Britain already faces and influx of 40,000 to 50,000, while India and Pakistan have their own problems. No one has any legal responsibility to stateless people.

It is possible that if stateless Asians can make their way to India, they will either be legally accepted or be able to disappear without trace among their 600 million countrymen. But no one is rushing to make a move. The British and Indian High Commissions in Kampala are awaiting instructions.

If no solution is found within the next few weeks, some 23,000 people nobody wants may be consigned to camps in Uganda to await transportation and rely on the awakening of compassion somewhere.

No dumping here, Uganda told

"The Times of India" News Service
Reprinted with permission, ©Times of India, August 22, 1972

NEW DELHI—THE Uganda government's threat to expel from that country its citizens of Asian origin is considered by official sources here as a clear violation of the Human Rights Declaration of the U.N.

It is asserted by these sources such a move would mean discrimination against one class of citizens. This could be called nothing less than a subtle form of racial discrimination.

The Uganda government has already been told that India would certainly not accept the citizens who are threatened with expulsion. It has been made very clear that they are the responsibility of the Uganda government and India could not be treated as a dumping ground.

It is pointed out, however, that no official intimation other than press reports about the fate of the Uganda citizens of Asian origin has been received.

REPERCUSSIONS

It is explained by these sources that India is concerned only with Indian citizens and in their case too India might insist that they must be permitted to repatriate their assets. India, these sources maintain, has to bear in mind the repercussions it might have in other countries where there are persons of Indian origin.

According to these sources it is very unlikely that many Asians in Uganda holding British passports would renounce their British citizenship. From India's experience in regard to Asians in Kenya, it could be reasonably said that no British passport-holder would give up his passport. It is also unlikely that these Indians would opt for India, but if they wanted a little time, India might consider the issue on humanitarian grounds.

Meanwhile, some officials have been flown from here to Kampala to strengthen the Indian mission and to assess the situation there.

Australian Reaction

News Compilation, August 23, 1972

CANBERRA,— The Australian Government yesterday rejected official British overtures for it to admit large numbers of displaced Ugandan Asians as migrants.

But Labor's spokesman on immigration (Senator Willesee) said a limited number of those to be expelled should be allowed into Australia— and given assisted passages if necessary.

The Minister for Immigration (Dr. Forbes) told Federal Parliament yesterday the Government would not depart from its policy of accepting only those settlers who could integrate readily into the Australian community.

Senator Willesee agreed that the number of "refugees' Australia could take would have to be restricted because of the present high unemployment.

Continued on Page 30

Man with 42,000 futures on his shoulders

By Christopher Warman
Reprinted with permission, ©Times Newspapers Limited, London, August 21, 1972

The plight of Uganda Asians facing expulsion by General Amin means more to Mr Praful Patel than just his already involved role as secretary of the all-party Committee on United Kingdom Citizenship.

For he is a Uganda Asian, born there in 1939 of Indian parents. His father, a trader, emigrated from Gujarat and, until Africanization forced the family wholesale business to close, worked in the centre of Jinja. Mr Patel was educated by British teachers and came to Britain in 1958.

His father returned to India last year and his brother chose to stay in Britain: a typical dispersal of a Uganda Asian family along age lines.

"Of course this affects me deeply. I am sentimentally involved in the problems that these families are facing", he said yesterday. He is well known among Asians in Uganda: indeed Patel is one of the most influential family names in the country.

He last visited his former home in 1968. He was deported from Kenya the next year and because that ban extended to Uganda, has not gone back. Now, however, Mr Patel is in almost daily telephone communication with his friends and leaders of the Asian community there.

"They seem afraid to talk about the problems, but I try to tell them that, although they may dislike what General Amin has done, they must get themselves organized. That is why we are gathering details of people's skills so that the 30,000 to 35,000 with British passports who are likely to come to Britain can be placed in the best possible way".

He added that perhaps 12,000 of the other Uganda Asians also to be expelled would probably come to Britain. The evidence of the skills of the British passport holders leads Mr Patel to believe that there will be no difficulty in their integration here.

There were 1,867 semi-skilled artisans from millers to motor mechanics, 1,604 skilled workers, 1,493 professional people, 1,070 technicians, and 5,000 traders: in other words, most of the 12,000 heads of family who may want to move to Britain were of semi-skilled status or higher.

"I am certain that, given the cooperation of the TUC and the Confederation of British Industry and the help of local councils, there will be absolutely no difficulty in dealing with this problem."

Mr Patel is shocked at the wholesale expulsions, although he saw some expulsions as likely. He said: "I never thought the Amin decision would be so drastic, causing great problems for the countries receiving them and economic disaster for Uganda.

"I have all sympathy for Africanization so long as it is planned. I am concerned with the aspirations of the African people. But Asians have made vital contribution to African territories and I do not believe that they have sabotaged Ugandan industry."

He does not claim to be a politician, perhaps because his strong views on race relations cut across party barriers, but he does believe he is "a political animal".

Certainly he thrives on his work for the all-party committee even though it causes occasional friction. He was more outspoken than some of the committee liked on the difficulties of what he calls "migronauts", those unfortunate people shuttled round the world and unable to stop.

He is happy to say that the issue of the Uganda Asians seems to have brought them all close together again, and is full of admiration for the Government's decisions. "They have acted with more humanity and compassion than the Labour Government and Mr Callaghan did on racial problems", he said.

Mr Patel sees the Ugandan issue as another "terrible" example of a form of racialism between brown and black people.

"It is part of a growing racialism and intolerance and can be equated exactly with racialism between black and white. It needs to be said. Here we have the poor Asians caught up in the crossfire between African nationalism and Powellite cynicism."

Apart from his work as committee secretary, he is also leader of three Indian groups in Britain and sees his work for them as the equivalent of an MP's constituency work. As if that is not enough, he is a business consultant and represents Indian companies in Britain.

His working day during the present troubles lasts from 7 am to 2 am and his business consultancy takes second place. He was busy at several meetings yesterday, lobbying and cajoling, trying to mobilize community and religious organizations in Britain to take action over those facing expulsion. Telegrams have been sent to the Government from more than one of these organizations to ensure that it realizes the depth of British concern over the affair.

Mr Patel, who is aged 33 and a bachelor, has no fears for the Uganda Asians' future here. "They will enrich Britain," he said." They tend to go where there are no great numbers of Asians. They will integrate very quickly.

"All they want is assurances about their house, job, and education for their children. They already have a good appreciation of all that is English, about English cricket, and they all know where Piccadilly Circus is."

UN to help Stateless Asians

News Compilation, August 21, 1972

GENEVA, Aug 20—The office of the United Nations High Commissioner for Refugees said today that if 23,000 Asians holding Ugandan nationality are expelled, as President Amin says they will, they will become stateless and so qualify in principle for assistance under the High Commissioner's mandate. Officials are awaiting confirmation from their representative in Kampala.

Ugandan Asian Expulsion: 90 Days and Beyond through the Eyes of the International Press

Continued from Page 25

Preparing for the Uganda Asians

A similar crisis occurred in 1967-68, when fears that the Commonwealth Immigration Act would pull up our drawbridge against them caused a panic inrush of British Asians from Kenya. But in the three months' peak period of that migration, not more than 15,000 arrived. This time there could be at least twice as many.

The Government's first aim in setting up a Resettlement Board to control the inflow of Ugandan Asians is clear and understandable. It wishes to prevent a backlash of white resentment by heading the newcomers away from the areas of coloured immigrant concentration which already exist and where a Ugandan influx might put an unbearable strain on housing, schools and other facilities. Predictable twitches of this backlash have already come from Mr Enoch Powell, the National Front and the Monday Club.

But there are also signs that these new immigrants command in advance a degree of public sympathy not shown for those who came in ahead of them.

Evidence of this new feeling is so far admittedly slight. A rural council in South Wales has offered the Ugandan Asians a few council houses. The Peterborough City Council is prepared to offer at least 50 more, if other local authorities—especially those in expanding towns—do the same. The Council leader, Mr Charles Swift, has called the crisis a responsibility which ought not to be shirked and is urging the Home Office and the Department of the Environment to summon a conference of local authorities to deal with it. A public relations firm invited to promote Uganda as a good place for investment and tourism has turned the contract down. But it seems clear that, in spite of General Amin's comic performances on television, and in spite of the case Uganda's Africans undoubtedly have against Asians whose success in business has impeded African advancement, there has been a public reaction in this country against the General's ruthlessness.

And now it seems plain that the General means to go the whole hog. Having already said he would be happier if all the Asians left his country, whether Ugandan nationals or not, yesterday in a startling speech he announced his intention to make this official policy. First he obliged all Asians who claimed Ugandan citizenship to check their papers with the authorities and crowds of them have been queuing all night to do this. Now he has declared that he will expel them all, even though by so doing he makes them stateless.

The General's intention to expel all the Asians has for days been a general fear in Uganda's Asian community and now it seems to have become a grim reality. It also appears that he means to keep the bulk of all Asian assets. Asians arriving in Britain are likely to have few resources of their own and the need for general help has become more pressing.

It was evidently in an attempt to ease this growing tension that the British Government on Friday backed up its announced policy of admitting British passport holders 'without question' by openly preparing to receive them in 'a humane and orderly way.' In this the Government has lagged behind Britain's voluntary organisations, both black and white, who moved into action as soon as General Amin delivered his 90-day ultimatum.

Led by the British Council of Churches, these bodies have formed themselves into a single operational unit called the Welfare Committee for Ugandan Asians. Their intention is to meet the newcomers at the door and to ease them through the first trying days of their life here. Bands of volunteers will be at the airports to offer guidance and, for those Asians who have no friends or relations to go to, church halls in the neighborhood are to be fitted out as temporary reception centres.

The voluntary bodies have the support of Asian community organisations in Britain. No conflict is seen between all this voluntary effort and the Government's plan. The two sides are to meet tomorrow to co-ordinate their efforts, but it is already clear that, while the volunteers will cope with the first impact of the Asian influx, the Government's resettlement board will deal with more enduring problems.

Even so, there is some anxiety on the voluntary front, in advance of tomorrow's meeting, about the Government's intentions. Although the Home Secretary, Mr Robert Carr, has said that persuasion alone will be used in an attempt to move Ugandan Asians into areas where there is room for them, there are fears that many may end up where they do not wish to be and away from their relations and friends.

The Runnymede Trust—a private body concerned with race relations—believes that dispersal ought to be organised on an individual basis before the Asians leave Uganda. The Dutch adopted this policy when they had to deal with 300,000 Indo-Dutch immigrants from Indonesia. Throughout the past week the Runnymede directors have been trying, so far in vain, to persuade the Foreign Office to back them (i.e., to give them effective protection against 'Amin's sergeants') in sending an expert team to Uganda at once, to gather every imaginable detail about each Asian householder wishing to settle in Britain. At this same time, a second team would investigate all job opportunities at this end, so that Ugandan skills might be related in advance to British needs.

There is also some concern about Mr Carr's suggestion that the Ugandans are likely to arrive here, not in a single mass but as manageable groups. This could, of course, mean simply that the Government hopes, against the odds, that General Amin will relax his eviction deadline or that ships, rather that aircraft, are to be the form of transport. But some of the voluntary leaders suspect that staging camps are contemplated along the migration route and to these there is almost universal opposition.

The general feeling is that staging camps, like refuge camps, tend to become permanent. A camp for Poles outside Cirencester which endured for 17 years is quoted as an example. Visualising a staging camp on some island in the middle of the Indian Ocean, possibly in the Seychelles, one Ugandan Asian already settled in Britain said he was afraid it might be used by the Government as a device for continuing the quota system.

But there seems to be at least some support for staging camps in India. The Indian Government has so far shown no overt interest in such a scheme, but it is thought that Mrs Gandhi may relent as General Amin increases the pressure. It seems likely that Britain would have to finance the camps, besides guaranteeing that those Ugandans who want to move on to Britain might do so in due course.

In fact, most experts agree that many of the British Asians due to be evicted from Uganda—perhaps half of them—will in the end choose to stay in India.

But avoiding all imaginable forms of delay is clearly the dominant ambition of those most concerned about the possible effects of the Ugandan influx on race relations here. They think it important that nothing should impede the known desire of East African Asians to get away from public notice and to merge themselves into the bourgeois landscape of Britain.

For what is coming now is a middle class invasion.

Most East African Asians are quite unlike the West Indian workers and the peasants from India and Pakistan who have come here ahead of them.

The very nature of the British presence, both in Kenya and Uganda, actively encouraged the Asians to adopt a middle-class role. In Kenya most of the white settlers wished only to be an expatriate landed gentry. In Uganda there were no white settlers on the land and the Asians found themselves coming second on the social scale—admittedly below a pretty wide gap—to the British official class. In both countries the labouring jobs were done, of course, by the Africans.

Young Asians were brought up in the British tradition and taught to admire British virtues, notably those now outmoded over here, like modesty, quietness and good manners. As one young East African Asian puts it: 'At school I was taught in English from the start. In fact, I failed Gujerati (his mother tongue) in the Senior Cambridge. I did Macbeth, Dickens and Tennyson. I wasn't taught Indian history, but the history of the British Empire.' He learned scouting from an English Rover who left him knowing more about the Yorkshire dales than he did about the Himalayas.

Within the last decade, many of these youngsters have come to Britain for their higher education. Typically, they have gone in for things like medicine, engineering, law and accountancy. Their working background in Uganda has been middle class. They have been shopkeepers, managers in commerce and industry, and even on farms; they have gone readily into the professions.

As a result, most of the Ugandans due to arrive here will pursue middle-class objectives. Those who have studied the recent incursion of Asians from Kenya see it as the most successful example of immigration in British history. They recoil from the ghetto life into which many of the poorer West Indians, Pakistanis and East Indians were forced in the 1950s and 1960s. So far their dispersal has been self-generated. Their ambition has been to join Britain's existing property-owning democracy, with a semi-detached house in the suburbs as their ideal home.

At the same time, self-reliance was almost forced upon their community in East Africa by British administrators who had no wish to favour them over the African masses. With limited help from their community organisations in Britain, they expect to make their own way and will apply themselves to this end with exceptional industry. There are already about 3,000 small Asian businesses in the London metropolitan area alone and British people who have to shop after 7 p.m. have reason to be grateful for their enterprise.

Most of them are Gujeratis, a people with more of the pioneering spirit than is common in India. Gujerati traders had established themselves in East Africa—even as far inland as Uganda—long before the first British explorer got there. If as a result of General Amin's intransigence the Ugandan Asians are obliged to arrive here in large batches and with little money, they will obviously need the help now offered to them by the Government and by voluntary workers. But the hope of most race relations experts is that absorption will be a rapid operation, doing nothing to hinder the readiness of these immigrants to take care of themselves.

Gen. Amin relents on expulsion of citizens

Standard Staff Reporter
Reprinted with permission, ©East African Standard, Nairobi, August 23, 1972

President Amin said in Kampala yesterday that Asians holding Ugandan citizenship would not be expelled from Uganda if they could prove their citizenship status.

Speaking at a luncheon in honour of the Sudanese Foreign Minister, Dr. Mansour Khaled, Gen. Amin said: "Asians who are Ugandan citizens will not be required to leave the country".

According to the Information Ministry, he said that under the second phase of his Government's programme to put the economy of Uganda under Ugandan control, the citizenship claims of all Asians holding Ugandan passports would be carefully checked.

Although there was misguided opposition from outside Uganda on the move to expel non-Ugandans from Uganda, Gen. Amin said the people of Uganda "firmly support him in what he is doing."

He made it clear that Asians who are Ugandan citizens would not be required to leave the country, but during the second phase to put the economy of Uganda under the control of Ugandans, he would carefully check the citizenship of all those claiming to be Ugandans.

"Those found to have dual citizenship will be given notice to leave the country," he added.

There was "nothing racist in what he was doing since his policy was designed to improve the economic position of Uganda."

He recalled that when the soldiers handed over power to him in 1971, they made eighteen points, and he has made sure that he implemented those points, one of which concerned the improvement of Uganda's economy.

"Is there room at the inn?"

News Compilation

London Area

Ealing: This borough has about 35,000 immigrants out of a population of 300,000—and they are predominantly Asian. About 4,000 East African Asians have settled in the past four years, and it is forecast that about 2,000 Ugandan Asians will make for Ealing.

Employment prospects are good because the Asians find work at Heathrow Airport or in London's service and transport industries. Housing prospects are reasonable but the biggest worry is education. In the last eight months Ealing registered 1,533 immigrant children, of which 509 were of East African Asians, a quarter of them from Uganda.

Brent: This borough has also put in a quick request for help because it is bound to be popular with Asian newcomers, with some 6,000 Asians already living there, mostly in the Wembley area. Brent has the largest immigrant population—7.4 per cent out of a population of 278,500—in the country. Brent would need at least £500,000 for emergency school accommodation in an already overcrowded situation. But jobs and housing are not crucial worries.

Midlands

Leicester: Population: 280,000. Immigrants: over 30,000. East African Asians: 6,000 Ugandan Asians who already account for a fifth of the city's immigrant population. The city has the highest percentage of immigrant children in secondary schools outside London. About 100 immigrant pupils arrive in the city each month.

Mr Tony Davies, Director of Education, said: "We are geared to cope with this sort of number but a sudden increase would be too much. We just haven't got the room."

The city is already sending hundreds of immigrant college students up to 30 miles outside the city for higher education.

There are 10,000 people on the housing waiting list out of a total population of 280,000. A reception committee for Ugandan refugees set up last week hopes to put up hundreds of families in properties earmarked for demolition and thousands more in the homes of the present Asian community.

Continued on Page 30

Advertisement

ANNOUNCEMENT

The British High Commission in Kampala wishes to announce that they are ready to proceed with the issue of entry certificates for the United Kingdom to those holders of British passports in Uganda who have previously applied for quota vouchers and to their dependants whose applications are already lodged with the High Commission.

To facilitate the smooth working of this operation, and in order to minimise inconvenience for all concerned, it is proposed to announce periodically in the "Uganda Argus" the High Commission reference numbers of those persons required to attend for final processing of their applications to settle in the United Kingdom.

The holders of the following reference numbers should attend at the High Commission on August 28 between 8 a.m. and 11.30 a.m., 2 p.m. and 4 p.m. bringing with them their valid passports and, where applicable, the passports of their dependants who have been notified to the High Commission.

High Commission reference numbers P63/19 to P63/79 inclusive; P64/4808 to P64/8212B inclusive, and P65/0043 to P65/5394 inclusive.

Quota voucher applicants other than those whose reference numbers have been quoted are asked not to attend at the High Commission until they are called forward in future public announcements.

Further announcements will follow with regard to the arrangements for dealing with applications from other British passport holders who wish to proceed to the United Kingdom.

SPECIAL CITY COUNCIL TO DISCUSS ASIANS

Reprinted with permission, ©Leicester Mercury, August 24, 1972

LEICESTER CONSERVATIVES have requisitioned a special meeting of the City Council to discuss the Ugandan Asian problem, which they describe as "one of the most serious emergencies the city has ever faced."

Some members of the Tory group are known to be worried about "wild mutterings" said to be going on in public houses and shops in some areas.

The Tories have called the emergency meeting of the council, which will probably take place next week, because they want immediate action and feel the "cosy talks" the Labour group are having between themselves and a few local immigrant spokesmen are quite inadequate .

Leader of the Conservative Group, Alderman Kenneth Bowder, said today: "The city as a whole must be consulted and the Government told what we as a City demand.

"We want action. We want it now. We want the people of Leicester as a whole to express a view to Central Government—and to do that with a loud clear voice with no delay.

"If we are to help the unfortunate Ugandan Asians, we must have assistance from the Central Government. A start must be half of the £4 million that General Amin must not now get—we need this in Leicester.

Meanwhile, a giant petition calling on the City Council to take all possible measures to prevent a large influx of Asians to Leicester because of the social and economic problems it would cause is circulating in rectories in the Evington Valley area.

It will be presented to the City Council's emergency meeting by Councillor Barrie Clayton, who expects it will have attracted many hundreds of signatures by the weekend.

'SILLY TALK'

He says of the petition: "This is one way the ordinary people of Leicester can make their feelings known to the council and ultimately the Government."

His brother, Councillor Michael Clayton added: "It is better for people to think seriously in terms of a petition than to engage in mutterings. There is a lot of wild and silly talk going on in supermarkets and pubs."

Councillors Barrie and Michael Clayton were among the Conservative members who have requisitioned the special council meeting. The others are Alderman Bowder, Alderman Reg Williamson, and Councillor Michael Cufflin.

Their requisition notice handed in to the Town Clerk, Mr. R. R. Thornton, calls for a meeting "at which the business shall be to consider all aspects of the impact on the city, its people, local services, employment and amenities of the arrival of further immigrants and, in particular the possible large numbers from Uganda.

Continued on Page 30

Ugandan Asian Expulsion: 90 Days and Beyond through the Eyes of the International Press

Continued from Page 27

Australian reaction

But he said 2000 was a possible number which Australia could absorb over some months.

He said the Government would be treating any migration applications from Uganda Asians on individual merits.

Dr. Forbes said the Government had acted in the interests of the Australian community. "We believe we have got to think of Australians first," he said.

In Australia-wide reaction to the plight of the Uganda Asians yesterday:

*The West Australian Premier (Mr. Tonkin) said he felt it was the State's duty to take some of the Asians to be expelled.

*The South Australian Premier (Mr. Dunstan) said he would welcome displaced Uganda Asians on a restricted basis.

*The Victorian Council of Churches urged the Federal Government to "respond in very positive terms to the desperate need of Asians in Uganda."

*Former Federal Labor leader Mr. Caldwell said it was "rubbish" to try to pressure the Government on this issue. Australia should not take any of the Uganda Asians, he said.

Continued from Page 29

SPECIAL CITY COUNCIL TO DISCUSS ASIANS

"Such council business to include the consideration of a motion that the Central Government shall make funds available now to assist with the reception of all future immigrants and also shall specifically assist with the provision of additional housing, so that the present waiting lists are not prejudiced, and also with the provision of additional job opportunity".

Alderman Bowder said of this notice: "We feel it is now high time there was a discussion which can be fully reported to the public. The proper place to do this is in the Council Chamber, where there can be a serious exchange of views account can be taken of the anxieties of Leicester people, and in which elected representatives can play their part.

"We have drawn up our notice in the widest possible terms so that if Labour want to co-operate with us in the wording of any subsequent motions for debate at the special meeting we will be very happy to discuss this serious matter with them.

"This is a matter where all parties and all citizens need to co-operate together to face what could be one of the most serious emergencies for Leicester for a long time if not for all time."

'RIDICULOUS'

Meanwhile the suggestion from Asian leaders that Leicester can take 1,000 Ugandan Asians has come in for strong criticism from other Asians.

Mr. Ramesh Jani, President of the Indian Art Circle, declared in a statement to the Leicester Mercury: "Their futile and irresponsible statements in the press have only caused uproar in the city and nothing else."

Some of the statements are "ridiculous" he said.

Pointing out that there has been no official Government statement on how many Asians Leicester will have to take, he added: "It's useless to say that we will make a place for 1,000 or 10,000 or 15,000 Asians when we are not sure whether we can accommodate them."

Leicester is not ready to take them all, he said, and the best way is to find out how many houses are available and then tell the government how many Leicester can take. He does not recommend slum houses.

"We do not want to turn our beautiful city into a slum city", he stressed.

Continued from Page 29

"Is there room at the inn?"

Coventry: Population: 340,000. Immigrants: 20,000 to 23,000. East African Asians 800 to 1,200, Asians 19,000. Expects 800 to 1,000 Ugandan Asians.

Mr Paul Stephenson, community relations officer, said that Coventry should be able to absorb the newcomers fairly easily. "Education will be no problem. Those of school age will be very skilled linguistically." A meeting of all East African Asians in the city has been called for tomorrow, when plans will be worked out and an advisory consultative committee set up.

Warley (includes Smethwick): Population: 164,000. Immigrants: 15,000. East African Asians: about 500. Asians: 9,000. Expects about 400 Ugandan Asians.

The Town Clerk's department said: "We are not under any housing pressure at the moment. We are coping without having anything to spare."

Wolverhampton: Population: 265,000. Immigrants: 22,000. East African Asians: 1,000. Asians: 12,000. Expects about 1,000 Ugandan Asians.

Mr Aaron Haynes, Community Relations Officer, made this appeal: "The British representatives in Kampala should be getting from potential arrivees the approximate areas in Britain in which they want to settle, so that local authorities can be alerted. Local education authorities should be told beforehand the number they will have to find places for."

There are 6,750 immigrant children in Wolverhampton's schools - 13.2 per cent.

Birmingham: Population: 1,013,000.

Immigrants: 55,000. East African Asians: 1,500. Asians: 25,000. Expects about 500 Ugandan Asians.

The city's schools at present have about 30,000 immigrant children. Councillor Mrs Sheila Wright, Education Committee chairman, said: "It will be a hard job throughout a fair proportion of the city to find extra school places."

Peterborough: The authority has written to Whitehall calling for a conference of local authorities to draw up a policy.

Council leader Coun. Charles Swift, said, "We could, if pressed, find at least 50 suitable properties in an emergency such as this, perhaps more, but other local authorities especially those in expanding towns must do the same.

Coun. Swift, who is also chairman of the Community Relations Committee at Peterborough, where one in ten of the population are immigrants, added: "We must avoid at all costs the creation of ghettoes: there must be complete integration."

North

Blackburn: (pop. 102,000) has 7,000 immigrants, mostly from India and Pakistan, with a very small number from East Africa. An influx from Uganda would be a strain on school places, as there has been a 16 per cent rise this year in immigrant school population.

Manchester: (population 560,000) has an immigrant population of 20,000 Asians of whom nearly 2,000 are from East Africa. The senior community relations officer, Mr Surenda Kumar, said: "I do not think there would be much of a strain on the educational system as the immigrant community is widely dispersed."

Bolton: (pop 155,000) has an immigrant community of between 9,000 and 10,000. Most are Indians with some Pakistanis. There are about 1,000 West Indians and 1,000 from East Africa. "We expect about 1,000 will come from Uganda to join relatives and friends already in Bolton", said Mr Abdul Qureshi, assistant community relations officer. He said that school accommodation was already overcrowding and no houses were available.

Huddersfield: (population 130,000) has about 6,000 Asians but only 20 or 30 families from East Africa. The town could find council house accommodation for about 20 or 30 more families.

Rhodesia out of Olympics

News Compilation, August 23, 1972

Rhodesia, whose entry in the 20th Olympic Games in Munich, West Germany had led to boycott threats by black African nations, was voted out of the 1972 summer games by the International Olympic Committee.

Rhodesia's entry was protested because of the country's racial policies. Rhodesia's entry had first touched off only a token opposition from smaller African nations, including Tanzania, Sierra Leon and Sudan. But the protest took on a new shape last week when Ethiopia and Kenya, the continent's two athletic powers, joined the boycott.

The threat of a boycott grew when a group of U.S. black athletes pledged in an unsigned statement to boycott the games if Rhodesia was allowed to compete.

The Games are scheduled to begin on August 26, 1972.

Page 30 *Ugandan Asian Expulsion: 90 Days and Beyond through the Eyes of the International Press*

'KEEP THEM OUT' MARCH

Protestors march in front of the Home Office.

Reproduced with permission,
©Robert Kemp/Times Newspapers Limited

'Enoch's right,' chant porters

By KEITH DEVES and BRIAN WESLEY
Reprinted with permission, ©Sun Newspapers Limited, London,
August 25, 1972

MEAT PORTERS and members of the National Front marched to protest against the "invasion of Asians" yesterday.

Police were taken by surprise as demonstrators stormed the Home Office. Later a spokesman said they had not been prepared for the "amazing alliance."

Scuffles broke out as 300 Nazi-saluting marchers were pushed back.

"Big Danny" Harmston, a porter who supports the ultra-right wing National Front, told marchers: "The Asians will never integrate.

"They are no more British than I am Japanese."

WARNING

The demonstration went on as Sir Charles Cunningham—the former civil servant heading an emergency board to deal with the Asian influx—spelled out a warning on the radio. Uganda Asians will be on their way "very soon" and in large numbers, he said. The first of the 40,000 immigrants is due next Thursday.

Sir Charles said "all persuasion available" would be used to guide Asians into areas of Britain not already strained by immigration.

But the board could not direct them to a particular area.

At the Home Office three marchers were allowed through police lines with a protest note.

It said "When will the Government take action to stop immigration?"

Passers-by cheered as the marchers chanted "Enoch, Enoch."

Coloured drivers were booed as the march turned away from Whitehall.

And along the embankment a group of coloured women were forced over a low wall into gardens.

Police said they had been carried over by the weight of marchers.

As the demonstrators passed the end of Fleet Street they chanted "liars, liars."

The biggest shouts and boos came when a lorry marked Mid-Asian Transport passed the demo.

Ugandan Asian Expulsion: 90 Days and Beyond through the Eyes of the International Press

ASIANS HERE PENNILESS: PLEA FOR AID

Reprinted with permission, ©Leicester Mercury, August 25, 1972

AS LEICESTER prepared to send a deputation to the Home Secretary, Mr. Robert Carr, to stress the serious consequences of an Asian influx, the full nature of the crisis which may face the city was underlined by the plight of the first family to arrive from Uganda.

They were penniless, having been stripped of money—and jewellery at Kampala airport, and the father and two sons had to be housed at Hillcrest while the mother and daughter went to relatives.

They had had their rings, watches and other jewellery seized by Ugandan Customs officers, and the father, an accountant, was not even allowed to keep the 40p which he had managed to take to the airport.

They were one of six families to arrive penniless in a week and with the fear that this situation may be multiplied many times in the coming weeks, Leicester is asking for financial and physical aid from the Government. Mr. Tom Bradley, MP for North-East Leicester, has sent a telegram to Mr. Carr asking him to receive a deputation as "the situation facing Leicester is critical."

Alderman Edward Marston, leader of the Labour Group and of the Council issued this statement following a meeting of his group's Policy Committee: "The decision of the Ugandan Government to expel Asians is a major tragedy for these people. The decision of the British Government to admit them to Britain is to be supported as a humane and necessary act.

"We believe, however, that the Government should be advised in the strongest possible terms that Leicester has extremely little room for any more arrivals either in housing, social and health services, or in the schools.

<u>TEMPORARY</u>

"In their own interests they should be urged to try to settle in other places which are less overcrowded.

"While emergency steps will be willingly taken to shelter and receive them here as a temporary measure, we can hold out very little promise to absorb many thousands of new arrivals on a permanent and satisfactory basis.

"The Ugandan Resettlement Board is also being acquainted with the difficulties of Leicester and is being asked to supply as much information as possible about the numbers, ages, etc. of those likely to come to Leicester."

The Leicester deputation will comprise the Lord Mayor, Alderman Stanley Tomlinson; the leader of the Labour Group and Council, Alderman Edward Marston; the leader of the Conservative group, Alderman Kenneth Bowder; the Labour assistant whip, Councillor Mrs. Janet Setchfield; and the Town Clerk Mr. R. R. Thornton.

Continued on Page 34

ASIANS CAN STAY WHERE THEY LIKE
Board powerless to aid crowded areas

By BRIAN SILK
Reprinted with permission, ©Telegraph Group Limited, London, August 25, 1972

THE resettlement board set up to deal with the Asian refugees from Uganda will be powerless to prevent many of them flooding into areas of Britain which already have big immigrant communities.

Sir Charles Cunningham, chairman of the board, made this clear yesterday, as cities and towns with high Asian populations called for urgent action to prevent their public services being overwhelmed by the newcomers from Uganda.

Sir Charles said his board could do no more than persuade the Ugandans to settle in areas which are not already under stress from immigration. "But we can't order people about and tell them where to go in this country," he said.

Many of the Asians could be expected to ignore the board's advice and settle in areas where Asian communities were already well established.

"The first phase of 15,000 due to come next month are most likely to have relatives in this country," said Sir Charles.

They had applied for entry vouchers before President Amin of Uganda decided to expel all Asians with British passports.

"Many of these will, of course, want to go to these areas which are already overcrowded.

Job of persuasion

"We have no power to require anyone not to go anywhere," said Sir Charles. "That would

Continued on Page 34

"We can't stop them swamping the ghettoes"
ASIANS - THE BIG FEAR

By BRIAN PARK and LEO CLANCY
Reprinted with permission, ©Daily Mail, London, August 25, 1972

THE Home Office said yesterday that it cannot prevent many of the 50,000 Uganda Asians due in Britain in the next few weeks from settling in areas which feel they already have as many immigrants as they can cope with.

But last night Sir Charles Cunningham, chairman of the new Asian Resettlement Board, suggested that financial inducement might be offered to steer the Asians where they could be more easily absorbed.

Sir Charles said: 'At this stage nothing can be ruled out. Certainly we will use all persuasion available. However, the Government will have to decide if, and for what purpose, public funds are used.'

'Remember this is a democratic country. We can't order people anywhere they don't want to go.'

Yesterday, councils throughout the country were planning to meet what they see as an emergency. London boroughs such as Ealing and Brent, and cities like Birmingham, Leicester and Bradford, fear that their housing and social service resources could be overwhelmed by the new influx.

Magnet

The city fears that its large East African Asian population will act as a magnet to the refugees.

Alderman Edward Marston, leader of the council, said last night: 'We are virtually full up. All our services are working to the limit. In their own interest, new arrivals should be urged to settle in other places less overcrowded.'

EALING, which includes the immigrant area of Southall, sent a deputation to Conservative Central Office yesterday.

Councillor John Telfer, leader of the council, said: 'We have such a massive problem already that we just cannot stand the influx of even another thousand.'

BIRMINGHAM will have a conference next week to assess the capacity of welfare services to deal with an anticipated 3,000 thousands Asians.

Councillor Stanley Yapp, a leader of the controlling Labour group said: 'We feel Birmingham has reached the limit of its ability to take more immigrants who might tend to settle in areas already over-burdened with immigrant problems.'

In *LONDON* yesterday, 500 market porters from Smithfield and Billingsgate joined National Front extremists to march from Smithfield to Whitehall and back, handing in a 'stop the immigrants' petition of the Home Office.

All the way they chanted: 'If you're black - go back. If you're white, you're all right'; and 'Two, four, six, eight - we don't want to integrate.'

They booed coloured passers-by and waved their banners menacingly at coloured bus and transport drivers.

Two of the leaders of the march were Smithfield porters Ron Taylor and Dennis 'Big Dan' Harmston. Both marched in support of Mr. Enoch Powell in 1968 after his 'rivers of blood speech,' and Mr. Harmston stood as a candidate for Sir Oswold Mosley's British Union Movement in the 1966 General Election.

VOLUNTEERS, including social workers, nurses and doctors, will be at Heathrow and Gatwick airport with £500 each to distribute to anyone arriving without enough money for immediate needs. They will also advise on where to stay, how to get there and where to obtain further advice.

Both cash and volunteers are provided by War on Want and Community Service Volunteers. Oxfam is also contributing to costs.

Page 32

Ugandan Asian Expulsion: 90 Days and Beyond through the Eyes of the International Press

Canada will take up to 5,000 Uganda Asians

By Guy Demarino
Reprinted with permission, ©Southam News Service, Canada,
August 25, 1972

Canada will accept up to 5,000 Uganda Asians within two months.

In announcing the cabinet decision Thursday "to offer an honorable place in Canadian life" to some of the 50,000 Asians ordered out of Uganda by early November, Prime Minister Trudeau said he has authorized Immigration Minister Mackasey to set up an emergency admission program.

The Trudeau announcement did not specify how many Ugandans would be allowed into Canada, but Mr. Mackasey later told Southam News Services he expected 3,000 Ugandans would take up Canada's offer to help immediately, and 1,000 or 2,000 more would do likewise as the program begins working.

There is no upper limit in the offer, said the minister, "but if all the developed Commonwealth countries do their share to help 5,000 people for Canada should be adequate," he said.

However, Canada would not be prepared to accept anywhere near the 15,000 to 18,000 Asians mentioned in recent news stories as a British suggestion to the Canadian government, Mr. Mackasey added.

May qualify

The prime minister announced that a team of immigration and health officials would fly to Uganda's capital, Kampala, to speed up the processing of the applicants. This, he said, would give Canada "a clearer impression of the numbers involved" and of "exceptional measures" which may be necessary to admit those unable to meet Canada's immigration qualifications.

Mr. Mackasey said he hoped all applicants would qualify under the immigration point system, but if necessary the system would be relaxed. He added that Canada is prepared to let the Ugandans in under its assisted passage scheme, under which the cost of travelling to Canada is advanced to the prospective immigrant and is repaid to the government later.

Entebbe Airport: Among the first to leave. Most of the Asians who left early had plans to leave even before the announcement to expel the Asians.

Reproduced with permission, ©Associated Press/Wide World Photos

Canada must help save Asians

Editorial
Reprinted with permission, ©Toronto Star syndicate,
August 25, 1972

Prime Minister Trudeau deserves credit for authorizing the admission to Canada, on an emergency basis, of Asians facing forcible expulsion from Uganda.

This is the humane course, and it also shows some political courage when there is much public opinion against further immigration at a time of high unemployment in Canada.

To bar the Ugandan Asians because of our unemployment problem would be short-sighted as well as unmerciful. There is much that governments can do to create more jobs for both present and new Canadians. And Canada's past experience is encouraging, for there is no doubt that immigrants have made a large new contribution to both economic growth and employment. It should be noted also that the Ugandan Asians appear to be exceptionally enterprising and self-reliant people.

The Asians are threatened by a wretched fate at the hands of a brutal African military dictator. They have been ordered to leave Uganda by the end of October, or face worse consequences. Emergency transport must therefore be provided, and the Asians will need some financial help. Canada's foreign aid program includes an annual payment to Uganda of about $1.5 million, and at least that amount should go to assisting the Asians instead of benefitting the oppressive Uganda government.

Uganda President Idi Amin says he had a message straight from God to throw the Asians out.

Continued on Page 36

Mackasey fears genocidal war

By Southam News Services
Reprinted with permission, ©Southam News Service, Canada,
August 25, 1972

Canada does not want to be held responsible for a possible massacre of Ugandans. Immigration Minister Mackasey said Thursday after the announcement that Canada would accept up to 5,000 Uganda Asians within two months.

Mr. Mackasey's statement was in answer to a question as to whether accepting the Ugandans would be interpreted as tacit approval of the expulsion.

"If a bunch of fanatics start a genocidal war against the Asians," he said, "we'd have it on our consciences. We are very concerned that the situation in Uganda could rapidly deteriorate."

He cited two precedents of large scale immigration to Canada, such as the 37,000 Hungarians accepted in the 1956-59 period and the 11,000 Czechs accepted in late 1968. He added that because the Uganda Asians fall mainly in the merchant or professional class, the problem of job-finding would not be as acute as some critics insist.

Many have cash

"No doubt there will be a backlash among some groups." Mr. Mackasey conceded. "But they (the Asians) are a people in need of help." He said there would not be a means test as such, but the point system includes ways of showing "the ability to support yourself."

In fact, for non-sponsored, independent immigrants having enough funds to establish a small business or store qualifies the applicant for 25 extra points—and 50 points means admission. Many of the Uganda Asians are said to have access to up to $25,000 each in cash deposited in banks outside Uganda.

Other cabinet sources said the discussion on the Asians' admittance was brief and the decision to allow them into Canada was generally supported by all ministers.

One of the things that the Canadian team flying to Uganda next week will have to organize is the means of transporting the new immigrants. Since they are apparently not allowed out of Uganda into neighboring countries, an airlift seems the only way. They could go to London, England and reach Canada from there, but chartered planes could be used for a direct flight to this continent.

Continued on Page 36

Continued from Page 32

ASIANS HERE PENNILESS: PLEA FOR AID

SATURATION

After the Labour Group decision the City Labour Party's Executive Committee met in the evening and approved the action to he taken.

Mr. Bradley said of his decision to send a telegram: "In Leicester we have reached saturation point and there is no possibility of the city coping with a further influx of immigrants without substantial Government assistance."

Dr. K. B. S. Seth, chairman of Leicester's British East African Subjects Association, said of the plight of the new arrivals: "This is typical 'of the harassment which Asians are already facing in Uganda, and the emergency has not yet begun."

"Customs officials in Uganda are taking what they can from Asian families, even those who were due to come here before the emergency but did not leave until afterward."

At Heathrow, the family was given train fare to Leicester and subsistence money for food.

In Leicester, the two women were given accommodation by relatives, but there was no room for the men.

At 11:30 p.m. last Friday night, they knocked on the door of Hillcrest Hospital, and were allowed to stay in the casualty ward, where there are 60 beds normally used for homeless people.

"The men were very well dressed. In the morning they were referred to a member of the Asian community and that was the last we saw of them" said a hospital spokesman.

Councillor David Taylor, vice chairman of the Social Services Committee, said Leicester could reach saturation if just another 20 Asians have to be put in Hillcrest.

He went on: "Yesterday, at a meeting of Labour councillors, people were bandying about figures of between 400 and 20,000.

One of the Indian leaders stated publicly that he could find homes for 500 of the Uganda Asians. He was asked last week to find homes for this family and they are now floating around Leicester. Need I say more?"

Councillor Taylor accused the Government of dragging its feet. Leicester fears that the city's large East African Asian population—estimated to number about 6,000—will act as a magnet to the refugees being expelled by President Amin.

FIRST QUESTION

Said Councillor Taylor: "There was a lot of pen pushing and form filling going on at the High Commission in Kampala.

"Surely, one of the first questions to be asked is whether people have relatives in England and where. If it is not on the form It damn well should be."

Mr. Anthony Simpson, prospective Parliamentary candidate for West Leicester, speaking to Conservatives in the city last night, said: "The problem which troubles all of us is undoubtedly that of the Ugandan Asians who were granted British passports at the time of independence by an inhumane and blatantly racialist Act (though not sufficiently racialist for Uganda to be banned from the Olympic Games).

President Amin has evicted a whole community. It is right that the British Government should accept the responsibility and honours its promises to these people.

"The speed of the Government's plans to receive them, and in particular Leicester's continuing responsible attitude in making the necessary preparations inspired by the Conservatives rather than the Labour group on the council, are in the highest traditions of humanity for which Britain is renowned. The focus of further strains on housing, schools and hospitals are very real but not insuperable."

PETITIONS

The Foreign Office today said that Britain is morally and legally responsible for the Asians expelled from Uganda.

A spokesman was commenting on reports that the Asians' right to come to Britain was taken away by a Labour Government Act of 1968.

He said that if the Asians had nowhere to go, Britain was obliged by international law to take them as this law had been built up by custom over the years.

But in Leicester dozens of petitions all protesting against the Ugandan Asians are being organised.

Yesterday an article in the Leicester Mercury described a giant petition which had been circulating in the factories in the Evinton Valley area. Councillor Barrie Clayton is to present it to the City Council.

Last night Mr. Clayton's phone hardly stopped ringing. This morning there were more phone calls and a stack of letters. Everyone wanted to know how they could sign the petition.

THE ONLY WAY

Mr. Clayton said today: "The original petition is now completed so I suggested that all those interested should start their own petitions. Any councillor, would, I am sure, be prepared to present it to the council. Most people agreed to do this".

One petition expressing the same protest was organised on Wednesday in the Parker Drive factory of the Bentley Engineering Company.

More than 350 signatures were collected, and the original is to be sent to 10 Downing Street. Copies are to go to Mr. Enoch Powell, the City Council and local MPs.

One of the organisers, Mr. Dave Chalk, said: "If the number of Uganda Asians quoted are allowed to enter the country, it will affect our future and our children's future with regard to education, employment and housing.

"We are not racialists, but we feel we have got to take steps to secure our children's future. A petition seems the only way to register our protest."

Continued from Page 32

ASIANS CAN STAY WHERE THEY LIKE

require legislation and is a matter for the Government.

"The possibility of such legislation is a matter of opinion, but I would not rate them very high myself.

"The board's job will be one of dissuasion and persuasion; to dissuade the Asians from going to those areas where the social services are under pressure and to persuade them to go to other areas by pointing out the advantages."

He said the Asians would be told of the advantages in schooling, housing and employment in areas not already under pressure. "Whether that kind of argument will persuade them one can only guess."

Advice on ship

The board will consider a suggestion that Asians should be brought to Britain by sea so that advice on resettlement could be given during the voyage. This would give them the opportunity to consider their future more carefully instead of hastily settling in an immigrant community after a short flight.

"But it is too late to make arrangements for transporting the first 15,000 by sea," he said. "Plans for transporting them by air are already going ahead."

With only a week to go before the Asians are due to start arriving in large numbers, steps to deal with them are being taken in districts which feel particularly threatened.

Call for aid

Eight Conservative councillors in Ealing called for Government financial aid to keep Ugandan Asians out of the borough.

In Leicester, an emergency meeting of the city council has been called for next week to discuss what local Conservatives described as "one of the most serious emergencies this city has ever faced."

In Birmingham, Ald Charles Collett asked for an emergency meeting of the city council. The arrival of many immigrants would cause Birmingham's social services to collapse, he said.

Official and voluntary welfare organisations in Birmingham are meeting to discuss the situation. The city's education, social welfare and health departments have been told to prepare reports on their ability to cope with more immigrants.

Councillor Stanley Yapp, Labour leader of the City council said: "We feel Birmingham has reached the limits of its ability to take more immigrants who might tend to settle in areas already overburdened with immigrant problems. This point will be put to the Government."

Manchester Corporation is having talks today with local community relations officers to consider the effect of a large influx of Asians on housing, welfare and education.

Charter flights

The seven airlines which have agreed to operate an emergency airlift from Uganda told the Government yesterday that they could supply sufficient aircraft to handle 15,000 people during September.

It is expected that about four flights a day will be needed to transport the 15,000. Besides two scheduled flights a day, the airlines say they can provide another three or four charter flights daily.

The suggestion that some of the Asians could be transported to Britain by sea came yesterday from Mr John Ennals, director of the Immigrant Advisory Committee.

He said: "The longer they take to travel the more time we have to prepare for suitable places for them to go and live and to work. And the longer the time local authorities have to find school classes and so on."

Mr Ennals, who is also a member of the Co-ordinating Committee for the Welfare of Evacuees from Uganda, said that voluntary advisory teams including medical personnel would be at Heathrow and Gatwick airports from September to meet arriving refugees.

Cash would also be supplied for the immediate needs of Asians in need, he said. The committee already had £4,000 to spend.

British laud Canada on offer to Asians:
"Thank you, Pierre"

Reprinted with permission,
©Canadian Press, August 26, 1972
Published in The Globe & Mail, Toronto

LONDON (CP)— A wave of highly favorable comment here has greeted Canada's decision to accept some of the Asians facing deportation from Uganda.

A Canadian High Commission spokesman said he could not remember a time when Canada figured more prominently in British news since the Suez crisis of 1956.

The British Government warmly welcomed the Canadian decision, announced Thursday, to accept some of the 50,000 Asians who hold British passports.

A Foreign Office spokesman described the move as "genuinely humane" and said he hoped the Canadian example would be followed by other Commonwealth governments.

Newspapers yesterday gave headline treatment to the action and some carried front page pictures of Prime Minister Pierre Trudeau. "Thank You, Pierre," said a headline in the Evening Standard.

However, some Canadian tourists interviewed in London were not so pleased with the decision. Diana Mohring, 27, of London, Ont., said she feared "these people will be used as political footballs by the opponents of Mr. Trudeau. They'll just get kicked around while the political parties fight it out at the next general election."

Canadian Prime Minister
Pierre Elliot Trudeau

Reproduced with permission,
©UPI/Corbis-Bettmann

Gerl Morris, 19, of Toronto, a visiting student, said the Asians might increase the unemployment problem in Canada. "But immigrants to Canada have to meet certain standards when they apply to come in and that should sort out part of the problem."

An editorial in the Evening News yesterday said Mr. Trudeau had stepped forward to champion a just but politically dangerous cause.

"This is a brave action by Trudeau. Canada today has an unemployment problem and the Trudeau Government must soon face an election. But he is prepared to stand by Britain and assist the homeless victims of brutal African oppression."

Meanwhile, a race relations leader here has resigned over the problem of the Asians. Bernard Perkins, 44-year-old chairman of the Greater London Council housing committee, decided to resign from the Community Relations Board that gives expert aid and advice to immigrants.

Mr. Perkins said he has fought against racialism all his life, but the influx of 40,000 or 50,000 Asians would do more to upset racial harmony than anything else which could happen.

'WELCOME TO LEICESTER' BOOKLET FOR UGANDA ASIANS

Reprinted with permission, ©Leicester Mercury, August 26, 1972

A BOOKLET called "Welcome to Leicester" is being distributed among Ugandan Asians in Kampala, claims Dr. Kundan Seth, a leader of Leicester's immigrant community.

And last night the Leicester British Asian Welfare Society decided to operate a rota system to ensure that some of their members are on hand to meet Asian families when they arrive in Leicester and to help them with money and accommodation where necessary.

Starting next Tuesday, 250 of the Asians already in Leicester will operate a four-hour rota from 6 a.m. to midnight each day, and they are asking British Rail and bus operators to set up reception offices at London Road station and St. Margaret's bus station.

The "Welcome to Leicester" booklet gives details of the city's education and welfare services—including where to obtain social security benefits—housing, social facilities, and English ways, and it is designed to help people adjust.

It mentions the fact that English people may find it difficult to get used to cooking smells or noisy neighbours, and that English people do not like to interfere with people's privacy.

It is published by the Commonwealth Citizens' Consultative Committee of the Council of Social Service, at 39 London Road, Leicester. According to an informant of Dr. Seth, it is being freely distributed in Kampala and London.

Dr. Seth said today that at present the Asian community in Leicester can offer homes to 500 people, providing they are given the services. There are 24 houses available and the rest of the people can be accommodated in other people's homes", he said.

"We are watching that we don't overcrowd the area", he stressed.

VOLUNTEERS

Another leader of the immigrant community Dr. M. A. J. Shakar, said: "I find it difficult to understand the attitude of the leaders of the City Council who say we cannot take one more British Asian.

Continued on Page 36

Petitions mount

Reprinted with permission, ©Leicester Mercury, August 26, 1972

THOUSANDS of residents in the city and county are organising and signing petitions in an attempt to stop the Ugandan Asians from coming to Leicester.

One Leicester housewife, Mrs. June Rich, of Palmerston Boulevard, has appealed to the public to raise a petition against the Ugandan Asians in their own street or road and send it to the Leicester City Council.

"If someone in every street in Leicester were to organise a petition in their own area, then we would have thousands of protesters," Mrs. Rich said.

Continued on Page 36

Advertisement

ANNOUNCEMENT

ALL Indian passport holders who are now in Kampala are requested to call at the Indian High Commission, Kampala, for furnishing additional particulars about themselves and their families. This applies also to those who may previously have already registered with the Indian High Commission. Heads of families or other responsible persons only need come in person together with passports of the remaining members of their families on Monday the 28th August, 1972, between 8 a.m. and 6 p.m.

2. Similar arrangements are being made for Indian Nationals outside Kampala. Details will be announced in the next days.

Continued from Page 33
Canada must help save Asians

His anti-Asian drive however seems as much motivated by greed for their property, which they will probably be compelled to leave behind.

The expelled Asians' only assets may be their education and skills. But they have been the backbone of Uganda's business community, as well as comprising most of that country's lawyers, doctors and teachers. Their forced departure seems likely to ruin Uganda, but could be Canada and other countries' gain.

Britain is opening its doors to Asians who have British citizenship, and some of the older people may go to India and Pakistan if they are accepted there. But there will still have to be a good deal of international co-operation if all the Asians are to be succored.

Canada has a duty as a wealthy Commonwealth country to play the fullest part in what is essentially a humane rescue operation. The Uganda dictator is unstable and unpredictable—his near neighbor, Tanzania President Julius Nyerere, calls him a "primitive animal" as well as a racist. Let us act swiftly and energetically, remembering that outside help proved to be too little and too late to save many German Jews from Hitler's massacres.

Continued from Page 33
Mackasey fears genocidal war

The Trudeau statement concluded that the humanitarian reasons given for the government decision would help Uganda and also Great Britain whose people "would otherwise be forced to share their already overcrowded island with a tide of involuntary immigrants."

Both the prime minister and Mr. Mackasey said the Uganda Asians would add to the cultural richness and variety of Canadian life and will make, together with other Asian immigrants already here, an "important contribution to Canadian society. "

Continued from Page 37
Metro's East Africans to help Asian refugees

Spadina riding and was speaking at a meeting at the International Institute on Davenport Road.

Other speakers at last night's meeting, attended by about 60 Asians, were R. W. McPhee, assistant director of the Ontario Human Rights Commission; R. C. Pratt, professor of political economy at the University of Toronto; and Peggy MacKenzie, head of reception services for the Ontario government.

Continued from Page 35
'WELCOME TO LEICESTER' BOOKLET FOR UGANDA ASIANS

"I feel once a man has been admitted here as a British citizen he is free to go where he wishes. Some have friends and relations in Leicester and will want to come here".

He forecast that "several thousand" would come to Leicester.

Commenting on the Asian Welfare Society's decision to set up a rota of members to meet immigrants arriving from Uganda, Dr. Seth, who is vice-president of the society, said: "There is no shortage of volunteers or transport, and a sub-committee has been formed to raise funds so that Asians coming to Leicester can be given immediate financial assistance."

Money will be collected from Asian households and substantial donations have already been promised. "European people will not be contacted, but if they wish to donate anything we would welcome it," said Dr. Seth.

"European organisations and individuals have already made offers of temporary accommodation," he added.

Meanwhile it was announced today that Labour and Conservatives will be united in their approach to the Uganda Asians issue at the emergency Leicester City Council meeting and in their visit to the Home Office, both of which will take place on Thursday.

Leaders of both groups met yesterday and agreed upon the wording of a joint resolution to be put to the council's special meeting.

The special meeting will follow a visit to London by deputation from the Corporation who on Thursday morning have an appointment with one or the more of the Home Secretary's deputies.

The resolution which will be moved by the Conservative group leader Alderman Kenneth Bowder and seconded by the Labour leader Alderman Edward Marston will say:

*That the council having considered all aspects of the impact on the City of Leicester, its people, local services, employment and amenities, of the possible arrival of large numbers of refugees from Uganda advise the Central Government:

*That the housing, social services, health and education services of the city are already stretched to capacity.

*Although emergency measures will willingly be taken to shelter and receive them as a temporary measure, the city can hold out little promise of absorbing any great numbers on a permanent and satisfactory basis.

*That before such emergency measures can realistically be considered, a great deal of more firm information than currently available is essential.

*That substantial financial and physical assistance will be required from national resources to enable the city to take such measures.

In view of the above, every effort be made through the Ugandan Resettlement Board to persuade the refugees that they should look elsewhere for permanent settlement.

The City Council will also be recommended to authorise the General Purposes Committee to take such action as becomes necessary in pursuance of this motion.

Alderman Bowder said after the agreement between the two groups on a joint approach: "It is most important that we show the city that we are working together on this most serious matter."

Members of the South Leicester Constituency Labour Party have passed a resolution pledging to do all they can to ease the problem of British Asians from Uganda and urging the Government to do all in their power to welcome them to Britain and in addition, to make substantial financial assistance to councils to whose areas the immigrants come.

British Midland Airways are to help in the airlift of Asians from Uganda, but the planes will not be landing at the East Midland Airport at Castle Donington.

Mr. Michael Bishop, managing director of the airline, said they would be using two Boeing 707 aircraft to fly the Asians but all of them would go to London.

Continued from Page 35
Petitions mount

Social problems

During the last few days Mrs. Rich has been collecting names in her own area and she claims that 99 per cent of the people who are asked are signing the petition, which appeals to the Lord Mayor and city councillors to take all possible measures to prevent further immigrants from becoming domiciled in the city because of the social and economic problems this would cause.

"It is time the public spoke up because it is the only way to solve the problem," Mrs. Rich said.

Some residents in Blaby were out this morning petitioning in the main Lutterworth Road shopping area and already after only a few days more than 500 people have signed a petition protesting against any Ugandan Asians coming to the area.

Response 'tremendous'

Mrs. Jean Jackson and Mrs. Margaret Taylor, both housewives in Blaby, plan to hold a silent demonstration outside the Town Hall on Thursday before a special meeting of the city council, when they will hand their petition in.

Mrs. Jackson, of the Five Winds Nurseries, Blaby, said this morning that the response from the public had been "tremendous".

Some people are also petitioning the Leicestershire Counts Council and this morning residents of Birstall were sending a petition with nearly 100 names on it to County Hall.

I won't be a burden, says first man to arrive

Reprinted with permission, ©Leicester Mercury, August 26, 1972

LEICESTER'S first Ugandan Asian immigrant since the crisis started said today that he will settle wherever he can find a house for himself and his three children. And he added: "We Asians will not be a burden to Britain."

Mr. Babulal Thakerar and his two sons Deenesh (16), Narendre (18) and daughter Shobhana (22) arrived in the country ten days ago, penniless after they had been forbidden to take money out of Uganda with them. He has three other children, a married daughter in Leicester, another in India and his eldest son still in Uganda.

At Heathrow they were given £4, and train tickets to Leicester, where they hoped to join his daughter Mrs. Urmita Tana who lives at 37 Garfield Street.

Still optimistic

However, the house was full, and Mr. Thakerar and his two sons found themselves sleeping with the tramps in the casual ward at Hlllcrest Hospital reception centre on their first night in England.

"When we awoke and looked around, we just couldn't believe what we saw and where we were. In the morning we saw the superintendent, who explained that this had been temporary accommodation. The following day we moved in with friends of my son-in-law", said Mr. Thakerar.

Mr. Thakerar, a Uganda businessman and trained accountant, has already signed on at the Labour Exchange and put his name down on the local housing list.

Continued on Page 38

From Kampala to Wimbledon

By Philip Short, Kampala
Reprinted with permission, ©Times Newspapers Limited, London, August 27, 1972

ROZAK DAMANI is 32. He has a well-paid job as production manager of a Kampala firm making suitcases, and is married with two small children. His parents were born in East Africa, and both he and his pretty 28-year-old wife, Gulshen, have spent all their lives in Uganda. "I didn't ever want to leave this country. This is my home," he says. "I applied for my citizenship in 1964, but I never even had a reply. Now we have no choice but to go."

Over the next few weeks the Damanis and thousands of other British Asian families like them will be leaving Uganda to make new lives in Britain.

The wrench of leaving is hardest on the older generation. Rozak Damani's 79-year-old grandmother came out to Zanzibar from Gujerat in India as a young girl. His 60-year-old father was born in Zanzibar. They cannot imagine any other life than that they have known in Africa.

When I talked to Rozak Damani and his wife in the bungalow they bought when they married seven years ago, I found them not so much bitter as sad. "Once the President had said it, I knew he would not change his mind," said Rozak. "He is stubborn. So now we are going to Britain."

One of his five brothers, Amir, has been living in Wimbledon for some years as a shop manager for a sportswear firm. "My brother, when he writes to us, he says, well, although things are not all right and the local people are not very happy— just come here and I'll fix you up. He doesn't really see any problems. But some people say that in the end it will get very bad, and perhaps be almost like South Africa."

Rozak was a teacher before joining the suitcase firm. He was trained in suitcase manufacture in Tanzania, then made study visits to Italy, West Germany and Switzerland. Last year he visited Britain to study the operations of the Revelation firm.

His factory has a staff of six Asians and 45 Africans, and a turnover of about £100,000 a year. What will happen when the Asians go?

"Oh, I think it may collapse," says Rozak. "I have been training three Africans—and they are very good, they know almost everything—but it is difficult for them to control the other people. We have an extension planned to make handbags and soft luggage. The machines are already installed. But nobody knows how to make these soft luggage goods except me—and when I go it's going to be a total loss."

Then there is the problem faced by all these Asians—the property they cannot take with them.

Two nearly new cars stand outside his bungalow. Pointing to one of them, Rozak says: "Someone is offering me £100 for that car. It's worth £1,100.

Continued on Page 38

95 Uganda repatriates find new home

By A Staff Reporter
Reprinted with permission, ©Times of India, August 27, 1972

FORTY-EIGHT British passport-holding Indian settlers in Uganda, who shunted back by the same ship which they had travelled to East Africa, were on arrival in Bombay on Saturday, relieved to know that they could still set up home in England.

When the Magul Line's *Mozaffari* docked at Ballard Pier, the Indians were given endorsements on their passports allowing them to apply for entry certificates to Britain to any British High Commission's office in India.

The contingent, including 27 women and nine children, had left Bombay by the Mozaffari on August 5, hoping to rejoin their families in Uganda. All of them were refused entry into Tanzania or Kenya as the ship touched the ports of Mombasa and Dar-es-Salaam. They were prevented from landing at either port on their way to Uganda.

Continued on Page 38

MORE ASIANS ARE STRANDED ON LINER AT MOMBASA

By NATION Reporter
Reprinted with permission, ©Daily Nation, Nairobi, August 28, 1972

MORE than 60 Indian and British passport-holding Asians were stranded aboard the liner Karanja in Mombasa at the weekend when Kenyan Immigration authorities refused them transit through Kenya to Uganda.

The Asians—37 Indians and 24 Britons— were stopped from disembarking when it was learned they intended travelling to Kampala.

Indian and British High Commission consular staff immediately went on board to discuss the situation with their nationals and later three British passport-holding Asians, formerly resident in Uganda flew directly to London.

"The British High Commission people were very helpful. Some relatives in Kenya paid for the three air tickets to London and the High Commission granted them the necessary entry permits," said a spokesman for the British-India shipping line.

"It must have been quite unexpected for the three who thought they were returning home to

Continued on Page 38

TORONTO, CANADA
Metro's East Africans to help Asian refugees

News Compilation, August 28, 1972

A Metro organization set up as a pressure group to get Canada to admit exiled East Asian Ugandans to Canada is redirecting its efforts to help those refugees who do come here.

The change in policy for the Association of East African Asians is a result of the federal government's decision to admit from 3,000 to 5,000 of the 50,000 East Asians ordered to leave Uganda.

The federal policy was outlined by Peter Stollery, director of the Canadian Institute on Public Affairs, who said unemployment would have to take second place to the plight of the refugees. Stollery is the Liberal candidate in

Continued on Page 36

Injustice in Uganda

Editorial
Reprinted with permission, ©Chicago Tribune, August 27, 1972

In African countries, justice did not replace injustice when black native rule succeeded white foreign imperialism. That truth has been illustrated many times in recent years, but seldom as vividly as now in Uganda. President Idi Amin of that country is persecuting residents of Asian ancestry. Though he claims there is "nothing racist" about what he is doing, the 55,000 Asians headed for expulsion in less than three months for no reason other than their ancestry know better.

Fortunately, so do enough Africans to have had some influence on President Amin. After Ugandan students and President Julius Nyerere of Tanzania had condemned Amin's decision to expel all Asians, Ugandan citizens as well as British

Continued on Page 38

Ugandan Asian Expulsion: 90 Days and Beyond through the Eyes of the International Press   *Page 37*

Continued from Page 37

I won't be a burden, says first man to arrive

"Above all I want to find a home for my family " he said. "I don't care where we live as long as we have a house and I can find work for myself, my son and daughter, and a school for the young boy."

Mr. Thakerar was forbidden to take any money out of Uganda but did manage to bring personal belongings. His eldest son Vinod, has remained in Kampala to tie up all the family affairs.

"He is going to try and sell our house, and belongings. However, with the situation as it is, I doubt he will make much money on them, and I will have lost over £1,500 because of the expulsion." said Mr. Thakerar.

Today Mr. Thakerar will be leaving his temporary home at 144 Harrison Road to join his daughter and 18-year-old son who have already gone to London to find a home and work.

"We will stay in London until we can find permanent accommodations," said Mr. Thakerar "My daughter has already got a job and my son will be going to college in Sussex."

Despite the difficulties of the last few weeks and the loss of his home, Mr. Thakerar is still optimistic that he will quickly settle in England.

"We Asians will not be a burden to Britain," he said. "We will work hard and increase the country's wealth."

Continued from Page 37

Injustice in Uganda

ones, Amin rescinded his order aimed at Ugandan nationals of Asian ancestry. But there are reports that the Ugandan government may deny on some technicality or another the citizenship of almost half the 25,000 Asians who consider themselves Ugandan nationals. There is little hope that the 55,000 Asians eligible for British passports will be spared being driven into exile.

Amin's racist persecution of Indians and Pakistanis is catastrophic not only for the exiles, but for the black majority which will lose the Asians' services if Amin carries out his ruthless plans. In Uganda, Asians have conducted 90 per cent of the country's commerce and supplied 80 per cent of the doctors, lawyers, and teachers. No country can afford to lose precipitately a high proportion of its professionals and businessmen. Ignorant Ugandans may cheer Amin's decrees now, but the loss of the services of the exiled Asians will prove a hardship to all who remain in the country.

The problem for Ugandan Asians is one for Britain, too. Motivated no doubt more by concern for white colonials than for the Asian residents of African countries, Britain years ago gave pledges to holders of British passports in Africa that it is now being called upon to redeem. Whether or not Britain wants tens of thousands of indigent Asians, Home Secretary Robert Carr said what an honorable man in his position had to say: "This is a problem we are determined to handle in a humane and orderly way."

Those naive enough to expect independence to be more just than imperialism have been disappointed again.

Continued from Page 37

95 Uganda repatriates find new home

ALL PROPERTY LOST

The vessel also brought 47 Uganda Indians possessing Indian passports, who are assured of a welcome in the land of their origin, but have lost all they owned, except their personnel effects permitted to be carried by the Ugandan authorities in two small suitcases or handbags. They related harrowing tales of woe to reporters on their arrival.

The British passport-holders had been uncertain about their future. Their fears were set at rest when immigration officers of the British Deputy High Commission in Bombay boarded the vessel and endorsed on their passports permission to apply for entry certificates to the U.K. Mr. R. F. Tidy, information officer of the commission, personally supervised the endorsement.

The Indians were also issued visas to stay in India for a period of two months.

Some of the British passport-holding Indians were to go back to Uganda after studies in India. They said they did not have any money to meet their expenses while in India and did not know how to contact their parents in Uganda. It was quite likely that a large number of Indians had already been expelled from Uganda, the said.

As for those who hold Indian passports, they appeared forlorn and dejected.

They wished to remain anonymous lest the members of their families in Uganda should be subjected to more harassment. One of the repatriates said that on the border check-post, the Indians returning to the country of their origin were subjected to the worst kind of humiliation. They were searched at bayonet point by military men.

Indians and other Asian settlers being uprooted from Uganda were not allowed to carry any valuables with them. Nor were they permitted to take away Uganda money. Their property was being auctioned and the proceeds forced to be deposited in government banks. All recoveries were forfeited to the government. Gold and jewellery too were being confiscated.

A member of the party said that another Indian who had hidden a piece of gold in a "laddu" was caught by the military picket at the border. He was whisked away near Kellmbro and was not heard of since. Probably he was shot dead, the narrator said.

An Indian who had been in Kampala for 12 years was witch-hunted for long just because he dared to criticise the Ugandan government's policy towards Asian settlers. He was at long last allowed to go back to India and brought to the border check-point with military escort.

The Indians had contributed a lot to the economic prosperity of Uganda, one of the repatriates claimed. Most of the British passport-holding Indians, who have returned, had return tickets with them. The others had their fare paid by their employers.

Mr. Kishenlal Handa, deputy manager of the Shipping Corporation of India, which had chartered the *Mozaffari,* was present at Ballard Pier to look after the welfare of the repatriates at the landing site.

Continued from Page 37

MORE ASIANS ARE STRANDED ON LINER AT MOMBASA

Kampala after a holiday in India and instead found themselves starting a new life in London."

The British High Commission official temporarily resident in Mombasa, Mr. Simmons, spent the latter half of the weekend in Nairobi discussing the situation with senior High Commission officials.

It was understood that "intensive diplomatic conversations" took place between officials in Mombasa, Nairobi and Kampala, but the weekend holiday temporarily delayed any final decisions being taken until this morning.

A spokesman for the Indian High Commission in Mombasa yesterday stated: "Of the 37 Indian nationals who have had to stay on board the Karanja, 11 are permanent residents in Uganda, while the remaining 26 are visitors to that country.

"It is our great hope that this morning we will hear something from Kampala and that at least the 11 permanent residents will be allowed back into Uganda.

"The Kenyan authorities obviously need an assurance that these people will in fact be allowed entry into Uganda should they be in transit through Kenya," he added.

Meanwhile, the remaining 21 British passport-holding Asians have been in touch with relatives in Kampala on the telephone and it seems likely that should they not get the necessary clearance into Uganda their cases will be taken up through the High Commission.

The Karanja sails for Durban this afternoon before returning on its round-trip to Bombay. Anyone still remaining onboard by evening will continue to Durban from where they can either be repatriated to India or resettled in Britain.

Continued from Page 37

From Kampala to Wimbledon

Although it has been announced that all Asian-owned real estate must be registered by next Thursday, the registration forms are still not available. But the point seems rather academic to Rozak. "Even if I do sell my house, even if I get £2,500 for it, what do I do with it? Only this morning, the banks are telling me that I can take only £50 with me for my family and myself."

So Rozak has become philosophical about his possessions. "I really don't care any more. We know that we are a hard-working people. If we are given a chance, a fair chance, in England, or anywhere, we can manage."

Wendy Hughes writes: In Wimbledon yesterday, Rozak Damani's brother Amir said: "I suppose three of my brothers may have to leave Uganda, but I have never thought of their arrival as creating any problems."

Even if Rozak Damani is allowed to bring very little money out of Uganda, Amir will not be worried. "I have a small flat over the shop in Wimbledon. This will be adequate until they can find their own places. And I would naturally help them financially if they need it, but there is no reason why Rozak should not start work at once."

Amir rejects any idea that his relatives might have to live on Social Security. "There would never be any question of such a thing. I do not believe in it and there would be no necessity for it," he says. "They are well-educated and professional people, and there are plenty of jobs here for skilled workers."

Frightened Asian asks: 'Is there a place in Canada for me?'

By GERALD UTTING
Star staff writer
Reprinted with permission, ©Toronto Star syndicate, August 29, 1972

KAMPALA, Uganda—Anywhere else in the world, Peter Patel would have it made.

But Patel, 38, is of Asian origin and here in Uganda he has until Nov. 7 to get out of the country.

The burly Patel is a rancher, the senior partner in a 5,800-acre beef and dairy farm not far from Kampala.

But since President Idi Amin announced that all non-Ugandan Asians must get out in three months, Patel has been living in fear. For Peter Patel is stateless.

He and his family do not hold British passports like most Asians here, nor are they Uganda citizens. They are simply regarded by the government as Asians, and they must get out. Where they go is their problem.

"It is terrible," Patel said today as he waited in the British consulate office where officials were frantically processing Asians for emigration. Britain has accepted responsibility for all Asians, about 55,000, ordered expelled by Amin. Canada has said it will admit several thousand, and immigration officials were expected to arrive from Ottawa this week.

"My parents were British subjects, but at the time of independence in 1962, my papers were lost," Patel said. "There is no way for me to prove I'm British."

"Now I will have to leave Uganda—who knows where for? I have to walk off the ranch just like that, with nothing to show for 10 years' work.

"My partner is an African, and I'll give him my share and hope that some day he will be able to help me.

"I would love to be able to go to Canada. Is there a place in Canada for a man like me? I know how to farm. I'm very willing to work, but I'll not have much money. I know they might let professional people into Canada, but I am only a farmer."

Amin, the 44-year-old strongman who seized power from former president Milton Obote in January, 1971, claims Asians are dominating and "sabotaging" Uganda's economy.

He has gradually expanded his expulsion order to include some of the 23,000 Asians holding Ugandan passports. All have been asked to prove their citizenship and many have been rejected on technicalities.

Practically all are like Patel who made a good living from his ranch but now faces the loss of almost everything he worked for.

The Uganda government has not officially said what it will permit the British Asians to take with them. Some say they have been told $143 is the limit.

Diplomats here say bank officials confirm this figure.

"It's a matter of high school arithmetic," said one diplomat. "We estimate the Ugandan foreign exchange reserves are enough to last for only two weeks to pay for imports. And that may be conservative.

"There is absolutely no way they could let 50,000 people take out their assets in full," he said.

"As a matter of fact, Gen. Amin said in a speech yesterday that Uganda insists the Asians must fly out in East African planes instead of foreign-owned planes.

Amin told troops in Jinja in Central Uganda that he made this decision because East African Airways is jointly owned by Kenya, Uganda and Tanzania. He said the three partner governments were "duty-bound to support it in every possible way."

But the diplomat here explained, "The East

Continued on Page 42

BRITAIN FREEZES £10M LOAN TO UGANDA

News Compilation, August 30, 1972

The British Government froze a £10m loan to Uganda in a major financial move against Idi Amin's regime.

In a carefully worded statement, avoiding any criticism of Uganda, the Foreign Office said: "a £10-million aid programme was agreed to in principle last year. At the time when the present trouble developed, it had not been agreed how the money should be paid. Action on the matter was then suspended and that is still the position."

The announcement was designed to warn President Idi Amin of Uganda that British assistance was imperiled because of his decision to expel Asians who hold British passports.

LET UGANDA ASIANS IN, SAY AUSTRALIAN BISHOPS

News Compilation, August 30, 1972

SYDNEY,—Some of the Asians expelled from Uganda should be allowed into Australia, despite the unemployment problem, the Australian Roman Catholic Episcopal Conference voted yesterday.

Breakfast at the station as 61 head for 'home'

By NATION Reporter
Reprinted with permission, ©Daily Nation, Nairobi, August 30, 1972

A GROUP of 61 Asians steamed into Nairobi Railway Station from Mombasa yesterday morning en route to Uganda—still "home" for many of them.

College graduates going to meet their parents mingled with rustic families on their way to join their breadwinners in Uganda. Some were on their first "foreign" trip to visit relatives and were almost penniless and unable to pay their rail fares.

Little children moaned for food as the party settled at the top end of the platform, loosely cordoned by police, Immigration and plainclothes men. Soon the concerned mothers unwrapped some food to give them a breakfast beside shunting trains.

Sitting on their trunks and baggage, some pondered their future or tried to figure out the immediate problem of finding some cash for their rail tickets.

"Would they allow us into Uganda?" was the question that still bothered most of them. Holding passports of Uganda, India, Britain or Pakistan, they wondered how long they would stay in their country of destination. They were all very appreciative of the cooperation and politeness of the Kenyan police and Immigration officers.

Mr. D. K. Ngini, the deputy director-general of the EA Railways Corporation, accompanied by four other top railway officials, was at the platform to sort out their ticket problems. A temporary ticket office was set up on the platform with a booking clerk to issue tickets as soon as the travellers could borrow money from friends.

British passport-holder Rasiklal T. Nathwani, had been given a visitor's pass to see his parents in Uganda. He was not sure whether he would be able to go back and finish his degree course at a Bombay college after the recent developments in Uganda.

Weather-beaten Swaran Singh, 46, was coming on holiday to Uganda for the first time to live with his nephew, a mason in Kampala. He felt he had been treated like a prisoner during the two days he spent on the liner Karanja, berthed in Mombasa.

Pretty Pramila D. Patel, a physics and chemistry graduate from Bombay, was going to see her parents. "Despite the news, I wanted to go back to my parents," she said. "I'll go where they go but I'm definitely not staying in Uganda. We have to go away."

John C. Pereira, an undergraduate from Goa, was going to Masaka to attend the wedding of his brother who is a teacher there. On his first trip from his homeland, John found the going "rather rough". He hoped things would be sorted out when he reached Uganda. Now he wanted to go back to Goa.

Three of the women who had husbands in Uganda have some relatives in India or Britain. Khatija Karmali, who has lived in Uganda for 12 years, regretted the sudden developments saying she would only wish to rejoin the family as they all wind up their business for Britain.

Most of the members of the group held their hopes on Britain, except for a few Pakistanis who said they would go back to Pakistan after seeing relatives in Kampala.

When the Kampala up-train chugged up on the platform the group talked of the railway their forefathers helped to build at the turn of the century which was now taking them on their "last journey home".

Ugandan Asian Expulsion: 90 Days and Beyond through the Eyes of the International Press

FIRST ASIANS FLY IN PENNILESS

Sir Alec to make TV broadcast

Reprinted with permission, ©Telegraph Group Limited, London, August 31, 1972

THE first 25 refugee Asian holders of British passports in Uganda flew into London yesterday penniless. They said President Amin's customs men had stripped them of every shilling—even money needed for drinks on the flight.

In an effort to divert the influx from centres already under pressure the Resettlement Board is including new towns in a list of areas it is selecting.

As an inducement to councils the Board is to offer repayment of "reasonable" expenditure, and financial help for housing is "not excluded." First reaction from several new towns was that it would be difficult to absorb the Asians.

A television broadcast to the nation tonight by Sir Alec Douglas-Home, Foreign and Commonwealth Secretary, is taken as an indication of Government alarm at public reaction to the expulsions.

Prince Sadruddin Aga Khan, United Nations High Commissioner for Refugees, assured Mr Godber in Geneva yesterday that Gen. Amin would be pressed to minimise expulsions.

Small group of 25 Ugandan Asians arrive penniless claiming Ugandan customs officers stripped them of every shilling - even money for beverages on the flight. Reproduced with permission, ©Associated Press/Wide World Photos

'Every shilling taken'

By BRIAN SILK

TWENTY-FIVE Ugandan Asians arrived at Heathrow airport penniless yesterday as the Government's Uganda Resettlement Board said it would ask selected areas without an immigrant problem to absorb families driven out by President Amin.

The Asians at Heathrow said there was now a complete bar on any money being taken out of Uganda. Some said they were hoping for assistance.

Mr Narshi Vadher, a microbiologist, who arrived with his family, said he had £2,500 in a bank in Uganda. But after filling in forms which were changed by the Ugandans he doubted he would get it. Every shilling was taken from his family as they boarded the plane.

Mr Vadher added: "I don't know what I shall do about the money. Perhaps there are some provisions being made by the British Government. My first task is to get myself a job."

Radio barred

Premilla Ladva, an 18-year-old secretary, said the Customs officers had taken £35 from the six in her family. "My sister and I are hoping to get work here but we have to rely on relatives until we find jobs," she said.

They had been refused permission to export even a tape recorder and a portable radio.

Mr Vishnu Fatania produced two receipts for 200 Uganda shillings, about £12, which he had to forfeit.

He said: "The instructions until yesterday were that we would be allowed to take out 100 shillings per passport, but there is now a new ruling and a complete ban on currency exports."

Mr Fatania and his wife and four children are going to stay with relatives in Leicester.

"Assaults & threats"

Mr Praful Patel, the Asian member of the resettlement board, has asked to see Sir Alec Douglas-Home, Foreign Secretary, about the treatment Asians are receiving in Uganda.

"I am getting reports all the time of assaults, plundering, threats and bullying," he said. "As I see it the situation can only get worse.

"The British Government's first priority is to protect the lives and property of its citizens. It is time this Government took steps to contact the Ugandans to put a stop to what is going on there."

The Uganda Resettlement Board is compiling a list of selected areas, including some new towns, which will be asked to absorb some of the expelled Asians.

This was announced yesterday by Sir Charles Cunningham, chairman of the board. He said the districts selected would be approached in the hope of taking pressure off big towns and cities with large immigrant populations.

In a number of cases new towns might be more easily able to offer accommodation and might have fewer difficulties in providing education and other social services, said Sir Charles.

The New Towns Commission said last night there was unlikely to be room for Ugandan Asians in the four completed new towns: Crawley, Hatfield, Hemel Hempstead and Welwyn Garden City.

A spokesman said: "The housing situation in these towns is already pretty acute with long waiting lists. It might be possible to find places for the Asians in the other new towns, which are still expanding."

Reactions from other towns differed. Spokesmen at Stevenage and Thetford insisted that housing and other facilities were scarce so that it would be difficult to absorb Asians. But Harlow and Corby, Northants, both said they could accommodate some.

At Harlow the urban council offered jobs and homes for three Ugandan Asian families, with a possibility of more later.

"We have no immediate housing problem as in older towns," said a spokesman. "We are a new town and build homes as industry grows."

Corby Town might accommodate five to 10 Asian families, if pressed to do so, Brig. Hugh Hamilton, general manager of Corby Development Corporation, confirmed last night.

Most new towns, however, stressed that lack of money for more housing would be a difficulty.

Financial help

Repeating that the board would have no power to direct Asians to particular districts, Sir Charles hinted at possible financial inducements, including subsidised housing. Financial help to buy or rent homes in areas not under stress was "not excluded."

The board will also try to coax towns without an immigrant problem to take Asians by reimbursing "any reasonable expenditure" immediately incurred.

Sir Charles's Board assumes the main airlift from Uganda will start on Sept. 12. But new problems may mean Asians will not arrive in any large number until much later.

Continued on Page 42

WHITEHALL TOLD: NO MORE –LEICESTER IS FULL UP

Reprinted with permission, ©Leicester Mercury, August 31, 1972

AS THEY LEFT the Home Office today after talks on Leicester's attitude to an influx of Ugandan Asians, the Corporation's deputation declared: "We told the Minister that Leicester is full up."

Leader of the City Council, Alderman Edward Marston, told a Leicester Mercury Civics Correspondent: "We urged that the Minister should use his influence to direct these people to other towns and cities where they would have more opportunities than in Leicester."

The deputation had spent nearly two hours emphasising Leicester's position—particularly the fact that services like housing, education, health and social services were already fully stretched—to Mr. David Lean, a deputy to the Home Secretary Mr. Robert Carr, who is on holiday in a remote part of Corfu.

Alderman Marston added: "Mr. Lane assured us that due consideration would be given by the Government to our very real problems.

"We were able to press on him that Leicester, as far as housing and services are concerned, is full up. And our schools and homes are overcrowded."

Ugandans seeking bargains from exiled Asians

By GERALD UTTING
Star staff writer
Reprinted with permission, ©Toronto Star syndicate, August 31, 1972

Kampala, Uganda—Africans have started going from door to door in the Asian areas here trying to buy the furniture and household goods of the Asian people who are being expelled by the Uganda government.

"They are offering from half to one-third of what the furniture, stoves, refrigerators and television sets are worth." said one Asian businessman. "Every day the price goes down. Every day is a day closer to our departure."

A conversation in a bank yesterday showed the uncertainty of the situation. A British Asian and a Ugandan Asian were waiting in a huge line-up of persons trying to get some foreign currency. They had been there for hours. Police strolled through the crowd and Askaris (guards) stood in strategic spots armed with rifles.

The British Asian was trying to sell his car to the Ugandan Asian, who may be allowed to stay under Amin's confusing expulsion order.

"It is worth 7,000 shillings ($1,000)." he said. "But I will give it to you for 3,000 shillings."

Continued on Page 42

DISASTER

Alderman Marston said that it had been pointed out to the deputation that the Asians could not be directed to particular places, but the Minister would do all possible to advise those intending to make for Leicester aware of the great difficulties they would face.

Asked if Mr. Lane had any promises of money or aid in housing, Alderman Marston commented: "He said this may be available."

Alderman Marston added: "Mr. Lane is going to pass on to Robert Carr all the information we have been able to give him."

Another member of the deputation, Alderman Kenneth Bowder, chairman of the Conservative group, said: "We told Mr. Lane that while as a city we were prepared to help in this great humanitarian disaster, we had already done all we could in absorbing immigrants and that other cities in the country should now make their contribution."

"The immigrants we already have we have learned to accept, and they are making a real contribution to our society but there is little room for any more."

Asked if he were satisfied with the way the talks had gone Alderman Bowder declared: "We are as satisfied as can be at this time."

Other members of the deputation were the Lord Mayor, Alderman Stanley Tomlinson; the assistant Labour Whip, Councillor Mrs. Jane Setchfield, and the Town Clerk, Mr. R. R. Thornton.

WORRIED

The deputation will report in detail on their Home Office takes to tonight's emergency meeting of the City Council, called to discuss what some members have described as "the city's greatest ever crisis".

After the meeting it was learned that a member of the Uganda Resettlement Board will visit Leicester shortly. No date has been set for the visit.

A Ugandan Asian Family who have arrived in Leicester penniless appealed today for action from the British Government to safe-guard their

Continued on Page 44

SCRAMBLE FOR BUSINESS
The big rush on forms starts

Reprinted with permission, ©Uganda Argus, August 31, 1972

THERE WAS A SCRAMBLE FOR APPLICATION FORMS FOR THE ACQUISITION OF BUSINESS BELONGING TO NON-UGANDAN ASIANS LEAVING UGANDA, AT THE MINISTRY OF COMMERCE AND INDUSTRY IN KAMPALA YESTERDAY.

This came as a result of President Amin's announcement on Tuesday at the Conference Centre that the long awaited forms could be obtained from the headquarters of Ministry of Commerce and Industry and the District commissioners' offices throughout the country.

It was learnt that the invasion of the Ministry by businessmen started early yesterday and the heavy morning rain soaked them to their skins.

Although each district got its forms many businessmen came from various parts up-country to get forms from the Ministry's headquarters. And it was not until very late that it was known that "Blue Forms" were for applicants while the "Pink forms" were for the out-going Asian businessmen.

Several anxious people, after getting the right forms, lined up to get the other types of forms—pink and yellow—thinking that by filling blue forms alone they would not have fulfilled Government's requirements.

The scuffle worsened as panic stricken Asians holding British passports queued at the Ministry for declaration forms for business and industrial interests in Uganda.

Most of them quite aged, feared that they would not get the forms.

According to one, "I thought these forms would never come and I was about to leave without selling my property."

As the tension heightened, the entrance door to the Ministry had to be closed and guarded by police while the officials of the Ministry issued forms through windows.

Across the road hundreds of Asians lined up for verification of their documents at the British High Commission and at the newly set up Passport Office at the Industrial Promotion Services building nearby.

The area between the I.P.S. building and Fresh Foods on Parliament Avenue was thus one of "confusion" one onlooker said.

As result, traffic came to almost a standstill throughout the working hours.

Meanwhile, an unprecedented shopping spree by people of all walks of life spread in Kampala yesterday. This was due to the fact that prices were extremely reduced and many shops were selling at special offer that one Phillips electric radio with two bands was selling at 35/-.

Several well known provision stores amazed shoppers when all of a sudden they turned into furniture marts and electronic appliance dealers.

Street loiters were seen busy in tubs looking for abandoned goods, and it was later said that many of them came out happy.

Ugandan Asian Expulsion: 90 Days and Beyond through the Eyes of the International Press

Continued from Page 40

FIRST ASIANS FLY IN PENNILESS

London experts do not consider East African Airways capable of mounting the airlift alone, except on a much-reduced scale and over a longer period.

So contingency plans for an airlift by seven British airlines are going ahead in spite of Gen Amin's declaration that all the Asians must be flown to Britain by East African Airways. A compromise is expected enabling British airlines and East African Airways to be used.

But British airlines still have no Government guarantee to cover cost of the operation, and unless this is given some of them intend to withdraw.

Uganda's dwindling foreign reserves are believed down to £6 million, and the airlines fear that Gen. Amin might forbid conversion to sterling of Ugandan currency they receive for fares.

BOAC said yesterday it could overcome this problem as it had a large operation in Uganda.

Currency difficulty

A Laker Airways spokesman said: "If the Government is not prepared to guarantee the fares, we would certainly not be able to take part. We have no outlets in Uganda and would have difficulty getting rid of Ugandan currency."

The Civil Aviation Authority, confirming no guarantee had been given, said the financial question had primarily to be taken up by airlines. But nothing was yet resolved. There were many complications.

If the Government took Gen. Amin at this word and withdrew from the airlift, leaving the field clear for East African Airways, the Asian operation would be spread over a longer period, considerable easing the pressure on Britain.

But, Government officials pointed out yesterday, this could also lead to increased hardship for Asians stripped of their assets while they queue for seats on the few available planes.

"Productive people"

Sir Charles said the resettlement board had taken very serious account of feeling in Britain about the number of Asians expected. He hoped that by receiving them sensibly the board would provide the "best answer to that apprehension."

He added: "They are British citizens. For the most part, as we understand it, they are people who can add to our productive capacity, can earn their living, and can become good citizens."

Asians arriving penniless would receive grants of money, and the Women's Royal Voluntary Service would issue extra clothing to those needing it. Temporary accommodation would be set up near airports for those Asians without immediate destinations.

Hostels, boarding houses, and private homes would be used for this purpose. The board already had offers from several hostels as well as private families.

A register of temporary accommodation is being established, and Sir Charles appealed for offers from people within a reasonable distance of an international airport. Those willing to accommodate refugees would receive rent.

A circular is being sent to local authorities. It says that any authority with reason to think a further substantial influx from overseas would create intractable problems I invited to let the board "have an urgent appreciation of the situation."

Sir Charles said it was too early to say what recommendations the board would make to the Government as a result of talks with local authorities. There was considerable room for discussion.

Continued from Page 41

Ugandans seeking bargains from exiled Asians

The Ugandan Asian said: "You will have to have it repaired."

"Who is repairing anything now?" asked the car owner.

"Oh, you are so right." said the Ugandan Asian. "Why do you care whether you sell me the car or just give it to me? You won't be allowed to take our any money anyway."

CAN'T CLOSE DOWN

Asian businessmen who want to hand over their thriving enterprises to African employees or friends have been told they cannot do so. Nor will they be permitted to close down their businesses.

Diplomats reported earlier this week that they had been unofficially told by foreign exchange officials that departing Asians would be allowed to take out 1,000 shillings ($143) in foreign currency.

"We will all be penniless." said one restaurant owner, who has a simple solution to his problems.

"I will just say to my African staff—and they are sad to see us go—'Well, goodbye. Thank you all for your good work. We will miss you.' Then I will walk out of the door in my suit and with a little luggage and that will be the end of it."

New electronic equipment, watches, cameras and other expensive portable items are selling at discount prices to Asians who either hope to stay—and thus see a bargain which may not be repeated—or expect to go and are buying goods to take out instead of cash.

Furniture and household effects were on display in stores—also at bargain prices as Asians started dumping their property. The price of an object seemed to depend on its size. Small valuable objects were selling well.

Continued from Page 39

Frightened Asian asks: 'Is there a place in Canada for me?

African airlines could not handle the traffic anyway, but it looks likely the main reason for Amin to take this position is to keep Uganda's foreign exchange reserves, which have to be paid in dollars.

"The foreign airlines don't want to be paid in Uganda shillings, for obvious reasons," he said.

The British consulate here started processing applications by Asians to enter Britain yesterday. The first of the cases it handled were Asians holding U.K. passports who had already gone through the initial application process.

500 LINE UP

There are 3,000 of these and 300 were dealt with yesterday. Others wait their turn. At any hour of the day a crowd of about 500 Asians lines up outside the British offices, only 100 yards from the Ugandan government complex.

The Ugandan Asians are the backbone of the merchant class of the country and even in their hour of distress, the commercial spirit that has driven them to the top was displayed here in the crowded streets.

One Indian-owned store circulated leaflets among those waiting saying "Going to U.K.? First things you will need there are a heavy overcoat and woolen suits. We have slashed our prices for clearing our final stock."

The Asians are patient, seemingly resigned to their fate.

"We are mostly of Indian origin, but we feel we are British, too," said one man, a student.

"We see that the British are sympathetic towards us. They are genuinely trying to help.

"The Ugandans we have been living with for many years are trying to throw us out. Now we know who our friends are.

"You can be sure we are one group of people who will never cause trouble to the country that is good enough to help us."

British officials have received dozens of phone calls asking for help in contacting Canadian immigration officials, who are known to be in Nairobi, preparing to come to Kampala.

"We will give Canada any help we can," said one British official. "Canada has agreed to help us out of this situation and we hope others will follow. But as of now we don't know exactly when the Canadians will be here."

Several Asians waiting to get into the British office expressed interest in going to Canada.

Biush Mistri, 22, a sales representative who has a Uganda passport said:

"At first the government said only British Asians must go. Then it said all Asians. Even Uganda citizens would be expelled. Now it says Uganda passport holders can stay if they're needed because of their skills.

"We do not know what the government really intends to do with us. All of us believe we have to leave while we can. Property, money—these things don't seem so important anymore.

'WHERE CAN I GO?'

"But where can I go? I will see the Canadians, to see if they will take me, but I am not a doctor or an architect.

"I know a little about business and sales. I'm willing to work very hard. Is that enough?

"Otherwise we'll have to go to the United Nations refugee organization. We are going to become refugees."

Bramob Patel, 24, who has just completed training in automobile engineering, said:

"I have British papers. I hope to get a job there, but if the Canadians come and open an office here, I would like to go there. I would do any work in the technical field."

'Not a single Ugandan shilling' to leave, airport notice says

From Michael Knipe
Reprinted with permission, ©Times Newspapers Limited, London,
September 1, 1972

Kampala, Aug 31—Lyons Maid ice-cream trucks and some shaded soft drink stalls did a roaring trade in Parliament Avenue here today as the bureaucratic process of the proposed Asian exodus floundered on. The atmosphere continued to be remarkably untense on the surface, with crowds of shirtsleeved Asians calmly doing business with African peanut vendors while engaging each other in animated conversations and waving a variety of pink, yellow and blue forms.

So far fewer Asians have taken advantage of the availability of British entry permits than was expected. The indications from the first four days of the British High Commission's permit-issuing exercise are that the influx into Britain may be considerably less than had been estimated.

Today 366 heads of families were called forward to receive the entry permits they had requested before President Amin's edict that all non-citizen Asians must leave Uganda by November 7. Of these, only 256 presented themselves at the emergency consular office. This brings the total who have received permits in the first four days to 880 heads of families, compared with 1,166 called forward.

It is uncertain what has happened to the missing 286 but British officials point out that the names of applicants on their files go back a couple of years and they may have emigrated elsewhere.

Family groups are averaging three people rather than five as had been expected, and this alone reduced the total number in the first group of Asians from 15,000 to 9,000.

The situation is a little less relaxed at Entebbe airport, where all departing passengers, not only Asians, are being thoroughly searched.

A notice warns passengers that *"not a single Ugandan shilling"* may be taken out. It restricts departing Asians to one ring, one watch, two bangles, one necklace and one pair of earrings.

The amount of foreign currency that can be taken out is restricted to £50 a head of family. Unaccompanied luggage is restricted to 200 kilograms of soft furnishings, and passengers can take 20kg of personal soft belongings.

ASIANS SEARCHED TO SKIN BY UGANDA CUSTOMS

By CHRISTOPHER MUNNION in Kampala
Reprinted with permission, ©Telegraph Group Limited, London,
September 1, 1972

ASIANS leaving Uganda are being permitted to take only £50 per family and a maximum of 485lb of personal effects, according to new Customs regulations posted at Entebbe international airport.

Rigorous checks, involving strip searches of men and women, are being conducted by Ugandan customs officials. All travellers on international flights are required to check in two hours before departure to allow for the search.

Customs regulations stipulate that the £50 allowance must be in foreign currency.

No Ugandan currency, even small change, may leave the country. Emigrants can take only one ring, one watch, two bangles, one necklace and one pair of earrings—nothing exceeding 15ct gold.

In addition, they can send out 440lb of soft furnishing, but no domestic hardware, and take 45lb of soft personal effects.

On several occasions I have watched Ugandan customs officials at close quarters searching departing Asians. The checks on personal effects have been protracted and meticulous but carried out in a proper manner.

No hostility

The officials I have observed have shown no more hostility than the impersonal brusqueness characteristic of the profession.

For personal searches two small temporary booths have been built in the tiny Customs hall. Men are searched by men and women by women. Intimate searches are made for possible concealed valuables.

But Asians are not the only people being searched. I had to undergo a polite but stringent examination two weeks ago, and a number of British and overseas businessmen have had the same experience.

Asians found to be carrying more than the permitted quota of jewellery or cash are given the option of having it confiscated or of handing it to a relative or friend seeing them off.

Asians leaving now are those whose entry vouchers under the normal quota system were approved before President Amin's expulsion decree.

CANADA
Farmer is willing to hire Asian

Reprinted with permission, ©Toronto Star syndicate,
August 31, 1972

OSHAWA—August Geisberger Jr., who farms 2,000 acres of land in this area, believes experienced farm workers among the Asians fleeing Uganda will find work in Canada.

After reading of the plight Peter Patel, who is being forced from the African country and the 5,800-acre farm he owns with a partner, Geisberger said yesterday he would be willing to hire the man for his farm and could supply an eight-room house for his family.

Star writer Gerald Utting, reporting from Uganda told of the plight of Patel, 38, and 60,000 other Asians who Uganda President Idi Amin said must get out of that country. Amin claims the Asians are dominating and "sabotaging" his country's economy.

Geisberger, son of a Swiss immigrant whose father started farming here 45 years ago, said there is a shortage of farm workers in Canada. He has a 200-head diary herd and besides feed for the cattle, grows cash crops such as tomatoes and sweet corn.

The farming would be different from Uganda, he said, but he and his partners—three brothers and a cousin—would be willing to train "anyone who is prepared to work".

"I know these people are going to have a difficult time," he said. "If there is any way to help, I'd like to do so."

Asians tell of passports cut, broken-glass haircuts

News Compilation, September 1, 1972

Stories of cruelty, haircuts with broken beer bottles, and arrests were told yesterday by Uganda Asian immigrants when they arrived at Heathrow. One man said there were violent scenes at Kampala when Asians found their passports had been cut up.

"There were long queues to get to the officials", he said. "I saw a Ugandan MP suddenly push two women as hard as he could. The fell to the floor and were injured.

"The authorities later admitted that they had been wrong in cutting the passports. In Kampala the police were armed with machine guns."

The Asians were reluctant to give their names. They said reports had reached Uganda of interviews given on Wednesday, and they were afraid for their relatives there.

A woman said: "The scenes at Kampala were terrible. Naturally all the Asians were anxious, and as the day wore on the scenes became more violent. People had been told that they had to go on a certain day to have their citizen status checked, but some passports had been collected and made invalid by cutting."

A boy aged 16 said he had been ordered to get his hair cut and that had been done to others with broken bottles. "I went straight to the barber's", he said. "It was no idle threat. Several people had been grabbed and had long hair and beard removed by the bottle treatment".

As they waited to leave for London the immigrants said they had been made to hand over all their money.

One said: "I went to the airport a few days ago to see someone off and the officials found a $5 American bill in an immigrant's suitcase. he was arrested and taken off to the cells."

About a dozen Asians arrived yesterday. Most appeared to be making for the Midlands.

Ugandan Asian Expulsion: 90 Days and Beyond through the Eyes of the International Press

BEHIND THE HEADLINES, WOMEN WHO GET THINGS DONE
Mrs Sheth sets about the Ugandan problem—personally

Jane McLoughlin
Reprinted with permission, ©Telegraph Group Limited, London,
September 1, 1972

OPINIONS are two a penny at the moment on the problems of the Asians being expelled from Uganda, and how we can help them as they arrive in this country. Mrs Indu Sheth is one woman who decided there had been enough talk about what to do; that it was time to take some action.

She knows better than most about the problems of resettlement. Six years ago she became a refugee when her lawyer husband was expelled from Kenya for political reasons. She arrived in London with her young children, unable to speak a word of English.

So Mrs Sheth, with her 12-year-old daughter Vandana, and son Sunil, 15, both on holiday from school, have started their own campaign to find homes for their Ugandan fellow Asians. They are knocking on doors at Edgware, Middlesex, where they live, seeking offers of accommodation.

"We started a fortnight or so ago, when we first knew the Asians would be coming. I go to my friends, ask them for any information they may have about possible housing, then go and look at what it is. I ask help from white people as well as Asians—everyone is helpful.

"But, so far, we are not doing very well. A three-bedroomed house, where perhaps two brothers with their families could live together, costs £30 a week. And the furniture—that is often very bad. We would not like to sit on some we have seen," says Mrs Sheth.

When Asians come to her through acquaintances here or in Africa, she is prepared to give them food and shelter in her own semi-detached, comfortably furnished home.

"We will keep them until they can move on. We will encourage them to disperse, to leave London. We have friends looking for accommodation in Wellingborough, Coventry, and the Manchester and Liverpool areas. We will tell the newcomers not to go to Birmingham or Leicester, which are already overcrowded."

Mrs Sheth has already proved that making door-to-door contact with people can work. Encouraged by her husband, who qualified in Britain, and holds open house at weekends so that Asians can come to him with any legal problems, she set aside her own shyness at the idea of making such direct contact with people, and went out to encourage Asian women new to this country, to go to English classes, run by volunteers in many areas.

"Asian women are very timid; they do not leave their homes or make contact outside of the family. In England, it is freer, but when I first go round and knock at the door, they refuse to come to classes until I promise that I will be there, too.

"The men and some of the children coming from Uganda will speak English, but very few of the women will. It is going to be a problem, and I will go round and ask them to learn about how the English do things—how to shop, use money, and about clinics and doctors.

"Timidity was something I had to get over myself."

Remembering her own experience, Mrs Sheth feels that somewhere to settle is a first priority for the Ugandan Asians; jobs must come later. She never imagined that Gen. Amin would allow Asian families to leave with much money, so it is no surprise to her that families are arriving penniless.

"We hear they have even taken women's gold jewellery, which their parents give them when they marry—gold which even our husbands have no right to take from us."

But she has no bitterness towards people who want to stop the Asians coming to this country: "They have their reasons, and they must be able to say what they think.

"We have found the British reserved, but not against us. Some of their habits were surprising at first—such as their feelings for dogs. But we understand that we have closer family links, and they have nothing to pour out their feelings on except dogs."

Mrs Sheth's efforts may seem dwarfed by the size of the problem. But she is not alone in helping in what may be a crisis area. Many of the Asians hope to go to North London, and a few local people are offering accommodation.

A doctor working part-time in clinics in Brent agrees that communication with Asian women can be difficult. "Sometimes they bring their husbands along as interpreters. They cannot even understand which way to place the baby for an injection, or understand feeding details.

"I think we will possibly have to provide chest X-rays to screen them for TB, and possibly have special clinics for immunisation which they may not have had."

Continued from Page 41
WHITEHALL TOLD: NO MORE – LEICESTER IS FULL UP

Ugandan bank accounts and other property left behind.

Mr. Harshi Vadher (32) arrived in Leicester yesterday with his wife ,Dhanu, and their daughter Bindu (3). He is staying with cousins at 88 Myrtle Road Leicester.

He said: "I want to help myself. I am a trained micro-biologist and I want to get such a job here but I can pick up a living at anything.

"But many Asians are worried about all the money and property they have left behind. The Government here could help people a lot if only they would make sure that all property—including gold and buildings—was registered with the Indian High Commission. I myself have £2,500 still in a bank account in Uganda."

Mr. Vadher said that his family were allowed to bring only clothes and used goods such as his typewriter.

No foreign currency was allowed out,. he was told.

TEACHING JOB
Mr. Vadher, a British passport holder, got a B.Sc. degree at Bombay University and went to Uganda as a micro-biologist. But he was told that he would not be allowed to work there in that job, since he was a British passport-holder, and Uganda did not recognise his degree.

After six months, he took a teaching job; but when that proved unsatisfactory, he joined his eldest brother in the family furniture business.

Leicester City Council and Indian leaders of the British Asian Welfare Society in Leicester were criticised today by the Indian Workers' Association over their treatment of the crisis.

Leicester branch of the association stated they were "appalled at the way in which the current situation is being exploited to encourage racist attitudes, and to increase insecurity among immigrants in this city."

The City Council statements of concern about strain on the social services had, the statement claimed, "inflamed public attitudes into hostility against Ugandan Asians who may wish to settle here."

DELAY
The Indian Workers' Association claim to know of only 70 families who wish to settle in Leicester from the first group leaving Uganda, and the association have given a firm offer of free hospitality to ten small families.

Sole responsibility for large numbers of Asians having to leave Uganda at this time is put on the British Government by the association.

They claim that the Government have been aware that this would happen since 1968 and the policy towards applicants for admission to Britain since that time has been one of delay.

If the Government had accepted applications in larger numbers throughout the period there would have been no emergency now and President Amin might not have had to take the decision to expel Asians, say the association.

The Gujarat Hindu Association in Leicester have decided to volunteer services to the incoming Ugandan Asians "on humanitarian grounds". The association said they will be willing to sit on any panel set up to help the Asians.

A number of petitions, bearing a total of more than 3,000 signatures, opposing the entry into Britain of the Ugandan Asians are to be handed to the Town Clerk of Leicester Mr. Robert Thornton today by Councillor Barry Clayton.

Councillor Clayton said: "Considering we have had a holiday period, it is remarkable that so many signatures have been collecting. An interesting number of immigrants have put their names to the petitions."

The documents will be forwarded to the General Purposes Committee, who meet next week.

AMIN URGED TO STOP HARSHNESS
'Our duty to take Asians'–Sir Alec

Reprinted with permission, ©Telegraph Group Limited, London, September 1, 1972

THE Foreign Office is to protest strongly to President Amin at any harsh treatment towards departing Ugandan Asians. A register of the assets they are forced to leave behind will be compiled by the British High Commission.

The departing Asians are being allowed to leave with only £50 per family, in non-Ugandan currency, under new Customs regulations. They can bring out only one ring, necklace, watch and pair of earrings and two bangles, none to exceed 15ct gold.

Sir Alec Douglas-Home, Foreign and Commonwealth Secretary, in a broadcast last night, appealed to the nation to perform its "clear duty" and face the great human problem with "our traditional calm and resource." Gen Amin's expulsion decision was "inhuman, unjust and unnecessary."

Several Midlands towns and cities said they could take no more immigrants. A delegation from Leicester told the Home Office their town was full up and social services already overloaded, while Birmingham called for the Asians to be spread throughout the country.

Asians' money seized

By FRANK ROBERTSON, Diplomat Staff

THE Foreign Office has instructed the British High Commission in Kampala to take up with the Ugandan Government all cases of departing British passport-holding Asians who are mistreated.

The High Commissioner has been told to make the "strongest possible representation" in proven cases of injustice, but it is admitted that they may well be ignored by Ugandan officials.

He will protest about the confiscation of the money of some Asians before they left Entebbe.

The Commission will open a register to enable Asians to record details of their property and other assets which they have had to leave behind.

Asians arriving at Heathrow from Uganda yesterday said they had to hand over their money at the airport. Several also complained that they had been grabbed and their long hair and beards cut off by broken bottles.

Little progress

Official efforts to get President Amin to act more reasonably have made little progress so far. Mr Richard Slater, the High Commissioner, has not been able to see the talkative President since Aug. 15.

Yesterday Mr Praful Patel, the Asian member of the Uganda Resettlement Board, had long discussions at the Foreign Office about the plight of the departing Asians bound for Britain.

He left memoranda covering their personal security, protection of their property, and searches and confiscations by Ugandan Customs officials at Entebbe.

Mr Patel was told that all Asians leaving for Britain could lodge details of property holding with the British High Commission.

He said afterwards: "There are so many individual cases of intimidation, bullying, threats and plundering reported by people coming here that I am generally worried about the situation.

"I am satisfied that the Foreign Office have the matters very much in their minds."

Last night the Foreign Office had received no further offers from other countries which had been asked to accept expelled Asians. To date India, Pakistan, Bangladesh, Canada and the Netherlands have said they will help.

ASIANS: Poll shows only 6 per cent want them allowed in now
YOUR VERDICT

Express Staff Reporter, DONALD SEAMAN
Reprinted with permission, ©Daily Express, London, September 1, 1972

The verdict of the British people on the issue of the expelled Ugandan Asians is today clear and overwhelming : Only six in every 100 want to see them allowed immediate entry to this country, according to a Harris Poll of Public Opinion.

Seventy one per cent of those questioned believe Britain will not benefit from becoming a more multi-racial society. And 51 per cent want to see all other immigration temporarily stopped if the Asians are allowed in en masse.

More than one person in three—38 per cent—would be willing for the British Government to pay for the Asians to be resettled in their ethnic homelands of India and Pakistan.

One in five thinks that if entry into Britain is allowed, it should be spread

Continued on Page 46

Advertisement

ANNOUNCEMENT

The Uganda High Commission in London wishes to announce that Asians who are currently in the United Kingdom and have been residing in Uganda are at liberty to return to Uganda to wind up their affairs. They will be required to leave Uganda by 7th November, 1972.

All Asians holding Uganda passports or claiming to be Uganda citizens are requested to call immediately at the Uganda High Commission, London with all the particulars relating to their citizenship and six passport size photographs.

Uganda-bound Asians refused entry in Kenya

Standard Staff Reporter, Mombasa
Reprinted with permission, ©East African Standard, Nairobi, September 1, 1972

Strict security measures were in force at Kilindini Harbour, Mombasa, as a team of immigration officials carried out checks on Asians with British and Indian passports bound for Uganda arrived on Saturday aboard a passenger ship, S.S. Karanja, and were refused entry into Kenya.

Policemen on guard asked people who waited to go into the ship for identity and the reason for going on board.

Many people, particularly those with relatives or friends among the passengers, were refused permission to see them.

The passengers affected were 40 Asians with Indian passports and 21 with British passports, excluding children. Cases of three passengers whose passports were issued in England were settled and allowed to disembark to fly to Britain after air tickets were brought to them on the ship by relatives.

Ten of the passengers were said to be residents of Uganda and the remaining people going to Uganda for the first time with valid visitors passes for periods ranging from one to six months.

When the ship arrived, immigration officers told the passengers that they were not allowed to enter Kenya and that they must not leave the ship.

Some of them were students who had completed their studies in India and were returning to join their parents in Uganda. Two people working with the East African Community, returning from leave with their families, were also refused to disembark.

An official from the office of the British High Commission, Mr. Symon, spent most of the morning on Saturday on board trying to help British passport-holders.

Some of the passengers complained that they were not informed of the situation in Kenya. Others said that they came to know this when they arrived at Karachi.

A woman holding a British

Continued on Page 46

Ugandan Asian Expulsion: 90 Days and Beyond through the Eyes of the International Press   *Page 45*

Asian crisis in Uganda

Editorial
Reprinted with permission, ©East African Standard, Nairobi,
September 1, 1972

Sorrowful stories are filtering through from Uganda about the scenes caused by President Amin's expulsion order against Asian-British passport holders.

Some of them are reported to be staging a hunger strike in the hope of winning an extension of the 90 days' notice to leave. A wild rush has developed among Asian traders to get rid of their stocks at knock-down prices and transfer their businesses; and among Africans to take over.

In any event, it looks as though they will have to leave behind whatever money they realise, or keep it to pay their fares in the forthcoming airlift. The first 15 to reach London arrived penniless. Heads of families had expected they would be allowed to take £15 for expenses during the journey. Even this trifling sum, they complained, had been confiscated at Entebbe Airport under a new restriction barring the export of all Ugandan currency.

Whatever the reliability of some of the rumours flowing from Uganda, there can be no doubt that families are being broken up and there is wide-spread distress among Asians. There are also disquieting stories about a number of people, including Ugandan Africans, who have been removed from their official posts or have not been seen in public for some time. Speculation is rife as to the fate suffered by some of those who have "disappeared" and not been brought to public trial.

In order to safeguard various sectors of the economy, which is taking a severe buffeting, many Asian experts are being allowed to stay on, in addition to those "professionals" who were reprieved by President Amin. On the other hand, companies are finding that, because of fear and uncertainty for the future, Asians who can stay on, or who are being expected to remain at their posts, would infinitely prefer to leave for the U.K., Canada or other destinations where arrangements are being made for their reception and placing in work.

This comment was written before the British Foreign Secretary, Sir Alec Douglas-Home, went on nationwide television last night to explain his Government's policy. He was expected to try to convert critics of the Conservative Party's attitude into believing that Britain has an unavoidable obligation to accept those holding U.K. passports who are thrown out.

On this point, the British Attorney-General has publicly explained that, under the 1948 law on British nationality, there is only one category of British citizen, whether from the U.K. or the colonies, or former dependencies. The U.K. has no alternative but to take in all those of its nationals who have nowhere to go; notwithstanding Mr. Powell and the demonstrators of dockland and areas like Smethwich and Wolverhampton. The newcomers are being advised to avoid "Asian settled areas" and become diluted among the indigenous British residents of other towns.

If all the Asians who flock out of Uganda arrive penniless, Britain's load of responsibility will be gravely increased, since the Welfare State will have to support them for some time to come.

President Amin says he has taught Britain a lesson and, if he was not quite so busy at the moment, would teach them another.

A soldier claiming to be "much better than most politicians in the world", he feels he has "all the British shaking so much" that he qualifies for a degree in philosophy (or should it be political science?).

Six months ago, he insists, the British High Commissioner in Kampala warned him that the U.K. Government would withhold a loan of £10,000,000 "if Uganda accepted aid from any other country" and he rejected the threat. This is the £10,000,000 he and his Foreign Minister, Mr. Kibedi, say was never forthcoming.

The loan was agreed last August in the form of a programme of aid spread over some years. Last Tuesday, the British Government announced that processing the programme would be suspended in view of the decision to expel some 50,000 Asian British subjects. In Whitehall, officials were saying the decision was made to appease irate British public opinion rather than as retaliation.

The rump of the existing programme, of which rather more than £1,000,000 remains to be expended, will continue unaltered by the decision to suspend further aid. Two critical problems for British policy are responsibility for the 1,000 or so Britons in Uganda, and the millions of British investment.

Sir Alec has not said so officially, but there is a growing feeling in London official circles that he will visit East Africa soon, in the footsteps of the unlucky Mr. Rippon. If he does so, he can receive only the same negative answers Mr. Rippon obtained. But it is re-assuring to Asians and the British alike that Tanzania, Zambia and Kenya have all restated a policy of dealing moderately with their problem populations and that Asians living in the three neighbouring countries have nothing to fear.

Continued from Page 45

YOUR VERDICT

over five years. Twenty one per cent think that if the Ugandan Asians are all admitted, all other immigration to this country should be restricted to people of British stock, such as Australians and New Zealanders.

STOP!

Those who believe Britain will not benefit by becoming more multi-racial, or are uncertain—a total of 86 per cent of all those questioned—were asked about their views on immigration generally.

Of these, one in four thinks it should be stopped completely.

Twenty-one percent feel that immigration should be restricted to those coming to Britain for education or training.

Thirteen percent say it should be restricted to people of British stock.

Twenty-four percent think immigration should be open to all—but that the numbers should be restricted.

The poll, the first detailed public opinion survey on the crisis, was carried out between August 21-28 among 1,958 voters in 120 constituencies throughout Britain.

Canadian election called

News Compilation, September 2, 1972

Canadian Prime Minister, Pierre Elliot Trudeau announced that a general federal election would be held on October 30, 1972. Robert L. Stanfield, leader of the Progressive Conservative opposition, welcomed the signal for a "long overdue election".

Continued from Page 45

Uganda-bound Asians refused entry in Kenya

passport, accompanied by her five-year-old daughter, said she had been in India on a three-month holiday and was returning to join her husband who owns a garage and her other seven children.

Another woman, accompanied by three young daughters, wept, saying that she had gone to Karachi for 11 days' holiday, her husband was a Ugandan citizen and she did not know what her fate would be.

The Karanja sails today afternoon and it is likely that all the Asians will have to return to India on the same ship.

It is understood that officials from the Indian High Commission are trying to see if some of the passengers could be allowed to proceed to Uganda.

Earlier this month Asians with British and Indian passports who arrived in Mombasa on aboard a chartered ship, Mozaffari, were served with letters declaring them prohibited immigrants by immigration officials and had to return to India on the same ship.

The first Ugandan Asians to have left Uganda since President Amin's expulsion order have told of searches at "bayonet point" by Ugandan border guards and refusal of permission to take any money with them.

The dozen or so who fled the country were part of a boatload of Asians forced to return to Bombay after being refused to land in Kenya or Tanzania on their way to Uganda.

They joined the ship, the S.S. Mozaffari, when it docked at Mombasa on August 16.

One of them told the Indian Press that an Indian who had hidden his valuables in some sweets had been taken away by guards and not seen again.

From Dar es Salaam, the East African Civil Aviation Board said that British carriers and East African Airways would share in the task of airlifting British Asians expelled from Uganda.

The board's Chairman, Mr. David Mwiraria, announced this in a statement following Press reports that a consortium of British airlines was planning to handle the airlift.

Mr. Mwiraria said he wished to state that the traffic involved "belongs to the U.K. and East Africa" and that under existing bilateral air services arrangements, "we expect the traffic to be uplifted by the licensed British carriers on the one hand and the E.A.A. on the other, on the basis of parity."

HEATH CALLS CRISIS TALKS ON ASIANS

Carr cuts holiday: RAF base prepared

Reprinted with permission, ©Telegraph Group Limited, London, September 2, 1972

MR HEATH is holding urgent talks on the Uganda Asians tonight with Sir Alec Douglas-Home, Foreign Secretary, and Mr Carr, Home Secretary. The Prime Minister is alarmed at the opposition to their admission to Britain and faces the prospect of a revolt by the Conservative party's Right wing, OUR POLITICAL STAFF writes.

Mr Carr is cutting short his holiday in Corfu to attend the talks, at Chequers, and to be at hand for the trouble in the prisons. The ministers will discuss what more can be done to allay public anxiety over the Asians.

Lord Foot, head of the welfare co-ordinating committee concerned with the Asians' arrival, attacked the Labour leadership of Mr Wilson and Mr Callaghan for not even "a whimper" over the Asians' plight. He also said he was distressed at the lack of tolerance and generosity by some of the public.

The former RAF Bomber Command base at Stradishall, Suffolk, closed in 1970, is being prepared as a short-stay accommodation centre, although it is not certain it will be needed. CHRISTOPHER MUNNION reported from Kampala that the final total of arriving Asians could well be less than half the original estimate of 55,000.

British Prime Minister Edward Heath
Reproduced with permission ©Archive Photos/Express News

Carr flies from Corfu

By DAVID HARRIS, Political Staff

MR HEATH, alarmed at the widespread opposition in Britain to the arrival of thousands of Asians from Uganda, is having a meeting at Chequers tonight with Sir Alec Douglas-Home, Foreign and Commonwealth Secretary, and Mr Carr, Home Secretary.

Mr Carr is cutting short his holiday in Corfu, mainly so that the can be at the meeting. Another factor in his decision to return home is the trouble in the prisons.

But it is being denied that Mr Heath ordered his recall following allegations that Mr Carr had been "kept in the dark" for some days about the mounting disturbances in the prisons because officials were anxious not to interrupt his holiday.

Mr Heath and Sir Alec will go to the Prime Minister's country residence after attending the funeral service for Prince William of Gloucester at Windsor today.

All-round view

Mr Carr will join them at Chequers after his special aircraft arrives at Northolt early this evening.

The three Ministers will review the whole situation over the Asians. In particular, they will

Continued on Page 48

AMIN 'THREATENS FAMILIES ALREADY IN UK'

Reprinted with permission, ©The Sun, London, September 2, 1972

ASIANS with Ugandan passports who already live in Britain fear that the long arm of the President Idi Amin threatens them even here.

For yesterday the Uganda High Commission in London demanded to see all those who claim to be Ugandan Citizens. An announcement in The Times directed them to take their passports and all citizenship papers to the High Commission in Trafalgar Square immediately. Many Asians fear that if they hand in their passports that will be the last they see of them.

Frightened

They are frightened of being left stateless. Mr. Praful Patel, secretary of the All-Party Committee on UK Citizenship warned, "There is a risk that their passports will be revoked." But at the High Commission a spokesman stated : "We do not mean to confiscate passports." He explained: "All British Asians must leave Uganda for good by November 7." "Some already in Britain claim Uganda citizenship. We want to verify their claims, that is all." "To do that we have to see their passports."

Settle

The Home Office says there are 4,000 Uganda passport holders in Britain at present. No one knows how many are Asians. The announcement also said that Uganda Asians in Britain were free to go home to settle up their affairs. But Mr. Patel, a member of the Uganda Resettlement Board warned: "Don't go unless you have to."

MAN LEFT £300,000 IN UGANDA

Reprinted with permission, ©Telegraph Group Limited, London, September 2, 1972

A UGANDA Asian who flew into Heathrow yesterday said he left £300,000 invested in Uganda. He owned two metal factories and was a coffee producer.

The man, Mr Habib Madatali, added: "The Government said that professional people and industrialists would be exempt from the expulsion order, but when I went for examination they said I had three months to leave because I did not have a Ugandan passport."

He was born in Uganda in 1922 and had a British passport. He hoped to get compensation.

Other Asians arriving at Heathrow said they had been closely searched before leaving Uganda. Several women complained that jewellery had been taken from them.

Bangles taken

Mrs Sushilie Vinod, a shopkeeper's wife, said: "They took six bracelets and several rings. All the women had to hand over their jewellery." Her young daughter had to give up inexpensive bangles she was wearing.

Mrs Chantinan Chandrekher, who flew in with her 12-month-old son, Alphis, said: "The Customs officials said we must give up the jewellery, apart from a ring, a necklace, a watch, a pair of earrings and two bangles. In fact, they mostly took bangles and bracelets. We managed to keep some of the rings."

Mr Basan Singh said that many were arriving broke because although the Asians were officially being allowed to leave with £50 a family in non-Uganda currency, it was taking weeks to get permission.

Keep to our standards says Cheltenham

By BRIAN SILK
Reprinted with permission, ©Telegraph Group Limited, London, September 2, 1972

MISS WINIFRED ALLARDYCE, secretary of Cheltenham Croquet Club and a public-spirited member of the local community, said yesterday she has no objection to a Ugandan Asian moving in next door to her home in Cleevelands Drive.

"Just so long as he conforms to the same sort of standards as we are used to here," she added.

A certain amount of anxiety spread among Miss Allardyce and her fellow Cheltonians when they awoke yesterday to find that someone living far away on the other side of the Cotswolds had nominated their spa as an ideal home for refugees from Uganda.

The idea came from the Archbishop of York, Dr Coggan, who had been pondering the problem of the Asians crowding into areas with already overloaded public services.

Dr Coggan suggested that the Asians should be invited to put down roots in other areas, for

Continued on Page 48

Race and Racism in East Africa

Editorial
Reprinted with permission, ©Washington Post, September 1, 1972

Over the century, from the great crowded centers of India and China, there has been a steady outward drift of emigrants. They sought their opportunities in the less highly developed, or less heavily populated, lands of Asia and Africa. Often they came as laborers, but quickly became tradesmen, merchants and technicians. Shopkeepers are not always popular with their customers, and when the differences of economic class are accentuated by differences of race and custom, they become a very vulnerable target.

In East Africa, over the past decade, a great many of the Asians have affronted the newly independent states by retaining their allegiances to the old colonial powers. Very often they have held onto their British passports, rather than taking citizenship in these countries where their families have lived for perhaps three generations.

Uganda, where the expulsion of the Asian minority will shortly create great suffering, is ruled by a demagogic and eccentric man. Like others who sought to shore up unstable governments, he has now resorted to the most flagrant racism. It is a familiar pattern. The melancholy drama now going forward in Uganda has been played many times over in the ten years with varying degrees of cruelty in countries all the way from Africa to Burma and Indochina. The Asians of East Africa can doubtless be faulted for a failure of political wisdom. The existence of a large and comparatively prosperous class of businessmen in permanent residence, but maintaining foreign citizenship, might give concern to countries much larger and, more confident than Uganda. But if the Ugandan Asians have erred, they are now paying an extremely harsh price for it.

About 90,000 of Uganda's 9 million people are Asians and three fourths of the Asians are not citizens. Currently Gen. Amin says that only the non-citizens must go, but he intends to run the rest through a process of verification of status that seems likely to leave a large number of them stateless. The British government is prepared to admit those with British passports, of which there are some 50,000. But the welcome even in Britain will be far from unanimous. Previous waves of Asian immigration have brought the race issue to British domestic politics, and elements in both parties are now bitterly protesting this addition to the Asian minority. Some of the refugees will go to India. Canada has offered to take about 5,000. The United States offers sympathy but its visa regulations, stressing professional and technical training, make it unlikely that more than perhaps 100 will actually be admitted. While the regulations can be waived, as a practical matter a waiver requires a degree of public pressure here that is altogether unlikely in this case. There is no lobby for the Asians.

Many of the departing Asians own houses and businesses, some of them substantial. Gen. Amin has promised compensation, but the promise is undercut by the obvious fact that Uganda does not begin to have the resources to pay market value. It looks as though the expulsions will be accompanied by one degree or another of confiscation.

The purpose of the expulsions is, as Gen. Amin puts it, to enable Africans to take over their own economy. Taking over an economy requires, unfortunately, a good deal more than walking into empty offices and shops. No economy can lose so large a part of its commercial class without going into decline. In Uganda, the first effect of the expulsions seems likely to be a sharp rise in unemployment.

Continued from Page 47

HEATH CALLS CRISIS TALKS ON ASIANS

look at the arrangements for dealing with the new arrivals and discuss what more can be done to allay public anxiety.

They realise that the Government now faces the prospect of a "revolt" led by Right-wingers inside the Conservative party.

Mr Heath is understood to have received an enormous postbag from people all over the country concerning the decision to admit the United Kingdom passport holders. There have been threats of resignations from Conservative workers.

Doubts on broadcast

The impression among MPs is that the ministerial broadcast on television on Thursday night by Sir Alec has done little to damp down the strong feelings in the country.

The Right-wing Monday Club is almost contemptuous of Sir Alec's attempt to reassure the public.

The split in the party could become the main feature of the Conservative. conference Blackpool next month.

Hopes began to grow in Whitehall last night that at least four foreign countries would take some of the Uganda Asians who would otherwise come to Britain.

Britain's diplomatic drive to seek the aid of other countries in dealing with the Asians to be expelled by President Amin has brought "expressions of interest" from America, West Germany, Fiji and Holland.

So far there have been no firm offers of entry permits. But Ministers clearly hope that the four countries and others will join Canada in agreeing to take some of the Asians.

Continued from Page 47

KEEP TO OUR STANDARDS SAY CHELTENHAM

example his own city of York, Norwich, Lincoln and Cheltenham.

Schools "bursting"

The Archbishop's solution did not go down too well with Miss Allardyce.

"I have nothing against them as Asians, but our schools are already bursting at the seams and we should probably get a lot of children who can't speak English."

Cheltenham, population 78,000, has only a tiny immigrant community, about 100 Indians and Pakistanis and enough Chinese to staff a dozen restaurants.

Ald. Charles Irving, a member of the Conservation-controlled Cheltenham Borough Council and prospective Conservative Parliamentary candidate for Kingswood, Bristol, said "The Archbishop must be stark staring bonkers to make statements of this kind without first finding out what the resources are.

"This sort of thing infuriates me. We are not racialists, but we couldn't absorb any number into our community. We have an unemployment situation and a housing problem. Our resources are stretched to the limit."

Another Cheltenham resident, Squadron Leader Thomas Hall, retired, who is secretary of Gloucestershire Royal British Legion, also went in for plain speaking.

"The friends I mix with are not in favour of affording help to cast-off foreigners who are prepared to accept the hospitality of this country and knife us in the back when it suits them," he said. "I don't think they would be popular here."

Not practical

In York Ald. William Burke, leader of the controlling Labour group on the council, said: "While I agree with the archbishop's noble sentiments he is not being very practical."

"The social services in York are woefully underdeveloped and sadly neglected. The housing situation is no better than it was 10 years ago and is getting worse."

In Norwich Councillor Mrs. Patricia Hollis, chairman of the city's housing committee, said: "It is not the people such as the Archbishop of York who make these big liberal gestures who have to pay the price.

"It is the people on the housing waiting list. We have 3,000 in Norwich."

Business life in Jinja takes new turn

Reprinted with permission, ©Uganda Argus, September 5, 1972

THE BUSINESS LIFE OF JINJA TOWN HAS TAKEN A NEW TURN FOLLOWING GENERAL AMIN'S EXPULSION ORDER TO ASIANS WHO ARE NON-CITIZENS OF UGANDA.

For the first time, since the colonial days, Asian traders are rounding off their businesses hurriedly and leaving shops empty in the town's business centre.

Evidence of this, is the first fact that all grocery and drapery shops formerly predominantly owned by them have declared clearance sale.

As a matter of fact two shops in this category are reported to be keeping less than one-quarter of the normal stock.

Continued on Page 50

Page 48

Ugandan Asian Expulsion: 90 Days and Beyond through the Eyes of the International Press

Petrol and food shortages as businesses close

From Michael Knipe
Reprinted with permission, ©Times Newspapers Limited, London, September 4, 1972

Kampala—Imperturbable Asians played cricket at the Muslim sports club here today while at the Lake Victoria Hotel, Entebbe, relaxed Asian family groups provided a good four-fifths of the lunchtime custom.

In other respects, however, the withdrawal of the Asian community from the national economic life is becoming increasingly apparent.

It is impossible to have bacon for breakfast here, because Asian controlled supplies from Kenya have stopped. And as Asian wholesalers in Kampala run down their stocks, because of their coming expulsion, various items are becoming harder to get. Even the best hotels in the city have minimal wine lists, and vermouths have disappeared from the shelves. A colleague let out a whoop of delight at lunch today because he had come across cheese on the menu.

Not surprisingly, there is something of a dearth of tourists in Uganda at present, but it is extremely difficult to hire a car here, as all the Asian-run car rental firms have closed.

At a petrol station this afternoon I could purchase only low grade fuel and the African attendant said blithely that he would probably run out of that by the end of this week.

"Our petrol is delivered by Asians", he said, "and they are all leaving." How did he feel about the exodus? "It is a good thing", he said beaming. "It will be difficult, but it is good that they are going."

Already in Tororo, near Uganda's eastern border, all the petrol stations are reported to have closed down except for one, which is owned by an African, who so far at least has supplies.

The effects of the decline in Asian business activity are being exacerbated by the fears of foreign traders over foreign exchange. The Nairobi Daily Nation said last week that the uncertainties could cause Kenyan and Tanzanian business houses to curtail exports to Uganda.

Twenty-five days have elapsed since President Amin imposed his three-month deadline and there is no sign yet of the airlift being mounted. The almost daily presidential directives on the matter seem to create even greater hurdles. The latest directive lays down that all requests for airline tickets to destinations outside East Africa must be cleared by the Bank of Uganda.

This is thought to be an attempt to prevent Asians from getting money out of the country by buying an expensive round-the-world ticket which could be turned in for a refund later.

Canadian officials are scheduled to arrive here tomorrow and United States officials later this week in connexion with the Asian exodus, but it is still not certain how many their respective governments are prepared to accept.

KAMPALA'S SIGN OF THE TIMES: One shopkeeper's attempt to clear his stock by bringing to the notice of potential refugees that their arrival in England will coincide with weather that they are not prepared for.

Reproduced with permission ©Archive Photos/Popperfoto

Free board offer to Uganda Asians

By DENNIS BARKER
Reprinted with permission, ©The Guardian, London, September 5, 1972

Associated Hotels, of which Sir Charles Cunningham, the chairman of the Government's Uganda Resettlement Board is a director, yesterday offered free accommodations to 100 Asian refugees for up to three months. It was the most dramatic offer yet in a slowly growing pattern of hopefulness towards the Ugandan Asians. Mr Keith Erskine, chairman and managing director of Securicor, a subsidiary of Associated Hotels, said that Securicor had many interests in Uganda. It had sympathy with the cause of the refugees.

Mr Erskine said there would be real hardship if the Asians had to endure the "semi-concentration camp" atmosphere of transit camps. Beds for 100 people would be only 4 per cent of the total accommodations.

"I do think that private enterprise must occasionally stop and think and help out for the public good," he said. Sir Charles Cunningham has said our offer will certainly be considered by the board."

Of the two problems facing the Asians—reception and resettlement—it was probably reception that was the more crucial, because the Asians had skills and could settle fairly well. "I am hoping our offer will start a sort of cascade. It would be quite easy for a small proportion of "the available hotel rooms to be put on one side. I hope our offer will be followed by offers of thousands of more beds."

Offers of help on a smaller scale continued to be made. Mr Iqbal Singh, of Wimbledon, London, the director of a property company, said

Continued on Page 50

Amin is more racist —Vorster

News Compilation, September 4, 1972

Bethlehem—SOUTH African racist Prime Minister John Vorster said here today that the expulsion of British Asians from Uganda was "the most immoral of acts", but hinted that South Africa would not accept any of them.

Addressing a meeting here, Vorster who said he felt sorry for the Asians—most of them Indians—being expelled by Amin, said various quarters had called on him to make a gesture towards them by inviting a number to settle in South Africa.

But it was not for him to do so, he said. It was the responsibility of India, a country which had through the years adopted "a pious, self-righteous attitude" towards other countries and which had especially fanned world enmity towards South Africa.

"Today India's chickens have come home to roost", he said.

"India, which has been so holy and pious about South Africa is not prepared to open its own doors to its people.

"But I and other countries must make a gesture", he added mockingly.

Vorster noted that Uganda had been one of the countries loudest in its condemnations of South Africa for racism, but was itself now committing a deed of the most flagrant racism.

Continued from Page 49

FREE BOARD OFFER

he was offering one of his houses free for three months. Mr Singh, who works in an advisory capacity with the Merton and Malden Citizen's Advice Bureau, said: "A few people locally have been against my offer, saying that I ought to have offered the house to the council, but I hope it will encourage other people to offer rooms and other accommodation."

Mr Culshan Singh Chuhan, a financier, of Coleman Street, Wolverhampton, has been advertising in Ugandan newspapers offering Asians accommodation in Wolverhampton, Leeds, Cardiff, and other areas with a high proportion of immigrants. He said yesterday he had received 4,000 requests for help.

Opposition to the coming arrivals was expressed by Mr Colin Jordan's British Movement, which urged air and transport workers who might be involved in resettling them to withhold their labour in an effort to prevent heir entry. The British Movement, which operates from the Midlands, has asked local authorities to tell the Government that they will not accept any more Asians.

Mr Carr's talks

The Home Secretary, Mr Carr, who has just returned from a Greek holiday, spent much of yesterday consulting with his junior Ministers and civil servants. At the end of the day, he saw Sir Charles Cunningham who will today- visit Leicester for talks about the fears of an excessive influx to the town.

Sir Charles will be accompanied by Mr Tom Critchley, directory of the board, and by Mr Praful Patel, the Asian member of the Resettlement Board. Mr Patel said yesterday that they would be meeting all the Asian organisations in the town and hoped also to visit the homes of Asians in Leicester.

Alderman Edward Marston, the Labour leader of the Leicester council, who will meet the party at the railway station, said yesterday: "I am confident we will convince the board that we cannot absorb any more." He led a deputation to the Home Office last week to make the same point.

Mr David Lane, Parliamentary Secretary at the Home Office, one of the junior Ministers who helped to brief the Home Secretary yesterday, said at Reading that the British people had received too little credit for the harmonious way immigrants had been absorbed during the fifties and sixties. "I want to pay tribute to the host community, particularly in urban areas where the strain has been the greatest." He added: "We are well aware of the public apprehension over the arrival of refugees from Uganda who hold British passports, but many of these fears and forecasts are exaggerated."

Our Political Staff adds: The Leader of the Opposition, Mr Wilson, left the Isles of Sicily for London at the end of his holiday. He will be back at work today. A meeting of the Shadow Cabinet has been called for next week to discuss the Ugandan Asian situation. There is criticism of Mr Wilson and Mr Callaghan among some Labour MPs for not making a public statement on the issue at an early stage.

So who's got room?

WHAT TOP PEOPLE THINK OF MR. JEREMY THORPE'S OFFER

By Alastair Wilson
Reprinted with permission, ©Daily Express, London, September 5, 1972

WOULD you put up an Asian family from Uganda in your spare room? Liberal leader Jeremy Thorpe would.

The offer he made on Sunday to let a refugee family use his Devon cottage got the support of the Archbishop of York, Dr. Coggan.

So the *Express* decided to find out in a snap poll what other top people thought.

MRS. JUDITH HART, former Labour Minister of State and M.P. for Lanark, said : "I think Mr. Thorpe's offer is a splendid idea.

"I wish I had two or three spare rooms to do likewise. Unfortunately, our home at the moment is rather full."

MR. MARK BONHAM CARTER, chairman of the Community Relations Commission, said : "I have been discussing this with my wife and we are quite ready to put someone up in the accommodations we have available in our London house."

MR. DONALD STEWART, the only Scottish National Party M.P., said from his home on the Island of Lewis: "No, I wouldn't take an Asian family in."

"We don't want England dumping its problems on us.

"I am against any further immigration into this country, regardless of colour.

"But I admire Mr. Thorpe for his offer. Far too many people are doing a lot of shouting about taking Asians in....but at the other people's expense."

LORD RHODES OF SADDLEWORTH, former Lord Lieutenant of Lancashire, M.P. for Ashton-under-Lyne from 1945 to 1964, and a Yorkshire industrialist, is not joining the home-for-an-Asian bandwagon.

"With the unemployment situation in this country as it is at present the influx of these Ugandan-Asians presents a very grave problem indeed," said 77-year-old Lord Rhodes.

"We are not as young as Jeremy Thorpe. We adopted a daughter, a Jewish girl, in 1938, and rescued her from the Hitler regime. She is now 46."

THE ARCHBISHOP OF YORK, Dr. Donald Coggan, said last night: "If necessary I would welcome a family of Asians at the palace, but the situation has not yet arisen.

"I think quite a few Asians may settle in York."

MR. MICHAEL BARNES, Labour M.P. Brentford and Chiswick, said: "I think Mr. Thorpe has made an admirable offer.

"I have a small flat and I haven't got room for an Asian family.

THE BISHOP OF LIVERPOOL, the Rt. Rev. Stuart Blanch, said: "We would of course welcome an Asian family, but it would mean us moving out of our home.

"I have a family of five and six bedrooms!"

MR. ANDREW FAULDS, Labour M.P. for Smethwick, said yesterday that he was prepared to have an Asian couple stay at his Stratford-upon-Avon home.

MAJOR DOUGLAS HOME, of Old Greenlaw, Berwickshire, brother of the Foreign Secretary, said: "I should think anyone with a large enough house and plenty of spare rooms would be willing to take an Asian family.

"Certainly I would if I had the room, but we already have an accommodation problem here with seven children arriving at weekends.

"We could hardly tell them: *'Sorry you can't come, there's an Asian family sleeping in your bed.'"*

Clan chief **DAME FLORAN MACLEOD**, of Macleod said from Dunnvegan Castle, on the Isle of Skye: "I would be delighted if I had a spare cottage." But I don't think they would appreciate spending the winter in Skye."

Continued from Page 48

Business life in Jinja takes new turn

A large number of shops situated on the main street of Jinja are barely empty. Most of the goods in them were purchased by the departing Asians themselves and well-to-do Ugandan Africans.

Although the President said that business must continue normally during the 90 days during which the Asians affected by the quit order must leave the country, it is believed that Asian businessmen have cancelled new orders and also pressed manufacturers to accept back goods which had been delivered to them.

As a result, according to well informed sources, sales figures in a prominent company in Jinja, have shown a big decline. The sources continue that only one prominent Ugandan African businessman in the town has been a regular buyer of this company's products.

It is not certain whether they are Asian businessmen in the town holding genuine Ugandan citizenship. But they are a few shops in the town owned by Asians and still operating normally.

Olympics suspended

Terrorists Kill 17 at Munich Olympics

News Compilation, September 6, 1972

Seventeen persons, among them 11 members of the Israeli Olympic team, were shot to death in a 23-hour drama, when Arab commandos broke into the Israeli dormitory at the Olympic village in Munich, West Germany. Nine of the Israelis, seized by their captors, were killed in an airport gun battle with the police. Also killed were five of the terrorists and one West German policeman.

Three terrorists were captured. In Cairo, an Arab guerrilla organization called Black September claimed responsibility for the attack. The games were suspended for a day.

Page 50

Ugandan Asian Expulsion: 90 Days and Beyond through the Eyes of the International Press

12 from Uganda held after jumping queue

By PETER THORNTON
Reprinted with permission, ©Telegraph Group Limited, London,
September 6, 1972

A PARTY of Ugandan Asians who fled from what they described as "terror" in Uganda, without visas or British entry documents, were being held at Heathrow Airport last night.

The group of 12, a man, three women and eight children, said they had bought tickets and boarded planes in Uganda "on the off-chance" of being allowed into Britain.

The Home Office said last night it was anxious that Asians waiting their turn in Uganda for entry permits to Britain should not panic and jump on the first plane out.

"While we appreciate there must be fear among the community out there, this would create more difficult problems at this end," said a spokesman.

The Asians detained at Heathrow yesterday all arrived with British passports. One women, Mrs Samiara Esmila who brought her three children with her, said her husband, an industrialist, had not been able to leave Uganda because his passport had been confiscated.

Refused to move

"On the way the plane landed in Kenya and we spent one and a half days in the airport lounge at Nairobi," she said.

"They told us we were going to be deported back to Kampala, but I refused to move, we have nowhere to go and we are penniless."

Mr Narinder Patel, a student, said the party had left because the situation in Uganda was a "dream-world."

"It is mad. Every day General Amin says he has had another dream and brings out new orders. It is a living hell and it is becoming impossible to get money or to get papers cleared."

A women with two young children said: "A few days ago I had been to the cinema with my two children and we were stopped by a soldier.

"We were forced to get out of the car at gunpoint and had to go to the army barracks. We were kept for four hours. Women are their targets."

Seven dissuaded

A family of seven—including four children—who flew to London last night on official entry vouchers, were dissuaded by welfare workers at Heathrow Airport from travelling to Leicester, where they said they had relatives, because of the city's attitude to overcrowding.

Temporary accommodation in London was arranged by the workers of the UK immigrants' advisory service. The family said they were penniless but prepared to go anywhere to find work.

ANNOUNCEMENT

CANADA-IMMIGRATION

The Canadian High Commission for Uganda announces that, commencing Wednesday, September 6, the Canada Immigration Office will make available Application forms, and will process Applicants, for permanent Admission to Canada.

Those Applicants who have Previously applied through the Canadian Regional Immigration Office at Beirut, Lebanon, will also have the opportunity to discuss their applications.

OFFICE HOURS:
MONDAY to FRIDAY

8.30 a.m. to 12.00 p.m. — 2 p.m. to 4 p.m;

ADDRESS:
I.P.S. Building, Parliament Road, Upper Level, KAMPALA.

Madhvani and his British manager arrested

News Compilation, September 6, 1972

UGANDA's leading Asian industrialist, Mr. Manubhai Madhvani has been arrested by troops and placed in "military custody." Mr. Madhvani's arrest was disclosed in a statement released after a meeting of the Defence Council under the chairmanship of President Amin.

Also under arrest in military custody is a Briton, Mr. Donald Stewart, who is manager of the Madhvani group's sugar factory at Kakira.

According to the statement, the two men are being held in connection with matters relating to the security of Uganda, external influences which are "sabotaging" Uganda's economy, and secret international arrangements by other countries against Uganda's security.

The Government has urged employees of the Madhvani group to continue working "with the same high morale—even if they get a new managing director."

UK asks 50 countries to help

News Compilation, September 5, 1972

Fifty foreign and Commonwealth countries have been approached by the British Government over the expulsion of Asians from Uganda.

They have been asked whether they can either accept Asians or help in any other way such as exerting pressure on President

---

Expellees
'India's responsibility'

"The Times of India" News Service
Reprinted with permission, ©Times of India, September 4, 1972

POONA, September 3: India will have to bear the responsibility for accommodating the refugees from Uganda, including those who hold British passports, a report submitted to the external affairs minister, Mr. Swaran Singh, by a former I.C.S. officer and now a member of Parliament, has suggested.

The report was drawn up on the advice of the foreign minister with the help of a group of Indians, including exministers in the Uganda government.

The recommendations are likely to be placed before Parliament when Mr. Swaran Singh is expected to make a statement on the crisis following President Idi Amin's expulsion of Asians from that country.

Many of the expelled persons of Indian origin feel that they may not be well received in Britain and that they would also face problems of adjustment to new conditions.

The report says that most of the expelled Asians could be rehabilitated in Gujarat, to which state they originally belonged. The problem of rehabilitation could be tackled both by the United Nations and the Indian government.

The report said it should not be difficult to absorb 80,000 Asians belonging to India. The "virile, enterprising and adventurous outlook" of these returning from Uganda should be an asset to India, it has been pointed out.

It has also been suggested that those holding British passports should be allowed to stay in India for two years, during which time they could decide about their future. Those who wish to migrate to the U.K. should be free to do so.

"LIBERALISE CUSTOMS" PLEA

A plea has also been made to liberalise customs and foreign exchange restrictions in the case of these persons. The government of India has also been urged to work out in collaboration with the United Kingdom, the question of moveable and immoveable property of the Uganda Indians.

The Uganda government should be asked to give adequate compensation for immoveable properties left behind by Indians.

The report also suggests that the government of India should undertake a census of Indians in other African countries like Kenya, Tanzania and Zambia, since these governments, too, might some day follow the example of Uganda.

Amin. The most intense diplomatic activity has been directed towards India, Pakistan and Bangladesh, countries in which the Uganda Asians would most likely want to settle. But many other governments, including those in Europe of the enlarged Ten and others in Latin America and Africa, have been formally approached.

As yet there have been few replies.

Ugandan Asian Expulsion: 90 Days and Beyond through the Eyes of the International Press

Uganda Asians in thousands seek Canada entry

By GERALD UTTING
Star staff writer
Reprinted with permission, ©Toronto Star syndicate, September 7, 1972

KAMPALA—Canada's immigration office opened here yesterday and by the time it closed 2,588 families seeking to go to Canada took out application forms.

They had a total of 3,549 dependants, which means that if all of the applicants are accepted, Canada will gain 6,137 Asian immigrants from one day's operation of the office.

Zavie Levine, a 26-year-old special assistant to Immigration Minister Bryce Mackasey, who came here to observe the situation for his boss, said, "For the first time in my life, I really saw what Canada means to people in other countries. I am really proud to be a Canadian."

There was a startling mixture of people in the line-up that greeted Canadian officials yesterday morning. There was a judge, there were doctors, police officials, lawyers, businessmen, housewives and students.

Asians were still lining up today to get applications.

Half a dozen guards directed the lines of people and a Ugandan policemen stationed himself inside the building.

Asians who completed their applications and were assigned interviews talked over their prospects with Canadian officers.

Levine said 80 persons expected to complete their interviews today.

GIVEN POINTS

The interviews last 20 minutes. The Canadian official then tells the applicant whether he has been accepted—subject to a medical examination for all members of his family. If he passes the medical test, supervised by Canadian doctors, the Asian is given a landed immigrant card and can make his way to Canada as soon as he gets clearance from the Uganda government.

The Asians must pass the regulations of the Canadian Immigration Act before they are approved for entry. Essentially they must satisfy the interviewing officer that they can get a job in Canada and integrate into Canadian society.

Applicants are awarded points for being in the age bracket in which they are most likely to find work; for education; for having relatives or sponsors in Canada; for job skills; for the place they want to settle; and for overall job prospects.

If an applicant can get 50 points, he passes and is allowed into Canada.

The Canadian system allows immigration officials some leeway in using their own judgement.

A successful Asian storekeeper in Kampala is likely to be able to get by in Canada even if he has not a good formal education, for instance.

ENGLISH OR FRENCH

Points are awarded to applicants if they can speak English or French, and that is one hurdle virtually all the Asians can clear.

They all seem to speak English fluently.

Hard times in Uganda for citizen Chawda

Michael Knipe
Reprinted with permission, ©Times Newspapers Limited, London, September 9, 1972

Arua, Uganda,—"The District Commissioner of the West Nile requests all traders and those intending to buy businesses from the departing Asians to report for briefing on how to fill in the forms in Chawda's Cinema Hall."

This notice broadcast by Uganda Radio attracted myself and a BBC colleague to this tiny community which lies at the geographic heart of the African continent. It is in the north-west of Uganda, only six miles from the Zaire Congo border and 30 miles from the Sudanese border, and it provides a vivid microcosm of the Asian problem of the West Nile district's total population of half a million. Only about 1,000 are Asians, but 900 of these live in Arua, the administrative capital, and they own about 90 per cent of the local businesses, to the frustration of the 12,000 African inhabitants.

It was here that President Amin was born and grew up. Key, the first of his four concurrent wives, still lives here and it is said in the town that she recently tried to buy Butane gas for her cooker, only to find that her supplier, an Asian, had sold out in readiness for his departure.

To get here we had a 350-mile journey, crossing first the Victoria Nile and then the Albert Nile. It was marked by the spectacle of grazing elephant herds and a constant flow of cars packed with Asian families traveling towards Kampala.

Two sleepy army sentries guarded the bridge across the Albert Nile, and at the town of Paokwach, a little further on, there was a barbed wire road block manned by wary policemen. Armed with our Uganda Government press passes, we were allowed through without difficulty, but Asians travelling the other way were having their cars thoroughly searched and their papers carefully scrutinized.

After miles of dirt road, tarmac resumes on the outskirts of Arua and a notice says that the Lions Club of the town extends a welcome. The orderliness of the ex-British colonial administrative buildings blends curiously with the shabby disarray of the Asian shopping centres, where Singer sewing machines clatter away on the doorsteps alongside open-air barbers and bicycle repairers. The film showing at Chawda's Cinema Hall is *A Lovely Way to Die,* but the prospect of taking over Asian businesses proved a worthy alternative attraction and a motley collection of Africans packed the hall in anticipation.

The District Commissioner explained in Swahili how prospective businessmen should fill in the forms, specifying the business they would like to take over and how much they would be prepared to pay for it. Then he gave the audience a fatherly pep-talk on the pitfalls of private enterprise. It would be no good, he said, giving products away to relatives. Even items wanted by the owners themselves should be paid for, otherwise the business would fail. These words drew knowing laughter. It would be no good, either, said the Commissioner, getting into the habit of closing the shop and going off drinking when people wanted to buy goods. This, too, would cause a business to fail.

As the meeting proceeded, we visited some of the nearby shops. A watery smile froze on the face of one plump, bespectacled Asian shopkeeper we tried to question. His eyes darted nervously to the Africans milling around his clothing store, and he shrugged. "You must understand", he muttered, "it is a very difficult situation. I cannot really talk to you." The reaction of another shopkeeper further down the road was precisely the opposite. Ignoring the Africans standing at his counter, he recounted bluntly how his Ugandan passport was seized and cancelled last week when he presented it to the authorities to have his citizenship verified. Then he blithely spelled out his name. The explanation for this contrasting attitude lay in the fact that this man expects to be on his way to England within weeks—penniless but safe.

Throughout all our conversations with both Asians and Africans, one name continued to recur—Raghuji Chawda, owner of the cinema hall, various garages, trading stores and 25 houses: indisputably the richest man in Arua. Remarkably, Mr Chawda was spoken of highly by both Africans and Asians. The Africans, who resent strongly the suggestion that the purge of Asians is racially motivated, hold up Mr Chawda as an example of the perfect Asian Ugandan patriot. He came to Uganda 39 years ago at the age of 12, adopted Ugandan citizenship at independence, and, the Africans pointed out, has invested all his profits in Uganda and not sent a shilling out of the country.

Furthermore he was a good friend of President Amin and was the first Asian to be given an award of the Second Republic.

This week Ugandan Asian citizens living in the West Nile have been summoned to Kampala with their complete families to verify that they are indeed citizens, and even the wealthy Mr Chawda, with his clear commitment to Uganda and his presidential award, is not immune from this bureaucratic appointment and the possible consequences.

11,000 Uganda Asians hoping to settle in Canada

By GERALD UTTING
Star staff writer
Reprinted with permission, ©Toronto Star syndicate, September 8, 1972

KAMPALA—In two days Canada may have picked up 11,000 prospective Asian immigrants in Uganda—6,000 more than Canada originally indicated it would take.

Canadian immigration chief Roger Vincent said last night that 2,032 persons—representing about 5,000 men, women and children—came to the Canadian immigration office here yesterday and picked up application forms.

The office opened Wednesday and 2,588 persons—representing 6,137 people including dependents—took application forms.

Eighty-six prospective immigrants were interviewed yesterday and a high proportion were given conditional acceptance as immigrants to Canada, Vincent said.

"Final approval depends on whether they pass the medical examination," he said.

The 85 Asians interviewed have 196 dependents.

However, Immigration Minister Bryce Mackasey told The Star from Montreal today the question of how many Asians that Canada should accept will be taken up by the cabinet early next week.

"We have to be fair to these people," he said. 'We have to assess their applications not only in a humanitarian light but also bearing in mind the likelihood that they can make a go of it in this country."

Mackasey said the cabinet has not set any hard quota and the previous estimates of 3,000 to 5,000 people were made in the expectation that "all countries, India and Pakistan, Australia and New Zealand, as well as Britain, would practice what they preach about human rights and assume their obligations."

The minister said the cabinet will have to set "hard policy" on the number to be admitted—"what we think the country can absorb in light of our own resources."

He said the government does not intend to skim off the cream of the applicants. "We are prepared to take a proper cross-section of these people."

Up to this morning, no applicants have been given final acceptance, but Asians who have been told they could go subject to medical examination were jubilant.

The interview took only five minutes, said one man who planned to go to Toronto where he has two sisters. Like many other Asians he declined to give his name, fearing that relatives left behind might be persecuted.

"The friendliness of the Canadian interviewers has really made a big impression. We are not used to government officials who want to help us," he said.

However, getting out of Uganda is going to be quite a problem for many of those accepted by

Continued on Page 54

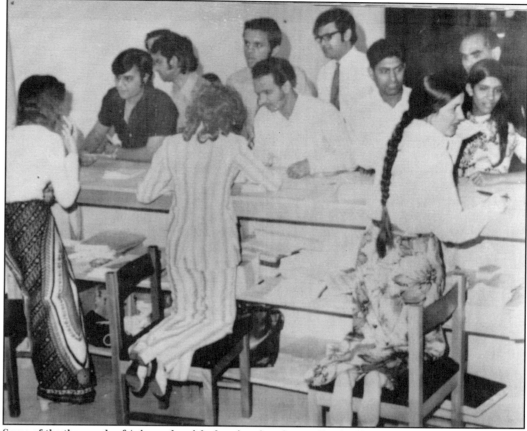

Some of the thousands of Asians who picked up immigration application forms at the temporary Canadian Immigration offices in Kampala.
Reproduced with permission, ©Associated Press/Wide World Photos

UGANDA'S ASIAN REFUGEES
Suffer the helpless to come unto us

Editorial
Reprinted with permission, ©Toronto Star syndicate, September 9, 1972

The thousands of Asian refugees lining up at Canada's immigration office in Kampala show us stark human desperation—and a Canadian opportunity.

In this distracted world nations are rarely able to co-operate even for the most commonsense purposes—such as the suppression of hijacking and terrorism. But there is nothing to stop a nation that has the resources and the compassion from performing a merciful act of rescue. Without a by-your-leave from anyone, such a country can make the world a little safer and more decent for helpless victims of inhumanity. That is Canada's opportunity now.

The Ugandan Asians are innocent, helpless victims. They have been ordered out of the country by General Idi Amin, a brutal racist dictator who could quite easily, for his own purposes, unleash a frenzy of bloodshed on these defenceless people.

Yet some Canadians, it seems, have turned their hearts cold and worry more about possible refugee competition for Canadian jobs. But if immigration really caused unemployment, this country would be mired in a permanent depression by now.

Let us now depart, callously and shortsightedly, from the generous tradition of the last quarter-century. From 1947 to 1952, Canada took in more than 165,000 persons displaced by war. In the same period it granted shelter to 4,527 Polish veterans. In 1956 it opened its arms to the Hungarian freedom fighters and over three years received 37,566 Hungarians. In 1968 and early 1969 it took 11,209 Czechs. Over the years Canada has also welcomed thousands of other stateless refugees, in addition to the hundreds of thousands of regular immigrants.

Nobody could deny that Canada is richer for having done so. Just look at the prosperity of this land—and consider the wealth of Ontario, which has received the lion's share of Canada's immigration. Immigrants bring not only skills and employment-sustaining consumption; they are also direct job-creators. From 1950 to 1962, Canada's immigration authorities kept track of 9,849 immigrants who went into business for themselves. These entrepreneurs created 44,749 jobs. Another 7,009 bought farms. Just one small example is the Sceptre Manufacturing Company in Toronto, founded by Evald Torokvei, a Swede who came here in 1948 and who today employs about 150 Canadians.

The fearful among us overlook the fact that the Ugandan Asians who are turning to Canada for help are being thrown out of their country precisely

Continued on Page 54

Ugandan Asian Expulsion: 90 Days and Beyond through the Eyes of the International Press

CROWDS CLASH ON ASIANS

Daily Telegraph Reporter
Reprinted with permission, ©Telegraph Group Limited, London, September 9, 1972

There were angry verbal clashes between two crowds of demonstrators outside Ealing Town Hall last night as the council held an emergency meeting about Ugandan Asians.

The meeting was held to debate fears that refugees would flood into Ealing's immigrant district of Southall, only a few miles from Heathrow.

About 50 local residents stood on the Town Hall steps to protest against any Asians settling in the borough. They carried placards saying: "Find homes for us first" and "Enoch Powell for Premier."

In the forecourt of the building 50 to 60 members of the Communist party, the Southall Young Socialists, and the Indian Workers' Association, had gathered to support the Asians.

Police stood by as the rival groups addressed each other through megaphones. No arrests were made.

Earlier the Labour mayor, Councillor Gordon Mason, was booed and jostled by Right-wing demonstrators as he left his car.

Ald. Robert Hetherington told the council the borough, with its high immigrant population, has been living on the edge of a volcano for several years.

The borough has about 33,000 immigrants, 22,000 of them in Southall.

RAF accommodation

Local authorities in Lincolnshire said yesterday they had not been told about plans to use RAF Hemswell as a reception centre for 800 Asians.

Mr Brian Eminson, deputy clerk of Gainsborough Rural District Council, eight miles away said: "No matter how sympathetic the council might be to these poor souls, there is nothing we can do. We have no vacancies."

Married quarters at Hemswell, which is no longer operational, has empty, unfurnished buildings which had been expected to be sold off.

The council at Lincoln, 10 miles away, where unemployment has been above the national average for the last four years, has said it will try to find jobs for between 40 and 50 Asians. It has already offered some accommodation.

Asian refugees arriving at Heathrow yesterday said that the Ugandan authorities were now refusing to register the births of Asian babies, presumably because they feared the children might try to claim Ugandan citizenship.

The Foreign Office said yesterday there was "no possibility" of newly-born babies being refused entry when they arrived in this country.

Continued from Page 53

Suffer the helpless to come unto us

because they are successful entrepreneurs and professional people. If they hadn't pulled themselves up by their bootstraps to where they are today, they wouldn't be the targets of Gen. Amin's cruel demagoguery. Obviously they will have a period of adjustment when they come to Canada, but their proven energies and resourcefulness will ensure their ultimate success in this country and their contribution to Canada's prosperity.

If, due to an unemployment problem that lies within the power of our government to correct, Canada were to spurn such energetic, educated people who will have no language problem here, this land would show itself to be not only heartless but extremely myopic. And the numbers game of how many refugees shall be invited is equally silly: If the trend of regular immigration for the first six months of this year continues, Canada could admit 10,000 Ugandan Asians and still not exceed last year's relatively low intake of 122,000.

Since Gen. Amin is obviously bent on expelling his victims without a penny, they will need help while they settle down here. Asians here are preparing to take this burden off the public, so far as they can; but other Canadians will have to lend a hand during the resettlement period. Let us not stint in this work of charity and mercy, from which our country will ultimately benefit.

Continued from Page 53

11,000 Uganda Asians hoping to settle in Canada

Canada. Flights to Europe are booked solidly already until Nov. 7, the date by which President Idi Amin has ordered 60,000 Asians holding foreign passports out of the country.

In addition, you cannot buy an airline ticket with Uganda shillings unless the Bank of Uganda—the government reserve bank—has given its written approval.

Applications are stacked up in the bank, which to put it mildly is not speedy.

Some people have to wait in up to 16 different line-ups to complete forms. Airline officials said no Asians have been issued tickets recently.

One Asian family which had expected to leave tonight for London discovered this morning that they will not be permitted to go because they have not completed all the processing.

The unwanted Asians who are accused by President Amin of sabotaging and dominating the Ugandan economy, must get approval for the disposal of their assets before they are permitted to leave the country. They must also get a tax clearance.

Several African civil servants, those supporting President Amin's expulsion decision, said they believe the expulsion deadline of Nov. 7 will have to be extended.

On top of this, British officials said there have been mass firings in the civil service and Uganda's creaky administrative machinery is grinding to a halt.

Until two nights ago, Asians were lavishly spending their remaining shillings at restaurants and night spots in Kampala.

But since the arrest of Uganda's wealthiest Asian industrialist, Manubhai Madhvani, Asians have virtually vanished after dark.

The industrialist was accused of sabotaging the economy of Uganda and of being involved in "secret international arrangements by other countries against Uganda's security."

The industrialist's British manager, Donald Stewart, was also arrested and accused of writing "a derogatory letter" about Uganda. The letter, sent to Stewart's wife in England, was intercepted by Ugandan police.

Neither man has been charged.

The Ugandan government, which was exposing alleged British "assassination plots" two days ago, has suddenly switched to denunciation of the Zambian president, Kenneth Kaunda.

A government statement yesterday called the Zambian leader a "black sheep" among African presidents for criticizing the expulsion of the Asians.

Immersed in religious affairs, Amin yesterday met the Ghanaian leader of the Redeemed Church of Uganda, the Rev. John Yeboka.

The priest told Amin that nobody is going to kill him because he is in the right direction of God.

The president invited Yeboka to a luncheon with the army command and told him to bring with him some of the dead people he supposedly has brought back to life.

One such person is a man who died on Wednesday at 4 p.m. and after prayers rose from the dead at 7 p.m., according to the official broadcasting service.

President Amin also took time out to ban the Saint Mark Path religion, a cult of Asian origin. To become a member you have to take medicine given by a cult leader.

A government announcement said the tutor at the national teachers' college and the wife of one of the hired officials of the commerce department had "run mad" after getting the religion.

President Amin said the religion is "very dangerous" to the health of the Ugandan people and told anyone who was aware of it being spread to call in the police.

IN TERROR-FILLED UGANDA, THE MACHINE-GUN LIVES

By GERALD UTTING
Star staff writer
Reprinted with permission, ©Toronto Star syndicate, September 12, 1972

NAIROBI, Kenya—The best thing about Uganda was leaving it.

As the jet heaved itself up into the sky from Entebbe airport, hurtling toward Kenya and away from the terror of Kampala, the tension began to drain away.

Idi Amin Dada, the giant Nubian president of Uganda, with his five wives and "oust the Asians" policy, began to seem more like a mythical ogre than the ever-present menace he had been for two weeks.

The Asians, frightened and panicky, often comical with their "oh my goodness me" brand of English, seemed braver in memory than they had been in the flesh. I could catch a jet out of Uganda. They could not—unless they were lucky enough to have a ticket paid for in foreign currency.

As the jet crossed the vastness of Lake Victoria and entered Kenya, the threat of the drunken soldiers and murderous secret police of Uganda seemed somehow shrunken. Were they still there terrorizing the people of Kampala, or had they somehow gone back to the pages of a cheap comic book.

A peasant society

It's hard to put the Uganda crisis in meaningful perspective. There is no rational explanation for Gen. Amin's policies. There is no careful purpose behind the brutalities of his troops.

You cannot explain Uganda today in the terms of Toronto. Idi Amin is not some kind of power-drunk Pierre Trudeau. The Asians he wants to drive out are not shopkeepers who run corner milk stores though many of them would like a chance to do just that.

The secret police are not even like those of Russia, though they are reputedly at least as brutal.

For Uganda is not a modern industrial state, but a medieval tribal and peasant society, with some of the institutions of the western world, such as bureaucratic government, troops with tanks and jets, a modern city centre.

The Asians, busy as bees by Uganda standards, knowing about modern things such as cash registers and currency manipulation, make up less than 1 per cent of the population.

They live well by the standards of the ordinary Ugandan. Some of them are rich. But the ordinary Ugandan is a peasant living on the land, growing a little corn and bananas, eating little meat. To him, a $10 transistor radio is a luxury, and the houses of the Asians are palaces.

Continued on Page 56

2:1 against Asians

News Compilation, September 11, 1972

A majority of people, by a margin of nearly two to one, think that the Uganda Asians should not be allowed to settle in Britain, according to a recent Poll carried out for the Daily Telegraph.

In response to the question: "Do you think that we should or should not let the Ugandan Asians settle in this country?", the answers were as follows:

Should..........................32%
Should not....................57%
Don't know....................11%

Showing the flag in South Eaton Place, a quiet Pimlico backwater, which was filled to capacity yesterday for a protest against the arrival of Ugandan Asians. "Heath out, Enoch in." shouted demonstrators outside No. 33— home of Mr Enoch Powell.

'Kill Amin plot' was my charity letter

By KEITH COLLING
Reprinted with permission, ©Daily Mail, London, September 11, 1972

Uganda's Amin regime has distorted the contents of a charity seeking letter from Britain into a "gun for hire" plot to kill the President, it was claimed yesterday.

The Ugandan Government alleged that a letter bearing a Leicester postmark from a Ugandan Asian named 'V. R. Bhati' offered a £50,000 reward to get rid of the President.

Leaders of the 6,000 Ugandan Asians already in Leicester denied knowledge of 'V. R. Bhati' or his alleged 'revolutionary Committee.' However, 24-year-old Mr Ramesh Jani, of Peebles Way, Leicester, a Ugandan Asian who is an official of an Indian arts circle, said: 'I am sure this allegation is a distortion of a letter I sent to Kampala.'

'I detest President Amin, but I do not want to kill anyone or hire an assassin.'

He wrote to a Ugandan Asian businessman, Mr Manubhi Madhvani, who employed the jailed Briton Donald Stewart as the managing director of his sugar business.

Mr Jani said he asked Mr Madhvani for a £10,000 donation for the arts circle, pointing out that much of this money would be used to help Asian refugees when they arrive in Britain.

'At the end of my letter I added a postscript, perhaps unwisely, which read "The days of President Amin must be numbered." '

He heard that the letter had been opened by Ugandan security officials— and now Mr Madhvani has been arrested.

Fear

President Amin canceled an important speech-making trip at the weekend because of his fear for his life. He has received from Uganda's Defense Council the insignia of Uganda's eight highest honours and medals—including the Order of the Source of the Nile.

Asians willing to go through the mill

By GILLIAN LINSCOTT
Reprinted with permission, ©The Guardian, London, September 9, 1972

Mr Prem Bhudia, formerly a salesman in Kenya, now a textile mill worker in Oldham, stretches out a left hand with fingers twisted and nails crushed, the result of an accident at the mill two years ago. He said: "If I'd been doing here the job I did in Kenya, I shouldn't have a hand like this."

Even the neat officeworkers's hand of his friend, Mr Vishnu Mohandas, once a cashier, now an operating theatre technician, has one finger bent slightly out of shape—from the time when he, too, worked in the mill. They speak without much bitterness. The point they are trying to make is that East African Asians are adaptable.

Both men, as officials of the local Indian Association, are making lists of families prepared to give homes to Uganda Asians if necessary.

They do not know how many, if any, of the Uganda refugees will come to Oldham.

There are probably about a thousand East African Asians in the town, many of them earlier refugees from Kenya and Tanzania. Other small towns of the industrial Northwest of England—Bolton, Rochdale, Ashton-under-Lyne—have East African Asian communities and are wondering how many of the new immigrants will join them.

So far Mr Mohandas knows of only four or five families likely to come to the town. From his own experience and that of his Kenyan friends, he believes that these and any other families who come will be no burden on society. He sits in the comfortable terrace house he owns, in the shadow of the mill chimney, a Hindu shrine in the corner of the room and explains: "We do not wait for things to be done for us. We help ourselves."

"People in England talk about the Uganda Asians taking their jobs, taking their houses, living on social security. They said the same about us when we came from Kenya."

"But whose jobs have we taken? In the mills you'll always see Asians on the night shifts, the shifts the English don't want to do. We don't take anyone's houses. We buy our own because nobody will rent houses to a coloured man, and we pay cash for them. Someone will borrow £300 from this friend, £200 from that friend, and get enough for a house."

Five years ago Mr Mohandas and most of his friends left Kenya in a hurry and without resources, in much the same circumstances as the Uganda Asians.

Twelve-hour shifts at the mills, seven days a week, laid the basis of comparative prosperity. Few of them found in Oldham the kind of jobs

they were doing in Kenya.

Engineers have become bus drivers and mill workers. A man with 16 years experience as a compositor also works at a mill. A more recent arrival from Kenya, a head of a school department who taught maths and English, clears frames on a mill night shift.

The school master has been accepted for a teaching diploma course in Manchester and in a year should be back at the blackboard. A young man who was a magistrate's clerk in Kenya has just become a magistrate's clerk again, after several years at the mill.

But work, rather than the status of the job, is what matters. Mr Mohandas says: "I tell people you must have things hard now if you want them soft later. I know about 130 East African Asian families here in Oldham, and only three of them on unemployment benefit."

"Two," Mr Bhudia interjects, "One of them found a job."

"Two then." Mr Mahandas says. "The point is, you can't buy houses cash down when you're on unemployment money. We have to work and the Uganda Asians will be the same. Our religion, you see, teaches that you must adapt your life according to circumstances."

Continued from Page 55

IN TERROR-FILLED UGANDA, THE MACHINE-GUN LIVES

Hunting and sailing

When the British arrived to colonize this essentially feudal society 70 years ago, they downgraded the black nobility and introduced Asians to do their bookkeeping and form an artisan class.

The British lived in spacious bungalows, with gardens full of flowering trees, had golf clubs, sailing clubs on Lake Victoria, and hunted wild animals for pleasure. The Asians prospered by hard work. The Africans watched from the countryside or went to the towns to work as unskilled servants.

When the British left in 1962, the new African politicians of the mould of President Milton Apollo Obote, ousted by Amin in a coup in January, 1971, simply took over the role of the British. But there were few of them who really knew what running a modern government was all about. They had to rely on the Asians to carry on the commerce of the land. Asians pay almost all the taxes in Uganda.

Obote ruled Uganda with a mixture of force and fraud, depending for his striking power on the Langi, his own large northern tribe.

Amin, who comes from the small Kakwa tribe, was able to form a coalition of officers from the West Nile region that was powerful enough to force Obote into exile.

Since Amin came to power, he has been dispensing ever more speedily with the old trappings of the colonial past—such as impartial courts—and depending on naked force. The police officers tried to resist the lawlessness of the president's methods and have been fired. Today in Kampala the soldier's submachine-gun has more weight than court decrees.

Outwardly, Kampala looks peaceful enough, and architecturally it is even impressive. But at night its streets are deserted. Asians are afraid to go out anymore.

"I don't know which is worse," said one Asian. "If the soldiers don't grab you and rough you up the kondos (bandit gangs) will stop you at a traffic light and take your car and your money."

The kondo menace in Kampala was one cause of Obote's downfall. In gangs of up to 30 armed with tommy-guns and pangas (great carved knives), they attack houses and communities almost at will. They cut the telephone wires and descend on a home, looting it. If the occupants show any signs of displeasure, they are killed.

"In the last days of Obote, they were robbing banks and stores and motorists in the main city centre every night," said a restaurant owner. "We all had to employ armed guards. There was a machine-gun battle right outside my restaurant one night.

"When Amin came to power he was welcomed. We hoped he would clean Uganda up. For a while the soldiers fought the kondos, shooting them down in the streets in cold blood when they were captured.

"Then the soldiers started to worry about other things. They started drinking when they got up and at night they were too drunk to chase kondos."

He demanded my ID

This reporter was stopped and questioned at length one day by three men in plain clothes while taking pictures in a slum against a backdrop of the parliament building.

One identified himself as a policeman, the second as an officer in military intelligence. The third, a private in the paratroopers, was drunkæand in charge of the team.

"It is against the law to take photographs here," said the policeman.

"Why are you collecting military information in our country?" asked the military intelligence officer. He demanded my identity papers.

He looked at a Toronto police press card and brightened. "Ah," he said. "You are a policeman, too, like us, from Toronto, Japan."

At first, Asians talked fairly openly about their anger at the Africans and their fears of a bloodbath when the soldiers get too impatient for loot to wait until they are gone.

The bureaucracy of Uganda is incredibly bungling and complex. Asians are not being issued airline tickets and cannot get foreign currency. It seems unlikely that clearance can be obtained for them to leave Uganda en masse before the Nov. 7 deadline imposed by President Amin.

"It is not so much a question of his mobs ordering us to be killed," said one Asian. He begged not to be identified, as did almost every Asian. "It is just that one day a drunken soldier will decide to start looting and will use his machine-gun. Then all the rest of the soldiers will start killing."

'You will have to go'

At the 18-storey Kampala International Hotel, there were rumors that the secret police came in the night and took people away from their rooms to be killed.

On my last day in Kampala, a friendly room clerk took me aside. He was shaking with fear. "The men from the ministry of security have been to the hotel asking where you were," he said. "You are in great danger. You will have to go to the airport if you can and get away from Uganda."

As I flew away from Entebbe, away from Uganda, a 19-year-old blonde girl in the next seat told me her parents worked for the United Nations in Uganda.

"The other day, while waterskiing, I found two bodies in the water," she said. "They had been shot to death.

"I loved Uganda, the people were so nice. But I am glad to be able to get out alive."

'To lead is not to lecture or cajole from a safe distance. To lead is to share'

ASIANS: POWELL LASHES HEATH

By WALTER TERRY, Political Editor
Reprinted with permission, ©Daily Mail, London, September 13, 1972

MR ENOCH POWELL, in one of the most unrelenting speeches of his career, delivered a ferocious attack on the Heath Government last night.

It was a Government, he said, which proved by its actions over the Ugandan Asians that it was totally out of touch with the people.

With savage irony, he chose to make his attack—on an issue which already had a large section of the Tory Party bubbling with discontent—at Pegwell Bay, Kent, within a couple of miles of the Prime Minister's birth place, Broadstairs.

How many Asians, he said, had the Government asked Broadstairs to take?

Let the Tory leaders show their sincerity over the problem by sharing it. That was the tenor of a speech which will have a devastating impact on a very sensitive situation.

One Minister after another, from the Prime Minister downwards, was picked off with scorn and anger. Underlying almost every word was contempt for what he called "the silence of connivance."

This was a reference to a favourite Powellite theme—that MPs, Fleet Street and Whitehall often conspire to ignore public opinion on race issues when it is thought inconvenient.

He said: 'Let those who would allay the nation's anxieties, and prove the fears of Leicester and Newham, Birmingham and Brent, Bradford and Huddersfield to be ill-founded or exaggerated, comment the like to their own supporters and demand that their own constituencies should be foremost to take a hand and share the toils, the benefits, the credit.

Feelings

'What have Broadstairs an Bexley (sorry Sidcup), what have Kinross and Hexham done wrong that they should be left out in the cold,' he asked in a reference which embraced not only the Prime Minister's home town, but also his constituency and the constituencies of Foreign Secretary Sir Alec Douglas - Home and Mr Geoffrey Rippon.

Mr Powell, speaking to the Ramsgate Round Table at the Viking Ship Hotel, showed no quarter to the Government's style, or lack of it.

He declared: 'In order to govern the people and to lead them, you must enter into their feelings and their fears and they must know that you enter them.'

His comment on Mr Heath: 'To lead is not to lecture or cajole from a safe distance. To lead is to share.'

Sir Peter Rawlinson, the Attorney-General, was shrugged aside simply as a lawyer put up to tell the country, wrongly, that it had no choice but to take the Ugandan Asians.

Mr Powell dismissed a TV broadcast by Sir Alec as a trick that fell flat on its face.

Mr Rippon?— He was merely the Minister sent to eat humble pie in Uganda.

As for the way the Government has handled the issue from start to finish, Mr Powell said: 'If the overriding purpose had been to humiliate the people of this country and show complete indifference to their interests, feelings, and wishes, the tactics could not have been better devised.'

Advertisement

CANADA
CANADIAN HIGH COMMISSION
IMMIGRATION SERVICE
INTERVIEWS

I.P.S. BUILDING, KAMPALA

Holders of the following reference numbers are invited to appear for interview Tuesday, SEPT. 12, 8.30 to 12.00 and 2.00 to 4.00.

8.30 to 10.30	10.30 to 12.00	2.00 to 3.00	3.00 to 4.00
62	123	173	241
70	126	176	247
74	127	176	254
79	128	183	255
83	135	184	257
86	139	188	258
87	144	191	261
88	145	224	264
89	146	225	267
98	151	230	268
	151	231	271
101	153	232	272
105	154	233	282
110	156	235	286
111	161	236	288
113	162		
115	163		
116	164		
117	166		
119	167		
120	170		

Wives and children under 18 must not appear. Only those heads of family or single persons whose REFERENCE NUMBERS appear above will be interviewed. All other holders of reference numbers will be invited through subsequent newspaper notices or contacted by mail. If you hold a reference number please refrain from contacting this office unless invited to do so.

Suburbia and the Asians next door

By MALCOLM STUART in Leicester on a city's undercover immigration anxieties
Reprinted with permission, ©The Guardian, London, September 12, 1972

Leicester is loudly campaigning to have Ugandan Asians directed away from the city on the grounds that the influx would strain its welfare and education facilities beyond capacity. Yet those families which have already arrived seem well capable of caring for themselves. So capable that this may be the real fear of Leicester. A large proportion of the newcomers are certain to be middle-class people with middle-class aspirations to good homes and the best available education for their children.

Until recently immigration has not been a middle-class concern in Leicester. Coloured people, still predominantly West Indian, mainly settled in Highfields, south of the city centre, and provided welcome labour for the more menial jobs. Indians and Pakistanis, direct from their sub-continent , arrived a little later and filled the vacancies in the prosperous hosiery industry.

It was not even a great problem for the elder residents of Highfields. The majority now live in new council estates. In fact there was no large-scale concern until Asians from East Africa started to arrive in the city in 1968.

An increasing number of these people are not interested in sharing a Victorian terraced house in Highfields. Many have owned substantial businesses in Nairobi or Kampala, and there seems some evidence to support General Amin's belief that they have quietly managed to export some of their capital over the past few years.

"And why not?" asked a 29-year-old economics graduate whose family had a textile factory in Kenya. "It was a question of getting some of it out or losing the lot. The usual method was over-invoicing. You simply paid too much to your foreign suppliers and they banked it for you. Now I have managed to buy an interest in a similar firm here. I cannot afford as large a house as my family had in Nairobi but, I have bought quite a pleasant place on the Leicester ring road.

"I get on very well with one neighbour, the other is a little more reserved. I get the impression that some people here are surprised, and in fact alarmed, that not every Indian wants to work on the buses."

Race Relations Act or not, Asians often find it necessary to send a white friend to inquire about new houses for sale. In fact it is the arrival of Asian families on new private housing estates that has been the most significant cause of middle-class anxiety.

A rising young executive with one of Leicester's larger knitwear companies was within two days of exchanging contracts on an £11,000 detached house in a new development last week when he discovered the homes on either side had been bought by Asians.

"The builders tried to hush it up but I'm afraid it's put me off," he said. "We really wanted that house. It would cost 20,000 in

Continued on Page 58

Ugandan Asian Expulsion: 90 Days and Beyond through the Eyes of the International Press

Amin plans concentration camps for Asians after deadline

News Compilation, September 14, 1972

President Idi Amin visited several military camps to examine possible areas where camps will be set up to accommodate non-citizen Asians who, without specific exemption by the Government, will not have removed themselves from Uganda by the November 8 deadline.

The affected people will have to be rounded up by the Security Forces and taken to these camps where they will be kept until the British Government allows them entry into their own Motherland, which is Britain according to the Government.

Uganda Asians to cross Kenya in closed trains—Moi

Kenya's Vice-President, Mr Daniel Arap Moi told parliament that the expelled Indians from Uganda who are travelling to the Port of Mombasa would be prohibited to leave their trains before they reach their destination. He added that special security measures are being prepared at stations all along the line.

One train a day will be reserved for the Indians according to the representative of the Shipping Corporation of India. The Indian ship, *State of Haryana* is expected to make at least three crossings to Bombay starting September 29th.

UGANDA ASIAN INFLUX COULD BE MET IF EACH CHURCH PROVIDED FOR ONE IMMIGRANT

Mr Walker, Secretary of State for the Environment, sought to introduce a sense of perspective into the impending influx of Ugandan Asians when he addressed the church leaders' conference here today. It was perhaps appropriate that he chose Birmingham for his forum, for the city has a large coloured population.

After he had been introduced by the Archbishop of York, Dr Coggan, who has offered accommodation for an Asian family at his home at Bishopsthorpe, Mr Walker said: "one has seen the reaction in this country by a large and vocal section of public feeling concerning the Ugandan Asians in terms of what problems this country can tackle, a very minor and unimportant effort could tackle this problem well. When you consider the churches represented at this gathering today, between them they have many more buildings than Ugandan Asians coming to this country.

"It is a reflection on how speedily and effectively a problem such as this can be solved if only each church made provision for one Ugandan Asian. I am not suggesting that they do this, but I am suggesting this indicates a small problem where the immediate reaction has been one of very considerable hostility to the Government for quite rightly meeting their obligations in this particular sphere.

Private home offers to Ugandan Asians

The Uganda Resettlement Board has received offers of more than 2,000 places in private homes all over Britain for the Asians expelled from Uganda.

This was disclosed after the board's third official meeting, held in London yesterday.

The meeting was attended by Mr Carr, the Home Secretary, who spent more than an hour discussing the latest reception and resettlement arrangements.

During the meeting Mr Carr referred to the help the Government intends to give to local authorities to help them to meet the extra costs directly attributable to receiving families expelled from Uganda.

One of the main topics of discussion was the difficulties facing both British Asian students from Uganda already studying in this country and that facing those who will be arriving here soon.

Mr Praful Patel, the only Asian member of the board, submitted a detailed plan for setting up a financial institution to help the Asians. To be run on the lines of a merchant bank, it would concentrate on providing loans to the expelled Asians on a commercial basis.

Support for the proposed institution is to be sought in the City and from wealthy Indians, Pakistanis and East African Asians already living in Britain. If the plan is accepted it will be run on business rather than charitable lines.

London's 32 boroughs are seeking an urgent meeting with the Home Secretary to discuss the difficulties they will face when the Uganda Asians arrive in Britain. They seek assurances that they will receive sufficient money and facilities to cope with the influx.

SWEDEN, NEW ZEALAND TO ACCEPT ASIANS

The Swedish and new Zealand governments have announced that they will accept 300 and 200 Asians from Uganda, respectively.

Premier Olaf Palme of Sweden said that Sweden wants "a fair amount of professionals, but it is not necessary for all of them to be skilled."

New Zealand's Foreign Affairs Minister Sir Keith Holyoake said that refugees possessing mainly professional and technical skills that are in demand there will be selected and not in the fields of existing unemployment.

U.S. urged to admit Uganda Asians

U.S. Senator Edward Kennedy and New York Representative Edward Koch have separately urged the Nixon administration to admit Asians from Uganda.

Mr. Kennedy said between 1,000 and 3,000 Asians should be allowed under the Attorney-General's power of "parole"—a power lately authorized for Soviet Jews.

Mr. Koch wants 5,000 Asians admitted without subjecting them to admission quotas. "By offering to accept 5,000 of these people, we hopefully will set an example for other countries to do the same," he added.

Continued from Page 57

Suburbia and the Asians next door

London, but we have pulled out. I have never thought of myself as a racialist. I don't think I would mind an Indian family on one side, but on both sides, well that's a ghetto.

" I find it a bit worrying. Although the city council is Labour controlled I think they are expressing all our feelings in saying we can't take any more. I don't think it would be so bad if they were just coming to work on the factory floor but something like a third of our design staff now are from East Africa. And look at the schools."

By "schools" Leicester's middle class mean the city's eight grammar schools. One of the best girls' schools, with an excellent university entrance rate, has started the autumn term with Asian girls occupying twenty per cent of the first form places; this in a city of perhaps 6,000 Asians out of a population of 273,000.

"The secondary moderns may have their language problems with children directly from India but the girls that come here are very bright and extremely hard working," said a science mistress at the school. "It will

be very interesting to see our GCE results in five years' time."

It is significant that there has been very little opposition to a hastily devised plan to make Leicester's secondary education comprehensive before its education services are merged with Leicestershire's in 1974. The feeling seems to be on some levels that coloured children will simply go to neighbourhood schools instead of traveling in to grammar schools.

In fact the merger will help end the totally artificial situation where 690 children, nearly all immigrants, have been unable to start school at all in the city this term, while schools in the county suburbs have vacant places.

"That is why I did my homework and chose to live in Wigston," said a former Kampala shopkeeper who arrived in this country three months ago and is now waiting for his family to join him." I went to public library and read the reference books," he explained.

Wigston, which is really part of Leicester has a pop-

ulation of 30,000 and has seen 5,000 private houses built since the war. In its entry in the municipal Year Book, the urban district council proudly states: "The town has excellent schools and was the first to operate the Leicestershire Plan for Secondary Education. Seven new schools have been built during the last few years (it lists a grammar, two high, one junior and five primary schools) and further educational projects are planned for the immediate future including a College of Further Education."

A house in Wigston is a prime ambition for a considerable number of up-and-coming Leicester people. If they cannot make Wigston then neighboring Oadby is a reasonable compromise. The Leicester area seems unlikely to receive the 15,000 Ugandan Asians that the city council have predicted but the very prosperity of the place will probably bring in more than the 1,000 that the existing Asian community forecast. And whether Leicester likes it or not, they too will have ambitions to settle in pleasant houses in Wigston and send their children off each morning in smart school uniforms.

Page 58 — *Ugandan Asian Expulsion: 90 Days and Beyond through the Eyes of the International Press*

How Canada moved fast in Uganda

By Peter Desbarats, Ottawa editor
Reprinted with permission, ©Toronto Star syndicate, September 14, 1972

OTTAWA—The letter-to-the-editor columns of metropolitan dailies, particularly in Toronto, and mail reaching his own office have indicated to Prime Minister Trudeau that no election issue at the moment involves Canadians as emotionally as the governments policy on the admission of Asians from Uganda.

No count on the Prime Minister's mail has been released but it is known to be running heavily against the direction of government policy. The Prime Minister's advisers haven't been surprised by this, nor by the fact that most of the critical letters come from Toronto and Hamilton, two cities that have received sufficient numbers of immigrants in recent years to noticeably alter the composition of their populations, and which can expect to receive a large proportion of the new arrivals from Uganda.

But it has been noted that these letters often appear to come from highly educated people in the professions rather than from workers who normally might be expected to voice the strongest concern about competition for employment. Letters favorable to the government's policy also appear to come mainly from business and professional people but are more evenly distributed across the country, the main points of origination being Montreal, Toronto and Vancouver.

Popular or not, the Trudeau government's response to events in Uganda in the past six weeks has been relatively swift, completely unequivocal and absolutely unique. The record in this respect, as disclosed by officials here, is clear.

Takes initiative

It began on Monday, Aug. 7, only three days after President Idi Amin's first pronouncement on his Asian subjects, when the Prime Minister's office took the initiative in maintaining contact with the situation in Uganda and co-ordinating the Canadian response.

The first inter-departmental meeting took place the following day, primarily involving the departments of external affairs and manpower and immigration. This enabled External Affairs Minister Mitchell Sharp to make his first statement on Uganda on Wednesday, Aug. 9, when he appealed to President Amin to reconsider his decision to expel an estimated 60,000 Asians from his country.

Continued on Page 60

Schools start with few Asian students

Reprinted with permission, ©Uganda Argus, September 15, 1972

KAMPALA CITY SCHOOLS HAVE OPENED FOR THE NEW TERM WITH VERY FEW ASIAN STUDENTS AND TEACHERS. THE FEW STUDENTS WHO HAD TURNED UP WERE ASKED TO GO HOME UNTIL TODAY TO ALLOW TEACHERS TO MAKE ARRANGEMENTS FOR UNAFFECTED STUDENTS BY THE EXPULSION ORDER, THIS WAS LEARNT YESTERDAY.

It was understood that many Asian schools—primary and secondary—were badly hit. Many teachers did not report for duty as they were allegedly busy queuing for tax clearance forms and other immigration documents.

But Mr James Kisubi, Senior Education Officer in the Ministry of Education denied knowledge of this.

He said: "The order has not affected our aided schools: all Government schools and their teachers are working normally."

The only problem experienced by the headmasters yesterday was assessing the number of pupils who were going back and those not returning to school at all.

Some pupils or students are leaving Uganda together with their parents; otherwise there is no problem at all. Teachers are still there and have started their work he said.

The investigations made in some schools however revealed that many pupils as well as teachers, mostly women, did not report for duty. This has not been attributed to families leaving the country as a result of President Amin's expulsion order.

It was also alleged that over 400 children in a certain primary school in Kampala had left. Some classes had only a handful of Asian pupils.

Most of these were Ugandan Asians and children of diplomats and

Continued on Page 60

U.S. delays Uganda loan over Amin note on Jews

News Compilation, September 15, 1972

The United States is holding up a projected $3 million loan to Uganda as a sign of displeasure over a recent statement by President Idi Amin supporting Hitler's slaughter of 6,000,000 Jews in World War II.

In messages to Secretary General Waldheim of the United Nations and to Premier Golda Meir of Israel, President Amin not only urged the removal of all Israelis from the Middle East to Britain, but endorsed Hitler's policies.

The State Department said this message was "deeply shocking and incomprehensible".

Advertisements

BANK OF UGANDA

ANNOUNCEMENT

All holders of British, Indian, Pakistan and Bangladesh passports who are required to leave Uganda by Decree No. 17 on or before the 7th November, 1972 are hereby notified that the purchase of air, land and sea tickets must be made only after they have obtained approval from the Bank of Uganda. The following documents must be presented for examination:—

(1) Passport
(2) Income Tax Clearance
(3) Evidence that a statement of assets and liabilities has been submitted to the Ministry of Commerce

(4) The head of every family unit must have applied for imigration treatment through his bankers

(5) Application for the purchase of air ticket

Non-citizens who have been exempted must produce evidence to that effect before their dependants' applications to purchase air tickets can be approved.

Tickets are available from East African Airways Corporation who have a temporary office on the premises of the Bank of Uganda.

The Exchange Control Department as well as the East African Airways Booking Office will be open from 8.00 A.M. to 12.30 P.M. and 2.00 P.M. to 6.30 P.M. from Monday to Sunday.

NOTICE TO PASSENGERS
ON KARANJA

Indian Citizens who have reservations Bombay on KARANJA sailing on September 19 are advised that if they intend to travel to Mombasa by Rail, they should do so only on the 17th September & not earlier. This will facilitate smooth transit through Kenya.

HIGH COMMISSION OFINDIA
KAMPALA

CANADA
CANADIAN HIGH COMMISSION
IMMIGRATION SERVICE

MEDICAL EXAMINATIONS
ISSUE OF IMMIGRANT VISAS
TRANSPORTATION ARRANGEMENTS

MEDICAL EXAMINATIONS OF PERSONS ACCEPTED FOR CANADA WILL START **MONDAY SEPT 18** FOR THOSE PERSONS INVITED ON THAT DAY AND SUBSEQUENT DAYS.

APPOINTMENTS

THOSE PERSONS WHO HAVE BEEN INTERVIEWED AND ACCEPTED **PRIOR TO MONDAY SEPT 18** SHOULD CONTACT THE CANADIAN IMMIGRATION OFFICE IN PERSON **TUESDAY SEPT 19** FROM 8:30 TO 12:00 FOR AN APPOINTMENT WITH REFERENCE TO THEIR MEDICAL EXAMINATION
APPLICANTS WHO WOULD BE PREPARED TO LEAVE FOR CANADA BY **SUNDAY SEPT 24** WILL BE GIVEN PRIORITY FOR THE MEDICAL EXAMINATION — IF MARRIED, THE WIFE AND CHILDREN IF RESIDING IN UGANDA MUST ACCOMPANY THEM.

VISAS AND TRANSPORTATION TO CANADA
PERSONS ISSUED VISAS WILL BE EXPECTED TO SIGNIFY THEIR READINESS TO DEPART FOR CANADA ABOARD CHARTERED FLIGHTS WHEN THE RELEVANT GOVERNMENT AND FORMALITIES ARE COMPLETED.

Ugandan Asian Expulsion: 90 Days and Beyond through the Eyes of the International Press

Sweden accepts 200-300 Asians

Editorial
Reprinted with permission, © Dagens Nyheter, Stockholm,
September 15, 1972
Translation courtesy of Dr. Charles Westin and Catarina Nyberg

Sweden accepts 200-300 Asians from Uganda according to what Prime Minister Olof Palme informed Prime Minister Heath. Furthermore, Sweden can give financial aid to contribute to the solution of the difficult refugee situation that arises when about 50,000 people—Indians and Pakistanis—are forced to head-over-heels leave their homes in Uganda, where many of them have been living for a couple of generations.

By accepting a limited number of Ugandan refugees, Sweden is committing an act of human solidarity and taking part in an international aid action, side by side with several other countries. As the Prime Minister pointed out, the Asians from Uganda can be included in the yearly quota of refugees that the National Board of Labour has taken on already as their responsibility; one can also assume that the Ugandan Asian refugees to a large extent are professionally trained. The majority of the refugees from Uganda—principally those with a British passport—are expected to leave for Great Britain; 20,000 - 30,000 it has been said. This figure can be said to be low for example compared to the number of immigrants from the West Indies. But the sudden flow from Uganda practically without any warning will inevitably create problems in a Great Britain that in recent years has tried to restrain immigration.

A couple of days ago the British Guardian published the complete wording of a telegram that Uganda's President Amin—the man behind the expulsion of the Asians—had sent to the UN Secretary General Kurt Waldheim with a copy to Prime Minister Golda Meir. In this telegram it was said among other things: "Germany is the place where Hitler, when he was the head of State and Supreme Commander, burned over six million Jews. This was so because Hitler and all of the German People knew that the Israelis are not people who work for the interest of the world, and this is the reason why the Israelis were burnt alive on German soil."

Formulations of this sort can only come from a sick mind.

Uganda denies Hitler statement delayed U.S. loan

News Compilation, September 16, 1972

A Ugandan Government statement tonight said that the United States Ambassador, Thomas P. Melady, had met President Idi Amin and denied Washington reports that a $3 million U.S. loan had been frozen because of Amin's recent statement praising Hitler's slaughter of Jews in World War II.

State Department officials reiterated that the decision to delay the loan was linked to Amin's remarks on the Jews.

Continued from Page 59

Schools start with few Asian students

British Asian teachers who were exempted by the order or by special permission.

The poor turn up in most schools was also attributed to the panic of some Asians after the announcement.

"Although some Asians were not affected, they show no inclination to send their children back to school," one of the teachers in a city school said.

Another teacher who did not like to disclose his name expressed his hope that the situation will come to normal soon.

He thought some parents were only confused by their brothers and friends who are leaving and did not know what to do.

It was also learnt from reliable sources that even though at the moment some teachers have reported on duty and are teaching, they are planning to leave within the next two or three months.

However, a number of headmasters of senior secondary schools declined to make any comment and referred to the Ministry of Education for any information in regarding teachers' problems.

Amin honours Asian athletes in his Olympic team

News Compilation, September 16, 1972

President Amin awarded Ugandan citizenship to all 18 Asian members of Uganda's Olympic Games team. The Asian sportsmen had won their citizenship, he said, because of their magnificent performance at the Games. The President delivered his gesture to the sportsmen at a State luncheon honouring the Olympic contingent on its return from Munich.

Continued from Page 59

How Canada moved fast in Uganda

The following week on Aug. 16, while Amin was altering his expulsion orders almost daily, the cabinet in Ottawa gave its first consideration to the question. It was less than two weeks after Amin's first statement. The matter was brought to cabinet on the personal direction of the Prime Minister, bypassing most of the normal preliminary steps.

There was no public statement after that meeting but Canada was apparently in a position then to respond positively, the following day, when Britain suggested to countries such as Canada and Australia that it would be grateful for help in coping with the large number of Asians expected to leave Uganda.

Emergency admissions

On Thursday, Aug. 24, the Uganda situation was brought before the full cabinet for the second time. The decision was then taken "to ease the effect of this humanitarian problem" by sending a special immigration team to Uganda "to institute a program of admission on an emergency basis."

There has been no further policy discussion by the cabinet since then, nor is there expected to be when the cabinet meets in Ottawa today, despite the unexpectedly large numbers of Asians who are now applying in Kampala for admission to Canada. A progress report probably will be presented to the cabinet next week.

In the meantime, a task force of officials from external affairs and manpower and immigration is meeting daily in Ottawa to implement the nuts and bolts of the policy decision.

This has been a complex task at times. The special immigration team, for instance, was delayed in Kenya for several days while procedures for its entry into Uganda were arranged. Once it arrived there, it discovered that no facilities were available for the medical examination of prospective immigrants.

Last Saturday, eight tons of medical equipment were loaded aboard an Air Canada stretched DC-8 in Montreal, to be taken to Europe and then flown by other carriers to Uganda. A team of seven military medical technicians was also sent to Kampala to operate the equipment.

The method of transporting the Asians from Uganda to Canada remains unclear. It seems likely now that Canada will have to arrange special charters at least between London and Canada. It also is expected that Canada will offer the Asians the same kind of special travel assistance, when necessary, as various refugee groups have received in the past.

No one yet knows when the first Asians will reach Canada.

To complicate diplomatic matters, it was only a few weeks ago that Canada's new high commissioner, William Olivier, arrived in Kenya to take up duties in a territory that includes Uganda. Before Olivier could see Amin, protocol required that he should present his credentials first to President Jomo Kenyatta of Kenya, but Kenyatta was away from Nairobi on vacation and known to dislike doing official business on his holidays.

As a gesture to Canada, Kenyatta agreed to receive Olivier in the small community of Nakuru, and this enabled the Canadian high commissioner to see Amin last Monday.

Australia hesitates

Canada's response to the situation in Uganda has been markedly different from that of Australia. While recognizing that "there exists a humanitarian problem of great magnitude" in Uganda, the Australian government has continued to do "business as usual" where immigration is concerned. In 1971, Australia admitted 2,696 "non-Europeans" and 6,054 "persons of mixed descent" as immigrants, the majority of them from Asian countries.

Despite the mail reaching the Prime Minister's office, Canada's public response to the emergency has tended to confirm the government's decision, and has certainly been different from the one in Britain. But it is too early to reach a conclusive verdict on this, or to estimate the importance of public reaction as far as the election is concerned.

'Desperate' Asians in Uganda: 'Like a stampede' to get out

Reprinted with permission, ©Toronto Star syndicate, September 15, 1972

Asians in Uganda are "absolutely desperate" to get out, 90 people making plans to welcome them as refugees were told last night—by a Ugandan immigrant.

"If you can visualize a stampede, that's what it's like," Adrienne de Souza told a meeting at the International Institute on Davenport Rd. "They are happy to go anywhere and take what you can give them. They don't care any more."

Miss de Souza, principal of St. Dorothy's Separate School in Etobicoke, came to Canada from Uganda in 1964. she returned for a visit this summer and found East Asian Ugandans "constantly at gunpoint and in fear of their lives" after the Ugandan government ordered thousands of them into exile on the grounds they were "economic saboteurs" hindering the progress of black Ugandans.

The meeting at the institute, a United Appeal organization that helps integrate immigrants was baffled by only two unknowns. Where and when the Asians will arrive.

Ottawa sources say that the first planeload of 145 may arrive in Montreal around Sept. 24. This means the first group to arrive in Toronto will probably land two of three days later. It's estimated that 70 percent of the Ugandans speak English.

At last night's meeting Gary Van Dop, representing the federal manpower and immigration department, urged everybody "to generate public acceptance of these people."

"It's the decent thing to do, despite the unemployment problems we have ourselves," said Van Dop, a native of The Netherlands.

Van Dop pleaded that there should be no clashes among the various ethnic groups in the operation to receive the Ugandan Asians. It was announced yesterday that there would be no limit on the number admitted, though earlier estimates had been 5,000 to 6,000.

"Let's leave the petty battles until after everyone is settled," Van Dop said.

Van Dop said temporary housing is the primary need and it would be useful if a central housing registry could list offers from the public.

"While we prepare for this awe-inspiring operation, let's not create false expectations among our Ugandan Asians," said Van Dop. "There's no need to paint a glowing picture. It's cruel to pretend the employment picture is rosy."

S. B. Shah, president of the East African Asian Association, said his 200 members are trying to launch a self-help program for the refugees.

Continued on Page 62

We're willing to take in Asians—council rebels

Reprinted with permission, ©Leicester Mercury, September 16, 1972

FOUR of the rebel Labour councillors who oppose Leicester City Council's "keep Asians out" policy say they are willing to take refugees into their own homes.

Nine councillors signed a letter to the Leicester Mercury saying they "wish to dissociate ourselves publicly from statements which suggest that Leicester is opposed to the arrival in the city of any Ugandan refugees."

Of the eight councillors contacted by the Leicester Mercury, one said he was prepared to take a family of the refugees, one could accommodate one or two and two said they would be willing to take one.

Councillor Den Corrall said they would take in an Asian family, Councillors Henry Dunphy said he could make room for one or two of the refugees and Councillors Bob Briant and Jim Marshall said they could accommodate one.

Councillor the Rev. Alan Billings and Councillor John Hall said they were not prepared to say what they would do and Councillor Mrs. Dorothy Davis and Councillor Jack Langman said they had no room in their homes.The ninth, Councillor Paul Kind, could not be contacted.

Continued on Page 62

Advertisement

AN IMPORTANT ANNOUNCEMENT ON BEHALF OF THE COUNCIL OF THE CITY OF LEICESTER, ENGLAND

The City Council of Leicester, England, believe that many families in Uganda are considering moving to Leicester.

If YOU are thinking of doing so, it is very important you should know that

PRESENT CONDITIONS IN THE CITY ARE VERY DIFFERENT FROM THOSE MET BY EARLIER SETTLERS. They are:-

HOUSING - several thousands of families are already on the Council's waiting list

EDUCATION - hundreds of children are awaiting places in the schools

SOCIAL AND HEALTH SERVICES - already stretched to the limit

IN YOUR OWN INTERESTS AND THOSE OF YOUR FAMILY YOU SHOULD ACCEPT THE ADVICE OF THE UGANDA RESETTLEMENT BOARD AND NOT COME TO LEICESTER

Asians: the city that says please come here

Derek Humphry reports from Peterborough
Reprinted with permission, ©Times Newspapers Limited, London,
September 17, 1972

AS SOON as Britain declared last month that it would honour its promise to admit Ugandan Asians holding British passports, the city of Peterborough wrote to Whitehall undertaking to accommodate 50 families. It was the first such offer, and hardly typical of the country's reaction. What has happened since?

NEWCOMERS are welcome in Peterborough. For years the city has been advertising for people to come and settle there. It is officially designated as an expanding industrial area, and its target is to increase its population from its present 89,000 to 185,000 during the next 15 years.

Houses are standing empty, and many people on the housing list feel free to be choosy and turn down offers that do not suit them. Several schools are full but most have room for extra pupils. And while there are 1,350 people registered unemployed in the city, there are 332 vacancies.

So far as immigration is concerned, Peterborough has an unusual history. At the end of the war many prisoners-of-war and displaced persons in camps in the Fens stayed on to work, mainly in the local brickworks. Peterborough has an estimated 4,000 Italians, 1,000 Poles, Lithuanians, Latvians and Germans, 1,300 West Indians, and 1,500 Asians. Its record of racial harmony is good.

This was the background when Peterborough made its offer of 50 homes to Asians. There was a reaction that startled the leader of the Labour council, Mr Charles Swift. Within days, hundreds of letters poured in, directed at him and at the town clerk, abusing them for their action. The letters came from all over Britain as well as from local people.

Councillor Swift's response was to send a written explanation to every protester who gave an address. He also sent something more unexpected—a housing application form. "If they qualify, they can come and live here," he said last week.

The biggest misunderstanding was over the houses that the 50 Asian families would be getting. They will not be moving into the new houses built by Peterborough Development Corporation, which requires the husband to have a job locally, but into empty houses awaiting demolition under local improvement schemes. If the Asians get jobs in the city and wish to apply for rehousing they will go on the list.

The protests demonstrated, in Councillor Swift's view, that racialism springs from ignorance. "Funny that nobody complains when we allocate a house to an Italian or German who may have fought against them in the last war," he says.

Last week, Colin Jordan's British Movement, which was last active in Peterborough during the 1968 anti-immigration campaign by Enoch Powell, started distributing leaflets urging people to create "no-go" areas in estates to which it was thought Asians might go.

To counter this campaign, the council is sending this week to every ratepayer a special edition of its newspaper, Focus, with explanations of its policy.

The education committee chairman writes in the paper: "Many parents have the impression that our schools are becoming overburdened with coloured immigrants. And while obviously some schools have a greater percentage, the facts are that Peterborough has only 600 coloured schoolchildren out of a total pupil population of 14,300."

Councillor Swift, a 42-year-old engine-driver, says in a hard-hitting article: "It would have been easy for me to jump on the anti-Asian bandwagon and say 'No immigrants here.' That is an easy way to win votes and it could have made me the most popular person in Peterborough. It would also have made me the most blatant hypocrite there is.

"I was brought up to care about people and to fight for what I believe is right. These Ugandan Asians are being thrown out of their homes, out of their country. They are turning to us for help. How can we refuse them?"

The liberality of Councillor Swift was dramatically emphasised last week by the decision of another "growth" town - Kings Lynn, 35 miles away on the A47. It has 165 new houses standing empty; but when the town council's lone Liberal member moved that 10 houses should be offered to Asians, he got only a single Tory supporter from among the council's 12 Tory and 12 Labour members.

One clue to this decision is that Kings Lynn has 3 per cent unemployment, which doubles in the winter. Another clue probably is that the town has no coloured residents, apart from a few doctors and nurses.

Continued from Page 61

'Desperate' Asians in Uganda: 'Like a stampede' to get out

Already they are searching for jobs and have an offer of 50 from a security company in and out of uniform.

He said other ethnic associations had promised financial help. Among those at last night's meeting were Czechs and Hungarians, Filipinos and Tibetans; Moslems and Hindus.

Dr. Freda Hawkins, from the federal department of the secretary of state and a British immigrant herself, said the Asians will arrive in a smooth flow, with a planeload every few days.

After immigration processing in Montreal, they would be dispatched to centres across the country. The government would try to place them with friends and relatives, at the same time trying to spread them across the country and not just in Montreal, Toronto and Vancouver.

Adults will get printed and illustrated information and their children will get information on the schools and what Canadian kids do in the winter months.

"There are a lot of children coming in," Dr. Hawkins said.

The secretary of state's department will also provide information leaflets for all voluntary and governmental groups on the sort of life the Asians have been used to in Uganda.

Calling for help from voluntary organizations and ethnic associations, Dr. Hawkins said the wives of the newcomers mustn't be left out and should be drawn in to community activities.

Russ Colombo, director of Ontario's citizenship branch, promised fast processing of the educational documents of the newcomers and outlined various provincial programs.

W. A. Boyce of Metro's social services department outlined what welfare payments would be available if needed and said cards should be available for drugs and dental treatment plus medical hospital coverage.

Continued from Page 61

We're willing to take in Asians—council rebels

Prosperous city

Their letter said: "We believe that a city as prosperous as Leicester, with relatively high employment, can and should along with Britain's other cities accept at least its fair share of refugees. We do not believe that our local authority services are so inefficient as to be unable to cope with the number of new-comers who are likely to succeed in finding permanent homes here bearing mind that if the city's housing is indeed full up then that fact alone will limit their numbers.

"We repudiate strongly the alarmist reports of those who should know better that the city is at risk and unable to cope with its problems. This image is false and causes needless alarm and even panic.

"We also deplore the picture that is being painted of Leicester" as a heartless even racist community, indifferent to the fate of the Ugandan refugees and hysterically determined to keep them from our door at all costs. Leicester's record of absorbing peacefully tens of thousands of Commonwealth immigrants is proof enough of the city's high standards of tolerance, efficiency and above all common sense.

Deputy Labour group leader Alderman Sidney Bridges said that the policy had been declared by the City Council in their resolution of a fortnight ago and it is pointless discussing the dissatisfaction of a minority. But the question of incoming Asians from Uganda might be discussed at a group meeting.

The Prime Minister, in a letter to Mr. John Farr, MP for the Harborough division, has said he realises the particular problems facing Leicester with the arrival of Asians from Uganda.

Two weeks ago Mr. Farr wrote to Mr. Heath suggesting that Ugandan Asians should be returned to the Asian country to which they naturally belong: with the aid of handsome financial incentives.

In Mr. Heath's reply he states "I do appreciate the problems caused by the arrival of Asians from Uganda in this country and the particular difficulties facing cities such as Leicester.

"It would, I think, be self-defeating to refuse to receive any of these immigrants whatever. This is not only a question of our existing obligations and commitments, although these are important, but there is also the practical consideration that we cannot obtain the help of other countries and international organisations unless we are prepared to admit some ourselves."

Estimates of the number and type of Ugandan Asians who plan to come to Leicester, which the Indian Social and Cultural Society has made from surveys undertaken in Leicester and Kampala, are not to be released for publication, the society committee has decided.

Page 62

Ugandan Asian Expulsion: 90 Days and Beyond through the Eyes of the International Press

Airlift gets under way tonight

from JOHN de St. JORRE: Kampala, 16 September
Reprinted with permission, ©The Observer, London, September 17, 1972

THE long-delayed airlift of British Asians to the United Kingdom will begin tomorrow night, East African aviation officials confirmed here today.

The first aircraft, a Boeing 707 of Donaldson Airways, under charter to East African Airways, will leave here tomorrow night and arrive at Stansted Airport, Essex, in the early hours of Monday morning with 180 Asian immigrants on board. Tickets, costing £100 each, were quickly sold out today.

The airlift consortium—East African Airways, BOAC, and British Caledonian—will initially operate 16 flights a week. At this rate, 20,000 Asians will be lifted to Britain before General Amin's deadline expires on 7 November. This should take care of all the British Asians still here, but allows no margin for the Stateless, of whom there may be as many as 15,000.

But use will also be made of spare seats on scheduled airlines and an earlier idea of diverting partially empty London-bound planes from Nairobi may be implemented.

Tomorrow, 100 Indian passport-holders will also be leaving Kampala, on a specially guarded train, for the Kenyan port of Mombasa, from where they will go by sea to India. A second contingent, 1,000-strong, will leave a week later by the same route.

The first charter flight—paid for by the Canadian Government—is also due to leave next week carrying 145 people.

The dispute between the British and Ugandan Governments over the airlift to the United Kingdom degenerated this week into a dangerous game of bluff, imposing a new strain on the tattered nerves of the Asian hostages.

Looked at from here, it seems that both sides were to blame. President Amin made the first move with his announcement that all non-citizen Asians still in Uganda after the deadline expires would be rounded up and put into camps. People are already calling them 'concentration camps.'

The British, in their turn, demanded that the Ugandans should remit the airlift fares in a hard, convertible currency and not in Ugandan shillings. The Ugandan Government promised that this would be done, but the British insisted on a guarantee, which they couldn't get. It is not known yet how the dispute has been resolved. The total cost of the operation is estimated at £3 million.

Britain's method of resisting Amin's blackmail was to go slow on the processing of the Asians' papers and sit tight on the financial side of the airlift. These tactics may have been politically correct, but from a humanitarian viewpoint they bore the seeds of disaster. Although President Amin often changes his mind, he has been implacable on the deadline for the Asians' departure. He emphasised it again this week when he met Mr Robert Gardner, the United Nations Secretary-General's special emissary.

The other point that he has made 'absolutely clear'—a favourite phrase in the Ugandan Government's litany—is that he now regards all the Asians, other than confirmed citizens and exempted professional men, to be Britain's responsibility. This means the 15,000 Stateless people will have to be out by the deadline or take their chance in the camps.

Britain, it seems, is not yet ready to face up to this harsh fact of life, hoping no doubt, that other countries and the United Nations will step in to share the burden. But, inevitably, this will be a slow process and time is running out rapidly.

Criticism of Britain's go-slow has come not only from the Ugandan Government. One of the Asian community leaders' major objections is that a large number of British passport holders, especially the older people, want to settle in India. The number in this category is put very high—at between 10,000 and 15,000.

The Indian Government will not give them entry visas unless their passports have first been validated for entry into Britain. The Asian argument—and it seems a reasonable one—is that if the British speeded up their processing, a lot more people could make arrangements now to go to India by train and ship.

There is also a psychological need which affects all the Asians here, even those who know for certain that they will be leaving soon. They are deeply grateful for Britain's decision to accept them; many of them understand Britain's difficulties, both at home and with Amin; and most praise the work of the High Commission. But what they would really like to hear is a little fighting talk of the kind Sir Alec Douglas-Home hands out to General Amin when white Britons are threatened.

At the moment, all they see are reports of welcoming placards at Heathrow Airport, reading 'Asians Out, Enoch In,' and half-page advertisements in the local paper telling them that Leicester, for one, doesn't want them.

The Asians are feeling their extreme vulnerability. Even those who are now being formally asked by the Ugandan Government to stay want to get out to almost anywhere by any means. The fear and anxiety about being left 'sitting on the fire,' as General Amin graphically described their dilemma this week, may diminish when the airlift gets moving, but it is unlikely to disappear until the last man, woman and child has gone.

Meanwhile relations between Britain and Uganda maintain a curious and erratic equilibrium. Donald Stewart, the imprisoned British businessman, is deported, but the Ugandan Government is told by its own courts to pay his costs. The British military team is kicked out, but Amin radios a goodwill message as they fly away.

But despite the terrifying talk of concentration camps and subversive elements, the shadow of Munich—Hitler's or Black September's—still has no place under Uganda's warm and sunny skies.

Secret plan to disperse Asians

News Compilation, September 17, 1972

Ugandan Asians who have nowhere to stay when they arrive in Britain this week will be discouraged from going to areas named in a secret "red list" drawn up by the Uganda Resettlement Board.

The Asians may be refused public funds unless they are prepared to go to a town on an alternative "green list" where their settlement is encouraged.

The names of the towns on the lists are being kept secret to avoid unwelcome publicity.

Carr: Act as neighbours to Asians

News Compilation, September 17, 1972

People in Britain were urged yesterday by Mr Robert Carr, the Home Secretary, to receive the banished Uganda Asians with "dignity and humanity". "It is your hearts, your minds, your good will, a little of your spare time I am asking for. In other words, I ask you to be neighbours to them," he said.

Uganda claims 'invasion by Tanzania'

News Compilation, September 18, 1972

Uganda claimed that invading Tanzanian troops had captured three towns and advanced to within 100 miles of Kampala. Tanzania claimed the fighting was between President Amin's troops and dissidents of a Uganda "People's Army".

A Uganda Government announcement said that the British had a plan to invade Uganda and that the incursion might be the beginning of this plan. The announcement claimed that there were many British spies in the country.

Canada Freezes Aid to Uganda

News Compilation, September 18, 1972

Canada has frozen its economic aid to Uganda in view of the mounting political crisis there, sources in the Government revealed. Uganda has not been officially informed because of the fear of possible reprisals against Canadians in Uganda.

Ugandan Asian Expulsion: 90 Days and Beyond through the Eyes of the International Press

How Mr Patel and Mr Jani came to town

by Dilip Hiro
Reprinted with permission, ©The Observer, London, September 17, 1972

SO FAR the Uganda Asians arriving in Britain, most of them Gujaratis, are living up to their reputation for initiative and self-help.

Of the 150 families who have come in since the beginning of the month, all but 15 had a destination to go to. Even those who have had to rely initially on voluntary or Government help have been anxious to stand on their own feet.

The case of two families—the Patels and the Janis—bear this out.

They were about the first to be helped by the voluntary Co-operation Committee for the Welfare of Evacuees from Uganda and the Government's Uganda Resettlement Board. Within a fortnight, Mr Patel has managed to find both work and a place to live in, while Mr Jani is about to secure a job.

Prafulbhai Patel is a small, slim man, 32 years old, with short hair and neat sideburns. Some months ago he sold his lorry and planned to take his money out of Uganda. But, in the end, he wasn't even permitted to take out the £50 in British travellers' cheques that were to be allowed to each departing non-citizen Asian family.

He and his family arrived penniless at Heathrow Airport on the evening of 2 September, a Saturday. He was expecting to be met by a relative living in Golders Green. The relative didn't turn up. Fortunately, a volunteer, from the Co-ordination Committee for the Welfare of Evacuees from Uganda, was on hand. He took Mr Patel, his wife and their two young daughters (aged three and one) to the office of the UK Immigrants' Advisory Service at the airport. Mr John Ennals, a member of the Co-ordination Committee, happened to be there. He took the Patels to his home in Buckinghamshire.

This is the diary of Mr Patel's stay in this country:—

Day One (Sunday): Phoned friends in London, none of them could be traced. Went to find Mr Raja, a friend living in Southall, but he was out.

Day Two (Monday): John Ennals took me to the social security office and employment exchange in Slough. He also contacted the Slough Community Relations Council. As a result, I moved to the house of Mr J. P. O. Benham, a master at Eton College. He allotted me two bedrooms.

Day Three (Tuesday): Mr Benham took me to Mr Raja's place, but again he was out.

Day Four (Wednesday): A reporter of a local weekly paper came to interview my host and myself. Mr Benham got us some Indian groceries, and we had our first Indian (vegetarian) meal since we left Uganda.

Day Five (Thursday): Cashed social security pay-slip at a local post office: got £5.50. Visited the East African Airways office to collect unaccompanied luggage; but it had not arrived. Met Mr Raja in Southall. He is planning to move to Leicester. He offered to accommodate me there and I decided to leave for Leicester on the Saturday.

Day Six (Friday): One Kanubhai Patel from Slough visited me. Originally from Uganda, he works as a clerk in the accounts department of a firm in Slough. He traced me from the news item in the local paper. He advised me *not* to go to Leicester, but to find a job in Slough.

Day Seven (Saturday): Rested.

Day Eight (Sunday): Visited Kanubhai at home. He gave me a map of Slough, and told me how to set about finding a job.

Day Nine (Monday): Again asked about my luggage, but was told it would be another two or three weeks. A nuisance, because all our pots and pans are there.

Day Ten (Tuesday): Search for a home continued. The fact that I have two small children and my wife is pregnant proved to be an extra handicap.

Day Eleven (Wednesday): Rain, Still searched for a home.

Day Twelve (Thursday): Success! Got a bed-sitting room in a house, owned by a fellow Patel, at £4 a week. Went to the employment exchange office, got £10.50. Visited three firms in the Trading Estate area. At the first, a confectionery firm, they said they wanted someone with "experience." At the second, a plastics concern, they said. "No vacancy." At the third—tube manufacturers—they asked me to fill in an application form and said they would let me know.

Day Thirteen (Friday): Visited more firms for a job. Success at last. Got a job as a punch-press operator at £19 a week. Moved to my bed-sitter.

When the Patel family arrived on 2 September, the Government's Uganda Resettlement Board was not in full operation. The Board appointed a man at Heathrow on 6 September, the day Jagdish Chandra Jani and his family arrived from Uganda.

Mr Jani is 36. He has slightly graying hair and an elegantly trimmed moustache. He wears dark glasses. He was an English teacher in Uganda and also owned a photographic studio which he sold last July. He got out £50 in British travellers' cheques.

On arrival at Heathrow, the Janis were led to the office of the UK Immigrants' Advisory Service by a volunteer of the Co-ordination Committee. The Resettlement Board's representative arrived after a few hours. While waiting, Mr Jani gave an interview to a news agency.

Finally, the Janis were taken to the Kensington Students' Centre, which is housed in the old Kensington Palace barracks.

Here is Mr Jani's diary:—

Day One (Thursday): On reading my story in a national paper, a relative in Nottingham sent a message through a cousin in Hounslow, telling me to go to Nottingham. This cousin tracked me down at the Student Centre the same evening. I decided against Nottingham, mainly because rail fares for the whole family—wife and four daughters—would have used up most of my money. We went to the cousin's place instead.

Day Two (Friday): Telephoned a photographic firm in Hemel Hempstead for a job. They said that I should try the following week. At the Student Centre, a warden, an ex-Army man who had spent some years in Kenya, brought us food from an Indian restaurant. Two representatives for the Resettlement Board interviewed us.

Day Three (Saturday): It had turned cold. Luckily, two old ladies from a women's organisation called and returned, within an hour, with warm clothes for us all. Bless them! The man from the Resettlement Board came with toys an a tricycle for the children. Indian groceries were brought in by a grocer from Hounslow.

Day Four (Sunday): Three more Asian families arrived at the centre. They were all small shopkeepers in Uganda.

Day Five (Monday): A representative of the social security department set up a temporary office at the centre. I collected £5.20 at a local post office.

Day Six (Tuesday): An official of the employment exchange arrived at the centre and interviewed those seeking jobs. I mentioned the firm in Hemel Hempstead. By late afternoon, they had an interview arranged for me the next day.

Day Seven (Wednesday): Had an interview with the firm's personnel manager. Told him of my experience of running a photographic studio. He was sympathetic and said he would give me a decision by Friday.

Day Eight (Thursday): Had a meeting of all the 10 Asian families, now accommodated at the Student Centre, to set down a code of conduct.

Day Nine (Friday): Got a message from the photographic firm that they will now let me have their decision on Monday. Now I must look for accommodation of my own.

Watergate Indictments

News Compilation, September 16, 1972

Washington, D.C.—In the midst of the presidential election, a federal grand jury indicted seven persons, including two former White House aides, on charges of conspiring to break into the Democratic national headquarters in Washington.

The indictment alleged burglary and possession of eavesdropping devices. All pleaded not guilty.

Israel retaliates

In retaliation for the slaying of 11 Israeli Olympic athletes in Munich last week, about 80 Israeli planes carried out air strikes against guerrilla bases in Syria and Lebanon. Reports indicate about 66 persons were killed, mostly civilians.

Asians face persuasion over areas

By MARTIN ADENEY
Reprinted with permission, ©The Guardian, London, September 18, 1972

The Uganda Resettlement Board has named areas where expelled Uganda Asians will be discouraged from settling. They include half of 32 boroughs of Greater London, six Midland centres with Birmingham, Leicestershire, Wolverhampton, and three West Riding towns.

In its guidance for counsellors the board calls on them to rely on persuasion and "a full presentation of those facts which make it undesirable that there should be a substantial further influx" to discourage Asians from going to these places.

But it says people proposing to go to an address listed on one of the areas who are not met by friends and have no money will not normally be provided with financial assistance to do so.

Where a specific address is given, but the other two conditions apply, the family will be housed in the board's temporary accommodation "while confirmation is sought from the town concerned that accommodation is in fact available."

Counsellors are also advised about families who have made arrangements for accommodation beforehand and have enough money to get to it. "Provided you are satisfied that the families are able to look after themselves, there will be not much more that you can do. Nevertheless you should again stress the problems that they will have to contend with if they persist in their intention to go there," the board advises.

The full list of places on the board's discouragement list is:

London: Brent, Camden, Ealing, Greenwich, Hackney, Haringey, Hammersmith, Islington, Kensington, Lambeth, Lewisham, Newham, Southwark, Tower Hamlets, Wandsworth, Westminster.

The Midlands: Birmingham, Smethwick, Leicester, Walsall, West Bromwich, Wolverhampton.

West Riding of Yorkshire: Bradford, Halifax, Huddersfield.

The Board explains its reasoning like this. "The Board have of course no power of direction. They must rely on persuasion and on a full presentation of those facts which make it undesirable that there should be a substantial further influx into these listed areas.

"The situation is that these areas are already overpopulated, and those who have settled there are now suffering from a severe shortage of housing. Jobs are likely to be as difficult to find as satisfactory accommodation.

"Further the social and medical services in these places are under great strain; and the present pressure on education facilities is such that there just would not be places in schools for the children of additional families. It is, therefore, in the interests of the newcomers, as well as those of existing Asian communities in this country, that future families arriving from Uganda should not attempt to go to such areas, but should plan to settle themselves elsewhere."

The Board said yesterday that local authorities in these areas had made it plain that they could not take any more Asians. But in some boroughs the news came as a surprise to local councillors.

Miss Hannah Stanton, who is Administrator of the Coordinating Committee for the Welfare of Evacuees from Uganda, said last night that she was concerned that people who arrived to find relatives had not turned up at the airport would be able to telephone them.

Talks could stop mass influx

by COLIN LEGUM, our Commonwealth Correspondent
Reprinted with permission, ©The Observer, London, September 17, 1972

THE success of the secret talks now going on in New Delhi with the Indian Government has encouraged the British Government to feel more hopeful about the chances of getting the Asians out of Uganda before the deadline.

If successfully completed, the talks could produce tow other major results. first, they could avoid a mass influx of Asians into Britain over a period of a few weeks. Secondly, they could make it easier to deal with the serious new problem which arose last week with General Amin's announcement that he regarded the so-called 'stateless' Asians as being Britain's responsibility.

The objective of the talks is to arrange with India for the mass of Ugandan Asians to be sent to Bombay. It will then be possible to determine the precise status of the Asians without harassment from Ugandan authorities or the pressures of a looming deadline.

The Indian Government has already agreed, in principle, to take the Ugandan Asians against a specific assurance that the British Government will accept ultimate responsibility for its British citizens.

The real problem that still remains to be dealt with in negotiations touches not on those who can clearly establish their right to hold British passports, but on the large category of Asians whose status is in doubt. This group—which may number about 15,000—comprises Asians who have tried over the years to have their claims to Ugandan citizenship established but have failed.

While Britain's legal position is clear that these so called stateless Asians are not her responsibility, she faces the moral dilemma that if they are not removed from Uganda they could find their way into Amin's concentration camps. Britain could then find herself attached internationally for cruel-heartedness in not saving them from Amin's clutches.

Ready for first special flight

By our own Reporter
Reprinted with permission, ©The Guardian, London, September 18, 1972

A formidable reception party, ranging from Sir Charles Cunningham, the chairman of the Resettlement Board, to old WRVS troupers with their tea and wads, will be standing by at Stansted Airport this morning to meet the first special flight in the airlift of Asians from Uganda.

The first test of the elaborate contingency plans that have been laid will find about 30 voluntary workers, including speakers of Gujarati, on hand at the Channel Airways building where the Asians will be processed.

A spokesman for the Resettlement Board made it clear last night that those Asians who are met by relations or friends will be able to go off with them immediately, wherever their destination.

But for people who are not met by acquaintances and have no firm plans, supplementary benefit assistance will not be available for travel to a list of places that includes Bradford, Birmingham, Leicester, Wolverhampton, and the London boroughs of Brent, Ealing, and Wandsworth.

No "deliberate block" was being put in the Asians' way other than discouraging them from going to these areas, which had been identified as those expected to find most difficulty in coping, said the spokesman. The board had told a number of local authorities such as Leicester quite openly that it would do everything it could to discourage people from going there.

The plan is that when the Asians arrive at Stansted, they will go through Customs and immigration in the normal way, and will then have to fill in a form—administered probably by voluntary workers drawn from local citizens' advice bureaux—to say whether or not they are being met by relatives and have homes and jobs to go to.

Welfare assistance, with hot drinks and clothing, if needed, will be available from the WRVS and the Red Cross, and St. John's Ambulancemen will be on hand.

After the sifting process, those with waiting relations will join them. Those whose plans are uncertain will have a coach waiting to take them to the old RAF camp at Stadishall, where the major task will begin of providing information about homes and jobs and matching them up with new arrivals' preferences, qualifications, and so on.

Among the voluntary agencies assisting, under the umbrella of the coordinating committee for the welfare of evacuees, will be people from Harlow Council of Social Service, members of the Society of Friends, community service volunteers, the International Voluntary Service, and United Nations representatives.

Asian refugees reach first base

By MARTIN ADENEY and MICHAEL LAKE
Reprinted with permission, ©The Guardian, London, September 19, 1972

IN THE chilly drizzle at Stansted the Asians managed to retain even more composure than the officials or the squads of milling journalists and cameramen there to meet them They queued patiently. No one burst into tears except the youngest children. They stoically approved of English weather and accepted the food offered—tea, cheese and apricot jam sandwiches, and fruit cake—rejecting only the tinned salmon.

Common to almost all the accounts of their departure from Kampala were stories of searches, if not at gunpoint, with guns being threatened, during the 13 miles to Entebbe Airport.

Some said there were as many as 11 separate checks. Almost all lost money and valuables. One retired civil servant said a £250 watch had been taken from him. Others lost cameras, bangles, and even rings from their fingers.

Mr S. M. Patel, a schoolmaster for 20 years and until recently headmaster at Busia, said £60 in Ugandan money and gold and valuables worth 10 times that had been taken. But his wife is already in Britain and he has managed to transfer £1,000 to a British bank.

The Ugandan authorities had insisted that he stay and teach. But he says he was threatened by the military. There is trouble and it is dreadful even for Europeans and British Asians. All are concerned for their lives and not money."

Others fearing reprisals were three brothers, members of one of the larger families at Stansted, who ran a haulage business. They would not give their names believing relatives still in Uganda would suffer.

The brothers, their wives, six children and an old mother clutching the children's hand like an aged Queen Victoria, said they had a distant friend in England but no other connection. But with an air of physical confidence the eldest brother added: "We are willing to do any work—petrol stations, garages, greasing, repairing, farming, anything."

By comparison the future seems to beckon Mr Jayantilae Pragji Umrania, a single civil engineer, aged 23. Last night he was already joking with other young Asians as he tried on a dressing-gown over his suit from the collection of second-hand clothes from the WRVS.

He has one sister in North London, but she was not at the airport to meet him. He preferred to go to Stradishall and take the advice of the resettlement board rather than go to see if his sister had any room.

Life is also likely to be little less difficult for Mrs Paraful Patel, a middle-aged widow with six children. In the two years since the death of her husband, she has run through what money he had left. Her eldest daughter, Bakasha, gave up a secretarial course to work as a bank clerk to keep the family.

Mrs Patel, her youngest daughter only four, arrived yesterday with just one contact—a sister who works as a secretary for British Rail who has a house in Tooting. Last night Mrs Patel was in the emergency accommodation at Stradishall, awaiting word from the sister.

Among those with nowhere to go was Mr Mansukhlal Kara, aged 33, his wife and child. "I have a friend at Golders Green and I sent him a telegram but he has not replied. We are tired but we will keep going. We can't afford to break down. All I want to do is to find a job somewhere. If work hard I will make it."

Mr Kara moved to Uganda from India 18 years ago. He had no trade but is now a skilled goldsmith and expects little difficulty in finding work.

Nor does Mr Manji Patel, a plumber, who arrived with his wife and three children to move in with relations in Blackburn. Mrs Patel had her bangles and rings taken by Ugandan soldiers. How did she feel now? "I am quite happy. I was not happy in the circumstances in Uganda. Everyone there is afraid of the army. We sold everything we had, but then the Government told us we could only bring £50 for a family of five. That is all we have."

One family which will not be occupying space in the city of Leicester for long is that of Mr R. J. Patani. He and his two brothers were at the airport to meet a fourth brother and his wife. Mr Patani said that the whole family would return to Leicester for a few days and then go on to Blackburn. Leicester is too crowded, he said. He prefers a smaller town and is prepared to sell his house to find one.

Many of those who arrived at Stansted praised the service they received on the flight from Entebbe and one man, acting as a kind of unofficial spokesman, said: "From the welcome we have received we think this place is going to be better."

Arriving in the chilly drizzle at Stansted Airport, the first of thousands expected over the next few weeks.
Reproduced with permission: Top photo ©Associated Press/World Wide Photos, bottom photo ©Times Newspapers Limited

Tea in England for Asian Exiles

By BRIAN PARK
Reprinted with permission, ©Daily Mail, London, September 19, 1972

Stansted Airport, England: Expelled Asians are given refreshments in the reception lounge following their arrival at the airport.
Reproduced with permission ©United Press International/Corbis-Bettmann

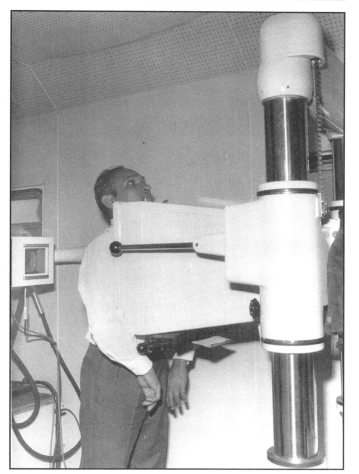

Unidentified Asian undergoes X-ray examination upon arrival.
Reproduced with permission ©Warhurst/Times Newspapers Limited

THE first of the exiled Asians arrived in Britain yesterday and divided 50-50 over their final destinations.

After a typically British welcome of tea and formalities at Stansted Airport in Essex, half went off to stay with relatives or friends, in spite of the Government's advice to keep clear of areas already full of immigrants.

The rest went off to the resettlement centre at Stradishall, in Suffolk, where Civil Servants will work out their future in less crowded areas.

In all, 189 arrived on the first Boeing 707 from Kampala. Another flight was arranged for yesterday, but it was suddenly cancelled without explanation.

Sir Charles Cunningham, chairman of the Uganda Resettlement Board, who was at the airport, said he was 'fairly satisfied' with how the first load had been dispersed.

Searched

'We have learned a lot of useful lessons today. We have tried our best to dissuade some of them from going to "red areas" but since they were determined and satisfied us that they had satisfactory accommodation we let them go.'

For the taxpayer, the first influx cost precisely £20 in Social Security grants helping 12 families on train journeys to their new homes.

The Asians came telling how they had been searched at gun point by Ugandan troops and all their money and jewellery taken.

And they asked for understanding and patience while they sort themselves out in Britain.

Mrs Terlochan Chana, 37, said: 'We were searched at gun point by troops on the way to Entebbe Airport. They took the rings off our fingers, all our bangles and necklaces—everything they could get their hands on. It was appalling.'

And Usher Mehta said: 'We are lucky to be alive. We can never ever repay Britain for this chance to go on living.'

'We hope people will be understanding if we crowd together at first, but soon we will stand on our own feet again. Just give us a little more of the kindness and understanding we have had today.'

Those who went to the old RAF base at Stadishall were given a meal of curries, chapatis, melon, chicken and vegetables, prepared by the WRVS and other voluntary workers.

Their quarters are furnished and heated and in communal rooms they can share television and radio.

Some families were a bit baffled by the coal fires. One man asked a voluntary worker politely if he could put the fire in his bedroom. 'As it is there I will be tonight and it is very cold.'

In London, building foreman Mr Karsah Patel, 43, went to stay at a friend's house in All Soul's Avenue, Brondesbury Park, N.W., with his 16-year-old son Kantilal.

'I'm sharing a bedroom here with my son until I move to Cardiff, where my brother lives,' he said. 'I don't know how I'm going to get some money together, but I am prepared to do anything in the building trade.'

Carpenter Mr Dhanji Patel, 30, who owns the house, said: 'I have sub-let two bedrooms upstairs to some friends, and it was they who met Mr Patel and his son at Stansted today. I'm quite prepared to have them living here with me until they can find somewhere to go.'

He added: 'There will be nine of us altogether here for about two weeks, but it shouldn't be too crowded. It's a pretty big house.'

1st Airlift From Uganda Gets British Welcome

By Bernard D. Nossiter
Washington Post Foreign Service
Reprinted with permission, ©Washington Post, September 19, 1972

STANSTED, England—A small brown-skinned boy in an oversized sweater waved his arm in greeting, then burst into tears as the first plane load of Asian refugees from Uganda arrived here in a chill drizzle this morning.

Some 193, mostly Indians and a scattering of Pakistanis—men, women and children—landed in a Boeing 707 to take up a new and strange life.

If the weather was cold, their reception was warm. Matronly British ladies in the prim blue and green uniforms of volunteer agencies distributed cookies, tea and sandwiches to mothers in saris, and gently led bewildered families through a maze of paperwork. Quakermen stopped tears with hard candies. Welfare officials distributed cash to the completely destitute, up to $45 for a family of six. Scores of photographers and newsmen swarmed over the dazed newcomers.

Gen. Idi Amin of Uganda has ordered the expulsion by Nov. 7 of more than 50,000 Asians—mostly of Indian and Pakistani descent—in his country who retained their British passports.

As many as 16 charter jet flights will be arriving here weekly to meet Amin's deadline. Perhaps 30,000 expelled Asians will settle in Britain and the rest will scatter from Canada to India, wherever they are taken in.

A small trickle of Ugandan Asians had already arrived before today's first full flight of refugees landed at Stansted, an airport 40 miles north of London. Like their predecessors, those who came today had been stripped of everything valuable that Ugandan soldiers could find.

The refugees were allowed to take with them 1,000 Ugandan shillings. But the Ugandan shilling is inconvertible—it cannot be exchanged for British pounds.

Many of the newcomers told of Ugandan soldiers yesterday seizing their gold bangles, rings, watches and cameras at road blocks on the road to the airport outside Kampala.

Twelve-year-old Inderajee Chana, pretty and pigtailed, said in a hushed voice that the soldiers "were rough: they were holding big guns."

Nibbling cookies and sipping tea, Inderajee said the soldiers had taken earrings from her mother, bracelets from her grandmother and rings from her 14-year-old sister.

Wind Up Affairs

She will be "a little frightened" of starting school in a new country, she said, but expects everything will be much better when her father, an architect, winds up his affairs in Kampala—and joins them in England.

Dark-haired Barveen Mughal, 23, wearing the red shalwar trousers of her native Karachi, was indignant over the 14 gold bangles she and her sister lost to the soldiers. She can take shorthand and type and hopes to land a job as a stenographer. Miss Mughal and her family will move into their brother's six-room house in Birmingham.

Stansted Airport: Making their way to the reception lounge. Reproduced with permission ©Associated Press/World Wide Photos

Like others of their countrymen who left the subcontinent for Africa and Southeast Asia, many of today's arrivals are resourceful and hardworking and have every intention of making their own way.

Meghji Patel, 35, in a dark business suit and glasses, spoke intently of finding work as an accountant. He had served an Italian firm in Kampala for seven years, but said he was "glad to get out." He and his wife hurriedly sold all their possessions at distress prices and he still has a sizable bank account in Uganda.

But he has few hopes of withdrawing his money and expects to start from scratch.

Sureschandra Trivedi, 40, a salesclerk who had lived in Kampala for 33 years, sat alone in a corner with his wife, four children from 18 to 9, and two gray parrots, all they had been able to take out.

He has no friends or relatives in England and, with about half of today's arrivals, will be put up temporarily in a former Royal Air Force barracks in Suffolk.

'I Want to Work'

Despite this bleak prospect, Trivedi, in shirt sleeves, stubble on his chin, insisted:

"It is nothing. Why should I worry, if I want to work. I am not afraid to do anything. Yes, I can work with my hands, too."

Representatives of 45 volunteer organizations as well as the government's newly created Uganda Resettlement Board were on hand to smooth the way for these first airlift arrivals.

From here on out, however, their reception may not be pleasant.

Several English Midland cities and London boroughs with immigrant populations have loudly complained that more newcomers would strain their schools, housing and jobs.

After the Sunday Times broke the story, the Resettlement Board acknowledged that it has marked Birmingham, Leicester and some other communities for special treatment. Officials are urging the refugees against settling in these places and will give no travel funds to those heading there.

About 3,000 Britons have offered room in their home to the Ugandan Asians. But many people here openly mouth a racist hostility toward them.

Just today, the Monday Club, a grouping of right-wing Conservative Party members of Parliament, issued a pamphlet on economic policy that said:

"The first priority for a responsible British government should be to launch a satisfactory repatriation program for the immigrants from incompatible races and cultures who should never have come here in the first place, have become a burden on our social services and who in the end will be the unwitting agents of social disruption."

However popular this view may be, the British establishment has closed ranks to provide a haven for the refugees. That, in the end, may prove to be decisive.

Half airlift Asians are homeless

By A. J. McILROY
Reprinted with permission, ©Telegraph Group Limited, London, September 19, 1972

Stansted Airport, England: Tired, weary and broke.   Reproduced with permission ©Associated Press/World Wide Photos

MORE than half of the 193 Asians who arrived at Stansted, Essex, yesterday at the start of the airlift from Uganda, had no friends or relatives to meet them and no homes to go to in Britain.

The 101 with nowhere else to go were taken to the reception centre established at the former RAF station at Stradishall, 25 miles from Stansted.

Two flights bringing about 400 more Asians expelled from Uganda are due at Stansted today. With more than 21,000 adults and children due to arrive in the airlift, the Uganda Resettlement Board is anxious in case too many have nowhere to go.

Travel aid

Although many of the Asians told of having money and valuables taken from them before leaving Uganda, social security officers at Stansted said they were surprised how few asked for money to help them to their destinations.

Twelve families were given travel aid. The social security officers paid out a total of about £25.

But this applied only to travel arrangements, the officials added. When the Asians reached their new homes they would be able to claim social security benefits in the normal way no matter where they settle.

The sums paid would correspond to amounts paid to any other British citizens in similar circumstances. If they had no income at all accommodation, food and clothing would be paid for.

After greeting the arrivals at Standsted Sir Charles Cunningham, chairman of the Uganda Resettlement Board, said it was powerless to stop the Asians from settling in overcrowded towns and cities anywhere in Britain.

Many of the Asians left Stansted yesterday for destinations in, or close to, areas listed by the board as places where they should be discouraged from settling.

Red areas

Painted red on a map the board has drawn up but is declining to publish in detail, these areas include half of the 32 boroughs of Greater London, six Midland towns, as well as Birmingham, Leicester and Wolverhampton, and three towns in the West Riding.

Sir Charles said these Asians had been met by relatives and friends or had satisfied the board's officers they had suitable accommodations. He could not conceal a note of anxiety when he read out the list of destinations—parts of London, including Tooting, Wembley, Blackburn, Leeds, Birmingham, Cardiff and Edinburgh.

All Ugandan Asians arriving at Stansted, even those with means to travel on independently, would be taken to Stradishall if they said they intended to settle in areas not recommended by the board. Efforts would be made at Stradishall to change their minds, Sir Charles added.

Uganda bombs Tanzanian town

News Compilation, September 19, 1972

A military spokesman confirmed that Ugandan aircraft had bombed the north-west Tanzanian town of Bukoba, on Lake Victoria, 20 miles south of the frontier. In response, the Tanzanian radio said about 1,000 Tanzanian troops are advancing towards the north-western frontier to repel any attack from Uganda.

Scores of Europeans were picked up by police and military officials. The number of British citizens held was believed to be as least 80 and the number of journalists detained rose to 14.

The British government denied Amin's allegation there was a British plan to invade Uganda and warned Uganda the "the whole of the Ugandan Government is entirely responsible for the safety of British subjects in Uganda."

'No, no, it's not the monsoon season, just an ordinary day.'

Reproduced with permission ©Daily Mail

Ugandan Asian Expulsion: 90 Days and Beyond through the Eyes of the International Press

UGANDAN ASIANS SAY THEY WANT TO SETTLE IN CITIES

By BRIAN SILK and HUGH DAVIES
Reprinted with permission, ©Telegraph Group Limited, London,
September 19, 1972

THE first Uganda Asians to be airlifted to Britain arrived in drizzling rain at Stansted Airport, Essex, yesterday. The 193 refugees, and two pet parrots, landed to find Sir Charles Cunningham, chairman of the Uganda Resettlement Board, waiting on the tarmac.

He shook hands with several passengers as they left the Boeing 707 which carried them from Entebbe, and told them: "I hope you will be very happy here.

"We'll do our best to settle you in."

First down the steps of the plane was Mr Kanji Karsan, 33, a building worker, wearing a second-hand British greatcoat and a green woollen balaclava.

He and his wife carried two bundles of clothing. Through an interpreter they told of being "grabbed" by soldiers at one of six roadblocks on the 23-mile journey by car from Kampala to Entebbe airport.

"I am penniless"

"I was dragged out of the car and stripped of my valuables and the little money I had," Mr Karsan said. "I am penniless and I have no plans."

Minutes before he boarded the plane a stranger approached him at Entebbe and thrust into his hand a book of addresses in Welwyn Garden City—his only contact with anybody in Britain.

He and his wife were planning to stay at the resettlement centre at the former RAF station at Stradishall, Suffolk, before deciding their future.

Last night there were 101 Asians at Stradishall, twice as many as resettlement officials expected. As they ate chicken curry and grilled fish cooked by women volunteers, coal fires were lit for them in houses and flats at the 700-acre base.

Job inquiries

When they arrived at the isolated camp, the Asians queued to have their identities and means listed by officials. Each had to be X-rayed.

Prospects for jobs and homes will be examined at detailed interviews beginning today.

Mr Eldon Griffiths, Parliamentary Under-Secretary in the Department of the Environment, who greeted the Asians at the camp, said overcrowding was not expected even though the draft would build up.

"We can take up to a thousand people here. Others can be accommodated at the two other camps we have prepared," he said.

Asian family arrives at London's Heathrow Airport on September 23, 1972. Mr. P. R. Patel (center), the father, was a supervisor at a soap factory in Kampala.
Reproduced with permission ©Associated Press/Wide world photos

Tiku and Chiku, the pet parrots of Viren and Hemant Trevedi, aged 8 and 10, settled down with them last night at the reception centre. There are no quarantine regulations for birds.

Coloured cards

At Stansted the Asians were divided into four groups, each identified by coloured cards—green for those being met by friends or relatives; blue for those going to an address on their own; pink for those needing assistance to travel to an address; and yellow for those going to the reception centre.

They were given a choice of egg, salmon, cheese or apricot jam sandwiches by the Women's Voluntary Service. Tables were laid out, with cups of tea and glasses of lime and orange juice. Children were offered sweets.

Ten, thousand disposable babies' nappies had been ordered. Shelves in a room were filled with overcoats and jerseys for Asians without warm clothes.

Then began the slow process of conducting heads of families through a small room containing four interviewers from the Citizens Advice Bureau.

The interviewers, each accompanied by an interpreter, attempted to persuade them to settle in areas not already swamped by immigrant communities.

Joining family

But many said they wanted to join relatives in the big cities and towns. One man sat down in front of a women interviewer and said he was joining relatives in Leicester.

"If you go there," the interviewer said, "we cannot help you. If you go to Leicester you won't be able to get a job or a house."

But after this had been explained to him by the interpreter the man insisted on going to Leicester.

He said he has no money and was given a pink card to show to the social security officials and a yellow card to show to the WRVS for warm clothing.

The next man said he was going to his brother's home in Cardiff. He was also given pink and yellow cards and a slip of paper to take to the medical examination team. "I'm sorry there's so much paper," the interviewer told him.

Shooting threat

As they waited to be interviewed other refugees sat over tea and sandwiches and told how their money and belongings had been plundered before they left Entebbe.

Mr Suryakant Patel said he had been a headmaster of a primary school for 20 years. He had been told by the government he had to stay in Uganda.

"But the Army threatened to shoot me if I did not leave the country," he said.

Forty Asians had been killed by Africans as they tried to cross the border a week ago, he added.

Tea and biscuits for apprehensive exiles

From Penny Symon, Stradishall, Suffolk, Sept 18
Reprinted with permission, ©Telegraph Group Limited, London, September 19, 1972

At 3:30 pm today two buses carrying 101 tired and apprehensive Asians and two parrots finally drew up on the parade ground here.

Stradishall, a former RAF station near Newmarket, disused for the past two years, had been waiting for them with teams of Red Cross and WRVS volunteers all day.

Messages from Stansted airport during the day had said about 25 people would be arriving at 1 pm, then the figure increased to 50, and so on.

Nobody knew why there was a delay. It was finally blamed on the press at Stansted and on the fact that the heads of the families were reluctant to say exactly how many dependants they had with them.

In order to forestall another similar scene, Mr Eldon Griffiths, Parliamentary Under-Secretary of State at the Department of the Environment and MP for Bury St Edmunds, held a press conference before the Asians arrived, to try to tell correspondents how to handle this end of the operation.

As there was time to kill, he was asked questions about housing, unemployment and whether the bringing of the Asians to Suffolk was a government scheme to encourage them to take a liking to the area and stay on rather than head for areas such as Leicester and Southall. He denied that it was.

When the Asians arrived the first people they saw apart from photographers were the WRVS staff who strode out of the reception centre to the buses with determined smiles, purposeful waves and shouts of "hullo".

The Asian women, wearing warm coats over their saris, smiled back with caution and the group was led into a large room where tea and biscuits were handed out.

Then confusion set in and Mr Griffiths chatted to them, held babies and told the press to go away, while volunteers tried to establish whether the new arrivals had been given medical checks at Stansted.

A pile of clothes collected by the WRVS was waiting in a neighbouring room, and one boy of eight found a pair of gloves several sizes too large and a women's silk head-scarf, both of which he put on proudly. He smiled for the first time since his arrival.

After medical checks and more delay, the families were taken to their allocated houses. There was a muddle here about the coal fires. Some had been lit and had been burning for two hours with nobody in the houses, while others were only lit when people moved in.

In a couple of houses the electricity did not work, and some families had obviously expected to find more than the table, chairs, beds and electric cooker waiting for them.

They would have appreciated some carpeting but were pleased at least with the bars of soap engraved "ER" waiting on their beds. They made the best of it, stoically, and said that it was better than nothing in the circumstances, and that the houses were adequate.

Stansted Airport, England: Sir Charles Cunningham (standing in the background), chairman of the Uganda Resettlement Board, talks to expelled Asians in the refreshment lounge prior to their departure to temporary accommodations at the RAF station in Stradishall. Reproduced with permission ©Times Newspapers Limited

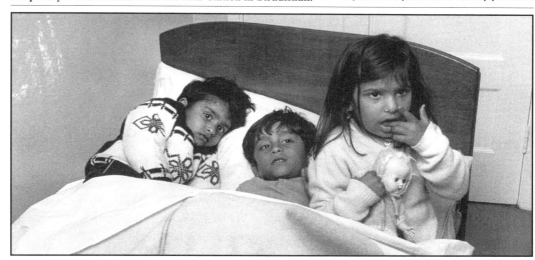

Wrapped in woollies to compensate for a sudden change of climate, three young members of an Asian family settle down for the first night's sleep at Stradishall. Reproduced with permission ©Warhurst/Times Newspapers Limited

One voluntary worker, struggling to light an obstinately smoking fire, said that voluntary workers were all very well but they could have done with some professionals.

Group Captain Frederick Rothwell, recently retired from the RAF, had been asked to take charge of the operation as he knew both East Africa and Stradishall. He said, after the families had been moved in, that he thought the operation had gone satisfactorily, and praised the work of the voluntary organizations.

"Of course, we had difficulties in the two weeks we had to prepare the station", he said. "We had difficulties with the sewage system and the heating. But I am sure all this will be ironed out.

"They have the basic essentials and in time will get flowers and decorations to make them feel a bit more homely." He added that the station could accommodate a thousand people, or more.

A meal of chicken or lamb curry, grilled fish, rice, vegetables and fruit was available today, prepared, by coincidence, by the same private caterers who cooked for the Tristan da Cunha islanders when they first landed here and were taken to an Army camp in Surrey.

Stradishall is intended as a short-stay station where people will be interviewed by government officials about their job expectations and plan about where they will go to live.

This will start tomorrow, and at the same time the volunteers will be gearing themselves again to deal with another possible influx from the afternoon flight, which is due at Stansted at 3:30 pm. Another flight is due on Wednesday; both will carry 174 people.

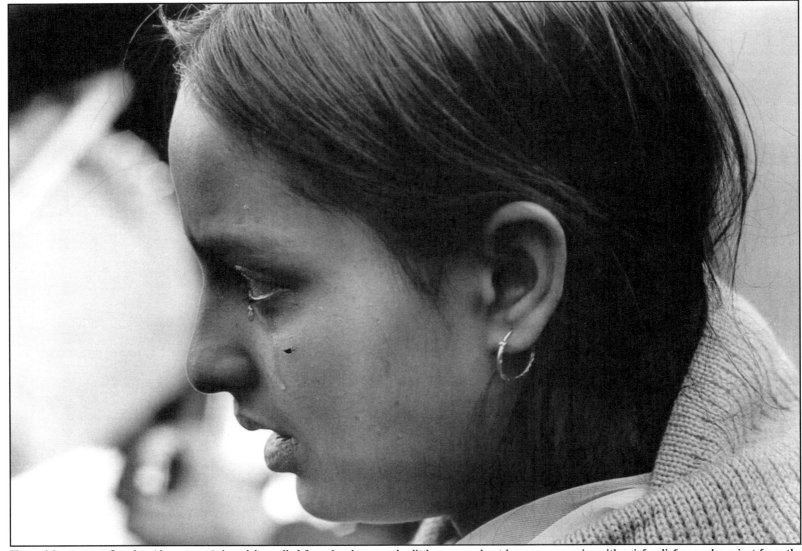

Here with a tear: at London Airport, an Asian girl expelled from her home and a little unsure about her new one, cries with grief, relief or perhaps just from the exhaustion of it all. Another ten plane loads of expelled Ugandans are expected by Tuesday. Reproduced with permission ©Michael Ward/Times Newspapers Limited

Scribbles in a grubby black book the only British 'contacts'

From Christopher Walker
Stansted, Sept 18
Reprinted with permission, ©Times Newspapers Limited, London,
September 19, 1972

Shortly after 12:30 today a tired, puzzled-looking Uganda Asian dressed in a secondhand army greatcoat and a green balaclava hat could be seen in the corner of an airport waiting room struggling to master the intricacies of an English telephone box.

In his hand was a grubby black notebook containing only a scribbled telephone number in Welwyn Garden City, another in Kensal Green and a third which claimed to be for "Hitrow Airport".

For Khanji Dhanji Karsan, the book, which had been hastily pushed into his hand last night by a complete stranger at Entebbe airport, contained his only contacts in Britain.

At the same time, in pouring rain outside the Uganda Resettlement Board headquarters here, Mr Surykant Patel was loading his suitcases into a friend's minibus which was waiting to drive him to Loughborough.

Although chosen at random, the two men demonstrate strikingly the widely varying situations of the expelled Uganda Asians who arrived here today.

Mr Karsan, a building worker aged 35, could manage only two or three words of English. Even for conversations with voluntary workers he was dependent on Gujarati translators.

With his new wife, Amina, a frightened but beautiful woman of 25, he had arrived in Britain with no friends, no money, no relatives and only the haziest ideas about the country where he found himself. The only reason that the heavy rain did not surprise him was that he had spent much of his early life in India.

Mr Patel, on the other hand, has been working for the past 20 years as the headmaster of a large primary school near the border between Uganda and Kenya. He was forced to leave it hurriedly 15 days ago after being threatened by members of the Ugandan Army who were camped near by.

"I was afraid for my life", he said. "I did not want to leave the school—after all, it was my life—but I had no alternative. Already there were reports that 40 other Asians had been killed near by when they tried to escape over the border to Kenya."

Mr Patel speaks perfect English and is clearly well educated. At the age of 42 he had built up the Busia Border School, which was exclusively for African children, out of money raised by voluntary contributions, and helped to lay the foundations himself.

"The education department tried to stop me leaving, because they fear a real shortage of teachers", he told me. "But I could see there was little alternative if I wanted to stay alive."

While Mr Karsan left Stansted this afternoon in a coach headed for the transit camp at Stradishall, with little hope other than the good will of an English building contractor who might employ him. Mr Patel had a very clear view of his ambitions.

"When I have settled in at the house at Loughborough I shall apply to take a diploma of education at the local college there", he said. With 20 years experience in charge of a school containing 300 children, he should not find it too hard.

Meanwhile Mr Karsan will try again tomorrow to get through to the telephone number in Kensal Green. He will still be without the slightest idea of whom he will be talking to if it is answered, or the identity of the man who handed him the notebook saying only: "If you need help in Britain, try ringing these numbers."

Amin stops BOAC airlift planes from landing in Uganda

By MARTIN WALKER
Reprinted with permission, ©The Guardian, London, September 20, 1972

The Ugandan airlift has been suspended for at least 48 hours. OBA staff at Entebbe Airport have been unofficially informed that the Ugandan authorities will not grant clearance for planes. "It is the political clearance we lack, not the operational," OACC said in London yesterday.

The initial British explanation for the standstill of the charter airlift of Ugandan Asians was that so few of them had so far applied to fly that they could easily be carried on the scheduled flights. But Britain was now seeking assurances from the Ugandan authorities that BOAC would get clearances to land at Entebbe, the Department of Trade and Industry said yesterday.

Volunteer workers and St. John Ambulance men were relieved of duties at Stansted Airport yesterday when the BOAC flight from Uganda was cancelled. Only 34 Asians were expected to arrive on the plane, which can carry almost 200. "We just don't know why there are so few; whether it is harassment or inability to obtain exit documents, or financial problems, or whatever." Mr Alan Foster, the resettlement board's coordinator at Stansted said.

BOAC has not yet sent its first charter airliner to Entebbe and will not do so until full clearance to land there has been obtained.

Eighty-eight Uganda Asians arrived at Heathrow Airport-London yesterday on East African Airways scheduled flights. Only 10 people, two families of five, out of 23 who arrived on the morning flight went to the resettlement board's hostel in Kensington. The others were being looked after by relatives and friends.

BOAC officials have been speculating whether their planes were being hindered by the Ugandan authorities in order to fill EAA planes, and improve their revenue. But airline and resettlement board officials were agreed that the delay in the airlift meant that the Asians' arrival would be concentrated into so little time that air and reception services would face a much greater strain than had been expected.

Arrangements have already been made at Stansted Airport to bring in yet more emergency lavatories and baggage tents to cope with the expected rush. "I envisage that even more space for their reception will be needed," Mr Alan Foster, of the resettlement board, said.

There is some slack to be taken up on scheduled flights before the charter airlift gets under way again, according to Mr J. Lusk, chief immigration officer at Gatwick Airport-London. He estimates that about 40 seats should be available on each scheduled flight, increasing to 60 when the rush of returning schoolchildren is over. But it would take almost a year to bring out the Uganda Asian community by scheduled flights, and General Amin's deadline for their departure has now less than two months to run.

Disconsolate people were waiting for their relatives to arrive at Stantsted yesterday and many of them went to the temporary residences at the former RAF airfield of Stansted to see whether their relatives had already arrived.

Jackie Leishman writes: Inspections of three empty military camps in the West country have been made by the Department of the Environment for the Uganda Resettlement Board in case extra emergency accommodation is needed for Uganda Asians. The camps are Houndstone, near Yeovil, Plaister Down, near Tavistock, and Heathfield, Honinton.

The board said yesterday that the inspection did not necessarily mean that the camps would be put to use. It was not that more Asians than expected had taken up the Government's offer of temporary accommodation after the first planeload arrived on Monday.

Nottingham corporation decided last night to warn the Uganda Resettlement Board that the city's social services were already stretched almost to breaking point. Councillor John Carroll, acting leader of the controlling Labour group, said: "If Asians have friends in Nottingham and they want to live here, then we have no power to prevent them. But they must realise that they are putting even more strain on a tense situation."

CANADA

No job favors for Asians says PM

Reprinted with permission, ©Canadian Press, 1972
Published in the ©Montreal Star, September 20, 1972

ST. CATHARINES—Ugandan refugees are not being guaranteed jobs "and certainly won't get them ahead of Canadians," Prime Minister Trudeau told a high school audience in this southern Ontario community yesterday.

"They are coming here and taking their chances as the rest of Canadians," the prime minister said during a question and answer period as he resumed campaigning.

Mr. Trudeau said he was sure the Asians from Uganda would find it difficult to settle in Canada but rejected one student's argument that refugees should be barred because of unemployment among Canadians.

"If Canada were to open its doors only when it was easy to do so, then we don't have much merit as a government and Canadians don't have much heart."

Mr. Trudeau said the refugees would take jobs Canadians will not accept. He said he had been told a number of jobs on the east coast, where unemployment is a chronic problem, "are going begging" because Maritimers won't take them.

"It's a fact that there are some jobs that Canadians don't like to do or don't snap up, and

---

INDIA

Indian from Uganda in a quandary

By A Staff Reporter
Reprinted with permission, ©Times of India, September 20, 1972

A UGANDAN citizen of Indian origin is in Bombay wondering how he will ever unite with his wife who is holding a British passport.

Mr. T. P. Suchak, a former president of the Indian National Congress in Uganda, has come to Bombay but fears that his wife might have to go to a camp in Uganda if he does not find a way out quickly.

Because Uganda is a commonwealth country, Mr. Suchak has been able to come to India for a temporary stay. He would like to settle down here.

His wife is a British passport-holder but she would not be able to go to Britain as unaccompanied women are not allowed to settle down there.

The Suchaks are not in a position to renounce their present citizenships as the Indian High Commission no longer accepts such requests.

"There are many people like me. We are frantically trying to find some way out. I have left property worth about Rs 10 lakhs in Uganda. We just want a place to settle down", he said.

More than half of the British passport-holders of Indian origin are willing to settle down in India if they got certain facilities from the government, it is learnt.

According to a rough estimate, the value of the property of the British and Ugandan citizens in Uganda is "several million pounds." But they are not allowed to take out of the country any valuables.

A source stated on Tuesday that British passport-holders and others leaving the country were allowed to carry with them household goods weighing only 200 kilos.

The source stated that the original Ugandans had been asked by the Idi Amin government to apply for the transfer of property left behind by the British and Indian passport -holders.

The Amin government was also likely to appoint a Ugandan managing director for the sugar factory belonging to that country's biggest industrialist, Mr. Manu Madhvani, it is stated.

Those leaving the country have been asked by the Ugandan government to submit a list of properties left behind. They are not allowed to sell or transfer any property.

The Ugandan government would later sell the property and has said it would hand over the amount to the rightful owners. "But we doubt whether it would ever happen."

Canadians don't like to do or don't snap up, and perhaps they will be taken by the Asians who want to settle here."

Mr. Trudeau hit the campaign trail yesterday after a two-day break in Ottawa. Mrs. Trudeau remained at home.

Ugandan Asian Expulsion: 90 Days and Beyond through the Eyes of the International Press

Amin seizes his Chief Justice
Amin's troops 'spread panic' in Kampala

By PATRICK KEATLEY, Diplomatic Correspondent
Reprinted with permission, ©The Guardian, London, September 22, 1972

Ugandan troops went on the rampage in some parts of Kampala, shooting and looting, according to witnesses who reached Athens Airport last night.

People thinking it was an invasion, scurried for the safety of shops and homes, and the whole operation of processing queues of desperate Asians for flights to Britain came to a halt as the queues melted away.

The road to the airport, 22 perilous miles from Kampala to Entebbe, has become an obstacle course with 10 roadblocks manned by trigger-happy soldiers, according to the travellers. In a day of apparent chaos, bringing Uganda inexorably closer to a breakdown of law and order, the Chief Justice was arrested at the High Court by armed men.

Witnesses said they were the dreaded Military Police who are outside the control of the civil police forces. But to compound the confusion, the official Government spokesman denied that the arrest had been carried out by any public official and issued a warning over Radio Uganda about the dangerous activities of "people posing as members of the security forces."

It was the more frightening, therefore, for the British community in Uganda to learn later that—although 44 British citizens had been released from the two main prisons in Kampala—a family of four, the Whitehorns, had been arrested at their home in a suburb and taken away at gunpoint by troops.

Inquiries

There is no obvious reason why Mr And Mrs Whitehorn and their two children, both under seven, should have been chosen for arrest. The troops appear to have searched the house and helped themselves. Last night the Whitehorns were reported to have been released.

Although there were no fresh reports of guerrilla activities in Southern Uganda, this was by far the worst day that the 100,000 citizens of Kampala have experienced since the invasion scare broke on Sunday.

The ultimate irony was General Amin's summoning of embassy representatives to his "Command Post" to remind them that he is absolutely determined that the mass migration of noncitizen Asians will be completed by midnight on November 7.

A few hours later, shooting broke out in the city and the queues of Asians at Ugandan Government offices disappeared. Processing at these offices has been moving at a snail's pace since Sunday, and there have not been enough Asians with completed documents to fill even one Boeing 707. The air lines whose charter operation to Britain came to a halt on Monday, have given up hope. A flight is scheduled for Monday.

In view of General Amin's calculated threat to diplomats about the deadline, the prospect for the majority of British Asians in Uganda after Nov. 8 is grim indeed.

There was little comfort for the Asians in the British High Commission announcement that 8,790 of them had now been cleared to enter Britain, 719 of them on Wednesday alone. The real hitch remains: getting through the Ugandan Government's treble queueing system.

First reports of shooting and panic in Kampala yesterday came from sources in Nairobi. Radio Uganda denied the shooting, but not that the streets had emptied and the shops had been closed.

Telephone messages to Nairobi spoke of indiscriminate firing, of lorries laden with troops roaring through the poorer parts of Kampala, particularly the industrial suburbs. In the centre, according to a British diplomat, no shooting was heard.

Later, at Athens Airport, travellers gave their accounts. One man said that his coach to Entebbe Airport had passed through 10 roadblocks manned by troops. At the first one, a few hundred yards from their hotel, they were stopped by an army patrol and told to go back. The officer said there was shooting on the airport road.

The passenger went on : "We could hear the shooting, but did not know who was involved. We could see soldiers and army officers taking jewels and other valuable belongings from men, women, and children. No one dared complain as the troops threatened to kill them if they said anything."

The airline passengers, most of them English-speaking who had settled in Uganda, also spoke about reports of soldiers raping women, particularly Asians.

There is no real doubt about the fate of the Chief Justice. Mr Benedicto Kiwanuka, Prime Minister of Uganda before his Conservative Party was defeated at the polls by the Obote forces.

Mr Kiwanuka had arrived for a sitting of the East African court of Appeal when men in the uniform of the Military Police—the units that operate the Makindye prison—arrived and handcuffed him. He was stripped of jacket and tie and led away.

Courageous

The Chief Justice courageously granted a writ of habeas corpus a fortnight ago in the case of Mr Donald Stewart, the British businessman arrested without cause and taken to Makindye. Before the judicial process could be completed, the army had released Mr Stewart and put him on a plane for Britain.

Mr Kiwanuka comes from the Masaka area in the South-west where there has been heavy fighting. A recent statement issued by the Defence Council, headed by General Amin, referred to "high ranking Government officials (who) prefer to confuse the people while pretending to pledge their loyalty."

There are still at least five British subjects and 12 others held in prison without charges.

Uganda Claims Victory

News Compilation, September 20, 1972

After a third day of fighting with Tanzanian troops, a Ugandan military spokesman announced that the invasion force had been 'completely routed'. Civilian casualties around Mbarara and Masaka were estimated to be about 150.

A British High Commission official was granted consular access to about 30 of the British citizens being detained in Kampala.

A Canadian tourist who had been detained for 30 hours by police in Kampala arrived in Nairobi last night. He reported that 65 Britons were being held in a bare room measuring 40 ft. by 20 ft. Women and young children were among those detained.

INDIA MAKES OFFER OF TEMPORARY STAYS

NEW DELHI, Thursday. INDIA has announced that British passport holders of Indian origin in Uganda who hold entry certificates to go to Britain can come to India for temporary stays.

An official spokesman said visas would be issued to such people by Indian Government representatives abroad. Their stay in India would not prejudice their right to go to Britain later, he added.

AUSTRIA TO TAKE ASIANS FROM UGANDA

VIENNA, Tuesday. TRADE Minister Dr. Josef Staribacher has indicated Austria will be prepared to accept skilled Asians expelled from Uganda on a temporary basis and under the same conditions as other foreign workers.

He said one of the conditions of employment in Austria was that the industry where Asians sought work really required extra labour.

Libyan airlift to help Amin forced to land in Sudan

News Compilation, September 21, 1972

Five aircraft carrying 399 Libyan troops to help president Amin were refused permission to fly over Sudan yesterday and had to land at Khartoum. The Sudanese government spokesman said they would not be allowed to continue to Entebbe. One plane is said to have carried a crated MiG-17 jet fighter.

President Amin threatened to invade Tanzania—to destroy military camps where, he said, the enemy was planning another invasion.

The Ugandan authorities announced that they had released all British journalists detained since the attack by dissident forces.

Government directs on cleared Asians:
NOT MORE THAN TWO DAYS

Reprinted with permission, ©Uganda Argus, September 23, 1972

MEMBERS OF THE UGANDA SECURITY FORCES HAVE BEEN DIRECTED BY THE GOVERNMENT TO ENSURE THAT ALL BRITISH ASIANS WHO HAVE BEEN CLEARED BY THE BANK OF UGANDA MUST NOT REMAIN IN THE COUNTRY FOR MORE THAN 48 HOURS (TWO DAYS), AND THAT WITH EFFECT FROM THE DATE WHEN SUCH ASIANS WERE GIVEN PERMISSION TO RETURN TO THEIR HOME COUNTRY, THEIR WORK PERMITS AND TRADING LICENCES ARE AUTOMATICALLY CANCELLED.

This follows reported allegations to the effect that the staff of the British High Commission in Kampala were slow in processing documents of the out-going British Asians.

Therefore, in order to make the position absolutely clear, Government yesterday gave details of the clearance and capacity which government possesses; the number of British-Asians so far processed by both the Bank of Uganda and the East African Income Tax Department, as well as the number of such people who have booked seats on flights arranged for them by the East African Airways and its partner British carriers.

Government has been informed by the British High Commission in Kampala that up to September 19, the number of British Asians issued with entry vouchers by the High Commission was 8,071.

Yet the position with regard to the British Asians cleared by the Bank of Uganda by the same date is 8,637. And furthermore, a comparative example of the rate at which the British High Commission and the Income Tax Department were clearing out-going Asians is illustrated by the following figures:

"Whereas on September 1, the British High Commission had issued 249 entry vouchers to the British nationals of Asian origin, the Income Tax Department cleared 284. On September 2, the British High Commission issued 71 entry vouchers against the Income Tax Department clearance of 229. On September 4, the High Commission issued 293 entry vouchers while the Income Tax Department cleared 315. As at September 14, the Income Tax Department was clearing 550 persons per day.

"The Bank of Uganda and Income Tax Department have adequate capacity for each to clear at least 1,500 out-going Asians per day. Unfortunately, only a few of these people are coming forward for clearance. If the British High Commission were issuing entry vouchers to their nationals of Asian origin at the same rate as Uganda is capable of clearing and if these British nationals were coming forward to be cleared by Uganda at that rate, Government is satisfied that all these British nationals would have been cleared and enabled to go back comfortably to Britain before the deadline of November 8.

Taking all these facts into consideration therefore, Government wishes to make it clear that no blame of any kind can justifiably be labeled against her for delaying the departure of these British nationals now in Uganda to their mother country. The clearing capacity of both the Bank of Uganda and the East African Income Tax Department is adequate to clear all the Asians who present themselves for clearance.

"It follows, therefore, that if the British High Commission issued entry vouchers to their nationals of Asian origin returning to Britain at the same rate as Uganda is able to clear and if these British nationals cleared, returned to Britain soon after obtaining clearance, all of them would easily have returned to their homeland by November 8. The fact that the British are not issuing vouchers to their nationals as speedily as they should has been supported by the complaints voiced by the Asians and reported in the Press on September 21.

Seats

"It will be noted that, in order to ensure that there are adequate seats to accommodate all the British Asians travelling within the specified time, East African Airways and its British partner carriers have put at the disposal of the out-going British Asians 16 extra flights per week to the United Kingdom.

"Furthermore the scheduled service which would not normally call at Entebbe on their way to United Kingdom are now being routed through Entebbe to provide additional seats for these people. In addition to all this, East African Airways services which normally terminated in other cities

Continued on Page 76

Airlift plane forced down in drama at Nairobi Airport

By NATION Reporter
Reprinted with permission, ©Daily Nation, Nairobi, September 23, 1972

FULL EMERGENCY measures had to be deployed at Embakasi Airport yesterday afternoon when an EAA Super VC-10 radioed to say its landing gear had locked soon after taking off from Entebbe Airport. The plane had left Nairobi yesterday morning heading for London via Entebbe and Rome. On board from Nairobi was Kenya's Minister for Agriculture, Mr. Jeremiah Nyagah, who was travelling to Gabon.

At Entebbe, the plane was kept waiting two hours for 140 British Asians to be cleared for the flight to London. The plane took off from Entebbe with the expelled Asians and a few other passengers, including Mr. Nyagah. The plane's gear locked soon after take off and the pilot decided to head for Embakasi for an emergency landing.

Fire engines and ambulances raced to the airport and took up position beside the runway. A few minutes later the giant plane touched down and landed safely. It had to be pulled back from the end of the runway by a tractor complete with its load of passengers and cargo.

The transit lounge was then filled with scores of expelled Asians who were given lunch by the EAA authorities while engineers worked on the plane to repair the locked gears.

Telling the NATION their story of how they left Uganda, some of the Asians said that they had reported at the EAA office in Kampala from where they were taken to the airport buses under police escort. They were made to pay an airport fee of 20/- instead of the normal feel of 10/ -, they said.

Continued on Page 76

Refugee dies after flight

TORONTO—An elderly woman, who arrived here Friday from Uganda with her grandson and his wife, died in a Toronto hospital Sunday.

The woman, who was more than 80, collapsed on the flight from London to Toronto—the last leg of her 8,000 mile journey from Uganda.

The woman and the young Ugandan Asian couple left Uganda on the pretext of taking a holiday. Carrying only one suitcase each and virtually penniless, they left behind a furnished three-bedroom apartment.

They asked reporters to withhold their names to protect relatives still living in Uganda.

The man, 33, was an insurance agent in Kampala and his wife, 26, an accounts clerk. They are staying here with another Ugandan couple, who immigrated more than a year ago.

The man said in an interview that Canadians should not fear that thousands of Asians being expelled from Uganda will come here and deprive Canadians of jobs.

Another Tanzanian town bombed
LIBYAN TROOPS ARRIVE IN UGANDA

News Compilation, September 23, 1972

A reported bombing today by a Ugandan aircraft of Mwanza, Tanzania's third largest town on the southern shores of Lake Victoria, has not been announced officially by the Ugandan authorities.

Eyewitnesses reported that thousands of residents of Mwanza were fleeing the town.

A Kenya radio report said the five Libyan aircraft carrying troops and arms to General Amin, which were detained in Khartoum, had now landed at Entebbe airport. Sources reported that they were released after they had given the impression they were returning to Tripoli, but instead, flying low, headed to Uganda.

"We are willing to do all kinds of jobs. I see that the prime minister of Canada said that some of us might work on farms picking fruit. There's nothing wrong with that."

Huge Uganda Air Lift Refused by Britain

News Compilation, September 24, 1972

The British government today refused to organize a massive air lift to meet the newest demands of Uganda's President Idi Amin. Amin gave Britain 48 hours to take away the 8,600 British Asians who have been cleared by the Uganda government of departure. The Foreign Office told the Uganda ambassador the demand was impossible and impractical to meet. The airlift has been disrupted by the intense security measures in force and because many families have been too afraid to run the gauntlet of eight Army roadblocks along the 20-mile route from Kampala to Entebbe airport.

Liberal Party to Campaign for Positive Welcome

By an overwhelming majority, the Liberal Party Assembly in Margate condemned "the racialist persecution of the Asians of Uganda by General Amin". The resolution welcomed the Asians to Britain and regretted the silence of the Labour Party.

The assembly also called on Liberal councillors and activists to campaign for their local authorities to provide facilities and a positive welcome for the refugees.

Heath to ease fear on Asians

Prime Minister Heath has planned to tour East Midlands in an effort to allay the anxieties of conservative voters. Significantly, Mr Heath has chosen to start his tour at Leicester, where the local council has announced that it cannot absorb any more immigrants from Uganda.

Continued from Page 75

Airlift plane forced down in drama at Nairobi Airport

Some who had been residents of up-country towns told our reporter they had been robbed of their money, wrist watches and other valuables.

At Kampala, those with money were asked to hand it over to the Customs Officers and were in return given receipts stating: "Such and such amount has been seized as liable to forfeiture under the East African Customs and Transfer Tax Management Act 1952 on the grounds that the amount was found in your possession contrary to section 146 of the Act."

Arriving on the same plane was Mr. Vincent Vivian Millett, a British national who had worked with the Ugandan Ministry of Agriculture, Forest and Co-operatives for the last 17 years.

Mr. Millett told the NATION that officials of the Ugandan Government arrived at his office in the morning and took him straight to the airport. He had been unable to say good-bye to anyone or even pack a suitcase.

He was put on the London-bound plane with nothing at all except his shirt and trousers.

Mr. Millett tried to contact the British High Commission officials in Nairobi but a NATION reporter had to give him the 2/ - to make the phone calls.

Exodus to Britain—Uganda Asians' Goal: New Life

By Joseph Cerutti
Chicago Tribune Press service
Reprinted with permission, ©Chicago Tribune, September 24, 1972

STRADISHALL, England, Sept. 23—This remote 700-acre disused British air force bomber base, 70 miles north-east of London, has been nicknamed Kampala New Town by local villagers.

Here more than half of the first British Asians thrown out of Uganda by President Idi Amin are getting their initial taste of life in England.

About 50,000 Asians holding British passports are due for expulsion by Nov. 7. The first batch arrived bewildered, confused, robbed of their last possessions, but thankful to have reached safety on a charter flight Sept. 18.

Some Have Accommodations

Those who had arranged to stay with friends or relatives already here headed for London, Cardiff, Blackburn, Birmingham, Leeds, Edinburgh, and Leicester, which already have large immigrant populations.

The remainder were bundled into buses and driven from Stanstead Airport to Stradishall, the first of six reception camps the British government is setting up to accommodate Asians with nowhere else to go.

The Asians share 27 houses used until two years ago by R.A.F. families. Emergency furnishings consist only of chairs, tables, and beds. The immigrants are dependent on government and voluntary workers for food, coal, and warm clothing. Many are penniless and rely on the Department of Social Security for pocket money. A television room is being set up in the main building and toys are being collected for children.

Jobs Sought

In another room used in wartime to brief pilots, the Asians, who include accountants, teachers, bricklayers, engineers, businessmen, and office workers, meet daily with Department of Employment officials to discuss job prospects. The big problem is linking jobs with accommodations. The feeling increases that many of the Asians still will be housed at Stradishall over Christmas.

Gohel Parshotta, 18, who arrived with five cents in his pocket and a small bundle of clothing under his arm, said: "Most of us are prepared to accept anything. We are just very thankful to be here."

Recurrent in the Asians' accounts of their

Continued on Page 77

Continued from Page 75

NOT MORE THAN TWO DAYS

in Europe have now been extended to London to cater for much people. These extra services are in addition to normal scheduled flights between Entebbe and London and are also available to carry some of the British Asians.

"It is, however, regrettable that a number of extra flights have had to be cancelled for various reasons. The most important of these are:

The failure of the British Asians to take up the seats available and the insistence on the part of the British Government that five days' notice be given for the special flights to enable them to give necessary landing rights and that the British High commission is not issuing sufficient entry vouchers.

"For example, the British Overseas Airways Corporation (BOAC) flight BA 702, scheduled to carry British Asians on September 19 and the British Overseas Airways Corporation flight BAC 72, scheduled for the same purpose to leave on September 20 we both cancelled because British authorities had refused them operating permits unless they gave five days' advance notice; and also because the two carriers did not have sufficient number of British Asians ready to leave for the United Kingdom.

The two flights had a total capacity of 346 seats which, unfortunately, have now been wasted. Furthermore, East African Airways EC 712 with a capacity of 120 seats was only able to take over 54 of the total passengers previously booked on the British Overseas Airways corporation cancelled flights. So, the greatest proportion of the 466 seats on the three flights on September 19 and 20, were eventually wasted.

Between September 20 and 24 BOAC British Caledonian Airways and East African Airways have a total of 581 seats available for the British Asians. However, by September 19, the three airlines had booked only 200 passengers, thus leaving 381 seats unoccupied.

"From the foregoing, it is clear that the outgoing British Asians are deliberately not coming forward to utilize the facilities made available to them. It should realize that all these services have been made available to return these people home at considerable expense to the Uganda tax-payer who has been milked by the same out-going British Asians for almost a century. The Uganda taxpayer cannot be expected to continue bearing this burden indefinitely. The British Asians who must leave this country are grossly mistaken if they believe that the patience of the Uganda tax-payer is inexhaustible.

"British Asians who are required to leave this country before November 8, are therefore, expected to leave immediately after obtaining their necessary clearance.

"Government has therefore, decided: that all British Asians who have been cleared by the Bank of Uganda will not be permitted to remain in the country for more than 48 hours. And that with effect from the date when such people have been given permission to return to their home country, their work permits and trading licenses are automatically canceled.

"Members of the Security Forces have therefore been directed to ensure that these decisions are fully complied with."

American in Uganda Jail Found Brutality and an Unlikely Esprit

By ANDREW TORCHIA
Reprinted with permission, ©Associated Press
Published in The New York Times, September 22, 1972

The writer of the following dispatch, an American correspondent based in Kenya, was seized last weekend, soon after arriving in Uganda, and arrived safely in England yesterday after being released.

LONDON, Sept. 21—Uganda soldiers pinned a man on the ground while a woman beat him with a rawhide whip—10, 20, 50 times until he screamed and writhed and the whip drew blood.

Thirty other soldiers—officers and men—shouldered around to watch. They laughed, enjoying the spectacle, and no one intervened. The beating went on for minutes—forever, it seemed—before the crowd dispersed and the screaming stopped.

This scene yesterday afternoon was for 13 Britons, Swedes, Americans and Canadians their last view of the Makindye military prison. None of us knew who the woman was or what the whipping was about. We stood silently in the hot sun at the prison gate, while guards handed back our shoes and money, and tried not to look.

Most of us had spent three days in Makindye and now we were being released from captivity by the Uganda Army. Ten, including six British and two Swedish newsmen, were being deported on a night flight to London. Three were freed in Kampala.

Many details of what went on in Makindye cannot be told. Disclosure could endanger others still imprisoned there without being charged and without hope of immediate release. One man has been inside more than a year.

Uganda soldiers and detectives, swarming around Kampala following a reported invasion Sunday from Tanzania, detained 150 or more Asians and whites, plus uncounted Africans suspected of disloyalty to President Idi Amin. As fear and suspicion mounted against whites and Asians, soldiers wielding submachine guns made arrests at a swimming pool and in a bedroom at midnight.

Many of those arrested were clubbed with rifle butts. Others were led from their cells and disappeared.

Troops trucked dozens of Uganda policemen into Makindye as prisoners—lending support to the belief that the fighting in southern Uganda resulted at least as much from feuds within the country as from the guerrilla invasion that General Amin had announced.

Some prisoners slept on bare concrete floors; others had blankets or thin mattresses. Meals were skimpy—sweet tea and dry bread for breakfast, cold baked beans or biscuits for lunch, meat scraps and a cold cornmeal dish for dinner.

Expecting a Spy

At the central police station in Kampala, more than 50 white men, women and children were kept in one room. Babies pants were hung on the window bars to dry and urine from adjoining cells ran on the floor. I was at the central police station only briefly, while being taken from my hotel to Makindye.

I was detained by three plainclothesmen during dinner Sunday night at a hilltop tourist hotel in Kampala. Where was my radio transmitter and where was my pistol, they asked, evidently expecting a spy. I was never formally charged or told what wrongdoing was suspected. The offense seemed to be that I was a foreign newsman who could not accept uncritically official pronouncements by Kampala on the fighting.

Makindye, on a hill four miles from Kampala, is a collection of one story buildings behind a double fence of barbed wire. Cows and chickens roam the grounds. Soldiers lie on the grass, cleaning their weapons.

Our building held up to 18 prisoners in seven 10-by-7-foot cells that were airy and clean, unlike the dank rooms at the central police station.

Wide Assortment of Prisoners

There were three Asian traders whose ivory exports had been blocked by the military. A young Tanzanian Army deserter was taken from his cell one day and did not return. Two Africans led twice-daily Roman Catholic prayer services for the Christian, Hindu and Moslem inmates.

Lionel, a British tea taster, asked if he could telephone the managing director of his company. He could not. Two Africans were beaten until they could not stand, covered with blankets and carried away, perhaps already dead.

Tony, a shy, bearded British student, was ill for two days after being hit with a rifle butt on the head. Bob, a British farmer, worried that his cows were not being milked.

And there was Manubhai Madhvani, the 43-year-old Asian head of Uganda's biggest industrial combine. Madhvani Enterprises employees more than 15,000 people and manufactures 19 products, from steel to sugar. Mr. Madhvani in prison more than two weeks but not formally charged, could lose it all in the Asian exodus.

Yet always cheerful and dignified, he calmed new arrivals. The morale of the whole cell block came to depend on him. "Come in and sit down, don't be formal," he would say, patting the floor of his cell. The walls, scarred with mottos carved by former prisoners, then seemed more like home.

Yesterday a tall plainclothesman led us out of Makindye and into two cars bound for the airport. He allowed a beer stop at a Kampala hotel. We bought him one.

On the plane, he counted noses and wished us a safe flight

"See you next year," someone shouted back. But he did not mean it.

Continued from Page 76

Exodus to Britain—Uganda Asians' Goal: New Life

departure from Kampala, the Ugandan capital, are stories of searches by armed soldiers. Some said there were 11 separate checks during the 13-mile trip to Entebbe Airport. Almost all lost money and valuables. One retired civil servant said a $600 watch had been taken from him. Others lost cameras, bangles, and necklaces. Rings were taken from the fingers of children.

Dilip Raeia, 26, holds a diploma of education from Makerere University in Kampala and for three years taught science at a senior school at Soroti, 215 miles from the city.

Raeia and his wife, Hansa, 26, who is seven months pregnant, have been married for 18 months. Their savings, worth about $3,750, they gave away before leaving Uganda because they could not bring the money with them.

"Now I have nothing but hope," Raeia said. "The baby is due in two months. I know it's a lot to expect but I would like to have found a home for my wife and child before the birth. I am look-ing forward to living here but if I cannot earn a decent wage, then I will try to see if I can get back to India from where my father emigrated to Uganda in 1923."

Others Offer Refuge

India has offered to take an unspecified number of British Asians on a temporary basis. Malawi is expected to host about 500, Sweden 300, New Zealand will take 200, and Canada will take an unspecified number.

Mansukhlal Kara, 33, here with his wife and child, has a friend living in London but has been unable to make contact.

Only Seeks Job

"We are tired but we will keep going," he said. "We can't afford to break down. All I want is a job. If I work hard, we'll make it."

Surykant Patel, a school-master for 20 years, said $150 in Ugandan money and valuables worth 10 times that had been taken from him before departure. Patel, who speaks perfect English, was principal at the Busia border school for African children. He left it hurriedly 15 days ago after being threatened by Ugandan soldiers camped nearby.

"I was afraid for my life," he said. "I did not want to leave the school but I had no alternative. Already there were reports that 40 other Asians had been killed nearby when they tried to escape over the border into Kenya."

For school girl Jayshree Mashru, 14, the flight from Uganda held terrifying memories. She said she was robbed by two soldiers who held a knife and a gun at her throat.

Feelings Summed Up

Her father, an accountant, who also brought his wife and three sons to England, summed up the philosophy of most Asians involved in the first refugee flight from Uganda.

"We don't like the idea of living in a military camp," he said. "We don't like losing the status we had in Uganda. But we do like being alive."

Ugandan Asian Expulsion: 90 Days and Beyond through the Eyes of the International Press

Sledgehammer murders

By CHRISTOPHER MUNNION
who arrived in London yesterday after four days in Kampala's notorious Makindye army barracks.
Reprinted with permission, ©Telegraph Group Limited, London, September 22, 1972

MAKINDYE is one of the seven hills of Kampala, but it is not on any tourist itinerary. It is the headquarters of Gen. Amin's much-feared military police force, and Ugandans, if they mention it at all, whisper in fear.

For many months there had been furtively-told stories of people being whisked from their beds or from the streets and taken to Makindye Barracks, never to be seen again.

There were tales of daily mass murders by bullet or sledge hammer, of irrational brutality and terror meted out to prisoners who had never been charged with any offence.

These were stories not easily verified without a personal visit, which few correspondents were prepared to undertake voluntarily.

But, as a result of Amin's purge against the British Press in Kampala, I and eight journalist colleagues found ourselves in the position this week of making an on-the-spot investigation—involuntarily.

For four days and three very long nights in the cells of Makindye we witnessed and experienced what can only be described as the total horror of Amin's military police.

We watched these brutalised and lawless soldiers indulge themselves off-handly in hourly violence on innocent prisoners, most of whom have little hope of release or recourse to any form of justice.

Amin "spooks"

Last Sunday dawned with the Presidential declaration of a Tanzanian invasion. Troops appeared on the streets of Kampala.

With them were the Amin "spooks"—the assortment of security police attached to at least four different organisations with which the Ugandan leader has surrounded himself in the face of the ever-apparent internal threat to his regime.

The British community in the capital, and in particular the overseas Press contingent based on the Kampala International Hotel, had been increasingly aware of sinister surveillance as the Presidential exhortations against Britain had become more shrill.

With the invasion panic, the security forces were given a free hand to move against Europeans.

On Sunday afternoon, I and colleagues John Fairhall of the *Guardian*, and John Harrison of the *Daily Express* were arrested by an extremely nervous and angry young policeman in the foyer of the hotel.

He made us sit at rifle pint and wait for his superiors who were upstairs searching the rooms of two Swedish journalists.

The Swedes, Lars Holmstrom and Kenneth Johansson, had arrived in Kampala that morning and had made the mistake of asking a hotel official to point out the Presidential residence from the roof of the 18-storey building.

They were arrested an hour later beside the hotel swimming pool.

Every word read

After their rooms had been searched, two uniformed policemen and two plain-clothes men, both casually carrying the Israeli-made machine pistols which identified them as Army security, led us to our rooms for searches of personal papers.

Any piece of paper which contains writing brands you as a spy in Uganda these days. Every word of every Ugandan Ministry of Information handout was read.

Why was *The Daily Telegraph* interested in the General's visit to Soroti? Was that where the British planned to assassinate him?

A duplicated British High Commission rundown on British aid to Uganda and a copy of Sir Alec Douglas-Home's statement to the nation on the Asian crisis were taken as proof of my identity as a British agent.

Searches of my colleagues' rooms revealed similar damning evidence. We were ordered to pack, pay our bills and, joined by Don McCullin, a freelance photographer, were bundled into the back of a Land Rover and driven to the central police station.

There the full pathos and absurdity of the anti-European drive was brought home. Groups of startled Whites, elderly couples, women with babies, youths in sports shirts, and worried wives crowded into the charge office.

Bewildered and nervous, they had been picked up as they sat at kerbside cafes.

"Every European found on the streets must be detained in a cell—President's orders," shouted a beefy police officer. But the dilemma of the desk sergeant was obvious.

Bullied by those strange young men from other security branches, he tried to protest but was himself threatened.

As the police station began to assume the appearance of a refugee camp, it became obvious from the shouting match that Uganda's usually well-disciplined uniformed police were in serious dispute with their brash gun-toting security colleagues.

Our fate was in the latter's hands. Again we were bundled with our luggage into the back of the Land-Rover, joined by the two Swedes and a British resident of Kampala, to hear the dread instruction to the driver: "Makindye!"

With blue lights flashing and the siren wailing, we were driven through the red lights in central Kampala and began the climb uphill to the barracks.

A few feet behind us, the security men followed in a police car, forcing traffic off the road and ensuring that none of us had a chance to jump off.

It was dusk as we swung into the Makindye Barracks compound. Having been curtly ordered to get out of the vehicle we found ourselves surrounded by the men of Makindye, swaggering, pot-bellied NCOs and grinning, glazed-eyed soldiers in full combat kit.

Within seconds our security escort had explained our presence in rapid Swahili. The word "assassination" featured several times.

Suddenly we were clubbed to the ground. Rifle butts hit the back of our necks, clubs were rammed into backs and swagger sticks chopped at shoulders.

In the dust, we were ordered to remove our shoes and double into the guardroom.

Leering soldiers

Soldiers stood around, sweating and leering , as we tumbled to the floor of the guardroom. One of them, a cigarette dangling from his mouth, ordered us to remove our socks. A corporal behind the desk began to make notes of our property in a disinterested way.

The operation was punctuated by angry shouts and the sounds of slapping and kicking outside. A plainclothes man, brandishing the inevitable machine-pistol, pushed an African in civilian clothes on top of our huddled and frightened group. None of the soldiers seemed to think this unusual.

Our fate seemed to take a slight turn for the better when the corporal received whispered instructions from a messenger.

He led us to a private interviewing room where his manner became comparatively pleasant. Painstakingly he recorded our money, watches and luggage. The order, it appeared, was to treat the wazungu—the whites—with care.

Whites only

What applied to us, however, was not to change the routine treatment of African and Asian prisoners, as we rapidly discovered when we were led to our respective cell blocks.

John Fairhall, the Swedes and I were led to Block A One, a 25ft. by 50ft. concrete building with barred windows set high in the wall—the only ventilation.

In bare feet we picked our way through the droppings of a herd of goats which grazed the barbed-wire compound surrounding the cell block.

Having stumbled through the single entrance—a heavy iron door—into the darkness we found willing hands offering space on the concrete floor and single blankets, the only sleeping facilities in the block.

These were our cell-mates, a friendly and, in the circumstances, amazingly cheerful group of 20

Africans anxious to hear our news from the outside and keen to advise us on prison routine.

There was not a criminal among them. None had been charged with any offence. Some had been inside for two months and they knew others among the 200 or so prisoners scattered throughout the compound who

Continued on Page 80

Uganda: The Outcast's Story

Reprinted with permission, ©Newsweek, Inc., September 25, 1972

The poignant drama has been played out in other times and other places. Now it is happening in Uganda, where as many as 55,000 British Asians face peremptory expulsion from the country. Under orders by Uganda's mercurial President Idi Amin, they are given no real choice at all: either they get out of the East African state by Nov. 8, or they will be rounded up and confined to "transit camps." In human terms, tens of thousands of Uganda's Asians face a sudden uprooting from the only homeland that most of them have ever known. And last week, a first group boarded an "immigrant special" airlift for Britain. They left fearful that, as people of Indian or Pakistani ancestry, the British might treat them as unwelcome "colored immigrants," but so far at least, their fears of a white backlash in Britain have proved members of the same family are already at the two ends of the migration. Last week, NEWSWEEK correspondents interviewed two brothers, one preparing to leave Kampala, the Ugandan capital, and the other already up against the odds of making it in London. Their stories:

'SO WHO AM I?'

Opening the door of his third-floor walk-up flat in Kampala, Jashbahr Patel glanced nervously down the stairwell to see if his visitor was being followed. he immediately reminded the visitor that he had agreed to an interview only on condition that his true identity be safeguarded (a request that has prompted NEWSWEEK to use a pseudonym). Patel's fear of reprisals should Ugandan authorities discover that he had talked to a foreign journalist seemed well-founded. All Kampala has heard of the case of a noted local Asian lawyer, Anil Clerk, whose name appeared in a notebook seized by the police from a British reporter. A week later, Clerk disappeared.

"This is what makes us worry so," Jashbahr Patel told correspondent Andrew Jaffe. "You're taken away and never seen again. We struggle and struggle to stay within the law because we don't want to give them an excuse, you know."

The plain, earnest face of Jashbahr Patel does not suggest a threat to anybody. He is 40 years old, a husband, father of four and a high-school teacher by profession. Born in what is now Tanzania, he was brought by his family to Uganda when he was 6 years old and was educated in Ugandan schools before being sent to India for university training. He received a British passport, the only type of travel document available to people living in what was then Britain's Uganda colony. When independence came to Uganda in 1962, he never bothered to apply for his citizenship papers in the new nation. Thus, like thousands of other Asians in Uganda, Patel placed himself in the ill-defined status of a "British passport holder" in an East African state.

"We are sort of trapped by history," he concedes. "We are British passport holders but not British citizens. All our passports carry a special 'D' stamp [indicating that they were issued in a British dependency or Commonwealth country]. We know we are not really wanted in Britain. And now we are not wanted here, either. What's more, I cannot go home to India, my family's motherland," Patel observed. "So who am I?"

According to the definition of President Amin, Asians in Uganda are "economic saboteurs." Jashbahr Patel looked out of his apartment window at the darkening street below, crowded with Africans and Asians returning from work. "It is true, as Amin says, that even today business and commerce here are in the hands of the Asians. You could say the Asian people have not helped the Africans to come up in business," he added thoughtfully. "But what about me? I was never a businessman. I am a teacher. Until now, I considered myself a Ugandan. When an African student came into my class, I worked just as hard to help him as I would for any Asian student."

By no stretch of the imagination can Patel be described as wealthy. Still, by local standards, he is comfortably well off. His teacher's salary brings in $2,352 annually, and he has accumulated some $1,400 in savings. He drives an eight-year-old car, and his apartment boasts electricity and indoor plumbing (though no hot water on tap). But because Amin has decreed that each expelled family may take out only the equivalent of about $140—with the government seizing the rest—the Patels will soon be virtually penniless. Nonetheless, Jashbahr Patel is among the luckier ones. As a teacher, he has been placed in an exempt classification and asked by the Ugandans to remain on his job until a replacement is found, thus sparing the Patel family the need to meet the Nov. 8 exit deadline. What's more, the Patels have already obtained a valid entry voucher to Britain. As things now stand, Patel hopes to leave with his family sometime in December.

Why won't Uganda's Asians fight for their right to remain to keep what is theirs? "It just isn't our way," said Jashbahr Patel. "When something like this happens, we say it's God's will. I will lose my job, my home, my car, my money and have to start again somewhere else." Patel paused, still determined to look on the bright side of things, and added: "You know we are lucky the British will take us in."

'A FRIENDLY ATMOSPHERE'

Jashbahr Patel's older brother, Kanti (also a pseudonym), left Uganda for Britain last December. "There was no real political trouble in Uganda then," Kanti Patel recalls. But he could see the handwriting on the wall. During all of his working career, Patel had been employed in civil service or government-related jobs. But two years ago, he was squeezed out of his post and replaced by a Ugandan black—all, explains Patel with a wry smile, as part of the Ugandan Government's policy of "Africanization." However much he and his family found life in East Africa to their taste, Patel decided there was no economic future for them there. Accordingly, the 42-year-old Patel, his wife and four children boarded a plane for the long flight to London.

They arrived with $750 and a few possessions but adapted to their new surroundings with aplomb. Before long, Mrs. Patel found work as a sorter in a laundry. And three and a half months of combing the want ads paid off for Kanti Patel in the form of a job with the Greater London Council processing parking tickets, which provides the family with an annual income of about $3,800. "I like the job, and it is a very friendly atmosphere in the

Continued on Page 80

Reproduced with permission ©Los Angeles Times

Continued from Page 79

Uganda: The Outcast's Story

office," says Kanti Patel, a short, stocky, unfailingly courteous man who speaks in a lilting East African accent. In addition, the Patels' 17-year-old daughter was accepted as a clerk-trainee in a neighborhood bank, and their three younger children found places almost immediately in a local school.

Despite the railings of some British politicians against a "new influx of colored immigrants"— and isolated signs of a white backlash among some segments of the British working class—the Patels insisted to NEWSWEEK'S Angus Deming that they have never yet encountered racial hostility in Britain. In fact, more than 50 voluntary organizations throughout Britain have been mobilized to take the penniless, confused Asians in hand the moment they arrive at London's airports. Empty barracks at three unused military bases have been readied for possible service as emergency lodging, and volunteers stand ready to supply transportation, warm clothes and even toys for the children. As of last week, only about 100 of Uganda's expelled Asians had reached Britain, and no one could be certain that everything would go smoothly when the big influx hits. For now at least, the response of most Britons to the new immigrants seems to be precisely the opposite of the hostility that had been predicted.

As it turned out for the Kanti Patels, their only complaint was directed at the slumlord—also an Asian—from whom they rent their tiny, two-room flat in north London at a rent of more than $30 a week. "Look at this place," said an outraged Patel. "My wife and I sleep here; our youngest boy has to sleep on that tiny day bed 3 feet away and the three other children have to sleep in the sitting room. We have to share the bathroom with the family downstairs. And yet, I suspect that this hateful landlord will demand more rent. Frankly, sir, some of the Asian landlords treat their own people very badly, indeed. They are clearly without mercy."

With his brother's family due to arrive in London shortly, Kanti Patel says he will do his best to help them get settled and find jobs. But he obviously has few resources to spare. The only luxury that he has allowed himself is a rented color-TV set. "The children kept telling me how much they wanted one," he said apologetically. "Now they're happy, so I'm happy and, oh well, it's only money." Eternal optimism seems to be a Patel family trait, and only occasionally does a sign of homesickness flicker across Kanti Patel's round, cheerful face. "I must confess that I don't find the weather here very agreeable," he said as he gazed at the gray London sky and the light drizzle falling outside. "Our second winter here is approaching. Just the thought of it is enough to make me chilly."

Continued from Page 78

Sledgehammer murders

had survived two years in Makindye with little hope of release.

Indentification or description of the many and varied personalities would lead inevitably to vicious retaliation but it can be recorded that they included a man whose sole offence was the purchase of a few household implements from an expelled Asian.

There was a trader from a neighbouring country who had been arrested by border guards, accused of smuggling and had his four-wheeled drive car appropriated by the guards of Makindye.

There were refugees from other African countries who had been snatched from their beds a month before and swallowed up by the barracks, their whereabouts unknown to anyone outside.

There were also four senior Ugandan police officers, dismissed by Amin in his purge of the force two weeks ago.

With some prescience of their fate, perhaps, they organise twice-daily Christian prayer services in a corner of the cell.

On Monday evening they were summoned outside "to the office" and instructed to leave their belongings in the cell. Five hours later the guards returned, to announce casually that the four had been killed and to take away their personal effects.

At midnight, the iron door, the sound of which brought instant and expectant dread to the faces of the inmates, opened to admit two Asians.

Caked with blood

The shirt of one was caked with blood. His chin was split. He had been stopped at a police road block near Kampala, ordered to lie face down on the verge and beaten by security men.

What had he done wrong? A shrug. Nothing more than getting stopped at a police road block.

Most of the blood on his shirt was from his friend who was so badly beaten he had to be taken to hospital. He hoped.

The other Asian, a slight, thin-faced man, sat shivering and speechless in a corner. He, too, had been beaten and relieved of his money by security police.

A sultry afternoon silence was broken by the shrieked commands of the guards outside. Prisoners from an adjoining cell block were ordered outside to unload several bodies from a truck.

The bodies, seen through a vent in our cell wall, were those of civilians. Later we heard the they died from sledgehammer blows to the skull.

This, it seems, is the favoured method of execution at Makindye. It is silent and prevents the panic among other prisoners that gunfire might cause.

We filed into the fading afternoon sun into the compound—the only time we were allowed out of the cell—to scoop our inedible dinner of stodgy maise and rancid meat from dustbins.

In an adjoining compound, the guards were enjoying themselves by making two half-caste teenagers perform athletic feats. The youngsters faltered and a soldier, spittle on lips, screamed abuse and brought his rifle-butt smacking on their skulls. It was a sound we heard frequently from within.

Dawn found the elderly Muslim in Cell Block One A already praying. We queued silently to use together the broken toilet. No towels. No soap. No toilet paper.

And Ulster, too

An African fellow-prisoner noticed us wince at the sound of a beating outside. He came over to apologise for African brutality. We comforted him by talking about Ulster.

The sporadic visits by the guards, often with no more purpose than to abuse a new prisoner, made relaxed sleep impossible, even when one became adjusted to the concrete floor.

In following their orders the guards had difficulty in restraining themselves with the Whites.

Lars Holmstrom, one of the Swedes, incurred the wrath of a junior officer when he misunderstood an instruction and failed to put his home address on a piece of paper.

A boot and a rifle butt were raised, restrained at the last minute and Holmstrom was made to lie full length and roll up and down the length of the cell several times.

Failure to communicate is extremely dangerous in Makindye.

Despair showed in our cell companions' faces when it became clear that we were to be released.

We assumed that someone in the Ugandan civil service realised the error of curbing Press activity by making correspondents privy to one of the country's darkest and most sinister institutions.

The Makindye establishment serves no social or military function at all.

As we were handed back our belongings and deportation orders at the prison gate, we learned that our colleagues had fared better.

They shared a cell block with Manubhai Madvhani, the Asian millionaire, industrialist, philosopher and benefactor, who was arrested a fortnight ago.

The Madvhani presence, they said, gave a lift to the morale of the whole cell block. He is cheerful, always dignified and resigned to whatever fate Amin decrees.

But even with the gates of Makindye behind us, the violence prevailed. Hard by the entrance, Ugandan soldiers held down a man while a woman whipped him repeatedly.

The man was screaming. The soldiers were laughing. No one intervened.

After only a few days at Makindye the scene did not seem to be that abnormal.

Page 80 | *Uganda Asian Expulsion: 90 Days and Beyond through the Eyes of the International Press*

Immigrants' terror: 'One word and we are dead'
AMIN'S RAMPAGING SOLDIERS HOLD ASIANS TO RANSOM

By HUGH DAVIES
Reprinted with permission, ©Telegraph Group Limited, London,
September 25, 1972

REFUGEES arriving at Stansted airport from Uganda yesterday told of Ugandan soldiers rampaging through villages, demanding ransom for hostages and of a youth dragged from his car to be machine-gunned to death.

Mr Ramam Patel, 42, a jeweller, who had fled with his son, said: "nobody dares to say anything. One word and we are dead, or one of our family vanishes."

Clutching bundles of belongings, 185 refugees were flown in on the second major airlift, all looked slightly happier than the 193 who had arrived six days before.

Although most of their money was taken at Entebbe airport, they had—unlike the first refugees—avoided the plundering activities of soldiers manning a series of roadblocks on the 20-mile journey from Kampala.

A week before, Asians were dragged from cars and many were assaulted and robbed of jewellery.

Armed police escort

On Saturday, refugees travelled in a convoy of 10 buses and were escorted through checkpoints by two truckloads of armed police.

Descriptions of life in Uganda given by the latest batch of refugees to arrive were far more harrowing than those of their predecessors.

The Mehta family—a mother, her daughter and three sons—told of a 24-year old friend, a shopkeeper, dragged from his Mercedes car at gunpoint in a Kampala street.

Hitesh Mehta, 16, said: "soldiers asked him why he was driving such a large car. Then he was taken off."

The family believe the youth was held in the notorious Makindye military barracks. On Friday, said Hitesh, the youth's relatives, who had begged the authorities for information, were told to go to Mulago hospital.

"There were six bodies in the mortuary, all marked with machine gun bullets. One was that of our friend."

The Mehtas had a few Ugandan shillings with them. Their blankets and clothes were wrapped in parcels.

Left in tears

The daughter said: "We left my father in tears at our home. He hopes to join us. But we have no idea when."

As the family were taken to the airport on Saturday afternoon, they said, buses passed them going towards Kampala carrying troops flying the Libyan flag.

Other Asians said Ugandan soldiers who had not been paid for two months were terrorising villages 50 miles from Kampala. Men were being taken as hostages and ransoms of 40,000 shillings (£2,000) demanded from their wives.

Without homes

From yesterday's flight 133 people without homes were taken to the Government's transit camp at Stradishall, Suffolk.

Others left for Harlow, Enfield, Oldham, Wisbech, Wellingborough, Harrow and Upper Norwood.

After satisfying Ugandan resettlement board officials they had settled addresses to go to several groups were allowed to leave for Government "red areas" already hard-pressed for amenities.

Sixteen Asians traveled to Birmingham, three to Leicester and 19 to London.

Lord Thorneycroft, a member of the Ugandan Resettlement Board, spent yesterday touring the former RAF camp at Stradishall, Suffolk, which by last night had become the temporary home of more than 400 Asians.

On a green, which the refugees have been using as a meeting place to sit and exchange experiences of their last days in Kampala, he spoke to Babu Patel, 24.

Mr Patel thanked him for "getting me a home." He added: "We will show our gratitude by deeds not words." He is hopeful of a job as a mechanic at Dagenham, providing he can find a place to live.

He is staying with his brother's family of five in one of the many blocks of red-bricked houses on the 700-acre site.

Bare furnishings

They have tried to make the place homey—a difficult job, they admit, without carpets and just bare furnishings of beds, tables and chairs.

Life at the camp revolves around the canteen where vegetable curry and rice is a favorite dish, and the house.

Although an Asian has established himself as a regular in the local inn, the Cherry Tree, where he drinks light ale, most of the men prefer to stay on the site.

They are anxious to be close to the Department of Employment office in case a job is found with that all-important extra—somewhere to live.

While the men have spent their days either at job interviews or walking the tree-lined paths of the camp their wives and children have been taken out by local people.

Residents of Haverhill, seven miles away, call to take them for car runs in the countryside or to the local market.

Pocket money is provided by the Department of Social Security and spent in a store near the camp on essential items such as toothpaste and soap.

Advertisement

ANNOUNCEMENT
CANADA

The Canadian High Commission announces that the first chartered flight by the Government of Canada (Air Canada) will depart Entebbe International Airport on Wednesday September 27.

All persons who have been booked by the Canadian Immigration Office for this first charter flight must assemble at the North Parking Lot (off Ternan Avenue) of the Kampala International Hotel at 8.00 a.m. Wednesday, September 27. Bus transportation to the airport will be provided for flight passengers ONLY. A charge of Sh. 15/- per person for transportation will be collected. An Airport Tax of Shs. 15/- will also be levied at the Airport.

Baggage Allowance is STRICTLY LIMITED to twenty (20) Kilograms per passenger (over two years) plus a small flight bag. No excess baggage will be allowed under any circumstances. Please note that the parking facilities of the Hotel are for patrons only and therefore flight passengers arriving at the Hotel in motor vehicles will not be able to PARK THERE.

Ugandan Asian Expulsion: 90 Days and Beyond through the Eyes of the International Press

Tickets now available at the Bank of Uganda

Reprinted with permission, ©Uganda Argus, September 26, 1972

A GOVERNMENT spokesman has stated that, in order to facilitate the acquisition of tickets by the departing Asians, arrangements have been made for air, rail and sea tickets to be available for sale in the premises of the Bank of Uganda.

All departing Asians are, therefore, expected to buy heir travelling tickets as soon as they have obtained their final exit clearance at the bank. They should, therefore, carry with them sufficient money at the time of obtaining final clearance with the Bank of Uganda so as to buy all the necessary tickets for themselves and members of their families before leaving the bank premises. The purchase of tickets there and then is obligatory.

The spokesman has further stated that Asians who have successfully verified their claims for Uganda citizenship and those who received specific exemption from the provisions of Decree No 17 of 1972 should report to the Immigration office, Kampala, to buy special identity cards to facilitate their continued stay and movements in Uganda.

The spokesman emphasised that this exercise is not for verification of claims for Uganda citizenship, since the period for verification of Uganda citizenship ended this month on the tenth. Requests to verify claims for Uganda citizenship will therefore, not be entertained under any circumstances.

Persons required to have identity cards, that is Uganda citizens of Asian origin and those who have received specific exemption when reporting to the Immigration office, to buy the special identity cards must take with them.

Photographs

(a) Two passport size photographs of themselves.

(b) Documentary proofs that they had successfully verified their claims for Uganda citizenship.

(c) Documentary proofs that they have received specific exemption from the provisions of the decree.

The cost of each identity card is 15/- and will be issued as follows—those employed in Government Departments, Government parastatal bodies, Co-operative Movement, the East African Community and international organisations should report between 7a.m. and 7 p.m. on Tuesday (today) and tomorrow.

All others should report between 7 a.m. and 7 p.m. from Thursday through to Tuesday October 3, including Saturday and Sunday.

MOI TELLS UGANDAN ASIANS TO GO FOR NEW IDENTITY CARDS

By NATION Reporter
Reprinted with permission, ©Daily Nation, Nairobi, September 27, 1972

KENYAN Vice-President Mr. Daniel arap Moi yesterday announced that Ugandan citizen Asians in Kenya must return to Uganda immediately to obtain their identity cards.

He also directed that Asian British passport holders who are residents of Uganda are required to report with their passports to the British High Commission in Nairobi to make arrangements for their inclusion in the Uganda quota of vouchers for them to travel to Britain at the appropriate time.

Mr. Moi requested that employers of these categories of Asians co-operate in the exercise to ensure that none of them were stranded in Kenya without the appropriate authority to enter either Uganda or Britain.

Meanwhile, President William Tolbert of Liberia has appealed to President Amin to ensure that Asians being expelled from Uganda suffer as little hardship as possible.

The Mombasa office of the Shipping Corporation of India announced last night that the State of Haryana due to sail for India on September 30 has no fewer than 300 vacant berths.

Expectations that this sailing would be confined to expelled Asians from Uganda have not materialised and those interested in availing of the unexpected availability of berths are asked to contact the shipping line's agents in Nairobi or Mombasa.

Toronto Families asked to open homes to Asians

News Compilation, September 27, 1972

TORONTO—Local residents have been asked to open their homes to Asian refugees from Uganda to help them settle in the city.

The Toronto reception committee, for the refugees—comprised of representatives from the local Asian community and the three levels of government—also is appealing for volunteers to help meet the refugees and show them around Toronto.

"We are looking for families—Canadian or Asian—who would be willing to take a refugee family into their home until they can get settled in more permanent accommodation," Anand Chopra, committee secretary, said Tuesday.

Mr. Chopra said the committee is compiling a list of employment opportunities and wants to hear from anyone who can offer a Ugandan refugee a job.

Ugandan aid groups set in 10 Canadian cities

News Compilation, September 27, 1972

OTTAWA—The state secretary's department announced today that special committees are being set up in 10 cities across Canada to help immigrants from Uganda get settled in new homes.

The department said the committees will included representatives of the federal and provincial governments, voluntary agencies and Asian communities. They will be formed in Montreal, Ottawa, Toronto, Hamilton, Windsor, Winnipeg, Edmonton, Regina, Vancouver and Victoria.

Their function will be to provide immigrants with information on housing, schools, transportation, credit, buying and orientation programs.

The department said the make-up of each committee will be announced soon.

Peace plan accepted by Uganda, Tanzania

News Compilation, September 26, 1972

Foreign Minister Omar Arteh of Somalia said today Tanzania and Uganda have accepted a five-point peace plan, details of which will be announced shortly. He added that a cease-fire already was in effect.

CANADA

Renovated military base first home
Curry, cots and counselling await Ugandan refugee flights

By NORMAN HARTLEY
Globe and Mail Reporter
Reprinted with permission, ©The Globe & Mail, Toronto,
September 28, 1972

MONTREAL—Curry, cots and counselling were all ready yesterday to receive the first planeload of Asian refugees from Uganda, due here early this morning.

The first plane, an Air Canada DC-8 with 145 Asians and two Canadian officials aboard, left Entebbe Airport in Uganda yesterday.

"We're treating the flight as a trial run to test out our hotel," a senior Canadian Armed Forces spokesman said. "I think everything is ready, but we don't do too many operations like this one."

The hotel is the Longue Pointe military base, a little-used former ordnance school in the east end of Montreal that has undergone hasty renovations in the 10 days.

Accommodation, food, medical and dental facilities and advice on everything from the climate in Edmonton to job opportunities in Vancouver are available. Officials of the Department of Manpower and Immigration, together with Armed Forces personnel, have turned almost the entire base into a reception area. "We can accommodate 600 refugees without becoming too crowded and we could push it to 1,000 if we really had to," a spokesman said.

Officials here hope, however, to keep the number of refugees in Longue Pointe at any one time below 600 and their target is to process each arrival and arrange transportation to his future home within 48 hours.

Canada will be receiving about 5,000 of the Ugandans, Bryce Mackasey, Manpower and Immigration Minister said yesterday.

"I think that's a pretty realistic figure based on the number of applications we have received," he said in Toronto.

Officials here are expecting an average of one planeload of about 160 refugees per day, with possibly two planes on Sundays. Seven flights are due in the coming week and by next week it is expected that there will be a regular daily flight.

At Longue Pointe yesterday, everyone who will be coming into contact with the refugees— military and civilian personnel, press and visitors—received a smallpox vaccination. A medical officer estimated that 600 to 1,000 people would be vaccinated during the day.

The first plane was due at 3:35 a.m. and the refugees were to be welcomed at Dorval Airport by Mr. Mackasey, then taken by bus the 20 miles to Longue Pointe. Over the next two days, they will receive clothing, food, $10 to $15 pocket money, advice on the next stage of their journey— and a chance to rest.

The army and civilian cooks have been given a crash course in preparing Indian food. "But I expect we'll get mostly requests for steak and bacon and eggs," one cook said with a smile.

Manpower counsellors from all regions have set up booths here and when the refugees have chosen their final destination, transportation will be arranged.

The refugees will receive loans to cover the cost of their fares inside the country, to be repaid at 6 per cent interest when they have settled in. They will not have to pay for their flights from Uganda.

Some jobs offered
First Ugandans arrive today

Reprinted with permission, ©Montreal Gazette, September 28, 1972

An Air Canada DC 8 jet bearing 145 British Asians from Uganda left Kampala airport yesterday afternoon and was to touch down at Montreal International airport before dawn this morning.

The flight begins a mercy airlift to a new life in Canada for several thousand Asians expelled by the African country.

The group—which included eight children— was seen off by Canadian High Commissioner William Olivier and was accompanied by two Canadian government officials. Another flight is slated to leave tomorrow and two more on Monday.

About 1,500 British Asians have been granted visas for Canada, but up to 5,000 or more are expected when the airlift comes to an end.

MACKASEY

Manpower and Immigration Minister Bryce Mackasey was to meet the group at the airport before they were bused to beds, meals and interviews with government officials at Longue Pointe army barracks east end Montreal.

Tejpal Thind, president of the India-Canada Association, said Montreal firms and individual had already offered the Ugandans 42 jobs and he was expecting more. He said 12 of the job offers

---

TORONTO   **Uganda Committee**
Group puts a roof over first family

Reprinted with permission, ©The Globe & Mail, Toronto,
September 28, 1972

Response to a request by the Toronto Uganda Committee for help in arranging temporary accommodation for the estimated 800 to 1,000 displaced Asians expected to come to Toronto has been "very good," according to the committee's secretary, Anand Chopra.

Mr. Chopra said yesterday over 200 calls offering aid had been received within the first of this committee's appeal.

"We have had offers of clothing, shelter and jobs, not only from Asians," he said.

"If the response continues, we'll be able to solve the problem easily."

Mr. Chopra said firms as far away as Guelph, Sarnia, and Hamilton had called with job prospects, as well as Toronto businesses.

The Toronto group had its first refugee family to look after yesterday when a man, his wife and child arrived at Toronto International Airport. The man, an accountant, said he had decided to leave Uganda before the Canadian charter flight departure "for personal reasons."

He refused to be photographed, and asked that his name not be printed.

Instead of waiting for today's Canadian federally-sponsored charter flight, he and his family took a flight to London, then flew to Toronto—at their own expense.

"One thing I want to say is that the Canadian immigration people in Kampala are wonderful. All the processing was smoothly done," he said.

Mr. Chopra said last night the family would be accommodated with one of the volunteers who had called the committee, and a job hunt would begin immediately.

He said the only problem facing the committee now is the shortage of bedding. "A lot of the volunteers need extra pillow, sheets and blankets." Mr. Chopra said the committee would arrange to pick up supplies if the donors would call 924-8401.

---

alone came from Canco Corporation. Most of the offers were for skilled technical help.

"I have heard from Manpower that they have many more jobs open for the Ugandans," said Thind, who is also appealing for clothing and emergency funds for the refugees, many whom were forced to leave their belongings in Uganda.

He said the first offers of help have come from Hungarians. "One Hungarian man told me he had been through the same thing before and wanted to do all he could to help," said Thind.

Thind can be reached at 931-7866.

Ultimatum not enforced

News Compilation, September 26, 1972

An order here making it compulsory for Asians to buy departure tickets on receiving exit clearance follows the ultimatum on Friday that departing Asians must leave the country within 48 hours of receiving clearance.

At least 8,000 have been cleared. Most of them are here, but there are no signs that the Government is enforcing it.

The effect of the ultimatum, however, has been a sharp speeding up of the departure rate. For the third successive day, the British High Commission has issued well over 1,000 entry certificates.

Ugandan Asian Expulsion: 90 Days and Beyond through the Eyes of the International Press

Ugandan Asians overwhelmed by welcome
Canadians sacrifice hockey to receive refugees

By NORMAN HARTLEY, Globe and Mail Reporter
Reprinted with permission, ©The Globe & Mail, Toronto,
September 29, 1972

MONTREAL—Perhaps the best tribute to the success of the opening day of Canada's Ugandan refugee operation yesterday was that it went on uninterrupted right through the Canada-Russia hockey game.

Despite the clearly unbearable temptations of three television sets bringing the match into the barracks assembly at Longue Pointe, the joint military-civilian team went on doggedly with the job of speeding the first 138 Asians on their way across Canada.

Most of the refugees did not appreciate the sacrifice but they had already gathered that the idea was to make them feel really welcome.

The refugees—the first of 5,000 officially expected by the end of October—were overwhelmed by their reception.

The armed forces and the Department of Manpower and Immigration found a lot of minor faults with their first day in the refugee business but the Ugandans found none.

"Even the Indian food was authentic," one woman said. "It was better than what I can cook at home. They thought of absolutely everything."

The armed forces had, in fact, brought in a Montreal Indian restaurant owner last week to give the military cooks two days of lessons.

"We certainly did not want to offend the refugees right on the first day by giving them food they were not allowed to eat because of their religious beliefs," an armed forces spokesman said.

From a dawn welcome at Dorval airport by Immigration Minister Bryce Mackasey throughout a day of resting, completing customs and immigration formalities and receiving advice on job opportunities, the Ugandans remained bewildered by the efforts made on their behalf.

"I don't know if we'll be able to keep this up over the coming weeks but we will certainly try," one senior officer said.

Because of the difficult and often brutal experiences some Asians had suffered at the hands of Uganda's military, the Canadian servicemen at Longue Pointe had received special briefings telling them not to behave in a military way if they could help it—and it worked, at least for the first day.

The armed forces had been told to expect 35 flights of about 160 refugees each at a rate of roughly one a day.

The friendly welcome and a day of bright sunshine helped but the mood of the first arrivals was one of relief, with much sadness and depression evident in the quieter moments of the day.

The break with Uganda came more easily for some than for others.

A 16-year-old student of a Kampala secondary school, Kaushik Patel, will have one of

Montreal International Airport: The first of some five thousand expelled Ugandan Asians expected to make Canada their home.
Reproduced with permission ©United Press International/Corbis Bettmann

the quickest transitions to a Canadian life.

He was met at Longue Pointe by his elder brother, Chan, a metals technician at Noranda, who came to Canada four years ago.

Within a couple of days, Kaushik will be a student at Noranda High School where he is already enrolled.

Many others came with no plan and some were still stunned at leaving both family and possessions behind.

"It's a really amazing feeling," one woman said, "We just walked out of our house, closed the doors and left everything inside as it was. Our relatives had already left for Britain. We just abandoned everything except our clothes and this radio."

Others gave household possessions away to servants. "I gave away a car," one civil servant said. "I couldn't sell it and it would have just been confiscated."

Many were afraid to give their names to the press and one man became terrified when a television cameraman started to film his family. "Many of us did not even tell our friends we were leaving, we were so afraid of being stopped," he said. "If those pictures are seen back in Uganda, it will cause terrible trouble for relatives still there."

One of the biggest losers was Sikander Jatha, who, with his brothers, abandoned a family business that employed 200 people and was founded by his grandfather in 1912.

"We had a beryllium mine about 240 miles from Kampala and a supermarket," he said.

Mr. Jatha was leaving for Vancouver with his young wife, Nargis. "I don't know what I will do, but I have done lots of jobs. I know the mining business and I used to manage a hotel and I've worked at the Toyota dealership in Kampala."

In the party yesterday were 24 families, including 48 children, and 42 single men and women.

When operations shut down at Longue Pointe at 5:15 p.m. yesterday, 90 of the 138 people had been dealt with and most of them left last night for their Canadian destinations. The other 48 should be on their way by this afternoon, a spokesman said.

Of the 90 cleared yesterday, 34 were classified as breadwinners—single people or heads of families. Of these there were 14 clerks, six from managerial positions, two engineers, two teachers, eight mechanics and technicians, a barber and a truck driver.

Their destinations were: Sarnia, 1; Montreal, 2; Cornwall, 1; Vancouver, 15; Calgary, 2; Toronto, 4; Winnipeg, 1; Edmonton, 3; Hamilton, 2; Scarborough, 1; London, 1; and Waterloo, 1.

CANADA

Fear for friends and relatives
Asians' silence says it all

By ANGELA FERRANTE
Reprinted with permission, ©Montreal Star, September 29, 1972

The exiled Ugandan Asians who arrived here yesterday to start new lives fear for the safety of those who remain behind.

Yesterday at the Longue Pointe Canadian Armed Forces base, where they went through immigration proceedings the tired Ugandans answered questions about their homeland with evasive eyes, nervous little laughs and thinly veiled sarcasm. None would venture to judge the actions of the Ugandan government which expelled them.

"We can say nothing until all our friends and families have left," one of them said.

One 29-year-old salesman from Kampala who refused to give his name said: "If I make a statement on how things are, it will not be good for the people still in Uganda. It might get them into trouble—they are my fellow brothers. I'm safe ...I'm in Canada. But what about them?"

He has been separated from his wife and three children for three months now. They had been in India on vacation when President Idi Amin gave his expulsion order and were not allowed return home.

Dressed neatly in a business suit and clasping his hands nervously, the young Ugandan said he did not know where he wanted to settle in Canada. But as soon as he gets a job and a house he will send for his wife.

Commenting on why the immigrants would not discuss the political situation in Uganda, he said that "we never decided all together that we would say nothing. We just felt it."

Mrs. Maureen D'Cunha wife of a senior auditor in the Ugandan civil service and mother of two, tried to explain why the people were so nervous about talking.

Silence explained

"Most people will wait for their friends to get out before saying anything that might jeopardize them. When the first Ugandans arrived in England, the English papers asked frank questions and got frank replies. But ever since, there has been a tightening up. You musts be very careful of what you write.

"Are the people scared? That's an understatement. They're terrified."

Mrs. D'Cunha and her husband made the decision to leave Uganda just six hours before the plane took off. They are Ugandan citizens and he worked for the government for most of his career.

"Everyone is trying to get out," Mrs. D'Cunha said. Every other day something happens. We were looking behind our shoulders all the way to the airport until we got into the plane. When the plane was three hours late, we thought the idea of leaving had been too good to be true."

The family left behind all their belongings, a house and money in the bank. They emigrated without even telling their servants or their friends.

Dr. K. Jokhani who is "stateless" according to Uganda, said, "I've always been stateless so I don't belong anywhere and that's all right."

Her parents, still in Uganda, have British citizenship, but Britain refused to extend it to her. On the point of being a citizen for the first time in a new country, the 25-year-old doctor said she will probably go to Vancouver, because of its mild climate.

All the Ugandans left with just personal belongings.

"The ladies were allowed to carry two bangles, a necklace and earrings," said 18-year-old Aju: She is just out of secretarial school and hopes to work in Toronto.

She said jokingly of her exile: "I didn't leave because I had to. I just felt like a change."

Dr. P. A. Amin said that those with property had to assess its value and give it into the ministry of commerce.

"They have promised to give it back later. They haven't told us how. If we hadn't registered the value of the property with them, they said the government could not be held responsible later on."

Some of the Ugandans were a bit more willing to talk about conditions back

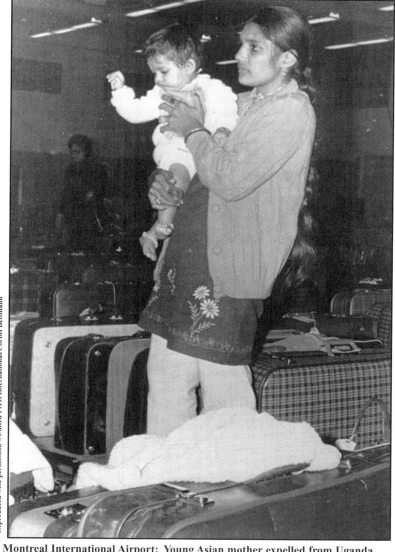

Montreal International Airport: Young Asian mother expelled from Uganda surrounded by luggage brought by the Asians on the first flight to Canada.

home. Rashida, a 26-year-old hairdresser, said: "things seemed quite calm but the people were always afraid. No one goes out after 6p.m. When a rumor starts flying, people go running home. It seems to be the safest place to go."

Dr. Amin said that while it is true people stay at home, "they do it because they want to. They are restricting themselves just to be on the safe side."

"Still those of us who must go out to work—as a doctor I had to work in the hospital—nothing happened to us," he said.

While their parents were going through the manpower screening program, about 43 children were playing ball outside or tag inside the gymnasium at the base.

The Ugandans, who started to go through manpower processing early in the afternoon after a few hours sleep, spoke mostly of broken up families, scattered to Britain and India or wherever a passport would take them. They also spoke of their gratitude to Canada.

"We are so proud to be in Canada," beamed Mrs. D'Cunha. "Yesterday it was my son's birthday—he was six—and he said the flight was the best birthday present anybody could give him."

"Canada was the one which made the first offer to us and the Canadians were the fastest workers in Uganda trying to get these people out."

"The Canadians who had not been involved with us and with no responsibility to us, just came to help us. That is why we are doubly overwhelmed by what you have done for us."

Asian who left everything he owned: 'What is money? I'm a strong man'

Reprinted with permission, ©Toronto Star syndicate, September 29, 1972

MONTREAL— "What is money, after all?" said Hamil Nagla. "I've got a brain. I've got hands. I've got a new home—Canada."

Nagla, 31, arrived penniless in Montreal yesterday from Uganda with his wife Jaya, 23, and sons Raju, 5 and Arun, 2.

"I worked as a hairdresser in Kampala (the Ugandan capital) for 13 years," he said last night over dinner provided for Asian refugees at the armed forces base mess hall at Longue Pointe.

"I had my own shop—the business was worth 25,000 bob (Ugandan shillings)."

That amount is worth $3,500 at the official exchange rate and bout $700 outside Uganda. But it is rare to find anyone wanting to by Ugandan currency.

"When I left Kampala to get on the Air Canada charter plane to Montreal I just walked out of my shop. I didn't even bother to close my door.

"Now I'm going to try my luck in Vancouver. I'm a strong man," said Nagla who is a slim, but wiry 5 feet 5 inches.

"If I can't get a job as a hairdresser I can work on a farm, drive a tractor, pick fruit—anything.

"I know nobody in Canada is going to rob me of my work and my country the way President (Idi) Amin has."

Asians leaving Uganda on the expulsion orders of Amin must leave all their property behind, thaking with them only about $140 in foreign currency.

EXCHANGE REFUSED

Nagla didn't even get that: "When I went to the Bank of Uganda (the government's central bank) they refused to let me change my shillings into foreign currency. They said: 'You are going to Canada. It is a very rich country. You don't need any money.' I told them they were thieves. They refused to give me anything."

It's a criminal offence in Uganda to try to take any shillings out of the country, so Nagla had to leave with no cash at all.

"I shouldn't have expected anything different," he said. "After all, they had already robbed me of my country.

"I was a Ugandan citizen. But when I went along to the authorities to have my papers checked they told me: 'We don't want barbers in our country.' They tore up my passport and citizenship papers and they told me to pack and up and get out.

"So now I am a stateless person.

"I couldn't argue with the officials. Most of them were soldiers with tommy-guns pointing at me.

"I'm afraid now that we Asians are going, the soldiers will start to turn on the Europeans. Two Sundays ago when there was a lot of trouble and shooting, I saw two soldiers beating an Italian in the street. They said he must be a spy because he could not speak good English."

Finishing a hearty meal of what Canadian army cooks figured was Asian-style curried rice, Nagla said: "Your soldiers don't look as frightening as troops in Uganda. They give us very nice dinners."

Continued on Page 87

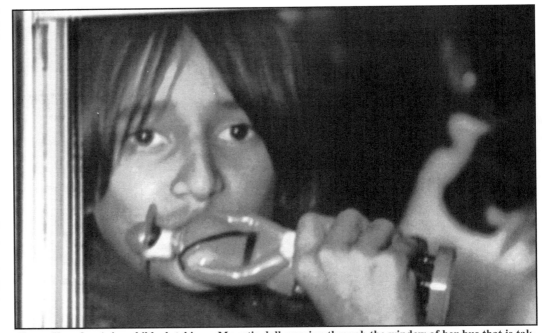

Above: Ugandan Asian child, clutching a Mountie doll, peering through the window of her bus that is taking her to Longue Pointe barracks from Montreal International Airport.
Below: Room, at the United Church of Canada in Hampsted, full of clothing and other goods donated by local citizens to be distributed to the Ugandan Asians. Reproduced with permission ©Pritchard/Sidaway/Gazette, Montreal

Ugandan couple like Canada because she 'really wants to help'

By Dennis Trudeau
Reprinted with permission, ©Canadian Press, 1972
Published in The Herald, Calgary, September 29, 1972

MONTREAL (CP) —Zul and Yasmin Rupani were married in Uganda 1-1/2 months ago—on the same day that President Idi Amin ordered all Asians out of the East African country.

Thursday, the young Asian couple, both accountants, were among 138 refugees in the first major group to arrive in Canada.

Two hours after their daybreak arrival, they were sipping coffee and eating cream cakes in a military gymnasium in east-end Montreal, waiting to be assigned temporary accommodations and thinking about their future in Canada.

" We like this country, you see," Mr. Rupani said, "a country that really wanted to help us."

They hope to go to Toronto where they have friends and will look for jobs.

They said they had heard "quite a bit" about Toronto.

As for the country they left, Yasmin said the political climate "was not really bad," but "people are trying to get out as fast as possible."

Both the Rupanis and another Ugandan couple had already made plans to leave their country before the expulsion order came.

LEFT POST

The second couple asked not to be identified because they still have relatives in Uganda and the husband had left his post as a senior agricultural officer without informing the government.

"We had foresight," the husband said, adding that they had already applied to Australia and Canada by the time the expulsion was announced. He was studying in Australia when the order came.

He holds a Ugandan passport while most of the refugees have British passports.

"I was also selected for Australia but I didn't like Australia," he said.

WANTS FARM

While they have not decided where they would like to go, the couple may choose Ontario which they said "has good soil."

'I would like to go to a small town and get a farming job," the agriculture officer said.

The two couples are typical of the Asian refugees encountered at the Longue Pointe military barracks where the immigration and manpower department has set up a reception centre for the Asians. Counsellors will help them decide on their final destination.

Both couples said they were relieved to be out of Uganda and happy to be in a country that "really wanted to help us."

Continued from Page 86

Asian says 'What is money?'

Nagla and his family with a loan of $30 from Canada Manpower and air tickets, were heading towards Vancouver and a possible job today.

"There's always something if you are ready to work hard," he said.

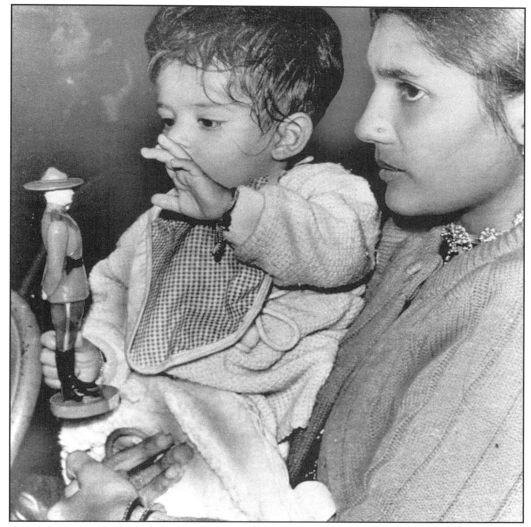

Above: Mrs Chiman Varu and her infant daughter Kishori arrived in Montreal this week. The child was presented with a Mountie Doll. Reproduced with permission ©Dick Darrell/Toronto Star Syndicate

Below: Arun Nagla, 2-1/2, works on a cupcake, while keeping an eye on the airport activity.

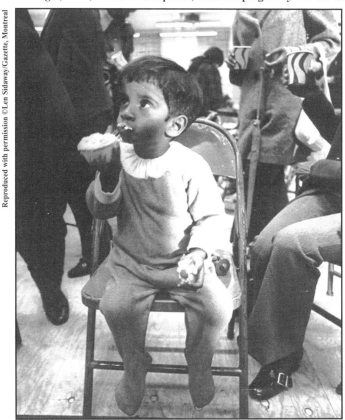

Reproduced with permission ©Len Sidaway/Gazette, Montreal

Ugandan Asian Expulsion: 90 Days and Beyond through the Eyes of the International Press

Asians' Exodus From Uganda Moves Slowly
Exile Invasion, Bureaucratic Red Tape, False Hopes Blamed for Airlift Delays

BY STANLEY MEISLER, Times Staff Writer
Reprinted with permission, ©Los Angeles Times, September 29, 1972

NAIROBI, Kenya—Vilified and harassed, the unwanted Asians are moving so slowly out of Uganda that some observers question whether they can meet President Idi Amin's expulsion deadline of Nov. 8.

Nevertheless, British officials in East Africa express confidence that the job can be done and that no British Asians will have to be herded into the military camps Amin has set aside for stragglers.

But, with the deadline only six weeks away, the main channel of exit, a special airlift, is barely under way. Relatively few Asians have left. Planes have left with seats unfilled.

Invasion Upset Airlift

There is no doubt that last week's mismanaged invasion by Ugandan exiles upset the airlift somewhat. But the invasion is not entirely to blame. The Ugandans and British have been blaming each other for the delays. And both—the Ugandans publicly and the British privately—have been blaming the Asians as well.

If the exodus accelerates from now on, the deadline can probably just be met. But only just. Much depends on the number of Asians in the expulsion. That vital statistic, however, is confused.

When Amin announced his expulsion of noncitizen Asians in 90 days, for "milking the economy of the country", it was assumed that there were 75,000 Asians in Uganda. Of these, 75,000 were believed to be British passport holders, 23,000 Ugandan citizens, and the rest Indian, Pakistani or stateless.

But Amin later decided to exempt some British Asians from his expulsion. They are the government technicians and private professionals sorely needed by Uganda. In fact, Amin's exemption was more like an edict. When some Asian professionals, sick of Uganda, decided to leave anyway, soldiers at the airport prevented their exit. The exact number exempted, however, is not known.

Tore Up Papers

At the same time, the Uganda government began a system of verifying the citizenship of Uganda Asians. For a variety of reasons, mainly technical and mostly arbitrary, officials began tearing up the citizenship papers of many Asians. The exact number is not known for sure, but some diplomats guess that half or even two-thirds of the citizens lost their citizenship. They became either British or stateless.

On top of all this the British ran stories a few weeks ago that talked of a steady, but quiet exodus of Asians from Uganda since the last census of 1969. Some articles said that there probably were 20,000 fewer Asians in Uganda than most people assumed. These stories, however, may have been somewhat off the mark, encouraged by British government officials who wanted to quiet fears in Britain about a "flood" of Asian immigrants.

Adding up all these uncertain pluses and minuses, an outsiders is left with the rather useless statistic that at the least, 35,000 Asians and, at the most, 60,000 Asians have to leave Uganda by Nov. 8. Perhaps the real figure is somewhere in the middle.

Price Haggling

Whatever the figure, most have to go by the airlift to Britain. But the airlift has taken weeks to organize, with the British and Ugandans arguing about the carriers and haggling about the price. Two weeks ago, it was agreed that East African Airways would handle half the flights while two British carriers, BOAC and British Caledonia, would handle the other half. The companies would fly 16 extra flights a week with a little more than 5,000 seats for Asian emigrants. The Asians also could fly out in any space available on the six regularly scheduled flights a week to London. The cost would be 2,000 Uganda shillings or $280 a seat.

The airlift began officially on Sept. 17 with a special flight of 193 Asians. But that was the day

Continued on Page 90

Life goes on as usual, or so it seems, in Uganda.   Reproduced with permission ©Archive Photos/Camera Press

Britain Seeks U.N. Help for Uganda Asians

BY DON SHANNON
Times Staff Writer
Reprinted with permission, ©Los Angeles Times, September 28, 1972

UNITED NATIONS—Britain asked all members of the United Nations Wednesday to take in Asians expelled from Uganda and to call on Ugandan President Idi Amin to extend his "arbitrary and inhuman deadline" of 90 days for the departure of 80,000 Asians.

The appeal was launched by British Foreign Secretary Sir Alec Douglas-Home in a speech to the General Assembly.

Delegates were surprised by the vehemence of the British attack on the actions of Gen. Amin, who has been described privately by some Britons as a "lunatic at large".

"This is an outrage against standards of human decency, in the face of which this assembly cannot remain silent," the British statesman declared. "These Asians have had their homes in Uganda, some of them for generations. They're now being ejected, stripped of most of their belongings and of their savings accumulated over many years."

Time Limit Assailed

Douglas-Home said earlier agreements for orderly evacuation of the Asians were "thrown out of the window" by Gen. Amin's fixing of a time limit.

"We do not accept that this deadline has any justification in law or in morality." Douglas-Home said in a voice edged with emotion, "We ask that the assembly debate this matter without delay and we are ready to table a resolution. I trust that it will be overwhelmingly accepted because, should this organization fail to do so, there's no one to whom any person, whatever the color of his skin, can turn for common justice."

Asian in Toronto finds a schoolmate

Reprinted with permission, ©Toronto Star syndicate, September 29, 1972

Twenty-six Ugandan Asians arrived at Union Station from Montreal at 7:30 this morning, carrying shopping bags and the only possessions they could carry.

Most of them were met by friends or relatives, but many refused to give their names, saying they still had relatives in Uganda and feared reprisal against them if they criticized the Ugandan government.

Subhash Chopra, whose family operates a boutique in Toronto, went down to the train "just to see them arrive—after all, they're my country people," and he met a schoolmate from Uganda.

The 24-year-old man, one who wouldn't give his name, plans to stay in Toronto and hopes to find work in marketing with an oil company, similar to the job he had back home.

He was wearing a Maple Leaf pin, which he said was given to each of the immigrants by the Canadian high commissioner in Uganda.

Mr. and Mrs. Mohammed Merchant, their son, Nieem, 9, and daughter, Sameena, 7, said they are going on by train to London to meet Mrs. Merchant's brother, Dr. Sadru Abatin.

They said that if the Canadian high commissioner had not escorted them to the aircraft in Uganda, the Ugandans would have taken they had.

They said they had no money, but another family said they did manage to get out a necklace, and watches with the personal possessions that they could carry.

This family, a husband, wife, daughter and the wife's sister, said they had left a new car behind, plus their home and all their furniture, but fled "because we were afraid of being killed."

A brother of the two women, a University of Toronto student, said their father and other members of the family were still in Uganda and they feared they would not be released.

The refugees who had no one meeting them and no place to stay were taken to the Canada Manpower office on Dundas St. E. to register while federal and provincial authorities made arrangements for their housing and meals.

Toronto lawyer Shanti Shah, chairman of the Asian committee in the city, said there had been a "tremendous response" from Canadians, offering housing, jobs and clothing for the Ugandans.

Representatives from the provincial citizenship branch of the Ministry of Social and Family Services talked with the refugees and will help the newcomers to get settled, a spokesman said.

Maurice Pinto was one of those who had no relative or friend to meet him but he appeared smiling and happy on his arrival.

"I would like to express my sincere appreciation to the Canadian people for their hospitality," he told The Star. "From our departure in Kampala to our destination here, everything was carried out with perfect co-ordination by so many of the various organizations and we hope to be citizens of credit to the Canadian nation."

Eleven of the 26 will be staying in Toronto, immigration authorities said, and the others are going to other western Ontario cities, including Kitchener, Guelph, London, Sarnia and Brantford.

Mrs. Jagdish Byas of Brampton met her sister, Mrs. Shobha Jani, and her 3-year-old daughter, Sonal, and said she would be taking them back to her home until they can get settled.

Mrs. Jani was an elementary school teacher in Uganda. She said she "just wanted to rest after three days of travelling."

All 26 were taken to breakfast in Union Station by immigration officials and Travellers Aid staff members, but some had less than an hour before catching other trains.

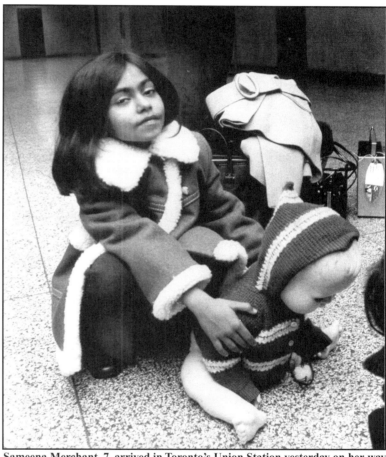

Sameena Merchant, 7, arrived in Toronto's Union Station yesterday on her way to London, Ontario.   Reproduced with permission ©Dick Darrell/Toronto Star Syndicate

Uganda Hits Plea for U.N. Debate on Asians

BY DON SHANNON
Times Staff Writer
Reprinted with permission, ©Los Angeles Times, September 29, 1972

UNITED NATIONS—Uganda protested Thursday against British demands for U.N. debate on the expulsion of Asian British subjects from the African state, contending that their lives are safe and that they will be paid for their lost property.

It appeared, however, that the Ugandan expulsion issue will join terrorism as a subject for assembly discussion later in the session.

Ugandan Ambassador G. S. Ibingira told the General Assembly's steering committee he opposed debate of his country's expulsion of Asians. he observed that Britain had never

Continued on Page 90

VANCOUVER, CANADA
City gets its first Ugandan refugees

Reprinted with permission, ©Vancouver Sun, September 29, 1972

After 25 hours of travelling, an exhausted family of four—the first Asians expelled from Uganda to arrive in B.C.—arrived at Vancouver International Airport Thursday night.

As dozens of flash bulbs went off, the youngest member of the family, a two-year-old boy, burst into tears. Although his five-year-old sister was silent, tears also ran down her cheeks.

"We are very, very tired," said their stylishly-dressed 30-year-old mother. Her husband is 27, an accountant. He did not want his name released for fear of repercussions by the Ugandan government against relatives still in that country.

Rod McDougall, acting coordinator for the movement of the Asian Ugandans, said the family had no money except what was given them by the government in Montreal.

They are meeting officials from the department of Manpower and immigration today to try to find accommodation and to discuss job qualifications, he said.

"We will provide them with financial assistance until they no longer need it," he said.

Asked if there is any limit on the length of time they can rely on government assistance, he said: "No. It's offered indefinitely."

"We are expecting more refugees every day of this week, in very large numbers," said Jacques Khouri, spokesman for Manpower and immigration. It could be in the thousands within the next month."

Khouri said most of them are entrepreneurs, many educated in England.

Coats, hats, gloves are needed for Asians

Reprinted with permission, ©Montreal Gazette, September 30, 1972

The response to requests for food clothes and money for Canada's newly arrived Ugandan Asians "has been fantastic," drive organizer Judy Duncan said yesterday. But she says people are donating too much of the wrong things—skirts and dresses.

PREFER SARIS

"These Asian women prefer saris," Mrs. Duncan said.

"We think local people, who have been extremely generous, should bear this in mind."

The drive started only a few days ago. Because she could not handle the organization alone, Mrs. Duncan, 29-year-old wife of a university mathematics professor, contacted the India-Canada Association of Montreal to help.

Three depots were set up immediately. And yesterday, the telephones did not stop ringing.

One depot is at the Queen Mary Road branch of the United Church of Canada; another is at the Hotel Provincial on Dorchester Blvd. West.

The third is in the basement of Mrs. Margaret Kingsford's home in the Town of Mount Royal. "People have been wonderful," she said. "I've got more stuff than I can handle."

"People are always marvelous in this kind of situation," she said. "And, of course, the Asians appreciate it as well as the organizers. But the public should know what is wanted. It'll save a lot of time.

"We really need coats, gloves and hats—in the way of clothes—and food and money. We have enough shoes and boots.-

"Many of the dresses people have given us have been really lovely—but of no use. We can't expect the Asians to change their style of dress."

Continued from Page 89

Uganda Hits Plea for U.N. Debate on Asians

protested when East African countries expelled black Africans from neighboring countries in the early post-colonial era.

Ibingira charged that Britain sought only to use the issue domestically to pacify Enoch Powell and his right-wing hotheads." Powell, a former Conservative cabinet member, has led the fight to block Asian and black immigration to Britain. Sir Colin Crow, British delegate, told the steering committee his government would ask the assembly to support Secretary General Kurt Waldheim's efforts to help the Asians and to urge Uganda to cooperate. Ibingira replied that the best way to help would be to avoid debate and let Waldheim proceed through his representative currently in Kampala, Robert K. A. Gardiner.

The steering committee adjourned overnight without a decision on the question but other speakers in Thursday's assembly backed Britain in condemning the expulsion of the Asians.

British Foreign Secretary Sir Alec Douglas - Home, in a news conference following the committee debate, rejected the Ugandan claim that the door to negotiations was open.

ASSESS NEEDS

Anyway, Mrs. Duncan says, before the drive began, the association enlisted a crew of Indian women to help assess the Asians' basic needs.

The clothes not given to the Asians, will have another use, Mrs. Duncan said. Some will be sent to the Douglas Hospital in Verdun and others handed to a United church organization concerned with helping North American Indians on reservations.

"Nothing'll be wasted," she said.

"And I'll tell you something else," Mrs. Duncan said. "The Canadian winter is going to be a new and hard experience for these people. That's why we would like more coats."

Continued from Page 88

Asians' Exodus From Uganda Moves Slowly

that the Ugandan exiles crossed the border from Tanzania in an attempt to overthrow Amin. The airlift sputtered after that. The second flight was canceled when only 34 Asians showed up at Entebbe airport in Uganda.

Empty Seats

By the end of the first week fewer than 1,000 Asians had flown to Britain on the airlift. That pace has increased during the second week to 450 a day. But airline officials report they have been canceling one special flight a day and there are still empty seats on the other flights.

There are probably several reasons for the desultory pace of the exodus.

According to a spokesman for the British Foreign Office, "There is a bureaucratic muddle on the Ugandan side." The Asians must receive clearance from the income tax department and approval for purchase of foreign exchange from the Bank of Uganda. At their best, in the most stable of countries, African bureaucracies move slowly.

But the Ugandan government denies that it is holding up the exodus. It claims that it has already cleared more than 8,000 Asians and is equipped to process 1,500 a day. Instead, the Ugandan blame British bureaucracy.

Some outsiders agree. They suspect the British were processing immigration papers for the Asians slowly in hopes that world pressure would persuade Amin to extend his deadline. But by Tuesday, the British High Commission in Kampala had announced it had cleared more than 13,000 Asians for entry to Britain. British spokesmen in Nairobi said the high commission in Kampala was now ready to process 10,000 immigration papers a week.

But whether or not the British and Ugandan bureaucracies are moving too slowly, it is clear that there are many more Asians cleared by both governments than have flown out so far.

Atrocities Cited

The Asians may simply have been afraid to travel to the airport, which Amin described as a plot to prevent the expulsion of the Asians. There have been numerous incidents of Ugandan soldiers abusing Asians. A few have been shot and killed. Many have been detained and others have been robbed and beaten.

Medical sources in Nairobi reported further evidence of the terrors of the route to the airport. One Asian woman, on a flight that stopped in Nairobi after leaving Kampala, had to be taken off the plane and hospitalized here. According to these medical reports, she had been raped five times by Ugandan soldiers manning the checkpoints on the road from Kampala to the airport at Entebbe.

In addition, some Asians may need more time to wind up their affairs, for many have well-stocked businesses and extensive property. The Asians may also have wanted to wait to see whether the invaders would succeed. A new Ugandan government, they may have felt, would rescind Amin's expulsion decree or at least extend the deadline.

New Regulations

This hesitancy by the Asians has angered the Uganda government and provoked it into new regulations to speed the exodus. It has announced that, after receiving clearance from the Bank of Uganda, Asians must buy their air tickets immediately and leave Uganda within 48 hours. When the government announced the 48-hour rule Friday, some outsiders thought this would be applied retroactively to the 8,000 already cleared. If so, they would have had to leave by last Sunday, an impossible task. But Sunday passed without any mass exodus or roundup of Asians.

The threat of invoking the rule, coupled with Amin's threat of putting laggards in military camps after Nov. 8, are sure to persuade many Asians that their best strategy now is to brave the possible harassment on the road to the airport and leave as soon as possible. The airlift to Britain is not the only means of exodus. The Canadian Government, at its own expense, intends to fly several thousand Asians to Canada for settlement there. The first Air Canada flight, with 134 Asians aboard, was due to leave this week.

In addition, several thousand Asians will leave for India, some by air and others by train through Kenya to the port of Mombasa, where they will board ships to Bombay. But these alternative routes do not ease much of the pressure on the main airlift to Britain. It clearly must quicken its pace considerably to beat the deadline.

British barracks placed into use before they are fully prepared

News Compilation, September 30, 1972

The recent influx of Asians filled the camp at Stradishall three days earlier than expected, requiring authorities to open the Hemswell before it was ready to receive anyone. Inadequate heating and a lack of adequate recreational facilities were among the problems facing the Asians arriving here. Hemswell is a four hour drive from Stansted Airport.

Ugandans see Canada life as welcome challenge

By GLEN ALLEN
Reprinted with permission, ©Glen Allen, September 30, 1972
Published in The Gazette, Montreal

Airlifted Ugandan Asians who stepped off Air Canada DC-8 into the chilly dawn of their new homeland yesterday are today sitting down to breakfast in a dozen Canadian cities, from one end of the country to the other.

Immigration officers said 90 of the 138 refugees had passed customs health and immigration checks and were on their way aboard trains and planes bound for their new homes in little more than 12 hours after their arrival.

All but two of the rest will be gone by this afternoon.

TOO EXCITED

The 90 men, women and children, many of whom hadn't slept for two days but were, said a department of immigration spokesman, "too excited to want to anything but head for their final destinations " were divided into 34 families and single adults.

Fifteen of those 34 chose to settle in Vancouver, nine in Toronto, three in Edmonton, two in Calgary, Hamilton, and Montreal and one each in Sarnia, Cornwall, Winnipeg, London and Waterloo.

"We expected the rush on Toronto," said

Continued on Page 92

Amin's reign of terror
'No words for what it was like'

Reprinted with permission, ©Montreal Gazette, September 30, 1972

Few of the Ugandan refugees would speak openly of what it was to be an Asian in President Amin's reign of terror.

Explained geography teacher Mohammed Ali: "We still have relatives and friends who haven't got out yet. What we say might cause trouble for them there."

But some could barely keep their bitter memories to themselves.

Said 34-year-old barber Hamir Nagla, tears welling up in his eyes, "there are no words for what it was like." Nagla had built up a business over 13 years. He lost it when ordered to leave the country and his bank account was frozen. He said, "they killed their own brothers, not just us."

He said the president warned that Asians left in the country after his deadline for departure "would be sitting on fires." He said that meant his army would be turned loose on Ugandan Asians.

Another said no Asians dared step out of their houses after 6 p.m. and that "they're already building a concentration camp. It was terrible and I'm not sure what was its cause. We didn't mix in politics. We didn't mix in what we shouldn't have."

A third said that on the day he left, an Asian driving on the highway outside Kampala was taken from his car and bayoneted by soldiers "or men dressed as soldiers." He said he witnessed the killing. "I think if you ask us after the deadline you will find plenty of people to tell you what it was really like."

Indian nationals expelled from Uganda have their papers examined by an officer of the ship State of Haryana prior to boarding at the Port of Mombasa, Kenya.
Reproduced with permission ©Associated Press/World Wide Photos

Indian group arrives to catch ship to Bombay

By NATION Reporter
Reprinted with permission, ©Daily Nation, Nairobi, September 30, 1972

MORE than 180 tired-looking Indian nationals expelled from Uganda arrived in Mombasa yesterday morning by special train on their way to India yesterday on board the State of Haryana.

Another special train-load of Indian nationals from Uganda is due in Mombasa this morning. It is estimated that about 550 Indians will leave on board the ship this evening.

The Indians travelled from Uganda to Mombasa under strict police and immigration escort. The expellees told stories of being mistreated on their way from Kampala to the Kenya border by military men. Some of them claimed that valuables, including wrist watches, radios and money, were forcibly taken away from them.

Hospital

One Asian was taken to hospital for treatment after he was hit with a stone by an unknown person between Kikuyu and Kibera station outside Nairobi. He is due to arrive this morning in Mombasa.

Most of the Indians were shopkeepers, craftsmen, artisans and contractors. They were served with tea at the shed No. 5 transit lounge by charitable organisations.

Speaking on behalf of his colleagues, Mr. Mawji M. Pindora, former building foreman at Kampala, said he saw soldiers of the Uganda Army robbing people of their valuables at Tororo.

Educated at the New Era School in Mombasa,

Continued on Page 92

Ugandans arrive in Calgary

Reprinted with permission, ©Calgary Herald, September 30, 1972

Manash Chakravarty became Calgary's newest resident and a father Friday.

The 25-year-old Chakraverty is one of the thousands of Ugandan Asians who have been forced to leave that African country. He was the first of the new immigrants to arrive in Calgary Friday night after a flight from Montreal. A young woman also arrived on a flight Friday night and several families arrived at the airport this morning.

The proud new father explained that his wife gave birth to a daughter, the couple's first child, in Calcutta, India.

"I am a bachelor of science graduate and I am looking for a job in the oil industry," he said on his arrival in the city.

Britain, Citing an 'African Initiative,' Suspends U.N. Bid for Uganda Debate

News Compilation, September 30, 1972

UNITED NATIONS, N.Y., Sept. 29—Britain today suspended her request for immediate General Assembly debate on the expulsion of some 50,000 to 60,000 Asians from Uganda.

The surprise move came in response to what Sir Colin Crowe, the British representative, called "an important African initiative" over the last 24 hours to resolve the issue in Uganda and avert a major clash at the United Nations.

It was understood that hurried private talks between African and Western delegates and foreign ministers here yesterday had resulted in agreement by President Mobutu Sese Seko of Zaire to intervene with President Idi Amin of Uganda.

First Ugandans arrive in Edmonton

By ERIC DENHOFF of the Journal
Reprinted with permission, ©Edmonton Journal, October 1, 1972

Accountant Nazmin Nanji, 20, read in the Uganda newspapers one morning that he and thousands of other Asians were to be expelled.

Nazmin, from Kampala, and an accountant friend Mohamed Nurani, 22, from Fort Portal, have arrived safely in Edmonton but are bewildered by the lives that lie ahead of them.

"Do you think we will like it here? You think it will be okay?" they asked.

"People have been very friendly and helpful. They say Edmonton is a good place. Do you think so?" Nazmin asked.

They took little with them when they left Uganda: "We were able to take no money out, only some clothes. But things look not so bad here.

"We have gone for interviews. I used to work for a firm—private—that has an Edmonton office and I have been there.

"Manpower is helping us. They have given us food and we have found a suite, so I think it will be good," said Mohamed.

Both are grateful to the federal immigration department and told of being driven from Kampala to the airport 20 miles away by the Canadian high commissioner to Uganda.

"It was very tense there, very uncertain. We were quite scared. It is hard on all those there," said Nazmin.

Asked where in Canada they would like to settle at the immigration interview in Uganda, Mr. Nanji said they told the officer: "Where do you think would be best, where do you think we could fill our stomachs?"

"I think, that if it isn't too cold yet, we can adjust to the climate. I hope so."

Another family of six refugees is expected to arrive in Edmonton Sunday.

Continued from Page 91

Indian group arrives to catch ship to Bombay

Mr. Pindora said they were glad to leave Uganda. "The situation there is just terrible. People live in fear everywhere," he said.

The skipper of the Haryana, Mr. A. A. Nazareth, a Goan, said he was supposed to be on leave but due to the emergency of the situation in Uganda, his leave had been cancelled.

"The ship was undergoing her annual survey in the dry-dock but the work had to be speeded up following the situation in Uganda which affected our nationals," Mr. Nazareth added.

The 42-year-old skipper said the ship was sailing straight to Bombay and "we may be back here anytime to pick up our people."

At the transit lounge to meet the arriving Indians were the Assistant High Commissioner of India, Mr. B. R. Sharma, police, immigration and Customs officers.

Mr. Sharma thanked the Kenya officials for the reception at the port. "I am sure these people are pleased in the way they have been received and I thank all those concerned," he said.

---

140 more exiles to arrive tonight

Reprinted with permission, ©Montreal Gazette, September 30, 1972

A second group of Asian refugees from Uganda is expected to arrive at Montreal International Airport shortly before 9 o'clock tonight. Immigration department of officials have a list of those coming in the Pacific Western Airlines aircraft but said, as in the first flight Thursday, there would be about 140 passengers

The last newcomers in the first flight—family bound for Calgary—were to leave the armed forces base at Longue Pointe this morning.

The family delayed its departure because an 18-year-old daughter—who celebrated her birthday yesterday with a birthday cake made by army cooks had found

---

Continued from Page 91

Ugandans see Canada life as welcome challenge

Manpower supervisor Mrs. Thelma O'Connor, "but the interest in British Columbia took us by surprise."

DISPERSED

Mrs. O'Connor said the Asians, most of whom are skilled workers or professionals, were either sent where they had friends, relatives or jobs already arranged, or simply where they wanted to go.

And this afternoon, just as military personnel tidy up Longue Pointe barracks in Montreal's East End, a camp that soldiers all but remodeled to house 5,000 Asians expected to land here in the next month, the jets of a second aircraft will be warming up to bring another flight of Asians to Montreal International Airport.

The second flight is expected tomorrow night. A third will arrive Monday, two will land on Wednesday and two more on Friday.

Yesterday's aircraft touched down at Dorval at 6:10 a.m. The bone-weary travellers, dressed in saris and other summer clothes too light for the 39-degree cold, were met by Minister of Manpower and Immigration Bryce Mackasey and his staff members.

Mackasey told them Canadians were "proud to open our hearts to you" and said "you are following in the footsteps of Hungarians, Czechs, Tibetans and others who have come to Canada after they were displaced as a result of turbulence in world events. I am sure you will greatly enrich our culture mosaic," he said.

There were 24 married couples, five infants, 43 children and 42 students and unmarried adults in the group. They were accountants and engineers, teachers, geologists, barbers, watchmakers and mechanics. Some were Ugandan citizens, some carried British passports and some were stateless. Some were Hindus and others were Moslems.

What they shared was life in a country that had rejected them and the decision to come halfway across the world to Canada.

"I have read that this is a very a vast country," said Naeem Ali, 9, who was clutching a plastic doll of a Royal Canadian Mounted policeman and a toy airplane. "But the only place I know about is in the far north— called Hay River." Naeem's father, Mohammed Ali said his children's weariness "has been overtaken by excitement."

NOT TIRED

A 20-year-old secretary named Avril Desoza had to be in Saskatoon by 9 a.m. Monday when she is to start a job at the University of Saskatchewan. "I don't really feel tired at all," she said. "Everything has been arranged so well everyone has been so good to us. You feel so good you don't feel tired.."

Rashida Jedha, a 26-year-old hairdresser who speaks both French and English was, as a Ugandan citizen, one of 30,000 Asians who aren't obliged to leave the country by Nov. 8.

"But I wanted to come anyway," said Miss Jedha. "I thought it would be nice to start all over again. I just

---

a job in Montreal and wanted to stay here. The family will fly west without her.

Of the 57 families and single working people on Thursday's plane, 20 went to Vancouver, nine to Toronto and only six stayed in Montreal. An immigration department official said yesterday the Ugandan Asians were being encouraged to head for smaller Canadian centres, but aside from one who is settling in Antigonish, N.S. and another who made for Athabaska, most are going to cities of 50,000 or more in population.

The department of manpower and immigration said 28 of the heads of families in the first flight were classed as clerks, 14 were technicians, seven were managers and others were doctors, teachers, a trucker, a barber and an economist.

---

hope people accept us. I read in the local paper that there was some opposition to our coming here."

Miss Jedha said she had met two French-Canadians once in Europe and had made friends with them. "I liked them very much and that was one reason I decided on Canada."

Nezmin Nanji, a young accountant heading for Edmonton last night, said many of the younger displaced Asians had chosen Canada over a choice of nations that included Australia, Brazil, Britain, India itself and some other African nations.

"Many people don't know Canada as any more than an outline on the map but it has a kind of reputation—we think it is a place to work hard and progress."

Highways Engineer Chimanlal Varu and his family of three almost didn't come at all. "My firm decided they needed me so they made an application to get an exemption for me. But I came anyways." Varu is used to working 12 hours a day in remote highway camps and says he is ready to work in bush camps in Canada if need be.

"I imagine this first year may be a little difficult. But when I am allowed to qualify as an engineer I don't think I'll have much trouble. My firm was an international one and has projects all over."

Varu, who says all he knows about Canada is that "it's a country that needs people," headed for Kitchener where he has a friend. Asked what effect the trip was having on his four-year-old son, Varu replied "he just thinks it's a trip to another part of town."

One of the few newcomers to settle in Montreal, watchmaker Abdeali Kamrudin had just left Tanzania for Uganda when the trouble began. "I never got to work at all. I went there because it had a future and now I am coming here because this has a bright future."

Kamrudin has already landed a job in the city and plans to send soon for his wife and three children in Tanzania.

The Asians breakfasted on coffee and cake at Longue Pointe barracks after being driven in buses from the airport. A curry lunch, prepared by 18 military cooks who had taken a crash course in Indian cookery from Mrs. Rani Khanna of Montreal's Maharajah Restaurant, was served shortly after noon.

SIX WEEKLY

The charter refugee flights may increase to six flights weekly until the deadline set by Uganda president Idi Amin for the departure of Asians from his country. About 1,500 visas have been issued in Kampala already.

None of the group interviewed they had trouble leaving the country, though bank accounts were frozen and belongings confiscated. Several said Canadian officials had made for an easy exit. The Canadians escorted them to the airplane. Two Canadian officials flew with the Asians on the 27-hour flight, which stopped in Athens and again in Paris for repairs to an engine.

MORE UGANDAN REFUGEES ARRIVE IN VANCOUVER

Family business, house confiscated

By BILL BACHOP
Reprinted with permission, ©Vancouver Sun, September 30, 1972

Hamir Nagla and his family left the rewards of 15 years' hard work behind when they boarded an aircraft two days ago to come to Canada.

There was Nagla's flourishing hairdressing business, the family's home and a late-model, air-conditioned U.S. car.

But the family also left something less attractive behind—the prospect of the internment in a prison camp in Uganda.

Nagla and his wife, Jaya, and their two children, Raju, 5, and Arun, 2, were among 25 Asians to arrive Friday in Vancouver after being expelled from Uganda.

"I didn't believe we were actually coming until we boarded the plane." Nagla said, after being met by Manpower and immigration officials at Vancouver International Airport.

Nagla said his business and his home and car were confiscated by the Ugandan authorities without compensation.

The Bank of Uganda, he said, also refused him permission to withdraw any money from his account to bring to Canada.

"I told them (bank officials) 'You are a bunch of bloody thieves' and they said 'Oh, you won't need any money—Canada's a rich country.' " Nagla said.

The Ugandan government, he said, appears to be deadly serious in its campaign to oust all people of Asian extraction from the country.

He said Asians who fail to leave the country by Nov. 8—the deadline set by the Uganda government—face the prospect of being imprisoned in a camp now built some 600 miles north of Kampala.

"It has electrified wire and a moat." he said.

Nagla said pictures of the camp have been shown to Asians on television to underline the government's intentions.

It's obvious, he said, that Ugandan authorities want to emulate the action taken by Libya, which two years ago expelled all persons of Italian ancestry.

And he said some 400 Libyan troops are now in Uganda.

Nagla said he had an income of about $450 Canadian from his business. But he isn't sure if he wants to stay in the trade here in Canada.

"I don't care," he said. "I'll work in a factory or with animals. I'll do anything."

Another of the party who arrived Friday, Nizar Nuraney, was a part-time schoolteacher in Uganda.

He and his wife Salma came with about $150 each and a few personal belongings.

Nuraney said they didn't suffer any personal harassment and the Ugandan authorities seemed "quite happy to see us go."

But he also said the Ugandan government is blunt about the poor prospects facing Asians who fail to leave. "They told us: 'you will know what it is like to sit on fire.' "

Nuraney said Canadian authorities have treated all the Asians coming to Canada "very well." And the group he arrived with was escorted to the aircraft by the Canadian high commissioner.

Vancouver auto dealer Tajdam Kassam, president of Impo Auto Sales 1972 Ltd., was on hand to meet seven relatives among the arrivals.

Kassam said he will find accommodation for them and help to smooth their path into a new life.

Kassam said in a telephone call to friends in the country he was told "it is raining very heavily"— a phrase he learned meant life for Asians is becoming more unpleasant.

And Rod McDougall, Manpower and immigration acting co-ordinator for the Asians arriving here in Vancouver, said every assistance will be given them to help them in job placement and in finding places to stay.

The Asians, he said, will be housed in hotels or motels while officials evaluate their job skills and prospects here in B.C.

"It's basically the same kind of assistance that is offered to any immigrant who arrives here in Canada to start a new life," he said.

McDougall added that arrivals will receive financial assistance until they are capable of making their own way.

OTTAWA, CANADA
Ugandan officials lenient with Canada-bound woman

By Catherine Jutras, Citizen staff writer
Reprinted with permission, ©Ottawa Citizen, September 30, 1972

"Now that I am here I don't really feel that I am far from Uganda," says Angela Dacosta, the first Ugandan Asian to arrive in Ottawa.

Her first impressions of Canada, seen from a train window, were strongly reminiscent of Kenya, Uganda's neighbor in East Africa—except for the climate.

Angela arrived from Montreal Friday afternoon to a joyful welcome from her 25-year-old sister, Aurea, who has lived here for 2-1/2 years.

Exhausted after a two-day travelling ordeal, the 31-year-old businesswoman nonetheless seemed calm and composed as she talked of the wrenching feeling of being ordered, with 55,000 fellow Asians, from the only home she has ever known.

The impact is stronger on her parents, who emigrated 35 years ago from Goa, on the west coast of India. Her father, 68, must give up his professional photography business and try to start again in India.

Angela had hoped to stay and help her family prepare for their journey to Goa in mid-October.

But she was among Asians with bank and income-tax clearance who were told at the beginning of this week they had just 48 hours to get out.

Angela, like the other 145 Ugandans on the 27-hour flight, was cleared through Canadian immigration and received landed-immigrant status at Montreal's Longue Pointe army base.

"The Canadian immigration officials have been tremendous," she said. "They couldn't have been better."

"We had a police escort from Kampala to Entebbe (the airport), so that we were not searched and of course our bus had a Canadian flag on it, which none of the others did."

Her conversations with Asians bound for other countries revealed those Canada-bound were the only ones not having any difficulty with Ugandan officials.

She was allowed to bring two suitcases, carrying a silver tea service in one and some clothes in the other. She was also allowed to wear "a few bits of gold" out of the country, unlike those going to other countries.

In Montreal, immigration officials furnished a warm coat and other clothing.

She had to leave between $300 and $400 in a Kampala bank account, along with most of her belongings.

·Angela had worked nine years for an import-export company, and was assistant manager for two years, after finishing secondary school and a secretarial course.

She would like to get a job in Canada, but not too soon. "I'd like to take about a month off to travel, relax and try to forget the turbulent events of the past month.

"We have been living in a very tense atmosphere," she said.

She considers herself lucky. Because of her sister's sponsorship, she did not have to wait in line for her departure papers, and knew that there was someone waiting for her.

"I feel most sorry for the other girls on the plane. They had no family and nowhere to go."

Most of the families on the flight were headed for Toronto or Vancouver.

"The children were excited as we approached Montreal, looking forward to the snow," but some of their elders suffered from homesickness.

The forced exodus came as a shock to most of the Asians, although relations with Ugandan President Idi Amin had been deteriorating for some time.

"The Africans are very sorry that it is happening," she said. Many of the Asians forced to leave were the most highly skilled workers in the country, and will be missed.

Angela has met General Amin because her company supplied equipment to the Ugandan army.

"I always found him a very nice person," she said, and was puzzled by his claim that God decreed the exodus to him in a dream.

Despite the tension and expulsion, she would like to go back, if only for a vacation. But she doesn't think it will ever be allowed.

Her parents and sister may rejoin Angela, and a brother, Bernard, who came to Canada a year ago to study at the University of Ottawa, after they settle their affairs in Goa.

Ugandan Asian Expulsion: 90 Days and Beyond through the Eyes of the International Press

RACISM AND HELPING HANDS

Ousted Uganda Asians Get Mixed Reception in Britain

By TOM LAMBERT
Times Staff Writer
Reprinted with permission, ©Los Angeles Times, October 2, 1972

LONDON—Worried but relieved, many of them broke, homeless and friendless on being plumped down in an alien homeland unenthusiastic about their coming, about 4,000 East Asian Britons have arrived here after being expelled from Uganda by its president, Gen. Idi Amin.

The new arrivals are the vanguard of thousands more who are entitled to and trying to come to Britain. Nobody knows how many will arrive ultimately, but estimates of those under expulsion order and eligible to come range from 30,000 to 55,000.

The British, who practice selective tolerance and generally have little use for foreigners or British immigrants with colored skins, have been welcoming the Asians with no great warmth or grace. However, a number of Britons have manifested a sincere sympathy for the newcomers and are trying to help them.

Thus, 38-year-old accountant Katilal Sheth, who arrived here two weeks ago from Uganda penniless; homeless, jobless and with a wife and three children has found a home and a bookkeeper's post with a building firm in Taunton. One of his compatriots from Kampala is working for a London pharmacist, another has resumed his Uganda trade as an auto mechanic with a British company.

But they are the exceptions.

There still are race-tainted, economic and other complaints from many Britons about the Asians and some "Wogs out" scrawls in London's subway corridors. And the British government still is scuttling about trying to deflect as many of the British passport carrying Uganda Asians as it can to any countries which will take them.

Australia, India, West Germany, Sweden, Canada and New Zealand are among some 15 nations which have indicated they will accept some of the Asians booted out by Amin on economic-racial grounds. The United States has been reported ready to accept about 1,000.

Chairman Sir Charles Cunningham of the Uganda Resettlement Board set up by the British government to help the newcomers said Saturday "we have a number of offers from local authorities (municipalities) for accommodations for families, also a number of offers of work." The work offers may number as many as 2,000.

Places in School

Some British schools are making places for young Uganda Asians, a British lawyers' group is trying to help place Asian barristers, and some British cities have offered limited numbers of houses and jobs.

The Leicester City Council, on the other hand, has made and is making no bones of its opposition to any Asian settlers. The council purchased a one-half page advertisement in a Uganda newspaper advising prospective immigrants in effect to stay away from Leicester.

The Asians, mostly of Indian heritage, have been coming here by air, some moving in with friends but most of them going to temporary resettlement camps at former military posts.

Although the British government knew a sizable number of the Asians might be coming, it seems to have been caught short in arranging enough temporary quarters for them and now is talking of opening more.

The arrivals are frightened, bewildered, uncertain and in many cases have been robbed of their property and valuables by Amin's soldiers or officials in Uganda.

Jashuantrl Raval, formerly an accountant in Kampala, said on arriving here the other day he had to abandon property and cash worth about $8,000 on leaving Uganda. But he said he had taken about $1,900 worth of gold and currency to the airport in the hope of bringing them along. Uganda airport authorities confiscated them.

Stripped of Jewelry

Tearfully, 26-year-old electrician Rajinder Singh reported he had "much trouble at Entebbe" airport at Kampala when Uganda officials found and stripped him of some gold jewelry he wanted to bring to Britain.

At least one Asian, 65-year-old tailor Nandlal Mehta managed to bring one possession with him from Kampala—one of the 10 sewing machines with which he had equipped his three Uganda tailor shops.

But when he arrived here, British customs officials impounded the sewing machine because the penniless Mehta was unable to pay $100 duty on it.

Less Robbery

The Asians arriving from Kampala the past few days seem to have been less subject to robbery by Ugandan officials and those who manage to sidestep Amin's soldiers seem to have been looted less thoroughly.

The Uganda expulsions have been carried out against a background of unrest in Kampala where Amin has been crying war with Tanzania, praising Hitler, apparently soliciting military help from Libya and proclaiming deadlines lines for the Asians he has expelled.

He has said they must clear Uganda by Nov. 8, and recently decreed they had to leave within 48 hours or be thrown into camps. The exodus is continuing, however, with up to 400 arriving here in Britain on some days.

Many Distraught

Understandably, those arriving here have been distraught. They have been cautioned on their arrival against settling in some areas of Britain. In some cases they have separated from families. But almost all have been physically well and grateful to be in Britain.

It is too early to fashion a profile of the arrivals, but one survey of some 1,500 showed about 25% of the men were merchants, with lesser percentages of teachers, clerks and skilled workers. Less than 5% were unskilled laborers, and only 2% were 60 years of age.

Sensing trouble, some Uganda Asians came to Britain before Amin expelled them. They include a 28-year-old Kampala shopkeeper who had been buying goods from a British producer, and overpaying him. The producer banked the excess money for the Asian and turned it over to him on his arrival. He recently bought into a small company here and purchased a house "quite modest, not as nice as my house in Kampala, but quite nice."

The arrivals thus far have caused no trouble. Some have shown a decided willingness to work their way out of the resettlement quarters into economic independence. One 28-year-old mother who had a house and two servants in Kampala now is trying to land a job as a kitchen helper in a British school.

Some Asians who have cleared Kampala with their families are bitter in their comments about Amin. "He is a madman, a madman," one of them said. But other arrivals with relatives still in Uganda are reluctant to talk about conditions there.

Generally, most of the arrivals are grateful to be in Britain, no longer subject to Amin's whims and hopeful of finding work or going into business and settling down.

"We will show our gratitude by deeds, not words," said a 24-year-old mechanic, Babu Patel.

U.S. to admit 1,000 Ugandan Asians

News Compilation, October 3, 1972

The United States will speed up entry procedures and admit 1,000 stateless Ugandan Asians, the State Department announced yesterday.

State Department spokesman Charles W. Bray said the "Attorney General will exercise his parole authority under the Immigration and Nationalization Act . . . so we can admit to the United States Ugandan Asians without valid claim to any citizenship."

The announcement came in response to a British request to assist in the resettlement of Asians.

Those admitted to the united States will be screened carefully. "We are making the selection of applicants with a careful eye to professional capabilities to insure that they will have means of self-support," Bray said. The stress on professional skills indicated the potential sensitivity of the issue given the continuing high rate of unemployment in the United States.

A State Department official familiar with the situation said that Ugandan Asians are, in general, "a very industrious, hard-working, well educated and by and large hard-driving people."

Big log-jam builds up in Asian transit camps

By Derek Humphry
Reprinted with permission, ©Times Newspapers Limited, London,
October 1, 1972

NEARLY 3,000 Asians are today relaxing in three transit camps in Britain deeply grateful—as they never tire of telling you—for the security and hospitality they have been given after the nightmare of their last two months in Uganda. But only now are immigration officials seeing how complex is the problem of getting them, and those still to follow, out of the camps and into homes and jobs.

One fundamental difficulty is how to match job offers to the availability of houses. Experts in the Department of Employment see no real problems in finding work for the Asians provided they are scattered widely. Every town has vacancies of a kind, and the Asians are willing to accept whatever is offered. The Board has received 1,295 offers of work from 369 employers.

Yet so far, only 500 homes have been offered by local councils. More are in the pipeline, but councillors have asked either that towns are not named, or that the number offered is left vague because they fear a backlash at the next local elections.

Nearly 3,000 people have offered temporary accommodation in private homes, but double this figure is likely to be needed so that the Asians can escape from the soul-destroying transit camps and get a foothold in the community.

In the two weeks since the Asians began to arrive, the DEP has been saying that the criteria for those wanting to leave the transit camps was securing a job. For instance, the DEP insisted on finding jobs for the breadwinners first. So far 12 Asians have been offered work in Peterborough, and the town is preparing homes for their families.

But by the end of last week it became apparent that a log-jam would build up in the camps if this policy of "job first" was followed meticulously. Some indications of the feared position is that the Uganda Resettlement Board is hastily preparing beds in 12 transit camps for up to 12,000 people. It is now virtually certain that 8,000 families about 25,000 people in all, will reach Britain by the end of next month.

A major switch in policy is to operate from this week. Accommodation lists will be opened with the jobs as second priority, but one proviso is still being attempted. Sir Charles Cunningham, Board chairman, explained: "We're going to try not to send to an area an Asian whose skills are similar to those of people already unemployed there."

Once they are out of the camps, the Asians will have access to the thousands of job vacancies which are never notified to the DEP, whose own register of jobs available numbered 205,000 at the beginning of this month. The official vacancy list represents about one-fifth of the true jobs market.

Another snag is that about only 1,000 Asians have gone their own way since arriving in Britain.

Continued on Page 96

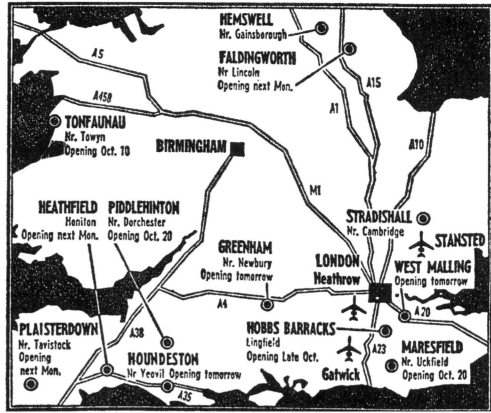

Map of current and potential Asian transit camps in Britain. Reproduced with permission ©Times Newspapers Limited

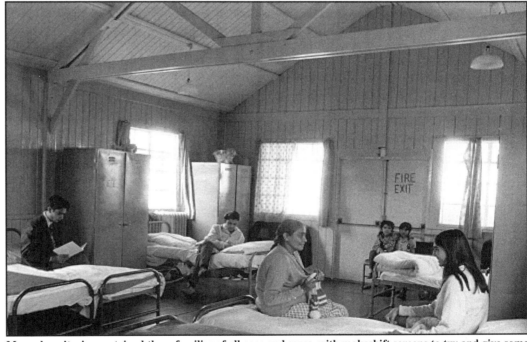

Many dormitories contained three families of all ages and sexes, with makeshift screens to try and give some privacy. Reproduced with permission ©Anthony Marshall/Telegraph group Limited

Asians find little help in getting a home

By Christopher Walker
Reprinted with permission, ©Times Newspapers Limited, London,
October 2, 1972

Two weeks ago, Mr Sureschandra Trivedi left his rented flat in the centre of Kampala for the last time. With his wife and four children he caught the first aircraft in the airlift bringing expelled Uganda Asians to Britain.

He arrived at Stansted airport with a few suitcases, an assortment of plastic holdalls filled with domestic goods and two pet African parrots. In his pocket was less than £30 in Uganda currency. With other Asians who had neither money nor an address in Britain, he was taken to Stradishall, the former RAF camp in a remote part of Suffolk.

Unlike the 1,600 refugees still at Stradishall today, Mr Trivedi and his family moved on Saturday into a rented terrace house in Willesden,

Continued on Page 96

Continued from Page 95

Big log-jam builds up in Asian transit camps

The Resettlement Board expected many more to do so, based on information from Kampala that the Asians were highly skilled and many had money in this country.

The reality seems to be that many of those with money abroad have generally opted for India or Pakistan, and that Canada, New Zealand, Australia and other countries are "creaming off" the professionals and technicians. So the British Government's attempts to persuade other countries to help reduce the number of Asians coming here is proving counter-productive in one respect, because we are not getting a cross-section of the skills and wealth of the refugees.

One reason why there was a miscalculation about the numbers who would need Government accommodation is that the Asians told the High Commission in Kampala the names of friends or relatives in Britain, assuming they could help. Many it turns out, do not have accommodation spare for a whole family.

From tomorrow a resettlement officer is to be installed in each camp to co-ordinate the work of the DEP (jobs) and Supplementary Benefits Commission (cash grants), and the Department of the Environment (housing). Every local authority is being asked to appoint a local resettlement officer to help the Asians after they are found homes. And the vague offers of housing must soon be made firm.

The desperate need to empty the camps as quickly as possible became obvious with last week's experience at Stradishall, a former RAF base, when it contained at least 1,600 people. It demonstrated that old military accommodation is unsuitable for women and children. The toilet and washing facilities are sparse. Families had to be squeezed into dormitories with one bath, a couple of wash basins and a few toilets between them. Within a few days the facilities were cracking up.

Many dormitories contained three families of all ages and sexes, with makeshift screens to try to give some privacy. There was nothing to do—the community centre had to be filled with beds—and the women sat on their beds talking while the men tramped the lanes getting their first acquaintance with the English countryside.

The standard of the food at Stradishall deteriorated rapidly once the overcrowding began. At lunch on Thursday, I found the food soggy and tasteless. For people accustomed to a highly spiced diet, it must have been even more depressing, and there was considerable wastage.

There was a shortage of interpreters, which the administrators will not admit to, believing that enough of the Asians speak English. In reality, their English is often not good enough to explain the more complicated problems with which their expulsion has faced them.

Despite the bad experience with the information from Kampala, too many officials involved in

Continued from Page 95

Asians find little help in getting a home

north London. This morning his daughter Saudimin, aged 17, will start her first day's work as a typist in an employment exchange in the West End.

Although grateful for the treatment he has received from the British, Mr Trivedi is critical of one vital aspect of the resettlement process. "On advice about jobs, there was no problem", he said. "But when it came to finding a house it was a very different matter. There did not seem to be anyone at Stradishall who could really help us with this."

Moving families out of transit camps is the most serious difficulty facing the resettlement board, which is why Mr Trivedi spent his last few hours at the camp giving advice to as many of his fellow refugees as he could find. "I told them they had to help themselves. Britain is too busy to do everything for us. If they just sit and wait, they could be there for ever."

In Uganda, Mr Trivedi, a Hindu, earned £1,500 a year as a shoe salesman. Apart from a little money sent to relatives in India, he sent a few cases of household possessions out of Uganda. "I had to give my Morris car away, because even if I had managed to sell it, the money would have been of no use." His eldest daughter passed five O levels recently and had just started a secretarial course. His three younger children were all at school.

Like many Asians arriving in the first wave of the airlift, he had first applied for an entry permit to Britain before the present crisis. "Ever since the Congo, we have realized that something would happen to us sooner or later, but we could not just run away—it is no good living in the forest if you are going to be afraid of the lions."

After spending a week at Stradishall, Mr Trivedi decided he would have to take action if he was going to find a house, his main priority. "I was offered a job with a Ford dealer in Dagenham, but what was the good as there was no house with it. Even if we wanted to, we would not be allowed to sleep in the streets", he said.

Equipped with travel vouchers for the train journey and about £12 in social security money Mr Trivedi and his daughter set out for London. She had an interview for her typist's job which had been arranged from Stradishall, while he spent four days househunting.

"Because we have children, it was very hard to find a place", he said. "But I did not come across any obvious hostility because we were Asian." He found few surprises in London except the cost of public transport. "Luckily a friend told me

about these Red Rover bus tickets—without them, I should have been sunk."

Eventually he found three furnished ground-floor rooms in a house in Willesden and paid a month's rent in advance with £70 borrowed from his younger brother. On Saturday he hired a mini-van and drove to Suffolk to collect his family and belongings and leave his new address with the resettlement board officials.

Willesden is in the borough of Brent, one of the "red list" districts which Asians have been advised to avoid. "We have all been told again and again that this is a red district, but I have found somewhere to live and that is what really matters", Mr Trivedi said yesterday.

This morning he will sign on at the local employment exchange and try to place his children in schools which are 15 minutes' walk from the house. "The most important thing is to finish the formalities first. There is no use in joining a new employer, and then having to go absent after a few days."

Friendly, good humoured and full of initiative, Mr Trivedi, like most Asians who have arrived recently, says he is prepared to do any type of work. Already he has noticed a vacancy sign outside a small printing works near his home, and will be inquiring about it this week.

After only a fortnight in Britain, he is a mine of information about housing and job possibilities in different parts of the country and has already applied in writing for a Greater London Council house in the overspill town of Wellingborough, Northamptonshire. Unlike many Asians still in transit camps, Mr Trivedi is beginning to settle quickly into a new way of life. "With a house, I am halfway on my feet and that is what really counts."

An Army camp in Tonfanau, near Towyn, in Merioneth, is being prepared for possible use by Uganda Asians. It can house 1,500 refugees.

The camp has not been used for many months. Electric cookers and heaters are being installed and huts are being partitioned so that families can be accommodated together.

In London yesterday the resettlement board said there were no immediate plans for the camp to be used. It would be kept in reserve because "it is somewhat remote".

the massive migration make assumptions about the Asians' capabilities or needs based on scanty knowledge or wishful thinking. This is likely to be balanced now that the Civil Service is responding to the offers of advice and help from welfare organisations and Asian groups with a wealth of expertise in this sort of problem.

Advertisement

DON'T ABANDON YOUR DOG OR CAT

ANY DEPARTING RESIDENT OF UGANDA WHO WISHES TO DISPOSE OF HIS/HER PET ANIMALS MAY BRING THEM TO THE FACULTY OF VETERINARY SCIENCE, MAKERERE UNIVERSITY, KAMPALA ON BOMBO ROAD ON THE LEFT SIDE PAST THE GAYAZA ROAD ROUNDABOUT. THEY WILL BE HUMANELY DISPOSED OF FOR A NOMINAL FEE. THIS SERVICE IS AVAILABLE, MONDAY THROUGH FRIDAY 10:00 - 12:00 A.M. and 2:00 - 3:00 P.M.

Ugandan Asian Expulsion: 90 Days and Beyond through the Eyes of the International Press

To India From Uganda: Story of Humiliation

Expelled Asians, Facing New Life With Little Hope, Tell of Petty Harassment

BY STANLEY MEISLER
Times Staff Writer
Reprinted with permission, ©Los Angeles Times, October 3, 1972

NAIROBI—Two trainloads of expelled Ugandan Asians came through Nairobi on their way to India last week with stories of petty harassment and greater humiliation.

One young man, angry, intense with tousled hair and open necked shirt, waved a long yellow sheet of paper from the window of his car in Nairobi station. It listed the items taken from him by soldiers when he boarded the train in his home town of Jinja in eastern Uganda.

The booty was five trousers, two bed sheets, six undershirts, six undershorts, three handkerchiefs, six pairs of socks, six water glasses, nine spoons, three batteries, one razor, one old five shilling coin, one wrist watch, and 15 packets of razor blades.

"So I don't have any underwear to travel," said the young man, an Indian citizen who had never lived in India. He had been born in Mogadiscio in Somalia 24 years ago and had moved to Jinja with his family when he was 8.

List Stamped

The soldiers had stamped his list with the date and their marker—"military police headquarters"—as if it were a receipt.

"I have the list," the young man said. "I am going to show it to everyone in India."

His father and sister had seen him off at the station in Jinja. They had not yet completed the laborious paper work involved in leaving under President Idi Amin's expulsion order. His sister is 13.

"The army people were touching her," the young man said. "They said she is my girl. They were just playing with her, just playing with her.

There is no life for Asians in Uganda, citizens or not."

What would he do in India?

"I was born in Africa," he replied. "I have never seen the place. We are going to start anew."

"I am just going there like water in an empty glass. I don't have anything there. I am just clean."

The trains were carrying the Asians across East Africa to the Kenya port of Mombasa, where a ship called the State of Haryana was waiting to take them to Bombay. The ship left Sunday.

These Asians were not typical of the tens of thousands who have to leave Uganda by Nov. 8 under Gen. Amin's expulsion decree.

Most of the Uganda Asians are British citizens who have either been born in Uganda or have lived there most of their lives. But the Asians on the refugee trains were almost all Indian citizens, most of whom are poorer, less educated in Uganda than the British Asians.

Like Calcutta

The scenes in the Nairobi station made it seem like a station in Calcutta, for the platform was packed with Asians from Nairobi, many in saris and turbans who had come to the station to hand fruit, bags of food, fruit coffee, and bottles of soda to the expelled Asians on board.

There were dining cars on board the special trains. But the soldiers had searched the Asians for Uganda currency and left them with no more than five shilling (70 cents) each. They also were allowed fifty pounds ($140) in travelers checks for use only in India.

"There is food on the train," said one Asian.

"But they are charging 10 shillings for a meal. Where are we going to get money?"

In Nairobi the Asians were not allowed to step off the trains.

The Kenya government wants to make sure that no Uganda Asian passing through Kenya tries to stay by hiding himself among the Asians of Kenya.

But the police let newsmen interview Asians through the windows.

One young man who speaks English in a halting way, said that he had accompanied his brother, a British citizen, to Entebbe Airport a few days ago where his brother boarded a plane for Britain.

At one roadblock, Ugandan soldiers ordered all men in the car to strip to their underwear so they could be searched more easily. The three women in the car were ordered to lie down on the ground.

Then, according to the young man, a soldier picked up a kiboko (a whip made of hippo hide) and announced that he would whip the women— "Five kibokos if they have a British passport, one if Indian."

The women were British Asians. The soldier, according to the young man, whipped the first woman twice. Then all the women began to cry and moan. When that happened, the soldier stopped and let them go on to Entebbe.

One heavy-set man said he had been beaten across the neck twice with a stick by a soldier because he had 10 shillings in his pocket. The Asian said the soldier told him, "You are a thief. Why keep your money in your pocket?"

An old man, his unshaven face grizzled with gray hair, pointed to the bare arms and neck of his wife. Asian women set off their silk saris with gold bracelets and necklaces so often that the sight was strange one. An interpreter explained that soldiers had snatched 300 grams of gold jewelry from the old couple.

Before telling these tales, almost all the Asians first said they had experienced "very little trouble." They had expected worse.

NOTICE

Advertisement

EAST AFRICAN AIRWAYS, BRITISH OVERSEAS AIRWAYS CORPORATION, BRITISH CALEDONIAN AIRWAYS AND AIR INDIA WOULD LIKE TO ADVISE ALL THE IMMIGRANT PASSENGERS AFFECTED BY THE EXPULSION DECREE THAT ENOUGH FLIGHTS HAVE BEEN ARRANGED FOR THEM TO TRAVEL TO THE UNITED KINGDOM, INDIA, PAKISTAN AND BANGLA DESH.

THE NUMBER AND SCHEDULES OF THE FLIGHTS ARE PLANNED WITH THE 8TH NOVEMBER DEADLINE IN MIND AND PASSENGERS ARE STRONGLY ADVISED TO MAKE FULL USE OF THE FACILITIES IMMEDIATELY.

IT IS STRONGLY EMPHASISED THAT SO FAR PROSPECTIVE PASSENGERS HAVE FAILED TO COME FORWARD TO BOOK AND THIS HAS CONSISTENTLY RESULTED IN CANCELLATION OF THE PLANNED FLIGHTS, DUE TO LACK OF SUFFICIENT LOADS.

EAST AFRICAN AIRWAYS, BRITISH OVERSEAS AIRWAYS CORPORATION, BRITISH CALEDONIAN AIRWAYS AND AIR INDIA WISH TO REMIND ALL PASSENGERS THAT IF THIS SITUATION CONTINUES, THERE WILL BE A LOT OF CONFUSION AND DIFFICULTIES TOWARDS THE END OF THE DEADLINE.

PROSPECTIVE PASSENGERS MUST THEREFORE AVOID POSTPONING THEIR DEPARTURE UNTIL THE LAST MOMENT, AND MUST THEREFORE COME FORWARD NOW AND BUY TICKETS IMMEDIATELY.

MEDICAL TREATMENT FOR ASIAN BEATEN BY SOLDIER

By NATION Reporter
Reprinted with permission, ©Daily Nation, Nairobi, October 2, 1972

MOMBASA Red Cross officials administered first aid treatment to former Kampala building contractor Mr. Ajit Singh, who arrived with 341 other Asian evacuees from Kampala at Kijindini Port over the weekend.

Mr. Ajit Singh had several stitches placed in a four-inch wound across his skull and also received treatment for severe back bruises. He told newsmen in Mombasa that he was beaten across the head with a steel rifle bult wielded by a Uganda Army soldier at Kampala Railway Station.

He was further kicked in lithe back by the soldier when he fell to the ground. Mombasa was the first point at which he was able to receive medical attention for his injuries.

Several of the train passengers also complained about the treatment meted out by Ugandan soldiers to passengers travelling by train between Kampala and Malaba on the Kenya border.

They claimed that Ugandan soldiers "looted" passenger baggage at several unscheduled stops along the line and that passengers were "beaten up" indiscriminately and "generally abused, both physically and verbally."

Together with an earlier trainload of 189 Indian nationals from Uganda, the weekend's 342 arrivals sailed on Saturday night for Bombay aboard the Shipping Corporation of India passenger vessel State of Haryana.

Finding a job is biggest worry for Ugandan immigrant

By Carol Hogg
[Herald Staff Writer]
Reprinted with permission, ©Calgary Herald, October 4, 1972

In less than a month he has lost his home, his car, his money, his job, his personal belongings and his dog.

But he's smiling. Why? Because he still has his life, his wife, his baby son, and a new chance in Canada—and for a Ugandan Asian refugee, that's a lot.

He is Mr. X—one of the first Ugandan refugees to settle in Calgary. He has asked reporters not to use his name or mention his profession for fear reprisals will be taken against his two brothers and his sister, still in Uganda.

"Brutal" is the word he uses to describe the treatment of Asians by the Ugandan army.

"It should not happen in the modern world."

Mr. X was vacationing in Canada when he heard the news that Asians were being expelled from Uganda.

"Everybody told me not to go back, that I would be crazy to return there. But I had to go back—to get my wife and baby."

While Mr. X was visiting Canada, his wife was staying with relatives in Kampala several miles from where she and Mr. X made their home, in the foothills.

Mr. X met her in Kampala. He was told there were 30 road-blocks set up between Kampala and their home.

"I told my wife that if she wished, I would try to go to our home to get some of our belongings, but that if I went I couldn't promise I would be able to return.

"She said we should not bother with our belongings. We should just save ourselves."

Mr. X laments the loss of personal things like photographs—and his dog, a tiny Pekinese called Tiger. He wishes he could see the roses he planted around his house in the spring.

The rest of his belongings he does not waste time worrying about—they can be replaced.

His wife regrets the beautiful saris and bangles she had to leave behind. But Mr. X has promised her new ones—plus some Canadian-style pant suits—just as soon as he finds a job.

A job is topmost on his mind. He is a professional man with a post-graduate degree and hopes to find a position suitable to his training—but he is willing to try something else.

"I need a job to help me forget what has happened."

He had to leave his diplomas in Uganda, but has sent for replacements from the universities involved.

"But that is a trivial thing, by comparison. When you are in a situation like in Uganda, you do not worry about your possessions. You just want to get out alive."

He tells horror stories of injustices, and mur-der, of an army on the rampage.

"I went to see an Asian travel agent I knew about getting airline tickets. Two days later he was missing. He was found later—murdered, and so horribly mutilated it was difficult to identify him.

"I know other stories, but they are not what you could put in a newspaper," he says.

He is bitter, but just happy to be alive, he says, and feels that at age 30, he is young enough to earn back many of the things he has lost.

He and his family arrived in Canada Thursday and in Calgary Saturday, where he is staying with Asian friends. He hopes to find a new life in this city. Like the other 5,000 or so Ugandan Asians Canada has accepted, he is grateful to be here.

"What I notice is how happy everyone is here. And the Canadian government has been wonderful."

Not even the stories about Calgary winters bother him—although it doesn't get colder than 60 above in Uganda.

"Let the winter come. At the moment all I'm worried about is finding a job."

Freedom baby

LITTLE JHANGIR MAKES IT A GREAT START TO LIFE IN BRITAIN

Reprinted with permission, ©Daily Mail, London, October 4, 1972

A LITTLE bit of history . . . that's Jhangir Tejani. For Jhangir, just two days old, is the first baby born in Britain to an Asian refugee from Uganda.

Yesterday he and his mother, 36-year-old Mrs Gulshankhan Tejani were both doing well, far from the turmoil and fear of their home country.

Attentive nurses fussed round him on his first public appearance in Ward A1 at Newmarket General Hospital, Suffolk. He was born on Monday night by Caesarean operation, but he weighs a healthy 6lb. 6oz. and the hospital said: 'Everything is quite satisfactory.'

Mrs Tejani, her husband Amirali, 37, and their five other children—two sons, three daughters—were among the first Asians to leave Uganda after General Amin's expulsion order. They are staying at the Government transit at RAF Stradishall, Suffolk.

There was more good news for the family yesterday. Mr Tejani, an embroiderer, learned that there was a good chance of finding a new home and a job by the time Jhangir is strong enough to leave hospital.

Ugandan Indians in Bombay

By A Staff Reporter
Reprinted with permission, ©Times of India, October 4, 1972

NINETY-TWO Uganda Indians holding Indian passports, who arrived in Bombay by ship on Tuesday, were ill-treated by armymen at every stage of their train journey from Uganda to the border of Kenya, and robbed of most of their belongings.

Mr. P. B. Bandiwadekar, acting as a spokesman of the repatriates told reporters aboard the B. I. liner, "Karania", that Ugandan soldiers pursued them all the way from Jinja, 79 km north of Kampala, forcing their entry into trains at regular intervals.

At Jinja, many Indians were deprived of their cash. Elsewhere, ornaments, wrist-watches, necklaces and chains of women were snatched: Shoes, tape-recorders and costly costumes were robbed.

At one station, the Uganda army officers dragged refugees who had not gone through the "immigration treatment" and asked them to crawl the entire length of the platform.

The "immigration treatment" is a procedure by which Asians forced out of Uganda are required to declare their assets before their departure from that country.

The former Indian settlers were allowed to carry with them personal effects valued at 10,000 shillings (Ugandan) and 1,000 shillings in bank drafts.

Ninety per cent of the refugees—most of whom were fitters, carpenters and masons—had very little by way of personal belongings.

A refugee said it was not true that property, money and other possessions of Asians had been confiscated by the Uganda government. They had been either frozen or blocked.

He also discounted the general belief that Asians had been confiscated by the Uganda government. They had been either frozen or blocked.

He also discounted the general belief that Asians were subjected to atrocities day in and day out. Only those people whom the Uganda authorities "did not particularly like for various reasons," were harassed, he added.

In certain cases, bank drafts officially released by the government were stolen by the armymen, it was stated.

The first batch of Uganda Indians to come by sea comprised 70 males, seven women and 15 children. They were shown the utmost courtesy and consideration by the Kenya police who escorted them from the border to the Kalindini harbour of Mombasa.

The Indian high commission in Nairobi extended all facilities to them and provided some pocket money for sundry expenses during their voyage.

This correspondent learnt that 15 Uganda residents of Pakistani origin, who landed in Karachi, did not receive any help from the Pakistani high commission either in Uganda or in Kenya. The Indian high commission did all it could to assist them in their repatriation.

The Maharashtra and Central governments have arranged for their temporary accommodation in Bombay before they leave for their respective places in India.

Two British-passport-holding Indians of Uganda who also arrived by the same ship, had their passports endorsed for entry into Britain by Mr. John Tidy, information officer in the deputy British high commission of Bombay.

Indian Stand at UN Pleases Africans

By M. V. KAMATH
"The Times of India" News Service
Reprinted with permission, ©Times of India, October 6, 1972

UNITED NATIONS, OCT. 5.

The unusually soft stand taken by India's foreign minister, Mr. Swaran Singh, towards the Ugandan government's determined policy to oust the Asians from the country at short notice has perplexed delegates here.

The Indian view seems to be that nothing can be gained by using strong words if they cannot be backed by meaningful action, especially when the Asians are still in Uganda and could conceivably be held as hostages, and any show of strong sentiments may trigger an anti-Asian wave in other African states.

In the circumstances, it is felt, a more conciliatory approach may be more fruitful and, at any rate, worth trying out.

This low-key approach to the crisis seems to have pleased many African delegations which warmly congratulated Mr. Swaran Singh after his address to the General Assembly.

It is, however, possible that they saw in Mr. Singh's soft approach a justification for Gen. Amin's behaviour. It is also possible that African delegations may have been pleased with the Foreign Minister's support to the struggle for independence in Namibia, Zimbabwe, Angola, Mozambique and Bissau.

While this is so, the continued needing of the U.S. by India on many issues, like Viet Nam and U.N. budgeting, is also perplexing observers here though it is conceded that Indian public opinion has been sorely tried last year.

At the same time, it is noted that the U.S. has been careful not to exacerbate matters further and there is a marked unwillingness on the part of U.S. officials to comment on Mr. Swaran Singh's speech.

Here, the Indian view seems to be that certain things that need to be said must be said, especially at the General Assembly forum, for the record.

Mr. Singh's address to the General Assembly has largely gone unnoticed in the U.S. press.

Confusion overDeadline

News Compilation, October 4, 1972

President Mobutu of Zaire said today that President Idi Amin had agreed to put back the deadline for the expulsion of non-Ugandan Asians. Mobutu had just returned from meeting Amin in Kampala.

However, a conflicting report from Kampala stated that Amin vowed to remain firm with the Nov. 8 deadline.

Addressing students at Makerere University in Kampala, he declared that it was a waste of time for other countries to try and negotiate changes in his decision expell non-Ugandan Asians.

He added: "No country should waste its time to come here and try to negotiate for the British."

Resettlement chief in Kampala

News Compilation, October 7, 1972

Sir Charles Cunningham, chairman of the Uganda Resettlement Board, has flown to Kampala in a personal attempt to ease the crisis over the placing of Asian families in homes and jobs in Britain.

He will tell the British High Commission that more detailed advance information is needed about the numbers, status and background of arriving refugee families. Without it the entire resettlement program is in danger of breaking down.

Film star entertains ousted Asians

News Compilation, October 7, 1972

Movie heart-throb Rajendra Kumar—described by fans as India's Richard Burton—was mobbed when appeared on a tour to entertain Asians expelled from Uganda. The 40-year old actor has made 56 films in 18 years.

Canadian Church Group Welcomes Ugandans

News Compilation, October 7, 1972

The Canadian Council of Churches sent a telegram to Canadian Prime Minister Trudeau commending him on the decision to admit Ugandan Asians.

The Council also appealed to fellow Canadians to "open their hearts and homes" to the Ugandan Asians. The Council also called upon Canadians "to try and understand the profound uncertainty and disturbance forced upon these refugees who have lost their homes and possessions and have had to move to a strange land and a cold climate".

Compassion—with Prudence

Editorial
Reprinted with permission, ©Chicago Tribune, October 5, 1972

A United States decision to admit 1,000 Asians ordered out of Uganda reflects a fine American tradition of helping the homeless and the persecuted, but in this instance we should act cautiously.

The refugees are among 50,000 Asians who have been told by Uganda's unpredictable President Idi Amin to leave by Nov. 8. Their only "crimes" are success in Uganda's business community and skins of a different color from that of the racist Amin.

Our country is right to feel compassion for innocent people being expelled from the only home they have ever known. But compassion isn't going to help them if it comes so prematurely as to encourage the expulsion that they are seeking to avoid. There is still a good chance that Amin can be dissuaded from his harsh decree [or be overthrown]. The pressure in this direction will be less effective if other nations move too quickly to receive the targets of his prejudice.

It is true that Britain has moved to grant or find havens for as many as possible of these unfortunates. But Britain has a special responsibility, since the 50,000 hold British passports.

However, London has not abandoned efforts to convince Amin he should temper his order. Foreign Secretary Douglas-Home has asked the United Nations to urge the African dictator to extend the expulsion deadline. President Sese Seko Mobutu of neighboring Zaire has visited Amin and says the Ugandan will do so. The Uganda Radio yesterday denied a change in deadline.

We must hope for more than an extension. The Asians' homes and businesses are in Uganda, and all of Uganda will suffer if they are forced to leave. The world has seen too many examples of successful minorities being harassed for their success.

If the world helps Amin get away with his wild plan, he will not be the last despot to try this. Racial persecution is contagious. We should do everything possible to control the current outbreak.

Advertisement

UNITED STATES OF AMERICA TO ADMIT LIMITED NUMBER OF STATELESS ASIAN

The United States of America will admit a limited number of stateless Asians to emigrate to the United States. First to be processed will be highly qualified members of the professions, scientists or artists and their dependants who are stateless.

Interviews will be conducted at the American Embassy, (Embassy House, Parliament St., Kampala,) beginning today, Friday, October 6, at 8 a.m. Only those members of the professions, scientists or artists who have previously submitted an application to the Embassy and who still desire to emigrate to the United States should come to the Embassy to determine if they still qualify. Interviews for those who have not previously applied will begin at 8 a.m. Saturday, October 7, and will continue daily until the maximum number is reached.

The following must be strictly adhered to:

(1) Only those who can comply with the qualifications listed should apply at this time.

(2) Only the principal applicant (not dependents) should come to the Embassy to file an application. He should bring supporting documents with him, such as educational certificates, documentation of professional skills and any other documents he may wish to submit as part of his application.

AMIN WATCHES AS ASIANS CHEERED AT GREAT PARADE

Reprinted with permission, ©Daily Nation, Nairobi, October 10, 1972

KAMPALA, Monday. A BEAMING President Amin today saluted several hundred Asians taking part for the first time in celebrations marking the anniversary of Uganda's Independence from Britain.

Asian men and children—and one solitary woman—joined their African fellow citizens in a ceremonial march-past at Kololo airstrip, near the city centre, where ten years ago today Britain handed over the instruments of independence.

They were preceded by troops, European, African and Asian veterans of the Second World War, nurses, university students and school children. But it was to the Asians that the biggest cheer went up.

All were Uganda citizens and will be staying after the exodus of the non-citizen Asians is completed in a month.

Last week General Amin helped to rehearse them for today's march-past, and he was clearly pleased both by the reception they were given and by the performance they gave.

Despite last month's invasion of Uganda, the atmosphere at the celebrations today was relaxed and the military was less in evidence than last January, when Ugandans celebrated the first anniversary of the army coup which brought General Amin to power

---

Advertisement

High Commission of India
KAMPALA

ANNOUNCEMENT

All Indian Citizens required to leave Uganda should immediately complete all departure formalities and make arrangements to leave Uganda well before November 7, 1972. They are advised not to delay their departure unnecessarily.

M.V. 'State of Haryana' is expected to sail for Bombay from Mombasa around **October 20, 1972.** Indian Citizens intending to travel by this ship should complete all formalities before **October 15,** 1972. A further announcement will be made soon about arrangements for booking passages. Those intending to travel by air should contact Air India/East African Airways bookings counters without delay.

All those 'exempted' Indian Citizens who are not leaving Uganda should inform the High Commission through post.

Soldiers start to check on shops in Kampala streets

From NATION Reporter: KAMPALA, Friday
Reprinted with permission, ©Daily Nation, Nairobi, October 7, 1972

THE Cabinet Sub-Committee and members of the Armed Forces have started a thorough check of every building in Kampala to find out who of the non-citizen outgoing Asians have not left the country.

This move follows a directive to that effect by President Amin. He directed that this week a check be started to find out who of the non-citizen Asians have not left the country.

The chairman of the Cabinet Sub-Committee who is also the Minister for Commerce and Industry, Mr. Wilson Lutara, and a member, the Minister for Minerals and Water Resources, Mr. Oryema, accompanied by members of the security forces yesterday made an on the spot check on some of the shops along Kampala Road.

In the progress of the exercise, both Ministers and members of the security forces found a number of Asians without identity cards or immigration documents. Those Asians found without these documents were taken away for further checking.

Both Ministers expressed concern over Asians they found still trading and working without work permits, despite recent Government statements to the effect that, as soon as the necessary exit clearance was obtained by any out-going Asians, their work permits and trading licences were cancelled.

Mr. Lutara stressed that in order to avoid the disruption of arrangements pertaining to the departure of non-citizen Asians, Government has decided that the institutions which process exit documents will remain open during the independence celebrations holiday period.

These institutions are: Bank of Uganda, the East African Income Tax Department and East African Airways Corporation offices. They will remain open from 8 a.m. to 7 p.m., and airport services at Entebbe will remain open 24 hours.

Mr. Lutara further states that in order to avoid any inconveniences to the Asians, Government therefore wishes to advise all persons who have been issued with identity cards, and those with foreign immigration documents, that they should carry these documents with them all the time.

The exercise will quickly cover Kampala and extend to other towns in the next few days.

Ugandan refugees in Toronto get together

News Compilation, October 10, 1972

The first social gathering for Ugandan Asians in Metro was held Saturday by members of the Uganda Committee who said they are preparing for a peak number of refugees in the weeks ahead.

So far, 793 of an anticipated 5,000 refugees have arrived in Canada since their expulsion from the East African country and about 150 have settled in the Metro area.

Shanty Shah, committee chairman, said "it's difficult for anyone to say how many will eventually be here but we can make the assumption that there will be from 1,200 to 1,500."

He said most of the recent Ugandans have friends and relatives to go to but future arrivals will include a majority with no connections at all.

Shah said about 200 Toronto families have offered to give a temporary home to the refugees and more are going to be needed. The committee has also collected about 250 job offers and has placed a dozen Ugandans.

T. N. Noormohamed is one who has just been given a job although not in his line of work. He was attending the party in the International Institute on Davenport Rd. with his wife and one-year-old daughter, Shahinoor.

He is an accountant with some British qualifications, and he estimates it will take about two years to qualify under Canadian regulations.

"I only hope the firms will give us a chance to get Canadian experience," Noormohamed said.

"I think we are getting used to the place very quickly," he added. "I am very surprised. People are kind."

School is the major concern of 14-year-old Narendra Panchal, who came with three sisters, 16, 18 and 22, to Toronto a week ago to join a brother and sister already living here.

His parents are expected from Uganda in December. He said they were sent ahead because "my parents worry about our safety and school was starting."

Anand Chopra, who meets refugees at Union Station almost daily, said there have been no real hardship cases but some girls between 12 and 20 are suffering a cultural problem.

Cut-price flats offered to Ugandan Asians

News Compilation, October 10, 1972

A property development company is offering 100 luxury flats at cut prices to Uganda Asians. It is knocking more than £2,000 off the original asking price of £8,000 for the four-bedroomed apartments, which are fully fitted with double glazing.

Other smaller flats in the block in Norton, a suburb of Stockton, Teesside, are offered at up to £1,500 less.

One building secretly had said it would offer 100 per cent mortgages.

PLUNDERED ASIANS NARRATE AMIN'S REIGN OF TERROR

By A Staff Reporter
Reprinted with permission, ©Times of India, October 10, 1972

FIVE hundred forty-six Indian passport-holders from Uganda arrived in Bombay by the Shipping Corporation's "State of Haryana" on Monday.

Like other groups which had come earlier, members of the present contingent too had a lot to tell of their trials and tribulations, of humiliation and sufferings to which they were subjected before and after their departure from Uganda.

They seemed to have experienced even greater hardships than the other batches as they were the first to leave the country after the outbreak of hostilities between Uganda and Tanzania.

Also arriving by the same ship were 46 British passport-holding and 19 Ugandan passport-holding Indians.

Of the Indian passport-holders, nearly half were women and children. Statewise, 70 per cent hailed from Gujarat and 20 per cent from Punjab. A few Goans and Maharashtrians were also among the lot. Kutchis constituted the bulk of the Gujarati element.

ADDITIONAL EXCUSE

The Uganda-Tanzania war provided an additional excuse to harass, pester and persecute Asians, one of them told reporters. A reign of terror was let loose by President Idi Amin in many parts of Uganda.

No Asian dared step out of his house after dusk. The Ugandan soldiers provoked themselves to a state of frenzy to beat up innocent Asians, it was stated.

Mr. Dharsi Ranchhod Katoria, a business man, his wife and two children, were shot by soldiers running amock at Wobubenzi. Mr. Katoria died in hospital, while his wife and children were still undergoing treatment for severe wounds.

Mr. Abdul Ebrahim Desai (35), showed a large wound on his right leg, inflicted by a Ugandan soldier at Tororo railway station on his way to Nairobi.

Tororo was the "worst" check-point and a good deal of the personal effects which the refugees had managed to keep with them after being robbed of their belongings at other "intercepting" stations, were snatched away by soldiers at the point of the gun.

Mr. Swaran Singh Bharaj, from Kapurthala, said a Sikh refugee happened to carry inside his turban a few shillings, his last savings. This provoked the Ugandan soldiers at Tororo to snatch

away the turbans of all Sikhs. No more "contraband" was discovered, but that did not prevent the trigger-happy armymen from forcing all the Sikhs to suffer the humiliation. Some were dragged and made to crawl, he said.

Swaran Singh, a fitter working in Kampala, was chagrined to find that his savings of Rs. 6,000 was "frozen" by his bank in Uganda, though he was entitled to draw the full amount for purchasing clothes and other necessities on "repatriation."

Of the 100 families and about 125 individuals, only 20 per cent were able to bring to India their entire personal belongings which were with them at the time of leaving their respective places in Uganda. The valuable articles such as watches, rings and jewellery were looted at one stage or other of their journey across Uganda to Kenya. Mr. Elias Mohamed Lohar (44) received a work permit valid for 12 months from a firm in Kampala. After two months of stay, he proceeded to Nairobi on a sight-seeing tour. While returning, he was stopped at the border by the Ugandan authorities and asked to go back where he came from. All his belongings had been left behind in Kampala and he roamed and roamed till he met some kindly Indians in Kenya who helped him to return to India.

Mrs. Kamalaben Vallabh said she and 12 other women, six men and 15 children formed themselves into a group, believing that safety lay in numbers. At Malawi, the Indian refugees who were on their way to complete their travel papers were surrounded by soldiers and their persons searched. One of the menfolk was beaten up because he was "impolite" to one of the soldiers.

ENOUGH OF IT

Mr. R. N. Trivedi, an engineer, who had settled down in Kampala for 40 years, had had "enough" of it. Even if he was paid a million rupees, he

would not set foot on Ugandan soil again.

Mr. Nanji D. Patel, a mechanic, has come back without a penny in his pocket.

Mr. S. K. Patel, president of the Brihad Bharatiya Samaj, and Mr. Babubhai Chinai met several of the refugees on board the ship, inquiring about their experiences.

The Central Maharashtra, Gujarat and Punjab governments have made provision for the temporary stay of the refugees in Bombay, their efforts being supplemented by the East African Indian Repatriates' Relief Committee organised by the Halai Lohaoa Mahajan.

TRANSIT OFFICE

A transit office has been opened at Sachivalaya. Temporary shelter is available to refugees at the MLAs' Hostel and the state Housing Board's colony at Bandra. The Mahajan wadi and other wadis at Thakurdwar have been made available by the relief committee.

The central rehabilitation department is contemplating the resettlement of the refugees without delay. Medical facilities, accommodation, internal travel facilities are all being looked after properly by various agencies. A cash allowance to last for 14 days for food and incidental expenses is being provided to each refugee.

Mr. R. F. Tidy, information officer in the deputy U.K. high commission in India, had the British passports of Indians validated for migration to the U.K.

The customs authorities went out of their way to expedite the clearance of baggage of the refugees. Mr. M.S. Kanwal, assistant customs collector, was present at Ballard Pier personally to supervise that the officers "went easy" with their belongings.

100 per cent mortgages for Ugandan Asians

News Compilation, October 10, 1972

Ugandan Asian refugees can buy homes in the London borough of Brent with up to 100 per cent council mortgages if a relative or a friend will act as guarantor, it was announced last night at a special meeting between councillors and local welfare organisations. Brent was listed as a "red" area that Asians were advised to avoid.

Advertisement

INTERGOVERNMENTAL COMMITTEE FOR
EUROPEAN MIGRATION (ICEM)
SOUTH AMERICA

NOTICE

TO UNITED KINGDOM PASSPORT HOLDERS
WITH ENTRY CERTIFICATES

A Mission is now established in Kampala with authority to process and accept for eventual settlement in South American countries a number of families or single persons now leaving Uganda. An opportunity is available which offers good prospects to those who wish to start a new life in developing countries. (Argentina, Bolivia, Brazil, Colombia, Ecuador, Uruguay, etc.)

Applicants should possess some skill in any of the following fields: Industrial Engineering, Electricity, Electronics, Chemistry, Textiles, Plastics, Machine and Tools, etc., or in Agriculture (rice, oil palm, etc.). There are also opportunities for Artisans in leather, copper, textiles, etc.

Assistance from ICEM (a specialised international agency acting on behalf of South American Governments,) will include : transport facilities, lodging and maintenance during initial settlement in South America, guaranteed placement and initial salary, free medical insurance and language tuition.

For detailed information, prospective candidates may contact a representative of the "Intergovernmental Committee for European Migration" (ICEM) from 9 a.m. to 5 p.m., every day except Sundays at the following address :

ICEM,
c o East African Development Bank Building
(First Floor).

THE MISSION EXPECTS TO BE HERE FOR
TWO WEEKS.

Advertisement

BRITISH HIGH COMMISSION

KAMPALA

THE PROGRAMME CALLING FORWARD BY NUMBERS ASIAN HEADS OF FAMILY HOLDING BRITISH PASSPORTS TO RECEIVE ENTRY CERTIFICATES FOR THE UNITED KINGDOM, WAS COMPLETED ON SATURDAY, OCTOBER 7th.

ANY HEAD OF FAMILY OR INDEPENDENT PERSON HOLDING A BRITISH PASSPORT WHO DID NOT ATTEND FOR INTERVIEW WHEN HIS NUMBER WAS CALLED SHOULD COME FORWARD **WITHOUT FAIL** ON MONDAY, OCTOBER 9th, TUESDAY, OCTOBER, 10th OR WEDNESDAY, OCTOBER, 11th, 1972. THE ENTRY CERTIFICATE OFFICE, J.P.S. BUILDING, KAMPALA, WILL BE OPEN FROM 8.00 A.M. UNTIL 6 P.M. ON THOSE DATES.

PASSPORTS AND DOCUMENTS, INCLUDING BIRTH, DEATH AND MARRIAGE CERTIFICATES RELATING TO ALL MEMBERS OF THE FAMILY, INCLUDING WIVES, YOUNG PERSONS UNDER THE AGE OF 21 AND AGED DEPENDENTS, SHOULD BE BROUGHT FOR INSPECTION.

IT WOULD ALSO ASSIST *IF THEY COULD BRING WITH THEM A NOTE OF THEIR EMPLOYERS* OR THEIR OWN INCOME TAX CODE NUMBER THIS WILL ASSIST THEIR APPLICATION TO THE UGANDA AUTHORITIES FOR TAX CLEARANCE.

Telephone enquiries regarding Entry Certificates -

KAMPALA 32554 or 32555

Ugandan Asian Expulsion: 90 Days and Beyond through the Eyes of the International Press

Win for 'middle way,' say Ministers

POWELL LOSES ON ASIANS

1,721-736 vote for Tory official policy line

By H. B. BOYNE, Political Correspondent
Reprinted with permission, ©Telegraph Group Limited, London,
October 13, 1972

BY a ballot vote of 1,721 to 736, the Conservative party conference last night rejected Mr Enoch Powell's attempt to argue that the Government's "precipitate acceptance of an unqualified duty" to admit the Uganda Asians was a departure from the party's declared policy on immigration.

But for the fact that a ballot vote was demanded, the majority against Mr Powell would have been much more impressive.

A reliable estimate was that not many more than 200 hands were raised against an amended motion which congratulated the Government for its swift action to accept responsibilities for the Asian refugees.

As it was, the Powellites were neither humbled nor crushed. On the figures, they could claim that nearly 30 per cent of the party support Mr Powell on the immigration issue.

Many constituency representatives who raised their hands against Mr Powell may have left the hall before the ballot, or perhaps failed to bring their ballot papers. But it is the figures that count on the record.

Ministers pleased

Ministers were in any case well satisfied with the result. In their view, it showed that the party, far from moving to the Right as Labour has moved to the Left, is firmly aligned on the "middle way" in British politics. As evidence of this, they cited its firm support of Government policy on law and order and on Ulster, as well as immigration.

The debate went against Mr Powell in the ratio

of at least five to three of the speakers called from the floor. His own speech was far from the most effective he has ever made at a party conference.

What really scuppered him was a television interview the night before in which he alleged that the Lord Chancellor, Lord Hailsham, was "deceiving" the British people and suggested that Sir Alec Douglas-Home, Foreign and Commonwealth Secretary, was possibly doing the same.

Mr David Hunt, chairman of the Young Conservatives, made extremely skillful use of this. His appeal to the conference to treat with contempt "that sort of slur on somebody we respect and admire" must have turned many waverers against Mr Powell.

Carr's reply

Mr Robert Carr, Home Secretary, in a brilliantly persuasive reply to the debate, also spurned Mr Powell's attack on the integrity of Lord Hailsham and Sir Alec in addition to rejecting all

his criticisms of the Government's policies and intentions.

He also quoted with great effect Winston Churchill's praise of the contribution the Asians had made to Britain's East African empire.

"President Amin may break faith with them— we shall not," be concluded passionately.

As he spoke, Mr Carr had not received confirmation of a report that President Amin intended to expel the British High Commissioner along with the last of the Asian passport holders. But he was probably thinking of this when he urged the conference to bear in mind the safety of the 7,000 British nationals working in Uganda.

The debate was the culmination of a day in which the Government's economic, housing, education, agriculture and VAT policies were all endorsed by large majorities.

British High Commissioner must leave by deadline

News Compilation, October 12, 1972

President Amin told Mr Richard Slater, the British High Commissioner in Kampala to leave with the last batch of Asians due to depart before the November 8 deadline.

Amin also announced that he was recalling Lieutenant-Colonel Lukakamwa, the Uganda High Commissioner in London. He said it was useless to keep a High Commissioner in Britain where there was a lot of propaganda against Uganda.

INDIA

Warm home-coming for evacuees

By A Staff Reporter
Reprinted with permission, ©Times of India, October 11, 1972

"FOR the first time in several weeks we had a sound sleep last night," an elderly couple, relaxing on a sofa after lunch, said on Tuesday. Their grown-up daughter was seated nearby, combing her hair.

The family was among the 546 Indian passport holders from Uganda who had arrived in the city by sea on Monday.

The husband said he was happy at the treatment he was getting . His elation was shared by the over 200 refugees who have been housed temporarily at Mahajanwadi, Thakurdwar, Bombay, in transit to their native towns. Most of them are from Gujarat.

As he was speaking, others were having their mid-day meal. It was a real Navratri feast provided by the East African Indian Repatriates Relief Committee.

POCKET ALLOWANCE

In other transit camps, too, including the one sponsored by the Brihad Bharatiya Samaj at Congress House, the repatriates were treated to a feast. Soon after lunch, most of them were busy preparing for their onward journey to destinations in Gujarat, Punjab, Haryana and Goa.

As they prepared for their departure, Union rehabilitation ministry officials distributed pocket allowances of about Rs. 40 to each family. The allowance is expected to last for a fortnight, enabling them to meet their food and incidental

expenses.

The railway fare is being paid by the Union government. These arrangements mark the beginning of a programme to resettle the repatriates.

Many of the repatriates are artisans—fitters, mechanics, carpenters, auto-repairers and masons. A large number of Goans and Keralites had served in Uganda as teachers, nurses, telephone operators and receptionists.

Gujaratis were mostly shop assistants, petty traders and government employees. The few emigrants from Pondicherry, U.P., Bahar, Haryana and Mysore, were also in the teaching profession.

Only a sprinkling of the repatriates were big-time business men and industrialists.

As the vast majority of Indian passport holders had migrated or gone to Uganda after India's independence, the wrench was not excessive. A very high percentage of them, over 90 per cent, have relatives in this country. They have no immediate problem of finding shelter.

The minority without close relatives will get top priority in the matter of rehabilitation, a government spokesman said.

Many of the repatriates told this reporter that this was just like another home-coming for them.

World News Headlines

Canadian Jobless rate hits 7.1%—a 10-year high. The Australian government announced that federal elections would be held on December 2, 1972.

Page 102

Ugandan Asian Expulsion: 90 Days and Beyond through the Eyes of the International Press

TORONTO, CANADA

Asian children here from Uganda long to see snow for the first time

By GERALD UTTING
Star staff writer
Reprinted with permission, ©Toronto Star syndicate, October 14, 1972

Iwona de Souza, 9, and her sisters, Deborah, 7, and Annabelle, 5, are waiting eagerly for the first snow of winter.

Asians from Kampala, Uganda, they have been debating ever since they arrived here as refugees Sept. 24 on the type of snowman they intend to build.

They have never seen snow, of course, and the prospect of the sort of winter that drives Canadians to Florida fills them with glee.

"It's all they talk about—their first snowman," said their mother, Lucy, 32.

The three girls have settled into Metro life without qualms. They all go to Nativity of Our Lord separate school on Saffron Crescent in Etobicoke, and have already apparently forgotten about the childhood dreads that were everyday reality back in Kampala.

"There we had to keep them in the house in case of trouble with the soldiers," said Lucy de Souza. "We never heard of them taking it out on children, but there were many incidents of adult Asians being mal-treated, so we couldn't take any chances.

"The children could see all that tension and they were afraid.

"Now they see how happy my husband Tom and I are to be here in Toronto and they can't help but feel happy, too.

"All we have had to worry about here has been finding a job and getting warm clothes. There we had worry about our lives."

Iwona came home the other night and was telling her family about her progress at school in homework. She said she had come second in her Grade 6 class at math—scoring 72 out of a possible 82 marks.

Deborah is in Grade 3 and Annabelle in Grade 1. The youngest de Souza, Clement Paul, is only 3 and plays with his mother in the Rymer Rd. home of her brother Percy D'Souza, a civil engineer who came to Toronto two years ago with his family of two boys and a girl.

The de Souza's and D'Souzas are of Goan origin, Catholics whose families

Continued on Page 104

Youngest new arrival from Uganda, Clement de Souza, 3, sits at table with father and mother, Mr. and Mrs. de Souza in the Etobicoke home of Mrs. de Souza's brother, Percy, who came to Canada two years ago.   Reproduced with permission ©F. Lennon/Toronto Star

61 cold Ugandans seek places to stay

Reprinted with permission, ©Toronto Star syndicate, October 18, 1972

Sixty-one Asian refugees from Uganda arrived in Toronto today and their first worry was trying to find a place to stay before looking for jobs.

Most complained of the cold—it was about 40—after getting off a train from Montreal.

"I love it here already, but it really is cold," said nurse Shainaz Pirani Karim Janmohamed. "But I'll get used to that."

Shainaz was met at the station by Dr. Donald A. Gibson, an orthopedic surgeon at the Hospital for Sick Children, who carried a neatly printed card with her name on it.

Gibson did research work in a hospital at Kampala, Uganda from 1952 to 1959, and that's where Shainaz was a nurse.

She won't have to worry about a place to stay because Gibson has arranged for her to stay at his home in Rosedale and also has a job for her at the Hospital for Sick Children.

Shainaz, whose parents, two brothers and a sister are still in Africa, is one of 1,000 Asian-Ugandans admitted into Canada since President Idi Amin ordered 60,000 of them to get out of the country by Nov. 8.

Immigration officials at Union Station said that most of the people who arrived today are professional workers, such as accountants and nurses.

Anand Chopra, secretary for the Uganda Committee of Toronto, said that host families are needed to help look after the immigrants until permanent accommodations can be found.

EDMONTON, CANADA

Ugandan committee seeks public support

Reprinted with permission, ©Edmonton Journal, October 16, 1972

The Ugandan Committee for Edmonton, set up to help Asian refugees expelled from Uganda is seeking public support. About 12 Ugandans have moved to Edmonton so far.

Dr. Ram K. Gupta, committee chairman, said that as the immigrants arrive in Edmonton they are met by representatives of Canada Manpower, which supports them financially for an indefinite time while trying to find them work.

The committee, with about 30 members, is trying to provide further services for the political exiles, such as decent clothing, cooking utensils and crockery, linen and furniture.

Dr. Gupta said: "More importantly, we would like to provide them with a human touch or emotional support." Each incoming family would be adopted by one or two Edmonton families. Adoption involved informal and frequent contacts to help them adjust to the new life.

Dr. Gupta said they have already planned a number of social events for 12 Ugandan refugees including a gathering with committee members and an invitation to a Pakistani Students' Association movie today; and a dinner organized by the Hindu Society Sunday evening.

Dr. Gupta said they don't know exactly how many refugees will come to Edmonton.

"We're guessing about 300 to 400, but that may be over five or six months."

The committee is seeking Edmontonians wanting to help with its project and programs, and people willing to offer their garages and basements for collection depots for clothing and other items.

Ugandan envoy tells of 200 death threats

News Compilation, October 16, 1972

THE Ugandan High Commissioner to Britain, Lieutenant-Colonel Samuel Lukakamwa, said here he has received more than 200 death threats to kill him, his family and commission staff during the past three months.

Colonel Lukakamwa, whose luxury London home is under constant police protection, said he was not personally worried by the threats but he was concerned for his family. He said he had not officially heard he was being recalled by his government—although earlier Ugandan Government radio reported that President Amin had announced the High Commissioner's recall.

Passports given to 'stateless British Asians'

By BRIAN SILK in Nairobi
Reprinted with permission, ©Telegraph Group Limited, London,
October 17, 1972

THE British High Commission in Kampala yesterday began the process of turning stateless Asians into British citizens in order to issue them with passports. To avoid confusion, officials pointed out that this did not mean there had been any change of policy.

The 80 Asians who went along to the High Commission yesterday were told that, contrary to any impression they might have formed the last time they called, they were not really stateless, and in fact never had been.

Now that this misunderstanding had been cleared up, Britain was able to offer passports to all 80 of them so that they could fly home.

The High Commission's exercise in semantics enabled the foreign office in London to deny that it was now prepared to allow stateless Asians into Britain.

There are between 10,000 and 15,000 Asians in Uganda who until now thought they were stateless, no doubt because no country was willing to accept them.

Citizenship revoked

All previously British citizens, they took out Ugandan citizenship after the country's independence in 1962 only to have this revoked by Gen. Amin in August.

The sense of statelessness increased when the British High Commission refused them entry vouchers and suggested they take their chances with the United Nations. Now, however, Britain has discovered that in many cases their earlier renunciation of British citizenship was not completed within the 90 days required by Ugandan law.

This was the main reason for several thousand losing their Ugandan nationality under Gen. Amin, who discovered the fact three months earlier. The Foreign Office therefore maintains that such people are still entitled to hold United Kingdom passports.

The point was explained to the Asians yesterday by an announcement in the Ugandan Press which said: "The British High Commission are now authorised to reconsider applications for United Kingdom passports from persons whose renunciation of United Kingdom citizenship did not effectively secure the retention of their Ugandan citizenship."

How many are in this category is not known although the Foreign Office says there are about 2,000 whose renunciation is uncertain. The Foreign Office obtained this information from the British High Commission in Kampala which insisted yesterday it had no idea of the number.

This is in spite of the fact that the High Commission has a list of names which it is using in calling forward the "stateless British Asians."

An airline official in Kampala who is working on the Asian airlift said he had been told by the High Commission to expect about 6,000 stateless people.

British officials in both London and Kampala point out that passports will be issued only to those who can show they are fully entitled to them. Hover, none of the 80 who called at the High Commission yesterday was refused a passport.

Entry vouchers were also issued to 422 wives and children whose heads of families are either Ugandan Asians or stateless.

Envoy leaves

The mathematics is becoming complicated at this stage in the airlift, as who is to say how many of these wives and children are also being allowed into Britain because their stateless husbands and fathers are not stateless any more?

Joining the Asians at Entebbe airport yesterday was Mr Richard Slater, British High Commissioner, and his wife, Barbara. Mr Slater has been recalled to London for consultation following Gen. Amin's decision to expel him when the last of the Asians have left.

The Slaters were unable to find a home in Kampala for their pet terrier Jack. Not wanting to leave him in Quarantine for six months, they have had the dog put down.

Continued from Page 103

Asian children here from Uganda long to see snow for the first time

come from the west coast area of India that was a colony of Portugal for more than 450 years until India annexed it in 1961.

The newest arrivals to Rymer Rd. say they have found no trouble fitting in the Canadian way of life. Tom de Souza had to walk out of his home in Uganda, abandoning virtually all his possessions and leaving a flourishing business as an insurance adjuster.

"We really like it here," he said. "We have forgotten Uganda, although I suppose the regrets will come after we have settled into our new country.

"I have got a job already. The children are in school. We have friends. Soon we hope to move in a home of our own. We plan to save to make up for some of the things we lost.

"But really, thanks be, I came out of Uganda with what's really important—my family."

De Souza, who left behind assets worth $90,000 in Uganda, arrived in Toronto with only $140 in cash—all the Uganda government would permit him to take out.

More efficiency

But he had permission from the Canadian government to become a landed immigrant, and made contact with a nationwide firm of insurance adjusters.

"I started work as a trainee insurance investigator in their Albion Mall branch Oct. 1," he said. "The pay is fair. I have a company car and I am studying insurance operations in Canada. In the next two years I hope to pass the examination and become a licensed insurance adjuster.

"I find the work here similar to what it was in Uganda, except things are much more efficient here. There is not so much red tape, so it really makes life much easier.

"What has really pleased me is the friendliness of Canadians. Asians going to Britain from Uganda are all afraid of meeting with prejudice because of the stories they have heard from there. But Canadians just don't seem to know the meaning of bigotry.

"Already the children have made friends. They come home after school and play and know they'll grow up here with wonderful futures in this peaceful Canada."

De Souza and his wife said that they knew it would get much colder, but "we'll just bundle up in big coats."

Lucy de Souza said that Canadian housewives needn't envy women such as herself, who had servants in her homeland.

"I don't think we need them here," she said.

There's a big difference in shopping with all your canned goods and frozen foods.

"There's such a range of things in the shops and life is made much easier. You just wouldn't even be able to dream about these things in Africa."

Start studying

Lucy is planning when her young son is a little older, to put him in a day care centre and start studying accountancy.

"She was a school teacher in Kampala," said her husband, "but she also has experience in accounting

work."

"You have everything here that we had in Africa and more," said Lucy. "You even have more fruit. We could never afford apples or peaches in Kampala, where apples are $4.25 a pound. Even though they grow coffee in Uganda, it is cheaper in Toronto.

"And there's everything you want in the way of spices for curries.

"In Kampala young children only go to school for half a day, but the children don't seem tired by the full day here. They seem to have a lot of energy in the afternoon and they still are wide awake to see my brother's TV at night. Of course, they love the shows and the many channels you have.

"In Kampala there is only one channel and all you see is General Amin making speeches. Even children don't want to watch him."

Misses sister

Lucy said there is only one thing she really misses—her sister. She and her husband had an interview recently and hope to be able to come to Canada.

Tom de Souza smiled when told some Canadians have suggested the Ugandan refugees might not be able to get jobs in Canada.

"The Canadian immigration isn't going to let in anyone like that," he said. "And I don't think that anyone who could make a living in poor Uganda will have any trouble finding a job in this fortunate country.

"Canadians are so lucky and I don't just mean as far as money is concerned. I had a good business in Kampala but I couldn't go out at night without being afraid. Here, I can go everywhere peacefully."

Ugandans flocking into areas that are hard pressed to cope

By Peter Evans
Home Affairs Correspondent
Reprinted with permission, ©Times Newspapers Limited, London,
October 19, 1972

In spite of the Uganda Resettlement Board's policy of trying to dissuade Asian refugees from going to "red" areas from which they are discouraged, many have continued to arrive in Leicester and the London borough of Brent.

This week Leicester had received 1,314, according to Alderman Edward Marston, leader of the Labour-controlled council, and the flow was continuing. Brent took more than a thousand, according to Alderman P. H. Hartley, the council leader.

Figures released last week by the board showed that Leicester was the most popular place after London. In London, Brent had attracted most. The board said yesterday that there was every sign that the Asians were showing the same pattern of settlement as indicated by last week's figures. About 16,000 had now arrived in Britain.

In Nottingham, a "green" city able to accept some Asians, Mr Andrew Main, the community relations officer, said that only 50 to 60 had arrived. "Accommodation has been offered by people in all walks of life", he added. "We have been feeding this information to the resettlement board, but not one offer has been taken up."

The board and the Government have no power to direct Asians to or from a place once they are in Britain, as was explained to Leicester. Two main reasons are given for the board's failure to persuade Asians to go where the authorities would like.

One is the pull of refugees towards other Uganda Asians settled here. This pull increases the longer refugees are stranded in camps. Many who registered after arrival in Leicester during the weekend were believed to have been fetched by friends from camps.

One family I met on the train to Leicester said they thought they would be better off with friends in the city rather than waiting in a camp for something to "turn up".

Jobs are another attraction. Unemployment in Leicester is well below the regional average and lower than in Nottingham, although Nottingham people have offered jobs for Asians. By the end of last week about 300 Asian men and 60 women had registered for employment in Leicester. About 40 had obtained jobs.

The inability of Leicester corporation to provide homes has not deterred Asians from arriving. Stories of overcrowding are spreading as friends put up refugees. In Brent, Mr Hartley told me: "We have made a pronouncement that we shall suspend the enforcement of regulations against overcrowding while the emergency lasts, say for six to nine months."

He thought the classifying of areas as "red"

Continued on Page 106

Refugees mentally, physically fit

By Susan Reister
Citizen Staff writer
Reprinted with permission, ©Ottawa Citizen, October 14, 1972

The Ugandan Asians arriving in Canada during the next few weeks are mentally and physically fit and concerned most about the Canadian climate and the elevation of certain cities.

After spending two weeks in Kampala, Dr. John Graham, a medical examiner with the department of national health and welfare, said that by the time he left Kampala on Wednesday the Canadian medical team had examined over 2,100 Asians.

He said the 20 Canadian medical personnel there would be able to examine the remaining 3,000 within the Nov. 7 expulsion deadline set by Ugandan President Idi Amin.

Dr. Graham said the medical staff conducted "as thorough as possible a medical examination under the circumstances." He said it was probably better than routine examinations because it was conducted by Canadian doctors. Normally, Canada has local medical personnel conduct examinations of prospective immigrants.

Chief concern

He said the main concern of the Asians "was the elevation and climate across Canada." The Asians generally lived in low-lying areas.

From his examinations, Dr. Graham said he found "generally what one would expect in a tropical country. There were very few exotic diseases and most people were very healthy.

No Asians were rejected as immigrants because of medical reasons, he added.

CANADA
Asians given a break

By Patrick Best
Citizen staff writer
Reprinted with permission, ©Ottawa Citizen, October 18, 1972

The Canadian government has dropped its usual immigration selection standard in an emergency move to get as many expelled Asians out of Uganda as possible before the Nov. 8 deadline set by President Amin.

Immigration Minister Mackasey revealed today the immigration rules had been relaxed as a "humanitarian gesture."

"As long as these Ugandan refugees don't limp we are accepting them," he added. "They are being persecuted and need a home. There is more to concern us now than the quality of the prospective immigrant."

The immigration team in Kampala is now clearing the way for all Asians who want to settle in Canada, including those who are stateless. The relaxed procedures relate to both the immigration point system and medical requirements.

Movement slowed

Immigration sources said they are very concerned over the fact that "roadblocks" of various forms are slowing down the movement of Asians accepted by Canada while en route to the airport at Entebbe, located about 20 miles from the capital of Kampala.

Some of the 156 Uganda exiles arriving at Montreal International Airport Tuesday reported seeing family members killed as they prepared to leave the country. Others were arrested by police.

Because of the fear of possible reprisals in their home country, the new arrivals hesitated to give any further details on the incidents. In a number of cases the actions were said to be carried out without the knowledge of President Amin's regime.

When the Trudeau government announced

Continued on Page 106

News briefs

News Compilation, October 16, 1972

Housing dispute: Mr Michael Crew, who on Saturday won a by-election at Basildon, Essex, after he had resigned as a Labour councillor over the issue of houses for Asian families, said yesterday that he will ask at the next council meeting for an assurance from the leader of the council that no preferential treatment will be given to Asians.

An overtime ban by Asians in factories and on buses to provide work for the Uganda refugees was urged yesterday by Mr Karter Singh Soar, senior vice-president of the Central Committee of Sikh Temples in Britain.

Group Travel, of Victoria, London, said last night that a Uganda Asian businessman who left before the present troubles began had offered free flights for pensioners to the Costa del Sol, in Spain, this winter as a gesture of thanks for British help for expelled Asians.

New 'emergency' school planned for Asians

Reprinted with permission, ©Leicester Mercury, October 19, 1972

With over 600 children currently awaiting school places, Leicester Education Department are considering the possibility of creating an emergency secondary school for Asians in the form of a group of mobile classrooms.

One of the sites being examined for the possible temporary school is a playing field at Davenport Road, Goodwood Estate, but no decision has yet been taken on this.

Leicester's Deputy Director of Education, Mr. D. E. Ramell said today that the possible mobile classroom school would be in addition to the decision to reopen the disused Belper Street school for Asian pupils.

Mr. Ramell said today: "It is true we are looking at a number of sites on which temporary accommodation can be put.

"The law says the local education authority must have school places for children. What is spent depends on building allocations, which in turn depend on Government approvals.

"So if an authority are allowed to build quickly it has got to be temporary accommodation.

Ugandan Asian Expulsion: 90 Days and Beyond through the Eyes of the International Press

Page 105

Asians encouraged to re-emigrate

News Compilation, October 21, 1972

To speed up the resettlement of Asian refugees attempts are being made to encourage some who have arrived in Britain to re-emigrate to other countries.

It was announced at a meeting of the Uganda Resettlement Board yesterday that posters printed in English and Gujerati are to be displayed in all reception camps. They give details of countries that have agreed to take Asians and tell how applications may be made.

Austria, New Zealand, Sweden, Guyana, Germany, Fiji, Australia, Canada and a number of dependent territories, including the Falkland Islands, are named on the poster.

The number of Asians the countries named are prepared to take and the qualifications they are laying down vary widely.

Offers made to date cover more than 8,000 people and members of the board are confident that a substantial number of them will be taken up.

After Canada's offer to take up to 6,000 refugees, the next most generous comes from Germany, which is prepared to take 1,000. Other countries are willing to take smaller numbers.

Continued from Page 105

Asians given a break

two months ago it would help Britain absorb the expelled Asians, it said that the usual immigration and medical standards would be observed. The sympathetic reception being given the Uganda refugees by the Canadian public is said to be a facto in the decision to relax the rules.

'Hate mail' gone

Mr. Mackasey said the "hate mail" he has been receiving on the Asian question "has dropped off to nothing. I used to be up to my neck in it."

President Amin says a house-to-house search will be made in his country after the Nov. 8 deadline to determine whether all the expelled Asians have left.

The flight arriving in Montreal Tuesday brought to 939 the total number of Uganda refugees who have come to Canada since the special airlift began Sept. 28.

The ninth planeload is due to arrive tonight, after which the schedule calls for daily flights until the end of October, with two flights a day in some cases.

University forms group to help Asian students

News Compilation, October 21, 1972

Dr. John Evans, president of the University of Toronto, said yesterday he has set up an advisory committee to help immigrants from Uganda who might want to study or work at the University.

The committee will be headed by Peter Russell, principal of Innis College.

Asians move in with Archbishop of York

From a Staff Reporter
York, Oct 19
Reprinted with permission, ©Times Newspapers Limited, London, October 20, 1972

The Archbishop of York, Dr Coggan, today introduced to the press the Uganda Asian family who have moved into the elegant thirteenth-century surrounds of Bishopthorpe Palace. Mr Muhammad Ali Fazal, aged 32, his wife, Pervin, aged 27, and their six-week-old daughter Irrun, arrived at the palace last night from Stradishall camp. They came to England last month from Kampala with only £50 and much uncertainty.

It was an informal conference at the palace with Dr Coggan firmly in control. Mr Fazal was born in India of Indian parents and taught mathematics, history and Islamic studies in Kampala. He graduated at Karachi University and holds a BA degree and a second degree in education.

Were the Fazals handpicked for Bishopthorpe? No, Dr Coggan replied; they met for the first time last night. What did Mr and Mrs Fazal feel when they found they were moving into a palace? "Very happy", Mr Fazal answered. "Deep shock", the archbishop boomed. Someone at Stradishall had simply told Mr Fazal that if he was interested there was someone who could give him a place to stay.

The new lodger beamed happily around the room while his wife sat calmly with little Irrun soundly asleep in her arms. Mr Fazal had trained in Islamic studies and comparative religion in Pakistan and could hardly have found a better place in which to make high-powered comparisons than the home of an archbishop.

Did he like the palace? "It is fairly big for me, much nicer than a flat."

Would the Fazals mind stepping outside for a photograph? Dr Coggan intervened, towering over the slim figure of Mr Fazal. "He has not got an overcoat yet and mine would not fit him", he declared.

The family will live in a self-contained flat in the palace, but have so far been having their meals with Dr and Mrs Coggan. It will be a rent-free arrangement until Mr Fazal finds a job, he hopes as a teacher, and can set up a new home for his family. He said he had applied to go to New Zealand, but had not heard from the New Zealand High Commission in London. He thought he would be happy to settle in York.

Dr Coggan said the arrangement was made after he had written to Sir Charles Cunninghan, chairman of the Uganda Asian Resettlement Board, announcing their willingness to take a family. He had publicly expressed concern about the plight of the Uganda Asians and encouraged people to provide homes for them, but no one had challenged him to do something about it personally.

How many Uganda Asians could he and the palace cope with? "Two and a half", Dr Coggan declared.

Dr Coggan's example seems to be spreading mildly in his own city. An urgent appeal for furniture went out today from social workers.

A spokesman said: "We have had some very generous offers of help and accommodation, and the first families are expected next week."

Babies arrive.—Eighteen babies were among 171 Uganda Asians who arrived at Hobbs barracks, Lingfield, Surrey, yesterday. Group Captain Peter Bird said more Asians were due to arrive daily until the camp had its full quota of 800.

Continued from Page 105

Ugandans flocking into areas that are hard pressed to cope

had been valuable. It had shielded Brent from the first impact. "In the long run I am almost certain that because we have a high number of Uganda Asians in Wembley we shall have by far the greatest share in the country."

There is, however, much criticism of the resettlement board, particularly regarding administrative coordination. The early failure of the computer to classify details collected in Uganda about the refugees is not forgotten. Arrivals could not be matched to information about them.

In Nottingham, Mr Main said information given to the board about offers of jobs and accommodation in the city did not seem to have been passed on to camps. Mr Vernon Clements, his assistant, had twice gone to Hemswell camp, Lincolnshire, and the information had not been sent there by the board.

There has been a shortage of detailed information about what financial help councils are sup-

posed to receive to offset costs of coping with refugees. In Leicester Mr Marston said a preliminary circular to local authorities on September 18 promised more detailed information at an early date.

Leicester and Brent are each being forced to open an old school. Leicester is spending £20,000 on repairs and refurbishing. In both places Asian children have to be provided with buses, but in Leicester there is a shortage of buses.

Meanwhile 553 children in Leicester, at last week's count, were not in school because places could not be found for them; 261 of them were refugees from Uganda.

Vietnam Peace Talks

News Compilation, October 21, 1972

U.S. Presidential adviser, Henry A. Kissinger and other U.S. officials met with South Vietnamese President Nguyen Van Thieu in Saigon to discuss a potential cease-fire accord.

MORE HIT BY DEADLINE ORDER

Now Amin tells Kenyan Asians to quit Uganda

From NATION Reporters
KAMPALA, Thursday
Reprinted with permission, ©Daily Nation, Nairobi, October 20, 1972

PRESIDENT Amin today extended his quit order to cover Asian citizens of Kenya, Tanzania and Zambia. They have to "remove themselves from Uganda" before the November 8 deadline.

President Amin announced his decision when he met Lt.-Col. Muhamud Aziz, who will act as commander of the Uganda Army during the absence of the acting commander, Col. Nyangweso, who is on a trip outside the country.

President Amin said that he had taken the decision in view of connections Asians from Kenya, Tanzania and Zambia, had with those affected by his quit order. Asians from the three countries had continued to enter Uganda by car and had taken advantage of the geographical positions at Kenya and Tanzania to smuggle goods out of Uganda.

The General claimed that there had been cases of Asians flying in from Zambia for the same purpose. President Amin assured Lt.-Col. Aziz that the Uganda Government, the Armed Forces, and the people were determined to win the economic war he had declared.

He urged Lt.-Col. Aziz to "be alert 24 hours a day" because it had been discovered that non-citizen Asians expelled from Uganda had now formed a syndicate with those not affected by the expulsion order to smuggle out currency.

The President yesterday warned that they are "wasting their time" making claims on buildings belonging to Asians ordered to quit Uganda.

Gen. Amin declared that the Government would not allow Indian and British banks which were "seizing" businesses and buildings belonging to departing Asians to frustrate its policy of transferring the economy of Uganda into the hands of Ugandans.

ASIAN 'REFUGEES' SAY THEY WERE ROBBED

Reprinted with permission, ©Daily Nation, Nairobi, October 20, 1972

THE Indian High Commissioner designate to Kenya, Mr. K. C. Nair, was among scores of Nairobi residents and social welfare workers who met about 340 Asians passing through Nairobi yesterday on their way to India from Uganda.

The Asians from Uganda stopped at Nairobi Railway Station where they were given food, dried milk, blankets, medical attention and clothes.

About 60 of the passengers, who joined this train at Mbale, said they were stripped bare by Uganda Police and Army personnel and their ornaments, watches, travellers' cheques and drafts were confiscated.

Two senior officials of the Indian High Commission in Kampala travelled with the train from Kampala along with a police escort and patrolled the entire train every couple of hours to see that all the passengers, mostly Indian nationals, were safe and unmolested.

The officials and police left the train at Tororo before it entered Kenya.

Passengers in the two bogles from Mbale, which mostly carried employees of the African Textile Mills, complained of the harsh treatment they suffered when they were thoroughly searched.

"When they liked anything they just took it away, after scattering all our belongings all over the place," said Ajit Singh a former resident of Kampala. "The lady inspectors took off all the gold ornaments which the womenfolk were wearing."

Manmoj Naik, a technician originally from Ahmedabad, said: "They took away our radios, tape recorders and even any used clothing which they fancied."

At Tororo, the entire train was again searched and any currency found on the passengers was taken way.

"Anybody protesting was badly beaten up," said Ratilal Hirji, a building supervisor who worked for Mowlem in Kampala. "They hit my younger brother, Zaverilal, on his left eye, badly bruising it, because as we were about to board the train in Kampala he went to buy a bottle of gripe water for a baby travelling with us."

At Jinja, when some passengers went to book their luggage, it was broken into and looted by Army personnel before the eyes of the owners, said a paper technician from that town.

Why 100 Asians rejected £40 jobs

Reprinted with permission, ©Daily Mail, London, October 21, 1972

A FIRM offered £40-a-week jobs and homes to 100 of the Asians expelled from Uganda.

But when the Asians at Stradishall camp, Suffolk, heard what the jobs were they turned them down unanimously.

For the firm which made the offer wanted the Asians to make pork and beef sausages, and it is contrary to their religion to handle these meats.

Problem

Last night Mr Neville Cheek, personnel manager of the firm, Scot Meat Products of Bletchley, Buckinghamshire, said: 'We thought we could help these people out because we have plenty of vacancies.

'We were all set to send people down to conduct interviews at the camp when we got a message from there saying that nobody would accept out offer.'

A spokesman at Stradishall, where more than half the 1,250 Asians are experienced factory workers, said: "The problem was that most of the people here are Hindus, and they are not allowed by their religion to work with these meats. Besides, half the people are vegetarians anyway.'

Advertisement

AMERICAN EMBASSY

OPEN SEVEN DAYS
A WEEK
TO PROCESS VISAS

The Embassy of the United States of America will be open

**8 a.m. to 7 p.m. daily
including Saturdays and Sundays**

to process applications of skilled, STATELESS Asians who wish to emigrate to the United States The Embassy is on the 6th Floor of Embassy House, Parliament St.

Skills of many categories will qualify Stateless Asians for Visas

To speed processing, applicants should bring to the first interview all documentation they have concerning skills, date and place of birth and, especially, documents attesting to statelessness.

Those persons who previously have applied for regular visas to emigrate to the United States under the professional—scientist—artist program are requested to come to the Embassy as soon as possible to verify their intentions.

Advertisement

DON'T ABANDON
YOUR DOG OR CAT

ANY DEPARTING RESIDENT OF UGANDA WHO WISHES TO DISPOSE OF HIS/HER PET ANIMALS MAY BRING THEM TO THE FACULTY OF VETERINARY SCIENCE, MAKERERE UNIVERSITY, KAMPALA ON BOMBO ROAD ON THE LEFT SIDE PAST THE GAYAZA ROAD ROUNDABOUT. THEY WILL BE HUMANELY DISPOSED OF FOR A NOMINAL FEE. THIS SERVICE IS AVAILABLE, MONDAY THROUGH FRIDAY 10:00 - 12:00 A.M. and 2:00 - 3:00 P.M.

SPECIAL ANALYSIS

Triumphs and failures

by COLIN LEGUM, ROBERT CHESSHYRE and DILIP HIRO
Reprinted with permission, ©The Observer, London, October 22, 1972

With only 17 days left to General Amin's deadline, it now seems certain that the last remaining 5,000 British Asians will be out of Uganda by 8 November.

The crisis has brought out something of the wartime spirit in the British people. Thirteen reception camps have been opened up since the first of the expected 25,000 refugees started to arrive just under two months ago. They are mostly well-run with good facilities. Soon there will be 20 of them.

Hundreds of volunteers are working all hours of the day and night, seven days a week. They have made it possible for the bureaucracy to meet this unique challenge.

So far, the chaotic conditions surrounding the immigrations of the 1950s and 1960s, which produced the ghettos of the West Indians and of the poorer Indians and Pakistanis, have been avoided.

Much of the credit for this goes to the immigrants themselves who—despite being uprooted in traumatic conditions of insecurity, physical ill-treatment and overnight impoverishment—have kept up their morale to a remarkable extent and, in many cases, have shown considerable initiative in adapting themselves to their new circumstances.

The first stage of the operation is almost completed, but the huge task of absorbing these 25,000 refugees into British society remains.

About 18,500 of the immigrants have arrived so far. Almost one-third have by-passed the reception centres, going straight from the airports to the homes of friends or relations (about 175,000 East African Asians are established here already).

About 3,000 of the immigrants have already left the camps—either because they have found temporary homes—though not necessarily jobs—or because they feel they must be more mobile, in the search for homes and jobs.

About 9,000 are still in the camps, and they will soon be joined by the remaining 5,000. Every day many venture out to see what they can find for themselves. They are given travel and subsistence allowances. Nobody, in principle, is discouraged from going anywhere—not even to the so-called 'red areas,' the towns listed as already carrying too high a proportion of immigrants.

But many prefer to stay in the camps, either because of feelings of insecurity because of fears that they will lose their right to subsistence or security benefits, or their chances of qualifying for homes or possible Government loans.

So far, there have been 3,108 offers of jobs from 841 employers—1,984 for men and 1,124 for women. Local authorities have offered 1,500 homes, while about 6,000 beds have been offered by private sources.

The Uganda Resettlement Board—the body set up to deal with the emergency—has had to abandon its earlier policy of trying to march jobs with homes. While still helping in the search for jobs, it now concentrates on finding suitable homes.

Although the Board is concentrating its efforts mainly on the so-called 'green areas' (towns with small immigrant communities and low unemployment), it seems to have accepted that it has lost any chance of steering immigrants away from the 'red areas.'

More than 2,000 newcomers have in fact gone, at least temporarily, to Leicester—the city which took space in Uganda newspapers to discourage more Asians from joining the 20,000 already there. Of these, about one-third are East African Asians.

Leicester is a magnet for immigrants for several reasons. Its unemployment rate (2.7 percent) is only two-thirds that of the West Midlands average. It has the highest employment rate (40 per cent) for women in the country—an added attraction for Asians who want to maximize family earnings. And the large East African Asian community already there is prospering in business: they own supermarkets, travel agencies, cash and carry stores, wholesale businesses and hotels.

About 1,800 of the new immigrants have moved into Greater London: 389 to Brent, 223 to Harrow, 166 to Ealing, 107 to Wandsworth and 890 to the other boroughs.

The Resettlement Board has both strong sup-

An outing for some Uganda Asian children near the transit camp in Kensington Church Street, London, where they were taken from Heathrow. Their "driver" is Mr Clive Halifax.

Reproduced with permission ©Times Newspapers Limited

in Asian camps

SPECIAL ANALYSIS

Television room at Houndstone, Somerset resettlement camp for Ugandan Asians. Reproduced with permission ©Telegraph Group Limited

Below: Stradishall resettlement camp- B.S. Jadhav, a compositor in Kampala before his expulsion, chats with his sons, Yanant, 18 (left), and Kiran, 15.

porters and strong critics among the voluntary organisations in the camps. Its supporters come mainly from the uniformed Women's Royal Voluntary Services and its critics from the voluntary Co-ordinating Committee for the Welfare of Evacuees from Uganda.

The WRVS has stayed out of the Co-ordinating Committee which links about 50 organisations: this has contributed to the strained relations between the WRVS and the Co-ordinating Committee in some of the camps.

The young volunteers are inclined to complain that 'pictures of long-haired yobboes doing their bit are never shown in the papers: it is always the ladies of the WRVS.'

Certainly, their approaches are different. Inevitably, this makes for friction. Complaints about the WRVS operations have been common.

There have been cases of people bringing carloads of good clothes to the camps, only to be told by a WRVS lady that they must be taken away again for 'correct sorting.'

Apparently, this means packing the clothes in bundles of five, folded according to WRVS regulations with no edges showing, and tied with a slip knot.

In one instance, Asian women and children were seen walking around a camp in the cold wearing only skimpy sandals, yet there were boxes of strong shoes in the WRVS clothing store.

The bulletins of the Co-ordinating Committee reflect a 'running battle', between the committed professionals with their keen sense of organisation and the enthusiastic amateur 'do-gooders.'

One bulletin, referring to the Resettlement Board's ruling that temporary accommodation must be vetted by the WRVS, commented: 'We are sorry over this delay when we have certain knowledge of jobs and houses in many areas.'

Eric Parsloe, the energetic and outspoken deputy secretary-general of International Voluntary Service, speaks of the 'woefully inadequate resources the Government are providing to tackle the practical problems.'

'The Civil Service,' he says 'must be put on a crisis footing. It is bogged down in regulations and a vast amount of red tape.'

At the core of the problem is the difference of approach between the voluntary workers and civil servants who follow well-defined rules. The result is time-consuming administrative battles between the two sides.

All volunteers tell stories of offers of accommodation made to the Resettlement Board that get swallowed up in the pipeline, 'because they come from areas of dense population that have school and housing problems.'

A well-established Indian businessman, who is trying to help, said: 'The refugees must be allowed into the established communities as soon as possible. It is there that they hear of the jobs that are not notified to employment exchanges.'

Steve Dey, IVS secretary-general, said: 'Initially the Board felt that the majority would have somewhere to go, would be skilled and

SPECIAL ANALYSIS

Triumphs and failures

have employment. That has now been proved wrong.' He complains of a lack of imagination at the top.

Mrs Mary Dines, general secretary of the Joint Committee for the Welfare of Immigrants, had other criticisms. She said Asians were being sent for jobs that were filled when they got there; that they were being filed in specific categories—'salesmen,' for example—when initially they might be prepared to do almost any work.

These criticisms look somewhat different when viewed from the offices of the Resettlement Board in London.

The chairman, Sir Charles Cunningham, a former Home Office Permanent Secretary, and his director, Mr Tom Critchley, are courteous. They greet criticisms with slightly raised eyebrows, apologising when they have to make a strong reply. They convey the impression of compassion.

First, we asked them about criticisms made by voluntary workers. They replied that some of the critics, like Parsloe, were not—in their opinion—speaking for voluntary workers generally. Relations with the various groups were good, they said, and there were representatives of the WRVS and the Co-ordinating Committee on the Board.

Sir Charles and Mr Critchley answered attacks on the Board's teams in the camps: 'They are not justified. The work of our senior teams is entirely praiseworthy from what we have seen. Civil servants are used to working hard.'

There is little doubt that the Board is as anxious as the voluntary workers to get the Asians into the community; but Sir Charles is conscious of his responsibility to lead them to places where there are opportunities for a full life, with decent schooling and housing as well as jobs. Thirty percent of the refugees are schoolchildren.

'For example, many of the men are motor mechanics,' says Sir Charles. 'It would be crazy to encourage a man to move out into temporary accommodation in an area where there is 23 percent unemployment among mechanics.

This is the thinking behind the creation of the 'red areas,' though the Board hate the use of the phrase.

Turning to the problems of establishing contact, with possible employers, Sir Charles and Mr Critchley said they did not believe it was significantly more difficult for those in the remoter camps. Rail warrants were issued, and it was possible for people to stay in a town. Sheffield was doing things the other way round: it was sending people into the camps to tell the Asians about opportunities in the city.

Sir Charles praised the support the Board was getting from the Government. 'We could not wish for more.' This refutes the Parsloe idea that resources are not forthcoming. Both Sir Charles and his director justly emphasised what had been achieved in eight weeks.

How do things seem to the newcomers in their

Young Uganda Asians strolling in the sunshine at the resettlement camp at Houndstone, Somerset.

Reproduced with permission ©Telegraph Group Limited

camps strewn around Britain?

One of the most remarkable aspects of the migration has been the good humour with which the Asians have endured their expulsion. We heard hardly one complaint in the camps; nor were any reported to us. All were philosophical about the loss of their possessions.

After a few hours in a camp, you begin to distinguish instinctively those who are going to become successful citizens in Britain and those with severe problems of qualification and adjustment who may become candidates for longer-term refugee camps.

There is a buoyancy, even a swagger, about the members of the first group. They are smartly dressed, European-style, speak good English, and have success stories to tell of their first few days as refugees.

A young man wearing a cashmere sweater and expensive grey flannels, with two strings of cowrie shells round his neck, said that he and his two brothers had got themselves fixed up with either a job or a place in college at Poole, Dorset, within ten days of arrival.

'We were told that there are not enough jobs to go round in England, said one of the brothers, who has found work with a bank. 'In fact there are. The English just won't do them.' The brothers plan to set up house in Dorset with their retired father. Eventually they hope to open a restaurant.

We spoke to an alert 18-year-old. His father had just got a job in Reading as a textile printer; the family had been offered a home; and he was to go to college to complete his 'A' level course. All had been arranged privately.

But such people are in a minority. The majority are those who will find it difficult to adjust. They might be seen shuffling round the camps, wrapped against the gusty October wind with grey wool scarves over their heads; or, more likely, lying on their bunks in the barrack-rooms, without even the curiosity to look up if someone comes in.

These people are mainly small traders, with no definable skill. They may be eaten up with family worries about stateless relatives who had to stay behind. Many can scarcely speak English, and are resigned and passive to their present predicament.

These are the people who will suffer from long periods in camps.

A father of eight was lying on his bed in mid-afternoon. Through a friend, he had been offered a job as a garage mechanic in Chiswick. But he claimed that the Social Security people at the camp had refused him a travel warrant on the grounds that Chiswick was 'red' area. Clearly, there had been a misunderstanding.

In the face of this set-back, this man was not prepared to go back and argue for a warrant. He was going to let the job go by default. He said

in Asian camps

SPECIAL ANALYSIS

Dhanji Karsan, 37, and his 23-year-old wife, Meghoai, look over the kitchen in their new home allocated to them at the old Royal Air Force Bomber Command base in Stradishall last month. They were among the first to arrive from Uganda and one of the first couples to be assigned a temporary home at Stradishall. Karsan has his address pinned to his coat. *Reproduced with permission ©Associated Press/World Wide Photos*

simply: 'They must find me a job.'

While most of the camps are likely to be cleared within a year or two, a hard core of immigrants unable to fend for themselves will remain. The Board, aware of this problem, is shaping its policies to allow for a few of the better-situated camps to be converted for this special category.

In the long run, these permanent casualties of General Amin's policies are likely to be best taken care of by their own community organisations.

One breakdown of the kind of work for which those in the camps are best qualified shows that 36 per cent have unskilled occupations (e.g., shop-keeping); 28 per cent have clerical qualifications, 13 per cent engineering and electrical qualification; 7 per cent are professionals (e.g., teachers, nurses, accountants); 6 per cent are technicians (e.g., draughtsmen, compositors, photographers, watchmakers); 3 per cent are qualified in building trades; 3 per cent are students.

At Stradishall refugee camp, in Suffolk, jobs have been found for 30 per cent of those in unskilled occupations; 28 per cent clerical; 14 per cent engineering and electrical; 1 per cent professionals; 3 per cent building tradesmen.

Our inquiries have shown that while a remarkable job is being done at both Governmental and voluntary levels, there are still weaknesses in the existing machinery and policies.

Several things should be done.

First, the pretence that it is possible to steer people away from 'red areas' should be officially abandoned.

Secondly, the Board's policy of encouraging people to enter the community as rapidly as possible should be clearly conveyed to both the immigrants and all the voluntary workers.

Thirdly, all local authorities should accept the Board's official advice to them—that they should provide 100 per cent mortgage loans to immigrants from their existing, adequate resources, and that, once granted, the first two years of repayment should be waived. These conditions are already available to non-immigrants, so there would be no reason for feelings that the new comers were being specially favoured.

An exceptionally high proportion of Asians want to become home-owners and are willing to make the necessary sacrifices to achieve their goal. Well over 80 per cent of East African Asians already established here have become house-owners. In this way, they contribute to rates in stead of being an added burden to local authorities.

Fourthly, the Resettlement Board should immediately enlist the help of private employment agencies to see how they can help.

Several agencies report that they made immediate approaches to the Resettlement Board, but 'didn't get much response.' But they are still keen to play an increasing role in the future.

The Brook Street Bureau has placed 11 people in London—including an accountant in its own office. The vacancy had existed for five months.

Fifthly, a scheme should be set up at once for providing loans on purely commercial terms for those immigrants wanting to start their own enterprises. More than a third of the newcomers are well qualified to run their own businesses.

A large proportion of immigrants have sufficient capital of their own, though it remains frozen in Uganda. Many still have bank accounts with three leading British commercial banks operating in Uganda—Barclays, Grindlays and Standard. These banks have, in the past, prospered from their Asian customers in Uganda; they know their creditworthiness.

The Resettlement Board now has a plan before it to create a consortium of bankers, insurance companies and businessmen to raise something like £10 million for immediate loans with the Government providing another £5-6 million by way of a loan.

Since it is now costing the Government £1,000,000 a month to maintain the existing camps, there may well be a saving in such an investment.

But the initial responses from the banks indicate that it is unlikely the scheme will get off the ground—unless the Prime Minister or Chancellor of the Exchequer intervenes.

All the banks involved said that assets and property in Uganda were largely irrelevant. 'Bankers are not pawnbrokers,' said one. 'They don't give credit without security. They give it to an individual.'

However, there is evidence that a man who did well in Uganda would get 'every co-operation' from the banks here.

OVER 700 OUSTED ASIANS HEAD FOR LIFE IN INDIA...

By NATION Reporter
Reprinted with permission, ©Daily Nation, Nairobi, October 23, 1972

THE State of Haryana, an Indian Government-owned passenger liner, was due to sail for Bombay last night after 24 hours' daily with 743 Indians expelled from Uganda on board.

The ship's departure was delayed because the baggage could not be loaded in time following the Kenyatta Day public holiday and some passengers had not received their baggage from Uganda by yesterday.

The State of Haryana will make another call at Mombasa early next month to pick up the last batch of Indian Nationals expelled from Uganda by President Amin. November 8 is the deadline when all non-wanted Asians must quit Uganda.

The 743 expelled Indians arrived in Mombasa from Uganda on Friday and Saturday by two special trains. More than 200 are children aged about 12 years and under.

The travellers spoke of having been mistreated, beaten and robbed of their cash and valuables by Uganda military men as they travelled by train in Uganda.

Some claimed their travellers' cheques were forcibly taken away from them and others said they were penniless.

The expelled Indians were met at Mombasa by Mr. B. Sharma, Assistant Indian High Commissioner and charitable organisations who provided them with food.

Members of the Red Cross provided them with 200 tins of milk powder and £100 worth of toys.

Meanwhile, about 1,250 British passport holders expelled from Uganda have arrived in India so far, according to the Minister of Labour and Rehabilitation, Mr. R. K. Khadilkar.

Indian Nationals arriving from Uganda total 2,848, Mr. Khadilkar said.

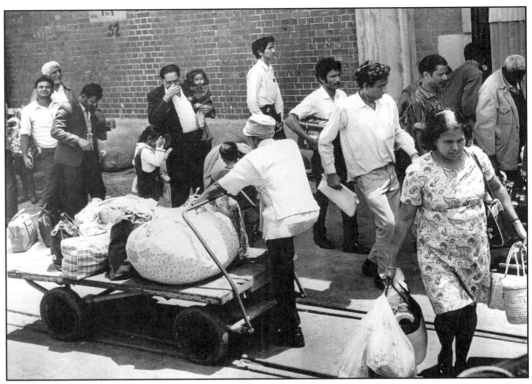

Port of Mombasa, Kenya: Asians lined up to board the State of Haryana, an Indian Government-owned passenger liner, due to sail for Bombay.
Reproduced with permission ©Associated Press/World Wide Photos

Asians complain of railway services

Reprinted with permission, ©East African Standard, Nairobi, October 23, 1972

Complaints against the East African Railways Corporation were raised on Saturday by some of the 407 Uganda Asians who arrived at Kilindini Harbour on a special train.

They were part of a total of 743 who started arriving in the port on Friday following their expulsion from Uganda by President Amin.

The complaints, raised through relatives and friends, concerned bedding and meals the Asians claimed they had paid for but never received.

The Asians, almost all of whom are Indian nationals, sailed for Bombay on Saturday night on the State of Haryana.

The Mombasa Red Cross Society, in addition to providing them with drugs for travel sickness, and for Malaria, also gave the travellers 200 tins of milk and £100 worth of toys for the children.

This latest departure of Uganda Asians brings the number of those who have passed through Mombasa to more than 1,400 in a month.

Anti-immigration MP provides a home for Asians

News Compilation, October 24, 1972

A family of Asian refugees from Uganda were settling down last night in the Hertfordshire home of Mr Peter Rost, Conservative MP for Derbyshire, South-east, who is a member of the Monday Club.

Mr Rost, aged 42, an opponent of the Government's immigration policy, is the first MP to take into his home any of the Asians who have arrived since the troubles in Uganda began.

He said last night: "I have given them a home for humanitarian reasons. They and all the other Asians thrown out of Uganda are the ones who are suffering. But this does not mean I have changed my views on immigration, or my criticism of the Government for not taking a tougher line with General Amin from the start."

His guests, who arrived by air from Uganda, are Mr and Mrs Karia who are in their sixties, their daughter-in-law, her two-month-old baby, and her sister. They have been given a three bedroom flat and a kitchen for as long as they need in Mr Rost's 24 room Victorian mansion in Dudswell, near Berkhamsted.

Mr Rost, who has four children, has appealed for other wealthy families living in big homes to open their doors to the homeless Asians. "I think we could help these people to settle down in areas where there are not already large immigrant communities", he said.

"Where I live is ideal, and several of my neighbours say they intend having Asians, but I do not think there is any danger of a ghetto establishing itself in the Hertfordshire stockbroker belt.

"The family we have taken in have suffered a great deal. The father is in hospital in London suffering from a stroke brought on by all the worry and his son has had to go to India. He is unable to join his wife and daughter because he does not have a British passport. None of my friends in the Monday Club have filed a motion calling on me to resign or anything, and I think most of them think I have done the right thing."

Amin hospitalized

News Compilation, October 24, 1972

President Idi Amin was advised by his doctors to have a complete rest. He is to continue to run the country from his hospital bed. The nature of his illness was not disclosed, but an official statement suggested he might be under treatment for some time.

Advertisement

AMERICAN EMBASSY KAMPALA

1ST FLIGHT INFORMATION

PERSONS INFORMED TO LEAVE ON FIRST FLIGHT SHOULD MAKE RESERVATIONS FOR EC FLIGHT 750 DEPARTING 27th OCTOBER AT 10.55 A.M.

Amin's Forced March

Reprinted with permission, ©Time Inc., October 23, 1972

Uganda celebrated the tenth anniversary of its independence from Britain last week. It was hardly an occasion for rejoicing. Under its unpredictable military ruler, General Idi ("Big Daddy") Amin Dada, the country has drifted closer and closer to chaos. It was an especially bitter holiday for Uganda's 10,000 Asian citizens, who have watched helplessly while Amin ordered the expulsion of tens of thousands of other Asians with British or Indian passports. Last week, after Amin "suggested" that they take part in the anniversary parade, the Asians responded with a pathetic gesture of "loyalty" to the regime that has set out to destroy them. TIME'S Peter Hawthorne was on hand to witness the event. His report:

A 21-gun salute set the pied crows to wheeling and wailing in the sky above Kololo Stadium in Kampala, Uganda's beautiful capital. As 2,000 soldiers led the British-style trooping of the colors, and the crowd sweated in the searing equatorial sun, General Amin flamboyantly conferred an array of honors on his distinguished visitors. The First Class Order of the Source of the Nile went to Somalia's General Mohamed Barre, while the Second Class Order of the same medal was bestowed upon the Sudanese Vice President, Major General Mohamed El-Bagir. Then Big Daddy decorated members of his own armed forces for meritorious service during the recent border skirmishes with Tanzania, handing out a seemingly endless number of "Distinguished

Continued on Page 114

Asians in 'squalid and dirty camp' claim rejected

DAILY TELEGRAPH REPORTER
Reprinted with permission, ©Telegraph Group Limited, London, October 25, 1972

ACCUSATIONS that Ugandan Asians were living in dirty and squalid conditions in a former Army camp were criticised yesterday. The claim was made by a doctor's wife, Mrs June Pepper, who is also a former nurse. She also claimed that the medical block was "a disgrace," and called for a top-level inquiry.

Mr William Pollock-Morris, senior regional Commandant of the Ugandan Resettlement Board, yesterday carried out an investigation at Heathfield Camp, Honiton, Devon.

After an exhaustive tour of the camp, where 1,060 Asians are billeted, Mr Pollock-Morris said he thought conditions were "as satisfactory as possible under the circumstances."

"It is not Hilton accommodation by any means and we would not pretend it was," he said.

Mr Pollock-Morris, a former East African senior district commissioner, said that all the camps in his area were meeting difficulty with keeping lavatory blocks clean. This stemmed from the unwillingness of high-caste Asians to clean lavatory blocks and from the tradition that their only responsibility was their own living quarters.

He said the medical block was clean and added that immediately before Mrs Pepper saw it there had been a large overnight intake of Asians through it.

In every society there were naturally clean and naturally dirty people. They were carrying out an intensive campaign to educate the Asians in the use of Western sanitary facilities and were subdividing lavatory blocks into smaller units for use by fewer families who would get their own keys.

Menial tasks

Another difficulty was that the Asians had been living a "middle class life" in Uganda, with servants to do menial tasks. "It is very much a problem in other camps but we feel we are not going to spoon feed them in every direction and it would be entirely wrong if we brought in Europeans to clean their lavatories," he said.

When Asians left Heathfield, and some 400 had already done so, they sometimes took with them the cleaning brushes, lavatory brushes and dustpans belonging to the camp. This had created temporary shortages.

No major changes in the administrative arrangements were needed and he praised the work done by both paid officials and voluntary workers from Honiton and the surrounding area.

Mr Albert Johnson, Honiton Town Clerk, strongly criticised both Mrs Pepper and Mr Peter Emery, Conservative MP for Honiton, and Under Secretary at the Department of Trade and Industry.

He said that Mrs Pepper, who is on Exeter City Council, had made a flying visit "of not more than five minutes," had not been present at the camp when work was to be done, but appeared to be "quite happy" to criticise afterwards.

Continued on Page 114

Advertisement

BRITISH HIGH COMMISSION
KAMPALA

FINAL NOTICE

There are only 13 days left until 7 November. If you hold a United Kingdom passport and are a head of family, an independent person or the wife of a Ugandan, Indian or stateless husband and you have not come forward for an entry certificate for the United Kingdom you must do so now

NO FURTHER ANNOUNCEMENT WILL BE MADE

Telephone enquiries regarding entry certificate Kampala 32554 or 32555

Ugandan Asian Expulsion: 90 Days and Beyond through the Eyes of the International Press

Continued from Page 113

Amin's Forced March

Service Orders," "Military Crosses," and "Victorious Service Crosses." During the lengthy ceremony an elderly Asian fainted and was carted off to an ambulance, betel-nut juice dripping like blood from his slack mouth.

While the crowd swayed and roared "Dada! Dada!" Amin barreled along, beaming as he inspected his troops, as well as boy scouts and youth leaguers. The Asian marchers brought up the tail end of the parade. As they shambled past, trying to get into step to the band's rendition of Old Folks at Home, African spectators laughed derisively.

There is a sort of Evelyn Waughtorn atmosphere in Kampala. While a vast crowd of Africans swarmed up Acacia Avenue toward the stadium, a lone white man carried on unperturbedly with his golf game on the course near by, his black caddy trotting dutifully by his side. Foreign journalists are definitely not welcome in the capital these days, and the few whites in the streets get curious stares, particularly if they are carrying cameras.

Many Asian families have moved into city hotels while they wait for flights to London or Bombay. Women and children are swathed in silk saris and wear whatever jewelry they own in order to prevent it from being stolen or confiscated; even the smallest child wears pearls in her ear lobes or nostrils. The men have developed a reflex of patting breast pockets to make sure their passports are still there. Strangers identify themselves to one another by mentioning the names of companies they were associated with "National Trading," says one women, referring to one of the country's largest wholesale merchants, "Desai Bros., General Dealers," says another.

At the East African Airways terminal, an Asian boy says proudly that he is going to Leicester, England. His exhausted father explains that he has read a warning from the city of Leicester that there is no more room for Asians. But what can he do? His only relatives are in Leicester, he says, so he must go there too. Another young man, an engineer, declares that he is going to Chicago, U.S.A.— he pronounces it "Shee-cago,"— where he has an uncle who is a "medical practitioner."

The exodus of the Asians has already had an obvious effect on the economy of Kampala. Jobless Africans are clamoring for work at the city's hotels, which are running short of bread, soap and even gin; one must drink vodka to immunize oneself against the mosquito bites. Restaurants guard their menus like gold: most of the printing in the city was done by Asians. In the commercial sector of Kampala, nearly 80% of the shops are now shut and barred; in some the stock can be seen gathering dust behind the steel mesh across the windows. There has been very little looting up to now, probably because the "duka-wallahs" (Asian shopkeepers) have always secured their stores as if they were Fort Knox.

But there will be looting soon, one departing storekeeper told me, as he padlocked his shop for the last time. "I'm leaving $40,000 worth of stock

FIRST AFRICANS TO BUY ENTEBBE SHOP
They resigned to take up business

BY LAWRENCE NYOMBI
Reprinted with permission, ©Uganda Argus, October 25, 1972

A MAKERERE UNIVERSITY LECTURER MR. E. SSERU-GOOTI-MAGABI AND HIS YOUNGER BROTHER WHO HAS BEEN A TEACHER, MR. A. KATABALWA-MAGABI, HAVE RESIGNED FROM PAID EMPLOYMENTS TO TAKE UP FULL-TIME BUSINESS IN ENTEBBE TOWN.

They have become the first Africans in the area to acquire one of the busiest business premises with a large building, sold to them by an outgoing non-Ugandan Asian citizen.

Telling how they managed to acquire the premises so soon, Mr. Sserugooti said that the building was first paid for by his family even before the economic war was declared. His family paid almost three quarters of the whole cost for the premises. The rest they were paying in instalments.

In 1969 Janthabhai Patel who owned the building began renting the premises for the Magabi family. They later started paying their instalments in an effort to attain full possession of business.

The economic war declaration was just a coincidence because the Magabi family were nearly completing paying off the remaining instalments.

In his response to the economic war by President Amin, Mr. Sserugooti decided to resign from St. Edward College, Bukumi, where he was both a mathematics and chemistry teacher.

When the third term began this year he had already put in his resignation.

Their business is now dealing in a variety of materials ranging from bicycle accessories, tools, farm equipment, building material for all general purposes to timber.

Commenting on the new business he said there are some problems to be overcome later. Such difficulties are attributed to capital badly

required to equip the shop to the best standard as may be demanded by the customers.

Some goods are not easy to find he said. Since a number of wholesale shops in Kampala are now closed, it would be a good idea if Government through the State Trading Corporation took immediate steps to begin importing such goods from where they could be found, Mr. Sserugooti suggested.

He said however that their shop had sold padlocks in a very satisfactory number, especially to the out-going Asians who even came from as far as Mbale and Tororo looking for them.

Arrangements for giving loans to African traders who have now taken over businesses should be made as soon as possible, he urged.

Asked whether he had some knowledge about business, Mr. Sserugooti said that he had already taken courses in bookkeeping and accounts. He added that with imagination and hard work he could manage successfully.

Mr. Sserugooti also holds a B.Sc degree from Makerere University, Kampala. His younger brother Katabalwa-Magabi was once a student at Mwiri College, Busoga. Later he was appointed shift production supervisor with Bread Limited in Jinja from where he resigned recently to participate in full-time business with his elder brother Sserugooti Magabi.

At present they can even offer transport with their pick-up vehicle to their customers, who happen to buy a lot of items from their shop.

Continued from Page 113

Asians in 'squalid and dirty camp' claim rejected
"Very poor"

Honiton and those concerned with the Asian's reception regarded her comments as "a personal slight". "It is equally disconcerting to note that the MP for Honiton has chosen also to make statements to the Press without the courtesy of discussing the position with the local health officials," he added.

Mrs Pepper was away from home yesterday but her husband, Dr B. J. Pepper, said: "She thought the medical block was very poor. She spent between one and one and a half hours in the camp, a perfectly adequate time to make a fair and unbiased assessment."

Mr Emery was away on Government business but his agent, Mr James Cobley, said the Minister had visited the camp before it opened, after 18 months of disuse, 17 days ago.

As a result of what he saw, Mr Emery spent 55 minutes telephoning Whitehall saying that if Heathfield was to be used for Asians then "let's get out fingers out."

Mr Emery had then visited the Town Clerk, Mr Johnson, and told him of his views. When he received Mrs Pepper's complaint, he acted as he would on any constituent's behalf and he would be visiting Heathfield at the weekend to see for himself.

in there," he said. "I can't eat it, I can't take it with me, so I leave it." He gestured down the street. "Already, see, there are the unemployed. I employed four Africans in my shop and two in my home. Now they have no jobs. Soon they will be hungry. Then they will find a way into my shop, if the soldiers don't get there first."

The Asians keep their eyes lowered—and perhaps their fingers crossed—as they pass the police and army roadblocks on the way to Entebbe Airport. It is little consolation to them to know that their forced departure is creating an economic crisis with which Amin's government is obviously incapable of coping, "I give the place three months," declares a Kenya businessman who can find no qualified Ugandan to run his Kampala-based company. "Amin may still have a country, but the country will have nothing." The Kenyan adds bitterly: "The general will probably only realize it when he finds he can't get any medals minted any more. The Asians even did that."

Page 114

Ugandan Asian Expulsion: 90 Days and Beyond through the Eyes of the International Press

U.N. ready to process stateless Asians

Standard Staff Reporter, Kampala
Reprinted with permission, ©East African Standard, Nairobi, October 27, 1972

Processing of stateless Asians to be expelled from Uganda should begin today by the U.N., according to reliable sources in Kampala last night.

They added that the Uganda Government and U.N. officials in the capital have agreed on arrangements for flying out of the country up to 5,000 Asians of uncertain nationality. However, until the U.N. Secretary-General's special envoy, Dr. Robert Gardiner, has a last meeting with Government officials, no announcement will be made.

The sources said the U.N. was determined to get all the stateless Asians out of the country by the November 8 deadline, and no effort would be spared to achieve this.

The Inter-Governmental Committee for European Migration and the International Committee of the Red Cross will be associated with the operation, which will, however, be a U.N. and Uganda Government affair.

The U.N. office, in association with the I.C.R.C. AND I.C.E.M., have established a centre in Kampala for all those in the category and who do not have valid travel documents.

Dr. Gardiner had more talks yesterday with Uganda authorities. On Wednesday he had talks with the representative of I.C.E.M., Mr. Christiansen, and with the I.C.R.C. representative, Mr. Frank Schmidt.

Advertisement

UNITED NATIONS CENTRE

FOR DOCUMENTATION ASSISTANCE AND TRANSPORTATION ARRANGEMENTS
(IN ASSOCIATION WITH ICRC AND ICEM)

To assist those members of the Asian Community who are of undetermined nationality and who are required to leave Uganda by 8 November, in accordance with Government Decree No. 17, the United Nations, in association with the I.C.R.C. and the I.C.E.M. have established a Centre at the following location:

**UPPER GROUND FLOOR
IPS BUILDING
KAMPALA**

All persons falling into the above-mentioned category, who do not have in their possession any valid travel document MUST report to the above address between 8 a.m. and 6 p.m. as from Saturday, 28 October.1972.

Those persons who have already been accepted by Canada, Switzerland, United States of America or any other country should not come.

Cases already registered by the I.C.E.M. should report to the above address when called by advertisement from the United Nations Centre.

Holders of the following I.C.E.M., reference numbers who have not yet been medically examined, are requested to report on the dates indicated:

SATURDAY 28 OCTOBER: 04/700 - 04/780
SUNDAY   29 OCTOBER: 04/781 - 04/897

EDMONTON, CANADA

200 Asian Ugandans expected here soon

Reprinted with permission, ©Edmonton Journal, October 25, 1972

The city can expect about 200 Asian refugees during the next three weeks according to the chairman of the volunteer Ugandan Committee of Edmonton.

Dr. Ram Gupta, and associate professor at the University of Alberta, made his prediction during an interview Tuesday.

He said there are about 20 to 25 Asian refugees in the city now.

Dr. Gupta said he is basing his prediction on the number of Ugandans expected to be absorbed by Canada—5,000—and statistics that show five per cent of immigrants settle in Edmonton.

Alberta is a good place for the newcomers to come, Dr. Gupta observed, because they will likely find jobs easier since the province's unemployment rate is very low.

On the other hand, he added, the cold climate doesn't suit the Ugandans and Edmonton's Pakistani-Indian community is small compared to eastern cities such as Montreal, Toronto and Ottawa.

In the eastern cities, he said, they may have friends they knew in Uganda.

The first refugees arrived in Edmonton 2-1/2 weeks ago. Of that 15-member group, all four who have tried to find work have found it.

"They're not the best jobs," Dr. Gupta said, "but still they're jobs."

The regional immigration office helps the newcomers find work, and a place to live.

Dr. Gupta's committee, meanwhile, helps the Ugandans become acclimatized to the city, takes them to movies and offers material assistance with such items as pots and pans and clothing.

The latest group of Ugandans arrived during the weekend.

Among them was a family of vegetarians who "had a hard time figuring out what to eat when they first arrived," according to Dr. Gupta.

Among the latest Ugandan arrivals: The 2,000th Ugandan Asian to immigrate to Canada arrived in Montreal International Airport last night. Mahem Somd and his family arrived on a CP charter flight along with 145 other Asians from Uganda. A spokesman for the department of immigration and manpower said last night's arrivals brought the number of Ugandan immigrants to Canada to 2,112 since the first flight arrived less than a month ago. At least 30 per cent of them have found jobs so far, the spokesman said. Reproduced with permission ©John Daggett/Gazette, Montreal

Why Army veteran Gurdit Singh feels he is British

From Michael Knipe
Kampala, Oct 26
Reprinted with permission, ©Times Newspapers Limited, London,
October 27, 1972

Arrangements to enable stateless Asians to leave Uganda were completed here today after weeks of protracted negotiations.

A United Nations centre is being established to provide the Asians with documentation, assistance and travel arrangements. No one is sure how many people have failed completely to find a country that will accept them, but current estimates range from a minimum of 2,000 to over 5,000.

Dr Robert Gardiner, the United Nations special envoy, Mr F. J. Homann-Herinberg from the United Nations High Commission for Refugees, Mr Frank Schmidt of the International Red Cross, and officials of the Inter-governmental Committee for European Migration have cooperated in the operation.

According to sources participating in the negotiations, the Uganda Government has been "very cooperative" and is providing the United Nations centre with temporary offices.

Once issued with travel documents the stateless Asians will be able to go to temporary reception centres.

It is understood here that Dr Kurt Waldheim, the United Nations Secretary-General, is attempting to mobilize financial assistance for the operation, which may get under way within a couple of days. Dr Waldheim is also understood to be handling arrangements for the establishment of reception centres. Italy and Austria have promised holiday camp facilities.

President Amin remained in hospital for a fourth day today and a brief medical bulletin said that his health continued to improve, and that he was continuing with his complete rest.

Meanwhile, one stateless Asian, Mr Sardar Gurdit Singh, a former British soldier, has discovered to his chagrin that bearing arms for the monarch does not provide one with an automatic right of entry to Britain.

Mr Gurdit Singh, who is 83, is a vigorous old man with an immaculate white turban and a steel-grey beard. He wears his African safari suit as smartly as if it were a full dress uniform.

Born in Patiala, India, he served in the Royal Navy from 1907 to 1914, and then transferred to the British Army. Joining the Patiala State Infantry and then the 82nd Punjabis, he saw active service on the North-West Frontier, and in Mesopotamia before retiring with the rank of corporal in 1922.

His ties with the British Army go much further back, however, through his family. His father served as an officer in the Patiala State Cavalry from 1867 to 1895. And before that his grandfather, Subadar Major Fujdar Singh, joined the 4th Sikh Infantry in 1847, receiving the Indian Order of Merit and the North-West Frontier Reward for Valour before he retired in 1872.

On his own retirement from the Army in 1922,

Mr Gurdit Singh came to Uganda, and in 1966 he renounced his British citizenship and became a Ugandan, but his Ugandan citizenship was cancelled last August.

Mr Gurdit Singh has three sons and three daughters living in East Africa, India and Britain, and could probably go as a dependant to live with any of them. He believes, however, that his family's record entitles him to some special consideration over and above mere immigration regulations.

Although his Army career is many years behind him, and he has had a successful life operating a transport business, Mr Gurdit Singh remains every inch a British military figure. Regularly on Remembrance Day he has been on duty selling poppies, wearing his own medals on his left breast, and his grandfather's on his right.

Last night he leafed fondly through his collections of photographs: reunions of old soldiers which in happier days included Europeans, Africans, and Asians, Government House garden parties, and pictures of himself shaking hands with the Queen Mother and the Duke of Kent, at Uganda's Independence Day celebrations, and Lord Mountbatten during a visit in 1960.

He remembers Lord Mountbatten saying that if he ever needed any assistance he should write to him, and he did so last month. Lord Mountbatten has been away in the Unites States, but in his absence General Sir Rodney Moore, the Deputy Grand President of the British Commonwealth Ex-Services League, wrote to the British High Commissioner in Kampala on Mr Gurdit Singh's behalf. Since then immigration officials here have advised Mr Gurdit Singh to resubmit his certificate of registration as a Uganda citizen, in case he is eligible for reclassification under the broad-

er terms of British entry announced two weeks ago.

For a proud octogenarian old soldier, however, that is not exactly the point. "I have always been very conscious of my family's long association with the British Army", he said, "and even though I've had Ugandan citizenship I have always felt very British. I don't want special consideration, I just feel I have a right...."

A British High Commission spokesman commented: "Regrettable as it may seem, there is no provision in the Immigration Act to take account of past military associations. However, Mr Gurdit Singh has been invited to submit further documentary evidence."

QUEEN DEPLORES EXPULSION OF ASIANS

News Compilation, October 28, 1972

LONDON-QUEEN ELIZABETH made a rare criticism of a Commonwealth country yesterday as she told Parliament her Government "deplores the action of the Government of Uganda in expelling residents of Asian descent."

The criticism of President Amin's Government, which has ordered the expulsion of all Asians by November 7, was contained in the Queen's speech formally closing the current session of Parliament. It was read for her in the House of Lords.

She said the British Government had made strong representations to the Uganda Government and had accepted the responsibility of admitting to Britain those Asians holding UK passports and wishing to reside here.

Tanya a Canadian but just by a month

Reprinted with permission, ©Vancouver Sun, October 31, 1972

If Tanya Dharamshi had been born a month earlier, she would be a Ugandan instead of a Canadian citizen. Tanya was born at the Royal Columbian Hospital, New Westminster, last Friday weighing six pounds, nine ounces.

One month earlier, on Sept. 27, her parents Nizar, 30, and Farida, 29, had left Kampala, Uganda—refugees from the government that had ordered all Asians out of the African country.

Nizar Dharamshi is a second generation Ugandan. His parents were also born in Kampala and are now in London, England. His brother is expected to arrive in Vancouver in the next few weeks.

Mrs. Dharamshi was born in Karachi, Pakistan, where she met her husband while he was at university. They have another daughter, five-year-old Farahnaaz.

Nizar taught Islamic history in Uganda but now seeks work as a bookkeeper.

Advertisement

CANADA

NOTICE TO PERSONS CLAIMING TO BE STATELESS

PERSONS CLAIMING TO BE 'STATELESS' AND WHO HAVE SUBMITTED AN APPLICATION AT THE CANADIAN IMMIGRATION OFFICE PRIOR TO THE DATE OF THIS ANNOUNCEMENT SHOULD APPEAR AT THE OFFICE WITH THEIR REFERENCE NUMBER.

THE FOLLOWING CONDITIONS ARE MOST IMPORTANT FOR THE PURPOSE OF OBTAINING AN INTERVIEW:

A. — DECLARATION ON THE ORIGINAL APPLICATION TO THE EFFECT THAT YOU WERE STATELESS.

B. — WRITTEN DECLARATION FROM THE BRITISH HIGH COMMISSION PASSPORT OFFICE AND THE PRINCIPAL IMMIGRATION OFFICER OF THEIR APPRECIATION OF YOUR REQUEST FOR ENTITLEMENT TO A PASSPORT BASED ON YOUR CLAIM TO EITHER UGANDA OR U.K.&C. CITIZENSHIP.

C. — OTHER CONSIDERATIONS DEEMED NECESSARY TO THE CANADIAN IMMIGRATION INTERVIEWER.

THERE IS NO NEED TO APPEAR UNLESS YOU ARE ABLE TO SATISFY REQUIREMENTS A AND B.

OFFICE HOURS — 8:30 — 12:30
2:00 — 5:00

A Fresh Start

Reprinted with permission, ©Time Inc., October 30, 1972

On former military bases now converted into refugee centers across Britain, thousands of Asians from Uganda last week wound up their ten-day celebration of Navratri, a Hindu festival of songs, prayer chants and dances in honor of an ancient war victory by the god Rama over the demons of the underworld. The incense and joss sticks were often lit at makeshift shrines on card tables, and the traditional ornate, hand-painted dancing sticks were replaced by plain wood dowels. Displaced and dispossessed, the refugees nonetheless found abundant reason to celebrate. Said one technical engineer, who arrived in London with his wife and seven children: "We are here. We are safe. We are happy."

So far 18,000 Asians of British citizenship have landed in England from Uganda as a result of General Idi Amin Dada's expulsion order. Several thousand more are resettling in Canada, India and some 27 other countries. The assets they have left behind, with little hope of full compensation, are estimated to be worth more than a billion dollars. Despite rumors of wealth secreted in Britain and Switzerland, many of the refugees have arrived, as one British social worker observed, "with only what they can stand up in."

As they left the Ugandan airport of Entebbe, the refugees said, they could see rows of their cargo crates still stacked beside the runway. Some of the crates had already been opened, exposed to the weather and carefully plucked over like boxes of fruit. Because they feared searches at roadblocks and airport customs, the refugees carried with them only the barest of personal belongings, often chosen in haste: a tennis racket, tape recorder, kitchen clock or guitar. Sakaria Rajendra, a student, wore 20 elephant-hair bracelets to give to people in England. One family, luckier than most, smuggled out a diamond valued at $10,000.

In Uganda, nearly all of the Asians had been prosperous (they are estimated to have controlled 80% of Uganda's economy). But still they complain remarkably little about their drastically diminished status. "Actually," says an engineer, "I was going to come earlier. The only difference is that I would have had some money and now I am penniless." Smiles an ex-merchant from Kampala: "The only thing I miss is my Citroen."

Family reunions are curiously without tears. A university student in a pinstriped suit awaits his father, a well-to-do Ugandan architect who will probably not qualify to practice in England. What are his emotions about this turn in his family's fortunes? "It's a bloody inconvenience," he replies. Adds a restaurant owner from Kampala: "There is no big problem. You only have to begin from scratch, work and earn, and slowly, slowly everything will be all right."

Though some of the refugees say that difficulties and harassment in Uganda have subsided, there are still occasional reports of random terror.

Continued on Page 118

4,000 STATELESS ASIANS TO FLY OUT TO EUROPE

Reprinted with permission, ©Daily Nation, Nairobi, November 1, 1972

GENEVA-ABOUT 4,000 stateless Asians will be flown to Europe by November 8, final date of their expulsion from Uganda, the Inter-governmental Committee for European Immigration—ICEM—announced today.

They will be put in transit camps before final resettlement in Europe and overseas, according to the organisation which handled to migration of Europeans to Latin America after the Second World War.

An ICEM spokesman told a news conference here the flights will be conducted by the regular airlines operating in the East African area, at rates which are reduced, but not as favourable as the charter flight rates.

Without going into details, he explained the airlines did not waive international rules granting them priority on these routes for the expelled Asians. He said the airlines agreed only to admit charter planes for these humanitarian flights when specifically ordered and paid for by a government.

The spokesman said Switzerland was the only country to order and pay for the flights for the 200 Asians it plans to bring to Zurich today and tomorrow to find permanent homes is this Alpine land.

The transport of the other Asian expellees is paid from international contributions and funds of the organisations involved in the exodus. ICEM organises the transport, the UN High Commission for Refugees and the International Red Cross Committee help with travel documents and other aspects.

An estimated total of 6,000 stateless Asians are in Uganda. ICEM plans to fly up to 700 per day to Europe beginning today. Canada is taking 2,000 stateless Asians, making its independent transport arrangements.

Of those going to Europe, 2,300 will find temporary haven in Italy, 1,200 in Austria and 300 in Belgium. Austria will keep 250 and Belgium 150 permanently.

Denmark has offered to take 40, Norway 200, Netherlands 300, the United States 1,000 and Argentina, Brazil and Colombia together 300, also permanently.

The UN Fund for Refugees has received 1.8 million dollars to help Asians leaving Uganda, a UN spokesman said in New York today.

Meanwhile, the first group of Ugandan Asian immigrants brought to New Zealand under Government auspices is expected in Wellington next Tuesday, the Minister of Immigration, Mr. David Thomson, said in a statement.

With only a week left before Amin's deadline, stateless Asians queue at the Kampala offices of the United Nations and the Inter-governmental Committee for European Immigration.

Reproduced courtesy of the office of the United Nations High Commissioner for Refugees

GRANTS TO HELP ASIANS NOT BIG ENOUGH—CLAIM

Reprinted with permission, ©Leicester Mercury, November 2, 1972

INITIAL reaction in Leicester to a Uganda Resettlement Board announcement today on payments to local authorities for the reception and settlement of Uganda Asian refugees was that they are "not enough".

City Council leader, Alderman Edward Marston, said: "While it is a move in the right direction, it does appear at first sight that these payments are nothing like what we will require."

The Board say they are prepared to reimburse local authorities for "reasonable and necessary expenditure" for one year from the dates first incurred.

These would be for:

* Hire of premises for the provision of services to Uganda Asians (£30 for each person).

* Staff specially recruited—for example extra teachers for teaching English (£40 per person).

* Travelling, overtime and subsistence allowances to existing members of local authority staff for work done for the Uganda Asians (no limit).

* Additional equipment specially bought for educational and similar services (£4 for each school pupil).

* Hire of school transport (£20 per pupil).

* Making habitable temporary accommodation (£30 for each person living in a particular house).

EXTRA STAFF

A 75 per cent grant will also be made by the Board for spending which results in projects being, undertaken with a life expectancy of more than three years, but not long term.

Examples include temporary classrooms or extra school trans-port. Grants will be subject to prior approval by the board.

Alderman Marston commented: "At first glance, these figures are not enough for Leicester.

"In the field of education, we have been told that it will cost the City Council £200 a child per year—just for bussing. This is one item alone. The cost of extra staff and buildings will be quite considerable.

"And the Director of Social Services in Leicester, Mr Thacker, told Sir Charles Cunningham, chairman of the Resettlement Board, when he visited the city, that we would require £6.50 per person per week for providing accommodation, plus extra staff".

City Education Director Mr Tony Davis told the Leicester Mercury: "My first impression is that one would have to query the insistence in the board's announcement that reimbursements would cover only one year."

"The £4 figure quoted to cover additional equipment, if it includes furniture, is a derisory sum. If it doesn't include furniture it is far from generous, but possible".

'REPAY LOANS'

The Board say that spending eligible for reimbursement must be incurred in reception or initial resettlement for which it can be shown there is an immediate need and which is outside the local authority's normal programme of expenditure and which would not have been spent but for the arrival of the refugees.

Grant claim forms for the period to March 31 next year will be sent to local authorities before the end of this financial year. Payments on account can be arranged in appropriate cases.

The Boards statement says that if dwellings made available to the newcomers require initial furnishings, the usual practice of seeking help from charitable or voluntary sources should be followed.

"Local authorities will also wish to know that in cases where the newcomers are receiving supplementary benefit, essential furniture which cannot be from the sources already mentioned can, for the time being, be provided by the Supplementary Benefit Commission."

Continued from Page 117

A Fresh Start

One father arrived in London only to receive a call telling him that his son, after driving him to the Ugandan airport, had been stopped by soldiers and slowly cut to death with machete-like panga knives. A businessman said that he left hurriedly after both is partners in a gas-station chain were stopped while carrying the week's receipts into Kampala, put into the trunk of a car and driven to a village where they were hanged.

Britons Approve.

Such excesses have helped make Amin Public Enemy No. 1 in the eyes of most Britons—and created some sympathy for the arriving Asians. Last week Amin called British High Commissioner Richard Slater into his office before live TV cameras and accused him of plotting against the Ugandan government; London angrily recalled its representative. Most Britons, according to a recent Harris poll, approve of Prime Minister Edward Heath's firm commitment to absorb the refugees.

Still, the Asians must find jobs in one of the worst and most prolonged periods of unemployment in Britain's postwar history. Before the influx, there were already 600,000 Asians in the country. Their coexistence with vocal pockets of racism was at best an uneasy one, and there were fears that the situation might be exacerbated by the new immigrants. Some quarters of the Asian community have rallied round, however. A group of prominent East African Asians already established in Britain have quietly assembled investment capital to assist the refugees in rebuilding their fortunes. They are urging them to avoid areas where there are already large Asian communities. Says Praful Patel, a business consultant who serves on the government-appointed Resettlement Board: "If they want to make a success of themselves in Britain, they have got to try to integrate as quickly as possible and avoid making little ghettos."

The path to integration has been somewhat eased—and their welcome made a little warmer—by new estimates that only some 26,000 Asians, instead of the 30,000 to 50,000 refugees originally expected, will immigrate to Britain. Even so, there will probably be another 5,000 Asians left behind, and they are the unluckiest of all. They earlier rejected British passports in favor of Ugandan citizenship, which has been arbitrarily revoked by Amin. They are now stateless. Britain has declined to consider restoring them to citizenship, and has referred their case to the United Nations High Commissioner for Refugees. But there is growing concern whether any international body can act swiftly enough to save them from being further victimized.

Liberals lose majority in Canada

In the closest federal election in Canadian history, the Liberal government emerged October 30 with 108 seats in the House of Commons, one less than the Progressive Conservatives.

EDMONTON, CANADA

EXILED ASIANS NEED HELP

Reprinted with permission, ©Edmonton Journal, November 2, 1972

Edmonton's small community of exiled Ugandan Asians still needs help.

Seventeen people have now arrived in the city, part of the expected influx of 5,000 immigrants to Canada following the expulsion order of Ugandan President Col. Idi Amin several months ago.

Blankets, linen, furniture, offers of transportation and jobs are needed, said Dr. Ram Gupta, member of the local committee recently formed to aid the exiles.

The committee would also like to borrow furniture for the use of refugees. It would be returned after the exiles have found work and become reasonably settled. It will be cleaned up before returned but lenders should expect "the usual amount of wear and tear."

People with cars who can spare a few hours to pick up and deliver donations are also needed, he said.

Although Canada Manpower and the committee do what they can to find suitable jobs for the exiles, potential employers could contact Manpower or the committee if they feel they have something to offer, he said.

While response from the public has been "reasonably good" to date, said Dr. Gupta, and donations of every kind continue to come in, the exiles' life in Edmonton since their arrival has been somewhat lacking in the "human touch".

Dinner invitations, periodic phone calls, or just "tea and chit-chat" would do much to help the Asians ease into Canadian life, he said.

The Uganda Committee is sponsored by the department of the secretary of state, and includes representation from such agencies as the YMCA, and Manpower as well as individuals.

USA

Asian Exiles From Uganda Arrive

By JOHN T. McQUISTON
Reprinted with permission, ©New York Times, November 3, 1972

Wearing warm clothing supplied in Rome by a Catholic relief agency, Vargala Kundan, his wife and their two teenaged children, weary but smiling, arrived at Kennedy International Airport last night, the first of 1,000 stateless Asians expelled from Uganda to be resettled throughout the United States.

Mr. Kundan, a 39-year-old accountant, and his family brought with them from their former home in Kampala, nine pieces of luggage, a transistor radio-tape recorder and the clothing they wore.

"We've left everything else we had behind, our property, everything," he told a crowd of officials from several relief agencies that had arranged for his family's flight to this country and a temporary home in Nyack, N.Y.

The Kundans were among 83 fellow Asians from the East African country—Hindus, Moslems and Ismailis—who arrived shortly before 10 P.M. on a Pan American flight. Within half an hour they began emerging from Customs, having been aided in advance by the International Committee for European Migration, an intergovernmental agency that placed the refugees aboard the plane in Rome, where they had arrived three days ago from Kampala, Uganda's capital.

On hand to greet the Kundans were members of the Tolstoy Foundation, a relief agency resettling nine other Asian Ugandans as well. Mr. Kundan said he had worked for the Exxon Corporation in Kampala and hoped to find a job with the oil company here.

Like Mr. Kundan, most of the adult members of the adult families are skilled professionals—carpenters, office managers, officers and teachers and an anthropology professor.

The United States Government has agreed to participate with other countries in taking 1,000 of the 50,000 persons who are being expelled from Uganda by next Wednesday by President Idi Amin, who has accused the Asians of "economic sabotage" of the country's commercial life.

The State Department has called on voluntary agencies to participate in the relocation program. Among them are the Lutheran Council, U.S.A., United States Catholic Conference, American Fund for Czechoslovak Refugees, the International Rescue Committee and the National Council of Churches.

Two more planes carrying Uganda refugees are scheduled to arrive at Kennedy Airport today.

ASIANS APPLY TO JOIN ARMY AND NAVY

News Compilation, November 2, 1972

Ugandan Asians from a refugee camp in Dartmoor have applied to join the Army and others are expressing interest in entering the Royal Navy.

Both Army and Navy spokesmen said there was no difficulty in accepting anyone who met the physical and educational requirements.

Penniless newlywed Asian couple gets 'palace' for honeymoon

News Compilation, November 4, 1972

A newlywed Ugandan Asian couple moved into their temporary home in Lambeth Palace yesterday. They were greeted by the Archbishop of Canterbury, Dr Ramsey, and Mrs Ramsey, who together with the Church Commissioners, have made available rent-free a small cottage to the two refugees, Mr and Mrs Sulikaralli Esmail.

Mr Esmail, aged 28, a former and qualified radio and television engineer, and his wife Zubunisa, aged 24, a typist, were married just before leaving Uganda on October 9.

Air Canada Uganda flight forced down

News Compilation, November 4, 1972

ST. JOHN'S, NEWFOUNDLAND—An Air Canada DC-8 with 140 Asians expelled from Uganda aboard left here for Montreal early today after repairs were made to an engine which lost oil pressure over the Atlantic on a flight from Paris.

An airline official said the aircraft landed here about midnight when instruments indicated engine trouble. The plane had flown from Uganda to Paris, where the crew was changed. The flight then resumed to Canada.

The passengers, who had been en route for 18 hours, did not leave the plane during the two-hour stopover here.

Advertisement

UNITED NATIONS CENTRE

FOR DOCUMENTATION ASSISTANCE AND TRANSPORTATION ARRANGEMENTS [IN ASSOCIATION WITH ICRC AND ICEM]

WARNING

The Red Cross Travel Document issued by the United Nations Centre to departing Asians can only be used for travel from Uganda up to the deadline of 8 November 1972.

Daily flights are available until 8 November 1972. If you have a Red Cross Travel Document you MUST purchase your ticket for IMMEDIATE DEPARTURE.

IN YOUR OWN INTERESTS DO NOT DELAY YOUR DEPARTURE ANY FURTHER

Amin tells Asian millionaire to get out

By DAVID LOSHAK in Nairobi
Reprinted with permission, ©Telegraph Group Limited, London, November 4, 1972

The millionaire Asian head of Uganda's largest industrial organisation, Mr Manubhai Madhvani, has been told by Gen. Amin that he must quit the country with his family by Wednesday.

Mr Madhvani, who is 48, has been granted a British passport and is expected to settle in England. His organisation employs 20,000 people in East Africa and has a £30 million annual turnover and a working capital of £20 million.

It includes:

* The Steel Corporation of East Africa, textile mills, a brewery, a match factory, tea estates.

* Other concerns manufacturing paper, sugar, glass and other products.

Gen. Amin said the whole organisation would be offered for sale to Africans in Uganda.

Mr Madhvani was imprisoned by Gen. Amin in September, accused of "industrial sabotage" and deprived of his Ugandan citizenship. On his release, after three weeks in Kampala's notorious Makinde jail, Gen. Amin said he would reconsider Mr Madhvani's status.

The decision now is that he must go on the grounds that his earlier renunciation of British citizenship had been made too late.

"Business loans" call

Gen. Amin said in Entebbe yesterday that Africans must take out loans and buy up enterprises left behind by departing Asians. The banks has plenty of money, he said, but no one was borrowing it.

The reason for this is, perhaps, that the banks are not inclined to advance large sums to Africans who have no security or know-how, particularly as many of the properties concerned are in any case being held by the banks as security for mortgages left unredeemed by departing Asians.

Early today he announced he was postponing action against "British imperialist domination" of Uganda's economy until the third week of this month. It was assumed he was referring to his directive that Ugandan Africans should start buying out British-owned estates in Western Uganda.

Nixon re-elected in landslide

News Compilation, November 5, 1972

President Richard M. Nixon, elected in 1968 with less than 50% of the vote, was re-elected with 97% of the vote. This was second in margin to Franklin D. Roosevelt who had 98% of the vote in 1936.

CAMP IMMIGRANTS TOLD NOT TO GET TOO COMFORTABLE

DAILY TELEGRAPH REPORTER
Reprinted with permission, ©Telegraph Group Limited, London, November 4, 1972

SOME "blunt advice" to Ugandan Asians not to linger needlessly in refugee camps, but to try to start new lives, is being given by Mr Praful Patel, an Asian member of the Government's Resettlement Board.

Mr Patel, who is making a special tour of the 16 camps to address refugees, said yesterday: "Life there is comfortable and I am urging people not to get too comfortable."

He was asked to visit the camps because of growing concern at the slowness of refugees to accept offers of homes and jobs and move out.

Since the influx began in mid-September, 19,000 Asians have been placed in camps. About 8,000 have moved on and 11,000 are still resident. Camp officials at Stradishall, Suffolk, estimate that about 120 of the 1,350 refugees have "no good reason" to stay here.

Mooning around

Major John Courtney, a former Indian Army officer who is camp administrator at Houndstone, Somerset, has said that many immigrants were not showing much initiative in getting jobs and seemed content to "moon around" the camp.

The Resettlement Board, however, is deliberately showing great tolerance to Asians reluctant to leave the camp. There is no question of any malingerers being forced to leave or having social security payments stopped, say officials.

Mr Patel said: "You must remember that these people came here feeling very insecure emotionally. But I am quite blunt in my advice to them, that nobody now should be sitting idly and not taking up the opportunities made to them."

Resettlement officers at the camps find that most refugees want to go to areas which already have large Asian populations. Many will not even consider moving to other areas.

Television room

A Daily Telegraph reporter who visited Stradishall on Thursday saw why refugees are loath to leave. At one of the recreation areas, the centrally-heated television room, young men relaxed, some with their feet up, in comfortable armchairs enjoying a drama programme.

Jayant Jdhav, 18, who has been at the camp a month, said: "In Uganda we only had one programme. Here we have several channels to choose from. However, I'm getting a bit bored, just sitting, sleeping and eating. I really want to work."

He said that his family was anxious to move on but it was difficult to find a house and a job.

Mr Zulfikar Mimji, 22, who was taking an afternoon stroll with friends on his 22nd day at the camp, said: "We have refused jobs with homes in Scotland. But this was not to avoid work. We just cannot face living in the cold.

"We want jobs in the south where the weather is warmer and where we have friends."

Generous facilities

The camp's facilities are generous now that initial overcrowding problems have been overcome. Refugees have a sporting choice of squash, badminton, volley ball, hockey or table tennis.

They can watch English films in a room adjacent to the television room. On Sundays a 20p-a-head outing is arranged to a cinema in Cambridge which shows Asian films. There is a morning and afternoon tea bar, and a sewing and craft room where electric sewing machines are provided.

This week the first edition of a weekly four-page camp newspaper, In Transit, was published, listing forthcoming events such as a firework display and tea parties.

Officials say that any refugee who shows signs of staying longer than necessary is "helped on" by being left out of community activities or excluded from sports teams.

Mr William Pollok-Morris, South-west Region Administrator, said that after a spell in a camp, where the Asians had no responsibilities and were cared for, there was a reluctance on the part of some to "take the plunge into the great wide world outside."

They had been out of circulation and felt like someone who had spent a long time in hospital, or been a prisoner of war and found it difficult to adjust.

Houndstone, the former Army camp near Yeovil where 836 Ugandan Asians are housed, is regarded by immigrants as an island of security for them, Mr Pollok-Morris said.

"They feel that if things go wrong they can fall back on that security."

Returned to camp

One family returned to Houndstone after leaving to live with relatives. They had found conditions too cramped. Often those who did leave wanted to know if there was an Asian community in the town they were going to.

At Houndstone, a Sikh father of six children who was a motor mechanic in Kampala said: "I am very happy to stay here. The food and the billet is good and I have no complaints."

A Muslim, married with two children, who was a Kampala businessman, said he had gone to London for a job but turned it down. "I was offered £1,100 a year but I found London too expensive. I also have to look after my father, mother and a brother."

A Sikh girl who is to become a student at Aberystwyth University said: "Some are afraid to move out because their only contact has been with Asians and people friendly to them."

Smooth flying with Operation Uganda

By Peter Desbarats, Ottawa editor
Reprinted with permission, ©Toronto Star syndicate, November 7, 1972

MONTREAL

The first planeload of Asians expelled from Uganda arrive in Montreal on Sept. 28, the last is scheduled to reach here tomorrow. During the 42-day airlift, Canada has received these new arrivals at an average rate of 100 a day.

Perhaps because of the election campaign, the entry of more than 4,200 Asians in little more than a month has gone almost unnoticed. Immigration in general was an issue in the campaign but specific references to the Ugandan immigrants were rare.

"It's gone as smoothly as anyone could have hoped," said an official of the Prime Minister's office last week. The official had been closely involved in the August decision to accept the immigrants.

"They've just faded into the woodwork," he said.

Despite the coincidence of the election campaign and Canadian sympathy for victims of racism in Uganda, this result has been more than a happy accident. It has been the calculated outcome of an elaborate government operation that will cost, according to unofficial estimates now being made in Ottawa, about $5 million.

The operation has been typically Canadian, in all its aspects, good and bad.

First, the good side.

For those Asians accepted by Canada's 40-member immigration and health unit in Uganda, the Canadian rescue operation has been efficient, humane and bountiful.

Free air transportation has been provided for all the immigrants from the Ugandan capital of Kampala to Montreal aboard chartered Air Canada and Pacific Western aircraft. (Early in the airlift, discriminating applicants soon learned that Pacific Western supplied free champagne on its flights compared with Air Canada's 18-hour "dry run" from Africa). Every flight also carried Canadian medical and immigration officers who did much of the routine processing of the immigrants en route.

Hot food and a bed

As soon as the planes landed, they were directed to a special section of Montreal's international airport where buses waited to take the Asians directly to Longue Pointe military base in the east end of the city.

Most of the arrivals were late at night or in the small hours of the morning. No matter what the hour, there was always a brief but formal ceremony of welcome for each group of immigrants when it reached the base. Then there was hot food and

bed for those who were able to sleep.

In the morning, the new arrivals received final clearance from immigration officials, selected their destination in Canada in consultation with Manpower officials, were given purchase orders for winter clothing to an average value of $40 per person, and loaned money for transportation within Canada.

At their final destination, they were met by local committees organized by Manpower centres and given temporary accommodation and allowances.

About 20 per cent of the Asians have elected to stay in Quebec, the rest are divided equally between Ontario and the rest of the country. The number who wanted to stay in Montreal was much lower in the first few weeks of the program and was a source of concern until one day, it increased suddenly and inexplicably.

2 views of Montreal

When officials investigated, they discovered that a traffic problem that day had rerouted the immigrants' bus from the airport to Longue Pointe. Instead of driving along the elevated trans-island expressway through dreary suburban and industrial areas, it had reached the city via the

Continued on Page 122

Advertisement

HIGH COMMISSION OF INDIA

KAMPALA

IMPORTANT NOTICE

TO PASSENGERS BOOKED ON

HARYANA & KARANJA

Passengers who have purchased rail tickets for travel to Mombasa on November 7 may please note that **a special train has been arranged** for them. The train will leave Kampala at **12 noon on November 7** and not at 4 p.m.

Canada Greets Uganda Exiles With Warmth

BY DON SHANNON, Times Staff Writer
Reprinted with permission, ©Los Angeles Times, November 5, 1972

TORONTO—At 6 a.m. on the morning of Oct. 11, Anil Lalani, general manager for Kodak Uganda, gave the keys of his comfortable house in Kampala to his father-in-law. With his wife, mother and infant son, Lalani got on a plane and flew to Montreal and a life of exile.

"I heard from my father-in-law later that the house had been stripped and my car taken before he got back that afternoon," Lalani said.

The young Asian and his family were among the first 2,000 given refuge in Canada after Uganda's President Idi Amin ordered the expulsion of some 50,000 Asians from the East African nation. Nearly one-third of these first arrivals chose Ontario province although they were free to go anywhere in the country. Toronto, Canada's largest city, already has an Asian population of 20,000.

One-Bedroom Apartment

Three weeks after arrival, home for the Lalani family was a cheerless one-bedroom apartment in suburban Toronto, sparsely furnished with second hand beds, a sofa and table from the Salvation Army.

"We were lucky," Lalani explained, gesturing toward the furniture. "We got out with $125 among the three of us and were able to buy this."

He said he was even more grateful that Canadian Kodak had offered him a job even before his departure from Uganda. Instead of managing a small of office with 14 employees, however, he is starting at the bottom in a plant that

employs 2,000.

"I think that's fair enough," Lalani said as his wife Shaida poured tea.

Native of Kenya

The younger woman wore a western dress, but her mother-in-law, Mrs. Shirani Lalani wore a sari. Born in Kenya, the older woman had lived most of her life in Uganda where her son was born.

The family belongs to the Ismaili sect of Islam and Lalani was educated partly in Pakistan and partly in West Germany. He returned to Uganda after his studies and regards himself as a Uganda citizen because he had renounced his British passport after colonial rule ended a decade ago.

"When I was called on to prove my citizenship, the only thing missing was the original certificate, but there was a duplicate in the government file," he said. "I was declared stateless along with my mother, although my wife's citizenship was confirmed."

Had Planned to Leave

Even if his papers had been judged acceptable, Lalani said he would have left anyway and had been planning his departure since last year when Amin began putting pressure on Asians.

"We were going to leave next summer after the cold winter here," the slim, bespectacled Asian said. "Every day at 5 we used to listen to the news and it kept getting worse."

Real concern swept through the Asian community, he said, when Asian members of

Continued on Page 122

Ugandan Asian Expulsion: 90 Days and Beyond through the Eyes of the International Press　　　　　　　　*Page 121*

Continued from Page 121

Smooth flying with Operation Uganda

Bonaventure Autoroute, providing the Asians with one spectacular view of downtown Montreal at night.

From then on, the Bonaventure Autoroute was used by all the buses and a significant number of Asians, particularly single young men and women, continued to select Montreal as their destination.

Operation Uganda has shown Canada's peacetime army at its best. The 20-hour "turnaround cycle for each group of immigrants arriving at Longue Pointe has been handled with detailed efficiency, with everything from curry in the military kitchen to diaper pins and rubber pants in the makeshift nursery.

Now that the operation is completed, it can be reported that there was one bomb scare triggered by a telephone call to the base at 9:15 p.m. one evening. The last of that day's group of Asians had just left Longue Pointe but the next group was scheduled to arrive at midnight. While contingency plans were made to accommodate the Asians elsewhere, the army moved hundreds of men to Longue Pointe and succeeded in declaring the base safe at 11:30 p.m. before the new group landed at the airport.

There was also a smallpox scare when doctors aboard one of the flights from Kampala discovered a baby with a suspicious-looking skin condition. A 24-bed isolation ward at Montreal's St. Justine Hospital had been set aside at the beginning of the operation for just such an emergency. The baby was taken directly from the plane to the hospital, and military officers routed one of the city's leading dermatologists from his bed and rushed him to the hospital. The specialist took one look at the baby and said it had an ordinary skin rash and everybody went to bed.

The calibre of the Asians has impressed everyone who has come into contact with them, including a rather hard-bitten information officer for the federal health department who still talks about the young immigrant who stepped into the freezing rain at Montreal airport wearing a blue blazer and clutching a tennis racket.

Spotting the information officer, the new arrival asked, "Play much tennis here, old man?"

"Not at this time of year," said the official.

The young man straightened his shoulders and stiffened his upper lip.

"Quite," he said.

The anecdote illustrates indirectly, the "other side" of Canada's humanitarian effort in Uganda. While more than 4,200 Asians were accepted some reports have stated that Canada turned down three out of four applicants in Uganda. Britain, with a much more difficult racial situation than Canada, has accepted more than five times as many Asians from Uganda.

"No doubt about it we've got the cream of the crop," said one official in Ottawa last week.

Continued from Page 121

Canada Greets Uganda Exiles With Warmth

Parliament disappeared several months ago. In the final weeks before their departure, he said, two friends were shot but his family was unharmed and his last close relative, a married sister, got out a week after Lalani's father-in-law.

Both Anil and Shaida confessed to nostalgia for their tropical homeland—especially the sunshine—but they are reconciled to never going back. The senior Mrs. Lalani, who understands English but is not a fluent speaker of it, said she left with no regrets and was curious to see a new country.

"Shopping is difficult here," Shaida reported. "Supermarkets are so big and far away, not like the little shops near the house in Kampala."

Both expressed surprise at the friendliness of Canadians. Lalani said he was prepared for some signs of resentment against newcomers because there had been criticism of the government decision to accept as many as 5,000 Uganda exiles at a time when unemployment here is above 7%.

"There's been nothing like that," he said. "Everywhere we go, people strike up conversations—it's really wonderful."

The young couple had high praise for the reception process at a Montreal army camp where an average of one flight a day has been bringing refugees since Sept. 27.

"At first, some of the people said 'Oh no, not soldiers again!' because the army in Uganda was the worst," Lalani said. "But we quickly found that these soldiers were different."

After an overnight train ride to Toronto, the refugees were greeted by members of the staff of the Toronto Manpower and Immigration Center and of the Uganda Asian Committee, volunteers from Toronto's Asian community, churches and civic groups.

Asad Shah, a Kenya-born lawyer who came to Canada on his own seven years ago, heads the committee.

Cites Calmness

"What has impressed me is the composure of the people," Shah said. "And all of them have said they were made to feel welcome by such little touches as having a birthday cake for a child who arrived on his birthday."

John Eckertt, Ontario regional coordinator for the refugee movement, said the government acquired valuable experience from the larger influx after the Hungarian uprising in 1956 and the 1968 inflow of Czech refugees. A building near Toronto's lakefront was hastily opened as a reception center and government volunteer workers greet the new arrivals here.

What Canada has done in Uganda, it has done well. It has done better than any comparable country with the exception of England, where special circumstances prevail. But has it done enough?

The government evidently believes that the Canadian consensus on this question is affirmative.

Job counselors interview men, teachers conduct orientation and English classes for women, some of whom need help in the language, and a day nursery cares for children while their parents are busy. The Asians received winter clothing in Montreal but additional clothing collected by churches is available at the center, along with furniture, currently the greatest need in getting the immigrants started in their new life.

Problem of Professional

Job training or retraining is offered by the federal manpower program, Eckertt said, and because the Asians were screened in Uganda for their skills they are expected to have little difficulty in finding work.

Many are professional men and for these there may be special problems, Shah said, explaining that qualifying for the Canadian bar would require a return to school for a Uganda lawyer. A young geologist, D. N. Zala, one of the first to reach Toronto and now a member of the reception committee, said he will have trouble finding a ‚job in his field.

"Lots of geologists are out of work here now," he said. "I have a master's degree from the university in Nairobi and even if I went back to school here and got a North American degree it would still be difficult."

Ice Hockey Matches

Tony Galasso, public relations director for the manpower center, said the cooperation between government and private agencies is speeding the adaptation process.

He recalled that the first arrivals got an immediate initiation into their new national sport, ice hockey with the climax of the Soviet-Canadian matches in Moscow.

"The soldiers at Long Pointe, the Montreal reception center, were watching the game on television and nearly took the roof off when Canada scored the winning goal," Galasso recalled. "The Asians must have wondered what was going on, but they all know now.

Recount results in Canadian election draw!

News Compilation, November 3, 1972

A November 2 recount added one seat to the Liberal party and resulted in an equal number of seats for the Liberal and Progressive Conservative parties. The final results were as follows:

Liberals - 109 (147 previously)

Progressive Conservatives - 109 (73)

New Democrats - 30 (25)

Others - 16 (13)

Prime Minister Pierre Elliot Trudeau announced his intention to remain in power.

The Conservative leader, Robert L. Stanfield, said that Trudeau had "lost the confidence of the people, and he should resign."

David Lewis of the New Democrats pledged to "make the new Parliament work."

Kampala criticisms studied

By JOHN EZARD
Reprinted with permission, ©The Guardian, London, November 6, 1972

THE FOREIGN OFFICE has cabled the British High Commission in Kampala asking if it has any record of a deaf Asian aged 30 who is alleged to have been barred from joining the rest of his family coming to Britain—although they are the only people in the world who know his private sign language.

The allegation is made in the latest of a series of highly critical documents about the British High Commission which an anonymous group of citizens in Kampala had been sending to Britain since early October.

It was forwarded to the Guardian by Mr Michael Dummett, Fellow of All Souls, who said last night that it showed that there was "a possibility of a very grave human tragedy" occurring to some Asians after President Amin's departure deadline expires on Wednesday.

He said that "extremely few" people in Britain were aware of the plight of stateless Asians or of the extent to which this was due to British Government and High Commission policy. His warning was endorsed yesterday by the Joint Council for the Welfare of Immigrants.

The first document was reported in the Guardian on October 12. The second was sent after categories of Asians eligible for passports were extended on October 15.

These alleged that the High Commission was

Continued on Page 124

Asians barred from returning to resettlement camps

By JOHN EZARD
Reprinted with permission, ©The Guardian, London, November 7, 1972

None of the 7,000 Uganda Asian refugees who have so far moved out of resettlement centres will be allowed to return except in cases of special hardship or distress. This order has been given confidentially by the Ugandan Resettlement Board to the heads of its 17 centres.

A ban on entry is also to be applied to the 5,000 refugees who have so far managed without centres. Responsibility for decisions on emergency admissions has been transferred from individual camps to the board's London headquarters.

The decision is described as a further step in the board's attempts to discourage some refugees from prematurely losing confidence in their ability to resettle outside camps.

The board said: "It is not a ruling so firm that things cannot be sorted out in the case of particular families. No one is going to be left in distressing circumstances." A spokesman added that the directive was not intended for publication and should not be misinterpreted.

However Miss Hannah Stanton, secretary of the Coordinating Committee for the Welfare of Evacuees, said last night that she was "extremely worried" that it would slow resettlement by frightening refugees away from temporary accommodation.

The directive was sent out after a board meeting on Friday. It begins: "It has been decided as a general policy that Asians who apply to enter your centre other than on their first entry to this country or to re-enter it, once having left it whether on your own arrangements or the board's resettlement arrangements, may not—repeat, not—be accepted by you."

Centre heads are to tell the board at once of "especially hard" cases or cases in which refusal would cause "serious distress or suffering." Heads should send a recommendation for action.

Miss Stanton said: "We welcomed the assurance that was given to us a few weeks ago that, if things broke down, evacuees could come back to centres. We were certainly assured this by the board. They have now gone back on this.

"Being able to return gave everybody confidence—not just the Asians but those who were offering the temporary accommodations. If things did get difficult, there was always a way out. I think now this will be difficult."

The board said concern had been expressed at Friday's meeting about "a few incidents when people were wanting to come back to camps, some no doubt for valid reasons, some for not such valid reasons. It was realised that problems might develop at some centres with the last of the new arrivals coming in. It is really a question of priorities of wanting to give priority to those coming in."

Later, after consulting the board's chairman, Sir Charles Cunningham, the spokesman added: "The board has consistently taken the view that it

Continued on Page 124

Advertisement

UNITED NATIONS CENTRE

All Asians due to leave Uganda under arrangements made by the United Nations Centre are requested to report at the

PATIDAR SAMAJ
Buganda Road,
Kampala.

on Tuesday, 7 November 1972 between 10.00 and 12.00 a.m.

Only heads of families and single persons should report.

UNITED NATIONS CENTRE

Those of the departing Asians who need special transportation arrangements to the Airport or special attention during the flight (handicapped in walking, mentally disturbed and advanced pregnancies) should contact the United Nations Chief Medical Officer immediately.

**IPS BUILDING
KAMPALA
TELEPHONE: 32463**

Ugandan Asian Expulsion: 90 Days and Beyond through the Eyes of the International Press

Continued from Page 123

Kampala criticisms studied

still making "impossible demands for documentation." It was refusing to accept affidavits of marriage and birth as substitutes from Asians who were too old to have been issued with certificates at the relevant time.

The third document reached Mr Dummett last month. The individual writer is described as independently "a man with an anti-Establishment bias who is nevertheless a trained observer and would have made effort to substantiate his information." He is said to be remaining anonymous "for obvious" reasons.

Asked to supply a reference to the writer's general veracity, Mr Dummett approached Dr Anthony Kenny, Fellow and Tutor in Philosophy at Balliol College, Oxford. Dr Kenny said last night: "I have good reason to think these documents have been sent by a personal friend on whose veracity one can rely."

The following are extracts from the document:

As the deadline for the expulsion of non-Ugandan Asians draws nearer, the High Commission appear to be becoming stricter, rather than more lenient, in their processing of dependants of British passport holders.

The following categories of dependants are still no nearer to obtaining their entry certificates to Britain:

1. Male students over 21 years of age, who do not hold British passports, are still being refused entry to Britain as dependants of British passport-holding parents.

One Ugandan Asian student celebrated his 21st birthday the week before last. Had the British High Commission been faster in processing his father's passport application this student would have been able to travel to Britain with his family. As its was, the father did not receive his passport until a few days after his son's 21st birthday. Thus, the son is forced to remain destitute in Uganda, while the rest of his family proceed to Britain.

2. Invalids aged over 21, who have indisputable medical evidence that they are unable to support themselves, are still being refused entry to Britain as dependants of British passport holders.

An example is a stateless 30-year-old, profoundly deaf man who communicates by a private sign language known only to his family. He has been refused an entry certificate as a dependant of his British passport-holding father. He must therefore remain behind, while the rest of his family proceed to Britain, severing his only means of communication with the outside world.

3. Evidence of dependancy. In spite of some assurances to the contrary, people are still being asked for documents which are really impossible to obtain, as evidence that they really are dependant on the person who supports them.

Only today, two weeks from the deadline—a 20-year-old boy was told to obtain a court order to certify that the person who has supported him since he was deserted by his parents is his legal guardian.

4. Dependants of British passport-holding

wives. The British press have publicised the fact that the British Government's policy of accepting British passport-holding wives but not their non-British husbands is separating wives from their husbands.

What is more disturbing is that the policy is also separating wives from their children. The criteria for giving entry certificates to dependants of British passport-holding males are strictly defined.

All unmarried daughters and all sons under the age of 21 are classified as dependant. The criteria for allowing children to accompany their British passport-holding mothers are much more arbitrary.

The only automatic qualification for dependency in this case seems to be that the child should hold his own British passport or be entered on his mother's passport.

In the case of one family, all children had British passports apart from the two who were stateless. The stateless daughter, aged 20, was given an entry certificate to accompany her mother to Britain.

But the son, aged 19, was refused on the grounds that he could "depend on himself." In another case all the children of a family were given entry certificates to accompany their mother to Britain—except for one 15-year-old girl, who happened to possess a Ugandan passport. She was told that she could stay in Uganda with her father, who also held a Ugandan passport.

The Foreign Office emphasised that the High Commission was carrying out British Government policy, not a policy of its own. Disputing the document's point 1, a spokesman said that entry permits were being issued for the purpose of study to dependants of passport holders.

On point 2, he said: "There is no policy on his type of case because it has never arisen as far as we are aware." But an inquiry had been sent to Kampala about the case mentioned.

On point 3 the Foreign Office said: "People are asked to provide evidence if there is reason to suppose there might be doubt."

On point 4 it was said: "There is no policy of

Continued from Page 123

Asians barred from returning to resettlement camps

is not generally in the interests of an Asian family which has moved into the community to return to life in a resettlement centre unless these are circumstances which exclude any alternative. There will, of course, be cases in which it is reasonable for a family which finds itself in difficulties to be readmitted. But the board believes that such cases should be few."

* Mr John Ennals, an executive member of the coordinating committee, said in Kampala yesterday that the British High Commission had worked long hours and had had a difficult task in granting entry visas. "But no one involved in the Asian exodus will ever forget the phenomenal rudeness and unconcern for human problems which has characterised some of the lower echelons of the British operation."

separating wives from their children." It was possible that, if the 19-year-old boy was working, he had been classified as a non-dependant.

The Foreign Office could not offer an explanation of the case of the girl of 15. But in general it was said that it was not the British Government which was splitting families. Passport-holding wives and dependants of non-passport-holding heads of families were not forced to come to Britain. The assumption behind British policy was that, after a period here, the dependants would naturally rejoin the breadwinners elsewhere.

Mrs Mary Dines, JCWI secretary, said the allegations of the document were "completely confirmed by everything we know. We have cases of people still in Uganda from whom impossible documentation is being demanded.

One Asian was in detention at Heathrow Airport - London because he was not being allowed in as a dependant of his older brothers to take up a place at Manchester University department of computer science.

A blind Asian, aged 60, was being barred from entry as a dependant of his son because he had not reached the retiring age of 65 at which a British Government considered a man became dependant.

Advertisement

THE EMBASSY OF THE UNITED STATES OF AMERICA

Announces the last flight of stateless Asians who hold visas to the United States. The time is as follows:

LAST FLIGHT

Departs Entebbe Wednesday November 8 at 02.00 a.m., AZ flight number 817

NOTE! NOTE!

All persons departing by this flight as given above should report to the IPS Building on November 7, 1972 at 10 p.m. There will be a special bus set up to take all these travellers to the airport and documents will be checked before departure of this bus. All concerned are urged to make this bus schedule without fail.

DOMINATION ENDS

BY CHRIS SERUNJOGI, REBECA KATUMBA AND PEREZ OWORI
Reprinted with permission, ©Uganda Argus, November 7, 1972

A last minute shopping spree in Kampala yesterday was described by many Ugandans as 'historic'. The high tempo of activity marked the day that saw the end of the domination of Uganda's economy by Asians, and the beginning of a new chapter of the country's economic independence.

All shops unaffected by the expulsion order—such as Deacons, Mukubi and Sons, and Anilyaliamany—were filled to capacity. The customers made long queues and spent several hours waiting to get into the shops.

At some shops, guards were employed to control the customers who were fighting for entry as there was insufficient space to accommodate the customers.

Inside some shops the heat made some customers faint . Many customers left some shops with tattered clothing—the result of scuffles at the entrances.

Several people had to leave shops without getting what they wanted as many of them were confused and could not differentiate between customers and shop attendants.

It was doubted yesterday whether Deacons had any stock for today.

Some rogues went into shops to use the spree as an excuse for stealing—and got caught red-handed with articles not paid for.

Few

By lunch-time yesterday, even a learner could drive in the main street of Kampala without difficulty. There were very few Asian cars hurrying home.

Many Ugandan workers took the lunchtime as a time for inspection of business premises which are in their plans for acquisition.

And while some were looking for business, other were looking for flats to rent.

Most of the immigration officials, technicians and doctors sent by the Canadian Government to Kampala to process entry certificates to the non-Ugandan Asians intending to settle in Canada have left after successfully completing their duties, an official from the Canadian High Commission disclosed yesterday.

He said that by tomorrow, all the team will have left. Most of them will go directly to Canada and a few will go to Nairobi to wait for a few days in case their assistance is needed in Kampala. Two thousand, five hundred have already flown to Canada on Canadian Government charter flights. The High Commission issued 6,000 entry permits to other non-citizen Asian.

The last flight will leave tomorrow for Canada, right on the nose of the deadline set by President Amin for the non -Ugandan Asians to leave Uganda.

It was said that most of the Asians going to Canada will have to start anew, but should not have problems fitting in to the new society. Many of the immigrants already have got jobs.

Yesterday, 10 Asians got their visas from the Canadian High Commission.

About six Asian families left Jinja by taxis for Entebbe Airport yesterday afternoon and were due to fly to Britain last night.

The group comprised 35 Asians, including children, who were affected by President Amin's expulsion decree.

As African taxi drivers were loading the luggage onto the car racks, some of the Asians burst into tears—attracting crowds.

Among the Asians was Mr Fatma, a Goan, who owned a grocery shop in the town centre. With him was his wife, their two children and his brother who was formerly employed by Dunlop East Africa Ltd. in Jinja.

Two families from Iganga in Busoga District are due to fly out today. The heads of these families were reported to have signed their declaration forms at the District Commission's Office, Busoga yesterday.

Before leaving Jinja, Mr Fatma said that although he was flying to Britain with his family, he wanted eventually to settle in Canada.

At the weekend, a fire broke out in a radio shop on Iganga Road, Jinja, causing serious damage to equipment and furniture.

According to Jinja Fire Brigade the incident was reported early on Saturday.

Among the goods damaged were radio and television sets, records and spare parts. Police are investigating. The value has not yet been established.

The shop is said to have belonged to a Mr Patel who has left the country.

Meanwhile, the Busoga District Team and Planning Committee met at the Jinja Town Council Chambers yesterday and drew up twelve proposals on how the economy should be handed over to Ugandan Africans.

The meeting, which was chaired by the Acting District Commissioner, Mr H. Gakuyo, will pass the proposals and recommendations to the Ministry of Public Service and Local Administration.

At another meeting plans were drawn up in respect of the forthcoming Remembrance Day celebrations on Saturday.

Mr Gakuyo also appealed to all residents of Jinja to decorate the town in readiness for the visit of the King of Saudi Arabia next week.

Outside the British High Commission grounds which has seen many Asian queues over the years, and particularly the last three months, there were no Asians to everybody's surprise.

At the beginning of the expulsion order, the staff at the office was reinforced by officials from Britain and wives of the Britons here in order to speed the documentation. *Continued on Page 126*

Asians to be counted—person by person

Reprinted with permission, ©Uganda Argus, November 7, 1972

President Amin has disclosed that he has directed the Minister of Public Service and Local Administrations and the Minister of Internal Affairs to make arrangements throughout Uganda to count physically all Asians in Uganda, starting on November 9.

The General made the disclosure when he met the Acting British High Commissioner to Uganda, Mr. J. D. Hennings, at the command Post.

The exercise, the President said is intended to find out Asians who are Uganda citizens and those who are not. The Asians in Kampala will be counted at Kololo Airstrip and Nakivubo Stadium Those in the Districts, will be counted at centres to be announced.

The exercise will also give a chance to Uganda citizen Asians to say which District they want to be sent, because they are going to be sent to the Districts to mix with Ugandans.

Report

The Asians, must report to the counting centres at 9 a.m.

The counting will be undertaken by officers from the Army, Police, Prisons, District Administrations and Town Councils.

The General told Mr. Hennings he had called him to clear three points.

FIRSTLY, the President wanted to know whether the British Asians will have cleared out of Uganda by the deadline (tomorrow).

The Acting British High commissioner told the President that the High Commission has completed the documentation of the British Asians. By today, the exercise will have been completed.

SECONDLY, the President wanted to ask him to give all details of the British people who own farms and private companies in Uganda. He wants to know their number, their families and where they are.

Mr. Hennings told the President that he intends to invite all British citizens to register with the High Commission, and when that is done, he will give the President the details.

THE THIRD POINT, said the General, was to inform Mr. Hennings that on November 20, 1972, he will have a meeting with the British representatives owning farms from all Districts of Uganda. The General suggested that about 15 from each District should attend the meeting at the International Conference Centre at 11a.m.

He will discuss with them the problems they are facing and their future in Uganda.

The conference, he said, will, therefore, be a very important one for the British.

Uganda, he said, is for the Ugandans, and they have to be the masters of their own affairs.

Ugandan Asian Expulsion: 90 Days and Beyond through the Eyes of the International Press

When East meets West in Suffolk

Reprinted with permission, ©Telegraph Group Limited, London, November 8, 1972

NORMAN RILEY looks into the problems of changing Asian refugees into British locals

STRADISHALL RAF base in West Suffolk, first of the 16 camps for Ugandan Asians, welcomed this week its last plane-load of 166 refugees.

The biggest of the centres set up by the Uganda Resettlement Board, near Stansted airport, it provides the best illustration of the complexities of an airlift without precedent.

Since Sept. 18 Stradishall has received some 3,200 of the 22,000 Asians expelled, penniless, by President Amin and flown to England on their British passports.

Of these 3,200, nearly 1,700 have by now left the camp, 900 of them to join relatives and friends in Peterborough, London, Leicester, Wolverhampton, Birmingham and other areas where there are already big Asian communities.

The rest are scattered in 40 localities, villages and towns, from Bath and Brighton in the south to Dalkeith and Edinburgh beyond the border. How many already have found both jobs and accommodation, or social security benefits locally worth up to £30 a week, is anybody's guess.

As long as they are at places like Stradishall, single people get £2 · 10 a week pocket money, married couples £3 · 50, dependent children according to age anything from 60p to £2 · 10 a week. This is in addition to three free meals a day—curried eggs, choice of vegetables for the vegetarians, lamb, rice, fish.

A round-the-clock staff at Stradishall, 30 strong from various government and local authority departments, has found jobs for 150 men in building, tailoring, nursing, watch repairing and office work.

This figure may not sound imposing, but it means the end of utter misery and hopelessness for 150 families—at least 750 people as Asian families go. And it takes no account of the efforts, regularly, day by day, for about 80 volunteer workers to make life tolerable in a cold climate for the older refugees who meander in cast-off overcoats round the camp, wondering what can possibly happen to them next.

Many of the men, with free travel warrants, go long distances to be interviewed for jobs—at, say, Wembley or Liverpool—but turn down offers of employment because they are so convinced their talents deserve something better. Some, recognised accountants in Kampala, are reconciled to at least two years' study in this country to qualify for the same professional accolade here.

Others, desperate, will accept almost any work, anywhere—and here's where the Resettlement Board's problems became a real tangle.

What do you do with a family of seven, including three crippled children and a grandmother who is blind?

The family ties are so strong that men from Stradishall—about 10 per cent of them claiming to be business or professional men who have lost everything, another 10 per cent skilled tradesman—will not leave for a job until they are sure of a home. Or they cannot hope for a home in some areas unless they first have a job, where there is often no job going.

The Board will not send families to housing accommodation which has not been approved by the local authorities. Its telex installation is busy all day sorting out offers of seemingly generous accommodation—and reminding would-be landlords of furnished accommodation that when they accept the rent they must also accept the fact that, under various rent Acts, they can't just as quickly get rid of their tenants whenever it suits them.

Group-Capt. Frederick Rothwell, only two days retired from the RAF, took over a care-and-maintenance RAF base where he was once wing commander (flying). His new sortie entailed assuring hundreds of refugees, with all their religious and dietetic prejudices, that there couldn't be a dozen different canteens to cater for them.

So at last the Moslem shadow falls, unheeded mainly, across the 90 per cent, eating Hindu food, and the various sects can eat or ignore the meat or fish or vegetables served on a two-shift basis by catering contractors with a staff of 60.

Many of the women know no English and show little inclination to learn it. About 200 children a day attend "acclimatisation" classes in the old lecture rooms draped round the empty hangers. "One or two as bright as buttons," a seconded West Suffolk teacher said. "Some know no English at all. Some, playing hookey in the living quarters, have to be winkled out and their parents told that attendance at school here is compulsory, whatever it was in Uganda."

Since the start all arriving families have had a medical screening. The verdict: "The majority are healthy, although there is some anaemia and diabetes. There is no evidence to show that any kind of exotic disease is being brought into the country. In fact the majority are at least as healthy as the resident United Kingdom population."

But there is still a 24-hours night and day health watch for unannounced departures, for families collected by car at odd hours by relatives and friends from all over the country.

The camp has an entertainments officer, the Rev. William Davies, vicar of Stradishall. He hadn't much time for do-gooding organisations that might sail in just once, collar a television programme and all the glory, and leave glowing with virtue and publicity. In a very thinly-populated area he now has a roster of 170 local families who entertain, every family and take them on trips to Cambridge or Newmarket by car, and for meals in their homes.

This works wonders with families who otherwise would have to spend four or five weeks in a kind of limbo during their stay in the camp.

Half a dozen young men have been placed in universities and technological colleges from Stradishall. A score of youngsters are preparing for their "O" and "A" level examinations at schools mainly in Bury St. Edmunds.

The big question is: How long will it be before all the elderly and infirm, the unskilled and unwilling from 16 centres have to be sorted out and provided for as the centres close down? The Board's hope is that the problem will cease to exit once 1,700 local authorities have all agreed to take just three Ugandan Asian families apiece.

Continued from Page 125

DOMINATION ENDS

Staff

Some of the temporary staff have been sent home as the level of work has been reduced.

About 28,000 people have been issued with entry certificates and it is hoped that by the deadline the whole lot will have left the country. Yesterday, 28 heads of family and 11 wives collected entry certificates.

A spokesman said that it is thought that the people who collect their certificates at the last minute might have wanted to stay on till the end or that they just never bothered.

Some Asians had abandoned their cars at the office. Police were called to take them away.

The British High Commission will have nothing to do with the abandoned property until they are asked by the Government.

At the United Nations office in Kampala, it was learnt that between 3,900 and 4,000 Asians have been documented as people of undetermined nationality. The number could be fewer because some Asians registered at more than one office and they might have been taken by another office.

Mr W. R. Prattley, the Resident Representative, said that the Asians will be going to Austria, Italy, Belgium and America. In the European countries they will be accommodated in transit camps.

Mr Prattley said that they wanted to take the whole lot, "and from the camps, other countries in Europe will have to select whom to take".

About a third of the total is under 16 years of age. Most cases have been straight-forward. There have been problems created by mixed marriages where the nationality of the children has been difficult to determine.

There have been problems of destitutes whose fairs will be paid. He cited a woman of 94 who was deaf and blind and almost crippled. Arrangements have been made to allow her to join her relatives in Kenya.

The temporary United Nations documentation office in the IPS building will probably close after the deadline. Nominal service will be maintained, in case some Asians turn up.

Mr Prattley said that 40 new cases cropped up yesterday. Some of the Asians might not have known about the order and that he planned to send out staff to look for such Asians.

Mr Prattley said that on the deadline, there will be ten special flights each with a capacity of 150 and 200 to make sure that they are all out.

We are making everything possible to see that we finish our work by Wednesday, he said.

Last minute offers from Malta, Morocco, Greece and Spain enable Red Cross to get 2,000 refugees away from Uganda on final day

Only 800 stateless Asians left as Amin deadline expires

From Michael Knipe, Kampala, Nov 8
Reprinted with permission, ©Times Newspapers Limited, London, November 9, 1972

About 800 stateless Asians were herded into two Sikh temples and a Hindu community centre here tonight as President Amin's 90-day time limit for the Asian expulsions expired.

Armed private guards were on duty to prevent any incidents but the Asians were regarded as being in the custody of the United Nations and no trouble was expected.

In the 24 hours leading up to the deadline the crisis produced a last-minute surge of desperately needed temporary accommodation in Malta, Morocco, Greece and Spain. This was enough to meet the demand and more than 2,000 Asians departed on a dozen airline flights, the highest number in one day since the Asian airlift began. United Nations and International Red Cross officials are confident that the remaining 800 will be safely away by Friday.

They are camping amid piles of suitcases and bundles of personal belongings in their makeshift quarters. At the Patidar Samaj Hindu community centre, there was an atmosphere of calm, controlled chaos.

Above the screams of young children, European volunteers shouted out flights as they became available while a few African helpers provided tea and carried messages. Asian applicants for the flights were escorted to the Bank of Uganda to buy their tickets and back to the community centre where they were issued with boarding passes.

A notice on a blackboard said: *"All passengers proceeding to transit camps in Austria should put on the warmest clothing they have. Shoes not sandals, overcoats, sweaters and pullovers if available and anything to keep your head warm. When you arrive the temperature will be around freezing"*. Some old Asians who have yet to experience freezing temperatures began delving into their battered suitcases for more readily available clothes.

"People with boarding cards for Austria, stand by", said a European helper. A harassed Asian asked a question. "The most important thing for you at the moment is to get you on a flight", replied the woman. Another Asian came up with a cardboard box containing about 20 hundred-shilling notes which he was donating to help buy tickets for those without funds. More than 100,000 shillings have been contributed in this

manner.

Of the countries accepting the stateless Asians on a temporary basis, Italy has taken 940. Belgium 400, Malta 200, Morocco 300, Greece 100, Spain 500 and Austria 1,500.

Among the last stragglers scooped up by the United Nations operation today have been some of the saddest cases. About 20 sick people, some of them just out of hospitals, have been helped on their way, including a number of mentally ill individuals. One woman suffered a miscarriage as she was about to depart and was taken to hospital.

The nearest thing to panic occurred last night among the Asians when lights went out over various parts of Kampala, including the Hindu community hall, for about an hour. Then later in the evening firing was heard. Some people counted at least 50 gunshots. There were no signs of emer-

gency measures, however, and the city, which had been celebrating the feast marking the end of Ramadan, remained calm.

President Amin said during a speech today that the shooting occurred when police opened fire indiscriminately, believing wrongly that there were some armed robbers in the Kololo suburb of the capital. Even some embassies believed fighting had broken out, said the President, but it was a false alarm. When the Army investigated they did so without firing a shot and found nothing untoward.

President Amin said that the power failure was due to a technical fault. The person who caused the confusion had been arrested and the police who opened fire would be asked to explain why they had wasted ammunition.

Continued on Page 128

Not one shop window has been smashed in Kampala in protest against Amin expulsions

Asians leave homes and wealth more in sorrow than in anger

From Michael Knipe, Kampala, Nov 7
Reprinted with permission, ©Times Newspapers Limited, London, November 8, 1972

I saw an angry Asian the other evening. It was in a Chinese restaurant, one of the handful of eating places still open here, and he was accosting other diners and berating an African waiter.

Flashing a large roll of green 100 shilling notes, he was forcefully buying rounds of drinks for everyone, slurring that the money was worthless to him because he was leaving "bloody Uganda" the next day. Moments later he was loudly demanding his change and accusing the waiter of stealing it.

His belligerence came from drink and although he clearly terrified the waiter, the diners—Europeans, Asians and Africans—suffered his interruptions with good humour.

During the past 90 days it has been possible to witness a whole gamut of emotions here as President Amin's harsh expulsion order has been put into effect. Anger, however, has been remarkably uncommon.

Forlorn women in saris with expressions of passive depression have sat crouched on their

haunches outside documentation offices; furtive little men with grey-brown faces have sweated nervously as they have tried to wheedle favours out of immigration officials.

Impassioned businessmen in smart mohair suits and Mercedes cars have bemoaned the loss of their fortunes, and whole families have cowered with fear at army roadblocks and government offices. And yet not one shop window has been smashed in retaliation.

Nine-tenths of Uganda's Asian community, certainly more than 40,000 people, have been evicted callously from their houses and the remainder face forceful resettlement in remote areas. But there has been scarcely one indignant sign of protest.

At the office block in Parliament Street where the British, Canadian and United Nations documentation has been carried out, crowds of Asians have sometimes totalled thousands, but there has never been any hint of violence, and there has been no need for police presence.

Continued on Page 128

Ugandan Asian Expulsion: 90 Days and Beyond through the Eyes of the International Press *Page 127*

Exodus of Uganda Asians Ends Calmly

By Jim Hoagland, Washington Post Foreign Service
Reprinted with permission, ©Washington Post, November 9, 1972

NAIROBI, Nov. 8—The mass expulsion of about 35,000 Asians from Uganda moved toward completion tonight as the deadline set by President Idi Amin for the last of them to leave expired in apparent calm.

An estimated 400 Asians were flown out today, virtually ending the six-week effort to transport them to more than a dozen countries that have offered permanent or temporary refuge. Among those leaving were the last of the 1,000 stateless Asians the United States agreed to accept.

Fears had been expressed in the international community that violence might erupt if all the Asians did not get out of the East African country by tonight's deadline. Amin had made a series of conflicting statements about what would happen to those who remained in the country, including a threat to put these Asians into special camps.

During the exodus, many of the departing Asians had been subjected to abuse by soldiers on the road to Entebbe International Airport outside Kampala, the capital of Uganda. There were reports that many had been stripped of their belongings and some killed. Also, some Asian women said they were raped.

But there were no reports of harassment of Asians today.

In a speech today, President Amin said that the expulsions had been "smooth and successful" and thanked the British government and the Asians themselves for having helped to make the operation a success. He promised that any Asians left after tonight would be "dealt with humanely."

About 1,100 stateless Asians remained in Kampala community halls that were converted tonight into United Nations departure centers, sources contacted by telephone in the Ugandan capital said.

United Nations officials raced to meet the deadline, which Amin had repeatedly stressed would not be extended, by finding countries that would guarantee to take the last group of stateless persons on a temporary basis.

Spain, Morocco and Greece offered them transit facilities, and Belgium increased the number of Asians it will accept. This meant that the deadline was technically met to the Ugandan government's satisfaction, according to unofficial reports.

Estimates of the number of Asians that would have to leave Uganda varied earlier from 35,000 to 60,000. The Ugandan government initially said that all of the 80,000 Asians it said had British passports would have to leave. But Amin later modified his order to allow Asian professionals to remain.

Britain claimed that only 40,000 Asians in Uganda were British citizens, while Uganda challenged the claim of many others who maintained they held citizenship. These claims and counter-claims left in doubt precisely how many Asians would be expelled.

In addition, some have been departing on their own, making it difficult to determine exactly how many Asians have now left the country.

According to informed estimates, about 10,000 Asians still remain in Uganda. They are divided about equally between Asians who could prove that they had been granted Uganda citizenship at independence in 1962 and those non-citizen Asians who were exempted from Amin's order because of their professional qualifications.

The remaining Asians have been ordered to report to government offices Thursday for a head count. The Ugandan citizens among them have been ordered by Amin to sell their property and move to African villages where they are supposed to mix with Africans.

Included in today's departures were about 180 Asians bound for Canada, which has taken early 4,000 of the expellees.

The stateless category covered Asians who were unable to prove that they held Ugandan or any foreign passport. Britain granted restricted citizenship rights to Uganda's Asians requesting them at independence and has had to absorb about 25,000 Asians since late September.

Another 4,500 have go to India, with the balance being divided between a number of other countries that accepted them on humanitarian grounds.

Canada, which began screening applicants for immigration early and established a detailed check list of qualifications, appears to have attracted a good number of Asians possessing top skills and capital to invest.

Continued from Page 127

Only 800 Stateless Asians left as Amin deadline expires

President Amin said there was no need for fear. "Nobody can attack us," he said. "If any enemy attacks these places he can be intercepted in a few minutes."

The President, who was congratulating ministers, army officers and government officials on the way they had conducted the expulsion order, said that if there were some Asians remaining who should have left, they would be dealt with humanely. "We are human beings and must not mistreat them", he said.

He also disclosed that he had ordered the expulsion of Mr Mahendra Metha, the owner of the second largest industrial complex in Uganda, which includes engineering plants, tea and coffee plantations and a 10,000-acre sugar estate.

Mr Metha had his Ugandan citizenship withdrawn on the ground that he was too late in renouncing his British citizenship. Last week President Amin refused to give citizenship to Mr Manubhai Madhvani, the head of the largest industrial complex in East Africa.

Today there were hardly any Asians to be seen in the streets of Kampala.

Continued from Page 127

Asians leave home and wealth more in sorrow than in anger

The meekness of the Asians has been matched by the moderation of the vast majority of Africans, who have not been inflamed by what President Amin calls their victory in this, the first battle of the economic war.

In banks, shops and hotels Asians and Africans have continued to serve one another courteously. One African civil servant threw a large farewell party with printed invitation cards last week for an Asian colleague.

In the Leopard's Lair nightclub on top of the International Hotel and at the Baraza Café on the terrace of the Grand Hotel, young Africans, Asians and Europeans have continued to mix socially as though they had never heard the term "Asian exodus".

All this has been in curious contrast to the government's fulminations at the "economic sabotage" by Asians, the threats of door-to-door searches and internment camps to speed the stragglers out of the country, and the grim tales told and believed by the Asians of atrocities, plundering of possessions, raping of women and the shooting of fathers, brothers and children.

It is difficult to judge the truth of the horror tales but most sober assessments point to only a few isolated incidents. It is equally hard to assess the degree of jubilation among Africans at the departure of the Asians.

In Kampala it is still difficult to tell how effective the exodus has been. About 75 per cent of the shops are locked and barred, some with goods still in the windows, others cleared out completely. Other businesses tick on under African management.

There are still plenty of Asian faces to be seen. Harassed Asian parents accompanied by wide-eyed children dressed immaculately for their journey to a new life, are still very much in evidence at the main hotel where African porters politely carry their baggage.

Reports from other parts of the country say that towns and villages are almost cleared of Asians. In some places, however, a few remain. Some have no wish to leave and intend to continue as they always have done, refusing to accept the inevitable, rather like people who will not make way for an impending motorway.

Overall, however, President Amin's audacious action to rid Uganda of its Asians within 90 days has been more successful than anyone imagined it could be.

By this evening the British High Commission had issued 28,039 entry certificates. Of these 23,840 have travelled to Britain by way of the air-lift operation. Another 6,000 have gone to India, 6,000 to Canada, about 1,000 to Pakistan and 1,000 to the United States. But of the 4,000 who have been registered as stateless there are about 1,500 for whom even temporary refuge has still to be found.

Today the last special train left Kampala taking about 150 Indian nationals, and a few Pakistan and British Asians to Mombasa, where two ships are to sail for Bombay in a few days.

At Entebbe Airport President Amin marked the last day of the exodus with a characteristic gesture. He met Asians leaving for Britain, who, according to Uganda radio, cheered him, shook hands with him and thanked him for being "tough with the British". They had been unable to go to Britain before, but now, thanks to President Amin, they were able to do so, the radio said.

Page 128 *Ugandan Asian Expulsion: 90 Days and Beyond through the Eyes of the International Press*

4,450 Asians now in Canada
Last Ugandan group arrives

Reprinted with permission, ©Montreal Gazette, November 9, 1972

A DC-8 stretch-jet carrying 200 Ugandan Asian refugees touched down at Montreal airport at Dorval early this morning and brought to an end Canada's mercy flights for the expelled Asians.

Today's final flight brings to about 4,450 the number of Asians to pass through a special reception centre at Longue Pointe Armed Forces base—a centre that will be dismantled tomorrow.

The first Ugandans stepped off an Air Canada jet to a new life in Canada on a chilly Thursday morning six weeks ago and like those that followed them were sent to jobs and homes across Canada by teams of manpower and immigration officials.

During the past few weeks, as the Nov. 8 deadline set by President Idi Amin approached, Canadian officials at Kampala speeded up the process, clearing more than 300 a day.

And Immigration officials expect to reach the objective, of 5,000 as others manage to leave the country on their own means. About 250 have already done so.

The hope and fears of the uprooted Asians, most of whom arrived with the barest of belongings, are graphically inscribed in terse notes tacked to a bulletin board in the cavernous drill hall used as the main reception centre.

"Proceeding to Prince Rupert tomorrow, try and join us," said one neatly-written slip.

"Worried about son, where is he going? Inform, if he wishes to come along here," said another note listing a Scarborough, Ont. forwarding address.

A simple plea, "If you can, try to come to Kamloops," advised another.

Robert Lefebvre, Administrator of the Uganda exiles program, explained that the new arrivals are offered a wide choice narrowed down to particular needs since many inter-related groups insisted on a common destination.

WELL QUALIFIED

He described the Ugandans as "exceptionally well qualified" and ready to accept any location. Many applied for the West coast because of the climate, he added, but distribution has evened out generally across Canada dictated by job openings.

Once selection is made, immigrants have their transportation paid with the provision for reimbursement in two years. the local manpower centre and welcoming committees ease the transition.

"We haven't lost one person yet," said Lefebvre, noting that immigrants frequently must make several connections en route to their new home.

Some 450 Ugandans have opted to stay in Quebec and a provincial training program is providing French lessons. Groups have already been successfully integrated in Farnham, Granby and Quebec City but most, including many professionals, have chosen Montreal for their new home.

BOON AND BANE

The high qualifications are both a boon and a bane to the newcomers, says Tejpal Thind, a long-time landed immigrant here who is active in an assistance committee.

They are in demand for their specialized work but employers stress Canadian experience. When they turn to lesser jobs their overqualification is a handicap, said Thind.

Despite the efforts of several interested groups, he estimated, only about 13 per cent had found jobs. Among the unemployed are economists, merchants who had their assets frozen and a heavy sprinkling of professionals.

During initial weeks immigrants, include whole families, are being put at YM and YWCAs and through special arrangement at the Queen's Hotel.

Capt. Jacques Charlebois, officer commanding a military medical team brought in from Valcartier Base to conduct physical checks, describes the newcomers as "a healthy lot."

STORK CAME CLOSE

Only a few cases of malaria have turned up, he said, but there have been at least three close shaves with the stork. "In the excitement of leaving some mothers seemed to have forgotten when pregnancy occurred.

Reproduced with permission, ©Robert Taylor/Montreal Gazette

Last of the exiled Ugandans: Bachibai Lalgi, 73 and totally blind, is guided from the airport building to an Armed Forces bus by her nephew, Firozali Janmohamed.

Now Amin gives 'marching orders' to Mehta chief

Reprinted with permission, ©Daily Nation, Nairobi, November 9, 1972

PRESIDENT Idi Amin today gave "marching orders" to another prominent Asian industrialist, Mr. Mahendra Mehta, who owns the giant Lugazi Sugar Factory situated about 28 miles from here.

Last week President Amin "ousted" Mr. Manubhai Madhvani, managing director of the Madhvani Group, when he announced that Mr. Madhvani was not a citizen and therefore he had to leave Uganda before the November 8 deadline.

Addressing a meeting of Ministers, Permanent Secretaries, senior Army officers and heads of departments today, President Amin said Mr. Mehta, a former Member of Parliament, was not a citizen and should leave Uganda tonight.

Meanwhile, 221 Uganda Asians passed through Nairobi yesterday on their way to various destinations outside Africa. Thousands of Kenya Asians turned up to greet them at Nairobi Railway Station.

Many presented the outgoing Asians with clothes and other gifts. Twenty of the travellers needed treatment for shock.

The Uganda Asians—125 adults and 96 children—were in transit to India and Pakistan. Among those travelling were three girls who said they had first boarded a train in Uganda bound for Mombasa on October 19. However, some soldiers of the Uganda Army took them away from the train to their barracks.

With the help of sympathetic soldiers they managed to escape from the barracks. They did not know what became of four other girls who were also taken to the barracks.

Mrs. Kokilaber G. Mathurhai said she had her 10-year-old son with her when the train left Kampala, and he had since disappeared.

"Two mothers gave birth at St. Justine Hospital only a few days after arrival and another became a mother hours after landing in Vancouver," said Charlebois.

Ugandan Asian Expulsion: 90 Days and Beyond through the Eyes of the International Press

Uganda refugees: the harsh results of honourable action

Christopher Walker
Reprinted with permission, ©Times Newspapers Limited, London, November 8, 1972

"Your chance to help one of Amin's victims. After 25 years with the Standard Bank, Mr Patel, now 47, seeks a job in London or Kent. The Big Five don't want to know. He'd keep your books as efficiently as a computer. He is also more human—so human he doesn't like living on the state."

The advertisement was tucked away on the classified pages of the New Statesman's latest issue. In sentiment, surname and initiative it reflects the predicament of many of the 25,000 Uganda Asians now in Britain.

The final total of refugees who have arrived here is far lower than many of the Government's critics said it would be, but the relief felt in official quarters is tempered by the fact that the most testing part of the resettlement process is still to come.

On August 18, Mr Carr told a press conference that special transit centres for the Asians would be set up only as a last resort. This morning he faces the reality that 16 of these centres—less euphemistically described as refugee camps—are already open, and there is a strong possibility that at least half will still be open next spring.

In spite of surveys conducted on its behalf in Kampala, the Uganda Resettlement Board—the ad hoc body set up to handle the crisis—was taken by surprise both by the large proportion of refugees needing temporary accommodation and by the rate at which they have been leaving the camps. "This is much slower than we bargained for", explained the chairman, Sir Charles Cunningham.

Of the 20,000 Asians transported by coach and train to the camps in far-flung parts of Britain, 12,500 remain. Many of these, because of language and other problems, are likely to be the most difficult to rehabilitate into a new society.

The majority of those who have already left the camp have not been resettled, but had not been able to make immediate contact at airports with relatives or friends. Many of them have gone to the "red" areas which the Asians were asked to avoid.

No official figures are given on how many Asians have actually been matched up with jobs and houses, but Asian sources in Britain estimate this at well under 1,500.

Realizing that many of the "reception centres" will be much more permanent than at first envisaged, the Board has started to put them on a more regular basis.

From the beginning of this week, all refugees who have found temporary employment locally have been asked to contribute to their upkeep. The charges range from £6 a week for man and wife down to £1.50 for children aged between two and 16. No decision has yet been made about whether or not to charge unemployed Asians out of their social security.

The costs of the resettlement programme have been estimated at more than £1 million a month. In an attempt to reduce costs and to induce a more independent attitude among the refugees remaining in the camps, the facility of free telephone calls has been withdrawn. I addition, camp administrators have been instructed not to permit Asians who have once moved out of a camp to re-enter, except in cases of extreme hardship.

In addition to the "self-help" maxim, the Board was also disturbed by a number of recent cases of refugees who had been found accommodation, but had left it to return to the more secure life of the camps.

A predominantly Civil Service organization not over adept at public relations, the resettlement Board has been criticized often. It has certainly given the impression of reacting to events rather than directing them, but on a number of occasions has found itself in a cleft stick. Six weeks ago it was being attacked because it was claimed that the camps were overcrowded and insanitary; now it is accused of making them too comfortable.

Certainly no one who has visited the camps could describe them as encouraging a long-term stay. All but one are former military establishments, usually bleak and isolated. As Sir Charles pointed out: "I find it hard to understand people who can describe a 200-yard walk to an outside toilet as 'comfortable'. What is apparent and far more difficult to counter is the security which many of the refugees find among their fellow countrymen. To many this contrasts starkly with the hostile welcome which they feel awaits them in areas where a large number of immigrants from East Africa are already established.

Bustling with voluntary workers and administered mainly be ex-Army and RAF officers who have come out of retirement, the camps present an example of British wartime spirit at its good-humoured best. What is by no means clear is just how much longer the workers, both paid and unpaid, will be expected to keep this up.

During the past fortnight, Mr Praful Patel, the one immigrant member of the Resettlement Board, and other Asian leaders have been deputed to make a whistle-stop tour of the camps to urge the remaining refugees to leave as soon as possible. Many of them regard this as a "last resort" for the board.

They claim that more than 40 per cent of the homeless Asians are small traders and businessmen who should be provided with loans to set up anew in Britain.

Talks have been going on with the major banks, but they are wary because they see little hope of the Asians' assets in Uganda being released by General Amin. Sir Charles explained: "Whether it is possible to go beyond our discussions and make public funds available for loans is a matter for the Government."

The Government has been widely praised in international circles for dealing honourably with a sensitive political problem. But part of the final judgment of its handling of the Uganda crisis still has to be made; it will rest on a head count of the number of figures in borrowed overcoats to be seen next winter still wandering aimlessly along roadsides in obscure spots like Stradishall, Tonfanau and Dartmoor.

500 EXPELLED ASIANS GIVEN TEMPORARY HOME AT MALTA

BY A STAFF REPORTER
Reprinted with permission, ©Times of Malta, November 9, 1972

The Malta Government answering a request by the United Nations High Commissioner for Refugees in Geneva at short notice, is providing temporary sanctuary to up to 500 stateless Asians expelled from Uganda by President Idi Amin.

The first group, 186 in all arrived late yesterday evening and were taken to Tigne Barracks where accommodation is being provided for them. Another batch of about the same number is expected to arrive today and smaller groups later. They are expected to remain in Malta for up to three months.

Prince Alfred Fur Lippe, Rome representative of the High Commissioner for Refugees, came to Malta on Tuesday evening to prepare the accommodation. He told journalists at Luqa Airport yesterday that Malta was one of the 22 countries asked by the U.N. Commission for Refugees to take in some of the 6,000 to 8,000 stateless Asians before President Amin's expulsion deadline at midnight last night.

In the words of Prince Lippe "the Maltese Government had most generously accepted to house as many as 500 refugees on condition that the High Commission undertakes to provide funds for their maintenance while in Malta and on the understanding that the Asians would not be allowed to work in Malta."

The Government had been given the guarantee that the Asians would leave Malta as soon as more permanent accommodation was found for them elsewhere.

Captain Malcolm Craig R.M.A., Military Attache at the Prime Minister's Office, who was also at Luqa Airport said that yesterday men from the Royal Malta Artillery and the Emergency Labour Corps moved into Tigne Barracks which has been unused for some time. They cleaned the barracks and prepared the accommodation.

They were followed by truckloads of blankets, beds, catering equipment and other necessary items. Captain Craig said that the Malta Land Force had given up their entire stock of blankets and beds which they do not require as they do not live in barracks.

The Army will set up a headquarters at Tigne Barracks whose task would be to look after the administration of the barracks and at the same time see to the needs of the refugees. Doctors will also be provided.

When the first planeload of Asians arrived late last night they were taken to the barracks in seven buses provided by the Government.

An army catering unit gave RAF the first hot meal and they were shown to their quarters.

Places have been found in various countries for the 6,000 stateless Asians who, unlike British passport holders, are not the responsibility of the British Government.

Bewildered, penniless, weary Asians safe at last

BY JOSEPH MERCIECA
Reprinted with permission, ©Times of Malta, November 10, 1972

As long as Tigne Barracks were not Ugandan soil, it was of little concern to 196 weary Asian refugees whether they were in Malta or Timbuktu. For the men, women and children strolling under a benign sun at the former mini-military town the important thing was that for the first time in weeks, if not months, they felt safe and sheltered even if penniless and dog-tired.

Their Journey to an Island they never heard of before began on Wednesday afternoon when, after much toing and froing, they were found seats on a "Boeing 707" of British Caledonian Airways to start the Journey from Entebbe to Luqa.

The first group arrived shortly before midnight on Wednesday/Thursday night. They were among 6,000 to 8,000 stateless Asians who were ordered to leave the East African country before midnight on Wednesday. Their only "crime" was that because of history. destiny and a measure of politics they were regarded as stateless.

Temporary accommodation

Of the total number of stateless Asians ordered out of the country where most of them had been born, Malta is providing sanctuary for between 400 and 500 people. A request for temporary accommodation had been made by the United Nations High Commissioner for Refugees to the Maltese Government and a positive reply, with guarantees made also by other recipient countries, was given by the Government.

Prince Alfred Fur Lippe, of Austria, who represents the U.N.H.C.R., flew to Malta on Tuesday and together with Capt. Malcolm Craig, the Military Attaché at the Prime Minister's Office, set up an organization to house and feed the refugees. Mrs. Mintoff, accompanied by Capt. Craig, visited Tigne to see for herself the arrangements made for the Asians.

Prince Lippe was up at Luqa when the first aircraft arrived to give a reassuring welcome. He had seen scenes like these and many worse ones before. During his 18 years with the United Nations he had been responsible for refugee problems during the Hungarian uprising in 1956; the invasion of Tibet, the invasion of Czechoslovakia and the recent Indian-Pakistani war.

Reassuring hand

The first two people to come through the aircraft's door at Luqa two elderly men, shaking and wide-eyed. They hesitated to make the first steps but then felt reassured as a Medical and Health official held them by the arm and gently led them to the R.M.A. and Police coaches waiting close by on the airport's apron. A team of doctors and nurses examined the passengers on the aircraft and some were given injections or inoculations.

The youngest passenger of them all was a tiny baby barely three weeks old. As a hostess carried the child from the aircraft the baby's young father forced a smile and hugged the baby.

Continued on Page 132

Stateless Ugandan Asians arrive at Vienna Airport in Austria. *Reproduced courtesy of UNHCR*

Uganda not written off by tycoon

By A Staff Reporter
Reprinted with permission, ©Times of India, November 10, 1972

MR. MANUBHAI MADHVANI, Uganda's biggest industrialist, who was expelled from the country along with other Asians by President Amin, has been staying quietly in Bombay since Saturday.

He is booked in the Dutch suite of the Taj Mahal Hotel and has spent a few days resting in Poona.

The elusive millionaire's presence in the city was not known to even his closest friends and associates.

On Thursday evening, on his return from Poona, when informed that this paper was trying to get in touch with him, Mr. Madhvani himself contacted the office.

He denied that he was hiding from the press. "I was only relaxing for a few days," he said. "Newspaper boys are my friends, they were in prison with me."

Mr. Madhvani looked relaxed, dressed in a white bush-shirt with brass buttons, and talked of Uganda with an air of nostalgia.

"We have still got confidence in Uganda, we have not written it off," he said.

Continued on Page 132

ASIANS' EXPULSION

Editorial
Reprinted with permission, ©Times of Malta, November 10, 1972

The deadline set by President IDI AMIN of Uganda for the expulsion of Afro-Asians from his country passed at midnight on Wednesday-Thursday, happily without any precipitate action on the part of the Ugandan authorities against those few still in the country.

This fact alone does not reduce the plight of a group of people about 30,000 in all. In three months they have been transplanted into countries all over the globe and have been reduced to pathetic straits prompting generosity from the governments of these countries and their peoples.

President Amin has expelled these people. He has grabbed their businesses, and prevented them from taking even the smallest possessions out of the country. They have no money and the prospects of recovering some of the possessions they have been forced to leave behind will be difficult and take time.

The gravity of the problem was brought home to Malta on Wednesday night when 200 of the Afro-Asians, technically stateless persons, were flown from Uganda and are now housed at Tigne Barracks. They were a sight which brought forth immediate sympathy from a people known through the ages for their generosity to those in need.

The Government's action in answering the humanitarian call of the U.N. Commission for Refugees to temporarily accommodate up to 500 of these Asians, is highly commended. So are the efforts of the Malta Land Force and all those who are extending a helping hand to these unfortunate people.

The question of the Afro-Asians does not end with the departure of the last groups from Uganda. General Amin may have achieved his immediate aims and some of his people may welcome his "Uganda for the Ugandans" pledge. But it makes him stand out among the few who, in this age of co-existence and cooperation, still choose to continue to discriminate against others in a most inhuman manner.

Continued from Page 131

Bewildered, penniless, weary Asians safe at last

Once the refugees were driven to Tigne they found Sisters and soldiers readily giving them hot drinks and sandwiches. They were then allocated to Quarters at Tigne Barracks which had been cleaned, and equipped with bedding during one day by the R.M.A. and some members of the E Emergency Labour Corps.

Refugees' thanks

The Prime Minister Mr. Mintoff, Mr. Lorry Sant, Minister of Public Building and Work, Dr. P. Holland and Mr. W. Abela, Parliamentary Secretaries went to Tigne at around 2 a.m. and met some of the refugees. There were also members of local Caritas Committee led by Fr. Fortunato Mizzi. Yesterday morning one of the early visitors to Tigne was Mrs. Burns DeBono, and other committee members of the Save the Children Fund.

At Tigne, the refugees yesterday mixed freely with visitors. A delegation of five men went up to Prince Lippe and on behalf of the whole group expressed their thanks to the Maltese Government and the U.N. High Commissioner for Refugees.

The refugees talked of the difficult months and of their uncertain future. Most of the family groups, a youth said, were now dispersed in various countries. It was no surprise that many of those in Malta were yesterday trying to get some stamps to be able to write to their next of kin.

After an informal documentation parade, Major K. Valenzia, R.M.A, who is in charge of the unusual operation at Tigne, conferred with his staff and representatives of the various nuclei amongst the refugees on the further practical arrangements required. Because of religion, composition of units and so forth various individual structures had to be set up. This included the catering organizations since some refugees are strict vegetarians, whilst others are less particular.

Officials at Tigne and members of local voluntary organizations were yesterday aware of the need for the refugees to indulge in recreative activities. It was hoped that voluntary bodies would come out to give a helping hand to these people for whom Malta is the end of a chapter, but not the end of their story.

Minister calls for a helping hand

In a Ministerial statement yesterday evening, Dr. A. Buttigieg Minister of Justice and Parliamentary Affairs described Malta's reception of the Asians from Uganda as "an act of charity and as a sign of solidarity with the United Nations and with all the human race without discrimination."

Dr. Buttigieg stated that it was neither an act intended to condemn any government nor to oblige any other government and made it clear that the Malta Government did not enter into the merits of the question.

Dr. Buttigieg also said that Malta has reserved the right that these refugees cannot stay in Malta for more than six months and cannot take up any employment.

The Minister urged the people to back up the Government act of charity with similar acts of their own. While he said that these people must not be looked upon as beggars but as victims of a great tragedy, he suggested that people should offer them presents, take them out for drives or to the cinema land invite them to their homes.

Immediate response

Following the appeal made by Dr. Buttigieg Mrs. T. Agius Ferrante set up a committee for the purpose of aiding the Asian refugees from Uganda.

Any contributions or donations can be addressed to Mrs. Agius Ferrante at No. 20, Magazine Street, Mdina All contributions will be acknowledged by receipt and forwarded through the proper channels

A soft drinks manufacturer company, has made the first contribution of 500 bottles of soft drinks.

Continued from Page 131

Uganda not written off by tycoon

Asked if his confidence was in Uganda or President Amin, he said, "Both."

He was careful about what he said about President Amin, who, before his (Mr. Madhvani's) arrest, was reported to be a great friend of his.

He said: "I believe in God, President Amin believes in God, I am sure he will be fair and reasonable to me and my family. I respect him."

But once in a while, the hurt could be seen. "I have left my home and everything there. I do not know my plans. I have to start a new life. But I am a young man." (Mr. Madhvani is 43 and looks younger.)

The Madhvani have a Rs. 50 cr. business in Uganda and their interests include steel, glass, sugar, beer and textiles.

Asked who was running the factories in his absence, he said they had good African executives in their employ. They were capable people, and if the government gave them proper support, they should keep the industries running.

He pointed out that what was happening in Uganda at the moment was an economic war. "You cannot deny that I am an Asian."

However, at the moment, Mr. Madhvani holds a British passport and will be soon leaving for London. The British passport has come to him through the strange rules that start operating when an entire section of the population is expelled.

He has been travelling on an Ugandan passport since 1964. However, when a dispute about his nationality arose, he left it to President Amin to decide.

It was on television that he heard that the President had refused him Ugandan citizenship and hence he had to revert to his former passport—British.

His three brothers hold British passports, but there is no expulsion order against them. The youngest, Mr. Mayur Madhvani, sporting long hair and looking very mod, is still a student in England. He flew down to Bombay to assist his brother. The two other brothers are on business tours in Europe.

Asked about the harassment of Asians, he said he personally had been well-treated. Even when he was in the Makindye jail for 22 days, they had treated him well.

Mr. Madhvani's wife, Jyoti, whom he had sent to her parents in Bombay earlier, said she was happy to be reunited with her husband. She had been very worried.

Amin takes roll-call of remaining Asians

By David Loshak in Nairobi
Reprinted with permission, ©Telegraph Group Limited, London, November 10, 1972

AN estimated 4,000 Asians still in Uganda went to special registration centres in Kampala and other towns yesterday for the physical count ordered by Gen. Amin immediately after his 90-day deadline for the expulsion of non-citizen Asians.

The number was less than expected. The Asians left are those with Ugandan nationality.

There were no complaints or reports of ill-treatment.

On Gen. Amin's orders, the Asians were told they will have to go to country areas to mix with African people. But they were not told when they would be required to leave.

The last of 1,300 stateless Asians still left in Uganda were flown out to transit camps in Europe yesterday. There were last-minute offers of accommodation from Spain, Greece, Malta, Austria and Belgium.

The streets of Kampala, normally busy, were deserted. Special offices at the British and Canadian High Commissions and at BOAC, where the evacuation operation has been carried out in the past three months, were closed down.

Refusing to leave

Mrs Mina Madhvani, a member of the millionaire Asian family which controlled Uganda's largest industrial organisation was still believed yesterday to be in her home near Kampala, refusing to leave the country. Her telephone was "off the hook."

Mrs Madhvani is the widow of Mr Jayant Madhvani, who died last year, and not, as reported yesterday, the wife of his brother, Mr Manubhai Madhvani.

Her nationality is not known. But if she is British, which is possible, she may be risking serious punishment by defying Gen. Amin's order to leave.

But Gen. Amin is believed to have a high personal regard for Mrs Madhvani and so far no known attempt has been made either to remove her from the house or oblige her to register.

Boys sent to mother

The British High Commission yesterday arranged for two Asian boys, aged eight and ten, who had been left by their parents, to rejoin their mother, now in Britain.

The mother left the children in the care of their father, but he abandoned them and went off with four other children by another marriage.

The boys made their own way to the British High Commission. They are the only two out of 23,000 Asians flown to Britain whose fares have been paid by the British Government.

High Commission denies reports of 'missing' Indians

By NATION Reporter
Reprinted with permission, ©Daily Nation, Nairobi, November 10, 1972

OFFICIALS at the Indian High Commission in Nairobi were last night in a state of confusion following reports from Mombasa that 20 Indian nationals were "missing" after boarding the last of the Asian "exodus" trains from Kampala to Mombasa two days ago.

A spokesman at the High Commission said 185 Indian nationals had boarded the train out of Uganda and that early yesterday morning the same number had arrived in Mombasa.

Earlier in the day Indian sources in Mombasa said it was feared 20 Indian nationals were not accounted for after leaving Uganda.

One of those who arrived in Mombasa said he has prepared a "Dossier of Death." The man, a doctor, claimed that over the last four months 1,164 Indian nationals, all males between the ages of 22 and 29 years have been executed by the Ugandan military forces.

Another man, who said he had been a temple guardian in Kampala, said 36 Indian girls between the ages of 15 and 25 years were either missing or dead after being kidnapped by soldiers.

Another doctor claimed that he had lost goods worth £3,000 during the train journey to the Kenyan border.

Concern was voiced for four Indian girls between the ages of 16 and 18 who were allegedly raped by Ugandan troops after being removed from the immigrant train Kakira.

Said a passenger: "We have reliable information that these girls in fact got back on board the train at Jinja after escaping somehow from Kakira, but they were again removed by the military personnel checking the train at Tororo."

Commenting on the arrivals, the India Assistant Commissioner in Mombasa, Mr. B. R. Sharma, said: "I should like to place on record our Government's deepest thanks to the sympathetic treatment by Kenyan Immigration, Customs, railways, harbours and police officials in Mombasa. Their co-operation throughout has been wonderful."

MINNEAPOLIS, USA

State groups prepared for 75 Uganda refugees

Reprinted with permission, ©Minneapolis Star, November 10, 1972

At least 75 Asian refugees expelled from Uganda by the government of Idi Amin will find homes and job interviews waiting for them when they arrive in Minnesota.

Lutheran congregations and two colleges in Minnesota have agreed to sponsor 20 refugee families long enough for the Asians to begin supporting themselves. Other congregations may join the program if more refugee families wish to come to Minnesota.

At least 12,000 of the expelled Asians were born in Uganda and had no citizenship in another country. President Nixon has waived immigration quotas to allow 2,000 of the refugees to enter the United States.

The participating congregations were recruited in less than two days by the Lutheran Social Service of Minnesota after the organization was asked to serve as a clearing house for the refugees. "We've had an amazing response, "says Dr. Morris Wee, coordinator of the program.

Each of 17 Twin Cities congregations has agreed to sponsor one family. The Zion Lutheran Church in Buffalo, Minn., will share responsibility for one family with the Buffalo Rotary Club. The remaining two refugee families will be supported by Gustavus Adolphus College, St. Peter, Minn., and Augsburg College of Minneapolis.

Most of the refugee families come from a middle-class background and are of Hindu or Moslem faith, according to Wee. The men are predominantly professionals, middle-management persons or merchants.

"We are trying to find the refugees a position that will match their level of skill," says Dr. Paul Schuessler, pastor of Pilgrim Lutheran Church in St. Paul, one of the participating congregations. He says the first overtures for jobs will be made to "management people" who are members of the congregation.

Dr. Alton Wedel says he was leading a meeting of the congregation in Mt. Olive Lutheran Church in Minneapolis when he received word of the refugees' plight. He threw the idea out to the congregation and they immediately agreed to help.

"A real-estate man in the congregation offered us a house right away," Wedel recalls. "Then a lot of people came forward offering a stove, a refrigerator and household utensils."

Many details have not yet been resolved. It isn't known whether the financial aid of the churches will be repaid when the refugees get back on their feet.

"We'll just have to wait and see how sensitive they are to receiving handouts," Wedel says.

Schuessler believes that a major responsibility of the churches will be to help the refugees adjust to their new life. "They're really going to be lost trying to establish new roots," he says.

The Mt. Olive congregation is setting up a committee to deal with readjustment problems. A home economist, a doctor, a banker and other specialists—all members of the congregation—will be available to advise the refugee family.

Most of the refugees are obligated by their religion to observe special holidays and dietary customs. Wee held an orientation meeting yesterday with representatives of all the participating congregations to make them aware of such problems.

Wee says that more refugee families are likely to come to Minnesota if this first effort is successful. The Lutheran Churches of the United States has a permanent apparatus to deal with refugees and is one of seven religious organizations asked by the U.S. State Department to handle the Uganda refugees.

Ugandan Asian Expulsion: 90 Days and Beyond through the Eyes of the International Press

The Last Ugandans... end of an immigration era

By Guy Demarino
Southam News Service
Reprinted with permission, ©Southam News Service,
Canada,
November 10, 1972

MONTREAL—When Bhadur Ali Kara stepped off an Air Canada plane into a cold, wet Montreal Thursday he made history.

He was the last immigrant to leave the last charter flight from Uganda to Canada. He made the total of Ugandan Asians forced out by president Idi Amin and accepted by Canada 4,348 people.

Mr. Kara, who is going to Vancouver with his wife to meet one brother and three sisters who all left Uganda this week at different times, may have made history in more ways than one.

Major waves

He may well be the last member of a group whose large scale immigration has been arranged by Canada, for a while at least. There have been three massive emigrations since the Second World War, but the influx of political refugees has never been criticized by as many Canadians as the last influx of Ugandans has been.

Between 1956-59, 37,189 Hungarians were welcomed to Canada after the unsuccessful Hungarian uprising in 1956; between September 1968 and January 1969, 11,209 Czechoslovaks arrived here, in similar circumstances. And now the 4,348 Uganda Asians, have arrived, augmented by about 200 who came on their own. Some with visas are now in England and are expected in the near future.

The official welcome, extended primarily by airline personnel during the flight and by Canadian immigration officials and by armed forces personnel at Montreal couldn't have been warmer.

Witness is one of the messages pinned on a bulletin board in Longue Pointe military base, where all arriving Ugandans are taken for the first night in Canada and where they exchange notes and addresses.

"We have received the best treatment we could get," wrote a Ugandan girl urging her relatives to follow her to Woodstock, Ont. And she advised them to listen to Manpower and Immigration personnel here. "It will be for your benefit."

But during the election campaign, many voices rising from the Canadian public were against the government's decision to let the Ugandans come to Canada, particularly at a time of high unemployment. Even Immigration Minister Mackasey admitted the Liberals may have lost a riding because of the Ugandans' entry.

Until the unemployment situation betters, and Canadians return to being the open-hearted, humanitarian people who accepted and absorbed 10 million immigrants since 1852, it seems unlikely that more massive scale emigration operations will be undertaken.

But no one can say for sure. There are 309,000 Asians in East Africa now who are afraid the same fate that befell their Uganda brethren is in store for them.

They too are afraid, the 190 Ugandans who arrived in Montreal early Thursday reported. And by comparison, the fear of not getting a job in Canada or even the fear of the cold climate, is nothing.

For some, like Mr. Kakira, jobs may be scarce. He worked as a storekeeper in a small Uganda town. Mr. Kakira, has only high school education and no particular skill. But he wasn't too worried. At the age of 30 and with no children to look after, the Muslim felt sure "God will help."

For others like Ramish Badiani, 30, getting a job in Canada should be no great problem. He holds a bachelor of science degree in chemistry and physics, and has worked in sugar refining for the last nine years. Hoping to settle in Ottawa but open to suggestion, Mr. Badiani has a well educated wife—a graduate sociologist—and a six-month-old girl.

Details first

Mrs. Badiani worried whether babysitters were available here, in case she found a job. Babysitters are small details compared with the cultural shock of being uprooted from a tropical African country to wintry Canada, but the small things caught the Ugandans' attention first.

Many, who had never been outside Uganda before, wondered at the right-hand traffic in Canada, as Uganda follows the British system of driving on the left. Others wondered at being helped by Canadian soldiers.

Shortly after being bussed to Longue Pointe, they were being told by an officer that "The armed forces here are a lot different than the ones from where you just left." The Ugandans politely applauded. But later on, as young soldiers were carrying the
Continued on Page 136

Reproduced with permission, ©Garth Pritchard/Montreal Gazette

Mrs. Varu and baby on arrival at Montral International Airport.

Problems 'seemed to dissolve' for family here for six weeks

Reprinted with permission, ©Montreal Gazette,
November 9, 1972

One of the first expelled Ugandan Asians to arrive in Montreal, Almir D'Cunha, has already planted roots in six short weeks.

The 36-year-old auditor quickly found a job locally, then, "leaving on good terms," moved on to a better paying one with a LaSalle accounting firm.

Now comfortably settled in a 6-1/2 room NDG apartment sparsely equipped with donated furniture, the articulate father of two glows with optimism over his future.

"Things are settling down beautifully. It was worrisome at first but our problems seemed to dissolve mainly because of all the unexpected aid."

Without classing himself as typical of the estimated group of 400 settled in the Montreal area, D'Cunha feels most have done surprisingly well and encountered few serious hurdles in adapting.

"We contact one another. There is mutual assistance but mostly in the form of advice. Everyone seems to be making their own way, nicely, thank you."

D'Cunha, with 19 years accounting experience, finds "very little" difference in work methods here. But he doesn't plan to stand still and is already keen on taking economics courses at university at night.

On the subject of food shopping, Maureen, D'Cunha's ebony-haired wife, grew expressive.

HAS LOTS OF TIME

"Problems? Are you kidding, with all those time-saving kitchen products? For a change I have time on my hands."

Six-year-old Mervyn has overcome his initial shyness at the immigrant language school and now spurns his mother's offer to accompany him, preferring instead two pals who call each morning.

The lad, like his four-year-old sister, is eagerly awaiting the Canadian winter.

"I know of no Ugandan who even thinks of returning, whatever the problem of the moment. Our choice is made, there is no time for feeling sorry for one's self," said Mrs. D'Cunha.

Britain deports Uganda Asians

by ROBERT CHESSHYRE and PETER DEELEY
Reprinted with permission, ©The Observer, London, November 12, 1972

BRITAIN is secretly deporting Ugandan Asians back to Kampala to an uncertain fate. At least five have been put on Entebbe—bound planes at Heathrow by immigration officials because they hold Uganda passports.

Eight more have been narrowly saved from deportation by the intervention of MPs and a member of the Lords, and another 24 face possible deportation. Some are being held in Pentonville Prison, London, while their cases are considered. Others are in detention centres and a few are held in resettlement camps.

Four are in police stations close to Stansted Airport, Essex. They were sent there by immigration authorities after they arrived in Britain on Thursday and have been warned they may be put on a plane out of Britain at any moment.

The deportations appear to conflict with the Government's stated policy of handling the refugee problem with compassion, but Mr David Lane, junior Home Office Minister in charge of the resettlement programme, said yesterday that no change of attitude was being considered.

It was only in the face of persistent OBSERV-ER inquiries that a Home Office official finally confirmed yesterday that a number of people had gone. How many he could not say because the files, he said, were locked up for the weekend.

Many of those people directly concerned with the resettlement of the refugees in this country were unaware until told by THE OBSERVER that any deportations had taken place.

Mr Praful Patel, the only Asian member of the Uganda Asians Resettlement Board, reacted with total disbelief until given the names of several Ugandan passport-holders who have been returned to Kampala. Lord Avebury (the former Liberal MP, Mr Eric Lubbuck) when told of the

Continued on Page 136

MORE ASIAN REFUGEES SETTLE IN TIGNE

By a Staff Reporter
Reprinted with permission, ©Times of Malta, November 11, 1972

Another 168 stateless refugees who have been expelled from Uganda were flown to Malta yesterday bringing the total of those being given sanctuary here to 364. A third group of refugees may arrive either today or tomorrow.

The second group arrived at Luqa shortly after 5 a.m. after being flown from Entebbe Airport, 15 miles from Kampala, on an aircraft chartered by the United Nations High Commissioner for Refugees.

The men, women and children who arrived yesterday were also taken to Tigne Barracks where the Officers and men of the Royal Malta Artillery have been working round the clock to make this humanitarian task as smooth as possible for the refugees.

Difficult months

Like the first group to arrive here, yesterday's arrivals told of the difficult months they have been through and the experiences of many unhappy incidents.

Whether men or women, young or old, all wanted to open their hearts but each and every one of them was anxious not to have their names quoted for fear of reprisals on relatives who may still be on Ugandan soil. Somehow, everyone's priority problem was to get stamps to write to relatives or friends who are in other countries or to attempt to find where the rest of their next of kin had been given sanctuary.

The task of trying to solve these immediate and other long term problems will be to a great measure entrusted to the Inter-Governmental Committee for European Migration (ICEM).

Dott. Enrico Pugi from ICEM's office in Rome left Malta yesterday afternoon after a 48 hour hectic stay during which he gave more than his fair share in seeing the refugees settling down. Dott. Pugi also interviewed many of the refugees to gather all possible information which could help towards their permanent settlement in other countries. The ICEM official is primarily an administrator but he was the only one available to come to Malta since the others are either spread in Italy and other recipient countries or in Uganda itself.

Public's response

As early as Thursday afternoon members of the public began to make sure that they contributed to make the refugees' plight easier. By yesterday morning Land Rover loads of clothing were collected. Private individuals and firms sent a wide assortment of presents to Tigne ranging from soft drinks and cigarettes to toys and games.

Tigne Barracks was again during yesterday visited also by members of the Social Action Movement who represent Caritas in Malta. Caritas in Malta, said a spokesman yesterday, had been requested by His Grace the Archbishop to give all possible assistance. Mgr. Gonzi promised all possible help by the Church when informed of the planned refugees' arrival in Malta by the Prime Minister, Mr. Mintoff.

The spokesman added that teams of nurses from the Sisters of Charity have been giving their assistance to the Asians at Tigne since the first group arrived on Wednesday night. The Dame di S. Lorenzo and the St. Aloysius Social Group ate looking after the refugees' clothing needs. Ursoline Creche Sisters are also helping Caritas to give all necessary help for the care of children. The Save the Children Fund have volunteered to take care of children and youths under the age of 18.

Generous donations

A Coordinating Committee has been formed under the chairmanship of Mrs. T. Agius Ferrante.

Mrs. Agius Ferrante said yesterday that the public's generosity has already been overwhelming. Generous donations in cash and in kind have been extremely encouraging and there were numerous individuals and bodies who offered hos-

Hunger strike threat by Asians at camp

By BRIAN SILK
Reprinted with permission, ©Telegraph Group Limited, London, November 11, 1972

UGANDAN Asians at a resettlement camp near Newbury, Berks, are threatening to go on hunger strike following complaints that a form of apartheid is being practiced there.

The 1,400 refugees at the Greenham Common camp share a canteen with about 300 staff and voluntary helpers. But they complain they have to crowd into one half of the canteen because they are not allowed to eat in the "European section."

The chairman of the camp's Asian committee yesterday sent a letter to the catering manager threatening the strike. The letter also said that unless the food was improved within 48 hours the Asians will go to a higher authority.

"Unwritten rule"

An English girl voluntary worker said last night there had been several problems since the camp opened, and there was considerable dissatisfaction about the canteen.

"There is a kitchen section down the middle, making two sections, one for Europeans and one for Asians. It is an unwritten rule that the Asians keep to their section, so they are eating in cramped conditions with long queues, while the Europeans are in comfortable conditions.

"The food has been unsatisfactory, and there have been many complaints about the quality. We no longer have anyone advising on Asian diet.

"The camp administration has attempted to solve these problems, but it is time the whole thing was cleared up."

Meeting arranged

A spokesman for the Ugandan Resettlement Board said last night: "The catering at the camp is done by an outside company. The Asian committee has sent a letter of dissent to the company and a meeting has been arranged between both to discuss the matter."

The spokesman confirmed that the canteen was divided into separate sections for Europeans and Asians, but added: "I'm sure this is for ease of operation rather that segregation."

pitality to the Asian refugees. The actual composition of the Committee was still being made with the object of creating a Fund for the stateless Asians.

An organization has been set up at Tigne Barracks to accept gifts in kind or in cash for the welfare of the Asian refugees. Clothing and other gifts will be gratefully received and acknowledged individually by the Officer in charge of the Refugees: Major K. J. Valenzia, R.M.A., Telephone Number 38788 or 38781.

Ugandan Asian Expulsion: 90 Days and Beyond through the Eyes of the International Press

Continued from Page 135

Britain deports Uganda Asians

situation, said: 'I don't know how this can have happened. It is monstrous and outrageous.'

The director of the United Kingdom Immigrants Advisory Service, Mr John Ennals, who returned yesterday after three weeks in Kampala, is to make immediate representations to the Home Office and the United Nations Commission for Refugees. 'I will be on the Minister's doorstep on Monday,' he said.

Mr Ennals described the deportations as 'scandalous and criminal.' He said he shuddered to think what would await people who had already been branded as traitors by General Amin.

'Britain and the United Nations have been sweating their guts to get these people out of a highly dangerous situation and here is the British Government sending them back in again.'

Mr Ennals was at Kololo Hill, near Kampala, on Thursday when all the Asians remaining in the country had to submit to a head count. He said it would be extremely dangerous for any Asian who was not now registered to return to Uganda.

'Anyone who fled would not know what to expect.'

Our inquires have established that those deported include a husband and wife in their sixties, a 16-year-old girl, a husband whose wife is a British passport holder and a 38-year-old man who has had to leave behind his wife and three young children.

Mrs Penny Leaver, a councillor in the London borough of Harrow, who heads the co-ordinating committee for Asian refugees in her area, first brought the deportations to light. She complained that a 17-year-old boy and his sister, aged 20, were about to be flown back because they held Uganda passports. They had come with their uncle and aunt who were British citizens.

Mr Bruce Douglas - Mann, Labour MP of Kensington North, took up their plight with the Home Office. Within a few hours the cases of another six people with deportation orders hanging over their heads were revealed.

What was not discovered until yesterday was that a number of people had already been returned. Mrs Leaver said: 'I think it is disgraceful that until someone starts to kick up a fuss nothing can be done to prevent these people from being deported.'

One of those returned is Mr Manilal Davda, 30, whose wife and three children are settling down in this country. Mrs Davda holds a British passport but her husband is a Ugandan.

According to Mrs Mary Dines, head of the Joint Council for the Welfare of Immigrants, it appears that Mr Davda was the victim of a communications breakdown between the Home Office and airport immigration officers. Throughout Mr Davda's stay here, the Home Office appeared to be treating his situation favorably. But he was suddenly taken from a resettlement camp nine days ago and put on a Sabena flight back to Entebbe.

His brother, Mr Laxmidas Davda, said that at the airport they pleaded with the immigration officials to postpone the deportation order. His brother and his family were in tears as he was taken on board the plane.

Laxmidas said that at one stage immigration officials asked him why his brother left Uganda.

'When I told them that people were getting killed there, they turned to me and said the same was happening in Northern Ireland, but that people weren't leaving there.'

Mr Davda, who did not wish to return to Kampala, got on the Sabena flight in Brussels, but was then put on another plane to Entebbe. He was last heard of there a week ago, but his brother had no news since.

Mrs Dines said that in another case a Mr Sodha, a Ugandan passport holder whose wife has a British passport, was sent back a fortnight ago. 'We also got to hear of a 16 year old girl who had been sent back. We heard of the case too late to be able to do anything and we don't even know her name.'

Welfare workers from the camps report cases of extreme hardship among those being held while deportation is considered. One Asian women at Greenham Common resettlement camp, near Newbury, Berkshire, who has seven children, was taken to hospital with complications over a further pregnancy. It took more than 24 hours before her husband, who was in Pentonville, was allowed to go to her bedside or to help her look after the children.

At Saffron Walden police station one Ugandan, Mr Babulal Jemwa, said he was being well treated but feared going back to Kampala, where his businesses have been confiscated.

Mr Jemwa is at Saffron Walden with a fellow Asian, Mr Narendra Patel, who is technically Stateless. The other two Asians held in a police station are at Harlow, new town. They have been allowed to see relatives, but were not permitted to talk to journalists.

Mr Jemwa is said by his family to be suffering from dangerously high blood pressure. He was treated yesterday by his sister-in-law, a doctor. He had been a member of the Ugandan Army and the Customs and Excise department, and believed he would be exempt from Amin's expulsion decree.

One of the considerations motivating the Government in its policy towards the refugees is the fear that by 'opening the door,' everyone with a Ugandan passport who does not like life under Amin will turn up. Ministers feel they have had a difficult enough job persuading the British people to accept those with British passports, and are privately pleased with the lack of tension the operation has so far caused.

Mr Lane, the Home Office Minister concerned, was unable to comment on the specific cases discovered by THE OBSERVER, because he was away from the office. He stressed, however, that each case was treated sympathetically and on an individual basis, and that no one would be sent back to a situation of extreme risk.

He said that the Government realised from the start that there would be complicated cases in which members of families held different passports. Borderline cases were examined within the framework of existing immigration laws. There

Continued from Page 134

The last Ugandans.....end of an Immigration era

Asians' suitcases to the new arrivals' quarters for a deserved sleep, the Ugandans couldn't believe the difference. Some kept shaking their heads in wonderment.

An eight-hour delay caused by mechanical problems meant the last group of Ugandan Asians never got to bed until mid-morning Thursday, after a 24-hour Entebbe-Fort Lamy-Chat-Paris-Halifax-Montreal flight.

But the excitement of being free again, free from fear of the police or the army, free from being robbed or beaten, free from being rudely ordered about, kept them wide awake while they should have been sleepy. The plane carried 47 families with 74 children among them. It had a 19-day-old baby and two 84-year-old grandmothers. It contained people who had to leave behind as much as $100,000 worth of house, cars, effects, and businesses.

It had people only allowed to take with them a suitcase or two of clothes, the odd radio or tape recorder, and a pound sterling in cash.

But, the Canadian government helps. It makes loans of about $50 to each family unit, more if there are more children, and it pays the train or plane tickets to the selected destination.

It helps them find jobs and accommodations, through ten special government committees in major cities across Canada. It provides hotel rooms, sometimes whole floors, for Ugandans on the move within Canada.

Cost $5 million?

And, of course, it has paid all transportation costs from Uganda to Canada. No total expenditure has been even estimated by government officials, and trying to find out what charter rates the government paid for the 31 flights from Africa which began Sept. 28 is a time-wasting effort.

Unofficial estimates put the total costs of the Uganda airlift and settlement in Canada at about $5 million for the government. Perhaps it is to avoid further backlash from the taxpayers that no dollar figures have been revealed yet.

So the great airlift has ended. The Canadian officials who went to Kampala to accept the applications and evaluate them have all returned, except two. The military base at Longue Pointe closes down this week, after serving as temporary hotel for the new arrivals. And the latter are dispersed across the country—about 20 per cent in Quebec, 40 per cent in Ontario, 30 per cent in B.C., the rest in the Maritimes and Western Canada.

All they need now are jobs, heavy clothes to survive the Canadian winter, and compassion and understanding from their fellow Canadians. It's likely they'll have all those things soon.

was no question of making a hard and fast rule that all those with Ugandan passports should be sent back.

Mr Lane said that there was no likelihood of a change in Government policy, and that the numbers being returned to Uganda were very small.

Homes without jobs, or jobs without homes, a problem for Asians in Wales

David Blundy
Reprinted with permission, ©Times Newspapers Limited, London, November 12, 1972

THE ASIANS in British resettlement camps look like facing a long hard winter - hardest of all perhaps, for 1,100 of them at Tonfanau in Merionethshire, an ex-army camp in a remote, bleak corner of Welsh-speaking North Wales. Tonfanau is squeezed between the mountains and the stormy Irish Sea.

Yesterday, Asians in overcoats and balaclava helmets huddled in queues waiting for their winter clothing.

The camp was closed down by the Army three years ago and reopened for Asians last month. Although it rates high for amenities, with huts for two schools, a recreation hall, a youth club, a play group and two canteens, the first Asians to arrive found it bewildering and slightly frightening.

They were particularly alarmed by a large sign saying "Beware of the firing range" and the barbed-wire fence. Many of them wanted to catch the train back to London. "We were warmly welcomed, though. They gave us blankets, they carried our luggage into the huts. We are very grateful," he said.

Some of the staff are puzzled by the decision of the Ugandan Resettlement Board to use this camp. It is in an area of high unemployment, miles away from any industrial centre and convenient only for other high unemployment areas like Lancashire. It is so remote that Asians going for interviews have to spend the night away.

The record for resettlement is good. Four hundred have found houses and jobs in the past month, but the flow is getting slower every day. The jobs advertised on the camp noticeboards show a hint of desperation—such as: "Skilled cobblers wanted in Vienna," and "Vacancies for general insurance underwriters in Addis Ababa." The Asians are largely willing to take any job available and three shopkeepers have just applied to be coalminers at Stoke-on-Trent.

The camp's resettlement officer said the main problem is matching jobs to houses. "We find houses in unemployment areas. When we find jobs, there are no houses."

An Asian teacher, Mr Harjinder Somotey, has a place at a Carmarthen teachers' training college, but there is accommodation for only one. "My wife and children will have to stay in the camp for at least another three months. It is 80 miles away. I will come back once a month."

An Asian photographer spent a fruitless day looking for a photographic agency in the local town of Towyn. One local council in Pwilheli declined to offer a council house to an Asian family, because, it said, they would feel out of place in a small Welsh town.

Although the local reaction to the Asians has been warm, Mr Somotey had his first taste of racial prejudice last week. "Please, what exactly is a wog?" he asked a voluntary worker.

Tonfanau has come in for some criticism from one of the Pwilheli councillors, Mr Victor Balma. "I visited the camp two weeks ago and I have never seen such primitive conditions. There were hardly any chairs. Women were sitting on the floor. There is only one electric fire in each hut and when a cold spell comes, it's going to be terrible."

The only people who are not complaining are the Asians themselves. I spoke to about 10 families. They all said facilities were adequate. "It is a little chilly, " they said, as their wooden hut rocked in the wind. "But the camp is well run. We are very happy."

Captain Freddy Fuller, the camp's administrator, who spent 25 years as warden of the Outward Bound school at Aberdovey is optimistic. "I hope that most of the people will have been resettled by next spring. Things have gone very well so far."

He resents criticism that the camp is remote and primitive. "They have the advantages of a rural life," says Captain Fuller. "They are not overtaken by the milling masses. The furniture is limited but this isn't a permanent camp. We want them out as soon as possible. All Mr Balma saw were the bricks and mortar. He did not see the joy of the place. If he thinks this is bleak, he ought to go and look at some of the Welsh villages."

Asian husbands reprieved

By JOHN WINDSOR
Reprinted with permission, ©The Guardian, London, November 11, 1972

An eleventh-hour intervention by Lord Avebury yesterday prevented seven Ugandan Asian men from being flown back to Uganda, leaving their families—all British passport holders—behind.

The Home Office was about to send the seven men—who fled here from Uganda with their families—on an 11:30 am flight from Heathrow Airport London. They would have been the first Ugandan Asians to be split up under the Foreign Office's ruling that Ugandan Asian mothers with British passports can bring their British children here but not their stateless or non-British husbands.

Lord Avebury telephoned Mr David Lane, Parliamentary Under-Secretary at the Home Office. He agreed temporarily to reprieve them. The Asians are now in Harmondsworth reception centre and Pentonville gaol while the Home Office takes their cases to the United Nations High Commissioner for Refugees, Prince Sadruddin Khan.

The Home Office said yesterday that a further 20 Asians were being detained while the Prince considers their plight. Mr Bruce Douglas-Mann, Labour MP for North Kensington, also persuaded the Home Office not to send back two orphans from Uganda, a boy aged 17 and his sister, aged

Great hospitality extended to refugees

By a Staff Reporter
Reprinted with permission, ©Times of Malta, November 13, 1972

A large number of Maltese families went to Tigne Barracks throughout yesterday to take out many of the Asian refugees who have been accommodated at the barracks by the Government.

The Maltese have shown great hospitality is the general feeling among refugees.

The locals' response to appeal for clothes and food stuffs has been described as "fantastic".

The Department of Information has asked the people not to send any more clothes. Two television sets and a number of books have been donated together with other necessary items.

One of the refugees said: "Today, Sunday, November 12 is our first day of freedom and enjoyment for several weeks and even months."

His Grace the Archbishop and the Minister of Health, Dr. D. Piscopo, visited the refugees on Saturday.

The Emergency Aid Commission of Caritas Malta has been informed that on a request by the Prime Minister's Office, the Emigrants' Commission had formed a Secretariat to help Ugandan refugees at present in Malta.

The Emergency Aid Commission has shown its readiness to collaborate with this secretariat and to meet regularly with the secretariat and with other organizations.

It has also suggested that if the Standing Conference of all organizations involved is set up representatives of the refugees and of the Camp's Administration should take part in it.

The Emergency Aid Commission was later informed that the office of the Prime Minister has set up a committee under the chairmanship of Col. Trigona.

Gifts will be received and acknowledged by the Officer in Charge of Refugees, Major K.J. Valenzia R.M.A. (Phone no. 38788 or 38791).

20. They were also detained at Harmondsworth.

Mr Givinji Ravji Thakvar, who is Stateless, has a wife and four children, all UK passport holders, who have been in a resettlement centre since their arrival on October 23. The fifth and eldest child, a son, Arvind, is over 21 and therefore Stateless. His case is also in doubt.

The other families arrived five days ago. The fathers are Ugandan citizens and the wives and children UK passport holders.

They are Mr Sadruddin Rahmatalla Alidina, who has one adopted son, aged 15. Mr Alidina is handicapped. He was refused entry to Canada because of his ailment. He is detained at Harmondsworth. His wife and son are at a resettlement centre in Lincoln.

Mr Hirmatlal Girdhal Hathi has a wife and four children; Mr Mahendra Gordandas Koteja a

Continued on Page 144

Ugandan Asian Expulsion: 90 Days and Beyond through the Eyes of the International Press

Kampala Exodus
Asian Quarter Like a Ghost Town

By Jim Hoagland
Washington Post Foreign Service
Reprinted with permission, ©Washington Post, November 13, 1972

KAMPALA, Nov. 12—Steel shutters are drawn in a long gray line across the store fronts of Williams Street, once a busy commercial area in Uganda's capital but now a drab collection of deserted dry-cleaning, grocery, clothing and other stores.

On one block, 71 out of 72 shops were closed yesterday. No one knows when or if they will reopen.

At the entrance to an office building, placards still advertise the professional services available inside. But the building is empty. Patel the accountant is gone. Shah the lawyer is gone. Narain the goldsmith is gone.

A survey of Kampala's streets establishes that, in fact, virtually all of the city's professional and commercial communities are gone, swept away in six weeks.

President Idi Amin's expulsion of about 42,000 Asians, which came to a relatively orderly end last week despite widespread fears of a potential racial pogrom, has left the economic and urban life of this East African country in a shambles.

As if their owners had been suddenly plucked up by a giant invisible hand that sought people but disdained property, thousands of shops and houses built up by the Asians in their seven decades on Kampala's hills stand silent and abandoned now, waiting to be taken over by eager new African owners.

Only a small group of fearful Asians remains in Kampala's Asian sections, which have been abruptly turned into miniature ghost towns where people do not venture out at night.

The expelled Asians have been driven from the pale, pastel-hued, cubically shaped houses they inhabited on Lugard Hill. Above the lush green grass and fragrant banana trees, washing still hangs on the line in some yards.

Forbidden to carry out most of their furniture, the Asians simply left it. At some houses, trucks driven by Africans were seen carting away pieces of furniture this weekend, although there has not been any major looting of houses or shops yet.

The doors of empty garages hang open. Many of the missing cars have been stolen by Ugandan soldiers or given to them by fearful Asians in exchange for promises of safe conduct to the airport.

Fewer than 1,500 Asians are reliably estimated to have turned up last week throughout the country for a head count ordered by President Amin. They have been exempted from the enforced exodus because they possess needed skills or because they proved they had obtained Ugandan citizenship.

Facing orders to dispose of their property— which in current conditions means abandoning

it—and to go live as Africans in the bush, the citizen Asians feel particularly isolated and vulnerable to Amin's quick shifts of mood.

One agreed with an outsider's evaluation that although most of the expelled Asians had desperately wanted to stay, those who did might turn out to be the unluckiest ones.

Even the stores that have been kept open by these Asians, or by the handful of Africans who already had acquired commercial property, are doing little business in the wake of the expulsion. The wholesale and distribution networks that were manned largely by Asians are teetering on the edge of breakdown as prices jump the shortages become more severe.

Shelves that a few months ago held shirts, tap recorders or canned milk are barren, and the answer to a customer's request for the razor blades, greeting cards or cheap ball-point pens is a uniform "out of stock" from the new African clerks who have just come on the job.

Despite this economic dislocation, Amin's decision to shatter the Asian-dominated commercial networks and to try to build new ones manned by black Ugandans appears to be popular with much of the African population.

Amin personally checked on the course of this self-proclaimed economic war against foreign interests yesterday morning by strolling along Kampala Road, the city's main shopping street. Wearing a dark blue suit, a red poppy in his lapel and a blue-striped shirt, the six-foot-five, 250-pound military leader beamed as he entered the shops that were open and noted that blacks had almost completely replaced the brown Asians behind the counters.

An enthusiastic street crowd of young men gathered around Amin and followed him from shop to shop. At a pharmacy, two Asians who had been exempted scurried out to shake hands with the president, who lectured them about not cheating Africans.

Whether the hasty expulsion of the Asians will continue to be a widely popular move once the economic realities of Uganda's new situation begin to bite harder is a key question for the future of Amin's military regime. It seized power in 1971 and has savagely repressed all potential opposition.

There are no signs that the government is planning any training program for the Africans, who are impatiently waiting for the shops and homes to be distributed. Experts here fear that the properties will be parceled out to those favoured by the military, and that the stocks left behind will be sold off and the stores then shut down.

Even more crucial is the employment picture in the towns. Young men who were clerks, domestic workers or salesmen for the Asians already lounge sullenly on Kampala's streets without work.

Experts estimate that each of the 8,000 Asian families who were expelled employed an average of five Africans. The majority of the estimated 40,000 Africans who have been left unemployed by the exodus are likely to be out of work for some time.

"I can foresee breadlines like those of 1932 in America unless the government does something fast," said one American resident.

Even where shops have been reopened, many of the Africans have been replaced as the new owner brings in his friends and family.

"The expulsion is still very popular with the people in the villages who never saw the Asians anyway. It is the African man in the town that will be hurt, although only few know it now," said an African resident.

What this man and many foreign observers fear is that Amin's bold move to "Africanize" Uganda's economy will succeed in an unfortunate sense: it could severely damage the economy, and force Ugandans to depend more and more on subsistence farming to survive, while Uganda's towns once viewed as models of Africa's ability to reproduce modern conveniences, sink into the kind of inefficiency and tawdriness that mark a number of Central and West African states.

The exodus of Asian professionals, coupled with Amin's systematic campaign of terror that has meant prison, death or exile for most of Uganda's top minds, has already shattered many of the country's major institutions.

One third of the students at Makerere University, once East Africa's most prestigious school, did not come back to class this year after vacations, apparently out of fear for their lives. These fears appeared to gain validity a few weeks ago when several of the university's top officials disappeared.

At Kampala's secondary school, the number of teachers dropped from 22 to 3 in one week as a result of the expulsion of the Asians. Only three doctors are said to be left working full-time at the main hospital in Kampala. The capital had a population of 500,000 before the Asian exodus.

The exodus cost Uganda 700 Asian teachers. The withdrawal of 107 American Peace Corps volunteers last month and the threats of many of the roughly 500 British instructors here to leave because of the internal turmoil have brought the country's' educational system to the brink of collapse.

But the immediate and obvious dislocation caused by Amin's expulsion of the Asians—the idea for which he says, came to him in a dream— may not have the sudden sharp impact that has been generally expected, some experts believe.

"Just as American bombing couldn't destroy North Vietnam's uncomplicated economy, Amin's disastrous policies won't really destroy Uganda's,

Continued on Page 140

A Home for Ugandans

Reprinted with permission, ©Time Inc., November 13, 1972

Arriving at New York's Kennedy Airport last week, they did not look much different from other passengers. The men wore business suits; the women were dressed in slacks or saris. Most of them spoke fluent English. But they were very special travelers: 82 Asians who had been peremptorily ordered out of Uganda by Strongman Idi Amin Dada, even though they were all citizens. Suddenly made stateless, they constituted the first wave of a group of 1,000 refugees that the U.S. has agreed to accept.

They were able to bring no property or possessions with them, and many had left part of their family behind; yet all of them seemed relieved to be in a country where they would no longer be the political scapegoats of a capricious dictator. Some had studied up on America. "I know the largest building is the Empire State," said Dolly Nasser, 23, a nurse. "And they are going to put even more stories on it." A bearded, wiry welder named Mahmood Ilani Mughal remarked: "I lost everything, but I am glad to be here. My two hands are here. They are my tools and I will rebuild again, with the help of Almighty God."

The effort to rescue the Ugandans has been one of the speediest operations in the history of U.S. immigration. Taking at face value Amin's dire threats of retribution if the Asians do not leave by Nov. 8, the U.S. invoked a special provision of the Immigration Law that permits the U.S. Attorney General to accept refugees under his "parole." Once they arrive in America they can apply for permanent residence and eventually citizenship.

Three weeks ago, a hastily called meeting of the seven major U.S. refugee agencies worked out plans to handle the Ugandans.* While some staffers searched for temporary homes and jobs for them, others went to Italy to talk to the exiles as they arrived at a transit camp near Naples. Lodging and work has been found for the refugees, though many will have to settle for less satisfactory jobs than the ones they left. Given their skills, they are not expected to have much trouble adjusting to the U.S. A bilingual tip sheet acquaints the Ugandans with some of the peculiarities of American life, such as its informality and addiction to cleanliness. Warns the sheet prissily: "It is highly advisable to air your apartments after you have prepared a highly seasoned Indian meal."

Compared with other waves of political exiles that have reached U.S. shores in recent years, the Ugandans are a mere ripple. Some 38,000 Hungarians have fled to the U.S., as well as more than 150,000 Cubans. But the Ugandans differ in that they are not refugees from Communist oppression. Nor do the Ugandans have large communities or coreligionists or fellow ethnics in the U.S. to plead their cause; there are few Ugandans living in America and not many Indians or Pakistanis. Still the U.S. might do more. Canada, for example, is admitting 2,000 Ugandans. There are still at least 6,000 Asians in Uganda desperately looking for some place in the world to go as the deadline hovers over them.

*Two agencies that specialize in resettling East European refugees—the American Fund for Czechoslovak Refugees and the Tolstoy Foundation—are each placing 100 Ugandans. The other 800 are equally divided among the United States Catholic Conference, the Lutheran Council, the Church World Service, United HIAS Service (Jewish) and the International Rescue Committee.

An Ugly Dream Comes True in Uganda

Reprinted with permission, ©Washington Post, November 16, 1972

The idea of expelling the thousands of Asians living in Uganda came to him, Uganda's General Amin has said, in a dream. It was an ugly dream and it has now come true. Up to a day or so ago, meeting the deadline the volatile leader had set for himself, he had dispossessed and expelled some 40,000 Asians, many of them residents of Uganda for two or three generations. The few thousand left behind—most of them with Ugandan citizenship—evidently are being dismissed from the towns and sent to rusticate in the bush. Whether they are more to be envied or pitied remains to be seen.

General Amin has done a good bit more than uproot thousands of individuals, stain his country's international standing, and supply white Africa and its sympathizers with a conspicuous and, to them, useful example of black racism. He has, by ousting the Asians, conducted an instant and massive social revolution, exporting virtually the entire middle class of Uganda. For it was the Asians, of course, who monopolized the commercial and professional life of the fledgling East African state for years past.

General Amin knows this better than anyone. That's exactly why he decided to "Africanize." The way is now clear for Africans to take over the shops, the offices, the houses, the bank accounts, the status of the Asians forced to flee. There are far from enough Africans in place or in training to take over these key economic positions. In the distribution of them, no little corruption and disorder can be expected. The economic dislocation is already substantial. The 40,000 African employees of the dispossessed Asians, for instance, are now by and large jobless. One wonders if the Ugandans' rejoicing in their acquisition of the spoils will survive their eventual realization of the damage to themselves they have done. It is a strange way to "develop."

Most of the uprooted Asians, having British passports, have been taken in by Britain, which, under the circumstances, is doing a creditable job trying to absorb them. Other European countries and Commonwealth members have taken some Asians; the United States accepted a few hundred. So many people, so many clans and groups, have been torn from their "homelands" in this century, and before. It is a deep misfortune that General Amin has seen fit to add, cruelly, to their numbers.

DUKE TOURS BRITISH RESETTLEMENT CAMP FOR UGANDA ASIANS

Reprinted with permission, ©Daily Nation, Nairobi, November 16, 1972

THE Royal Family's interest in the welfare of the Asians who have gone to Britain after their expulsion from Uganda was demonstrated yesterday when the Duke of Edinburgh visited the Resettlement Centre at West Malling in South-East England.

During his one-hour visit to the centre, the Duke chatted to a number of the Asians, visited their men's hall, the headquarters of Toc H, one of the British voluntary organisations which is doing much to help the refugees, the junior school of the camp for young Asian children and two of the accommodation blocks where refugees live.

Frequently the Duke was applauded as he walked around the camp watched by many of the 750 Asians who are still quartered there. At the entrance to the men's hall he was given the traditional Hindu greeting by Mrs Madhvi Pattni, who arrived in England from Kampala just under a month ago.

Mrs Pattni strewed rice and rose petals in his path as he entered, holding at the same time a tray on which two joss-sticks were burning.

Mrs. Pattni has already found a job in nearby Maidstone, with Britain's Department of Health and Social Security but she is still at the camp and

Continued on Page 144

Reproduced with permission, ©R. K. Laxman/Times of India

Fate Brings 2 Ugandans, Bewildered, to Washington

By Eugene L Meyer
Washington Post Staff Writer
Reprinted with permission, ©Washington Post, November 18, 1972

Suchet Singh 22, and Surender Singh. 37, are not related except by fate.

Both are of Indian ancestry and both were born in the East African country of Tanzania. Separately, they migrated to neighboring Uganda.

Neither had journeyed from East Africa and neither had wanted to. But yesterday they arrived here in Washington, looking both bewildered and relieved, facing an uncertain future, but nonetheless a future, in a new country.

Suchet and Surender are among some 5,000 people left "stateless" when Uganda President Idi Amin last August ordered the ouster of about 80,000 Asians from the country. Most Asians, of Indian and Pakistani origin, held British passports and were reluctantly accepted into the United Kingdom. There were others, however, with neither British passports nor Uganda citizenship.

Surender and Suchet fell into this latter group.

"I always felt I belonged in East Africa. I thought I would live in East Africa forever," Suchet said.

"I think there's no more future in Uganda for anybody," he said. "The Africans aren't very happy with what the government is doing. It may be popular with the Army, but not with everybody . . . People are just being arrested. If you're brown, you've had it."

Suchet professes little interest in politics, but he had an explanation for Amin's policies: "I think he must have gone nuts, or something."

Yesterday, both Suchet and Surender were thankful to be here, unaccustomed to the cold weather, vague about their future. Surender wore a green overcoat given him by Hias, a Jewish social agency that is helping the pair get settled.

Hias, founded as the Hebrew Immigration Aid Society at the turn of the century, checked them into Hartnett Hall, a low cost interfaith rooming house at 1426 21st St. NW, near Dupont Circle.

Carrying two pieces of luggage each, they had arrived in New York Thursday, spent the night at an airport motel, and were flown here yesterday morning. They were among 26 Ugandans aided by Hias, one of seven charitable agencies resettling the refugees here in cooperation with the U.S. government. The United States has agreed to accept the refugees as a "humanitarian" gesture, according to the State Department.

The two men had left Uganda Nov. 5 for a "staging area" near Naples, Italy. There, they had joined 1,000 stateless Ugandans destined for America and 3,000 to 4,000 others bound for other countries. Roughly half of those immigrating to the United States are already here.

Suchet is from Kilembe, a copper-mining town of 10,000 in the mountains of western Uganda, where he said he had worked in the mines and as a mechanical engineer. His family had come to East Africa from India in 1925, and to Uganda in 1958.

His parents are still in Uganda, his father exempted from the ouster order because of his British citizenship and technical skills. One broth-er has gone to Canada, another to Italy.

Suchet expects his parents to leave, too. "They only stayed for one reason," he said. "That was because the three of us were stateless. They wanted us to go first."

Suchet went to school with Africans (his mother is one) and he says most of his friends were African.

Surender wears a turban, thin beard and Islamic bracelets around his right wrist. While Suchet graduated from high school, Surender had no formal education. He learned to read and write in a Moslem mosque.

He was an auto mechanic, earning $40 a month, in Mbrara, an army town in southern Uganda, scene of a barracks tribal massacre in June, 1971. When the ouster order came, Surender went to Kampala, Uganda's capital where he tried without success to get a British passport.

"I went back (to Mbrara) and found that my boss had gone to Canada," he said. He, too, then left.

Now, Suchet and Surender both say they want jobs. Suchet, who had planned to go to college in Uganda would also like to study here, if possible.

Do they hope to return, someday, to Uganda? Surender shook his head. Suchet said, "I don't know. I can't take a chance to go back again."

But if politics were to change, if Amin's policies were reversed? Again, Surender shook his head, and Suchet said, "I wouldn't go back. It might happen again."

ST. PAUL, USA

Exiles to settle in area

By JOHN LUNDQUIST, Associated Press Writer
Reprinted with permission, ©Associated Press
Published in the St. Paul Pioneer Press, November 18, 1972

Sixty-two Asians ousted by Uganda militants are to arrive in Minneapolis Tuesday night, most of them to be resettled under sponsorship of Lutheran congregations.

Pastors and laymen from nearly a score of Twin Cities area congregations met at Lutheran Social Service Friday and responsibility was assigned for the 11 families and six individuals.

Citizens of Buffalo in Wright County are assuming charge of a family of five, and Gustavus Adolphus College will take in a 22-year-old student and his brother.

The remainder, including accounts clerk Mohammed Ahmed, his wife and seven children, are assigned to 18 area congregations.

"You have each helped to save one Uganda family from death or camps," Dr. Morris Wee, who is in charge of the resettlement project locally, told the ministers.

Asians in the former British colony of East Africa were ordered expelled by Uganda leaders by Nov. 8. A background paper issued by the Lutheran Council in the U.S.A. said up to 75,000 were ordered ousted and that 1,000 are being admitted to the United States.

The council is among seven Protestant, Jewish and Catholic agencies taking responsibility for the refugees.

The Council's Department of Immigration and Refugee Services stated that about half of the 1,000 are from business, finance and banking families who have sufficient funds outside Uganda to make a new start. The remainder need resettlement assistance.

Those coming to the Twin Cities are in the latter category. Their job descriptions include shopkeeper, electrician, clerk, salesman, high school teacher, radio-TV repairman and accountant.

Ahmed's family of nine will be under auspices of three downtown congregations in Minneapolis.

Congregations were advised their first responsibility is to line up employment and housing for the newcomers.

"Congregations should determine how the breadwinner can obtain immediate employment enabling him to earn his own way and pay his own bills," the council memorandum states.

"This group, we are informed, has never known welfare and will work hard to provide for themselves and their families."

"At a time when we Americans hang our heads because of our international reputation, it feels good to reach down and take someone's hand across the ocean and give them a fresh start."

The 62 refugees, now in staging areas at Rome, will fly to the Twin Cities via New York.

Continued from Page 138

Asian Quarter Like a Ghost Town

which is based on growing enough corn and bananas for everybody to eat," said one observer.

And for the moment, Amin's African followers are still eagerly eyeing the businesses and houses the Asians have been forced to leave behind. They also hope to get cut in on the large bank accounts that the Asians could not touch, except for necessities, after Amin announced the expulsion in August.

Such hopes are bolstered by one story being told by foreigners and Africans in Kampala. A member of the Madhvani family, which includes the richest Asians in East Africa, withdrew 16,000 shillings ($2,300) to purchase airplane tickets, the last withdrawal he could make. "You can keep the other 26 million shillings," he glibly told the teller as he walked away.

However much outsiders see dangers ahead for Amin's course, the general this weekend seemed unperturbed by them. After inspecting a dozen shops on Kampala Road and delivering his talks to the new African managers on the joys of capitalism, he suddenly hopped on an aging and crowded city bus that happened to pass by.

He invited the crowd to join him, and more than 50 smiling youths jammed onto the sagging vehicle. Then the bus bearing a grinning Idi Amin and his happy followers, who had no idea where he was taking them, bounced off through Kampala's mostly deserted streets.

Page 140   *Ugandan Asian Expulsion: 90 Days and Beyond through the Eyes of the International Press*

MINNEAPOLIS-ST. PAUL, USA
62 Ugandan immigrants arrive to start new lives

By Howard Erickson
Staff Writer
Reprinted with permission, ©Minneapolis Tribune, November 22, 1972

Bedazzled by flashbulbs and TV cameras, 62 very tired refugees from the East African nation of Uganda arrived in the Twin Cities Tuesday evening to make new homes in Minnesota.

Weary after 22 hours of travel from temporary quarters in Naples, Italy, the 11 immigrant families were too sleepy to say much at Minneapolis-St. Paul International Airport last night, despite their excitement.

Greeting them were members of more than a dozen Lutheran churches and colleges, who have arranged furnished apartments and job interviews for the new Minnesotans since word came less than two weeks ago that the group would arrive.

"We called it Operation Hectic," said the Rev. Einar Oberg of Gustavus Adolphus parish, 1509 27th Av. NE.

"The people responded just amazingly," Mr. Oberg said. "We collected bedroom furniture, pots and pans and enough money for two months' rent just by standing the ushers at the door on Sunday."

Other pastors reported equally eager and generous responses in their congregations.

Mount Olivet parish, 5025 Knox Av. S., learned that Abu Ahmed Bachelani's wife spoke no English and tracked down women who speak Swahili to take her grocery shopping—an example of the resources in a large church, said the Rev. Harian Robbins.

A job at Bergin Wholesale Fruit Co. offered by another parishioner, awaits the 48-year-old Bachelani.

"The people are very hospitable. I thank them very much," said the Bachelanis' 18-year-old son, Mohamed Ali, looking handsome in a new sportcoat still creased from its Refugee Relief packing case.

"I'm really humble," he added in precise English with a trace of a British accent. "I hear that it is very cold here, and that you have a great holiday tomorrow or the next day—Thanksgiving it is called."

The Bachelanis and their seven children, aged 11 months to 22 years, have been invited to spend Thanksgiving with the elderly residents of Mount Olivet Home. They are being housed for the first two weeks at the Guest House Motel downtown, until they can move into a three-bedroom home at 49th St. and Knox Av. S.

"They are not wealthy people, the folks who donated the house for four

Continued on Page 142

A Ugandan Asian mother holds her crying son as she and 61 other Ugandan Asians were greeted by members of a Lutheran church at the Minneapolis-St. Paul International Airport.   Reproduced with permission ©Associated Press/ World Wide Photos

Expelled Ugandan Family Provided St. Paul Home

By GEORGE RICE
Staff Writer
Reprinted with permission, ©St. Paul Pioneer Press, November 22, 1972

Just over three months ago, Ismail Ahmed Munshi, 44, master of education, college lecturer, part owner of a private college in Kampala, Uganda received a curt notice from the government.

It informed him that his application for Ugandan citizenship had been turned down and that he must depart from Uganda forthwith.

Munshi was, not surprised. He knew that he and the thousands of others of Asian Indian extraction in the African nation were ticketed for expulsion, and that the Ugandan Government would expropriate their property.

What he had no way of knowing, however, was that on a chilly November night he and his family—wife, three daughters and a son—would be settling in a new home in St. Paul.

The Munshis and 59 other Ugandan expellees arrived Tuesday night at Minneapolis-St. Paul International Airport from New York, under the sponsorship of Lutheran Social Service of Minnesota.

Altogether, Minnesota Lutherans are sponsoring 73 expellees—20 families.

When they stepped of off the Northwest Airlines 747 the Munshis were greeted by a large, homemade sign, white letters on a red background, spelling out "Welcome to Ismail and Hurbai Munshi and Family."

Holding the sign aloft was Jerry Klingner, 1688 Ashland Ave. He was flanked by two pastors: the Rev. E. K. Bentley, of Immanuel Lutheran Church, and the Rev. Paul E. Schuessler, pastor of Pilgrim Lutheran Church.

The two churches are co-sponsors of the Munshis. Immanuel Church is ALC (American Lutheran Church); Pilgrim is a Missouri Synod congregation.

Klingner, who acted as coordinator for the two churches and is a member at Immanuel, said the two congregations learned they would be sponsoring the Munshis only last Friday.

In the intervening few days, a house was rented, furniture was acquired and food collected—much of the food through the efforts of St. Odilia Catholic Church of Shoreview. (It seems the Munshis' new landlord had a relative who belonged to St. Odilia's.)

Moreover, the sponsors have at least three leads for employment for Munshi at Twin Cities colleges.

An hour after their arrival Tuesday, Munshi and his family—wife, Hurbai (42), daughters

Continued on Page 144

Just-arrived Ugandan family in city still has fears, but now not of death

By JOHN CARMAN
Minneapolis Star Staff Writer
Reprinted with permission, ©Minneapolis Star, November 23, 1972

Twice in the past three months, soldiers forced their way into Jagdish Trivedi's home at gunpoint.

With good reason, he feared for his life and the lives of his wife and two small children.

Trivedi still has private fears, but now they are of a different sort. His apprehensions now center on finding a job and beginning a new life.

Trivedi, 27, is one of 62 refugees from Uganda who landed Tuesday night at Minneapolis-St. Paul International Airport after being expelled from the East African nation.

They are among 75,000 Ugandans of Asian descent ordered out of the country by President Idi Amin, a dictator who has expressed admiration for Adolph Hitler.

For the moment, Trivedi and his family are wards of Christ Lutheran Church in Minneapolis, which has moved them into an apartment at 2022 Park Av.

While a color television loaned by a parishioner showed "Hollywood Squares" in the background, Trivedi sat on a couch in his apartment last night and told his story.

He has a basic command of the English language, but he is unaccustomed to speaking it, and much of what he said was difficult to understand.

Trivedi said he was born in India. His family moved to Uganda when he was only a year old, and he had lived there since. For 10 years, he was an auto electrician for a large firm in Jinja, a city of about 40,000 just north of Lake Victoria.

His wife, Shakuntla, 19, also is of Asian ancestry. Their children are Jiten, a 1-1/2-year-old boy, and Nimish, a 6-months-old girl.

Trivedi said that he learned from newspaper and radio announcements a few months ago that noncitizens and citizens like himself who were of Asian origin had three months to leave Uganda.

The reason for the expulsion was that other Ugandans resented what was described as their domination of the former British colony's commercial life.

Within a month, soldiers "came and asked when you are leaving, and they stole the money we had in the house," Trivedi said.

He said soldiers came to his rented house once shortly after 9 p.m. The second occasion, they roused him from bed at about 6 a.m.

Both times, Trivedi said, the soldiers appeared to have been drunk on waragi, a Ugandan liquor. Trivedi was lucky. Asian friends of his were beaten, and he wasn't. Some were beaten to death, he said.

Trivedi sought travel papers to India and to Britain. He said both nations refused his family refuge. "No other country was ready to accept us," he said, besides the United States. He talked to American officials in Uganda.

"We don't know anything," he said. "We have not seen the country. We are new to the country. They told me it would be all right, not to worry."

The planeload of Ugandans that landed in the Twin Cities, after stops in Rome, Naples and New York, was part of a group of 2,000 refugees admitted to the United States.

While they were en route, the Lutheran Social Service of Minnesota was making preparations for them here. More than a dozen Lutheran churches in the Twin Cities area are sponsoring individual families.

Because of the resources of the churches, immediate prospects for the immigrants are good. Many of the newcomers were shopkeepers at home. One was a banker. Most already have job interviews scheduled.

Trivedi, who never before had heard of Minneapolis, would like to find work here as an auto electrician. He plans on staying in the United States and wants his family to become citizens.

Trivedi had to leave his car and household goods in Uganda. He and his family were given winter clothing in Naples.

While his wife was taken grocery shopping yesterday by Christ Church parishioners, Trivedi set out on his own for a walk around his new neighborhood. The walk exposed him to the coming winter climate in Minnesota.

"When in the morning I went out it was too cold," he said, "so I turned back in half and hour."

A Ugandan Asian family waits quietly for their host family upon their arrival at the Minneapolis-St. Paul International Airport.

Reproduced with permission ©Associated Press/ World Wide Photos

Continued from Page 141

62 Ugandan immigrants arrive to start new lives

months," Pastor Robbins said. "But their new house in Bloomington is ready to move into, and the old one isn't sold yet. So when they heard they could help…"

Bachelani was running a draperies shop with three partners in Mbale, Uganda, when the new nationalist government of Gen. Idi Amin proclaimed its new policy of native control of the economy.

The nine Bachelanis are among 75,000 Ugandans, mostly merchant and professional families, of Hindu and Moslem religion and Indian or Pakistani descent—who were forced to leave. Of 12,000 who were stateless and had no place to go, 2,000 are being admitted to the United States. Immigration quotas were waived by special order of President Nixon.

Requests from the Lutheran Council-U.S.A. immigration service that Twin Cities congregations sponsor 20 new families were announced Nov. 9.

"Our Committee on Social Ministries accepted the request Nov. 12 and we announced it in church that same day," said Mr. Oberg of Gustavus Adolphus parish.

"The chairwoman, Mrs. Edward Femrite, said it's the first time she never had to ask anyone to help—she just answered the phone."

Amin victims wait to go to Norway

From Penny Symon
Rome, Nov 26
Reprinted with permission, ©Times Newspapers Limited, London,
November 27, 1972

There is a map of Norway prominently placed on the wall in La Villa, a comfortable hotel just outside Rome. The hotel is usually quiet out of season, but now anxious people cluster round that map, looking for Oslo and Bergen and asking each other constantly what life is like there.

None of them really knows, because they are all stateless Uganda Asians in transit, staying here at the expense of the International Committee for European Migration.

The Norwegian mission was one of the first to arrive in Uganda after General Amin's expulsion order and many stateless Asians chose to go there to be, as they said, on the safe side in case no other missions came to offer them a country. They leave on Friday.

For about 33 of 106 people here, the other reason for choosing Norway was its closeness to Britain. These people's wives, children or close relatives are British passport holders and are now in Britain. They themselves do not hold British passports. As Uganda citizens, they had Uganda passports many of which, with other documents, were seized by the army.

They are being well looked after here, and a bus is available to take them in and out of Rome three times a day. The food is good, if a little strange to them.

The men with wives in Britain say that if they cannot go to Britain too they hope that the Norwegian authorities will allow their wives in. But they have been warned that this could take time. They are planning holidays in Britain as soon as they can.

Today they were visited by one of the vice-chairmen of the Coordinating Committee for the Welfare of Evacuees from Uganda, Mr Habib Habib, and by Mrs Mary Dines of the Joint Council for the Welfare of Immigrants. Both had come from London to collect details which they will eventually present to the British Government to support arguments that Asians with dependants in Britain will be allowed in.

The moment that Mr Habib and Mrs Dines arrived a crowd gathered round to tell them exactly where their wives and other relatives were in Britain. A queue quickly formed, and masses of details were taken down.

Mr Himatlal Bhanubhai, aged 32, who ran a radio repair shop in Kampala, showed me an address book, in which was written his wife's name, care of Hobbs Barracks, East Grinstead. His three children were there too and he was very worried about them and his wife who was not well.

"She had a British passport, and I had a Uganda one which was seized. So I sent her to Britain with the children. I have several well off relatives living there and I am the only one left. I am going to Norway, but obviously I would much rather come to Britain to join my family."

Mr Jayanti Jani, also 32, and an accountant, is in a similar position. His wife had a British passport and is now living with her parents in Islington. Mr Jani took Uganda citizenship in 1962. "I am going to Norway, but of course I would prefer Britain. I have been told that I will have to wait about a year for my wife to join me in Norway, so naturally I hope to be able to go to Britain to join her and my baby."

The Asians all hope that the coordinating committee can help, but some feel it is a hopeless situation. "These people are only raising the Asians' hopes and wasting their time", said Mr Mustaque Jaffer, aged 24.

Mr. Madhvani says he wants to return—but with honour

Standard Staff Reporte
Reprinted with permission, ©East African Standard, Nairobi,
November 24, 1972

London.—Mr. Manubhai Madhvani, head of the Madhvani industrial empire which the Uganda Government now controls, said in an interview in London: "I love Uganda. I would like to return there with honour, respect and dignity but not otherwise."

Mr. Madhvani, who has just joined other members of his family in Britain after a period in India, following his expulsion from Uganda, claimed that President Amin had deliberately prevented his becoming a Uganda citizen.

He had applied for Ugandan nationality in 1963 but was unable to renounce his British citizenship during the 90-day period because he was abroad, he said, but the Uganda Government still granted his application and he was given a Ugandan passport.

Over the years he had repeatedly reminded the authorities in Kampala that he had been unable to relinquish British citizenship as the law required, but there was no problem until Gen. Amin took action against the Asians last August. After his release from three weeks in Makindye Prison he was summoned before Gen. Amin who asked him whether he was a Ugandan citizen.

"I told him I had applied for verification and the matter was with his Minister," he said. "I also told President Amin that I loved Uganda and wanted to remain a Ugandan citizen."

It was only after the General declared in a speech on October 27 that he had refused him citizenship that he surrendered his Ugandan passport for a British one. A few days later the President announced that as Mr. Madhvani had chosen British citizenship he would have to leave. Mr. Madhvani said he was confident that Gen. Amin would honour his promise to pay compensation for his business although he had blocked his application for citizenship.

"I believe he will pay compensation and prove he is a man of his word. He has, of course, shown he is a man of his word up till now," he added.

Contrasting responses to Uganda

Editorial
Reprinted with permission, ©Minneapolis Tribune, November 27, 1972

The welcome given to 62 Ugandan refugees who arrived in the Twin Cities Tuesday was an uplifting bit of news for the Thanksgiving weekend. Lutheran churches in the area rose in splendid form to meet the occasion by helping the expelled Ugandans with food, housing and job opportunities. We would like to be able to add that the problems of Uganda are being approached in a similar spirit of pragmatism and good will at the upper reaches of American government. But for reasons that have just come to light, the role of the Nixon administration in this African tragedy begins to look more and more distasteful.

Those 62 who have come to Minnesota are among the 2,000 admitted to the United States out of the more than 42,000 that Uganda's erratic strongman, Idi Amin, ejected during the past three months. It was an act of undisguised racism. Amin simply wanted to get rid of all Asian Ugandan citizens—those of Indian or Pakistani origin—at the same time confiscating most of their savings and property.

Amin achieved further world notice in September by writing a rambling, sometimes incoherent letter to Israeli Prime Minister Golda Meir explaining how Hitler had the right idea for dealing with Jews and suggesting that all Jews in Israel now be sent to Britain. The other day, with the United States mounting a drive for international action against aerial hijacking, Amin announced his praise for the hijackers.

In short, Uganda's present government must rank near the bottom of the list of those that the United States wishes to encourage. Amin's deportation of Asian Ugandans stripped the country of a high percentage of skilled tradesmen, professionals and managers. That exercise in nation-wrecking together with Amin's disregard for some of his country's own citizens and his outrageous attitudes toward others, seemed to us this fall abundant justification for the suspension of U.S. eco-

nomic aid to Uganda. That is what the State Department said was being done as an indication of American displeasure with Amin.

A Washington Post report Sunday from Kampala, Uganda's capital, tells a different story. Amin was apparently assured by the American ambassador, on instructions from the State Department, that any slight delay in $6 million in loans was for technical, not policy, reasons. American officials in Kampala now seem convinced that the loans will go through about as scheduled and, indeed, ought to. Their reasoning is that the loans are for good purposes: teacher training and animal husbandry. They were initiat

Continued on Page 144

Ugandan Asian Expulsion: 90 Days and Beyond through the Eyes of the International Press   *Page 143*

Stateless refugees wait and worry in Italy

From Penny Symon
Naples, Nov 29
Reprinted with permission, ©Times Newspapers Limited, London,
November 30, 1972

There is a similarity between the Centro Canzanella refugee camp here and the Uganda Resettlement Board's Stradishall centre in Britain. In spite of the flowers and the sun and Signor Benito Giannotta, the Italian director, who is an extremely patient and helpful man, Asians sit in worried groups discussing their uncertain plans and the whereabouts of their luggage, which has not yet arrived from Uganda.

The difference here is that the 386 people are all stateless, and about 15 per cent of them have their wives and children in Britain. Another 30 per cent have parents, brothers and sisters, and other close relatives.

So far, 300 of them have applied for entry into the United States because they do not want to be stranded here. They hope that their families will eventually join them, but would obviously prefer to go to Britain. The rest are undecided.

There are six agencies helping them to make arrangements, and their stay here is being financed by the Italian authorities, who are doing everything possible to make the rather bare rooms more comfortable. They have also provided teachers.

The main complaint is the slowness of Italy's postal and telephone system. They have allowed the Asians to cook their own food, and a small army of woman volunteers have been recruited.

Yesterday's visit here by Mr Habib Habib, the vice-chairman of the Coordinating Committee for the Welfare of Evacuees from Uganda, to gather detailed information about those people with relatives in Britain in the hope that his committee can persuade the British Government to allow them in, has raised people's hopes. His colleague, Mrs Mary Dines, of the Joint Council for the Welfare of Immigrants, is visiting the three centres in Lecce, near Brindisi, where 700 Asians are staying.

As soon as Mr Habib arrived, the queue formed. The Asians were anxious to tell us all about their problems. One said he would like to stay in Italy because he had heard that Britain was very overcrowded. Another, a civil servant, said that he wanted to go to Britain because his wife and six children were there.

Continued from Page 139

Duke tours British resettlement camp for Uganda Asians

very much involved in organising social activities there.

Her case is typical of many of the Uganda Asians in the British resettlement camp who have found jobs in Britain easier to acquire than living accommodation.

The Duke was received at the camp by Major B. J. Arrowsmith, the resettlement administrator and regional administrator of the south-east of England.

Also present to greet him was the camp's medical officer, Dr. Aziz, and representatives of voluntary organisations.

West Malling, a former Royal Air Force fighter station which was in the front line during the Battle of Britain in 1940, was unoccupied for seven years before it was reopened as a resettlement centre on October 4.

Because of the swiftness of the action needed following President Amin's expulsion order the administering authorities were given just five days to equip the camp and arrange heating, bedding and feeding facilities.

Since the camp was opened 1,082 Asian refugees have arrived there. Accommodation and employment have already been found for 326 of them, leaving 756 still in the camp.

Continued from Page 137

Asian husbands reprieved

wife and one child and Mr Praful Chandra Kanani a wife and two children; Mr Mahendra Naranda Kateja's wife expects a baby in December. Mr Harish Gordandas Koteja has a wife and two children.

Mr Douglas-Mann said the treatment of the orphans, Alinu and Nargis Sangi, was atrocious. Neither had a UK passport nor an entry permit when they arrived with their uncle and aunt five days ago. Their brother, Mr Amin Sanji, aged 26, who works in a supermarket delicatessen, offered to support them and let them live in his home in Bayswater.

"When I last saw Nargis she was crying and saying 'don't let them send us back. We'll both be killed.' The fear of being sent back has made her physically ill—she can't eat," Mr Sanji said yesterday.

"The Home Office was well aware that they are here to study. They have all the papers with them. If they go back now, the Ugandan Government won't accept them. But they will return in two or three years time, after completing their studies. I want them to have a good education here, and I have paid deposits for their fees at London schools."

Cars of expelled Asians returned to Uganda

Standard Staff Reporter
Reprinted with permission, ©East African Standard, Nairobi,
November 30, 1972

Mombasa—Goods belonging to non-citizen Asians who left Uganda under the expulsion order of President Amin and sent to Mombasa for shipping to the owners might not be forwarded to the original destinations following instructions from the Uganda Government, according to reports reaching Mombasa yesterday.

The reports linked these instructions with the visit last weekend to Mombasa by a team of Ugandan officials.

Sixteen cars out of 22 belonging to the Asian expellees, which were not cleared by the Uganda authorities, were returned to Uganda on Tuesday afternoon from Mombasa, the sources said.

The fate of six other cars still lying at New Azania Service Station, Mombasa, is still unknown. It is understood that a local Ugandan Government institution has written to a Mombasa firm of advocates, acting on behalf of the expellees, informing it of the return of the cars to Uganda.

The sources said that between 3,000 and 4,000 baggages belonging to expelled Asians were still lying at Mombasa godowns.

They were brought to Mombasa for shipping and it was feared that they might now not be forwarded following new instructions from Uganda. Most of them should have been shipped to Britain or India by now, the sources stated.

Continued from Page 141

Expelled Ugandan family provided St. Paul home

Rukuya (20), Razia (19), and Zohra (16), and son Shebhaz (10)— were in their four-bedroom-and-den home at 731 Virginia St.

On the table was food and drink. There were two television sets and a stereo. All the bedrooms were furnished.

"It was more than we could ever expect," was all Munshi was able to say as he surveyed what his new Lutheran and Catholic American friends had done.

The Munshis are Moslems.

Continued from Page 143

Contrasting reponses to Uganda

ed under a previous Ugandan government. They will give the United States more influence with Amin. Besides, the argument continues, an American failure to support Amin might provoke a coup that could bring in a still worse government

Our concern would be this: Does it seem likely that the best interests of either Americans or Ugandans are furthered by U.S. financial assistance for a regime whose apparent incompetence is exceeded only by its demonstrated indifference to basic human rights? An endorsement of present U.S. aid policy in Uganda would seem to require answering yes to that question.

Czech case different
Govt. won't help Ugandans with tuition fees

By Patrick Best
Citizen staff writer
Reprinted with permission, ©Ottawa Citizen, November 30, 1972

Ugandan Asian students who have been offered places in Canadian universities will get no help from the federal government for their tuition fees.

The government rejected the argument of Ugandan Asian committees that the students should be treated in the same way as the Czechoslovakian immigrants who came here in 1968.

Forced out

This means that virtually all of the more than 100 Asian students who had planned to continue their studies at Canadian universities will be forced to withdraw due to lack of funds. Six of them were due to attend Ottawa universities.

One was enrolled in U of O's medical faculty.

The 4,420 Asians who came to Canada in emergency airlifts after expulsion from Uganda were not allowed to bring any money or valuables with them. Ugandan students in Toronto had sent a telegram to Prime Minister Trudeau asking that they be declared eligible for special grants.

"The situation in which the Ugandan Asians find themselves is not parallel with that of the Czechs in 1968," said a manpower and immigration department official.

"The Czechs were true refugees in that they fled their homeland to seek asylum in other countries," he added. "Ugandan Asians were selected in their home country for admission to Canada as landed immigrants.

"They were given entry visas on the understanding that they would join the work force on arrival in Canada. None were admitted as students. But they were made aware that they could continue their university studies if and when they had saved enough money to do so."

Under the special arrangements made for the Czech refugees in 1968, students received federal loan grants of $1,200. The Association of Universities and Colleges of Canada co-operated by finding universities willing to provide "tuition-free" studies.

As landed immigrants Ugandan Asian students are not eligible for grants under the Ontario student awards program until they have been residents of the province for a year.

Rajat Naj. Chairman of Ottawa's Ugandan Asian Committee, said that the federal government's decision "puts us in a very frustrating position."

"The decision seems to have come right from the top," he added. "The students barely have enough to live on at the moment and we don't know where to turn to now."

He expressed surprise that the government would provide the same "fine treatment" for Ugandan Asians as it did for the Czechs, but draw the line when it came to student grants."

WIVES PLEAD WITH BRITAIN 'LET OUR HUSBANDS IN. . .'

Reprinted with permission, ©Daily Nation, Nairobi, December 12, 1972

LONDON-A GROUP of British Asian women pleaded in a letter today that their "stateless" husbands now living in European camps be permited to come to Britain.

The group of 24 women said they were speaking for many others who were in a similar position since leaving Uganda to come to Britain in recent months.

In a letter to The Times newspaper they said that a "cruel and inhuman decision" was separating them from their husbands who now were in United Nations' refugee camps in Belgium, Austria or Italy.

They said their husbands were "stateless" because they had become Ugandan citizens a few years ago before President Amin ordered all non-citizens expelled some months ago.

The women appealed to British wives and mothers "to try to imagine our misery and anguish as we sit from day-to-day wondering what will ever happen to us. And when will we ever see our husbands again, when our children will know that they still have a father?"

The letter continued: "We appeal to British people we do not wish to live off the State any longer, but while our husbands are refused admission to Britain there is little hope of most of us being able to work. Most of us are trying to raise families of young children. Our husbands on the other hand, are working men of all skills and professions.

"We make a desperate appeal to the Home Secretary." The letter concluded, "Please try to consider our miserable plight and save us by allowing our husbands (a relatively small number) to come to Britain and support us. Help us to make our lives worth living again."

EDMONTON, CANADA
Most Ugandans here are now employed

Reprinted with permission, ©Edmonton Journal, December 15, 1972

More than 30 of the employable Ugandan Asians living in Edmonton have found permanent jobs says George McIntosh, Manpower Centre information officer.

Mr. McIntosh said most are working in sales or clerical jobs but several tradesmen have been placed.

Of the 16 unemployed, he said, one had a part-time job which folded and three other men are trying to buy their own business. Prospects for those who are not employed still look good as employers are still contacting the centre.

Recent figures from Ottawa show that more than 1,040 of the 2,200 Asians, who registered for work when they arrived in Canada, are now working.

Kampala takes over 'Uganda Argus'

Standard Staff Reporter
Reprinted with permission, ©East African Standard, Nairobi, December 2, 1972

The Uganda Government yesterday took over the *Uganda Argus* and renamed it the *Voice of Uganda.*

A Government spokesman announced that with effect from yesterday the "*Uganda Argus* newspaper" had been taken over by the Government and will be managed by the Ministry of Information and Broadcasting.

The Ministry has also instructed the existing staff of the paper to report for duty as usual.

Later, the Minister of Information and Broadcasting, Mr. V. Naburri, accompanied by his Permanent Secretary, Mr. Emojong, the Under-Secretary, Mr. Ekodeo, and other officials of the Ministry went to the *Uganda Argus* offices to convey to the staff of the paper of the Government's decision.

He said that the take-over of the paper is not peculiar as this has been done in other countries, though in different ways.

He warned the staff against frustrating the Government decision. He asked them to co-operate with his Ministry for the smooth running of the paper.

Earlier this week, President Amin complained that the paper had published an incorrect report of a sugar shortage. He warned that if it persisted in publishing such reports it would be closed down.

The *Uganda Argus* was founded in 1955 and was marked down for nationalisation by the previous Ugandan Government of ex-President Milton Obote.

An armed police guard was put outside the premises of the *Uganda Argus* last night after the announcement of the take-over. The police checked all persons entering the building.

Fate of personal baggage left by ousted Asians at Kilindini unknown

By NATION Reporter
Reprinted with permission, ©Daily Nation, Nairobi, December 1, 1972

MORE than 15 vehicles worth thousands of pounds, belonging to expelled Uganda Asians and railed to Mombasa for shipment overseas, have been returned to Kampala on the instructions of the Uganda Government.

This was learned in Mombasa yesterday following the disclosure that the owner of one of the vehicles now living in Britain, intends taking legal action against the Ugandan Government's Kilindini port clearing agents, N. T. C. Transocean (Uganda) Ltd.

In a "final demand" notice sent to Transocean on behalf of the vehicle owner, the Ugandan shipping agency was cited for its "unilateral action" and return of the vehicle, or financial compensation for its "loss" was demanded.

Ugandan Asian Expulsion: 90 Days and Beyond through the Eyes of the International Press

NEW YORK CITY

2 Asian Refugees Here Recall the Tension and Harassment of Their Last Days in Uganda

BY DEIRDRE CARMODY
Reprinted with permission, ©New York Times, December 10, 1972

Ramesh Tara pushed back his chair, smiled at his wife and his host and said: "I am very, very relaxed. It is the first time I have been able to relax since it began."

That was a little more than a month ago. Mr. Tara, a 28-year-old Indian, had just arrived from his native Uganda with his wife and 2-year-old son, and had found refuge in a comfortable house in suburban New Jersey. They were among 75,000 Asians living in Uganda who were stripped of their property and their savings and sent into exile by Maj. Gen. Idi Amin, the Uganda President.

The 90-day deadline President Amin set for leaving the country is well past, and most of the Asians have left Uganda. But Mr. Tara will not allow his real name or other highly specific information about him to be used for publication until all of his relatives are safe in other countries.

Seemed Carefree

The refugees have few doubts that Asians remaining in Uganda illegally will be persecuted or even murdered. President Amin made his own feelings clear when he sent a telegram in September to United Nations Secretary General Kurt Waldheim, expressing approval of Hitler's extermination of six million Jews.

But Mr. Tara did not seem like a man who had just emerged from a nightmare. He wrestled on the living room floor with his son, who squealed with delight. He jumped up, grabbed his camera and snapped a picture. Then he flopped down on the sofa next to his wife, who was talking about their last days in Uganda.

"I was not eating. I was not sleeping," she said. "We talked and talked and we went to bed so late every night. Then we could never sleep. When I asked my husband a question, he would never answer because he was tense all the time."

The Tara family, originally from the Punjab region in India, had been in Uganda for four generations. Like many Indian merchants, Mr. Tara's grandfather moved to Kampala, the capital of Uganda, to set up a shop. Then one by one other members of his family followed and started businesses of their own.

Their shops prospered and proliferated, and in time the family began to buy property in the villages. Mr. Tara attended private school—there is no public education in Uganda—until he was 20.

Then his father, feeling there was a limited future in being a shopkeeper, sent him out to seek a job.

Worked as Sales Manager

Mr. Tara found work as a salesman for an international company. In a few years, he was managing a branch office and handling sales for a 300-mile area. Promotions and raises came quickly; in a one-year period, he says, sales under his supervision increased from the equivalent of $1,500 to $10,000.

He married a young Indian girl who had been born in Uganda also, and they lived in a pleasant house in a village outside Kampala. He drove a foreign car, played tennis in the afternoons and, like the rest of his family, began to invest his money in property.

"We lived an easy, luxurious life," he says. "We never had to suffer anything."

The evening of Aug. 7, Mr. Tara went out as usual to join some Indian friends for a walk. He learned that General Amin had ordered all Asians holding British passports expelled from the country. (Later that order was amended to include almost all Asians.)

"We were shocked, but we also thought that this was a joke, that he would change this around," Mr. Tara said. "You cannot believe that the entire Asian population would have to leave the country."

Then the lines began to form in Kampala in front of banks and rail and air ticket offices as 75,000 Asians prepared for exile. Mr. Tara joined 23,000 Asians who were Uganda citizens in the mile-long line at the immigration office. For some, the wait was as long as two days. People who lived nearby brought food, but some of those in line fainted, old people collapsed and some of them died.

Inside the office there was confusion as Asians tried to have their passports verified. Immigration office clerks, many of them Indians who were themselves standing in lines, had been replaced by Africans unfamiliar with the procedures.

Shoved by Soldiers

To expedite things, soldiers outside were given the power to verify passports. The soldiers then walked down the line of Asians, shoving them with the butts of their guns, verifying some passports and rejecting others at whim. Indians whose passports were inside had their citizenship nullified because they did not have their passports in hand.

In the end, 1,000 Asians were permitted to remain in Uganda, and 500 Asian professionals were ordered to stay in the interest of the economy.

Mr. Tara's passport was snatched by a soldier and he was told he would have to leave the country. From that moment, he was subjected to harassment by the soldiers swarming all over Kampala because he had neither passport nor verification of his citizenship.

"I was worried all the time," he recalled. "Everybody was depressed. I would have died out of tension if I had had to stay there another week."

On Oct. 31, Mr. Tara flew out of Kampala with his wife and his son, taking their clothes, towels, sheets and blankets in five suitcases. His wife wrapped all of her gold jewelry in a handkerchief and carried it in her hand. The government had confiscated all their property and savings, which Mr. Tara estimates were worth $50,000.

The Tara family is among the 1,000 stateless Asians the United States has said it will take in. To date, 872 of them have arrived. Mr. Tara says he was willing to go to any country that would accept him, as long as he could keep his family together.

About seven out of 10 Asians arriving here sent their wives and families to India or to England, according to Charles Sternberg, executive director of the International Rescue Committee, one of seven organizations helping the refugees here. He said legislation would be needed to allow these Asians to bring their families.

Met by Committee

The Tara family flew to Rome and then came to New York, where they were met by committee members, brought to Manhattan and put up in a hotel. There, Mrs. Tara, who is a vegetarian, took out the rice, flour and special spices she had brought along and cooked an Indian meal on the hotplate in the room.

"Then we went out and we were happy looking at the buildings, the cars, the lights," she said. "We just thought that we were lucky being in America."

The first thing Mr. Tara did the next morning was buy a newspaper and begin looking for a job as a salesman. The Taras were visited in their hotel by Dr. Roshan Chaddha, president of the Association of Indians in America, 663 Fifth Avenue near 53rd Street, who is helping to find foster families for the displaced Asians. Later, he invited the Taras to stay with him at his home in New Jersey.

Moves to Queens

Once his family was safely settled in Dr. Chaddha's house, Mr. Tara resumed his search for a job as a salesman. He found one shortly with an office and photographic-supply company in Flushing, Queens, where he earns about $150 a week and hopes to be on commission soon.

He has moved his family into a furnished studio apartment in Elmhurst, Queens, in a building where there are eight other Indian families. The suitcases were unpacked for the first time, the sheets and blankets from Uganda have taken their place on the bed, and the cupboards have been stacked with crockery brought from home. The new life has begun.

Kneeling on the living room floor, Mr. Tara threw fake punches at his son, who ducked, punched back and rolled on the floor with glee.

"Look at him—the future Golden Glove champion," Mr. Tara said with a grin. "He'll grow up to be a Yankee."

CHICAGO, USA
Ugandans Find Hope Here

Reprinted with permission, ©Chicago Tribune, December 14, 1972

For 14 years, Mahmood Dhanji and his father ran a grocery store in Kampala, Uganda. Business was good, life was good, and even the money was good.

But suddenly all that ended with President Idi Amin's order expelling more than 20,000 Asians who either held British passports or whose Ugandan citizenship was challenged.

Live in Wilmette Now

Today, Mahmood, his wife, and three small children—one of them a victim of a rare blood disease—literally live on charity in the home of a Wilmette family.

In somewhat halting English, Mahmood told how he has gone from supermart to supermart looking for a job in the only trade he knows.

"They say I fill out a form. And then they say no job is available immediately," he said.

"I will keep looking, I know I will get a job. If I can't get job in a grocery, then I'll get a job some place."

Family has $200

The family has a bankroll of $200. The money and some warm clothing was given to them by the International Rescue Committee during a stop-over in Rome.

Everything else was left in the neat little house on the Kampala street where Mahmood, 33, his father, his two brothers and family of his wife, Rosmir, 24, all had neat little houses.

"We had worked hard," Mahmood said angrily. "Fourteen years, we had the grocery. Living was easier. Then, it was gone—just like that."

Arrive Nov. 25

The Dhanjis arrived here Nov. 25. The Wilmette family had notified the local chapter of the Indian League that a small apartment behind their home would be available to house a stateless Asian Ugandan for as long as needed.

Last month, the United States agreed to accept 1,000 of the stateless individuals. So far, 26 have arrived in Chicago.

Mahmood, though he is technically Indian, has never seen India. He was born in Mombasa, Kenya, and went to school in Zanzibar. He moved to Uganda in 1958. The following year, Mahmood opened the grocery store.

Friends in Alaska

When he was ordered to leave Kampala, Mahmood said he applied for an American visa because "everybody say 'Nice place, no trouble, and they treat you polite. The life of the children will be bright'."

Besides, he added, he has friends in Alaska—obviously not realizing the distance from Chicago to Alaska.

The adjustment to the new life, despite all the helping hands, has been difficult in other ways.

Has Rare Blood Disease

Rosmir doesn't leave the house because it is so cold outside and everything is so bewildering—the people, the strange street, the timer on the stove,

the automatic ice-maker in the refrigerator.

The two older children, Siddika, 6, and Mossie, 3, speak no English. Their major source of amusement is the television set. And the baby, Sukkina, 7 months, is busy just being a baby.

Siddika suffers from a rare blood disease. She has just learned to walk and each month she must be taken to a hospital to receive a blood transfusion.

"We took her to the hospital the day after we arrived," Mahmood said. "We didn't pay nothing but I sign some more forms."

SWEDEN
The Sawjani Family
Their lives begin in a gray barrack.

By Rune B. Axelsson

Reprinted with permission, © Rune B. Axelsson/ Dagens Nyheter, Stockholm, December 13, 1972

Translation courtesy of Dr. Charles Westin and Catarina Nyberg

Life begins in Alvesta. This is the hope of the 140 Indians who have been expelled from Uganda and now arrived at the Board of Labour's foreign camp in the County of Småland. A month ago they were persecuted but wealthy. They had cars, houses, businesses, industries and bus companies in their native country.

Today they are taken care of in Alvesta, but impoverished. They have not brought any material wealth with them. But they are eager to start all over again.

The Kantilal Sawjani family is a typical example of the destinies of a few hundred Ugandan refugees' journey to Sweden, through the mediation of the UN High Commissioner for Refugees.

Father, 42, was a business man in the textile industry in the town of Jinja. His wife Hemlata came to Uganda from India as a two-year-old. She is a trained dress maker. They have three children, 13-year-old Mita, 11-year-old Aashitkumar and one-year-old Mitkulmar.

Within two, three nights they arranged their escape. The industry is deserted, the flat abandoned, the car is at a parking place.

Only Clothes

"Every time we passed a town on our way out of Uganda, our luggage was searched through several times," 13-year-old Mita says.

"Each time we were forced to leave our most valuable belongings, such as jewelry, radio, TV, etc. Today, all we have left is just about our own clothes."

After years of agony, hardship and suffering, the Indians from Uganda are still almost relieved to have escaped from there. They talk in a calm and matter-of-fact manner about the past—even about torture, maltreatment and assassinations.

The head of the family is one of those who managed to bring his personal documents out of the country. Absentmindedly he flicks through the now probably worthless bank papers that show that he used to be a wealthy man, that he had large savings that would have been more than enough to start over again anywhere in the world. He has no hope of ever getting any money back.

"Me and my wife have asked for work at a textile and garment factory," says Kantilal.

"Otherwise we will take on employment at a car factory, or anything. Anyway, we can not become businessmen until we have learnt the Swedish language."

Thirteen-year-old Mita is interested in school. She is wondering whether she could start Swedish school already after New Year. That would be fun, she thinks.

Gray Barrack

They arrived in Alvesta on Monday night. They were accommodated at the Board of Labour's barrack camp. The family disposes of two rooms, mostly consisting of beds and a table by the window. The walls are gray.

"This is still our chance for a new beginning. We shall take it, the Sawjani family says. All over the camp feverish activity prevails. Housemaids, nurses, directors and assistants are all busy as in an ant hill to organise everything."

Alvesta is a community on the map on the wall that was worn out by thumbs already on the first day. The newly arrived guests are queuing up for pocket money so that they can write to their friends and business associates and tell them that they are safe.

Maybe a house?

"Do you think it is possible for me to get money from the two life insurances, for which I have paid premium in Uganda, but which are in Indian and American companies? Then I might be able to buy a house here," says Kantilal.

Wife Hemlata is rushing off for a lesson in Swedish child care. Nurse Dahlia Andersson shows how to change diapers made of wadding and whipping children's food. She is assisted by Surya Gussing, who is Swahili-speaking and from Kenya, but employed by the Board of Labour.

"It is important that those who come here can learn how to take care of their children with Swedish facilities," Dahlia Andersson says.

"Otherwise they will not like it here, not trust us. When we took wet cotton cloths away from them instead of diapers this was perceived by many as if the world was falling apart for them."

"Each group has its special problems," says the Director Bo Möller at the Board of Labour camp in Alvesta. "We are expecting them to stay here for three months. We shall use this time to teach them what they need to know to be able to adjust to Swedish living conditions. We shall even try to entertain ourselves with plays and different field trips."

An elderly man passes by the map on the wall. He chose to come to Sweden instead of going to Canada with his son. This is the second time he is expelled out of an African country. He has business associates here in Sweden from whom he has been importing goods. Now he wants to see if he can help them with the export business.

Continued on Page 148

Ugandan Asian Expulsion: 90 Days and Beyond through the Eyes of the International Press

Stateless Asians Wait in Austria, Elsewhere
Future of Uganda's Exiles Poses Problem for Countries Who Gave Them Refuge

BY ROBERT CHESSYRE
Exclusive to The Times from the London Observer
Reprinted with permission, ©The Observer, London, December 14, 1972

VIENNA—An international crisis is gathering over the future of the stateless Ugandan Asians who were accepted for temporary refuge by European countries following their expulsion by President Idi Amin.

Nearly half those, now with no country, are here in Austria.

The crisis is twofold. Not enough nations have yet come forward with offers of permanent homes for the expelled Asians. Unless 2,000 places are provided by the end of the year, the United Nations High Commission for Refugees will have exhausted its special fund. And most of the stateless still look toward Britain for their eventual homes—whatever the official policy.

Countries like Austria, which made immediate offers of sanctuary, are facing the prospect of caring for long-stay stateless groups. Next time such an emergency occurs they may not volunteer so swiftly. It is a problem that also confronts Italy, Malta, Morocco, Spain, Belgium and Greece.

Traditional Role

It was largely because of Austria's traditional role as Europe's main refugee center that the majority came here. Standing on the borders of the Eastern bloc, she took in the first flood of refugees from Hungary in 1956, and Czechoslovakia in 1968.

If Britain sticks to her intention to reunite families now in British resettlement camps with stateless breadwinners when they finally achieve permanent homes, the numbers who will need to be taken in by other countries will be much greater than 2,000.

Pressure from welfare groups concerned with Asian resettlement in Britain will grow on the government to accept those whose immediate families have British passports.

At the largest refugee center 20 miles from here, where 700 Asians are housed, 150 of the men have their wives and children in Britain and another 150 have their closest relatives there.

Britain, First Choice

They all want to go to Britain. While they think they have a chance, many seem unlikely to accept offers of permanent settlement elsewhere.

A four-man Dutch delegation has been relatively successful in persuading Asians to accept the 250 places available to them in Holland. But one senses that this is mainly because the Netherlands is close to Britain. There are fears that the Swedish team due here will not find takers for all the 300 homes they have to offer.

The Danes have agreed to take a few Asians who are physically handicapped. The Austrians themselves are offering 200 permanent places.

This leaves 700 here whose prospects seem dismal.

The Asians crowd around any British visitor as soon as he arrives at one of the camps. My notebook was grabbed by people eager to write down for me the names of wives and children already in British resettlement camps.

One brought out a telegram from Southall: "Reknar is very sick, come soon." Another produced records of his four children's impressive achievements at school. "If I stay and work in Austria," he asked, "could they finish their education in Britain?"

A 24-year-old with a small beard and volatile hands told me quite bitterly: "I am the equivalent of head of family. My widowed mother, my younger brothers and sisters are in Britain. If I'd been four years younger, I could have gone in as a dependent. Now they are stranded, with no one to care for them."

Others there in a long, low concrete hut southwest of this city include Asians who have lately made the headlines by being deported from Britain.

Some of the stateless—though very few of them—have money. One asked the Dutch delegation if he could use his $12,500 to start a restaurant in the Netherlands. Another, ironically, owns a house in Enfield, Eng.

Barrack Blocks

The main camp is at a place called Traiskirchen. Here the Asians live in tall, battered barrack blocks built for soldiers of the Austro-Hungarian empire. They were used later by Hitler's troops, then by Stalin's. Today, besides the Asians, they house 900 East Europeans also seeking asylum in the West.

The three blocks—one pink, one gray and one ochre—are surrounded by high wire fences. It is difficult for visitors to get in; the authorities are on guard against agents of the East European secret police. Austrian police in gray uniforms stand at the entrance to the dining hall. I asked why they were there. "There are always police at refugee camps," I was told, "because sometimes there is trouble."

The Asians seem the last people to cause it. But to some extent they do—because they cannot make up their minds. When I was there, a coach had been waiting since 8 a.m. to take a group of them to temporary work on a sewerage pipeline. At 1 p.m. it had still not gone. Men were leaping on and off, driven into hopeless indecision by the fear that by taking one course of action they might jeopardize another.

Some in Village

Another large collection of Asians—200 of them—are at the village of Neuhaus in lower Austria. They keep themselves warm by stuffing big logs into ancient iron stoves and are jollied along by an Austrian woman with a riveting laugh.

She did refugee work during the Austrian civil war of 1934 and seems to have been at it ever since.

At Neuhaus the Asians' own leader is a thin, quiet spokesman who was Ford's main dealer in Uganda. He said his family was then worth more than $2.5 million. Now he organizes entertainment and hopes to start lessons for the children.

The rest of the Asians are scattered among several out-of-season hotels along the Danube in upper Austria. In spring and summer these places are filled with German tourists.

The Austrian government is allowed a daily amount for the maintenance of each Asian by the U.N. commission. The U.N.'s Austrian representative urges that nations offering permanent homes should not do so in a selective way.

"The Austrians did not select," he said, "when it was a question of saving life. Countries coming forward to help must not pick and choose, but should simply take people by numbers. Otherwise, Austria will be left with the duds. It has happened before."

He believes that the Asians will start moving in a better frame of mind once they accept the fact that Britain is not open to them as a permanent home.

And he added: "In 20 years I have never met a better crowd of refugees."

Continued from Page 147

Ugandans find hope here

The Dhanjis and their "host family" eat both lunch and dinner together. At noon, Rosmir cooks the traditional curries and other spicy dinners, but at night, it's American-style food cooked by an American housewife.

Hamburger Causes Woe

"We had tuna casserole and spaghetti and hamburger," Rosmir said. The hamburger caused a slight misunderstanding until the Dhanjis, who are Muslims, learned it was not made from forbidden pork.

Still, the main problem is a job for Mahmood. "I go to school. I learn better English. I get a job," he said.

And there must be jobs, housing and host families for the other Asian Ugandans already here and expected to come in the next month.

Hopes for Help

The going has been slow, admits Sangayya Hiremath, president of the local India League. But he is hoping that as the Wilmette family opened its home and heart to the Dhanjis, so will others.

Anyone willing to offer housing or a job to the refugees should contact Hiremath at the league offices, telephone 485-5162.

Many Uganda Asians face homelessness says London survey

By Derek Humphry
Reprinted with permission, ©Times Newspapers Limited, London, December 17, 1972

THOUSANDS of Asians who were forced out of Uganda by General Amin are finding it increasingly difficult to settle down in Britain. This is revealed in survey by International Voluntary Service in the London districts of Camden, Brent, Ealing and Wandsworth—four districts which were classified as "red" by the Government because they were already overcrowded and had huge waiting lists for homes.

The Government asked the Asian refugees not to live in those areas, but this policy was thwarted by: hostility in less crowded districts to the Asians joining them; the low rate of housing and offers of jobs; and the Government's refusal to order people where to live. A large proportion of the refugees have ended up in "red" areas.

International Voluntary Service organised the survey in conjunction with Co-ordinating Committee for the Welfare of Evacuees from Uganda—the group of 65 churches, welfare and charitable bodies who have been helping the Uganda Resettlement Board.

The report says the Resettlement Board did an effective job of receiving the Asians, but points out that not only are there 9,000 still living in 14 camps but the situation facing many outside "is a justifiable cause of anxiety."

Altogether 21,000 Uganda Asians used the board's reception centres, but many for only a few days. The board helped 4,500 to find accommodation and the Department of Employment found jobs for 2,100.

IVS workers surveyed 1,039 Asians in Camden, Ealing, Brent and Wandsworth, comprising 219 families. It found that 57 per cent of the individuals had tried to "make it" themselves by avoiding the camps.

The survey then broke down the Asians into those "settled" (permanent housing and clear plans for the future) and "unsettled" (living temporarily with relatives in unsatisfactory conditions and with no plans).

It found that 76 per cent were unsettled; with those in the borough of Ealing, which includes Southall, by far the most unsatisfactory. In the four boroughs there were 484 Asians facing ending of tenancies, eviction, or living in seriously overcrowded and inadequate conditions.

In Camden, a family of six was living in one room. They were ineligible for help because the husband was not a United Kingdom passport holder, while the rest of his family were. About one third of the Uganda Asian families in the borough had one member in a job. Of the 172 Asians surveyed in Camden, 122 were not settled.

About 1,000 Asian refugees have gone to Ealing. Out of 654 checked by IVS, 67 had moved away, 139 could be considered settled and 372 unsettled.

In Brent, there were 179 Asians unsettled and only 15 settled. Of the unsettled, 12 were under threat of eviction. Out of 112 employable people, only 42 had jobs. Some families were paying large rents—£30 a week was common.

In Wandsworth, 74 per cent were unsettled, and 39 per cent of them were either facing eviction or had unsatisfactory accommodation. Thirty-three Asians had found work and 56 were still job hunting.

The report adds: "In several cases in Wandsworth families are paying more than half of their income towards the rent. A dire example was the family whose income was £19; rent £16."

A continual criticism of the Resettlement Board has been its reluctance to take up offers of 7,000 beds in private homes. It accepted 1,600 offers, but the others were in areas considered too remote from chances of employment, or in the "red" overcrowded areas.

The IVS survey looked at 200 private accommodation offers and found that 30 per cent were still available, 22 per cent had not been checked out by the board, 13 per cent were in use, and five per cent had been used once.

The IVS report says that many Asians labelled by the board as "resettled" are, in fact, in dire need. It recommends that the board should urgently consider accepting continuing responsibility for assisting all Uganda Asians with problems.

But the board said yesterday that it did not have the facilities for after-care, which was left to local authorities. "As yet we have had no reports from them."

IVS says an effective counselling service is essential in the camps and outside, and it will play its part in this. "The problems of the London boroughs have now reached crisis proportions and 'solutions' are almost impossible," the report adds.

Another Cabinet decision is now required to resettle the Asians effectively. "There should be additional grants for permanent housing, bearing in mind the current housing crises outlined in numerous Shelter reports. The Asians have shown the necessary personal initiative. Many local authorities have shown immense goodwill. But do the Cabinet and Parliament have the political will to provide the necessary leadership and resources."

A traditional English Christmas for Asians in camps

From Penny Symon, West Malling, Kent, Dec 18
Reprinted with permission, ©Times Newspapers Limited, London, December 19, 1972

Father Christmas, 17-stone and riding on a "sleigh" converted from an airfield trolley, will enter the dining hall of the Uganda Asian resettlement camp here on Boxing Day to distribute presents to 266 children. In real life he is Mr Charles Buckett, the camp's catering manager. Tomorrow he takes delivery of turkeys for the traditional Christmas dinner, which he and a staff of 30 will prepare for the Asians on Christmas Day.

Mr Buckett said: "There will be no curry at all on that day; and the Asians who are vegetarians have said they will sample a little bit of turkey. They are all very excited about it."

A woman member of Mr Buckett's staff, 16-stone and 6ft 3in tall, has volunteered to play an ugly fairy. "It is wonderful how everyone is joining in", Mr Buckett said.

Most of the 561 Asians here are Hindus, the rest are Muslims and Sikhs, and there are five Roman Catholic families. Although Christmas has no religious significance for most of them, there are events planned in all the 14 resettlement camps. The 9,000 Asians in them are only too pleased to join in something they have never experienced, and which they see as part of the British way of life.

The only drawback, so far as the children are concerned, is the lack of snow.

Here, as in all the camps, a very full programme of events is planned. On Christmas morning each of the 4,000 children in camps will receive a bag of toys collected and given by the Variety Club of Great Britain, which is also collecting toys, and new clothing, and arranging outings and parties.

Sixty children from this camp were taken to a pantomime in London. There have been carol services and visits to town near by to admire the decorated streets.

On Boxing Day, after Mr Buckett's entry with the presents, many of which have been given by local churches, there will be a Punch and Judy show, a magician, a skiffle group, Indian films and cartoons.

"Local people have been very generous. One shopkeeper has given us 60lb of boiled sweets. The response has been wonderful", Major Colin Landells, the camp's deputy administrator, said.

Many Asians had received invitations to local homes at Christmas, he said, but he thought it would be better for them to stay together in the camp. "We are not stopping them going out: but I think they will have a better time all together here", he said.

But although most of the children are excited about the toys they will receive, all Mrs Prabhavanti Popat's eight-year-old son wants for Christmas is his father. He was crying today, as usual; his 10-year-old sister is constantly upset, too. They keep asking when their father will come.

Mr Gorhandus Popat is in a camp for stateless Asians in Vienna. He was refused permission to enter Britain because he gave up British citizenship for Ugandan in 1962. Mrs Popat, a British passport holder, writes to him daily.

There are 26 wives without their husbands in this camp. Many of the husbands are in the same predicament as Mr Popat. And many of the other camps also have wives in this situation.

Canon John Collins appealed to his congregation in St Paul's Cathedral yesterday to write to the Prime Minister asking him to allow the stateless husbands into Britain to rejoin their families. He has already written to Mr Heath.

Ugandan Asian Expulsion: 90 Days and Beyond through the Eyes of the International Press

Ugandan Asians find Canadian winter cold but people very warm

Reprinted with permission, ©Canadian Press, 1972
Published in the Ottawa Citizen, December 23, 1972

Canada's 4,878 Ugandan Asians are brimming with gratitude for a warm welcome by Canadians. However, Canadian winters and Christmas madness have left them cool,— but interested.

Because most of the Asians belong to religious groups which don't celebrate Christmas, many have been standing on the sidelines during the holiday season, watching with wide eyed interest as Canadians jam stores and shopping centres in the annual Yuletide rush.

Many of the Asians—mostly Moslems and Hindus—are familiar with Christmas only through white Christian missionaries in Uganda. Those who will be recognizing Christmas have found Canadian traditions "a pleasant surprise."

"At home, we don't have the family feast," says Zulfikar Alibhai, one of the 10 Asians who settled in St. John's, Nfld.

"In Uganda usually everybody goes to church in the morning Christmas day, then to the pub at night. . . the next day it's as if it never happened."

But while white Christians are a familiar sight in Uganda, white Christmasses aren't—many of Canada's new arrivals have never experienced temperatures below 75 degrees fahrenheit.

H. M. Gupta, chairman of the Regina Hindu Association, describes the reaction of the 26 Asians living there to three nights of below zero temperatures: "They couldn't believe that it could be so cold."

Bhanumati Patel, a newcomer to Portage La Prairie, Man. says:

"We came here with the intention of starting from the beginning. If we can just get used to the climate we'll be all right."

'Scared of slipping'

Ram Gupta, chairman of the Edmonton Hindu Society says the 140 expelled Asians who settled there find winter "not a very pleasant experience. They're scared of going out of the house because they might slip or catch a cold."

One Asian girl who came to Ottawa can sympathize. She recently slipped on an icy sidewalk, fracturing her knee.

But on the whole the first Canadian winter has offered the Asian expellees more ups than downs.

The department of manpower and immigration reports that of the 4,878 men, women and children who had arrived in Canada from Uganda by Dec. 15, about 1,400 have found work, 850 are awaiting jobs, 2,400—including dependent family members—are receiving temporary adjustment assistance and 200 are enrolled In manpower training courses with 111 on the course waiting lists.

By Dec. 15, the department reports, there were 10 Asians in Newfoundland, 146 in Nova Scotia, 70 in New Brunswick and 15 in Prince Edward Island. Six hundred and forty had settled in Quebec, 2,001 in Ontario, 214 in Manitoba, 573 in Saskatchewan, 225 in Alberta and 1,358 in British Columbia.

More eligible to come

About 1,500 Ugandans are still eligible to come to Canada because immigration officials in Kampala handed out about 6,300 visas. However, they may he visiting relatives on the way to Canada or have chosen another country to settle in.

Eleven welcoming committees, jointly funded by the secretary of state, provincial and municipal governments, were set up in major centres across the country, many before the first planeload of Asians arrived at Montreal Sept. 28. Only a few Asians remain in temporary living quarters in hotels and motels.

The emotional adjustment for the Asians is something else. The 90 days in Uganda between President Amin's, announcement of the expulsion and the Nov. 8 deadline he set were filled with grief. Many still fear for the safety of relatives and friends left behind.

Most of the Asians, however, have managed to remain optimistic about their future in Canada.

Coming to Canada for one young man was "like coming from Hell to Heaven. The people are so nice . . . should have come to Canada a long time ago."

AT HOME: The Rev. David Payne stands at the top of the staircase in Uganda Immigrant House with new arrivals and at bottom is one of his helpers, Sister Lucille Dumais of the Inter-Faith Welcoming Committee.
Reproduced with permission, ©Morris Edwards/Montreal Gazette

Ugandan Asians who left 'will not be allowed to return . . .'

Reprinted with permission, ©Daily Nation, Nairobi, December 18, 1972

KAMPALA, Sunday

UGANDA citizen Asians who left here when non-citizen Asians were expelled earlier this year will not be allowed to return, a Government spokesman announced today. He added that their property and businesses would be treated in the same way as those belonging to non-citizen Asians, and allocated to Ugandan Africans.

"It has been decided that the Ugandan citizens of Asian origin who abandoned their businesses and properties and left the country after the launching of the economic war will not be allowed to return," the spokesman said.

"There businesses in Uganda will be treated as those of the non-citizen Asians, and therefore advertised and allocated to successful Ugandan African applicants.

The spokesman went on to warn that Ugandan Africans would not be allowed to form companies in which non-Ugandans had a stake because this would "perpetuate the practice of window-dressing which the Asians who have now left were practicing."

The spokesman said that if the Government discovered that this directive had been ignored, the registration of the companies concerned and their trading licences would be cancelled. The Ugandans involved would also be regarded as "saboteurs of Uganda's economy," he said.

Ugandan family feels guilty it can't give on Christmas

By Terry Farrell
Staff Writer
Reprinted with permission, ©Minneapolis Tribune, December 25, 1972

This is the first year that the dark-skinned man, his wife and seven children have had a Christmas tree.

And they feel profoundly guilty about it.

For the man is Abu Bachelani, a Muslim, and one of the 75 Ugandan refugees who came to Minnesota last month. And for Bachelani and his family the tree, given them by friends in Minneapolis, represents a time in which they are forced to receive without reciprocating.

Bachelani's 17-year-old son expressed their feeling:

"Due to some financial difficulties we couldn't give Christmas gifts to those who gave to us — we're really ashamed of this."

The Bachelanis' tale is Horatio Alger's in reverse. They were fourth and fifth-generation Ugandans. Their "forefathers"—the children's great-great-grandfathers—went from India to the East African country 150 years ago, when Uganda, like India, was a British colony. They worked hard and became well-to-do merchants.

The owner of two fabric shops and a grocery store, Abu Ahmed, 48, was constantly busy with his businesses, traveling often from his home in Mbale into the bush country.

Gen. Idi Amin, who became president of Uganda after a coup in early 1971, changed all that. He declared that Uganda should be controlled economically by black men and decreed that most of the Ugandan-Asians, who were the entrenched mercantile and white-collar classes, had to leave the country by Nov. 8.

Holding no British passports, the Bachelanis could not go to England as did some 27,000 of the 75,000 Asians forced to leave. The Bachelanis instead chose the United States, one of the handful of nations that agreed to accommodate the refugees.

"We came to the U.S.," explained 17-year-old son, Mohamed Ali, "because of the language . . . Besides, there was no other place to go."

Except for Mrs. Bachelani, the family members have a working knowledge of "British," the language of Ugandan commerce. Mohamed Ali, who studied English in school, speaks the language most fluently.

Channeled to the Twin Cities by the Lutheran Council-USA immigration service, the Bachelanis are one of 20 Ugandan families of Asian descent who came to Minnesota Nov. 21.

Seventeen of the families have been supported by the Lutheran congregations in the metropolitan area. Two have been supported by Gustavus Adolphus and Augsburg Colleges. The twentieth family, in Buffalo, Minn., is sponsored by a Lutheran congregation there and by the Buffalo Rotary Club.

"The people of the church and neighbors are very hospitable and humble and they helped us in each and every way," said Mohamed Ali as his father nodded in agreement.

The congregation of Mount Olivet Lutheran Church, 5025 Knox Av. S., footed the bill for the Bachelanis' 16-day stay in a motel, found them a house at 4920 Knox Av. S., and aided Bachelani in his search for a job. Two weeks ago he got his first, cleaning up in Dayton's department store.

The Bachelanis, like others of the Asian immigrants interviewed this weekend, are settling into their American lives perhaps as well as can be expected given the flip-flop in their social and economic conditions.

There have been difficulties.

Muslims celebrate their Sabbath on a Friday. But, said Bachelani, "I can't do anything here."

He must rise at 4 a.m. and take the bus to be on the job by 6 a.m. He can not find the time—or place—to pray five times a day as prescribed by the Islam faith. So, he does nothing.

Food is another problem, both for the Muslim immigrants—who are the majority of the arrivals—and for the Hindus. Muslims eat no meat from pigs and are supposed to eat only meat from animals killed by Muslims.

Hussein Hirji-Walji, 22-year-old father of one, and some others in the Twin Cities get meat through a cooperative they joined. The meat is that of cows killed by a St. Paul Muslim and stored in a freezer until it is needed.

The Bachelanis, however buy meat at the local Red Owl. "Otherwise, we'd starve." Said Mohamed Ali.

Hindus are vegetarians. Many vegetarian provisions have been donated to them by the church groups, said Ramesh Joshi, 25. The supply of rice, beans, peas and corn given him more than a month ago has not yet been depleted.

And there are the minor irritants that may build a mosaic of life that is at best interesting, at worst difficult: Learning to drive on the right-hand side of the road; "pro-Noun-see-a-shun," as one immigrant phrased the language difficulty; American slang; and 20-below weather when one is used to temperatures that range from 68 to 78 degrees.

The immigrants watch TV; go to dinners at friends houses; some continue the hunt for jobs. They have aspirations and plans for the future.

At the Bachelanis, Mohamed Ali said he would like to finish 12th grade and then "go to university."

"But due to some financial difficulties I have to work now. I don't know how long it will take before I can go to school."

'Let these people in' plea to Britain

Reprinted with permission, ©Daily Nation, Nairobi, December 23, 1972

LONDON, Friday—HUNDREDS of stateless Ugandan Asians presently in European transit camps should be allowed to enter Britain, the committee which is co-ordinating efforts for their welfare said today.

The committee says that the United Nations camps in Italy and Austria hold "orphan" children stranded without parents and hundreds of husbands on whom relatives already in Britain depend.

Members who visited some of the 2,000 refugees there found 315 husbands with families in Britain, the Co-ordinating Committee for the Welfare of Ugandan Evacuees said.

Mrs. Mary Dines, one of the visitors, said she saw at least 30 children aged between five and 17 who were alone in the camps without mother or father.

One or both of their parents were either lost or still in Uganda, and the children could only legally enter Britain if both their parents were already there, Mrs. Dines said.

Mr. Douglas Tulbe, chairman of the committee, said they hoped for an urgent meeting with British Home Secretary Robert Carr, to press particularly for the admission of husbands with dependents in Britain.

The Guardian newspaper also said today stateless Ugandan Asian husbands, stranded in Europe and unable to join wives who are British citizens, should be allowed in.

The newspaper said that more than 200 Asian families are affected in this way. Describing the plight of the fathers, the paper said: "Refused passage on the British airlift which carried their wives and children to Britain, they were forced to travel to Europe.

"There they have remained in isolated refugee camps, cut off from their families, their only hope of reunion being a change of heart by the British government."

The paper said the government's only gesture came when, during a recent House of Lords debate, it was suggested that the wives and children might be sent to Ecuador or Bolivia.

Ugandan Asian Expulsion: 90 Days and Beyond through the Eyes of the International Press   *Page 151*

EDMONTON, CANADA

Snow and Christmas lights delight Ugandans in city

Reprinted with permission, ©Edmonton Journal, December 26, 1972

For Canadians Christmas is an exciting time of year but for the recently arrived Ugandan refugees now living in the country it is all very bewildering.

Some of them know about Christmas but have never celebrated it.

In Edmonton, many of the 128 expelled Ugandans had their first taste of Christmas at a party and dinner Saturday night. The affair, sponsored by the Ugandan Committee of Edmonton, Catholic, United, Anglican and Unitarian churches, was attended by more than 200 Ugandans and Edmontonians.

The food—provided by churches and individuals—included all the trimmings from pickles through turkey with dressing and there were lots of candies and oranges for the children.

Looking around the brightly decorated church hall in the basement of McDougall United Church Jalaladin Dhanji, of 10659 107 St., said much of the Christmas tradition was new to him although he knew some of it because of the British he knew in Uganda.

Mr. Dhanji, his wife and two sons in November explained that most of the Ugandans are members of the Khoja sect of the Mohammedan religion and their main holiday is Khushiali. On this day, he said, the brother invites his sister and her family to his house for a feast and they exchange gifts.

But in Uganda there are no street decorations, no Christmas trees and his kids had never seen Santa Claus.

Another thing entirely new to him is snow.

"I never saw snow, except in movies, until I got here," he said. Which is not too unusual since the lowest temperature he ever experienced was 75 degrees above zero.

All the children at the party received presents. For the younger ones there were small stockings of oranges and candies, while all the kids five years old and up were presented with a gift voucher from Woodward's for a pair of skates.

Donna Archibald, whose group Gold Bar Neighbor got together with three churches and provided enough food for 90 people at the dinner, said the main idea for the party was to provide an opportunity for Edmontonians to meet the Ugandans and we hope they will establish friendships."

"We're also trying to stress to the Ugandans that different religions can work together.

Dr. Ram Gupta, chairman of the Ugandan Committee of Edmonton, said after the dinner, that although most of the refugees are getting settled they are still facing some problems. The most acute problem, he said, was that some still had relatives left in Uganda and they don't know if they are alive or dead. Others have members of their families in England, Pakistan, India and other European countries.

Another problem facing them is either finding employment or switching to a more appropriate job. The last Canada Manpower figure revealed that in Edmonton 30 of the 46 employable persons had found work.

Many, Dr. Gupta said, are having trouble adjusting to the winter.

Winter for them "is not a very pleasant experience.

"They're scared of going out of the house because they might slip or catch a cold," he said.

Ugandan refugees making adjustment to new life

By JOHN LUNDQUIST
Associated Press Writer
Reprinted with permission, ©Minneapolis Star, December 25, 1972

A CHRISTMAS TREE in a Moslem family's parlor may seem strange, but it is symbolic of the adjustments being made by Husein Hirji-Walji, 21-year-old head of a family of seven.

The tree and Christmas season are no stranger to 75 Uganda refugees who have arrived in this area since Nov. 21 than are cold weather, the necessity for dressing warmly or the types of food that can be obtained in Minnesota.

Nor is the adjustment of Husein and his family any greater than that of Sat Paul Chada, who only a few months ago was a wealthy man with a thousand sawmill employees under his supervision, and three personal servants in his home.

He is awaiting word here that he has passed a physical examination and can have a job as a coin box checker for the bus company.

The 75 refugees, most of them of Asiatic birth or extraction, received orders a few months ago from Idi Amin, dictatorial president of Uganda, to be out of the country by Nov. 8.

The alternative was internment in a concentration camp or, for many of them, death by torture.

Lutheran Social Service of Minnesota handled arrangements for the group that came here. All are relocated in the Twin Cities with the exception of a family of five the city of Buffalo, Minn., is sponsoring; and two brothers sponsored by Gustavus Adolphus College at St. Peter.

The job of finding homes, jobs and clothes and of helping the newcomers adapt to American food has fallen largely on church congregations, although several businesses have helped with supplies and employment.

Walji has imposing head-of-family responsibilities. Living with him in a first-floor duplex near the downtown area are his wife, Kaniz, 17, and their month-and-a-half old daughter Batul; his mother, Fatmabai, and three brothers, Shabir, 19, Hasanain, 17, and Zulfikar, 14.

Augustana Lutheran Church, three blocks away, is shepherding this family, with support from four churches in Bloomington.

Hussein had a job at Northwestern National Bank in downtown Minneapolis within a week of his Nov. 29 arrival.

He is studying electricity at Vocational High School. He works part-time and Shabir works full-time in Augustana Home for senior citizens. The younger boy, "Zully," goes to school where he gets special help in making the transition to American life.

Hussein's teen-age wife gets help in tending her baby and housekeeping in the six-room duplex from her mother-in-law.

"It is hard to get used to the cold outside," she admits, recalling recent record low temperatures of -20.

Because Moslems do not eat commercially slaughtered meat, the family has arranged, through a friend, to get a supply slaughtered by a Moslem in St. Paul.

Mohammed Ahmed, a former textile shopkeeper and accounts clerk, heads a family of nine. He's 42, spare at about 115 pounds and has boys that range taller than him. The youths are 20, 19 and 18, while four girls range from 7 to 14.

They're under the wing of two churches, Central Lutheran and Mount Olive. Ken Born, a realtor and member of Mt. Olive, arranged to have the family move into a one-and-a-half story Cape Cod style home in St. Louis Park. Central Lutheran is paying the rent for three months and a layman is handling utilities up to $100 a month.

Ahmed hops on a bus or walks 3 miles in milder weather to his job as a night manager at a grocery store on Excelsior Blvd.

The eldest son has landed a job as carpenter at a sash and door firm, and the other children are attending school.

Mrs. "Mim" Wedel, wife of Pastor Alton Wedel of Mount Olive, is a home economist and is coaching the mother and daughters in making American foods palatable.

A group of three young men includes Sat Paul Chada and Rameschandran Joshi, who are Hindus, and Vicky Fernandez, a Catholic of Portuguese and Ugandan parentage. They room in a modern apartment building in Fridley.

With the aid of three churches, they're also trying to find employment. Chada is awaiting word on a physical exam he had last week.

Page 152   *Ugandan Asian Expulsion: 90 Days and Beyond through the Eyes of the International Press*

AUSTRIA BRIGHTENS UP CHRISTMAS FOR ASIAN REFUGEES

Reprinted with permission, ©Daily Nation, Nairobi, December 27, 1972

VIENNA, Tuesday—A BLEAK Christmas in Austria for some 900 Ugandan Asians was brightened by gifts of candy and clothes—and for some a dinner with the Austrian Roman Catholic primate.

United Nations refugee officials say they would have liked to make it a bonanza celebration but funds are badly depleted.

The Asians in Austria are one of the largest contingents of the 3,500 stateless expelled from Uganda last month now living in refugee camps throughout Western Europe supported by the United Nations.

The majority have no immediate prospect of a permanent home and UN officials here say countries appear to be showing little interest in taking them.

Although the Austrians have made every effort to cater efficiently for their needs they are still isolated by language, culture and climate.

The UN allows 28/- a day to cover basic everyday requirements, and occasional extras.

The overall upkeep throughout Western Europe is costing about £30,000 daily and officials say funds will be non-existent by February.

"It's really serious," commented one refugee official. "We can't use extra funds for Christmas candies for it's out of our budget."

However, clever economising by refugee centres here, bolstered with small extras provided by the international community in Vienna and the Austrian authorities, meant Christmas was Christmas—even for Muslims and Hindus.

All Asians in Austria got a small Christmas package of sweets and some clothes.

In the week preceding Christmas, Asian children joined East European refugees at parties and received small bundles of toys from an Austrian Santa Claus.

Religious differences were forgotten and religious authorities in Catholic Austria went out of their way to ease the plight of the Asians.

Some of the refugees working in Austria complain of low wages and of work which they say is beneath their social standing.

Some living in the Traiskirchen Camp, 16 miles south of Vienna, went to the Southern Austrian province of Carinthia to work in factories and as labourers.

They complained bitterly of the wintry climate and their incomes, and said the labourers' tools were cursed in their religion. Many also faced great language difficulties.

"They tell us they are traders and intellectuals and don't want to be employees," a representative of the UN High Commission here told reporters.

"Integration is a slow process. They didn't like their jobs, they felt isolated and weren't satisfied with the money," he added.

"Things can't be settled in one day," say camp officials. "We realised there would be problems but we have to get these clearly in focus."

U.S. Urged to Take More Uganda Asians

News Compilation, January 8, 1973

UNITED NATIONS, N.Y., Jan. 7—United Nations and United States officials have been told that 1,800 stateless Asians expelled from Uganda last fall are still waiting in European camps for resettlement and that their predicament is becoming grave.

Their plight was underscored by John F. Thomas, director general of Intergovernmental Committee for European Migration, who flew here from Europe last week in the hope that the United States could be induced to accept 200 to 300 Asian families in addition to the 1,000 refugees it has already accepted.

Mr. Thomas met here with Secretary General Waldheim, in Washington, with Secretary of State William P. Rogers and influential Congressmen and, finally, with representatives of the seven private Christian, Jewish and nondenominational agencies that have found homes and jobs for refugees who arrived last fall. Twenty-seven-thousand Asians who held British passports were admitted by Britain, leaving Mr. Thomas's committee and the United Nations to care for 6,600 stateless persons.

Mr. Thomas said that the chances that Washington would agree to admit more families were good. He said that the agencies concerned understand that unless the Asians are settled promptly, they may be forgotten and become in time, impersonal "cases," not people.

Response Was Swift

When the first call for help for the Uganda Asians came, the response from the agencies was swift. One agency, the Lutheran Council in the United States, received offers of help from 400 congregations in four days.

"We had many Midwestern congregations calling which had to look in their atlases to locate Uganda," said Donald Anderson of the Lutheran Immigration and Refugee Service. "We didn't know if the families would be black, brown, white or mixed. There were no problems."

Mr. Anderson added emphatically that the Lutherans had only a share of the program shouldered by the seven. The six others are United HIAS Service, a Jewish organization; the United States Catholic Conference; Church World Service, which is Protestant; and the Tolstoy Foundation, the International Rescue Committee and the American Fund for Czechoslovak Refugees.

300 Asian husbands to be allowed into UK

News Compilation, February 23, 1973

Mr Carr, Home Secretary, has decided "as an act of humanity" to allow into Britain about 300 Asian husbands expelled from Uganda to be reunited with their families here.

Many of the men renounced their British passports when they took out or attempted to take out Uganda citizenship. But they were made stateless by President Amin's expulsion orders.

Their wives, who had kept their British rights and had not tried to become Ugandan, were allowed into Britain with their children. They have been without a breadwinner and many were thrown upon British resources.

Mr Carr said in a parliamentary written reply yesterday that, unlike responsibility which had been accepted for Asians with United Kingdom passports expelled from Uganda, Britain had none similarly for others expelled. Some went to third countries and others to camps in Europe organized by Prince Sadruddin Aga Khan, United Nations High Commissioner for Refugees.

Mr Carr went on: "The high commissioner has today informed me that, of the 3,600 refugees from Uganda accepted into his camps in Europe, he has already succeeded in placing 1,100 in 16 different countries. About a thousand others are being processed for permanent settlement." The High Commissioner was discussing with various governments the resettlement of the remaining 1,500 still in European transit camps.

Mr Carr said he had also told the high commissioner that "we shall look sympathetically at about a hundred other Ugandan refugees who have arrived in this country, but have not yet been admitted for settlement, and also at a smaller number in Europe whose circumstances present strong compassionate features."

Aided Hungarians in '56

To Mr. Thomas, "it was a gigantic interfaith undertaking—truly ecumenical."

"The Uganda program was conducted as an emergency operation much like the program that Mr. Thomas's committee conducted in 1956 to help 200,000 Hungarians who had fled their country. Much of his organization's efforts, Mr. Thomas says, are less dramatic—moving, for instance, Europeans who want to make a new life overseas.

Many of them head for Australia or Latin America.

Ugandan Asian Expulsion: 90 Days and Beyond through the Eyes of the International Press   *Page 153*

Uganda Asians still present difficulties as Stradishall refugee camp closes

From Christopher Walker
Stradishall, March 21
Reprinted with permission, ©Times Newspapers Limited, London, March 22, 1973

An emotive reminder of Britain's continuing efforts to cope with the difficulties caused by the enforced arrival of 27,000 Uganda Asian refugees was provided today when the resettlement centre here was closed. From next month it will be taken over by the Home Office and turned into an open prison.

The former RAF base at Stradishall, Suffolk, with its barrack blocks and neat terraces of houses, was the first transit camp to be opened by the Uganda Resettlement Board last September. This morning it became the eleventh camp to close, leaving five to accommodate the 3,638 refugees still to move into the community.

The speed with which the refugees have left the camps has come as a welcome surprise to officials and confounded the predictions of some pessimists. But a survey I have just completed of the remaining camps scattered in remote corners of Lincolnshire, Kent, Berkshire and Warwickshire shows that many of the most difficult cases remain.

This view was confirmed by Mr Reginald Davies, a former Director of Civil Aviation in East Africa, who is now the board's administrator for the Northeast. He has overall responsibility for the two Lincolnshire camps, Faldingworth and Hemswell, which are the ones likely to remain on a long-term basis.

Mr Davies, who has more than 800 refugees in his care, said today: "Things are going to get tougher and tougher from now on. We are very much into the hard core in both camps, particularly after the concentration of Asians from other centres which have been closed."

In every camp large families, classed as those needing houses with four bedrooms or more, are presenting the greatest difficulties. At Faldingworth, half the 487 refugees still unplaced are in families of seven or more. A recent calculation shows that only 2.8 per cent of the board's remaining list of council houses can take large families.

Efforts have been made to persuade the larger families to split up but, because of the Asian's traditionally strong family ties, these have been unsuccessful.

Mr Mohamed Mughal, aged 55, a former game warden and garage owner, rejoined his family recently from a stateless refugee camp in Austria. He has two wives and 13 children aged between 17 and two. The wives and their children are now living in separate blocks on the USAF base at Greenham Common.

Once the owner of five cars and a professional big game hunter, Mr Mughal's only valuable possession is a jacket made of leopard and goat skins. He is a proud man, who is obviously unhappy to have to take any form of charity but insists that his wives must live in houses within a few hundred yards of each other.

At the camp, he divides his day between playing billiards and reading Gujerati papers and books, and seems to have given up all hope of finding a job. "The officials are trying to send me to a house in Scotland but I will not go there", he said. "Three friends of mine who did, wrote and told me it would be suicide, it is so cold there."

Group Captain Peter Bird, administrator at the resettlement camp at Lingfield, Surrey, which closed on January 12, 1973, saying goodbye to Uganda Asians who were moving to another camp near Newbury, Berkshire.
Reproduced with permission, ©Times Newspapers Limited

Persuading refugees to take up the many offers of housing in Scotland has proved difficult. Of the 315 houses offered by local authorities north of the border, only 130 have been claimed. One at Wick, complete will full coal cellar and larder provided by the Rotary Club and the attraction of a small Asian community, has been offered at all camps since November but there have been no takers.

"A friend of mine said that they call us brown dogs up there", one young Asian student said.

Every camp notice board has letters from Asians happily resettled in Scotland on prominent display; Scottish evenings and film shows have been organized and elaborate attempts made to convince refugees the climate is habitable.

The difficulty of placing the elderly is something officials can do little about at present. With about 200 refugees leaving the camps each week they are still concentrating on the more manageable difficulties. One resettlement officer said: "When we get down to the really hard core in two or three camps, the top brass in London is obviously going to have a lot of hard thinking to do."

Although most of the refugees feel indebted to the Government there are signs that this is beginning to wear off among some, particularly those who have been forced to make a number of moves.

At Hemswell, I was surrounded by a crowd of more that thirty angrily shouting complaints. Mr Rasul Ali, a student aged 20, whose father is in a Swedish refugee camp said: "I would like to ask why they are transferring us from one camp to another. If they tell us to move again, we will sit down and refuse to go anywhere."

The cost so far of the resettlement and reception process is estimated at around £7m, but I understand that at least one board member feels that too little is being done to find out what has happened to refugees once in the community.

RESETTLEMENT CENTRE STATISTICS

Centre	Date of Opening	Date of Closing	Capacity (Initial/revised)
Kensington	6 September, 1972	23 February, 1973	250
Stradishall	18 September, 1972	24 March, 1973	2,000/1,500
Hemswell	28 September, 1972	5 October, 1973	1,150/950
Houndstone	30 September, 1972	16 February, 1973	950
Greenham Common	1 October, 1972	30 June, 1973	1,600/1,400
West Malling	4 October, 1972	15 January, 1974	840
Tonfanau	7 October, 1972	28 February, 1973	1,400
Heathfield	9 October, 1972	2 February, 1973	1,200/1,100
Faldingworth	11 October, 1972	15 May, 1973	685
Lingfield	13 October, 1972	15 January, 1973	950
Plasterdown	15 October, 1972	13 December, 1972	800
Maresfield	17 October, 1972	28 February, 1973	650
Piddlehinton	19 October, 1972	24 November, 1972	500/400
Doniford	23 October, 1972	19 March, 1973	1,225/1,125
Raleigh Hall	27 October, 1972	20 January, 1973	430
Gaydon	28 October, 1972	16 July, 1973	830

Amin's Uganda Features Unique Public Giveaways

By Andrew Torchia
Reprinted with permission, ©Associated Press
Published in The Washington Post, March 11, 1973

NAIROBI, Kenya—It was a slow, sunny day in Kampala, the kind of day when Ugandans doze under banana palms oblivious to their government's directives against miniskirts and gun-carrying imperialist agents posing as Christian missionaries.

President Idi Amin was about to give away a hotel, but he hadn't decided to whom. The man who expelled 40,000 Asians from his country has been masterminding the distribution of perhaps $400 million worth of Asian property to black Ugandans. The distribution of some 3,500 abandoned businesses is nearly complete.

Gen. Amin, driving his own Jeep through downtown Kampala, decided to intervene personally in the allocation of the Speke Hotel, which was worth $125,000 in the busy days before Amin banned tourists.

According to witnesses, Amin spoke extemporaneously in English and Swahili to a large group of applicants. Uganda owes a lot to its security offers, who are responsible men and should be rewarded for their service, the president said.

Amin paused and surveyed the crowd as if making up his mind. Suddenly he pointed to a Lt. Col. Bogere and said: "There's a responsible man who should have this hotel."

Witnesses said Bogere, chief army medical officer and one of the few in the audience who had not been brandishing blue-and-white forms applying for the Speke, looked around as if to say: Who, me?

Bureaucracy has been cut to a minimum in the property distribution aimed at creating an instant new African middle class that operates, if not entirely owns, Uganda's commercial enterprises.

Applicants carrying proof of citizenship and their bank balances gather on the sidewalk. A Cabinet minister arrives in a limousine and open-neck shirt. Applicants thrust their forms forward and shout down each other's claims as if attending an auction. The minister moves down the block, giving away a business every few minutes.

New proprietors get front door keys on the spot.

As formerly Asian-owned shops reopen gradually, there are disappointments on both sides of the counters. Some new storekeepers find nearly no stock on hand to sell. Customers accuse some Ugandans who took over shops of trying to make a killing by profiteering on scarce items.

If the government sticks to its promises of compensation for dispossessed Asians, the new shopkeepers will eventually have to pay up. Meanwhile, the government has assumed long-term control of thousands of abandoned properties, and there are difficult questions concerning taxes and rents to be paid by the new operators, and prior bank mortgages to be honored.

Canada raises Uganda quota

By GUY DEMARINO
Reprinted with permission, ©Southam News Service, Canada, June 7, 1973

OTTAWA—Canada, which accepted 5,500 Ugandan refugees late last year, has agreed to accept a few more—and they are starting to come.

Of the 1,500 people still housed in Austrian refugee transit camps, after being expelled from Uganda last fall, 70 have already received permission to come and are due to arrive this month.

Another 280 applications still outstanding are being processed, with the eventual arrivals due to be completed within the next three months.

However, Manpower and Immigration Minister Robert Andras said yesterday he does not expect, nor would he want, all those awaiting for resettlement in Austria to emigrate to Canada.

The ones being allowed to come, he said, are "special consideration" cases of family reunifications or other such hardship cases. Some of those being allowed to come, in fact, have relatives who came to Canada during last winter's massive airlift of Ugandan Asians to Montreal.

"It's only a trickle," said Mr. Andras. And this time, unless a special request is made, Canada will not pay for the transportation of the additional refugees from Austria. During the 1972 airlift Canada had chartered special aircraft for the purpose and had paid for them, spending about $4 million to receive and resettle the 5,500 Uganda Asians.

Canada has received representations concerning the plight of those in the Austrian transit camps from the United Nations refugee commission, Mr. Andras said, but I can't be expected to accommodate them all. It is understood that other nations are in the process of accepting some of those remaining refugees.

Many of them are stateless, which permits a relaxation of the standard Canadian immigration regulations, and almost all of them waited in Uganda until the last moment, hoping that President Idi Amin's expulsion order might be rescinded.

WASHINGTON, D.C <u>Family Settles Down in Oxon Hill</u>

Presbyterians Aid Ugandans

By Alice Bonner
Washington Post Staff Writer
Reprinted with permission, ©Washington Post, June, 22, 1973

A family of Ugandan refugees arriving here last week as charges of an Oxon Hill United Presbyterian church, found comfort and the promise of security for the first time in seven months.

Rajabali Bhimji, his wife, Maleksultan, her 71-year-old mother and the couple's four children had been living in an Italian refugee camp since last November. With only one week's preparation, members of the Southminister United Presbyterian Church rallied to meet their adopted family's immediate needs of clothing, food and housing and the long-range needs such as jobs for the adults and schooling for the children.

"Our goal is to help them become independent as soon as possible to get them settled in their own apartment and adapted to the community," said the Rev. Richard E. Ittner, Southminister's pastor.

Although they arrived in this country penniless, their air fare paid by the Church World Service, the Bhimjis are not helpless. Bhimji, a professional tailor, and his wife, a seamstress, left behind a 22-year-old business in Uganda.

Far from being poor, they owned three houses and two automobiles where they lived in Mpigi, a town of about 150 near the Ugandan capital city Kampala, the elder daughter, Rosie explained. They could take only their personal belongings when they left Uganda, she said.

Rosie, a self-assured 18-year-old, was an accounting student in Uganda and hopes to continue her training here, she said. In addition to English, taught in Ugandan schools, and her native Indian tongue, Gujarati, she speaks French and Swahili, learned from Asian, African and Hindu schoolmates, and Italian, learned in the refugee camp near Naples.

Her mother and grandmother speak no English and the father very little, so Rosie has become the family spokesperson and interpreter.

The Bhimjis are not bitter over their dispossessed state, and harbor no longing to return to Uganda, she said, only hope for their future in the United States.

"My heart is broken over what happened to us, but if we returned it would just happen again," she said. "The church people have been so nice to us that it (the past) doesn't matter."

"It is very nice here, we even have a swimming pool," added Shafic, 16, speaking of the William Ross home where the Bhimjis are temporarily housed.

"This family's spirit is amazing, considering the way they have been uprooted." said Jan Klein, who with her husband Jody, heads the church's refugee resettlement committee.

"It was the highlight of my seven-year ministry in this area to see the Bhimjis arrive at the airport and to see the church mobilize in an effort of compassion for people not of our culture," Mr.

Ittner said.

The refugee family are not Christians: they are Moslems of the Ismaili sect.

"We have made every effort to see that they pursue their own religious preference including taking them to a mosque in Washington on Sunday," the Presbyterian pastor said.

"Their religion doesn't allow them to eat pork, and we are careful to respect that when various church members invite the family for dinner," Jody Klein said.

"Our involvement is simply that we are concerned about people and about justice. The main thing we wanted to do was get them out of the camp," Mr. Ittner said.

The United Presbyterian Church nationally has helped 75 Ugandans, temporarily sheltered in European countries where they were airlifted by the U.N. last fall, to enter this country.

Ugandan Asian Expulsion: 90 Days and Beyond through the Eyes of the International Press   *Page 155*

Canada's welcome: Ugandans find a place to call home

By E. KAYE FULTON
Star staff writer
Reprinted with permission, ©Toronto Star syndicate, July 23, 1973

Less than a year ago Jagdish Patel had a thriving gas station business and the only law practice in northern Uganda.

With, he says, an annual income of more than $24,000 and a sprawling four-bedroom house, he was considered one of the elite in the small town of Gulu.

Today Patel puts in a 12-hour day as a land title searcher at $125 a week, and goes home to a small basement apartment in Scarborough. His is the story of many Ugandan Asians. Instead of going from rags to riches, he has lost not only his money, but his business, his home and his country.

The 38-year-old Ugandan, his wife, Bharti, and two sons are among some 660 Asians, expelled from Uganda last year by President Idi Amin Dada, who have settled in Metro Toronto.

Finding a suitable job in a country with an unemployment problem was no easy task for Patel, who was told in job interviews that he was either over-qualified or inexperience in the Canadian way of life.

Assisted by Operation Arrival, a government-sponsored program designed to help the newcomers find jobs, housing and other personal necessities, Patel tackled the problem of supporting his family with the same energy that all his fellow refugees in Canada have displayed.

Canadian officials have been astonished by their enterprise. Of the 660 Ugandans in Toronto, Operation arrival reports that 92 per cent of the heads of households are now employed, all are housed, and there is not one case of welfare.

While fewer than half of the immigrants—described by a Canadian immigration official as "the cream of the crop"— have found jobs in their own field of employment, Operation Arrival officials say there is a general feeling of satisfaction with the jobs they did find.

Patel's attitude toward his family's new life and his need to support them reflects the feelings of many of the Ugandans. "We like to work," he said. "It was a bit of a shock to find out it would be difficult to make ends meet even though I knew I might not make much money at first.

"But while I don't particularly like my new job it is still a good beginning for me. I would go into any job provided I was sure I could support my family. I don't care how much money I make."

Patel, a British citizen, learned that his qualifications as a lawyer were not recognized in Canada, but he has decided to seek requalification in December, a process that will take about three years.

Forced to leave $100,000 behind in Ugandan bank accounts, he was allowed to bring only $110 plus a few articles of clothing to Canada.

But his main concern now is to see that his family adjusts to their new and bewildering life.

"It will be easier for my two sons to adjust," he said. "Already they have picked up a Canadian accent and a few native expressions. They are beginning to forget about life in Uganda.

"Over there we had a comfortable living. My wife had a full-time housekeeper and my sons had numerous playmates they will probably never see again," he said.

"But there was always the threat to our security. Twice before I felt I was threatened by armed guards in my office. My family was told we would be put in a concentration camp. If I had stayed any longer I wouldn't be alive today."

Patel has accepted the fact with equanimity. "Sure it was difficult to leave such a good life," he added. "But I feel that in the long run it will be better for my children. Here they can be secure."

Patel's two children, round-eyed and shy in front of strangers, are easily adapting to their new life.

Nine-year-old Mayank, a student at Corvette Junior Public School, came first in his Grade 3 class last year, a commendable feat considering he started in March. He is taking special summer courses to catch up on background material for next year.

Nimish, 6, will enter Grade 1 this fall. Both boys are fluent in English and are active in soccer, football and Mayank's new-found love, hockey.

Mrs. Patel, from Anand, India, is finding it more difficult to adjust since she spends most of her time at home.

Since coming to Canada, Mrs. Patel, who has degrees in science and education, has suffered severe arthritis in her hands from the cold weather and will be unable to work for at least six months. Medical bills for treatments add to their financial burden.

Coming from a town of 3,500, the Patels find Toronto life "very pressing and very cosmopolitan."

They still have some connections with their old country, as friends drop over to their apartment to talk over old times and plan their future.

Byarali Somani, 36, who once owned a hardware business in Kampala, the capital of Uganda, now works in a factory in Toronto.

Another friend, Mawji Mohamed Jaffer, 29, left behind a dairy farm and plantation that employed 150 people, and is at present searching for a job in Toronto.

They don't expect to see their homes again.

"But we should be grateful that our families are still intact," Patel said. "So many families were separated. My dream now is to get Canadian citizenship and bring over my parents, who are both in London, England, to share our new home."

Where Uganda's Asian refugees went	
Britain	27,000
Canada	6,175
United States	1,600
Austria	70 (plus 1,500 in transit)
Sweden	319
The Netherlands	253
Belgium	30 families (plus 428 in transit)
Denmark	small number of handicapped people
Norway	114
Sweden	300
Switzerland	200

No more Ugandans here—Andras

By GUY DEMARINO
Reprinted with permission, ©Southam News Service, Canada, July 9, 1973

OTTAWA—The federal government has no intention to allow any more Uganda Asians into Canada, Manpower and Immigration Minister Robert Andras said Monday.

He told newsmen that his department had not prepared, nor was it planning, any special program of admission for any of the 4,000 Ugandans presently in a temporary refugee camp in Austria, and apparently anxious to settle in Canada.

Mr. Andras said that if they wished to apply under Canada's immigration rules "we would examine their applications," but indicated no special concession would be granted to them.

He made no reference to the anti-immigration backlash of the past federal election campaign, but said: "There's unemployment in Canada now, you know?" The minister added that only in the case of families being split up—with some members already in Canada and some in Austria—some relaxation of the immigration rules would be considered.

"They didn't apply to me," he replied when asked whether any representation had been made to the Canadian government on behalf of the Ugandans still in European refugee camps. he also denied that the United Nations, as alleged, had been pressuring Canada to accept some of those refugees.

The same day Mr. Andras indicated the government's unwillingness to accept any more immigrants from Uganda, the Commons was given an idea of the cost of bringing 4,425 Ugandans to Canada last fall, via an emergency airlift program.

Supplementary estimates tabled Monday by Treasury Board President C. M. Drury showed that $3,965,000 was set aside by the government as the cost of "assistance to Asians from Uganda."

Cost breakdowns were not given, but the largest single cost will certainly be the chartering of the aircrafts that brought 4,425 Uganda Asians to Montreal. At about $60,000 per plane, the cost of 27 special charters would be $1.6 million.

Beside those brought into Canada by charter, another 453 Ugandans came on their own, making the total of arrivals from that African country 4,878. About 6,000 Canadian visas were given out.

$1 million for one Ugandan but rejection for others

By CHERYL HAWKES
CP Staff Writer
Reprinted with permission, ©Canadian Press, August 3, 1973

Madatali Bardai flashes a ready smile behind the counter of his East Indian grocery store in Toronto. "Business is very good here in Canada. Yes, so easy to make business." "Why," he adds "in three years I will be a millionaire."

Mr. Bardai had the same kind of store before in Kampala, Uganda. He employed 35 people, he says, and he worked eight hours a day. He lived in a new $50,000 home and he drove to work in one of his seven cars. Now, the 35-year-old father of two runs his small Toronto store with the help of his wife Shamin. Together, they work 16 hours a day, living in a rented apartment above. "But those 16 hours are many times more happy than those eight in Kampala he says.

Looks all day

The Bardais are among the 5,657 Asians who arrived last fall after their expulsion from Uganda by President Idi Amin. They are among the happier statistics, what immigration officials like to describe as one huge success. Of the 2,500 who arrived looking for work, fewer than 400 are said to be still jobless.

For that group Canada has not been a bright new life. Take Pyarali Lalani, 41, a Kampala retailer who has hunted fruitlessly for work in Toronto since his arrival. "Phone him either very early in the morning or late at night," cautions a friend. "He looks for jobs all day."

He arrived penniless last autumn, forced to leave his capital behind. Now, at 7:30 a.m., he was preparing for another day's job hunting. His wife had been working for four days and his daughter, 16, since last November with an insurance company. "I don't like her to work.. I want her to go back to school. She was in Grade 12 in Uganda.

For Mr. Lalani, initial optimism has diminished and he wonders. "I think it is because of my skin, you know."

There are store signs seeking workers sometimes but "when I ask the manager about that job, he says: 'There are no jobs here.' " And he has been told repeatedly he needs Canadian experience.

A cop-out

Government officials agree that is a common roadblock for Asians seeking jobs. Says one: "It's a catch-all phrase, the great cop-out when some potential employer doesn't like the look of someone, and it doesn't violate the Human Rights Code."

Still, the over-all economic absorption rate has been high. The Ugandan themselves have helped ensure that. "The Ugandan Asians have been very good refugees," Freda Hawkins says. Dr. Hawkins was one of two national co-ordinators overseeing the entire movement of the expelled Asians. She is a senior immigration consultant with the secretary of state.

They're cheerful, polite and friendly. They've settled in with a minimum of complaint and a willingness to take various kinds of employment and get started. "It's very obvious that this is a community with a lot of drive."

Many—even those with Ugandan citizenship who were officially entitled to stay—foresaw the expulsion and made arrangements to get some of their wealth out of the country.

Madat Shariff, 33, began looking for a business as soon as he arrived in Toronto last fall with his wife and their 15-month-old daughter.

Business Oriented

He formed a partnership with another refugee, Umed Jess and a Canadian and set up an importing business similar to the one he ran in Kampala.

"The vast majority of these people are business-oriented," says Dave Ashby of Toronto, a director at the Ontario Welcome House. "This was the major factor which led to their expulsion from Uganda, wasn't it? They practically owned the country." The influx of experienced people will be good for the country, Mr. Ashby said. "They'll make good—no doubt about it."

The rush of Ugandans in the fall has slowed to a trickle. Now, many of the newcomers are considering sponsoring other members of their families—who are in Britain or transit camps in Europe.

Manisha Vyas is looking forward to a family reunion in Canada. A sparkly immaculately-groomed 20-year-old Manisha was the only member of her family holding a British passport. She watched the rest of the family shipped off to refugee camps in Europe and then boarded a plane alone for Canada.

A former secretary, Manisha now works as a clerk in the accounts branch of an Ottawa department store. She has sponsored the family's entry into Britain and they are settled in London. Manisha met her roommate, Rosemin Kara, 22, on one of the 31 chartered planes the government used to bring the Asians here. They decided to come to Ottawa, where Rosemin works as a keypunch operator in a data centre.

The government spent close to $4 million on the movement and settlement of the Ugandans. By far the largest expense was the chartered flight from Kampala. Other costs were inland transportation from the special reception centre at Longue Pointe, Que., to other centres, hotel accommodation and living expenses while the Ugandans looked for housing and jobs. Included in the over-all cost was the $20,000 the government spent on 11 welcoming committees set up across the country to assist the newcomers during the first six months. Funds for the centres also came from provincial governments and voluntary agencies.

The Ugandans have generally become well established here in a short time. But for most, the move to Canada represents a long step down the economic ladder—a fact they accept cheerfully.

Mr. Bardai recalled the family's departure. My wife was crying and sobbing. We practically had to carry her onto the plane. She did not want to leave. "We lived in our new house only two months. I left behind seven brand new cars . . . so many things . . . so much to leave behind. But we are happy here, yes, much happier."

A few Ugandans have insisted on repaying all expenses incurred on their behalf including the charter flight from Kampala, immigration officials say. The overseas flight was definitely free, says Ranjit Hall, chief of immigrant and migrant settlement in the immigration department. The rest is repayable "sometime, but we are not pushing."

Toronto got the lions share of the refugees. More Ugandans actually settled in Vancouver, 1,400 compared with Toronto's 805. But most of the 2,400 Asians who went to Ontario passed through Toronto on their way to smaller centres. Montreal received about a major share of the 700 who settled in Quebec. Two hundred and seventy-five settled in the Maritimes and slightly more than 600 went to the three Prairie provinces.

Education has not been a problem. Besides coming from an affluent urban environment, almost all speak English and some speak French. By June, 130 were enrolled in manpower training courses, with about 30 on waiting lists. Adapting to the new environment—the Canadian winter excluded—has been generally easy for the adults and even easier for their children.

Asked how his children like school, Mr. Bardai laughs. "My children? Why I think they are half Canadian already."

Andras praises Asians

News Compilation, November 2, 1973

OTTAWA—Ugandans who came to Canada a year ago following expulsion from their homeland by Gen. Idi Amin have made a rapid and successful adjustment to Canadian life, Immigration Minister Robert Andras said Thursday.

"Most of these immigrants are now employed in almost every type of industry or endeavor; some in jobs commensurate with their professional qualifications, while others are undertaking their own business enterprises.

"Only 83 Ugandans are currently registered as seeking employment, a fact which offers conclusive evidence of the positive attitude, initiative and skills that these people possess," Mr. Andras said in a news release.

Of the 5,761 Ugandan immigrants, only 142, including dependents, still are receiving financial assistance, he said.

This compared with the 3,300 who were temporarily assisted after their arrival last year.

Ugandan Asian Expulsion: 90 Days and Beyond through the Eyes of the International Press

Ugandan refugees: A success story

'They helped themselves,' says a neighbor. 'They didn't sit and cry'

By JACK BREHL, Star Staff Writer
Reprinted with permission, ©Toronto Star syndicate, May 15, 1975

BELLEVILLE, ONTARIO, CANADA

Amirali Damji feels a special poignancy when he reads of the fears of refugees from Viet Nam.

Not quite three years ago, a Ugandan soldier threateningly held a pistol to Damji's head.

At the time, Damji had his own drapery store in Mbale, with $100,000 worth of stock, and owned three houses.

He, and his wife and three children and his mother were forced to flee Uganda, with $120 and what suitcases they could take on the chartered airliner. He locked his store door, gave the key to an agent, a Ugandan African lawyer, and hasn't heard a word about his property since.

"I don't know if he's alive or dead," he says.

"But at least," he adds, referring to the fears in Viet Nam, "we did escape safely, with our lives."

Canada sent planes to bring over 6,000 Ugandan refugees. Bryce Mackasey, then minister of manpower and immigration, met the first ones and presented the children with toy Mounties and teddy bears. The refugees were loaned money for transportation in Canada, and given purchase orders worth about $40 per person for winter clothing in Canada.

Federal and provincial officials worked closely together and with local committees to counsel, plan orientation programs, line up jobs and shelter.

Then the tumult and the shouting died, as tumult and shouting have a way of doing. The speeches and special ceremonies ended. Most of us forgot about the refugees.

Just fine

Two and a half years later, how are they doing?
Just fine, generally, it turns out.
Surprise. Something has worked the way it was supposed to.

"An unqualified success," says Shantichandra Shah, a Scarborough lawyer who was chairman of the Metro Toronto committee set up to work with the 660 Ugandan refugees who went there. Success stories abound. Almost no refugee is out of work; many now own their own businesses.

Federal manpower officials are making a detailed follow-up study. So far it is incomplete and confidential. But they can say: "The unemployment rate is just about zero. So far as we know, none are on welfare. These were extremely able people, many of them entrepreneurs, and they stepped off the planes looking for work."

Both refugees and Canada gained, it seemed.

Belleville's a pretty good place to talk to the refugees. For one thing, they are not hard to find. There are only four families here. Originally, more than a dozen came here, as a conscious effort was made to spread the refugees widely in Canada. But from here and other small cities, there has been a pronounced shift to the metropolitan areas.

It's understandable. That's where friends, relatives and coreligionists are, and business opportunities.

Balibir Manku, the first arrival in Belleville, a former accountant with a French oil firm, has gone on to become an auditor in Toronto with the provincial sales tax division. Madat Hajiani, who worked in a variety store here, now has his own grocery and post office branch in west Toronto. Mohan Sond is now an accountant in an Ottawa bank.

For another thing, it is sort of intriguing to think of Belleville as the warm-hearted host town for dark-skinned refugees. It has 35,000 residents and is in traditionalist-minded United Empire Loyalist country; there are not many mosques around and while there are 20 million Ismaili Moslems, religious followers of the Aga Khan, in the world, it's doubtful any lived here before Akbar Mawani hove on the scene in 1972. There have been times when to be strangers in small-town Ontario was not the surest route to comfort.

Yet Akbar's wife, Gulshan, can say: "Everything has been good, nothing has been bad."

Fair tribute

This is a fair tribute, considering that she and Akbar are among the very few Ugandan refugees who are unemployed right now. Akbar lost his job as an accountant in early March when the legal firm he worked for broke up; Gulshan was one of 450 workers laid off by Northern Electric four months ago. He had been making $150 a week, she $160 a week.

He has written 40 applications for work. They are concerned but not panicky yet; they are saving people and "do not smoke or drink, which gives us a certain economic advantage," says Akbar.

What Belleville had was people, like Jim Staveley and Fred Deacon and Kathy Cunningham, Jack McIntosh and Barbara Trupp.

Akbar and Gulshan Mawani and their three daughters were trying to get settled on their first day in a Belleville apartment when there was a knock. It was Kathryn Cunningham, who is married to a security guard, and who lived across the hall, and who was a pretty typical Bellevillian, UEL back to when her great-great-great-great-grandfather settled nearby in 1787.

She wanted to know if she could be of any help— "How," asks her husband, Norris, "could anyone pass by a family in that predicament?"— and she was. She would take them shopping and explain Canadian things and even teach Gulshan ordinary chores.

"Why, do you know when she came here poor Gulshan hardly knew how to iron or wash dishes," says Mrs. Cunningham with a resonant laugh.

That was not an uncommon problem. Many of the virtually penniless refugees had been successful merchants and businessmen; their wives were used to servants and possessions. At Masaka, Akbar was head of the science department at a government school; he and Gulshan had two servants, two cars.

The shift from affluence to initial penury at age 41 was traumatic. "At Masaka, I was secretary of the community welfare society, people

came to me for help. Here, people were giving us clothes and furniture," Akbar says.

Akbar's qualifications as a teacher were not accepted here. He decided to go to Loyalist College to study accounting (he completed his two-year course in three semesters and ranked first in his class).

Gulshan got a job as a sewing machine operator at Fred Deacon's sportswear plant. She started work on Dec. 22 and three days later, on Christmas Day, "Mr. Deacon and his brothers came to our apartment. They must have had nearly $100 worth of gifts for us—flowers, clothing, food, toys."

Amirali Damji had a somewhat similar experience. Within two weeks he got a job as a salesman in Jack McIntosh's drapery store, the second oldest business in Belleville. McIntosh found an apartment for the Damji family and furnished it.

Barbara Trupp, of the Seventh Day Adventist church, was everywhere, the refugees recall, arranging clothing donations, dinner invitations. For months, the Mawanis had dinner out once a week with local families.

First person

Jim Staveley was the first person most of the refugees had much to do with at first. He is 69, and was a counsellor with the local Manpower office. He knows everyone in the Belleville-Trenton area and he is involved in many community activities. His present consuming interest is development of the Quinte-Hastings Recreational Trail, which has 600 miles of present and potential trails.

He was retired but the Ugandan program was his second call out of retirement. Earlier he had been in charge of the successful settlement of 60 Tibetan refugees in the area.

Staveley says there wasn't much trouble winning acceptance for the refugees because they were both able and willing. Norris Cunningham also remarks: "They helped themselves, they didn't just lie down and cry, they just needed some guidance and then they did it themselves."

The other two families in Belleville are:

—The Jamals. Ahmed, his sister, Nasim, and his brother, Shiraz, all were working within a week of arriving. Their family had owned a car dealership and other businesses in Jinja. Ahmed, who managed a bus company in Uganda, is a mechanic here.

—The Kamrus. Lila Kamru, a 23-year-old bachelor, brought his mother and sister. He is an apprentice plumber.

The refugee families all say they have run into no hostility whatever. Their children have fitted in well at school.

They have had their first wedding in Canada: Nasim Jamal, who met and married Damji's brother, Nizar. They live in Toronto.

And they've had their first baby born in Canada, a son of Ahmed Jamal.

Continued on Page 159

Hard work key to success in Canada—East Asians

By DON THOMAS
Reprinted with permission, ©Edmonton Journal, November 29, 1976

Get a job, any job to give yourself an income while you learn the language and the customs of your new home.

Work hard.

Accept that Canada is going to be your new home and avoid forming cliques that put distance between yourselves and your new neighbors.

That's the advice offered Vietnamese refugees from people who came here themselves as refugees six years ago when Idi Amin ordered East Asians out of Uganda.

Between September, 1972 and March, 1973, about 200 Ugandans came here, 90 per cent of them Ismaili Moslems with backgrounds largely in business and technology.

Within six months of their arrival, most were self-supporting, most had jobs and their own accommodation, says Dr. Ram Gupta, former chairman of the Uganda Committee.

"They are a highly enterprising group," says Dr. Gupta.

His committee was disbanded in April, 1973, because there was no more need for it .

Some of the Ugandans have come very far indeed.

Take Nazmin Nanji, 26, of 15801 89th Avenue, the first to arrive in Edmonton. He had only the $10 in his pocket that immigrations officials gave him when he landed at Montreal.

Today he owns seven small stores and an import-export distributorship with warehouses in Edmonton and Toronto. He employs 30 people and has real estate interests as far as Denver.

"Canada is a country that has accepted me." He says. "When I walk down the street, people accept me as a Canadian, not as a foreigner."

Success hasn't come easily to Nab Nanji. For the first few years he worked seven days a week. He still goes to work at 7a.m. and fills in for workers who are absent.

"I was willing to take a gamble," he says. "If I saw something that was a 50-50 risk. I would want to take it. There is so much potential in this country."

But what counted when he needed it, he says, was help from the people of Edmonton.

"The friends I made here then gave me the moral support, helped me to adjust to the conditions. Moral support, that's what you need to make the adjustment."

Mr. Nanji married in 1976 and recently became a father for the first time. Last year, he became a Canadian citizen.

Had Idi Amin not come to power, Azim Jeraj, of 9444 73rd Street, eventually would have taken over a family empire including tea and sugar plantations, a factory and other businesses.

All were confiscated by the Ugandan government and Mr. Jeraj and his family came to Edmonton with only a modest sum deposited in a British bank.

For a while, he helped his father run a small gift shop, then he was in partnership at a Langley, B.C. motel and for a year he worked as a carpenter.

Today he's an insurance agent for New York Life where he has climbed into the circle of the Million Dollar Round Table of agents writing more than $1.25 million a year in policies.

Last year he married an Ismaili girl from Tanzania who is studying computer science at the University of Alberta and this year he became a Canadian citizen.

His advice to the Vietnamese refugees is to work hard, and to accept that Canada is your new home.

"Don't stick to your own community, don't make a group of your own." Says Azim Sarangi, 25, chief accountant at F.G. Bradley Co. Ltd., a meat processing firm.

"If we just stuck to our own community, we wouldn't have been looked on very well. It doesn't create a good impression on the Canadians. Explain your culture."

Mr. Sarangi's parents were in retail and wholesale businesses in Uganda and were "very, very rich." They landed in Montreal with $70.

His first job here was as a warehouseman earning $310 a month. Later he got an accounting job at Northern Canada Power Commission and started at F.G. Bradley as an accounting clerk.

In August he married a girl studying computer science at the U of A. He has a sister in St. Albert who's a teacher, a brother in Edmonton who's a geologist, and in the U.S., a brother who's a medical doctor and a married sister.

"At first we stayed with my sister in St. Albert. We had some major problems at first but the people in St. Albert were just super."

Nizar Hudda is a partner with Taj Kassam in The Leather Place with five stores in Edmonton and one each in Red Deer and Regina.

Taj Kassam came to Edmonton early in 1971.

Mr. Hudda had been a partner in a men's wear store in Kampala. When he came to Edmonton he first worked in a bottling plant, then leased and ran a Mohawk service station.

He and his wife both worked there, putting in 14 to 16 hours a day before selling out and buying into The Leather Place.

Mr. Kassam had a car dealership in Kampala and managed to sell much of his property there before leaving.

When he came to Canada, he arrived in Vancouver and tried to get into the car business. No one would have him.

One man told him that while he was well-qualified, he would be a lousy salesman because of his color.

Later Mr. Kassam set up a used car business of his own and the same man, now unemployed, came looking for a job. Mr. Kassam felt obliged to say he was overqualified.

Mr. Hudda's advice to the Vietnamese is to "take a job, anything you can get as long as you can make a living. Even if you are an accountant or doctor, get a job first."

Adjusting to the cold is hard for Ugandans

Reprinted with permission, ©Edmonton Journal, January 15, 1974

In Uganda, the cool clear waters of Lake Victoria sparkle under sunny, hot weather year-round.

There are 150 Ugandans, in 50 families, living in Edmonton now whose only chance for a January swim is at an indoor heated pool, sheltered from the 20 degree below zero temperatures outside.

Nazim Nanji, 21, an accountant at Alberta Giftwares Ltd., used to count swimming in the lake that forms the source of the Nile River, among his favorite past times.

Since being expelled from his East-African homeland in 1972 along with thousands of other Asians living there, Mr. Nanji has had to adapt to a completely different set of climatic conditions.

This is his second winter in Edmonton, and he said yesterday he's become used to the cold.

Last winter was a different story.

"It was tough," he said.

"Then, he didn't have a car to get around in. He had to wait for buses, and walk where he wanted to go. That meant wearing thermal underwear. This year, having a car means no thermal underwear; just going out of the house to get to the car, then a second short trip from car to office.

He admitted last winter was "a surprise" to him.

But now that he has adjusted to the cold he wants to learn to skate. Only his workload on a university course towards certification as a registered industrial accountant is stopping him, he said.

Mubarak Ali, also 21 and an accountant at the Northern Canada Power Commission, said his first winter was also one of adjustment.

"Last winter I found it cold," he said. "this winter it doesn't seem as bad."

He said those of his countrymen most bothered by the cold are the older ones. These include his parents, who are in their 40's.

One senior member of the Ugandan community who doesn't find the winters too bad, is D. D. "Dec" Kapoor, a security officer at the Provincial Museum and Archives of Alberta, and father of two.

Continued from Page 158

Uganda refugees: A success story

Their children are making plans. Anis Mawani, who is completing Grade 13, wants to study architecture. Shiraz Jamal, 24, has just finished his accountancy course at Loyalist College. Nadir Damji, 19, who recently completed Grade 13, wants to go to college to study restaurant and hotel management.

The three Mawani girls are Girl Guides and their mother, Gulshan, was a Guider in Belleville—as she was in Uganda—until she went on to shift work.

Still, there is not yet an impression of roots having been put in place. All four families still are renting. There is a pull towards Toronto, where there are thousands of Moslems.

"We are still trying to get settled," says Shiraz Jamal. "It's not that we are homesick, or that anybody's missing anything; it's just fine here.

"But you don't start from scratch, start all over, and get settled in a couple of years."

Ugandan Asian Expulsion: 90 Days and Beyond through the Eyes of the International Press

'Took cream for crummy jobs'
Canada blasted for Ugandan Aid

Reprinted with permission, ©Canadian Press, July 26, 1978

OTTAWA (CP-Special)— An article published in a British professional journal states that Canada, through selective humanitarianism, skimmed off "the cream of the crop" when President Idi Amin expelled 52,000 Asians from Uganda in 1972.

One of the authors said he felt it was "a cynical attempt—certainly utilitarian—on Canada's part to find people to fill low-grade jobs that native Canadians did not want."

In Ottawa, James S. Cross, who was acting assistant deputy minister of immigration at the time, said: "It's just not true."

He said everything happened so fast, it was impossible for Canada to be selective.

The article, by Cecil Pereira of the University of Winnipeg; Bert Adams, University of Wisconsin, and Mike Bristow, of the Social Science Research Council of the University of Bristol, compares the status of the 29,500 Ugandan Asians who settled in Britain to the 6,500 who went to Canada and the 10,000 who went to India.

In a telephone interview, Bristow said Canada deliberately "excluded the sick, unemployable and unskilled."

Instead, it selected young, well-educated healthy Ugandan Asians who could "settle into Canadian society more easily," he said.

However, he said, it would be wrong to assume that this emphasis on skill meant that the immigrants got jobs equivalent to their skills.

Instead, interviews showed that 90 per cent of the immigrants had obtained jobs in Canada that were "below their qualifications."

Commenting on the accusation that most of the immigrants wound up under-employed, Cross said "this happens with every refugee movement."

He said however that within two or three years of their arrival, most of the refugees were in the types of jobs for which they were best suited.

A news statement by Routledge and Kegan Paul, publishers of the journal Ethnic and Racial Studies, quotes the report as saying that "most Ugandan Asian refugees believed that they had been selected to settle in Canada."

"In contrast, most Canadian citizens and government officials believed that immigration procedures had been relaxed to respond to a human need.

"A few well-informed officials, however, believed that Canada acted out of self-interest, not out of consideration for the refugees' plight.

Canada showed heart on Ugandans

Editorial
Reprinted with permission, ©Toronto Star syndicate, July 27, 1978

Perhaps we don't deserve any medals for doing the decent thing, but Canadians sure don't deserve to be characterized as cynical and selfish for having opened their doors to Ugandan Asian refugees in 1972.

In what looks like a new version of a study that has been rattling around for some years, three academics in an English journal accuse Canada of skimming "the cream of the crop" of the 52,000 Asians driven out of Uganda by President Idi Amin and using them to fill low-grade jobs that native Canadians didn't want. The writers are Cecil Pereira of the University of Manitoba, Bert Adams of the University of Wisconsin and Mike Bristow of the University of Bristol.

The study makes it sound as if we hypocritically paraded our humanitarian virtues while callously exploiting the poor refugees.

Well, the study is wrong.

If you think back to 1972, you will recall that the Ugandan dictator gave the Asians only a short time to leave the country or face his unpredictable wrath.

While many of them held British, Indian or Pakistani passports, thousands of them were stateless persons with nowhere to go.

The United Nations High Commission for Refugees appealed to Canada to take as many of the "hard core" stateless refugees as possible.

And we did. We took 645 of them, more than Britain, India or any of the other Commonwealth countries. We did more than that. We admitted more than 6,500 Asian Ugandans in a very brief period of time.

And we did it well. We sent special planes for them. We set up a special staging area outside Montreal where refugee families received free medical treatment, orientation lectures on Canada and language classes.

When they scattered across the country, local citizen committees greeted them, helped them find housing, advised them on jobs. In fact, it went so well that immigration expert Dr. Freda Hawkins of the University of Toronto described it as a model that should be copied for all immigrants.

Meanwhile, unemployment was rising in Canada. Some Canadians were alarmed and argued that with a 6 per cent unemployment rate Canada should not be admitting refugees.

But Prime Minister Trudeau replied that if Canada were to open its doors only when it was easy to do so then "we don't have much merit as a government and Canadians don't have much heart if that is their attitude."

Yes, we did pick young, healthy, well-educated heads of families because we believed they could adapt to Canadian ways most easily. But we also included the sick, the old and the frail members of their families.

And yes, many of these fine people were underemployed. Businessmen did end up sometimes working in factories and engineers were

Uganda Beckons, but Those Exiled Are Cautious

By DANIEL J. WAKIN
Reprinted with permission, ©Associated Press, April 25, 1993

Africa: Some are invited to reclaim their property. But successful recovery has been mixed because of residents' resistance and an ailing economy.

KAMPALA, Uganda—On Sept. 21, 1972, Kiran Bhimjiyani fled with nothing but a suitcase, abandoning his sports car and a warehouse full of peppers and tea.

The import-exporter was among 70,000 Asians expelled by dictator Idi Amin so he could "Africanize" the economy. Most were of Indian descent, and many were citizens.

Now, Bhimjiyani and a few other Indians are returning, invited to reclaim their property by a government desperate to revive the shattered economy. Their success in recovering property has been mixed, and some have met resistance from black Ugandans.

Jim McCoy, an American adviser to the Departed Asians' Property Custodian Board, said early this year that 2,700 claims had been received for about 7,000 Asian-owned businesses, and 1,740 properties had been rejected.

Among the recovered properties are sugar plantations, textile mills and breweries—large operations that President Yoweri Museveni hopes will spur the economy.

Only 500 to 1,000 of the Asians intend to live in Uganda. Many have settled into new lives in England, Canada and the United States. Others worry about Uganda's history of instability.

They also encounter problems, however sincere the government's invitation.

"There's a lot of resentment from the local people," Bhimjiyani said. "I will probably give it six months."

He spoke of harassment by government bureaucracies and the reluctance of black Ugandan businessmen to by goods from an Asian. Asians report some threats from black Ugandans who took over the abandoned properties.

Tenants of property returned to Asians face eviction or higher rents. Many simply do not pay for lack of money, and there is little a landlord can do. Half of the non-payers are government offices and officials.

One such landlord in Suresh Ghelani, who works as an accountant in London. The government internal security department occupies two of his family's houses.

"What is the point of saying, 'Come back, take your

Continued on Page 162

employed as draftsmen. However, it isn't because we wanted it that way. It was because they had to take their chances with the rest of us in weathering hard times.

We aren't auditioning for the role of angels, but looking back, we sure did a bang-up job on behalf of the Ugandan refugees. What's more we're glad, because they sure made fine citizens for Canada.

Ethnic Discord
Asians Return to Hope and Hostility in Uganda

By TAMMERLIN DRUMMOND
Times STAFF WRITER
Reprinted with permission, ©Los Angeles Times, August 17, 1993

Expelled 20 years ago by Idi Amin, they are starting to reclaim their land and property. But much has changed since they left.

KAMPALA, Uganda—Sherahi Jaffer had just opened a $1.5-million hotel in downtown Kampala when Idi Amin ordered all Asians to leave the country within 90 days.

"Someone from the military had told me I was a fool to build the hotel because they were just going to take it away from me," said Jaffer, 68, the Ugandan-born son of an Indian cotton trader who immigrated around the turn of the century. "But I never thought they would just take our property without compensating us and throw us out."

Yet on Aug. 9, 1972, Amin did just that. Accusing Asians—namely Indian and Pakistani immigrants—of exploiting blacks and "milking the economy," the former dictator stripped them of everything they owned, then deported them. More than a third of the 70,000 people affected were Ugandan citizens.

Jaffer, then a member of Parliament, joined the Asian exodus to Canada, Britain, the United States and India. Accompanied by his wife and six children, he eventually resettled in British Columbia and bought a poultry farm there.

Now he is among the 2,000 Asians who have returned to Uganda under a new government policy to reclaim the land and buildings that they left behind two decades ago. The 8,000 properties affected—now worth about $800 million—include mansions, apartment buildings, commercial complexes and tea and sugar plantations, many of which are empty and in a state of utter disrepair.

The official policy to return expropriated property actually began in 1982 under then-President Milton Obote. But it was only last year when the World Bank threatened to withhold a $125-million structural adjustment loan to Uganda that government officials began acting in earnest. Hoping to finally close this chapter in the nation's history, the authorities have set an Oct. 30 deadline for submitting claims. After that, any property that has not been spoken for will be auctioned off.

Many Ugandans believe the return of Asian investors is a crucial step toward rebuilding a nation still reeling from decades of civil war. Up until 1972, Asian entrepreneurs and industrialists were the backbone of the Ugandan economy, controlling key areas of trade and commerce.

But others resent the Asians' return to their former positions of economic dominance.

"A lot of people are bitter because Asians are taking back what they thought had become theirs." said Margaret Ndekera, a 35-year-old black Ugandan businesswoman. "Some people have even burned up buildings when they found out that they were going to be repossessed."

So far, about 2,000 of the confiscated properties have been returned to their pre-1972 owners. Entire blocks in downtown Kampala have changed hands, sparking a renovation frenzy.

But more than half of the properties have yet to be claimed, according to the Departed Asians Property Custodian Board, a government-appointed panel that acts on compensation requests.

Mumtaz Kassam, an Asian attorney who represents dozens of clients seeking repossession, insists that government officials should be doing more to locate the legal owners.

"We've asked them to at least make up lists with the addresses of the properties, but they say it would cost too much," said Kassam, 36, who first returned in 1986 to reclaim her family's 200-acre coffee farm outside Entebbe.

Forming a potentially volatile backdrop to the government's policy are racial tensions rooted in Uganda's colonial past.

Long before the arrival of the British in the late 19th Century, Indian merchants based in Zanzibar controlled much of the trade between East Africa, the Arabian peninsula and India. In later years, British colonials imported indentured Indians to build the Ugandan railway.

From the late 19th Century to the end of World War II, a key element of British colonial strategy was to promote the entry of Asians into the commercial sector while at the same time blocking the development of African trade. While Asians were granted exclusive rights to buy and market local produce, blacks were denied the same opportunities and relegated to peasant farming.

Over time, the gulf between the two classes widened, fueling anti-Asian sentiment. And by 1972, the pent-up frustration of black Africans were ripe for exploitation by Amin.

"Amin spoke the language of nationalism," Mahmood Mamdani, an Asian political scientist, said in a 1992 speech. "At a stroke, the 1972 expropriation sliced off the dome of local privilege. . . ," added Mamdani, who was himself expelled.

But the move also plunged the country into economic chaos.

Many firms quickly collapsed due to lack of capital, dwindling inventories and a lack of business experience on the part of the new owners. Within three years, the government was faced with a slew of bankrupt businesses and an economy in shambles.

"Shops were given to people who didn't even know where to order the new inventories from," Ndekera said. "Everyone just thought the money was coming from heaven."

Still, despite the terror that Amin would later unleash on the Ugandan people, many black Ugandans hold up the 1972 expulsions as one of the few positive legacies of his regime. For the first time, they argue, black Africans had access to commercial markets.

Amin used the Asian properties to create an elaborate system of political patronage. He doled out the choicest sites to the military and distributed the leftovers in a national lottery. Each successive government in turn redistributed the properties to its own political supporters. Consequently, many of the homes and businesses are now occupied by civil servants and military officers.

The repossessions have pitted these current occupants—many of whom have been renting from the government for as little as 10% of market value—against the returning owners.

In some cases, the two sides have managed to resolve their differences. But other times negotiations have ended in eviction. Some tenants have flatly refused to budge, even threatening violence, according to some Asian owners.

Meanwhile, many tenants complain that owners have raised rents to force them out. But owners like industrialist Mayur Madhvani counter that all they are asking for is a fair return on their investment.

"What we're saying is let us fix up the property to make it better for you, and then after that we'll have to charge you some more rent," said Madhvani, 44, one of five brothers who own a multimillion-dollar empire that includes a 22,000-acre sugar factory, a brewery, textile business and other assorted real estate. We not saying we want to throw you out."

Yet for tenants like Shaban Matovu, the end result is often just that.

Back in 1973, Matovu said, the government gave him a license to operate a restaurant in a building downtown that had once belonged to an Asian businessman. For the past 20 years, he said, he has kept up the building and invested $65,000 of his own money in equipment.

But on July 12, the owners appeared with a court order telling him to vacate the premises. On a recent afternoon, two men armed with shotguns guarded the entry denying access to the two-story complex.

"I came back one day to find it all locked up and chained," Matovu said. "I didn't even have a chance to get my things out."

Despite the more than 2,000 properties repossessed so far, only about 400 Asians have come back to stay. Most of these are businessmen and industrialists who left millions of dollars of assets behind.

"Most people come, sell off their property and go back to wherever they came from," said Ruth Namirembe Ohje, a spokeswoman for the Departed Asians Property Custodian Board. "I guess many of them don't want a repeat of their experience in 1972."

Ugandan Asian Expulsion: 90 Days and Beyond through the Eyes of the International Press

Expelled Asians take wary step back to Uganda

Reprinted with permission, ©Telegraph Group Limited, London, September 15, 1995

Some of the thousands who fled from Idi Amin's terror have returned, but they have learned to be cautious, Louise Tunbridge reports from Jinja.

MAYUR Madhvani's business card bears the Mahdvani family logo—a gilded cog wheel—and seven company addresses: two in Uganda, five abroad.

Their expulsion from Uganda by Idi Amin has taught a lesson of caution to Asians, like them, who have returned. Never again will they commit quite so much to one place.

The former 70,000-strong Asian community now numbers no more than 5,000. Most have gone for good.

Those who did come back keep one foot outside the East African country, mindful of the horrors of the past and every wary of the future on the volatile continent.

Private security guards man the barrier at the start of the immaculate dual carriageway leading to the 20,000-acre Kakira estate, the original heart of the Madhvani empire, just outside the town of Jinja.

The spacious family residence, known as "the bungalow", conceals its rather garish decor behind thick, flowering bushes.

Mr Madhvani, 46, was born in this house and fled to England with the rest of the family in 1972. No Madhvani children have been born here since then, however, and none is likely to be. His children are still in England, mere holiday visitors to the old homestead.

"When we left, we expanded our business interests. We're no longer having just Uganda as our base," he says. "We're coming and going here. If there's stability, the way the kids talk is like Uganda is the family base. They'll be investors here, they'll come and see their assets, see whether they're doing well."

They certainly are. Their derelict industries handed back by the government have sprung back to life. Today, the Madhvanis contribute 14 per cent of Uganda's economy and pay eight per cent of tax revenue.

Kakira sugar factory, the core of the business, crushes 3,000 tons of cane a day, cut by hand by labourers in the vast plantation. The panoply of companies include Nile Breweries, two tea estates, soap and oil factories, a steel mill and packaging plant. About 80,000 people depend on Kakira for their livelihood. It is a town within a town, with 11 primary schools, a 100-bed hospital, welfare shop and recreational facilities for employees.

The group is shortly to be listed on the local stock exchange. "Our thinking has changed," admits Mr Madhvani. "We see ourselves as custodians for the general public. Let them feel part of it. Once you're involved, you protect it more."

Visibly orchestrating the return of the Asians is the hand of President Museveni, who has bent some of his own rules to win them back.

Impatient to increase the flow of private capi-tal to the still convalescent economy, he dismisses the need for Asians to go into partnership with indigenous Ugandans.

"I look at Asians as very friendly forces," he says. "Some of these Asians and foreign investors are a hundred times more useful than hundreds of Ugandans."

He has close personal links with the Asian business community. A member of the Madhvani dynasty, Nimisha Madhvani-Chandaria, has been appointed first secretary to Uganda's embassy in Washington, with the brief of attracting and promoting new investment.

But in the trading areas of Kampala there is a bitter feeling among Ugandan merchants that the government is selling off the family silver. "We're not happy, we Africans," said a shopkeeper. "It's shameful to see this economy. We're not self-dependent. Asians are taking all the money from us and we're looked at as slaves in our own country."

Rents have been increased by as much as 10 times by Asians returning to reclaim and rehabilitate their property. Far from appreciating the injection of private capital, many Ugandans resent the government's policy of not compensating the Asians and keeping them out.

The accusation of "economic imperialism" levelled at the Asians by Idi Amin 23 years ago still strikes a disturbing chord.

But the majority of small Asian traders expelled from Uganda found better lives in Britain or other countries. Unlike the Madhvanis, they have neither the money nor the desire to return.

Continued from Page 160

Uganda Beckons, but Those Exiled Are Cautious

properties,' and at the end of that, all you have seen in two years is struggle?" he asked.

Amin's declared purpose in establishing the Custodian Board was to care for the abandoned properties, but it soon became a symbol of corruption.

Museveni has shown resolve in cleaning up the board, which an unusually candid government report called "conduit for distributing political favors." Its progress in returning property was a condition for $130 million in credit from the World Bank.

Ghelani was an early beneficiary of the reforms. He first visited Uganda in 1991 and recovered his properties more than a year ago. In a slow, sad voice he told of his life in Uganda and the sense of loss.

"The way it was left, it was beautiful, absolutely perfect, a beautiful place," said the accountant, who fled at age 18, "When we came back, it seemed to be in ruins."

Kampala has indeed fallen on hard times. Red dust is everywhere, dead traffic lights tilt at crazy angles, sidewalks are broken, many buildings are pocked by gunfire and only 20% of the city has electricity.

The decline, accelerated by civil war, began with the expulsion of the Asians, who owned most of downtown Kampala. They were widely viewed as Uganda's economic backbone, accounting for $1 billion in property and business. But they rarely mixed with the black Ugandans.

Bitterness lingers.

Ghelani says many of the Asians were citizens like himself, often the third generation within the country.

Uganda: An inspiration for the continent

News Compilation, April 25, 1996

Uganda has replaced Ghana as the model reformer in Africa, according to a report in the *Financial Times,* London. The paper notes that the highest growth rate in Africa is turning a country once associated with disaster into an inspiration for the continent. The return of Uganda Asians expelled by Idi Amin, coupled with greater confidence in the economy has seen the return of capital. One of the most striking examples of the reversal of the disastrous nationalisation policy is the revival of the Madhvani family agro-industrial group of companies with assets in Uganda standing at more than $200m.

There are obstacles to investment, housing is difficult to obtain, expensive power supplies are inadequate and erratic and the road and rail network remains weak.

AIDS related diseases have reached disastrous levels, but emphasis on AIDS education may be leading to a decline in HIV cases.

Uganda's economic reform still has along way to go and must overcome many obstacles, but she can draw on an extraordinary range of natural resources to help overcome challenges and fuel further growth.

Amin leads a quiet life in Saudi Arabia

News Compilation, 1996

JEDDAH, Saudi Arabia—Exiled former Ugandan dictator Idi Amin lives a quiet life in an attractive marble villa with about nine of his more than 40 children. He goes to the local Bukhsan mosque every week for prayers.

While many have sighted him pushing his shopping cart or walking to prayers and others have gone up to him over the years, he keeps to himself, rarely granting interviews.

In a rare interview with the Ugandan government-owned newspaper, *The New Vision*, he said that he had no interest in returning to Uganda.

"I'm not badly off at all," Amin said in the interview. Amin said he would not accept any overtures from Museveni because the Ugandan leader had consistently insulted him.

"It would be ridiculous for people who keep calling me a buffoon and dictator to invite me back," Amin told *The New Vision.*

"My father was so much for Uganda that every penny he had, he invested in here," Ghelani said. "There was nothing that he took out."

"The only worry that we had was, please, get out alive. Things were happening so fast. There were people who were killed . . . . .People looted on their way to the airport."

Those who left "were in their prime at the time," said another who came back, Atul Radia. "Suddenly, they had to flee their country and became beggars."

SPECIAL REPORT

How they did it

Resettlement of Asians from Uganda in Europe and North America

Published by the Office of the United Nations High Commissioner for Refugees
May 1973

Reproduced courtesy of UNHCR

List of contents
Introduction
Austria
Belgium
Canada
Denmark
The Netherlands
Norway
Sweden
Switzerland
United States of America

According to UNHCR practice, family names of individual cases are not given in this report

Government contributions to resettlement expenses of Uganda Asians at 1 May 1973

Country	$US
Australia	142,790
Belgium	123,456
Denmark	500,000
Fed. Rep. Germany	220,126
Finland	50,000
Japan	10,000
Netherlands	154,321
New Zealand	17,865
Norway	303,260
Sweden	210,526
United Kingdom	586,584
U.S.A	500,000
Total	**$2,819,198**

UNHCR is the Office of the United Nations Commissioner for Refugees

UNHCR has to main functions:

Protection—to promote and safeguard the rights of refugees in such vital fields as employment, education, residence, freedom of movement and security against being returned to a country where their life or liberty would be endangered because of persecution.

Material Assistance—to assist governments of countries of asylum in the task of making refugees self-supporting as rapidly as possible.

Though UNHCR is sometimes called upon by governments to provide emergency relief, its assistance is intended primarily to promote permanent solutions to the problems of refugees through voluntary repatriation, local integration or settlement in another country.

United Nations
High Commissioner for Refugees
Palais des Nations
CH-1211 Geneva 10 Switzerland

Introduction

Shailesh M. stepped up to the mound and faced the batter. The pressure was on. There were two boys out, and the count was two strikes and one ball. With a motion that owed a heavy debt to his training as a cricket bowler, Shailesh pitched. The ball came in hard and fast—too fast for the batter who reacted a split second too late and struck out. Shailesh's pitching had again retired the opposing side, to the delight of the girls in the cheering section.

First as a student and now as an athlete in an unfamiliar sport, Shailesh, a displaced Asian from Uganda, was proving himself and was winning the respect and friendship of his American schoolmates.

Shailesh is representative of the some 5,900 Asians of undetermined nationality who had to leave Uganda at short notice in November 1972 and who as of mid-April were in the process of settling in nearly a score of countries. "How They Did It" is the story of a cross-section of Asians who went to the main countries of resettlement in Europe and North America but the title could also apply to the organizations and people who have helped the Asians to help themselves, demonstrating anew the value of an international mechanism capable of organizing the migration of uprooted persons on an emergency basis.

Notwithstanding the encouraging results that the Asians have achieved thus far, it was clear in mid-April that a final collective effort would be needed to ensure the settlement of some 1,900 Asians still in European transit centres at that time. With the goodwill which abounds and the expertise available to translate it swiftly into specific measures—and above all given the fibre of the people themselves—it is inconceivable that the international community should fail to offer a reasonable solution to each and every one of these individuals and families.

The Asians in East Africa are a heterogeneous group drawn from various places throughout the sub-continent that are now part of India or Pakistan. Though overwhelmingly Hindu or Moslem they also include Christians from the former Portuguese enclave of Goa. Asians and Arab traders had sailed their dhows across the Indian Ocean from the earliest times, but the first great surge in immigration came at the end of the 19th century when 32,000 Asians arrived from 1896 to 1901 to build the railway across Kenya and Uganda to link Kampala and Mombasa. Some 6,500 decided to settle as craftsmen or employees in the administration.

In Uganda, Indians from the Bombay area developed cotton ginning mills and sugar plantations. Ten times more numerous than the Europeans, Asians established prosperous businesses and reached important administrative and economic positions. As in other parts of East Africa, they also managed to obtain certain political rights ahead of Africans. In 1949, however, the British authorities imposed a number of restrictions on immigration of Asians to East Africa, and instituted certain economic measures aimed at reducing their control over major industries. Thus in Uganda, where Asians controlled 90 per cent of the cotton mills, these were purchased in 1952-53 by the Government and offered to Africans.

When Uganda obtained her independence in 1962, large numbers of Asians were given the opportunity of becoming Ugandan citizens. Not all, however, availed themselves of this opportunity within the time limit which was stipulated.

In all the newly-independent East African countries, more or less severe restrictions were little by little imposed both on immigration and on residence of non-citizens. Doubtless a great number, having obtained British passports, hoped to be able if necessary to withdraw to or settle in the United Kingdom.

Repercussions in the United Kingdom

However, the growing number of immigrants to the United Kingdom, not only from Africa but also from the West Indies, led the British Government, in its turn, to impose restrictive measures in 1968. Under the new law on immigration only 1,500 British passport holders from the Commonwealth were permitted to settle in Great Britain per year.

In Kenya, steps were being taken to provoke accelerated departures of non-citizens, but on a progressive scale. In Uganda, pressures for similar measures were also building up. Nevertheless, the order given in the summer of 1972 by the Chief of State, General Idi Amin, that all non-citizen Asians should leave within three months, came as a shock. Of the thousands of people affected, many were totally unprepared for a rapid departure. While some were able to make advance arrangements to ensure their own resettlement elsewhere, others could only put their fate in the hands of the country—the United Kingdom in most cases—which had given them a passport. Those holding no passport had nowhere to turn.

In these dramatic circumstances, the United Kingdom agreed to waive temporarily the quota fixed under the 1968 law and admitted some 27,000 British passport-holding Uganda Asians. At the same time, the British Government appealed to a number of countries to accept the expelled Asians as immigrants. Certain of these countries, in particular Canada and the United States, reacted positively to this appeal and arranged to select thousands of candidates for immigration on the spot, in Kampala. A large part of those admitted by Canada were British passport holders while those accepted by the USA were Asians of undetermined nationality. The former travelled direct starting in September, while the latter transited through Italy, starting in November.

Emergency evacuation

There remained all those who held neither Ugandan citizenship nor a British passport. Although their exact number was not known, they amounted to several thousand. They too had to leave the country before the deadline, fixed at 7 November 1972. In order to comply, they needed valid travel documents, a country of temporary asylum (if a permanent one could not be arranged), and the means to travel there in time. With this in view, the Uganda Government turned

Continued from Page 165

Introduction

to the United Nations Secretary General, Mr. Kurt Waldheim, with a request for the assistance of the world body to Asians of undetermined nationality. On 23 October, a mission composed of Mr. Robert Gardiner, Executive Secretary of the UN Economic Commission for Africa, and Mr. F. J. Homann-Herimberg, Regional Representative of the United Nations High Commissioner for Refugees in New York, arrived in Kampala, to join Mr. Winston Prattley, Resident Representative of the United Nations Development Programme.

As a result of their negotiations with the Uganda authorities, Mr. Prattley was made responsible for organizing an emergency evacuation operation.

It was agreed that the International Committee of the Red Cross (ICRC) would deliver travel documents to those requiring them, and that the Intergovernmental Committee for European Migration (ICEM) would arrange transportation to temporary or permanent resettlement countries. In the interim, at the request of the Secretary-General, the High Commissioner for Refugees, Sadruddin Aga Khan, appealed to the international community for assistance, in the form of offers of resettlement places, or of temporary residence permits, and funds to pay for the transport and the care and maintenance of the evacuees until such time as they could be permanently resettled.

Temporary residence

In response to the High Commissioner's urgent appeal for transit accommodation, a swift response was received from seven European countries—Austria, Belgium, Greece, Italy, Malta, Morocco and Spain. Within 12 days, more than 3,600 persons were transported to five of these havens (the offers of Greece and Morocco did not need to be taken up). The Asians "in transit" were placed in refugee reception centres, youth hostels, hotels, holiday centres and even disused military barracks. In each country, UNHCR entered into an agreement with the responsible authorities, under which the latter undertook to provide accommodation, food and medical care against an all-inclusive per capita payment by UNHCR. While Government bodies assumed the main responsibility for caring for the transitees in Austria, Italy and Malta, voluntary agencies took the lead in Belgium and Spain.

Permanent resettlement

These interim measures were a palliative. The main continuing aim remained to find permanent places of settlement. As the High Commissioner, Sadruddin Aga Khan, told the press in New York on 10 November: *"The worst thing that could happen to any of them would be that they remain too long in limbo in transit centres. Any serious situation of that kind has been avoided since the unhappy postwar days when so many camps in Europe were filled with displaced persons."*

By that time Canada and the United States had already been in the field in Uganda, closely fol-

lowed by Switzerland and Denmark. Once the move to Europe was completed, attention turned to the transit centres. Norway, the Netherlands and Sweden came forward to offer permanent settlement opportunities along with Belgium and Austria who agreed to let some of the transitees remain. A number of Latin American States announced their readiness to consider applications from candidates satisfying the criteria applicable under their regular immigration programmes.

Time passes

By the beginning of February, some 1,100 persons had left the temporary transit centres. Several hundred others were waiting to know whether they had been accepted by countries to which they had applied for resettlement. But almost 2000 others had no immediate prospect of migrating. Among them, many hoped to go to an English-speaking area, where they felt they could settle more easily; with this in mind, they had made requests for visas for Canada or the United States. Hundreds of others were separated from their families and could not take a decision committing them for the future until this primordial problem was solved. Most were heads of family who had tried, too late, to obtain Uganda citizenship, and whose wives and children, on the strength of their British passports, had gone to the United Kingdom. Others had members of their family scattered among different countries: in transit in Europe, in Canada, in India, in Kenya. And then there were the aged, the infirm, the handicapped. In some cases, young people refused to accept migration offers because they were not permitted to take with them a sick mother or a brother suffering from tuberculosis. To guide and advise the Asians on the difficult choices that confronted them, UNHCR officials went to the transit centres to counsel the transitees.

The High Commissioner's action

At UNHCR headquarters in Geneva, a special task force was created under the responsibility of Mr. John Kelly, Deputy Director of the Protection Division, to handle the Uganda Asians problem. It was this unit that acted as a clearing house for information on schemes put forward by Governments and also kept the voluntary agencies abreast of developments. Meanwhile efforts were being made to raise the substantial funds needed to cover care and maintenance of the transitees ($400,000 a month was being spent for this purpose at the height of the operation) as well as their transportation. By March 31, some $2.8 million had been contributed by 12 Governments in response to the High Commissioner's special appeal.

In mid-January the High Commissioner himself visited the temporary transit centres in Austria, Belgium, Italy and the Netherlands. In his meetings with the Asians, he encouraged them to be patient and assured them that he would continue to spare no effort to find them permanent new homes and reunite divided families.

A few days later, the High Commissioner went to London, Washington and Ottawa to discuss with the authorities at the highest level the possibilities for further resettlement places in their respective countries. The results of these conversations were to prove most positive. On 23 February, the British Government announced that it was prepared to admit the heads of families of undetermined nationality whose wives and children had already been admitted to the United Kingdom, as well as a certain number of persons whose circumstances presented strong compassionate features. On 9 April, the United States Government in its turn announced a new special quota. Canada declared that it would examine with particular care all requests from Uganda Asians, especially those coming from members of divided families.

Meanwhile, Australia and New Zealand also announced special schemes which a few weeks later were in both cases greatly enlarged following the visit of a member of the High Commissioner's staff. Likewise the original programmes of Denmark and Switzerland were expanded so that by early April there was a kind of humanitarian chain reaction in progress. The High Commissioner, while welcoming this series of gestures, stressed that the continuance of care and maintenance for those Asians still in transit centres could never be considered a solution and urged that a renewed effort be made to accord settlement opportunities to the entire residual group. *"Both on humanitarian and economic grounds, this is the only reasonable conclusion," he said. "There is really no viable alternative."*

Austria

Of the five European countries which took in the Uganda Asians on a transit basis, Austria accepted the largest number—some 1,500 persons. Soon after their arrival in November and December, selection missions from the Netherlands and Sweden started choosing likely candidates for resettlement; under their respective quotas, Sweden accepted 319 persons and the Netherlands 253.

Following the decision by the British authorities to admit heads of families whose British passport holding dependents were resident in the United Kingdom, another 160 persons left Austria. Counting those who had emigrated to other countries, 756 persons remained in Austria on 31 March 1973, still awaiting resettlement opportunities. The majority had expressed their desire to go to an English-speaking country: the United Kingdom, Canada, the United States, and also Australia and New Zealand. At mid-April, there were more than 420 applicants for Canada. The Asians' hope, even slight, of being able to join relatives or friends in one of these countries explains the relative reluctance on their part to accept Austria's offer of permanent resettlement places. In fact, only some 70 persons had chosen this solution to their problems.

In the meantime, the balance are still living in the transit centres—half at the Traiskirchen refugee reception centre near Vienna and in two rest-homes in lower Austria (Neuhaus and Reichenau an der Rax); and the other half in hotels at Wallsee (Lower Austria), Saxen and St. Nicholas (Upper Austria) and in a home for the handicapped at Thalem, near Salzburg. This dispersion, due to the lack of suitable accommodation in and around the Austrian capital, has at times caused difficulties, particularly in informing and counselling the Asians.

The task of caring for the Asians was split up among voluntary agencies along geographical lines: the World Council of Churches for those living in Lower Austria, and Caritas, in co-operation with the International Catholic Migration Commission, for the others.

As soon as the Asians arrived these agencies made themselves responsible for their welfare, distributing warm clothing, taking care of individual cases, especially those who wished to find jobs or settle permanently in Austria. Later, they helped to check and support the Asians' applications for admission to other countries, through consulates or selection missions. This constituted a follow-up to the work of a UNHCR official who spent two months in Austria keeping a constant watch on the day-to-day developments of the impatiently awaited resettlement offers.

The Austrian Government, for its part, is doing its utmost to find solutions to the problems facing those Asians wishing to settle in the country. The most acute is housing; job opportunities are most easily available in and around Vienna, but unfortunately this is the area where accommodation is the most difficult to find.

As will be seen from the following case-history, a family with three members having found jobs is still living at Traiskirchen; here, the authorities are in the process of arranging comfortable accommodation in an apartment block for families who wish to settle in Austria.

Continued on Page 168

Above: Arrival at Vienna Airport and suddenly there was the cold Austrian winter. Warm socks and shoes were welcome gifts upon arrival.

Below: In the corner of one of the rooms of Austria's Traiskirchen transit centre, four youngsters enjoy a typical European game of Ludo ("Mensch argere dich nicht"), designed to teach acceptance of bad luck.

Continued from Page 167

Austria

"Figyelem, figyelem, Kovacs Karoly jojjon a Lagerleitung-ba!"

(Attention, Attention: calling Kovacs Karoly, come to the office, please).

Nothing strange about an announcement in Hungarian over the loudspeaker system at the Traiskirchen refugee reception centre—except that the voice was that of an Asian girl from Uganda, Shamira A.

She arrived at Traiskirchen in November 1972 with her father, mother, brother and two small sisters. A few days later, the family members capable of earning their living started looking for jobs. Shamira was immediately hired by the administration of the centre, where she serves as interpreter, fills out forms and does all sorts of useful odd jobs. Rajabali, the father, who had been a bicycle merchant and mechanic, looked for a job in his own field, but had difficulty finding one because of the language problem. He and his son Shafik finally were able to find employment in a nearby metallurgical plant. The younger girls, Nouvaz, 11, and Nailin, 13, are going to school in the neighbourhood and have quickly picked up German—and with the Lower Austrian accent! They are often invited by their schoolmates, and life for them is almost back to normal. Not so for all the members of the family, however, as they still live six to a small room in the Traiskirchen centre. The housing problem in this area is not easy to solve, even for an Austrian. Landlords insist on high down-payments for most rented accommodation, and neither the Government nor the voluntary agencies have yet been able to establish a fund to cover such expenses. It is hoped to find an apartment for Rajabali and his family in a municipal housing complex now under construction. When it is ready, Shamira hopes to resume her studies, as does her brother Shafik, who should have finished his secondary education this year.

In the meantime, these are busy days for the whole family. They are up at 5 a.m., so that Rajabali and Shafik can catch the bus which takes them to their jobs at the Thormetall plant. At 8 a.m. it is the children's turn to leave for school. Shamira, in her spare time, is studying German with a tape recorder. Each Saturday, she accompanies her father and brother to the home of a secretary in the plant, who gives them German lessons. The mother, Shirinkhanu, has some time to dream, when she has finished the housework—but even in her dreams she is mainly concerned with finding ways of improving their lot. Why shouldn't she use her cooking talents, once she has her own kitchen, to offer some new exotic taste thrills to the many *gastronomes* of cosmopolitan Vienna? They are always on the lookout for new restaurants, and her dishes are even spicier than the Viennese! One can dream, and thanks to the sympathetic welcome given to the Asians, among them the M. family, some of these dreams may well come true.

Belgium

Belgium originally agreed to receive on a temporary basis 428 Uganda Asians of undetermined nationality. They arrived on November 8 and 9, 1972, and were offered hospitality at the holiday centre at Zon en Zee, at Westend, under the auspices of *Caritas Catholica and Entr'aide Socialiste.* The cost of maintenance is being paid by UNHCR, while the above-named voluntary agencies are contributing some US$ 12,500 for medical expenses and transportation inside Belgium.

By government decision of October 27, 1972, 30 families were selected for permanent settlement at the end of November by the National Labour Board and the voluntary agencies. An amount of some US$ 123,000 was allocated by the Government to UNHCR to cover resettlement costs incurred by the voluntary agencies for the permanent resettlement of the Asians. The task of providing employment and accommodation was entrusted to the following four voluntary agencies: *Caritas Catholica, Entr'aide Socialiste, Entr'aide Ecumenique and Solidarite liberale internationale* .

Large families form the majority of the Uganda Asians who have accepted the offer to settle in Belgium. All 30 families now being integrated total some 175 persons (including 80 children), originating sometimes from other countries, in particular the United Kingdom. Like some other resettlement countries, Belgium has granted refugee status to the families admitted for permanent settlement. By March 30, 50 persons had found an employment.

The *Visseries et Trefileries Reunies,* a wire- and screw-cutting factory, was the first company to show concern for the people uprooted from Uganda and, in January, offered nine jobs for unskilled labourers in its laminating plant at Machelen, near Brussels. *"This is hard work, not a pastry shop,"* the likely candidates were warned.

Nothing actually obliged the job-seekers to accept on the spot the first job they were offered which might mean a complete change from their past activity and an adaptation to a rhythm of work for which they were not prepared. Nine men, however, eventually accepted. A few days later, they departed from Zon en Zee, leaving their families behind. They were to live temporarily in accommodation put at their disposal by the factory. Their performance was considered satisfactory and a few weeks later the factory offered another seven posts which were filled at once.

"At first glance, I found them a bit slight," explained Mr. Stuckens, the staff manager. *"Short, frail, small hands... Around here, when the rollers have to be loaded, size is important, and strength, too! But there were hardly any problems. Now that their families have joined them and they have their own home, they are in high spirits..."*

"A proof of their will to succeed is their assiduity at the Flemish language course organized in the factory for the benefit of the Asians to improve the knowledge acquired in the courses

they had attended in Zon en Zee," notes Miss Strypstein, a Caritas welfare officer in charge of their integration.

"The most skilful of all..."

Mr. Natwarlal P., 40, a father of eight children, aged three to 14, belongs to the first group employed by VST. It is quite natural that he, like his fellow-countrymen was particularly attracted by the high salary offered by the company: BF 75 per hour, plus 20 for groupwork, plus special bonuses. With a large family and him the only breadwinner the amount of money on the wage-slip is of vital importance. Mr. P., however, unlike his fellow-countrymen, had the advantage of being familiar with this kind of work. At Machelen, he very soon proved to be very competent, capable of operating a machine on his own and, when working with others, of training teammates. *"The only serious problem for Mr. P. was the change from English measurements to the metric system,"* says the staff manager. *"We find him to be a particularly skilful and conscientious worker, and we can fully trust him."*

The Machelen plant works around the clock. Mr. P. is part of the shift which starts work at 2 p.m. For a few weeks he has been living with his family in the five-room apartment of a three-storey house in Halle, ten minutes' train ride from the factory. The rent amounts to BF 3,000, including heating, gas and electricity. It is not a mere matter of luck that the rent is so cheap. The flats are located in a former convent that was made available gratis by the Diocese and rents could then be adapted to the needs and means of this family and of a Moroccan family, accommodated on the floor above. A young Belgian couple also lives there; both wife and husband are teachers who have decided to help immigrants. During an initial period, this kind of help is essential; it includes services to cope with daily life, such as shopping, various application forms to fill out, medical care, registering of the children at school... *"Apart from the usefulness of this type of help it is even more important to make the newcomers feel they are not isolated. I believe we have succeeded. We are visiting each other. We call each other by our first names. The P. children are invited to their schoolmates' families, who, in turn, come and see them."* And the friendly neighbour adds: *"What touches us most is their good will. The Moroccan from the floor above spontaneously offered to paint the flat for the P. family. And Mrs. P., in turn, offered to babysit for us during the day."*

Such relationships are no more than natural. But the mere fact that they could be established right from the day the P.s arrived at Halle, saved them from the early hardships of adaptation, from ignorance or fears, which, of course, may be dispelled sooner or later but which often undermine the precious optimism newcomers so badly need.

Though efficient welfare services exist on a local level all over Belgium, Mr. De Brandt, the secretary general of the Belgian Caritas Catholica considers of primary importance the friendly help

Continued on Page 169

Above: Mumtaz, Arif and Zinnat B. on their way home from school.

Below: Abdul B. and his son Mustak found work with a Belgiun wholesale dealer in home decoration material.

Continued from Page 168

provided by volunteers whom Caritas seeks to recruit wherever large families settle. Indeed, the presence of these sponsors is not the only stimulating or regulating factor which determines the social and economic progress of the newcomers. The substantial material assistance provided by the agency in charge of their integration is meant to ensure that their standard of living is similar to that of their neighbours, and at a level which the immigrants can be expected to maintain in the future.

Mr. De Brandt indicates that furniture is given free to families moving into permanent accommodation. He also paid out BF 2,400 to the P. family. "This amount corresponds to two months' family allowance which this family is entitled to. Now that the basic conditions are met and the application forms filled out, the further allowances will be paid by the social security office. The P.s, like the other families, should, as they start working, benefit from the same advantages as Belgian workers."

Various trades are practised by Uganda Asians in Belgium: Two jewellers got the same job they had in Uganda, four weavers are employed in a rope factory at Ostend; three work in a supermarket, four as waiters, two as storemen... We went to see these two at their place of work and at their home. There we were welcomed by Ammanula B.

"Frankly speaking, I didn't really know where Belgium was on the map. When we left Kampala, I actually thought we were going to land in Italy. We arrived at Brussels airport and went on to Westend, where we stayed for three months in very comfortable living conditions. However, we all were worried about our future and wanted to start working again as soon as possible and live a normal life."

Ammanula, 19, is the third son of Mr. Abdul B. They are a family of ten and at present resettled in Hasselt, a small industrial town ten miles from Brussels.

"How lucky we are to be all together here," he says, overflowing with gratitude. "Everything was ready for us when we came here. Thirty people were here to welcome us... And in the fridge we found food for at least a fortnight."

His father and one of his brothers are employed by a wholesale dealer in material for home decorating. This job, and the large, comfortable flat, were found for them by Sister Marie C., a nun of the order of Scheut, who works for Caritas. Sister Marie's family owns the business; they only needed one employee there, and first hired Mustak, the young brother, as a storekeeper. And then, learning that his father Abdul, who owned lorries in Uganda, knew something about mechanics, they thought they might employ him as a van driver or a maintenance mechanic. His problem, at this stage, is still the language. This is why father and son—who already understands Flemish—still work side by side. Mustak, who is only 17, earns BF 57 per hour, his father 66. "The elder B. has quite a few skills," says the employer. "He can operate a drilling-machine, handle a saw as well as a plane; he can do carpentry work, too. You just have to explain to him—in English at the moment—what he has to do, and he does it. Anyway, father and son always do their job well, and when they have finished they go and ask the boss for more work to do."

Father and son are both timid and reserved. They nevertheless readily agreed to be filmed at work. They did not believe that they deserved all that publicity. Much more relaxed at home, as they welcomed their visitors, they answered questions. "Of course we are happy! How could it be otherwise?" says Mr. B. "Think that a month ago, we didn't know what was going to become of us."

But the most talkative of the family is Ammanula, the student. He explains that as he and his elder sister had more aptitude for academic work, the family decided that he should go on with the medical training he had started in Kampala. A fortnight ago, he was given an opportunity to go to London for an exam. If he passes, he will try to get a scholarship to continue his studies, preferably in England.

"Of course I want to settle here. I am learning Flemish and French. If I pass my diploma in England, I can always take the necessary exams to be able to practise in Belgium..."

His elder sister lives in England where she is married. Two other sisters were given an opportunity to go there to finish their "O-levels" (Secondary School final exams). They will come and join the family, too, when they graduate. Two younger sisters and a small brother attend the nearest primary school. We met the girls coming out, surrounded by classmates. How do they feel? They are not deaf and dumb any more, the teachers, and above all, the classmates, see to that. It started with a smile, a ball game, shouts of joy. Soon, the bit of Flemish, learnt at Zon en Zee bursts out spontaneously. *"It's us who do the shopping now!"* Bread? "Brood!" And butter? *"Boter."*

The Belgian girls around break into laughter. And the mothers, watching at a distance, can't help smiling, too.

Canada

Canada sent a selection mission to Uganda early in September, some two months before the November 7 deadline. Under this special programme, visas were issued to 6,175 Asians of various nationalities of whom some 4,200 were flown directly to Canada on flights financed by the Canadian Government. A further some 1,400 left at their own expense and arrived in Canada after stopping off to visit relatives en route (mostly in the U. K.). Among these some 5,600, who had arrived by 31 March about 1,370 were of undetermined nationality. Under new arrangements Canada is accepting further Uganda Asians of undetermined nationality from the transit centres in Europe, and by 12 April, 183 had been admitted.

The Canadian intake, apart from being large, abounds in skilled professional people in a wide variety of fields representing a "windfall" in terms of expensively trained manpower. One evening in April 1973 the Asians hobnobbing at the New Canadians Services counselling office in Ottawa included a mechanical engineer who was working on gyroscope development for the Canadian Navy and Air Force, a pharmacologist holding a postgraduate diploma from London University doing advanced work in toxicology and environmental studies, and his wife, an agricultural chemist.

Sometimes several months were needed to place Asians of this calibre in their specialized sectors of activity, but by April 1973 thanks to the Department of Manpower and Immigration and to private organizations, suitable jobs had been found for nearly all persons whose skills were immediately transferable, particularly technicians and accountants. For some professions, notably teachers, there have been problems of accreditation and of domestic oversupply, and in these cases the Asians have been helped to undergo retraining. For example, women teachers are converting themselves into secretaries for whom there is a strong demand on the labour market. Intensive English courses have also been arranged for men who held managerial positions in Uganda, where most of their business was conducted in Gujerati and Swahili, in order to enable them to be placed in Canada in posts commensurate with their experience.

While the Government has had primary responsibility for settling the Asians, they have, in common with other immigrants, benefited from the activity of private organizations who have worked closely with the local branches of the Department of Manpower and Immigration. Representative of these is the New Canadians Services which is manned from early morning to 10 at night by highly capable volunteers, many of whom have had professional experience as social workers and all of whom are extremely knowledgeable in advising the Asians on all aspects of life in Canada, from how to find a better apartment to where to buy curry.

Mrs. Colleen Polsuns, the Chairman of the N.C.S., reports that in general the Canadian people have responded in an extremely positive way.

The V. Family, with three wage earners, has a comfortable home in Ottawa.

"I believe all Canadians who have come in contact with the Asians from Uganda have been favourably impressed," she says. *"To be sure, Canada has given them a chance to start a new life after a particularly trying ordeal and the Asians appreciate this. But they are by no means coming empty-handed. By their will to work and intelligence they are already enhancing and enriching Canada's multi-cultural society."*

UNHCR is actively furthering the continued flow of Asians from the transit centres to Canada by contributing a substantial proportion of a Loan Fund being used to finance transatlantic flights organized by the Intergovernmental Committee for European Migration.

Sadruddin V.

The Sadruddin V. family were selected in Uganda and came directly to Ottawa in September 1972. Mrs. V. and two of her three children—Shelina 7, and Azmina 5—arrived first and then her son, Farouk, 17, with her mother-in-law, and, finally, her husband. Before leaving Uganda they had lost everything of value. Mr. V. never refers to this difficult period in their lives. Soft-spoken but firm, he has concentrated all his energy and determination on proving his worth again in Canada—a challenge which, however formidable it might have seemed at first, he now appears to enjoy, for the tide has definitely turned in his favour.

In Kampala he had his own filling station. Now he is working his way up in the shipping department of a large typewriter company that offers much greater long-term scope. His wife, who in Kampala was accustomed to having servants, faced up immediately to realities of the do-it-yourself life in the New World and, in addition to taking care of the house and doing the cooking, she went out to work in an architectural supply firm. Her mother-in-law is too old to be a very active help at home but she can baby-sit which is a great boon.

The third wage-earner in the family, young Farouk, has a clerical job in a department store. With their combined incomes the V's are on their way to becoming firmly established. They live in a modest duplex apartment in the middle-class Bay Shore district, about 20 minutes from the centre of town. However, it takes a lot of money to maintain a household of six persons, and in common with many other Canadian housewives Mrs. V. joined whole-heartedly in the recent meat boycott to protest against the rising cost of living.

As yet, the V's do not have a car. Travelling to work by bus, Sadruddin is away from 7 in the morning until 7 at night. His wife also takes the bus, but having less far to go, arrives home in time to prepare dinner.

Farouk's best friend is a boy about his age named Don, who lives a few doors away. In their leisure time they go over to the Bay Shore Country Club to play pool or basketball. Farouk, a lean 6' 2", plays guard on the Bay Shore team and was one of the top scorers in the past season.

Shelina goes to the local public school and is now doing well after overcoming initial difficulties caused by the fact that she was not used to studying in English. She is becoming immersed in all the usual activities that captivate a little Canadian girl, including the traditional sugaring-off party. This takes place in the spring when the maple sap begins to run, and a few weeks ago Shelina went off with her class for a day's excursion in the woods to see how maple syrup is made and, better yet, to taste it.

"From the very moment I arrived—a mother alone with two children in a strange country—everyone in Canada was so wonderful", Mrs. V. recounts. *"They told me not to worry, that my husband and the rest of the family would soon be joining us.*

"The people in Manpower and New Canadians Services helped us find jobs and a nice place to live almost at once. We have really been very lucky."

The V's have not abandoned their customs and

Continued on Page 171

Gooli works near the famous Canadian Parliament building in Ottawa

Continued from Page 170

traditions. Mrs. V. finds all the spices needed to cook the same pungent dishes her family relished in Kampala. At home the family still speak Gujerati and once a week they gather for worship with other members of their religion living in Ottawa. But Canada is their home.

Gooli and Amirali A.

Gooli A. is a soft-spoken woman in her early thirties with a gentle manner that makes her singularly unobtrusive, yet in only a few months she has established herself as one of the most efficient secretaries in the Department of Secretary of State in Ottawa. *"She was so good I 'stole' her from a colleague"*, explains her boss, Miss Jennifer McQueen, a young administrator in the Citizens Cultures section which seeks to protect and promote the cultural identity of the various ethnic groups that make up Canada's population.

"What impresses me most about her, though," she continued, *"is her cheerfulness. She is always smiling and good-natured and you would never guess that only a few months ago she, her husband and her little boy had to leave home and start life all over again in a strange country."*

Gooli had help in that her brother had already been in Canada for four years as a teacher in Ottawa Technical High School, and his assistance was of great value in the first few weeks after the A's arrived.

While Gooli's experience as a secretary in Barclay's Bank in Kampala led to her being hired by the Canadian Government almost immediately, it was more difficult to place her husband. He had owned and managed a small grocery store in Uganda, but his command of English was not as good as it might have been. Under the auspices of the Department of Manpower and Immigration he was enrolled in a retraining course at Algonquin College. He is making steady progress and in the relatively near future will be ready for a job in business.

"Everyone has been so kind in Canada", Gooli recalls, *"not only in the office but in everyday life. I remember once soon after arriving I was in the supermarket near where we live and a woman I hadn't met before came up to ask how I was getting along. It was a cold winter day and she wondered how I was standing the change in climate. I told her I had to be especially careful about our little boy, Munaf. In Uganda he was used to running around with practically no clothes on, and here I have to bundle him up in snowsuits. I thought no more about the conversation but a half-hour later there was a knock on the door and the same woman, whose name I didn't even know, appeared with her arms full of warm clothing for Munaf. How can anyone help being grateful to wonderful people like this?".*

Gooli and Amirali live, with Munaf—now 18 months old— in a neat one-bedroom apartment in a modern high-rise development outside Ottawa. Especially with her husband not drawing a salary at present, Gooli keeps very close track of her daily expenditure. The one service she does not have to pay for is baby-sitting. Every morning she leaves Munaf with Violette, a warm-hearted French-Canadian woman who lives in the next building. Violette's own son is grown up and studying medicine abroad. "Munaf takes his place," Violette explains. "Looking after him is really a treat for me."

Mrs. Malek M.

Mrs. M. was widowed in Uganda during the turmoil that preceded the November 7 deadline. When she arrived in Ottawa on October 25 with her three-year-old daughter, Jameela, she was grief-stricken and completely bereft. She had been a school-teacher, but her credentials were not recognized, and there is in any case an oversupply of teachers in Ontario. Thus she was—and will be for some time—completely dependent on aid from the Manpower and Immigration Department and the New Canadians Services. The latter was particularly helpful in finding a room for her and her child with a Canadian family. Mrs. M. cannot

Denmark

Denmark, though a small country of less than 5 million inhabitants, has for many years displayed a marked interest in refugees. In spite of its geographical situation, it has become a country of asylum for thousands of exiles originating from more than 20 countries all over the world. When Denmark learned about the expulsion of the Uganda Asians, the Government on the advice of the Danish Refugee Council, which groups a dozen voluntary agencies, such as the Danish Red Cross, the Danish Interchurch Aid, Caritas Denmark, and Save the Children Fund, immediately decided to receive a number of them. The possibilities for jobs and accommodation being limited, it could only be a small number, but, in return, preference would be given to handicapped individuals or families including a handicapped person. The first sixteen were admitted directly from Kampala, after a selection carried out jointly by the Council and the Ministry of Social Affairs, based on dossiers which had been prepared by Dr. Cleve Schou, chief medical officer of ICEM. They arrived on November 7, and were put up in a hotel in Copenhagen, where the Refugee Council usually accommodates newly-arrived refugees. Later on, more handicapped Asians arrived from the various transit centres in Europe: Malta (five persons), Spain (eight) and Italy (eight). In February, the Danish Government, in addition to its important contribution to UNHCR of US$ 500,000 towards the cost of transport, and care and maintenance of the Asians in these countries, decided to accept another 100 persons; again, handicapped persons will be given preference.

"Some of the Asians we have accepted were TB cases," reports Mr. Piel Christensen, the secretary general of the Danish Refugee Council. *"After a three months' stay in a sanatorium, we can now consider them as cured. But we also have people with incurable diseases, mental cases who will have to be put into a home."*

No Asian has yet been offered a job. Several families, however, have already been accommodated. Ten days ago, one of them, the Ch. family,

Continued on Page 172

speak highly enough of the kindness of the Peter Harkness family and the way in which they have adopted her as part of their own household.

This has helped greatly to offset her loneliness. Soon after her arrival, Mrs. M. was advised to take a secretarial course, which she is now doing under the auspices of the Department of Manpower and Immigration, and by August she will be in a position to hold down a full-time job. Till then she will continue to draw $63 per week from the Government.

Mrs. M's position as a woman alone with a child in a strange country after a particularly cruel loss, was especially vulnerable but the welcome she has received in Canada has given her a new lease on life, and she is now facing the future with confidence.

Learning the language in Denmark.

Continued from Page 171

Denmark

was able to move into a flat at Albertslund, some seven miles out of Copenhagen. Mr. Ramzanali Ch. and his wife Gulshan have five children. Two of them arrived with their parents from Kampala, two sons came from England where they were studying and the fifth is on his way... Today, however, the family has grown: Mrs. Ch.'s sister, her husband and two children have come from Sweden for a visit; they are at present living at the reception centre at Moheda. A joyful family gathering, to which Mr. Ch. would have liked to add his two brothers, who also landed in Sweden, two others in England, a sister in Switzerland and another in Kenya. *"Our family is scattered all over Europe,"* he says. *"Fortunately, the distances are not too great. We shall be able to meet from time to time."*

Registered as handicapped because of a heart disease, Mr. Ch. says he already feels much better after the treatment he has been receiving since his arrival in Denmark. He is impatiently waiting for the results of the last medical checkup, which should allow him to start looking for a job. In Kampala, Mr. Ch. owned a transport business and would like to be able to use his experience. For the moment, however, he can do no more than study Danish, just like his fellow countrymen. Like them, he receives allowances from the Danish Refugee Council. For the time being, the rent for the four-room flat which the family occupies in a new building, is paid by the Council. Mr. Ch. will start paying for it when his salary and that of his children enable him to do so.

The family receives an allowance of 1,330 crowns which is equivalent to what the State pays to pensioners, plus 212 crowns per child. This is enough to live on, considering that, among other things, schooling for the children and medical care are free.

Back in Uganda, Mr. Ch. was an active member of the Ismaili community. Today, he is interested in bringing together members of this Moslem sect living in the area. He asked for and obtained permission from the spiritual leader of the community to gather the members at his home for Friday prayers. Later, he hopes to set up a small mosque. Mr. Ch. feels optimistic. He says that he is not afraid of the future. Quite the opposite; he considers himself fortunate to live in Denmark now, and he is full of praise for the kindness and generosity shown to him and his family.

On our return to Copenhagen, Mr. Christensen suggests we should visit two other places where we can meet Asians from Uganda. We start with the language school, set up by the Danish Refugee Council. We find the people we are looking for in two classrooms. In one of them, the students are all in booths wearing earphones, while a teacher, who is a real technician, gives them an audio-visual lesson. In another room, the teacher is writing on the blackboard. He asks each pupil the following question: "Talte hun dansk?" The pupil repeats the sentence, and then has to answer: "Ja, hun talte dansk." Which means (if you haven't guessed): "Did she speak Danish?"—"Yes, she spoke Danish." The pronunciation is even more difficult than you believe, which is why the young girls prefer to whisper. The teacher, however, is optimistic. "We have only been doing it for 100 hours. With four hours a day five times a week, there should soon be noticeable progress. The main thing is to get rid of shyness."

At the Hotel Corona, Danish, of course, is spoken; but to an equal extent Slavonic languages, Spanish and Portuguese, and lately Swahili and Gujerati. Refugees from all over the world, plus the Asians from Uganda, live there. "We would like to meet little Harish," we ask at the reception. He arrives a few minutes later. He is a boy of twelve whom the Danes selected in Malta. He had come there without parents and is probably an orphan, at least according to what the people say who used to know him in Kampala. He is a lively and mischievous youngster who easily made friends in Malta; but rebellious, too. We might be able to look for a Danish family to adopt him." He also likes us to take his photograph; on condition,

Netherlands

In November 1972, in response to the High Commissioner's appeal, the Netherlands Government sent a selection mission to Austria to choose some 250 Asians from among those in the transit centres.

A former World Health Organization staff member, Dr. Fred Vorst, joined the mission to assure the Asians that they could be given proper medical care once in the Netherlands. For certain families, this was a very necessary precaution: one included a 16-year-old mentally handicapped girl; another, a paralysed young man; in yet another family including eight children, the mother was chronically ill, and the father was worried as to whether he could care for the family in the Netherlands.

In the space of one week, 50 families totalling 253 persons had received visas, and between 24 November and 1 December they were flown from Vienna to Amsterdam. Some 180 persons were immediately accommodated in bungalows rented by the Government at Rabbit Hill summer resort, at Nieuw Milligen, near Apeldoorn. Other summer residences at Bennekom, in Gelderland province—also closed for the winter—were used to house 70 other new arrivals.

Joint efforts were immediately undertaken by the Government, the voluntary agencies grouped in the Netherlands National Federation for Assistance to Refugees *(Stichting Nederlandse Federatie voor Vluchtelingenhulp)* and the UNHCR Representative in The Hague, to find jobs and permanent homes for the Asians.

Starting on 8 December, all the Asians attended intensive Dutch language classes, five hours a day. Even the women, who first thought the classes were "for men only", agreed to attend, and nurseries were organized to help out those who had small children to care for. School-age children were sent to school, and soon struck up friendships leading to reciprocal invitations to play with their Dutch schoolmates.

Children and adults alike received approximately $250 to buy clothing; one enterprising draper even offered to take the Asians by minibus to his shop and gave them a big discount on all purchases!

The Netherlands Government established a special budget amounting to $860,000 to cover the care and maintenance of the Asians until they were fully settled. It also took a most generous attitude towards the problem of families which were split up in the rush to leave Uganda. As Mr.

Continued on Page 173

though, that we send it to him. "Of course!" The promise will be kept.

Other wishes, other demands, less easy to express, haunt the minds of many a boarder at the Corona. Exiles and uprooted people from all over the world, they rub elbows, they talk, they put their heads together, they make plans. What says the oracle? in the nearby harbour, the blast of a hooter. After having met with a squall, a ship is back in quiet waters.

Norway

It was in Italy that the Norwegian mission selected a group of 114 Uganda Asians of undetermined nationality. Large families and single people. Eighty of them were at first put up in three hotels in Oslo and 33 in Bergen. The task of receiving and settling the Asians was assigned to the Norwegian Refugee Council, which draws on substantial government funds set aside for this purpose. As well as providing the other necessities, these funds cover care and maintenance and financially support the newly arrived during the initial months when they start working and get established.

At Bergen, the first encounter with a member of the group of Asians settled here may well take place at the desk of the most elegant hotel in town. The employee who, after dinner, hands you your key, does not look Norwegian at all. As a matter of fact, his name is Ashikussin A. He was born in Kampala 21 years ago. He arrived with the rest of the group from Rome on December 1, 1972, with his parents and three sisters. Like his fellow-countrymen, Ashikussin took advantage of the two months' acclimatization period imposed on all newcomers by the Norwegian Refugee Council to take an intensive Norwegian language course—five hours a day. Since he had experience in the hotel trade—he was head of the reception desk of a hotel in Kampala—he asked for and obtained, with the help of the Norwegian Refugee Council, this job which suits him perfectly. He is quite aware of the immediate advantages and the possibilities for advancement. He works at night and at present earns 2,200 crowns; but he knows that promotion prospects depend on him. All he has to do is improve his knowledge of Norwegian. English, however, is just as important for his job.

"I really was lucky to be given a chance to use my knowledge and experience," Ashikussin explains. At home, satisfaction and optimism prevail. His father, who is an accountant, has not yet found a job, but Fatima, 24, is working in a chocolate factory and Amatuzohira, 19, in a bank. Shanaze, 17, was admitted to the oldest and most respected secondary school, the Bergen Katedralskole. Shanaze is pretty and cheerful; everybody likes her and the same is true for Harjit and Manjit S., two Asian boys of about the same age. They are of Hindu religion, whilst she is a Moslem; but who makes a distinction here? Among the Asians at Bergen, there are also Sikhs and Catholics. . . They all volunteered when the Norwegian mission came to select candidates at the Hotel Villa near Rome. *"The only thing I regret is that we couldn't take everybody,"* says Mr. Wilhelm Boe, secretary general of the Norwegian Refugee Council.

"We arrived on December 1st; it was raining cats and dogs. Many of the women had nothing but their sari and a pair of sandals to wear; we had to walk in ankle-deep water," says Shanaze. An event which today is recalled with pleasure. Another memory: the snow that eventually started to fall, and first tries on skis. But most of the time

Continued on Page 174

High Commissioner for Refugees, Sadruddin Aga Khan in Canzanella colony near Naples, Italy, with Senator Lodovico Montini, President of the A.A.I., the Italian International Aid Administration.

Continued from Page 172

Netherlands

Henk van der Bie, spokesman of the Ministry of Culture and Social Affairs, put it: *"If a man has six children, and officially you only anticipated four, what would you do with the two others?"* The answer of the authorities was—you take all members of a divided family. When the High Commissioner visited the Netherlands in January 1973, he learned to his satisfaction that some 60 family members not included in the original selection had arrived or were en route, much to the joy of their relatives.

The efforts on the part of the Ministry of Labour and the Federation for Assistance to Refugees to find jobs for the Asians soon started to pay off. There was a variety of offers, from a chain of Department Stores which made a dozen jobs available after a pre-employment training course, to a restaurant owner who had decided to open an Indian restaurant, and went to Nieuw Milligen to recruit qualified personnel... Clerks, accountants, mechanics, electricians, bank and insurance company employees, to mention but a few, all found new futures opening up for them.

Meanwhile, the search was going on for suitable housing accommodation for the Asians; the UNHCR Representative contacted 22 municipalities, located for the most part in eastern Holland, and by the end of March, all the new immigrants had been found homes. Some 70 per cent have individual dwellings, while the rest are in apartments. Almost all are new lodgings, and to enable the Asians to pay relatively high rentals, they are receiving housing grants for at least the first year. According to Mr. van der Bie, there are few problems. There might be difficulties with four or five families, but the policy was not to select only those without problems—neither the large families nor even those including a handicapped person were to be excluded; the main condition was that these people were set on building a new future in the Netherlands.

Three Asians are in mental hospitals where they are receiving appropriate treatment. A young paralysis case has been admitted to the Het Dorp village for the handicapped near Arnhem.

From different parts of the Netherlands come reports on how the Asians are faring. Take, for instance, the F. family: they are living in a comfortable apartment at Almelo, in Overijsel province. There are four in the family: Shabbir, 34, his wife Fatima, and their two daughters, Mahbooba and Batulhai. Shabbir, a former shopkeeper with accounting experience, is busy learning Dutch and has been in contact with a firm where he hopes to get a job in the near future. Fatima, his smiling wife, is already active in voluntary work in a committee formed to help the 14 Asian families at Almelo. She helps to smooth out their difficulties and solve the thousand and one small day-to-day problems that are bound to come up.

She has already made friends with a number of Dutch families, and her charming elder daughter, Mahbooba, has done likewise at school.

Or, take Sumanlal P., also living at Almelo. This 26-year-old electrician who had been in charge of the electrical system in a factory in Kampala, is sure of getting a good job in Holland, where his trade is much in demand. Recently married, he and his young wife Parvatiben could hardly believe their luck when they were told that the National Federation for Assistance to Refugees had arranged for him to take a special training course at Almelo which will permit him to get a better job than those open to him with only his practical experience.

As for Ramesh J., former senior executive in a bank in Kampala, he came to the Netherlands with his wife Saraswati and their children, Sandeep, eight, Manish, five, and Sonal, one-and-a-half. Luck was with them, too—Ramesh has found a good job in a bank in Amsterdam. Active and competent, he is having no difficulty adapting to his new surroundings; as for Saraswati, life in this big, cosmopolitan city where fate has brought her suits her perfectly, and she has no time to be homesick.

Continued from Page 173

Norway

it rains in Bergen, just like today.

Together with Mr. Boe, we went to see the A's at home. They have a flat in a modern housing development in one of Bergen's new suburbs. It lies behind a mountain and is linked to the town by a tunnel which seems nearly as long as the one that runs under Mt. Blanc. Above the door there is an inscription in Arabic: a wish of happiness. Inside, a large room with a view over the valley. Three bedrooms and a beautifully-equipped kitchen, enough to make the most demanding housewife envious: refrigerator, washing-machine and electric airing-cupboard. *"It's always raining here,"* says Mr. Boe, who has known Bergen since his childhood. *"The laundry has got to dry somewhere!"* As a matter of fact, all the flats here are equipped in the same way.

The rent for the first month is paid by the Norwegian Refugee Council. For the next six months, it will amount to only 400 crowns; only afterwards will the family have to pay the full rent, i.e. 600 crowns. With three salaries in the family, the A's will be quite able to manage. However, after three months of employment, they will have to start paying taxes. The scale is progressive: 35% of the total to start with, and, a year later, the full amount. On the other hand, economically weak families will benefit from the social welfare scheme whereby allowances are paid for every child or aged person who is unable to work.

Mrs. A. serves tea and spicy biscuits. The conversation turns to cooking. Of course, everybody in the family prefers Indian food. *"What, you don't like fish pudding?"* Mr. Boe pretends to be surprised. *"Yes, of course we do; it's very good,"* replies Ashikussin, *"we have it quite often at the hotel canteen. It lacks pepper, though."* *"I distribute Norwegian recipes,"* says Mr. Flemming Bjorn Olsen, who is in charge of the integration of Asians in Bergen. *"Not really to put them off their traditional dishes, but just to help them to cook cheaper meals."*

This, however, is not Mr. Olsen's only job. With the help of the municipal welfare office, he looked for and found jobs for the Asians whom the Council and the authorities had decided to resettle at Bergen: two tailors, a car mechanic, two welders who work at the shipyard. . . Before they could be employed they attended an accelerated vocational training course and proved to be very skilful. *"Can you imagine that I haven't yet found a job for an electrician? As if we had too many of them here in Bergen!"*

The mechanic is called Jose-Honorato M. He is a bachelor. His mother and sister live in Goa, from where his grandparents had originally emigrated to Uganda. In Uganda, he owned a garage; he organized safaris, too. He works at the Opel garage in Bergen. We met him on the third floor, in the new cars department.

"I check the cars before delivery. As you see, I also polish them. That's just a start. Later on, when I have proved my skills, I'll move on to the repairs department and earn more money." Jose-Honorato's problem is that he wants to send some money to his mother and sister. Asked if he wants them to join him in Norway, he answers: *"Later on, perhaps, if things work out that way."*

Elsewhere in Bergen, a hilly town, like Rome and like Kampala, on the first floor of an old building in the business centre, there is a small tailor's shop. There you can meet the best adapted, the happiest of all the Asians: his name is Chagantal Zina S. Tape measure round his neck, scissors in hand, he practises his peaceful craft which after all, might be called an art. He is about to finish off a regional costume, worn in the Hardanger district. It looks like a hunting dress, with adornments, a yellow waistcoat and a grey and green jacket. Just for fun he tries it on. It suits him beautifully. A true Norwegian. His colleague who is nearly 80 but who looks 20 years younger shows him how to dance: lift one leg and slap your thigh... Mr. S. says he is a happy man. Happy, because he can practise his profession, because his colleagues and boss consider him as a friend; happy also, because his wife, daughter and younger son will be arriving from Bombay tomorrow. The elder son who came to Bergen with him, has found a job as well; he works in a hosiery factory.

"I am immensely grateful to all those who helped us to come to Norway and get settled here. Hjertelig tak!"

Business lecture at local bank

Sweden

The admission of refugees, which has been a tradition in Sweden is considered there a humanitarian task and is carried out with generosity and efficiency.

When the Swedish Government, in answer to the High Commissioner's appeal, offered to admit 300 persons of undetermined nationality, the quota was filled within a few days. The Swedish mission which went to Austria, accepted 319 who went to Sweden in the course of December. More recently, 88 holders of British passports staying in England, applied in turn for migration to Sweden.

Contrary to the practice in the other European and Scandinavian countries, the Swedish authorities themselves take care of the reception, employment, accommodation and integration of the immigrants, without calling upon voluntary agencies. For this purpose, the Labour Market Board of the Ministry of Labour has set up two resettlement centres, one at Alvesta and one at Moheda, in the south-east of the country. The refugees remain there for two to four months before they take up either vocational training or a job. During their stay, they attend Swedish language courses, in order to be able to make themselves understood.

By April, there were still 275 Uganda Asians living at the centres, accommodated in comfortable, friendly little houses painted in yellow, amidst meadows, pine and birchwoods.

"You brought the sun to Sweden" said the hosts. In fact, never has Smaland known such a mild winter and such an early spring. *"Frankly speaking, we were afraid for these people, used to a hot climate, because of the hard winters here,"* says Mr. Bo Muller director of the Alvesta centre. *"Warm clothing, of course, was ready for them."*

Climate and food, in fact, were the administration's main preoccupations. In the refectory, a self-service was set up so that everybody should choose his own food. Various menus had been prepared to conform with the eating habits and religious requirements. *"Mostly, these requirements are strictly observed. But not by all of them. We noticed that quite a few people, especially the younger ones, willingly have a try at every dish."*

The teaching of the language, which is not an easy task, is carried out systematically and according to the latest methods. Younger people, of course, learn more easily, but the older people don't give up trying. As an incentive, the pupils get four crowns per day for attending the courses.

Continued on Page 175

Switzerland

At the end of September 1972, the British Government approached a number of countries, asking them to admit Asians forced to leave Uganda at short notice. In response, Switzerland, as early as October 11, declared itself ready to admit 200 persons who had neither British passports nor Ugandan nationality. Also since then, the Swiss Government has set aside a substantial fund to cover expenses for the resettlement of the Asians, for transport, temporary care and maintenance and integration. The largest sum, US$ 185,750, is allotted to integration.

A mission composed of representatives from the Police and Justice Department and from the Federal Administration for Industry and Labour went to Kampala. They had been instructed to give preference to families with at least one skilled member able to find employment in Switzerland. However families including aged or handicapped persons requiring social welfare support, were not to be excluded.

This latter provision was interpreted in a particularly liberal way especially when Switzerland decided to complete its initial quota with Asians from Spain and Italy. Ten were admitted in April, consisting of five severely handicapped persons and a family with a chronically sick father. None of these would easily have found another country willing to receive them.

Temporary resettlement

The Police and Justice Department had the over-all responsibility for admission of the refugees. One of its tasks was to establish lists of localities, willing to accept a group of Uganda Asians. The Swiss Red Cross took charge of the temporary accommodation of the newly arrived. They were flown directly from Kampala to Zurich, where they arrived on November 2 and 3. They were immediately directed to five reception centres in the cantons of Berne, Saint Gall and Neuchatel, where they were to remain for a period ranging from one to three months. There they would familiarize themselves with living conditions in Switzerland and start learning the language (for most of them it would be German). At the same time, preliminary steps would be taken to arrange for their permanent settlement.

A few months went by and everything worked out according to plan. In most cases, the immigrants endeavoured to establish contacts with the local population. Several of them even insisted on starting work right away, albeit on a temporary basis. Welfare officers undertook to inform them of laws and regulations, the educational system, wage scales, taxation; mothers attended courses in childcare and domestic science.

Integration

The Central Office for Swiss Aid to Refugees was put in charge of the integration of the Asians, under its auspices, six voluntary agencies shared the caseload: Swiss Caritas (50 persons); Swiss Union of Jewish Welfare Committees (45) Swiss Protestant Relief Work (40) Workers Welfare Societies (35), Christian Movement for Peace (20) and Commission for Orthodox Refugees (10).

The Central Office had established dossiers, mentioning professional qualifications, in view of placing the Asians in different Cantons, depending on the employment possibilities.

The Office also undertook to advertise through the press the needs of the Asians for jobs and accommodation.

A large family

The V. family is the largest of the Asian families resettled in Switzerland: it totals 13 persons. The father, Ismail, three adult sons and a daughter are working. The other girls and boys are at school, except for the small daughter of Hassan, Ismail's eldest son.

The task of settling them fell to the Swiss Union of Jewish Welfare Committees. *"It was no small problem,"* says Mrs. Edith Zweig, the welfare officer in charge. *"We had to find in the same area adequate jobs for five members of the family, as well as accommodation for all of them."*

With the help of information obtained by the Central Office, suitable accommodation was found in St. Margrethen, a town at the junction of the Austrian and German borders. With its huge fuel tanks, saw-mills, workshops and huge trucks from Eastern Europe passing through, it is a typical border town, cosmopolitan and lively. The day of our visit happened to be carnival day. Children were wearing fancy dress.

"Which of the masks could be hiding one of the V. children?" we asked ourselves, trying to ferret out their address. But they were all at home, awaiting the visitors. *"We had to find a separate house for them,"* explains Mrs. Zweig. There it was, on a hillside, overlooking the town. Big, but rather rundown, it needed repair, and a bathroom. The V's had wanted to give a hand, too; *"Not*

Continued on Page 176

Continued from Page 174

Sweden

Apart from the language courses, the stay in the resettlement centres also serves other purposes. The immigrants get all the necessary information as regards living conditions in Sweden, regulations to be observed and welfare benefits to which they are entitled. Generally speaking, refugees get the same benefits as the Swedes. Furthermore, special funds are allotted by the Labour Market Board to various categories of refugees (to which the Asians from Uganda are assimilated). Thus, for instance, they may obtain loans as soon as they start working. These loans, advances on their future salaries, will help them to buy furniture or anything else they may need for their permanent settlement. The system provides for the local welfare funds to guarantee the rent in case of difficulties. Allowances are paid to those who are still unemployed and to those who are too old to work. Immigrants may enter primary, secondary and high schools on the same conditions as Swedish nationals. Medical care is free.

The administration of the resettlement centres and the County Labour Boards find jobs and accommodation for the families settling in Sweden. In Municipal Housing, the rent is fixed by regulation. The only problem, sometimes a major one, may be that of finding in the same town a working place, accommodation, medical care for handicapped members of the family and schooling facilities for the children.

Particular attention is paid to the trade the immigrants may be called upon to exercise. Guided tours are frequently organized for groups to various factories, where the newcomers can observe workshops on the spot, learn about time and motion, hours of work and wage scales.

"In this group of Uganda Asians, we have unfortunately not found the skilled people for whom there is a large demand," says Mr. Wilhelm Mohl in Moheda. *"Offers mostly come from industry. This is why we encourage the job seekers to attend vocational training courses. Not far from here, at Vaxjo, there exists a vocational training centre for lathe-operators, welders, mechanics, panel-beaters, etc. The course lasts approximately four months: eight weeks of general subjects, and ten to twelve weeks at the workshop."* A first group was already attending these courses, and the next day another thirty was due to leave for Vaxjo.

Their departure was the occasion for a party given at the Moheda centre by the Asians for the Swedish staff. The Asians had taken over the kitchen and prepared "chapati", curry and a variety of other typically Indian dishes.

"We went easy on the spices so that our guests should not become addicted. Red pepper is like a drug. If you take to it, you can't live without afterwards!" says a joyful gentleman in his sixties, Mr. Paresh S. Dynamic and talkative, he had attended a lecture in the afternoon, held by a local bank for those Asians who might be interested to know about commercial and credit regulations applicable to them if they wanted to open their own businesses. *"The information was not too encouraging,"* he says, *"for people who have no capital of their own, which is the case for most of us.*

"At present, yes. But who knows, things might change," a younger man points out. Mr. S. had owned a cattle farm and was familiar with operating and maintaining tractors and other machinery. *"Being experienced in mechanics, I applied for a vocational training course at Vaxjo. After working for a few years in a garage, I might take over the management of a petrol station, and even start up a small repair shop."*

After a few months' stay, despondency gives way to optimism. Children are born, young people get engaged. Will the Asians have more difficulties in adapting than other groups of refugees resettled in Sweden? *"I don't think so,"* says Mr. Nickolausson, the director of the Moheda centre. *"For the past ten years, Sweden has been getting used to living with foreigners of all origins: Turks, Albanians, Lebanese... We have factories like Volvo in Goteborg, where more than 30% of the workers are foreigners. We do our best to help them to adapt as quickly as possible."* Proudly, he shows us a newspaper clipping about a group of gypsies that arrived from France some time ago. The headline says: *"Tenacity opens the doors of dreamland."*

Ugandan Asian Expulsion: 90 Days and Beyond through the Eyes of the International Press

United States of America

The 1,000 Asians of undetermined nationality who were selected by the United States in Kampala in the autumn of 1972 under a special programme have been advancing toward settlement with exceptional speed, thus vindicating the decision of the Administration to admit them as an exceptional measure, in view of the urgency of the situation, on "parole" outside regular immigration procedures. Subsequently a further some 100 Asians entered individually from transit centres in Europe under regular criteria. Helped by the good results achieved with the first arrivals, the negotiations between Secretary of State William Rogers and the High Commissioner led to a new special quota of 500, also on "parole", being announced in April 1973.

The main impetus for settling the Asians who have already been admitted, at the local level—and for supporting within the USA, UNHCR's appeal to the Government to undertake the second special scheme—has come from voluntary agencies many of which are Christian or Jewish in affiliation. The seven participants have been American Fund for Czechoslovak Refugees, International Rescue Committee, Lutheran World Federation, Migration and Refugee Services-United States Catholic Conference, Tolstoy Foundation, United HIAS Service, World Council of Churches. The fact that the vast majority of the Asians—being Hindu or Moslem—are neither, has in no way curbed the enthusiasm with which Churches and Synagogues across the country have responded in arranging accommodation and jobs for the expellees. In one rural congregation of only 200 people, most of whom a few months ago would have been hard put to find Uganda on the map, there were offers to sponsor 10 Asians. In the end, there were not enough cases to go around, and they took only six. Asked to explain such an effort in favour of persons with whom his parish has no ethnic or religious ties, the pastor replied, *"This project has brought people together who had never worked together before and united them in a common cause. It has been marvellous to see their readiness to meet the distress of their fellow men, not because they have the same colour skin or go to the same Church, but simply because they need help. And if you want an explanation, in my opinion it is a clear case of the Holy Spirit at work."*

The economic position of the Asians is becoming stronger every month. In many families there are several wage-earners, and they are living frugally, paying off the initial loans received from the Agencies and building up savings as they had done in Uganda. They are also making a strong effort to adapt their life-style to that of Americans. For example, in deference to their neighbours who may not share their fondness for the smell of curry, Asians have followed the recommendations of social workers and take care to give their apartments a thorough airing after each meal.

Assimilation is of course quickest for children who have made friends at school and have already adopted American idioms and accents to a surprising extent. On the whole, the Asians with their natural reserve have reached an accommodation with the more extrovert American personality and have come to realize that there is no ulterior motive behind the generosity with which they have been welcomed. They see moreover that their success depends only on their abilities. And as keen businessmen they have grasped the fact that in the

Rashmi V. greets his wife after a separation of six months, during which their baby daughter, Rakhee, was born.

Continued from Page 175

Switzerland

everything is fixed yet," they apologize. The kitchen for sure was ready and soon 15 people were asked to sit down to a meal: the family and the visitors; among them were two cameramen who were going to film them. The loud sound of a piece of oriental music recorded in Kampala gave them the impression of still being there. *"A pity you can't also record the smell of spices on tape,"* said young Mustafa.

A little later, we went to see the father and his son Hassan at the garage where they work. Screwdriver in hand, Hassan was bending over a recalcitrant engine. His colleague with blond, bushy hair, spoke to him. But what language is he talking? Hassan smiles. He understands Swiss German, even the joke! For the film, Ismail was asked to pour oil into the engine of a new car. That is actually his job. In Uganda, he owned a garage, and today he does not feel lost among all those shiny cars which he must get ready for delivery.

Sadik works in a factory for metal door and window frames. His brother Abdul found a job in another factory nearby. Independent by nature, he prefers to live by himself. One of the daughters works in a grocery store at St. Margrethen. She lives with her employers and also helps in the house. She earns SF 600 per month. Adding up all the other salaries (Ismail 1,000, Hassan 1,300, Sadik 1,200), the family's monthly income amounts to SF 4,100 (appr. US$ 1,270). The expenses are as follows: rent: 800; food: 1,600; heating: 150; social security: 270; sickness fund: 180; instalments for furniture and TV set: 1000. Total: SF 4,000. Just enough to make both ends meet.

However, they all expect their first salary increase very soon. Should temporary difficulties arise the Voluntary Agency will not hesitate to step in.

Here in Switzerland, as in the other countries, the usual meeting place for the Asians is the language course. The Migros Club at Saint Gall has organized courses for them twice a week at 6 p.m, attended by about 20 people, coming from as far as St. Margrethen, like the V's. Here they can exchange information and news, and learn about friends from Kampala and those they have met in the reception centres. Since last month, almost all of them are settled in some 20 different towns and villages.

Those with jobs are electricians, gardeners, storemen. One is a technician, working in a water purification plant; three women are skilled dressmakers, one is a trained secretary, another an X-ray assistant. For the time being, quite a number of them have been hired as unskilled labourers, like Abdul or Sadik V. But what they consider most important is to have found a job and to earn money, even if the salary is not as high as that of Mr. N. As an insurance expert, he was immediately engaged by a Swiss company and earns several thousand francs a month.

Some families have special reasons for rejoicing. They obtained from the Police and Justice Department an authorization to have a member of their family join them, who had either left Uganda before them, or not been able to leave at the same time. So far, 20 visas have been granted, and ten children, wives or grandparents have already arrived, gratifying fully the hopes and wishes of these uprooted families.

Shailesh M. stood first in his class in math among 22 fourth graders at Summit Valley Elementary School.

United States their talents and industry can in time bring them much greater material rewards than they might ever have hoped to achieve in Uganda.

Rashmi V.

One of the most unfortunate aspects of the expulsion and uprooting of Asians from Uganda was that many families were broken up in the great dispersal. Most holders of British passports, which included many women and children, went to the United Kingdom, while often the heads of families who, some time before, had decided to opt for Ugandan nationality, found to their dismay that they had undertaken the procedure too late.

Rashmi V., an accountant in his late 20's, was one of the Asians in the latter category who was selected by the United States in Kampala. His wife, Kundan, on the strength of her British passport had flown to the United Kingdom a month before to await the birth of their child, which was due in the latter part of January or early February, in the care of a brother and sister-in-law living in London.

Rashmi also had good luck in being settled in the Harrisburg area. He was hired by Tressler Lutheran Service Associates and was welcomed as a roomer with one of the Organization's staff members. Early this year the wheels were set in motion to enable Kundan to rejoin him, together with their new-born daughter, Rakhee.

As spring came, Rashmi became increasingly impatient. Finally, he was informed that his wife and daughter would arrive on 29 March at 4.30 p.m.

On that Thursday when he arrived for work he found his office decorated with signs bearing slogans such as "Together again at last", "Today you are a family man". Rashmi took all this good-natured joshing in his stride, and his reserve never left him, right up to the moment that the plane taxied to a halt and he stepped forward to help Kundan and her infant alight. In that second, however, his composure evaporated and his face broke into a broad smile of untrammeled joy and pride. Rashmi had been reunited with his wife and he had held his baby daughter for the first time—and the United States had gained another family.

Salehbhai R.

Within a week after three generations of the Salehbhai R. clan arrived in Harrisburg, Pennsylvania, on Election Day, 1972, all three adult males had been hired by Grimms Electronic Shop and were earning a combined total of $1,300 per month. The father repairs transistors, one son aged 26 works on cassettes and the other, 25, fixes car radios—specialized skills that are in tremendous demand in a country where practically every household owns at least one of each of these appliances. *"We could use some more men like them, I can tell you,"* says Mrs. Grimm who has been running the business with her son and daughter-in-law since Mr. Grimm's death a few years ago. *"Always on time, never any noise and absolutely dependable in what they do."*

For the R's there is thus basically no change in their occupations, except that in Kampala they were their own bosses.

Sponsored by a relatively wealthy parish in Mechanicsburg, a suburb of Harrisburg, the R's live in a typical American house, complete with front porch, on West Main Street. Because they came almost directly from Kampala with only a six-day stay in a transit centre near Naples, the transition was particularly abrupt and, in a certain sense, unreal.

"One day we were in the East African sun and then all of a sudden it was the first time we saw snow," explains Liqata, the bachelor son. *"I was so excited I went out to play in it."*

The R's landed just in time for Thanksgiving Day. A family from the Church invited the whole clan to share their traditional Turkey dinner.

"It was Thanksgiving for us, too," Liqata said. *"From the very start we have had a lot to be grateful for. . . good jobs, a nice place to live, and everyone trying to help us."*

His brother, Inayatali, who forms part of the same household together with his wife and two young children, misses the wide circle of male cronies with whom he used to spend leisure hours playing cards or conversing in Uganda and realizes this type of social life takes time to build up in a new country. But it will surely come.

The member of the family making the fastest adjustment to American life is, without doubt, 13-year-old Hasina, whose flashing smile has helped her win a host of friends at Mechanicsburg Junior High. The principal reports that her academic performance is completely satisfactory, and she is certainly one of the most popular girls in the eighth grade. Hasina's classmates often walk home with her after school in the afternoon and are somewhat mystified to hear her conversing with her mother and sister-in-law in Gujerati, which is the language spoken at home. The adult R. women maintain the traditional Indian manner of cooking and take pride in donning their elegant saris when they go out to the local supermarket. One senses they do this somewhat in self-defense against the strong current of a way of life that is so different from what they knew in Uganda. But as the years go by and Hasina and her two little cousins, now two and eight, grow up, exerting an ever-growing American influence on their relatives, there is no doubt that the R's will become a prototype of something which does not yet exist in American society: an Asian-American household.

Prabashankar M.

The settlement of the Prabashankar M. family was sponsored by the small congregation in Pennsylvania mentioned above. Within a matter of days a parishioner had offered a small two-storey house next to her farm; it was in somewhat decrepit condition but a group of volunteers made up of professional carpenters and painters fell to work refurbishing the downstairs and converting what was essentially an attic into pleasant living quarters. The M's—two adults and four children under 10—arrived in November to find the house ready and fully equipped with stove, refrigerator and all other standard household equipment. *"We had so many appliances flowing in from donors,"* Pastor B. Penrose Hoover recalls, *"that I could hardly keep track of them."*

Mr. M. had been an accountant with Barclays Bank in Kampala. At first there was some difficulty in finding him the same kind of employment and his first job was as a packer in a poultry processing plant. All the time he kept an eye open for a chance to get back to his own field. One day he spied an ad asking for an auditor at the National Central Bank in Lancaster and, without telling anyone, he went over to investigate, was interviewed and got the job. His employer agreed that such an opportunity was too good to turn down and without any hard feelings allowed him to leave. Since then Mr. M. has proved his worth as a member of a flying team of auditors that makes spot checks on branches of the company throughout the area, a highly responsible position which speaks well for his training and integrity. His boss, Mr. S. W. Bomberger, reports that Mr. M. is carrying out his duties in a most satisfactory manner and estimates that the United States and the Bank have acquired, in Mr. M., skills entailing some $35,000 worth of education.

The eldest child, Shailesh, takes after his father in his flair for figures and stands first in his class in math among 22 fourth-graders at Summit Valley Elementary School. He is also developing into a fine athlete. This spring is his first baseball season but already he has successfully adapted his cricket style and more than holds his own with his classmates.

Shailesh serves as the family interpreter when his father is not at home, as his mother speaks little English and the other children—a 5-year-old boy and two 8-month old twins—are too young to be of help.

Mrs. M. has had difficulties with a bone in one of her feet and has had to undergo a minor operation. As all the Asians were enrolled in a Health Insurance Scheme upon arrival, this expense is covered and will not play havoc with the family budget, which is already fairly tight because of the reimbursement on the loan received from the Agency and the instalment payments on a second-hand car, which is an absolute necessity for Mr. M's work. During her stay in the hospital, parishioners again rose to the challenge and took turns looking after the children and cooking for the family.

END OF UNHCR REPORT

<u>Acknowledgments</u>

Thanks to:

*the newspapers, wire services and photo agencies who waived or reduced their copyright reproduction fees to make this publication feasible.

*the library and photo department at the Offices of the United Nations High Commissioner for Refugees in Geneva, Switzerland.

*family, friends and associates for their assistance and support.

Special thanks to my wife for her assistance, support and encouragement and to my 4-year-old daughter for her patience during the preparation of this book. It is for children that this bit of history must be preserved.

The following blank pages are provided for you to record your own experiences to share with future generations. You can place photographs, newspaper clippings and handwritten memoirs here.

Page 180

Page 181

Page 182